Interpersonal Encounters

Connecting Through Communication

Laura K. Guerrero

Arizona State University

Bree McEwan

University of Toronto Mississauga

SAGE

Los Angeles | London | New Delhi
Singapore | Washington DC | Melbourne

FOR INFORMATION:

SAGE Publications, Inc.
2455 Teller Road
Thousand Oaks, California 91320
E-mail: order@sagepub.com

SAGE Publications Ltd.
1 Oliver's Yard
55 City Road
London, EC1Y 1SP
United Kingdom

SAGE Publications India Pvt. Ltd.
B 1/I 1 Mohan Cooperative Industrial Area
Mathura Road, New Delhi 110 044
India

SAGE Publications Asia-Pacific Pte. Ltd.
18 Cross Street #10-10/11/12
China Square Central
Singapore 048423

Printed in Canada

Library of Congress Control Number: 2022902222

ISBN (pbk) 978-1-4522-7019-7 | ISBN (loose-leaf) 978-1-0718-5924-7

Acquisitions Editor: Lily Norton

Content Development Editor:
Jennifer Jovin-Bernstein

Development Editor: Kathryn Abbott

Editorial Assistants:
Sarah Wilson, Sam Diaz

Production Editor: Rebecca Lee

Typesetter: diacriTech

Cover Designer: Janet Kiesel

Marketing Manager: Victoria Velasquez

This book is printed on acid-free paper.

22 23 24 25 26 10 9 8 7 6 5 4 3 2 1

BRIEF CONTENTS

CONTENTS

PREFACE

We are excited and honored to release the first edition of *Interpersonal Encounters: Connecting Through Communication*. This book is a collaboration designed to be relevant to today's students while being true to the current core research in interpersonal communication and related fields. The structure and content in this book are also designed to meet a need for an introductory book on interpersonal communication that focuses uniquely on interaction in interpersonal encounters from a functional perspective, as we explain next. We strongly believe that being an effective communicator is a key skill in both personal and professional contexts. People who have better social and personal relationships also report being more physically and mentally healthy. Students in business-related fields learn that developing their "soft" skills is critically important for success in the workplace with clients and co-workers. Indeed, interpersonal skills are frequently cited as one of the most valued sets of skills within organizations. Being able to make good impressions, manage conversations, influence others, and deal effectively with conflict and transgressions, along with other topics covered in this book, translates into skills that cut across various contexts. In fact, we challenge students and instructors to think about how some of the issues discussed in this book work across contexts as well as how they might differ. We also challenge students to try to think outside of their own perspective to better understand their own biases and tendencies related to communication.

APPROACH

This book takes a functional approach to the study of interpersonal communication. By "functional" we mean that we focus on what communication *does* or, in other words, some of the functions it fulfills, within interpersonal interaction. At many universities and colleges, students learn about general concepts related to nonverbal communication, verbal communication, and listening in an introduction to communication course and/or public speaking course. There are also courses at most universities in context areas such as family, workplace, or relational communication. Students have told us that much of what they learn in their introductory interpersonal classes is redundant to what they have learned in these other courses. Thus, to provide a unique look at introductory concepts, this book does not include stand-alone chapters on topics such as nonverbal communication, listening, language, family communication, and so forth. Instead, we focus our efforts on showing students what communication—both verbal and nonverbal— *does* in their lives.

After the introductory chapter, the remaining chapters delve into topics such as how people perform identities, manage impressions, communicate across cultures, manage conversations, express emotions, influence others, develop relationships, maintain quality relationships, manage conflict, cope with transgressions, and, finally, end relationships. Of course, communication functions to do more than what we cover in this book. Our choice for chapters was guided by the research on interpersonal communication to date. Indeed, one of the primary goals for this book was that it be both research based and practical. Within each chapter, our goal is to provide students with research-based knowledge that will help them understand themselves and others better as communicators. When appropriate, we also give students information that will help them build their level of interpersonal skill. To that end, we strived to provide students with both the seminal and current research on each topic and to flesh out some of the practical applications that research has for their lives. We also recognize that interpersonal encounters are deeply influenced by factors related to our identities, including race, gender, sexual orientation, and culture. Within this text, we do not bracket these influences into specific chapters or box features. Rather, we have attempted to weave scholarship representing diverse authors and study participants throughout the text in the same manner that identity and context are woven through our interpersonal interactions. We also call on ourselves and our fellow interpersonal scholars to prioritize diversity, equity, and inclusion in future interpersonal scholarship to create even greater knowledge and understanding of interpersonal communication processes. The special features within the book are also designed to help students think more deeply about interpersonal communication and develop their skills.

ORGANIZATION

Between an introductory chapter and a capstone chapter, *Interpersonal Encounters* is organized in a format that moves from looking at the self to looking at how people communicate in social and personal relationships. We believe that the breakdown of chapters reflects the research in the field of interpersonal communication. Following the introductory chapter, Chapters 2 and 3 take an in-depth look at how people communicate their identities, form impressions of others, and manage their own first impressions. The next chapter (Chapter 4, "Communicating Interpersonally Across Cultures") focuses on broadening students' perspectives so they think outside of their self-concept and experiences to communicate better in intercultural interactions. The next three chapters (Chapters 5–7) focus on three essential functions of communication—conversation, emotion, and social influence. These three areas have received considerable attention from researchers, given their centrality to what communication is used to do in people's everyday lives. The next five chapters (Chapters 8–12) center on social and personal relationships—from their development and maintenance, to coping with conflict and transgressions, and finally, to ending relationships. Finally, the book ends with a capstone chapter (Chapter 13). The goal of this concluding chapter is to provide students with some overall principles to take away from the course. These take-home messages come from looking across all the previous chapters to summarize major principles that are central to being more effective communicators in interpersonal interactions. Each of the previous chapters also ends with principles, so this is a way to give students an overarching set of final principles that will help them pull everything they have learned together.

FEATURES

When planning the features for this book, we kept our pedagogical goals in mind. Specifically, our primary goal was to provide students with a book that was both research based and practical. We also talked to our students to get ideas of the kind of features they find useful in textbooks. This led us to create the following features for this book.

Opening Scenarios: Each chapter begins with a vignette that provides an example of some of the concepts that will be discussed. The example is referred to multiple times within the chapter as a kind of mini case study. Students appreciate these types of scenarios when they are relatable and put concepts in context, which was our goal in creating them.

Skill Builders: Most chapters include at least one Skill Builder box that describes various interpersonal skills, often with recommendations for ways to develop or refine those skills. Many of these boxes end with questions that students can use to think about their skills and ways to improve them.

"I Didn't Know That!": These boxes highlight something that students might not know or expect to be true. An important part of critical thinking is for students to be able to evaluate the various messages they are bombarded with about interpersonal interactions, both from social media and the popular press. While some of this information is valid, some is also questionable. These boxes not only point out some information students might not know or expect, but they also teach them the importance of researching before believing everything they read as fact.

"What Would You Do?": These boxes present students with different situations or scenarios and ask them what they would do in those situations. Most of these boxes include an ethical dimension as well as practical concerns. For example, these boxes deal with issues such as when it is appropriate to fake emotion or engage in deception, and how to break up with someone in a kind but firm manner.

Principles: Each chapter ends with principles that tie together some of the ideas and concepts students learned. Students find these kinds of summarizing principles helpful in developing a "big picture" understanding of interpersonal communication.

Key Terms and Glossary: Each chapter includes a key term list. Each term also appears in the glossary at the end of the book. While the principles help give students a "big picture" understanding of ideas, being able to define concepts gives them the specifics they need to pull everything together.

Reflection Questions: There is a set of reflection questions at the end of each chapter. These questions ask students to think about their own communication and/or reflect on key issues in the chapter. The reflection questions would also be appropriate for discussion boards or as prompts for short reflection papers.

TEACHING RESOURCES

This text includes an array of instructor teaching materials designed to save you time and to help you keep students engaged. To learn more, visit sagepub.com or contact your SAGE representative at **sagepub.com/findmyrep**.

ACKNOWLEDGMENTS

No matter how passionate you are about a topic like interpersonal communication, it is still a challenge to find the time to work on a new book when you are busy with many professional and family activities. This book has been a product of patience, collaboration, and a strong desire to write the kind of introductory book that would get our undergraduates as excited about interpersonal communication as we were when we first discovered it and still are today. This book became a reality because of the hard work, dedication, and support of many people.

First, from both of us: We would like to thank the team at SAGE for all their hard work, patience, and creativity: Lily Norton, Acquisitions Editor; Jennifer Jovin-Bernstein, Senior Content Development Editor; Kathryn Abbott, Development Editor; Sarah Wilson and Sam Diaz, Editorial Assistants; and Rebecca Lee, Production Editor.

Second, from Laura: I would first and foremost like to thank Bree. When I was first asked to write an introductory-level interpersonal book in the tradition of my upper-division book (*Close Encounters*), I was crazy enough to think that I could write it on my own. It quickly became apparent that if I did that, the book wouldn't be published until 2030. (Well, maybe it wouldn't have been that bad… but still.) When I considered who to ask to co-author the new book with me, Bree came to mind because of her knowledge, writing skills, and our shared teaching philosophy. I'm so glad she accepted the invitation. This book has truly been an equal partnership and I value all of Bree's contributions more than I can say. I would also like to acknowledge my daughters, Gabrielle and Kristiana, who were instrumental in two ways. First, they were always available to read excerpts to make sure they really did reflect how Gen Z communicates, and, second, they helped with some of the photos. On that note, I would like to also thank them and their friends who appear in some of the book's photos: Natalie Greenberg, Noor Fahim, Avery Duane, and Ally Nash. Last but not least, I would like to give a huge shout-out to my PhD advisor, Judee Burgoon, whose use of the functional approach as a way to conceptualize nonverbal communication was influential in my thinking about how to structure this book.

Third, from Bree: When Laura called me to ask if I was interested in being her co-author, I knew I would have a supportive co-author in Laura and that we had a clear and shared vision about the type of textbook we wished was available for the interpersonal course. I am so thrilled that she asked me to come along on this journey with her. I would also like to thank my undergraduate interpersonal students from my time at DePaul University, who readily accepted the role of reading in-process chapters and providing excellent feedback that improved the overall feel and accessibility of the book. In addition, I would also like to acknowledge my family—my husband, Colin, who among many talents also keeps the small McEwans occupied when I need to research and write, and the small McEwans themselves (Branwen, Oriana, and Cael) who provide me with a unique perspective on how people learn and develop interpersonal behaviors.

Finally, from both of us again: We would like to thank many of our colleagues, both in the Hugh Downs School of Human Communication and in the College of Communication at DePaul University, for their support and for sometimes letting us float ideas or ask them about their understanding of concepts. We would also like to acknowledge the book's reviewers:

M.E. Achterman, Seattle Pacific University

Shae Adkins, Lone Star College-North Harris

Christine Armstrong, Northampton Community College

Gale R. Burtch, Ivy Tech Community College

Chantele Carr, Estrella Mountain Community College

Rueyling Chuang, California State University, San Bernardino

Dr. Sheila Cuffy, Purdue University at Fort Wayne

Amber Davies-Sloan, Yavapai College

Jane Elmes-Crahall, Wilkes University

Vanessa Ferguson, Mott Community College

Michelle Givertz, California State University, Chico

Dr. Trey Guinn, University of Incarnate Word

Taewook Ham, University of Georgia

Meredith Harrigan, SUNY Geneseo

Betty Kennan, Radford University

Ben Krueger, Northern Arizona University

Jenna McNallie, Augsburg College

Ines Petrovic-Mundzic, Thomas Nelson Community College

Owen Pillion, College of Southern Neva

Evelyn Plummer, Seton Hall University

Matthew Seyfried, Tompkins Cortland Community College

Brandy Stamper, UNC Charlotte

Zuoming Wang, University of North Texas

Alesia Woszidlo, University of Kansas

Gordon Alley Young, Kingsborough Community College

Phyllis S. Zrzavy, Franklin Pierce University

And last, but definitely not least, we would like to thank our students! This includes both our undergraduate and graduate students over the years. The undergraduate students we have taught give us suggestions, help us determine what is helpful and important to them, and keep us enthusiastic about teaching interpersonal communication. Many of the graduate students we work with teach the introductory interpersonal communication course. Their feedback about what works and does not work in their classes has been invaluable while writing this book. It is our hope that this book makes a difference for the next generation of students.

—L. K. G.

—B. L. M.

ABOUT THE AUTHORS

Laura K. Guerrero (PhD, University of Arizona, 1994) is a professor in the Hugh Downs School of Human Communication at Arizona State University, where she teaches courses in relational communication, nonverbal communication, conflict, emotional communication, research methods, and data analysis. She has also taught at the Pennsylvania State University and San Diego State University. Her research focuses on communication in close relationships, such as those between romantic partners, friends, and family members. Her research has examined both the "bright side" of personal relationships, including nonverbal intimacy, forgiveness, relational maintenance, and communication skill, and the "dark side" of personal relationships, including jealousy, hurtful events, conflict, and anger. Dr. Guerrero has published more than 100 journal articles and chapters related to these topics. In addition to *Close Encounters*, her book credits include *Nonverbal Communication in Close Relationships* (co-authored with K. Floyd), *Nonverbal Communication* (co-authored with J. Burgoon & V. Manusov), *The Handbook of Communication and Emotion* (co-edited with P. Andersen), and *The Nonverbal Communication Reader* (co-edited with M. Hecht). She has received several research awards, including the Early Career Achievement Award from the International Association for Relationship Research, the Dickens Research Award from the Western States Communication Association, and the Outstanding Doctoral Dissertation Award from the Interpersonal Communication Division of The International Communication Association. Dr. Guerrero serves on editorial boards for several top journals in communication and relationships. She enjoys traveling and exploring new places (especially with her daughters), writing fiction (when not writing nonfiction), and taking long walks in the mountains or on the beach.

Bree McEwan (PhD, Arizona State University, 2009) is an associate professor in the Institute of Communication, Culture, Information, and Technology at the University of Toronto Mississauga where she teaches courses on research methods and mediated communication. She has also taught at DePaul University and Western Illinois University. Her research focuses on the intersection between interpersonal and communication technology, with a particular interest in how people manage and maintain networked social relationships. She has published articles related to these topics in journals such as *Communication Monographs*, *Annals of the International Communication Association*, *New Media & Society*, and *Social Media + Society*. Her other book is *Navigating New Media Networks: Understanding and Managing Communication Challenges in a Networked Society* (Lexington). She is a recent winner of the Outstanding Article Award from the Human Communication and Technology Division of the National Communication Association and the Outstanding Contribution to Communication Science from the Communication Science and Biology Division of the International Communication Association. She serves on the boards of *Human Communication &Technology*, *Communication Studies*, *Communication Reports*, and the *Journal of Social and Personal Relationships*. She enjoys spending time with her husband (Colin) and her children (Branwen, Oriana, and Cael), leads two Girl Scout troops, and loves reading and her daily yoga practice.

1 UNDERSTANDING INTERPERSONAL COMMUNICATION

WHAT YOU'LL LEARN...

When you have finished the chapter, you should be able to do the following:

1.1 Define interpersonal communication.

1.2 Describe the various components within a transactional model of communication.

1.3 Describe the different codes/elements of nonverbal and verbal communication.

1.4 Be able to describe different types of communication and behavior and how they vary in terms of intent and reception.

1.5 Explain what it means to be a competent communicator.

Sydney is nervous and excited as she waits to be checked into her dorm room at her new university. She looks around at the other new students in line. Are they as nervous as she is? Some of them are quiet and look a little anxious, but others are already chatting and getting to know one another. Sydney doesn't want anyone to think she is nervous, so she tries to look calm. At one point she pulls her cell phone out and sends a couple of messages to friends from high school so that she isn't just standing there looking around. When Sydney gets to the front of the line, a friendly looking young woman smiles and asks for her name. "Sydney Coleman," she replies. The woman introduces herself as Hannah and tells her that she is one of the residence hall assistants. Hannah looks Sydney's name up, hands her a small envelope with a key, and then starts giving her directions to her room. There is so much noise behind them, however, that Sydney can't hear the directions. Seeing the confusion on Sydney's face, Hannah pauses, leans forward, and repeats the directions a little more loudly. Sydney thanks Hannah and heads off to find her room, excited to start a new adventure in her life.

Humans are social creatures. Indeed, one of the primary ways humans differ from the rest of the animal kingdom is that people can communicate with one another in highly sophisticated ways, such as being able to provide one another with detailed directions or flash someone a meaningful look. The ability to communicate effectively is a highly developed skill that improves people's lives by affording them more opportunities and better relationships. For Sydney, her new life as a college student is likely to be a more positive experience if she has the communication skills necessary to meet new people, get along with her dormmates, and develop new friendships. Ironically, however, the average person receives very little, if any, formal training on how to communicate verbally and nonverbally. Think of all the time you have spent in classrooms learning to read and write. In comparison, you have probably had little, if any, education regarding how to communicate verbally and nonverbally during interactions with others. Yet most people spend as much time communicating with others as they do reading and writing, and much of people's writing is done in the context of communicating via sources such as text messaging or email.

In the 21st century, communication has, in some ways, become even more complicated because of all the technology people have at their disposal. Being a good communicator not only entails being able to converse with others in face-to-face contexts, but it also requires being able to understand the art of communicating via channels such as text messaging, social media, and email. Various means of communication are literally at people's fingertips. The prevalence and availability of different forms of communication can lead people to take their skills for granted and to see communication as simple and intuitive rather than complicated and in need of practice.

Whether people are interacting face-to-face or through technology, communication makes things happen. If you want to meet someone, start a relationship, join a group, persuade someone to do something, obtain a new job, understand someone from a different culture, or change something you don't like in a relationship, you need communication to reach your goal. Sydney will need communication to navigate through her new environment, make new friends, and succeed as a student. This is why this book takes a functional approach to interpersonal communication. A functional approach is grounded in the idea that communication makes things happen; this approach focuses on how people use communication to fulfill goals and accomplish everyday tasks. The functional approach also examines what nonverbal and verbal messages mean in a given context (Burgoon et al., 2013; Patterson, 1983).

The remaining chapters in this book focus on different functions of interpersonal communication, such as how communication helps people display identity, make positive impressions, develop relationships, maintain relationships, express and manage emotion, and engage in constructive conflict management, among other topics. To provide a foundation for these topics, this chapter describes the general process of communication.

WHAT IS INTERPERSONAL COMMUNICATION?

At a basic level, **interpersonal communication** involves the exchange of nonverbal and verbal messages between people who have some level of personal or social connection with one another. There are three key ideas embodied in this definition. First, messages are at the heart of the communication process. **Messages** are the information that is being exchanged. Messages can be verbal or nonverbal. In fact, people can use verbal and nonverbal communication at the same time or in sequences to send particular messages. For example, imagine that upon meeting her dormmate, Sydney smiles shyly and glances downward before looking up at her and saying, "Hi. It's nice to finally meet you in person." How would you interpret Sydney's communication? You might surmise she is a little shy or anxious but also excited to meet her new dormmate. Notice that it is the package of verbal and nonverbal messages that creates meaning in situations such as this.

Second, the term **exchange** is critical within this definition. For communication to occur, some scholars believe that the minimum requirement is that a sender must intentionally direct a message toward a receiver (Motley, 1990). Other scholars argue that the minimum requirement is that a receiver must attend to or interpret a message (Andersen, 1991). The idea of exchange captures this. For interpersonal communication to occur, there must be some level of exchange that includes a sender and a receiver. Either a sender must direct a message toward a receiver, or a receiver must attend to something another person says or does and interpret that message. Many behaviors go unnoticed by others or, even if they are noticed, no meaning is attached to them. Think about all the behaviors you engage in while sitting in a classroom listening to a lecture. You probably take notes, get restless and fidget, rearrange your legs under your desk, or stretch at some point. If no one notices any of these behaviors or attaches meaning to them, you are not communicating with anyone.

Third, not all communication between people qualifies as interpersonal communication; interpersonal communication occurs between those who have (or would like to have) some type of social or personal connection with each other. So, hitting the chat button on Amazon's website and asking a customer service representative about the process for exchanging a defective item would not be classified as interpersonal communication in most situations. Instead, this is a business transaction where you would simply be exchanging basic and impersonal information with no intention of ever interacting again or building any type of real connection with the representative.

As this example illustrates, interpersonal communication involves exchanging information that is personal rather than impersonal. This is what helps distinguish interpersonal communication from more generic forms of communication. For instance, when you buy groceries, you interact with the cashier. Pleasantries such as, "Did you find everything you needed?" and "Yes, thank you," might be exchanged, but the interaction is likely to follow a typical script for how people act when checking out at a grocery store. Now imagine instead that you know something personal about the cashier. The last time you were in her line you saw a bunch of kids excitedly waving at her and calling out, "Hi, Miss Jada!" This prompted a short conversation where you learned that in addition to being a cashier, Jada babysits a group of kids after school for a couple of hours every day and also takes a couple of night classes at the university. The next time Jada rings up your purchases, you ask her if she is still babysitting and how her classes are going. Then you both disclose that you are struggling to balance everything in your lives. When she hands you your receipt, she says "Good luck with everything," You reply "You too," and then you take your bags and go. Most people would agree that there is a qualitative difference between this interaction and the typical way most people communicate with a cashier at a grocery store—it is more interpersonal and less scripted.

As this scenario shows, communication is more personal when it involves going outside of the traditional script for a given interaction, usually because people have gained personal knowledge of one another. This makes the communication unique. When people have a unique relational history, including shared experiences, inside jokes, or knowledge of private information, their history shapes how they communicate with each other, much as in the example with Jada.

Another way that personal communication differs from impersonal communication is the type of influence people have on one another. The more people influence one another's thoughts, emotions, and behaviors, the more personal the interaction is. Think about the interactions in the checkout line described earlier. In the first interaction, only behavior would be affected. The cashier would greet you, you would respond, they would eventually hand you the receipt, and you would probably say "thanks" and leave. In the second interaction, you might feel anxious when talking about trying to balance everything in your life but then feel a sense of comfort knowing that Jada is in a similar situation. Indeed, you might think that Jada is even busier than you are, which could motivate you to do better. This second interaction is clearly more personal than the first.

Your unshared thoughts are considered intrapersonal rather than interpersonal communication. Interpersonal communication involves an exchange of messages between a sender and a receiver. If no receiver is present, interpersonal communication cannot take place.

iStock/splendens

The definition of interpersonal communication as "an exchange of messages between people" still leaves some room for interpretation. Traditionally, communication with oneself, such as Sydney thinking, "I'm nervous but I'll get through this," has been defined as **intrapersonal communication**. There is little disagreement regarding this definition. There is, however, some disagreement about *how many people* are involved in interpersonal communication. Some communication researchers believe interpersonal communication involves two people, group communication involves three or more people, and public communication involves one person talking to many. While this might be an easy way to classify different levels of communication, using the number of people involved in the interaction misses what truly distinguishes interpersonal communication from other types of communication—the personal nature of the communication. Think about this: If you are having a personal conversation with a close friend and another close friend walks over and joins you, how does the situation change? Rather than communicating within a dyad, you are now communicating within a small group. Does this mean that the conversation among these three friends is no longer considered interpersonal communication? We would suggest that it is still interpersonal communication because of the types of messages being exchanged, but it is interpersonal communication within a small group rather than within a dyad. From this perspective, communication within a family, friend group, or broader social network can be considered interpersonal communication.

A MODEL OF INTERPERSONAL COMMUNICATION

When interpersonal communication was first studied in college classrooms, most students were introduced to a linear model of communication that included a sender, a receiver, and a message that is delivered through a specific channel, such as through written or spoken words (Berlo, 1960; Shannon & Weaver, 1949). While these elements of the communication process are still important, they are no longer considered separate from one another. Communicators are both sender and receiver in most interactions, and the message one person sends may provide feedback to another person. Thus, communication is best viewed as a dynamic process that involves a series of moves and countermoves between people who are (sometimes simultaneously) sending and receiving multiple messages. The **transactional model of communication** (Barnlund, 2008; Watzlawick et al., 1967) is based on these ideas. This model (see Figure 1.1) includes the following elements: communicators, encoding and decoding, message, feedback, channel, field of experience, and noise.

FIGURE 1.1 ■ The Process of Communication

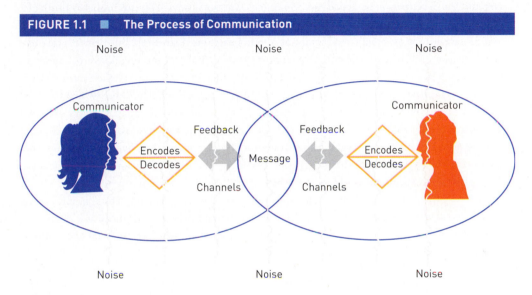

Communicators: Encoding and Decoding

During the communication process, **communicators** are actively involved in sending and receiving messages. Being a sender involves **encoding** messages. To encode a message, you need to take an idea or information and translate it into a code that you can use to communicate that message. Codes include words as well as nonverbal behaviors, such as smiling, gesturing, or using a sarcastic tone of voice. Some messages are encoded strategically. In these cases, you may carefully plan what you are going to say and how you are going to say it. Other messages are encoded spontaneously, as a natural reaction to something. You might laugh at a friend's funny remark or yell out an obscenity when you stub your toe.

Being a receiver involves **decoding** messages. To decode a message, you attend to and interpret the words or behaviors of another person. Put another way, you make sense of and attach meaning to the messages produced by someone. When a message has a clear meaning within a given context, the decoding process can be straightforward. For example, messages such as telling someone to turn left at a stop sign, smiling when receiving an especially nice gift, and speaking in a nervous-sounding voice are likely to be interpreted similarly by most receivers. Other messages are more ambiguous and difficult to interpret correctly. Extended eye contact can be intended to show affection or to intimidate someone. Asking an acquaintance "Are you talking to anyone right now?" could be interpreted as a simple question, an attempt at small talk, or a sign of romantic interest. During the communication process, decoding is hit and miss. You are likely to interpret a lot of messages correctly, but you are also likely to misinterpret some messages. A classic study by Noller (1980) helps illustrate this point. In this study, husbands tended to interpret their wives' vocal tones as unpleasant or hostile when the wives actually considered their tones to be neutral. When husbands overestimated the amount of negativity in their wives' voices, both husbands and wives reported being less satisfied in their relationships.

Sometimes the roles of sender and receiver, and the activities of encoding and decoding, are distinguishable, but more often they overlap. Think about what the communication process would look like if you could freeze it by taking a photo. In the photo, would one person be encoding and the other person be decoding? Sometimes, but not always. You can probably think of a time when these roles were, at least temporarily, distinct. For example, one friend might be listening carefully as the other friend is talking about something distressing. But even in a case like this, the friend who is in the listening (or receiving) role may also be sending nonverbal messages by trying to look empathetic and concerned. The sending and receiving roles are most distinct when communication is delayed. Snapchatting and texting are examples of this. When you send a snap or compose a text, you are in the sender role; when you look at a snap or read a text, you are in the receiver role. However, during most communication transactions, these roles overlap; people send and receive messages at the same time. For example, when Sydney walks into her new dormitory, she smiles so that she appears friendly and relaxed rather than nervous (encoding) while looking around at others to see how they are acting and reacting to her (decoding). This is why the transactional model uses the more general term "communicators" to refer to the people in the model rather than classifying one person as a sender and the other as a receiver, as the linear model did. The transitional model emphasizes that most interpersonal communication involves simultaneous sending and receiving.

In this instance, who appears to be in the sending role and who appears to be in the receiving role? How might this change throughout the interaction?

iStock/gradyreese

Messages

Messages are at the heart of the communication process because they contain the information that people exchange during an interaction. Multiple messages are often exchanged during an interaction. In her brief interaction with Sydney, Hannah sent messages related to friendliness (by smiling), authority (by saying she was a residence hall assistant), and competence (by adjusting her message so Sydney would understand the directions).

Notice that messages can be either verbal or nonverbal. The information people exchange through verbal and nonverbal messages allows people to share thoughts, emotions, and ideas. Of course, not all messages are exchanged in ways that produce shared meaning between communicators. For example, directions may not be fully comprehended or a friendly smile may be interpreted as condescending. This is one reason why people commonly give and look for feedback from others. **Feedback** refers to the messages you receive from others in response to your communication as well as the messages you send to others in response to their communication. In the interaction between Sydney and Hannah, feedback plays a critical role in creating shared meaning. Hannah sees that Sydney looks confused and adjusts her communication by leaning forward and repeating the directions. The confusion on Sydney's face provided valuable feedback that Hannah used to communicate more effectively. Sydney then responds by thanking her, which provides further feedback that Hannah has accomplished her goal of helping Sydney. Many of the messages people send provide this type of feedback.

The other essential component related to messages is the **channel** of communication. The channel is the means by which a message is sent from sender to receiver. When most people think about interpersonal communication, they envision face-to-face communication between people. However, communication can occur in many other channels, including writing, talking on the phone, texting, Snapchatting, emailing, Facetiming, and posting messages on social media, just to name a few channels. When technology is part of the channel, the communication is referred to as **mediated communication**.

The channel of communication matters. Think about how you might wish a friend a happy birthday. Do you post a message on your friend's Facebook or Twitter page? Is this different than sending your friend a card or calling your friend on the phone to say happy birthday? Or perhaps you decide to post something on Instagram or to Facetime your friend. Most people would agree that you would choose the channel based on a number of different factors, including convenience, how close you are to the friend, and what you wanted to communicate beyond just saying "Happy Birthday." Indeed, the channel can shape the kind of message you send. For a friend's birthday, you might post a collage of photos showcasing some of your memories together on your Instagram story. Or you could post a video on your Twitter account with a song in the background and a happy birthday message. These types of messages are public and show others that you are close. On the other hand, you could send a direct message to your friend, keeping it private. Or you could Facetime and have an extended private conversation that could get highly personal. The choices people make about the channels they use are influenced by the type of messages they wish to exchange.

It is important to recognize that verbal and nonverbal messages are embedded within broader channels of communication. For example, in face-to-face interaction and some mediated forms of communication, such as Facetime, people say words and display facial expressions. When communicating via other forms of mediated communication, such as email and text messaging, people type words and use emoticons (such as winking or smiling faces). Thus, both verbal and nonverbal channels are present whether communication is face-to-face or through technology.

People can communicate through multiple channels simultaneously. This mother and daughter are using their faces, hands, webcam, and laptop to video chat with someone.

iStock/fizkes

The difference is not as much about the distinction between face-to-face and mediated communication as it is about the degree to which people see one another while interacting and the degree to which messages are synchronous. During face-to-face communication and when communicating using technologies that allow partners to see one another, a wider variety of nonverbal cues are available for both encoding and decoding. Communication is also more synchronous when people can see and/or hear one another, meaning that it occurs in real time with the possibility of continuous feedback. Face-to-face communication where people are physically present, live interactions using media (such as Facetime, Zoom, or Skype), and voice-to-voice conversations on the telephone are all examples of synchronous communication. On the other hand, when people communicate using computer-mediated channels such as email, text messaging, and Snapchatting, as well as social networking sites such as Instagram, Facebook, and Twitter, they have more control over the interaction. They can carefully compose and revise a message before sending it, they can decide what photos (if any) to post, and they can delay responding to someone if they are not sure what to write or what picture to send.

Field of Experience and Noise

Finally, two other components of the transactional model are field of experience and noise. Every person brings a unique set of perceptions, attitudes, beliefs, and experiences to the communication table, which is sometimes referred to as a **field of experience**. This helps explain why two people might interpret the same message differently. Imagine that when Hannah paused, leaned forward, and repeated the directions, Sydney took this behavior as an indication that Hannah thought she was stupid and needed to hear the directions twice. Based on her experiences, this interpretation may make sense. Perhaps Sydney had a parent who always repeated everything because she thought Sydney would not get the message the first time. As a result, Sydney would be prone to misinterpret Hannah's message that way, whereas another person with a different set of experiences would be grateful that Hannah repeated the message.

Field of experience also includes (1) your cultural background and history of interactions with specific people and (2) your interactional partner's culture and history of interactions with you. Imagine going to the airport to pick up a business associate who is from a different country. When you extend your hand to shake hers, there is an awkward pause, after which she smiles awkwardly and shakes your hand. If she is from a culture where people bow rather than shake hands, she may have interpreted your handshake as overly forward. On the other hand, if she is from a culture where people commonly hug or kiss cheeks upon greeting, she may have regarded your handshake as too formal. Either way, her field of experience impacts how she interprets and responds to your handshake.

Words can also be interpreted very differently depending on culture. To illustrate this, Agar (2012) gave an example of a conversation he had with a friend from Austria. She asked him what a "date" was. It became clear that she understood how people in the United States used the word in sentences, such as saying they were going on date, and that she also understood that the word "date" could refer to a day or a piece of fruit, but she still did not grasp the full meaning of the word as used by people from the United States. Agar (2012) explained that despite his best efforts, it was challenging to explain the US concept of a date to her. As he put it:

> I started to answer, and the more I talked the more lost I became in how Americans see men and women, how they see relationships, intimacy—a host of connected assumptions that I'd never put into words before. And I was only trying to handle straight dates. It was quite different from her Austrian understanding of men and women and what they are to each other. For a while she looked at me as if I'd just stepped out of a flying saucer, until she finally decided I was serious. (p. 15)

Even within the United States, the words "date" and "dating" differ in meaning depending on a person's background. For example, there are generational differences in what it means to be "dating." For younger generations, this can mean that you are in a relationship; for older generations, it can mean that you are casually going out with someone and seeing where things go. The point is that people's backgrounds heavily influence how verbal and nonverbal messages are decoded.

Similarly, your history of interactions influences how you interpret messages. If one of your friends is acting shy and not talking much at a party, you might think nothing of it because this is how your friend normally acts. With a different friend, however, you might correctly assume that he is upset or depressed since he is usually outgoing at parties. Sometimes, field of experience helps people interpret messages more accurately; other times, it leads to messages being misinterpreted.

Noise can lead people to either misinterpret or completely miss messages. **Noise** occurs when something interferes with the sending or receiving of messages, often reducing the degree to which there is shared meaning between communicators. Noise can be external, such as when fans are cheering at a football game and you cannot hear what your friends are saying, or when you get distracted and cannot concentrate on the lecture after seeing people walking outside from your classroom window. Noise can also be internal, such as when you have trouble listening or comprehending messages because you have a headache, are preoccupied with something (such as a speech you have to give), or are daydreaming about a loved one. In sum, anything that distracts you from the messages you are sending or receiving is a form of noise that can reduce shared meaning during an interaction.

TYPES OF MESSAGES

As you already learned, communication is composed of both nonverbal and verbal messages. But you may not know that nonverbal messages often constitute more of the meaning in a given interaction than do verbal messages. One reason for this is that nonverbal communication is **multimodal**. This means that we can communicate through more than one nonverbal mode or channel simultaneously. For example, you can wave, smile, and move toward someone all at the same time. In contrast, we can only say one word at a time. Next, we define nonverbal communication and review the various channels or "codes" that make up nonverbal communication.

Nonverbal Messages

Nonverbal communication has been defined various ways (Burgoon et al., 2022). When people hear the term "nonverbal communication," they typically think of body language. However, nonverbal communication includes much more than this. **Nonverbal communication** comprises nonlinguistic behaviors that are sent or received during the communication process. The key concept here is "nonlinguistic." While it might be tempting to think that nonverbal communication includes all messages that are not spoken, this is too simplistic. Instead, it is more accurate to think of nonverbal messages as behaviors that are not directly related to words, whether spoken or unspoken. For instance, American Sign Language is an unspoken language, but it is based on words. Therefore, many people consider it language rather than nonverbal communication. **Language** is a method of human communication that uses words. Nonverbal communication, in contrast, uses nonlinguistic forms of communication.

I DIDN'T KNOW THAT!
THE ROLE NONVERBAL BEHAVIOR PLAYS IN THE COMMUNICATION PROCESS

As we grow up, we spend a considerable portion of our time in school learning the rules for speaking and writing language. In contrast, most people never get any formal training in how to communicate effectively nonverbally. Therefore, it might surprise you to learn that in many interactions, nonverbal communication carries more meaning than verbal communication. If this fact does not surprise you, you may have heard the estimate that 93 percent of all meaning in communication is derived from nonverbal cues, leaving only 7 percent of the meaning residing in verbal cues. A more conservative estimate is that around 66 percent (or two-thirds) of the meaning in most interactions is gleaned from nonverbal as opposed to verbal cues (Burgoon et al., 2022).

So which estimate is right? The answer is that it depends on the context. When people are trying to figure out a person's emotions, they are much more likely to look at nonverbal cues such as facial expressions than verbal statements. Similarly, when people are making first impressions, verbal communication is often scripted and superficial, so impressions are formed largely based on nonverbal cues such as appearance and facial expression. However, there are also times when verbal communication is dominant. For example, when you are listening to a lecture in class, you key in on what the professor is saying so that you understand the information. Regardless, nonverbal messages play a vital role in creating meaning across interactions. So, the next time you hear someone say that nonverbal communication is trivial, you can tell that person that nonverbal cues actually communicate as much or more than words do in many situations.

Another way to define nonverbal communication is to look at the codes that constitute it. A **code** is a set of signals that is transmitted through a particular medium or channel. Nonverbal communication consists of the following codes: kinesics, vocalics, proxemics, haptics, appearance and adornment, artifacts and environmental cues, and chronemic cues. Next, we define each of these codes and discuss some of the key research related to them.

Kinesics

This code is similar to what people commonly refer to as body language. **Kinesics** includes facial expressions, body movements, and eye behavior, such as smiling, posture, and pupil dilation. Researchers have classified kinesic behavior into five categories: emblems, illustrators, affect displays, regulators, and adaptors (Ekman & Friesen, 1969). **Emblems** are behaviors that substitute for words. Examples include waving to say "hello" and crossing one's fingers to say "good luck." **Illustrators** are kinesic behaviors that describe or emphasize something. You might pretend to swing a bat, point left while giving directions, or indicate how tall something is by reaching into the air. **Affect displays** show emotion. Smiling to show happiness, slumping when depressed, and clenching your fist when angry are all examples. **Regulators** help manage interaction and include behavior such as raising your hand when you want to speak, avoiding eye contact when you want someone else to speak, and leaning backward when you are content to let someone else do the talking. Finally, **adaptors** are idiosyncratic behaviors that people engage in, often by habit, when they are nervous or restless. Tapping a pencil on a desk, playing with one's hair or jewelry, and shaking one's leg nervously are all adaptors.

The same kinesic behavior can be classified in different ways. For example, this hand gesture is an emblem that means "stop," but the woman in the picture is also using it as a regulator to stop an interaction and an affect display to show her negative emotion.

iStock/Tharakorn

Vocalics

The **vocalics** code includes the way words are spoken, along with pauses and silences that occur during an interaction. Vocalic behaviors such as vocal pitch, loudness, accent, tone, and speed have all been studied, as have vocalizations such as crying and sighing. Researchers have studied baby talk as a form of flirtation and have shown that softer, higher-pitched voices communicate affection and intimacy (Burgoon et al., 2022). Vocalized pauses, such as saying "um" when nervous, are also part of the vocalic code. Research has shown that vocalic behaviors are difficult to control and, therefore, might provide useful information when trying to determine how a person feels.

Proxemics

The **proxemics** code revolves around the use of space, including conversational distances and territory. People have been shown to guard and defend their territories, especially their personal belongings and private spaces, such as their bedrooms. You might mark your territory with a "do not disturb" sign or put your backpack on your desk to reserve it. These are territorial markers that help you regulate your privacy. People also use different conversational distances depending on the type of interaction they are having (Hall, 1990). In the United States, the **intimate zone** stretches from 0 to 18 inches. This close distancing is typically reserved for interactions with close friends and loved ones or conversations about very personal issues. The edge of the intimate zone also demarcates your **personal space bubble**, which is an invisible, adjustable bubble of space that you carry around with you. People usually respect this space and do not enter it unless they are invited to or have a particularly close relationship with you. The **personal zone** in the United States ranges from 18 inches to 4 feet. This is where most of our social interactions with casual friends, acquaintances, and sometimes co-workers occur. The **social zone** runs from 4 to 12 feet and is the distance at which many impersonal conversations take place. The idea of social distance took on a new meaning in 2020 during the COVID-19 pandemic when people were asked to keep a distance of at least 6 feet between themselves and others in public places. The social zone became the "new norm" in many ways. Finally, the **public zone** starts at 12 feet and expands out from there. This zone is where public forms of communication, such as a professor lecturing or a boss giving a presentation, frequently occur. Keep in mind that these conversational zones are specific to the United States. In other parts of the world, these zones can either be larger or smaller, so it is important not to assume that proxemic norms within one given culture translate to another culture.

Haptics

The **haptics** code references touch as a form of communication. Touch and proxemics are related to each other; the distancing between people helps define whether touch will or should occur. Considerable research has shown that touch is an essential ingredient for healthy social and physical development. Early work demonstrated that children in orphanages tended to get sicker and engage in more antisocial behavior if they were not touched (Montagu, 1978). Recent work has shown that affectionate touch, such as hugging and kissing, is related to a number of health benefits, such as decreases in stress hormones, increases in oxytocin (a hormone that promotes a positive mood), and decreases in blood pressure and blood sugar (Floyd, 2006; Floyd et al., 2005, 2009). Touch is a particularly powerful nonverbal code. On the one hand, touch can communicate messages related to intimacy, affection, and support; on the other hand, touch can be violent.

These two women are communicating within the intimate zone and might easily touch. What assumptions might you make about their relationship based on this? What other nonverbal cues are they displaying that affect how you would perceive their relationship?

iStock/Drazen Zigic

These shoppers in Peru are following social distancing guidelines during the COVID-19 pandemic in 2020 by standing within Hall's social zone, at around 6 feet apart. How do you think this spacing affects the shopping experience? How different would spacing have looked if this was taken prior to the pandemic?

Sebastian Enriquez/AFP via Getty Images

Appearance and Adornment

Physical attributes such as height, weight, and attractiveness, as well as adornments such as clothing, perfume, and tattoos, all fall under the appearance and adornment code. Research has shown that people make judgments based on appearance cues. For example, as discussed in Chapter 3, when people are especially good-looking, others tend to attribute all sorts of positive internal characteristics to them (outgoing, fun, intelligent) but also some negative characteristics (superficial, conceited). Fortunately, how people communicate also makes a difference (Albada et al., 2002). If you have a fun, positive interaction with someone, you are likely to rate that person as more attractive than you would if your interaction with them had been awkward or boring. Additionally, other aspects of our appearance, such as the clothing we choose to wear, can communicate messages about the type of person we are.

Artifacts and Environmental Cues

The environment and objects in the environment, such as furniture and pictures, can set the tone for certain times of interaction. Think about the difference between going to a football game with friends versus a play. The game is likely noisy and crowded, so you and your friends are more likely to talk loudly. Whether your team is winning or losing will also affect your moods and therefore your communication. At the play, you will likely be focused on the stage. You and your friends might exchange looks or whisper a comment or two. Sometimes, we intentionally manipulate the environment to create a particular atmosphere for interaction, such as lighting a fire in the fireplace and playing soft music to make a date more romantic.

Chronemic Cues

The use of time to communicate messages, or **chronemics**, is one of the less obvious nonverbal codes. Nonetheless, time can send powerful interpersonal messages. Think about how you feel if someone shows up really early to the party you are hosting or really late for a date. What if someone starts taking longer than usual to reply to your Snapchat messages or leaves you on "read" for a while before answering your text? Such behavior can cause uncertainty or conflict within relationships. Other chronemic behaviors, such as spending extra time with someone or cutting a visit short, also send strong messages about the type of relationship we have with someone.

People sometimes read a lot into time. If someone is not answering your messages, you might wonder what it means to the point of continually looking at your phone to see if a new message is there or even checking someone's Snapchat score to see if they have been on the phone.

iStock/Prostock-Studio

Verbal Messages

Verbal communication comprises spoken or written words that are sent or received during the communication process. Language organizes words so that they represent things, thoughts, emotions, and abstract ideas. Specifically, **language** is a system of words that is made up of letters or symbols that work together in a structured way to convey meaning. Several types of rules govern the way language is structured and understood. **Constitutive rules** tell us what words represent (Searle, 1969) . For example, a tree could be called an "oogley" but in the English language, a tree (or a thing with a trunk, branches, and leaves) is called a "tree." This also illustrates the arbitrary nature of most words. There is no reason why a tree is called "tree" instead of "oogley." Over time, the word "tree" emerged. Notice also that the words used to describe a tree—such as "trunk," "branches," and "leaves"—are also arbitrary. **Phonological rules** tell people how to pronounce words within a given language. The word "branch" is pronounced differently in the United States versus Scotland, for example.

Syntactic, semantic, and pragmatic rules also govern language. **Syntax** involves the way words are arranged to form sentences. Different languages have different syntactic rules. In English, for example, adjectives come before nouns. So English speakers say "the green tree." But in some languages, such as Spanish and French, the adjective follows the noun, so speakers would say "el árbol verde" or "l'arbre vert," which translates to "the tree green." This is just one example of many syntactic differences among languages.

Semantics refers to the way people interpret and attach meaning to words and sentences. Importantly, when applying semantic rules, meaning is determined by looking at the other words and phrases within a conversation. Some words can have multiple meanings, such as a branch referring to the branch of a tree or a bank branch, or the idea that a person needs to "branch" out. The other words in a sentence help people know the correct interpretation. Connotation and denotation are also related to semantics. The **denotative meaning** of a word is its basic dictionary definition. For example, words like mansion, castle, and hovel could all be defined as dwellings where people live. The **connotative meaning** of a word is more subjective and contextual, and it includes feelings and states that we associate with a particular word. A mansion might be associated with wealth, a castle with royalty, and a hovel with poverty.

Finally, **pragmatics** is also associated with meaning, but in this case, meaning is gleaned through context, such as the situation or place where the interaction is occurring, the person who is speaking, or the relationship between the communicators. So if Su Lin tells James, "You seem cold," she could be referring to his body temperature or his attitude toward her. Based on the situation, James may be able to interpret Su Lin's comment correctly. If the room is cold and James is shivering, he might say "yeah" and then get himself a blanket. If he and Su Lin had an argument and he has been giving her the cold shoulder, he should know that she is talking about his behavior toward her.

These rules govern all language. Some types of language, however, are specific to certain relationships. Personal idioms and slang are examples of this. These, and other types of language that reflect and define interpersonal interaction, are discussed next.

Personal Idioms

Idioms are words or groups of words that have a special meaning that is not readily deducible. For example, English phrases such as "in a New York minute" or "you can't judge a book by its cover" have meaning beyond what the words themselves mean. When bilingual or multilingual speakers hear such phrases in English, they are often confused because the literal meaning does not make sense and they are not privy to the special meaning. **Personal idioms** are a subcategory of idioms that have special meaning known only to those in certain relationships or social groups. Common examples are nicknames, expressions of affection, and special names for others (Hopper et al., 1981). For example, Sydney might call her boyfriend "Boo," tell her best friend that she looks especially good by simply saying "slay," or refer to a guy that she and another friend dislike as "the snake." Outsiders are unlikely to understand the meaning of these terms (or know who "the snake" is); therefore, the use of these types of personal idioms signifies that people have unique relationships.

Slang and acronyms, which are abbreviations such as GOAT in this photo, tend to be understood by certain groups and not others. Identify the slang in this text message exchange. What are some of the common terms you and your friends use that are unique to your group or generation?

Courtesy of Laura Guerrero

Slang

Like personal idioms, **slang** encompasses informal words and phrases that are used more in speech than in writing and are only understood by certain people. However, while the meaning attached to personal idioms comes from within a relationship, circle of friends, or family members, the meaning attached to slang is understood by a broader group, such as those from the same generation or cultural group. Sydney and her college friends will likely understand what it means when one of them says, "I'm low-key down for that" or "That party was lit," but their parents or grandparents may not. Slang is typically temporary in nature and can change rapidly. Because of this, using and understanding slang indicates that people belong to a particular group, which can help create feelings of connectedness.

By the same token, slang can also create division and misunderstanding. Even people within the same generation sometimes define slang terms differently, as a perusal of *Urban Dictionary* will tell you. One study conducted at a high school found that slang reinforced some social and racial divisions between students. For example, many Black students said the term "jock" was a verb that meant to "hit on" or "flirt," whereas white students saw it as a noun to mean "athlete" (Bucholtz, 2012, p. 284). Black students also tended to interpret the term "notch" as something you would call someone who is attractive, making it a compliment, whereas white girls thought the term was derogatory. As you are reading these, you may or may not be familiar with these slang terms because they change quickly. This is part of why adolescents and young adults see slang as part of being cool; you have to be current to understand it (Bucholtz, 2012).

Storytelling

Verbal communication is also used to tell stories about people's relationships. These "stories are vehicles through which individuals link themselves as relational partners and characterize their joint relational identity" (Burleson et al., 2000, p. 253). People tell stories about how they first met, endured hardships, went on vacation, broke up and got back together again, attended a special event, and so forth. Sharing these stories with others and referring to elements of these stories within conversations with one another creates a sense of uniqueness and relational history that helps people define their relationships.

Verbal Tense

Storytelling is one way to remember and honor the history of a relationship. The use of past, present, and future tense can also do so. Talking in the past tense about what "we used to do" can showcase the stability of a relationship. Using present tense indicates that people are currently connected. Even simple statements, such as "I'm having so much fun right now," can express positive sentiments about how a current interaction is going. Finally, using future tense can be a significant indicator that a relationship is moving in a positive trajectory or that two people are (or are moving toward being) committed to one another or being long-term friends. For example, if Sydney's new dormmate starts talking about going to a concert in November, this statement shows a commitment to keep their new friendship in good standing until then.

Pronoun Use

Even the simple use of pronouns can reflect or affect the type of relationship that people share (Bartlett Ellis et al., 2016; Wiener & Mehrabian, 1968). One distinction is between "you" and "I." The context matters here. Using the "you" pronoun when making positive statements about another person makes the message personal. For example, Sydney might tell her new roommate, "You are really pretty," which would be perceived more positively than "I think you are really pretty." On the other hand, there are times when using the "I" pronoun allows people to take ownership of their statements rather than blaming the other person. Think about someone telling you that "you are so frustrating" versus "I feel so frustrated." When people hear the first statement, they are likely to feel insulted and get defensive. By contrast, the second statement is less threatening and may even prompt empathy.

SKILL BUILDER
USING "I" VERSUS "YOU" PRONOUNS

Sometimes it is better to use "I" pronouns. This is especially the case when you are discussing negative feelings or behaviors. If you own the behavior, it comes across as less critical and threatening, plus you "own" your thoughts and feelings rather than blaming your partner for them. By using "I" pronouns in these cases, you may also prompt your partner to feel empathy for you. This could lead to a conversation about how to fix the issues that are causing your negative thoughts or feelings.

"You" Statements That Show Blame	"I" Statements That Show Ownership
You make me feel really bad.	I feel really bad.
You are always so judgmental.	I feel like I'm being judged.
You are so confusing.	I am confused.
You are ruining everything.	I feel like everything is ruined.

There are cases, however, when using "you" statements is more effective than using "I" statements. These situations generally involve giving compliments and validating the other person. Look at the following statements. When you compliment someone directly by using the "you" pronoun, the statement comes across as a fact. When you change it to an "I" statement, this qualifies it. In other words, the person may think, "Okay, you think I'm kind but that doesn't mean others do, too." "You" statements are also especially effective when they give a person credit for something positive, such as making you feel happy.

"You" Statements That Give Direct Credit	"I" Statements That Fail to Give Direct Credit
You are so kind.	I think you are really kind.
You are good at that.	I think you are good at that.
You make me happy.	I am happy.
You make me feel so much better.	I feel so much better.

"We" is another pronoun that is significant within interpersonal interaction. When friends, couples, and family members use the pronoun "we," it not only symbolizes that they are a unit but also reflects that they are close and share a satisfying relationship (Dreyer et al., 1987; Honeycutt, 1999). In workplace relationships, "we" statements can create a sense of teamwork and community. Similarly, imagine one of your teachers saying, "We are going to talk about effective communication today" versus "I am going to talk about effective communication today." The first statement implies that the class is a unit and encourages discussion. The second statement implies that the teacher is in charge and will be lecturing without as much input from the class. Think of times when it would be more appropriate to use the "I" pronoun and others when it would be more appropriate to use the "we" pronoun. Can you think of a time when using one of these pronouns made you feel blamed or left out?

TYPES OF COMMUNICATION

As noted previously, encoding and decoding are important components within the communication process. Messages must either be encoded or decoded for communication to occur. In fact, researchers have debated what types of messages count as communication, in part by looking at issues related to encoding and decoding (Andersen, 1991; Motley, 1990). One of these issues is whether a message was encoded with intent. In other words, did someone send a message with the intent that someone would see and interpret it? The other issue is whether a message was actually received and interpreted by someone. When these two issues are considered, six possibilities emerge, as shown in Figure 1.2 (Guerrero & Floyd, 2006).

FIGURE 1.2 ■ Types of Communication and Behavior			
	Message Not Interpreted	Message Interpreted Inaccurately	Message Interpreted Accurately
Message Sent With Intent	**Attempted communication**	**Miscommunication**	**Successful communication**
Message Sent Without Intent	**Unattended behavior**	**Misinterpretation**	**Accidental communication**

Note that although these forms of communication are presented in isolation as if only one message occurs between two people in sending and receiving roles, the process of communication is more complex than this, with multiple messages being exchanged and people occupying the dual roles of sender and receiver. Nonetheless, understanding these types of communication helps describe the different types of messages that constitute the communication process. This model also suggests that there are things that people do and say that do not qualify as a message and instead are unattended behaviors.

Attempted Communication

Attempted communication occurs when a message that is sent with intent is not received. Sometimes this happens because the intended receiver simply misses the message. Have you ever tried to signal to someone that you wanted to end an interaction or leave a party, but the person didn't get the hint? Perhaps you used leave-taking behaviors such as looking at the time on your cell phone and saying something like "it's getting late" but the person just kept on talking. If the person was oblivious to the fact that you wanted to go, then your attempt at communication failed. Communication can fail for other reasons. You might call to your roommate and not get a response because he or she is listening to music with earphones on, or a room might be so noisy that you can't hear a message, as was the case when Hannah was trying to give Sydney directions.

Miscommunication

Miscommunication occurs when a message is sent with intent but is interpreted inaccurately. This form of communication occurs quite frequently. Perhaps a smile that you meant to be merely polite is interpreted as flirtatious, or a question that you posed out of interest is taken as a challenge. These are examples of miscommunication. Sometimes miscommunication occurs because people are too quick to jump to conclusions or because they think they know someone better than they do. Gottman (1994) discussed the concept of **mindreading** as a potential problem in relationships. Mindreading occurs when people assume they know how their partner is thinking or feeling. Oftentimes, these kinds of assumptions are wrong and can lead to miscommunication.

Successful Communication

Successful communication occurs when a person sends a message with intent and a receiver attends to and interprets that message correctly. This type of communication is often considered ideal because there is shared meaning. In other words, the sender and receiver agree regarding the meaning of a message. When Sydney thanks Hannah, both women interpret Sydney's words as a polite expression of gratitude. Since this is what Sydney meant to convey, the words have shared meaning and successful communication has occurred. Most interactions do not result in 100 percent shared meaning since communicators cannot get inside one another's heads, but people sometimes get close to that goal. Successful communication is the prototypical type of communication and is what most people think of as "good" communication.

Unattended Behavior

Unattended behavior is not considered important within the communication process because it does not involve encoding or decoding. With unattended behavior, people emit behaviors unintentionally, and no one notices or interprets those behaviors as meaningful. As you are reading this chapter, you are blinking but you probably didn't even realize that until now. Behaviors such as normal blinking are unintentional, automatic behaviors that neither senders nor receivers tend to notice. Similarly, behaviors that are not directed at anyone and go unnoticed, such as stretching your legs under your desk where no one can see them, are unattended behaviors that are not part of the communication process. At a minimum, then, verbal and nonverbal behaviors need to be either encoded or decoded for them to count as communication. This is why the terms "behavior" and "communication" are not synonymous; many behaviors go unnoticed and do not constitute communication.

Misinterpretation

Misinterpretation occurs when a sender does not intentionally send a message, yet something the sender says or does is interpreted incorrectly by a receiver. If you are having a bad day and some of the negativity that you are feeling shows in your face, a friend might think you are mad at them when you are not. Similarly, if you are tired and having trouble paying attention to what others are saying, people might think that you are uninterested in the topic at hand when you would actually be excited about the topic if you weren't so tired. The key here is that the sender did not mean to send a message, but the receiver attached meaning to the sender's behavior anyway, and the meaning they attached was wrong.

Accidental Communication

Accidental communication occurs when a sender does not intend to send a message, yet a receiver still notices and correctly interprets the sender's behavior. In the scenario at the beginning of this chapter, Sydney tries to cover up her nervousness by looking calm and keeping herself busy by sending messages on her cell phone. Her intention is to send out the message that she is composed and confident. However, suppose that a few of the other students see the worry in her eyes and notice that she is a little fidgety before reaching for her cell phone. They correctly interpret her behavior as reflecting nervousness. In this case, Sydney did not intend to show people she was nervous, yet some people still interpreted her behavior that way. Such is the case with accidental communication.

Spontaneous expressions may not be directed to anyone, yet these unintentional actions can still send very clear messages about how someone is feeling.

Alex Livesey/Getty Images

COMMUNICATION COMPETENCE

Take another look at the boxes in Figure 1.2. Which type of communication is likely considered most competent? Most people would say successful communication because the message was decoded accurately and shared meaning was created. Shared meaning is often the primary goal of communication because people usually need to get their point across to reach other goals, including self-presentational goals, relational goals, and instrumental goals (Clark & Delia, 1979). **Self-presentational goals** revolve around presenting yourself in a positive way so people accept and like you. **Relational goals** involve being able to successfully navigate relationships, including being able to initiate, develop, maintain, and end relationships. Finally, **instrumental goals** involve being able to get tasks done, including getting someone to help you with something, changing someone's opinion, and resisting someone else's attempts to influence you. In many cases, reaching these goals requires at least some degree of shared meaning between sender and receiver.

Within the context of interpersonal interaction, **communication competence** refers to the degree to which a person successfully uses communication to meet goals. Moreover, competent communication is characterized as effective and appropriate. Communication is *effective* when it achieves the goal or task it is directed toward (Spitzberg & Cupach, 2012). Sometimes goals are simple, such as appearing friendly by saying "hi" to an acquaintance. Other times, goals are complex, such as managing conflict with a co-worker or telling someone you would rather stay friends than start a romantic relationship. Communication is *appropriate* when it tactful and polite and does not violate social norms, rules, or expectations (Spitzberg & Cupach, 2012). So, forcing someone to do something they do not want to do is effective but not appropriate. On the other hand, being too polite to stand up for yourself during a conflict situation may be appropriate, but it is not effective.

To better understand the process of communication competence, Spitzberg and Cupach (1984) advanced the component model of competence. This model includes *motivation*, *knowledge*, and *skill*. Motivation and knowledge are precursors to being able to communicate competently (Spitzberg & Cupach, 1984, 1989). To be competent communicators, people must be motivated to approach people and situations and then act. They must also have the knowledge to be competent communicators. Just being motivated to communicate is not enough; you have to know *how* to communicate. Having knowledge about social norms as well as personal knowledge about the person with whom you are communicating is part of this. Such knowledge helps a communicator make good decisions about how to act in effective and appropriate ways. Skill is then necessary to carry out those actions. People who have communication skills know how to adapt their communication so that they say and do the right things within a given situation.

Different skills are also relevant based on the situation. Thus, throughout this book, we will be discussing various skills related to particular topics. For example, we will discuss emotional intelligence in Chapter 6 on emotions and conflict management skills in Chapter 10 on conflict. For now, we review six fundamental skills that help communicators be more competent: encoding ability and expressiveness, decoding ability, interaction management, composure, attentiveness and empathy, and adaptability (see Figure 1.3).

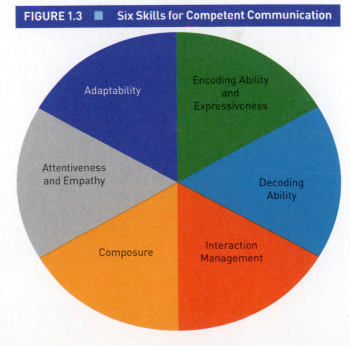

FIGURE 1.3 ■ Six Skills for Competent Communication

- Adaptability
- Encoding Ability and Expressiveness
- Decoding Ability
- Interaction Management
- Composure
- Attentiveness and Empathy

Encoding Ability and Expressiveness

Some people are especially good at expressing themselves in ways that show their feelings and allow them to connect with others (Riggio, 1986). Good encoders also manage their expressions to hide feelings that might be seen as inappropriate. People who are high in encoding ability tend to be extroverted and expressive and have large social networks. They are also adept at monitoring their behavior and influencing others (Burgoon et al., 2022). Encoding ability is related to the broader skill of expressiveness, which includes being open, articulate, nonverbally dynamic, and likeable (Spitzberg, 2015).

Decoding Ability

People who are skilled in decoding are observant and able to interpret the behaviors of others correctly. They are good at sizing up people and making favorable first impressions, and they also tend to be highly sociable (Burgoon et al., 2022). Being able to decode communication accurately leads to less miscommunication and misinterpretation. Research suggests that encoding and decoding abilities are related and that, on average, women are better at encoding and decoding nonverbal behavior than are men (Burgoon et al., 2022). As you will learn later in this book, it is also important to recognize that messages have different meanings depending on culture and context. Good decoders try to look beyond their own field of experience when interpreting messages and check for understanding.

Interaction Management

Being able to manage or coordinate interaction is another critical communication skill (Backlund & Morreales, 2015; Capella, 1994). This includes engaging in smooth turn-taking, speaking when appropriate, and knowing when to listen to others. Individuals with this skill can also direct the flow of an interaction by introducing new topics and shifting away from old ones, asking questions, interrupting when necessary, using an appropriate amount of talk time, and changing the intonation of one's voice (Spitzberg, 2015; Spitzberg & Cupach, 1984). Being able to manage interaction in these ways helps people facilitate the type of communication that helps them reach their goals.

Composure

Most people have been in situations where it was difficult to stay composed. You can probably recall times when you were nervous, uncomfortable, or angry, and the people around you could readily see those feelings despite your efforts to look calm and composed. Although there are times when nervousness is endearing and anger is justifiable, there are also times when it is in people's best interest to look composed. Behaviors such as speaking in a calm and confident voice, having an open posture, speaking fluently, and using expressive rather than nervous gestures (such as fidgeting) give an impression of composure and confidence (Spitzberg, 2015). People who display such behaviors, especially when under stress or pressure, are rated as good leaders and seen as assertive and persuasive.

Attentiveness and Empathy

Competent communicators make other people feel valued. They act interested in what others are saying and are supportive and empathetic (Backlund & Morreales, 2015; Spitzberg, 2015).

People show attentiveness through listening, nodding to show agreement, using backchanneling cues such as "Aha!," being expressive and animated, leaning forward, and giving eye contact (Coker & Burgoon, 1987; Spitzberg, 2015). These behaviors show that a person is an active participant in a conversation. They also validate the other communicator by making them feel like what they have to say is important. Empathy, which is a "social and emotional skill that helps us feel and understand the emotions, circumstances, intentions, thoughts, and needs of others, such that we can offer sensitive, perceptive, and appropriate communication and support" goes a step further (McLaren, 2013, p. 27). There are two specific components of empathy—affective and cognitive (Lawrence et al., 2004). **Affective empathy** involves feeling what others feel, whereas **cognitive empathy** involves being able to put oneself in another person's place to understand that person's perspective. When people experience empathy, they better understand others, which makes them better at decoding as well as crafting appropriate messages that lead to shared meaning.

Listening attentively and providing support are cornerstones for being a competent communicator.

iStock/Jgalione

Adaptability

Finally, being able to adapt one's communication based on context is a highly important communication skill. Context involves a number of factors, including (a) the situation, (b) the other communicator's personality, (c) the type of relationship you have with the other communicator, and (d) culture. The best communicators are flexible and mindful in how they communicate based on these factors (Backlund & Morreale, 2015; Wrench & Punyanunt-Carter, 2015). They look for feedback from receivers so they can adjust their behavior as necessary. Having empathy and being skilled in decoding contribute to adaptability, which shows how the different aspects of communication competence work together.

PRINCIPLES OF THE COMMUNICATION PROCESS

At the end of each chapter in this book, we provide principles that help tie together or expand on some of the key concepts within the chapter. The principles discussed next all focus on some aspect of the process of communication that highlights the nature of interpersonal interaction.

Principle 1. Communication is a dynamic process that is irreversible and unrepeatable.
Communication involves much more than a simple exchange of information. It is a complex process filled with moves and countermoves, with communicators simultaneously engaging in the sending and receiving of messages. Communication within a given interaction is constantly changing, as are people's interpretations of one another. Yet despite the dynamic nature of communication, once words have been spoken or behaviors have been displayed, they cannot be taken back. This shows the irreversible nature of communication. Everyone has encountered a situation where they wish they could take something they said or did back, but it cannot be done. Communication is also unrepeatable. The exact circumstances of any interaction, including people's thoughts, moods, and feelings, cannot be repeated. In addition, reactions will be different if something has been communicated previously. Therefore, it is impossible to completely recreate any communication situation.

Principle 2. The channel of communication affects communication.
In this chapter, we have emphasized that interpersonal communication is composed of both nonverbal and verbal messages that can be exchanged through face-to-face or mediated channels. Nonverbal and verbal messages can work together or separately to create meaning. Sometimes these messages are consistent, making it relatively easy to determine their meaning. Other times, nonverbal messages contradict one another or are at odds with verbal messages, making it more challenging to determine the meaning behind them. The distinction between face-to-face and mediated communication is also important, although the more important distinctions are based on the degree to which people see one another while interacting and the degree to which messages are synchronous.

Principle 3. Communication can be intentional or unintentional.
As discussed earlier in this chapter, some forms of message exchange—such as those classified as attempted communication, miscommunication, and successful communication—involve intentional encoding. In these cases, a message is directed toward a receiver. Other forms of message exchange—such as misinterpretation and accidental communication—occur when people attach meaning to behaviors that were emitted spontaneously, without any intention to direct them to a receiver. Ignoring any of these types of message exchange would paint an incomplete picture of the communication process. Attempted communication may lead to frustration, which could then lead to conflict. Miscommunication could lead people to be at cross-purposes. Misinterpretation could lead a receiver to engage in behavior that is unwanted by the sender. And accidental communication could increase understanding between people. Thus, both intentional and unintentional communication play important roles in the communication process.

Principle 4. Not all behavior is communication.
It may be tempting to think that since communication can be intentional or unintentional, all behavior is communication. Sometimes people misinterpret Watzlawick, Beavin, and Jackson's famous statement that "one cannot not communicate" as meaning exactly that (Watzlawick et al., 1967). However, the statement that "one cannot not communicate" actually refers to the

idea that if you are interacting with someone, that person is going to attach meaning to something you do or say, even if you do not intend to send a message. This is different from saying everything we do is communication. Indeed, take another look at Figure 1.2. Unattended behavior occurs when people engage in spontaneous behavior that no one notices or attaches meaning to. This is not communication. Communication involves either sending a message with intent by directing it toward a potential receiver or having a message interpreted by someone.

Principle 5. Communication varies in terms of competence.

As mentioned previously, competent communication is effective and appropriate. Effective communication helps people reach their goals. Appropriate communication is polite and conforms to norms. Creating shared meaning is often a prerequisite for competent communication to occur. Think again about the boxes in Figure 1.2. Both successful communication and accidental communication are high in shared meaning because the receiver interpreted the message correctly. In some cases, accidental communication may inadvertently help people reach goals. For example, if Sydney is nervous about meeting her new dormmates, she might have the goal of looking and feeling less nervous. Her new dormmates could pick up on her nervousness and try to make her feel more at home. As a result of their friendly interaction, Sydney then feels more comfortable.

CONCLUSION

Communication will help Sydney flourish in her new environment. Sydney will likely use a wide variety of communication channels to make new friends and maintain contact with her old ones. Face-to-face communication may be the typical form of communication with her dormmates, whereas snapping and texting may be common with other students she meets on campus as well as with old friends she does not want to lose touch with. For Sydney to maximize her communication competence in her new environment, she needs knowledge of the rules and rituals within her dormitory and her university. Having skills related to encoding, decoding, conversational management, conversational interest, empathy, and adaptability are all key ingredients in the recipe for Sydney to be a competent communicator.

CHAPTER 1 STUDY GUIDE

KEY TERMS

Identify and explain the meaning of each of the following key terms.

accidental communication

adaptors

affect displays

affective empathy

attempted communication

channel

chronemics

code

cognitive empathy

communication competence

communicators

connotative meaning

constitutive rules

decoding

denotative meaning

emblems

encoding

exchange

feedback

field of experience

haptics

illustrators

instrumental goals

interpersonal communication

intimate zone

intrapersonal communication

kinesics

language

mediated communication

messages

mindreading

miscommunication

misinterpretation

multimodal

noise

nonverbal communication

personal idioms

personal space bubble

personal zone

phonological rules

pragmatics

proxemics

public zone

regulators

relational goals

self-presentational goals

semantics

slang

social zone

successful communication

syntax

transactional model of communication

unattended behavior

vocalics

REFLECTION QUESTIONS

1. Think of all the ways you communicate on a daily basis, including face-to-face and on your phone. How does the channel of communication (for example, texting vs. face-to-face vs. social media) influence the communication process? Are certain channels better for some types of communication than others? Explain.

2. How powerful do you think nonverbal communication is in everyday interaction? Think about the interactions you have had over the past 24 hours. How did you use nonverbal communication in both your face-to-face and phone interactions?

3. Think about the forms of communication and behavior in Figure 1.2. Give an example of each of these. How often do you think communication would be classified as "successful" according to this figure? What are some common causes of miscommunication and misinterpretation?

4. Imagine that a friend finds out you are taking a communication class and wants some tips for how to be a better communicator. What would you tell your friend? Be specific.

2 PERFORMING THE SELF

WHAT YOU'LL LEARN...

When you have finished the chapter, you should be able to do the following:

2.1 Identify the difference between self-concept and identity performances.

2.2 Explain how identities are performed.

2.3 Explain the influence of context and audience on identity.

2.4 Describe different cognitive biases related to our perception of our self and others.

2.5 Articulate the tenets of self-expansion theory.

Kara opened her eyes on a Saturday morning, happy to be back at home for the weekend. She had just turned in a major paper the day before. She worked very hard on it, as she hoped to get into her professor's selective senior seminar the following year. Today, she was looking forward to a lazy day at home, followed by her good friend Janna's birthday party. Kara spent the day having coffee with her mom and playing some competitive rounds of rummy with her little brother. Throughout the day, Kara sent some snaps to her best friend with possible outfits for the evening. After dinner, Kara started getting ready. After Kara did her makeup, she thought she looked pretty cute so she took a selfie and posted it on her Instagram story. Posting the picture reminded her that she needed to tweet a current event for her computer-mediated communication course. Kara found a New York Times article and posted it with her public account @KaraPWilliams. Then she switched to her private Twitter @KissesfromKara and tweeted, "It's gonna get lit 2night! #turnt #jannababy #21." As Kara left for the party, she stopped to scribble herself a note reminding her to pack her closed-toe shoes for her internship interview next week.

Kara's concerns and behaviors, as described above, all focus on how she understands herself and performs her understanding of self for others (identity). Our understanding of self is our **self-concept** and the way we perform that understanding of self is our **identity**. The questions "Who are we?" and "Who am I?" have been enduring and important philosophical inquiries for scholars. The answers to these questions are heavily intertwined with processes of communication. Perceptions of self-concept are grounded in communication. How others respond to us influences our sense of self. In addition, our identities are performances that are transmitted to our friends, family, and other social audience members through communication. As we learned in Chapter 1, a key characteristic of interpersonal communication is learning about others. Thus, understanding self-concept and identity performance is key to becoming a more competent interpersonal communicator.

SELF-CONCEPT

Self-concept is how people internally understand who they think they are (Oyserman & Markus, 1998). Self-concepts have multiple dimensions and are derived from the information we have about ourselves gleaned from experiences, relationships, social roles, beliefs, and abilities (Gore & Cross, 2014). Perhaps you volunteer for youth programs and have an award-winning cookie recipe. Or you might be a business student and have aspirations of playing professional golf. Perhaps you are all of these things. Your particular combination of traits and how you organize them internally is your self-concept. Your self-concept is your personal answer to the question: Who are you?

Interpersonal communication scholars generally believe that people build their self-concept through communication with others. Our relationships define us as a daughter, son, friend, employee, group member, or student. Our social roles emerge from the communication we have with others in our social networks. The social roles and categories we can and do enact are grounded in communication with other social network members (Pennington, 2000). Our abilities are even encouraged or hindered by the way that others around us communicate about those abilities. For example, your perception of your artistic abilities is likely based on the way people have responded to your artistic attempts.

Symbolic Interactionism

Symbolic interactionism is a foundational concept for interpersonal communication scholarship on aspects of the self. Symbolic interactionists argue that people develop meaning for

objects, messages, and others through social interaction (Blumer, 1969; Mead, 1922). These meanings then influence how people act toward those objects, messages, and other people. For example, we learn to use a fork based on how other people around us use a fork. We might have learned to hold a fork differently if we lived in a different part of the world or we might have learned to use a completely different eating utensil, like chopsticks. In the Disney movie, *The Little Mermaid,* we see Ariel learning about human objects from a seagull who makes up his own interpretations. When Scuttle tells Ariel that a fork is a dinglehopper and for brushing hair, she believes him and acts toward the object—brushing her hair—based on that interaction. The point here is that the way we act toward forks is based on what we have learned from others about forks. The same goes for other objects, language, and people, including ourselves. Just as we learn how to use a fork based on how other people around us use that fork, we learn who we are through how the people around us communicate with us.

Cooley (1902), an early symbolic interactionist, argued that our internal sense of self derives from how we imagine others experience us. This reflection is the **looking-glass self**. The looking-glass self concept suggests that we come to know our self through how we think others perceive us, considering how others might think of our appearance, actions, and place

Our interactions with others give objects meaning. We see this fork as an eating utensil, not a dinglehopper as Ariel was led to believe it was.

in the social world. These perceived mental perceptions serve as a mirror that allows us to perceive our self as a specific social entity.

Mead (1934) expanded on the looking-glass self by arguing that people create an internal representation of the presumed attitudes and perceptions of their social groups called the **generalized other**. The generalized other is our perception of how other members of our communities view the social world. Instead of trying to think of how our individual social connections might perceive us, we come up with a more general perception of how our social groups as a whole might perceive us. The concept is abstract in that there is no single person that we are imagining but rather the opinions that people in our social network might typically hold regarding who we are. People then consider these imagined general opinions in developing their own self-concept.

The ability to have separate conceptions of our self, others, and how others view our self and hold feelings and attitudes about our self is critical to the development of a social self. This process is also fundamental to the concept of **theory of mind** (Wellman, 1992). Individuals have a theory of mind when they are able to understand that

1. an individual or being has mental states,

2. others have mental states,

3. these mental states are different from each other, and

4. we can influence the mental states of others.

Our ability to have theory of mind allows us to understand that (a) others are separate individuals whom we hold representations of within our own mind and (b) other people have representations of us within *their* mind. Thus, your own self-concept is influenced by the communication of others, since their communication gives you insight into the representations people have of you. Theory of mind is essentially the idea that people understand that we have the ability to influence the minds of others through communication. Thus, theory of mind is an important concept for several interpersonal communication phenomena, including conflict management, persuasion, empathy, perspective-taking, and deception, all of which you will learn about in this book.

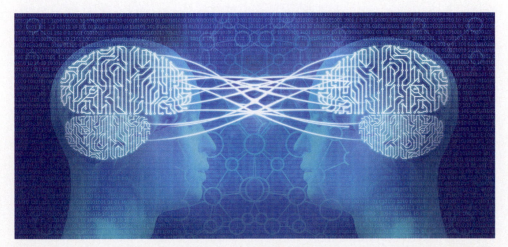

Having a theory of mind entails understanding that other people have different mental states than you do, and realizing that what you say and do affects other people's mental states.

iStock/Maxiphoto

Although these foundational theories of self-concept were developed early in the twentieth century, there is more modern evidence that highlights the way these perceptions of self develop. Over time, children incorporate an understanding of how other people see them into their self-concept. Research suggests that as children develop, their sense of self is increasingly connected to how they are viewed by others around them (Cole et al., 2001; Wigfield et al., 1997). When children play, which often involves taking on the roles of others through fantasy play or imitating parents when playing with dolls or action figures, they are in the beginning stage of differentiating others and the self (Mead, 1922). Later, social games allow for further practice at socialization as children not only consider how others will behave but also learn to accept, play by, and discard various subjective, social-rule systems.

In line with Mead's theories, research has found that in the prekindergarten years of childhood, most children have highly positive and optimistic self-perceptions (Eccles et al., 1984). Upon questioning, young children are likely to tell you that they are the best in their class. This overestimation of self is unsurprising, given that up to this point most small children have experienced a social world primarily consisting of family and close family friends who constantly reiterate positive messages ("You're so smart! You can do it!") to young children. Over time, children begin to experience a wider audience of peers and schoolteachers. The assessments presented by peers and teachers are quite likely less adoring than those of children's parents. By the third grade, children usually develop a more realistic sense of self.

Research on racial identity has also shown that people are influenced both by how they see themselves as well as how they believe others see them. **Racial identity** is "the part of a person's self-concept that is related to their racial membership, including the significance someone puts on race in defining their self" as well their interpretation of what it means to be a member of their race (Minniear & Soliz, 2019, p. 329). Racial identities can be connected to a kind of *double consciousness*, where people are aware of who they really are versus who other people stereotype them to be. In one study, college students who identified themselves as Black discussed how they struggled with being proud of their race, not wanting race to define everything about them, and being aware that they could be discriminated against or stereotyped because of their race. Two women in the study gave an example of this type of struggle by explaining a situation where they had "wanted to express their opinions and beliefs about racism and discrimination, but they also did not want to be seen as 'angry Black women'" (Minniear & Soliz, 2019, p. 329). These types of identity struggles extend to other groups as well. The key point is that our identities and communication are shaped not only by how we see ourselves but also by how we believe other people see us.

Personality and Communication

Another way to consider the internal self is the idea of personality. Although there are many definitions of personality, it can be thought of as the way the self organizes its view of its characteristics and presents those characteristics to others (Eysenck, 1947).

One common way that personality is measured is by using the Big Five inventory (John & Srivastava, 1999). The Big Five consists of five different factors: extraversion, agreeableness, conscientiousness, neuroticism, and intellectual openness. **Extraversion** refers to how talkative, assertive, and energetic a person is. **Agreeableness** is being good-natured, cooperative, and trustworthy. **Conscientiousness** is shown through being orderly, responsible, and dependable. People who score high on **neuroticism** are nervous, worry, and are easily upset. Intellectual **openness** is being intellectual, imaginative, and open-minded.

Although psychologists often classify these as internal traits, a close examination suggests that at least three of the five are communication styles (extroversion, conscientiousness, and agreeableness). In addition, personality constructs change over time due to feedback and communication within our social world. A recent longitudinal study compared people's personality constructs measured in their adolescence (when they were 14 years old) and then 63 years later. The researchers found that there was very little correlation between the participants' personality traits in their adolescence and their golden years (Harris et al., 2016). These and other findings on personality constructs suggest support for the symbolic interactionism perspective, in that personality appears to be malleable over time and might largely depend on the communication that we have with others. For example, people who marry similar others find that their personality constructs change less over time than those who marry dissimilar others. The dissimilar partners find that their personality traits converge over time (Caspi & Herbener, 1990).

Individuals who have been happily married for a long time have often become more similar to each other.

iStock/jonya

Nevertheless, the Big Five has been shown to correlate with a variety of communication variables (Correa et al., 2010; Hazel et al., 2014; Heisel et al., 2003; Hostetter & Potthoff, 2012; Itzchakov et al., 2014). For example, extraversion is negatively correlated with communication behaviors such as reticence (a hesitation to speak out) and verbal aggressiveness but positively correlated with social internet use. All Big Five characteristics except for neuroticism are correlated with preferring to communicate with people who have constructive listening styles. Extroverts and neurotics both produce more representational gestures (gestures that reinforce the verbal content of the message), but those with neurotic tendencies have difficulty getting others to like them and want to spend time with them, whereas extroversion is positively associated with this type of affinity seeking.

IDENTITY

While our self-concept is our internal consideration of who we are, our identities are the external communication of aspects of that self for a variety of social audiences. Jackson (2002) called identities codes of personhood with our identities constructed through interactions with others. The **dramaturgical perspective** proposes that our performance of aspects of ourselves is a key component of how other people learn who we are (Goffman, 1959). We represent ourselves through performative behaviors that influence others' opinions of ourselves. Throughout his explanation of the dramaturgical perspective, Goffman relies on explanatory metaphors of actors, performances, and theaters. The identity performances we give in social encounters are the "lines" or roles that people take, much like actors performing their lines in a play. We perform our self through verbal and nonverbal behaviors while taking into consideration the appropriate performance for a particular social audience and context.

Identity Performances

Two different types of social performances occur in everyday life—performances *given* and performances *given off* (Goffman, 1967). **Performances given** refers to the ways that people use verbal and nonverbal cues to portray their identity to others. **Performances given off** are the way that others receive our identity performances. Consider Kara at the beginning of this chapter. As Kara carefully chooses her outfit for the party, she is likely trying to show people particular aspects of herself. Perhaps Kara thinks her outfit shows that she is fun, on trend, and fits in with her particular group. Her outfit helps her give a specific type of performance. However, when Kara gets to the party, her outfit might not be perceived in the manner she intends—a bold choice in shoes is seen by her former classmates as trying too hard, or her makeup might be considered too heavy for a casual get-together. The other partygoers' reactions to her appearance are the *performances given off* by Kara. At times, performances *given* and *given off* may match. For example, if Kara wears sensible shoes and a suit to her job interview to appear professional and polished and is, in fact, seen as polished and professional by her interviewer, her performance *given* and *given off* match. At other times, such as in our party example, the reception of our identity performance may not match the way that we intended to be perceived. In other words, the performance given is not actually the one given off.

In addition, social performances are often tailored for a specific audience (Altheide, 2000). Kara from our opening story, for example, is likely to consider a very different outfit for the audience at her friend's birthday party than she did for her internship interview that required formal closed-toe shoes. To follow Goffman's metaphor of the theater, different audiences and stages require different performances.

Like Shakespeare's idea that life is a stage, Goffman likened self-presentation to performing various roles based on what is appropriate for a particular audience and context.

iStock/amphotora

Face

Our **face** is a combination of the person who we believe ourselves to be and the identity performances that we believe would be supported and approved by social groups that are important to us (Goffman, 1967). Face depends on three intertwined streams of information related to our self:

1. Our understanding of our internal self;

2. Our perception of how the audience we are presenting our self to sees us; and

3. Any external information, such as having a college degree that is relevant to the particular face one is trying to portray.

If we again consider Kara's interview, the impression that she can make depends in part on her outfit, presentation, and answers to the interviewer's questions. Her "face" also depends on what the interviewer thinks she knows about Kara. The interviewer's perception could come from a previous interaction at a career fair or her general impression of the college-aged interns hired by the company. In addition, external evidence supports the image Kara is able to present. If the interviewer has Kara's transcripts showing low grades in political science classes, Kara will not be able to take the line that she's a whiz at understanding and implementing political theory. These external representations of self through the perceptions of others and evidence are particularly important to how Kara's *face* is perceived. Goffman argues that who we are is not lodged within our body but rather is a product of the events of interpersonal encounters and how the events of these encounters are experienced and perceived.

There are times when we may find ourselves *out of face*—acting in a way that is inconsistent with the image we generally portray to the world. When we are *out of face* due to our own behavior, this is **shameless**. Imagine Kara shows up for her interview smelling of alcohol or wearing an outfit that is more appropriate for a nightclub than a professional setting. This performance would be a shameless one because Kara herself has made performative choices that are not in line with the face she would like to take (being a desirable internship candidate). On the other hand, there are times when others may communicate in a way that does not support our chosen line. These others may "call us out," so to speak. Imagine again that Kara shows up at her interview and finds that a friend of hers is the receptionist. If her receptionist friend tells Kara's interviewer that Kara is irresponsible, then she is not supporting Kara's interview persona in a way that is **heartless**. In both cases, Kara finds herself in wrong-face. To be heartless in this manner is sometimes necessary; one can imagine issues of being a witness to a crime, needing to speak up regarding racism or sexism, or wanting to prevent a boss from hiring a truly irresponsible candidate. Often, we fall back on politeness norms to construct these interactions. At other times, society as a whole has constructed laws to protect whistleblowers and witnesses or developed a different set of norms for settings such as a courtroom. These processes allow one's face to be breached and yet at the same time reinforce the idea that to be heartless is not normative behavior.

Politeness and Face

Other scholars have argued that there may be specific ways that people communicate to protect each other's face. There are two types of face: positive and negative (Brown & Levinson, 1987). **Positive face** is the socially appropriate self-image people wish to present to others. Although negative face seems like it might include when you want to make a negative impression, that is not the definition. Rather **negative face** is the idea that we all would like to make autonomous decisions regarding how we behave in the world. Of course, we are interdependent with others and cannot be fully autonomous.

Sometimes we make certain communication choices, called **politeness strategies**, to recognize the face needs of others (Brown & Levinson, 1987). Politeness strategies are used when people need to communicate some act or intention that is face threatening. **Face threats** are communicative actions that might harm someone's positive or negative face. Positive face threats include actions such as needing to critique someone, perhaps a formal critique in reviewing someone's work, or something more casual such as telling a friend that a shade of lipstick doesn't quite work for her or the cologne he splashes on before a big date doesn't smell as good as he thinks it does. Positive face threats may also include engaging in disagreements, bringing up divisive or emotional topics, or blatant noncooperation in communicative interactions such as interrupting or ignoring someone. These are all face threatening because they are actions (or inactions) that do not support the positive line that the co-interactant is attempting to take.

Negative face threats are threatening because they request that someone behave how the speaker wishes them to behave rather than allowing full autonomy on the part of the hearer. However, to get along in our social world, we all have to navigate receiving and sending negative face threats. An order given by a superior may be face threatening, as might a request from a friend. You might feel some level of irritation when reminded by a roommate to put your dishes away, not necessarily because the roommate is wrong about the dishes but because the request is a face-threatening act in that the roommate is asking you to complete the task on their schedule rather than your own. Other types of negative face threats include communication behaviors such as offering advice or making an offer. Although these may be viewed as cooperative types of communication, advice can be face threatening if it suggests the advice receiver is not fully capable of making the best decision. An offer to help may be intended positively, but it also indicates that the receiver needs help and that they may feel obligated to return the help at some future date. (See Chapter 11 for suggestions on offering more effective social support.)

Not all face-threatening actions are equally severe. How a message is perceived is likely dependent on the power difference between the person communicating the face threat and the message recipient as well as the relationship between them. Your boss can tell you to perform some task in a way that would be inappropriate if you tried to tell your boss what to do. A close friend is likely to be viewed as more appropriate when telling you that your outfit isn't flattering than the same message delivered by a rival. In this way, the relationship frames our own and others' identity performances to affect how a message is perceived. Politeness strategies are the communication choices people make to minimize face threats and make messages more socially palatable.

In these cases, we can see how politeness strategies are useful for taking the edge off of the potential negative effects of face-threatening acts. Politeness strategies include a wide array of linguistic choices. Brown and Levinson (1987) called these choices redressive actions. **Redressive actions** are communicative choices that people use to form messages that are viewed as more appropriate or polite. Using politeness markers such as "please," "thank you," and "I'm sorry" helps people realize that you know your request may be face threatening and that you recognize that they are autonomous individuals who can say yes or no. A face-threatening action that does not include any redressive action is considered bald-on-record. **Bald-on-record** strategies typically involve simply stating something critical or making a demand. A bald-on-record, positive face threat might be "That cologne really stinks" or "You have way too much makeup on." Redressive actions for these statements might include attending to the hearer's desires. For example, instead of saying "that cologne really stinks," you might say, "I think you have another cologne that smells better than that." Examples of bald-on-record negative face threats might include a sibling saying "Give me that!" or a roommate telling you "Do the dishes." These strategies can be considered quite rude for both positive and negative face threats. A redressive action for a negative face threat can be as simple as saying "please." Other negative politeness strategies include noting that you are incurring a debt ("It would really help me out if you'd do the dishes") or giving deference ("I know you're really busy, but could you handle the dishes tonight?").

Saying "please" can be a simple yet effective way to soften a request that might otherwise threaten someone's negative face.

iStock/master1305

Pointing out a role relationship such as supervisor-subordinate or professor-student may also make a negative face threat such as a critique or request feel less threatening. Other linguistic choices include hedging ("I know you're busy but…"), attending to the hearer's other face needs ("You should wear less makeup. You are so naturally pretty."), or joking around ("Formal denim! Are you trying to bring back the 90s?"). Redressive action can also be communicated through nonverbal cues such as trying to appear friendly rather than threatening when making a request or using vocal tone to sound unsure while hedging (Trees & Manusov, 1998).

Another fairly sophisticated strategy to soften the blow of potentially face-threatening communication is to go off-record. **Off-record** strategies are messages formed in such a way that the face threat cannot be directly attributed to the speaker. Let's think about what this strategy might sound like. Perhaps you would like a ride home from class and instead of demanding a ride (a bald-on-record strategy) from your classmate ("Give me a ride") or using redressive action ("Please give me a ride"), you say to your friend, "It's so cold outside. I'm really not looking forward to waiting for the bus." Your friend might then choose to offer you a ride, but if they do not, you both have a face-saving out—you weren't really asking, and they did not really have to say no. Of course, linguistic choices related to politeness are embedded within a particular culture. Different cultures may view different communication choices as more or less appropriate for performing politeness (Jenkins & Dragojevic, 2013).

Off-record strategies are common in the interpersonal phenomena of flirting. Stating bald-on-record utterances such as "I like you," "I want to spend time with you," and "I want to have sex with you" can all be face-threatening acts. Using off-record strategies allows potential partners to keep things lighthearted and fun while avoiding threatening the face of either party. Of course, as you may have noticed, this also makes it more difficult to decode the true intentions of a flirting partner ("Are they just being fun? Do they really like you?"). Research has found that both flirtatious communication and the rejecting of flirtation involve indirect, nonverbal, and off-record strategies (Goodboy & Brann, 2010; Hall et al., 2010).

People rarely choose to engage in bald-on-record strategies, and when they do, these strategies are often viewed negatively or as aggressive by their communication partners (Dillard et al., 1997; Trees & Manusov, 1998). At times, people may state that they value the bluntness or authenticity of bald-on-record statements and, in some cases, bald-on-record strategies are seen as more effective (Goldsmith & MacGeorge, 2000). However, in actual interactions, politeness strategies are often seen as a more appropriate way to achieve communication goals (Blum-Kulka, 1989). Indeed, the choice to use or not use politeness strategies serves as a specific type of identity choice.

At other times, people's reaction to a face threat involves reassessing how they consider the social audience. For example, Bell and Hastings (2011) found that while members of interracial couples who experienced excessive staring or negative comments would sometimes respond by smiling or staring back, they also used noninteractive strategies to minimize their perception of the face threat. For example, partners reported ignoring the face threat, rationalizing the threat by telling themselves that the opinions of people other than their partner do not matter, or reframing the face threat by articulating that people who might view their relationship negatively did not matter to their perception of self and their relationship.

SKILL BUILDER
POLITENESS

For many of us, our parents first teach us how to be polite. Parents dutifully train their toddlers to say "please" and "thank you," they caution their teenagers to watch their tone, and they remind a 9-year-old to ask rather than demand. However, when asked the inevitable question *why* (Why should one be polite?), the answer is so ingrained in our language and culture that many parents may fall back on the old stand-by—"Because I said so!"

The idea of *face* helps explain why people use certain language markers. It can also help us better understand politeness and perhaps be more skilled communicators. In many cases, the less polite version of a request is the shorter, seemingly more effective version. Why say something like "Is that the salt?" when what you really mean is "Hand me the salt"? Why hedge a request to a co-worker by saying, "If you're not busy, would you mind filling out this report?" when we mean "You have to fill out this report." In these cases, people are trying to manage multiple face goals. Although we need the report, our co-worker is more likely to provide it if we recognize in our message that our co-worker is a busy person who likely has better things to do. Indirect questions, hedges, and other politeness markers indicate the respect we have for the other person's autonomy and identity. In addition, people can react badly to others not treating them with the respect they feel they deserve. Your parents told you to ask rather than demand because it is irritating to be told what to do by a 9-year-old. Your co-workers react badly to demands because they signal you think of yourself as superior rather than equal.

We can also run into problems when we do not understand indirect requests and negations for what they really mean. If we are asking someone on a date or trying to get a job interview and we are repeatedly told "maybe later" or they use some other way of indirectly saying no, we may not get the "hint." Consider the following scenarios: What different ways might you phrase your message to appear polite? Do your strategies make your message less effective? What redressive actions do your messages employ?

1. After the end of the semester, you receive a text from a classmate that you suspected had a crush on you asking if you would like to see a movie. You are not really interested in dating this person but know that you will likely see them again in future classes.

2. You receive an unexpected parking ticket and realize that if you pay the parking ticket, you will be short on rent money. You decide to ask your sister if she might loan you some money. How do you frame your request? Do your strategies change if you are asking your parents for money? What about a friend?

3. Recently you were promoted to assistant manager of the retail store you work for. The promotion comes with more responsibility and more money. However, you have made friends with many of your co-workers and now you are in charge of assigning tasks to them. You come into work today and the back stockroom is a disaster. You need to ask two of your friend-colleagues to fix it and you know that no one likes this task.

THE MANY FACETS OF IDENTITY

Thus far we have been speaking of the self as if it were a single coherent entity that is in some way performed for others. However, careful consideration of the dramaturgical perspective illuminates that different identities and faces are likely performed for various audiences in different social contexts. Many scholars have considered the idea that the self might contain many facets. As far back as 1890, James argued that "Properly speaking, *a man has as many social selves as there are individuals to recognize him* and carry an image of him in their mind" (James, 1890, p. 294). (And, of course, we would argue the same is true regardless of one's gender.) However, James also noticed that these image-carrying individuals can be considered as more coherent groups or audiences such as "friends," "teachers," or "employers." Freud (1949) famously argued that people have an id, an ego, and a superego. Others have considered that we may perform particular selves for particular audiences (Altheide, 2000).

The Crystallized Self

More recently, some scholars (Altheide, 2000; Tracy & Trethewey, 2005) have considered the self as not just containing different facets but also as selves growing and creating different facets in response to the social environment—much in the way that a crystal grows. This metaphor of the

Like a crystal, our identities are composed of many everchanging layers, facets, and dimensions, all of which look different depending on the angle from which they are viewed.

iStock/kbeis

crystallized self allows people to think of the different performances, or lines that we take, as different facets of self. In this view, the self does not have some authentic core and no one facet of self is more or less authentic than any other facet. For example, in some contexts, a person may perform the role of mother; in another context, that person takes a professional role; in yet another, perhaps they are a marathoner. None of these particular selves are more or less real than any of the others; they are all simply different performances. We are all made up of these collections of performances, but we are no less real or authentic when performing our job, spending time with family, or maintaining our friendships.

The metaphor of the crystallized self also helps us consider how different facets of self are privileged by different audiences. For example, in the US, people often put great weight on the importance of the corporate labor market and may be especially concerned with their identity performances as they relate to how they are viewed in the workplace. An example of privileging the workplace in regard to identity performances is messaging and campaigns devoted to persuading teenagers to be careful with what they communicate on social media. Often at the heart of these campaigns is a concern that performances that seem appropriate to youth based on their peer audiences will be seen as inappropriate to future employers.

The idea of the crystalized self encourages us to play with both the language that surrounds our sense of self as well as the actual experiences in which we engage. By exploring new avenues of self, people may be able to develop meaningfully and grow new facets of their crystallized self, allowing for a richer and deeper experience of one's self and society. Selves are able to reflect on their construction, accept or resist societal narratives related to the self, and choose particular performances of identity. The ability to seek out new experiences and audiences is ultimately a fairly privileged position—not everyone will have the resources to pursue self-growth in this way. For example, one's ability to engage in meaningful work may be enabled by people working in low-paid childcare positions (Tracy & Trethewey, 2005, p. 180). Thus, it is important to keep in mind the way that our own performances of self may restrict or be enabled by systems that restrict the performances of others.

The ability to claim particular identity performances or not be questioned regarding identity performances is also privileged. Drummond and Orbe (2009) found that Black and Hispanic focus groups discussed negotiating identity gaps in a way that white participants did not. The identity gaps were centered on questions that challenged people's perceptions of their personal identity and their identity in relation to others. For example, these participants reported experiencing the question "Where are you from?" This question highlights an identity gap where people perceived themselves as locals, but others assumed a foreign identity erroneously based on their physical appearance. White participants did not experience this type of identity gap.

Monitoring Identity Performances

Although all of us have multifaceted selves, people may be better or worse at creating identity performances that are seen as appropriate for different contexts. People may need to **self-monitor** or adapt the communication and emotional expressions to particular contexts. Self-monitoring may lead people to change their behavior in one of the following ways (Snyder, 1974):

1. Intensify their true emotions. For example, you might try to look more upset when a parent informs you of the passing of a distant relative because you know your parent is more deeply distraught.

2. Communicate emotions that an individual may not be actually feeling. An example of this might be the child who learns to appear contrite when caught with their hand in the cookie jar regardless of their actual feelings.

3. Conceal inappropriate emotional states. Perhaps you have been pleased when your partner's favorite (but very old and tattered) t-shirt is destroyed in the laundry but offered condolences and made overtures to empathize with their sadness.

Each of these examples illustrates attempts to monitor and adjust our emotional displays and show an appropriate face to a particular audience. (See Chapter 6 for more on ways that people manage emotions.)

Self-monitoring goes beyond just emotional displays. The concept has two additional factors. First, self-monitoring requires an ability and willingness to be other-directed in considering the production of interpersonal messages. The communication choices of high self-monitors reflect their concerns for behaving in a socially appropriate manner and addressing the face needs of others. The second factor is related to the idea of extraversion. High self-monitors tend to have an aptitude for crafting public performances of communication (Gangestead & Snyder, 2000). The influence of these two factors—an appreciation of the social audience and the ability to perform appropriately—leads high self-monitors to perform better on a variety of communication tasks. High self-monitors are very responsive to the opinions of others and the norms of particular social situations (Gangestead & Snyder, 2000). High self-monitors tend to be better conversationalists than low self-monitors. They are more active, more focused on their conversational partner, more likely to reciprocate self-disclosures, and more adept at pacing conversations (Dabbs et al., 1980; Ickes & Barnes, 1977; Schaffer et al., 1982). High self-monitors are also better at using humor (Turner, 1980).

The ability to self-monitor also influences performance in the workplace. High self-monitors are more likely than low self-monitors to be promoted to management (Kilduff & Day, 1994). High self-monitors are better able to build and actively leverage their professional social networks (Mehra et al., 2001). High self-monitors become more important in their work networks over time. In contrast, low self-monitors were found to have weaker connections to others in their workplace even after a lengthy period of employment.

Low self-monitors may also have difficulty adapting to different situational contexts. Their communication is driven primarily by their internal states rather than contextual norms or requirements (Gangestead & Snyder, 2000). However, low self-monitors may engage in more intimacy and authenticity in their relationships (Rowatt, et al., 1998). Low self-monitors are less concerned with social comparison information. Thus, they are less likely than high self-monitors to focus on superficial aspects of relationships such as peer status or external attractiveness (Oyamot et al., 2010).

Identity Performances Online

Today, we do a considerable amount of our identity work online. Although many of the same principles of self and identity apply, mediation changes identity performances in ways that James, Goffman, and Mead likely never dreamed of. Online performances of self may be less like the stage performances that Goffman described and more like an exhibition of artifacts in our personal museum of the self (Hogan, 2010). People find themselves in the role of a curator, picking and choosing different identity artifacts to place online in order to showcase particular identity performances. Moreover, people often tailor their identity performances for various social media. For example, the selfie Kara posted on Instagram might have to pass a different test (for example, be especially cute) than would something funny she would post on her Finsta (fake Instagram), just as the professional identity she projects on LinkedIn is likely to be very different than the side of herself she shows in videos with friends on TikTok.

Furthermore, different types of online spaces facilitate different processes related to identity development. Online spaces may be more fixed or flexible in relation to how identity performances and social audiences are structured in online channels (McEwan, 2015). The idea of fixed and flexible refers directly to how identity performances are structured in different online spaces.

This type of picture is more likely to appear on an Instagram or Snapchat story than on an Instagram feed. How might these women change the way they take photos throughout the day to present different identities on various social media platforms?

iStock/Drazen_

Fixed Network Spaces

Identity performances that occur in **fixed network spaces** recognize a single consistent entity behind the identity performance. Often this performance is tied to an embodied, physical self. Sites such as Facebook or LinkedIn are examples of fixed identity spaces because people have to perform a self that is coherent and consistent. These identity performances have to be coherent in that all of the facets of self that are performed in this space make sense with each other. Identity performances have to be consistent in that they make sense to the various audiences that will see them. Otherwise, users may experience **context collapse**. Context collapse is what happens when social audience members that exist in different spaces offline and thus would receive different identity performances are lumped together in a single audience due to the structure of the social media platform (Marwick & boyd, 2011). For example, if you have friended co-workers on Facebook, you might need to be careful about not complaining about work on Facebook.

Many times, young people turn to fairly sophisticated communication strategies to manage context collapse (boyd, 2014). They might engage in **social steganography** by choosing words and phrases that are intentionally vague to people (such as parents or teachers) who lack the shared knowledge and context to fully understand the meaning of the messages (boyd & Marwick, 2011). Youth often tend to fragment their audiences, using Facebook more sparingly as a catch-all type of site and then saving more social messages for platforms where they have connected only with close friends such as Snapchat or Tumblr. In the opening vignette, notice that Kara had two Twitter accounts—a public account, @KaraPWilliams, and a private account, @KissesfromKara. She can present different facets of her identity on each of these accounts as a way to manage context collapse.

Flexible Network Spaces

Another way people may attempt to avoid context collapse is to choose **flexible network spaces**— online platforms that allow for anonymity or pseudonymity. People may interact with each other either anonymously or using a pseudonym or user handle. Flexible identities can be created, performed, and discarded easily. Online message boards or massive multiplayer online games are examples of spaces where people perform flexible identities. The flexibleness allows people to interact with others using identity performances that are not tied to offline selves or the perception of others within a fixed social network. The infamous image chat boards of 4chan and its successor 8chan might be the most "pure" example of flexible network space. On these boards, everyone goes by the user handle "Anonymous" and thus each of their identity performances lasts no longer than a single post. More popular flexible networks would include spaces like reddit.com where users can choose one or several pseudonymous handles.

One concern for flexible identity spaces is that people might experience **online disinhibition**. The feeling of anonymity may encourage people to behave in ways that they would refrain from in offline communication contexts (Suler, 2004). Online disinhibition can be benign or toxic (Suler, 2004). A benign form of online disinhibition would be a space where people might feel more comfortable expressing emotions or engaging in self-disclosure online than offline. Teenagers might reach out in online communities to express or experiment with new identities (Valkenberg et al., 2005). People with serious illness might disclose in online support groups in order to not burden their families with their worries. Toxic online disinhibition occurs when people consider anonymity as a license to be rude, overly critical, or threatening. Toxic inhibition can lead to online spaces that close down online debate and relationship building.

WHAT WOULD YOU DO?
JOB SEEKERS (AND TRAVELERS) ASKED FOR SOCIAL MEDIA PASSWORDS

In 2011, the Associated Press (AP) ran a story about employers asking for Facebook passwords. Previously, employers may have performed Google searches or browsed the public portions of social media accounts. In this case, the Department of Corrections (DoC) for the State of Maryland asked correctional officer, Robert Collins, specifically for his password. The password allowed the DoC to search through all of Collins's postings and his friendship network. Although it was unclear how many employers were engaging in the practice, the AP article was taken fairly seriously. By 2014, 30 state laws had been passed prohibiting employers from requesting access to social media passwords.

Reactions to password requests were mixed. A set of over 4,000 Yahoo! News comments provides some insight into public reaction (see McEwan & Flood, 2018). Some people argued that asking for social media passwords is fair game for employers. After all, they argued, if you've got nothing to hide, then why should you be worried? Some took this argument further, saying that they felt asking for passwords was fair because they would hate if someone who was on drugs or engaging in illicit behavior got a job instead of them. Others worried that handing over social media passwords gives employers too much power. There were concerns about private information but also that certain network connections (for example, someone who grew up in a bad neighborhood) might cause them problems. Some suggested resistance strategies, including walking out of an interview, trying to publicize companies who engaged in the strategy, and trying to get legislation passed against the practice.

Social media is a place where multiple facets of identity are performed. Should employers be able to access all aspects of a potential employee's identity? Would you feel comfortable working for a company that asked for Facebook passwords? How might you react in an interview if you were asked for your social media passwords? Would you engage in a resistance strategy? Would you be upset if someone with an unsavory social media profile was hired for a job over you?

PERCEPTION AND BIASES

As should be clear by now, the self and its identities are negotiations between our internal cognitions and our external social networks. Despite the multifaceted nature of our identity performances, there is evidence that people strive toward **cognitive consistency** in how they view the world around them. People generally want the world to make sense and for the people around them to behave in a predictable manner.

The human brain is structured to use heuristics to make sense of the world. Heuristics are simple decision rules that allow us to make decisions quickly (Chaiken, 1987). For example, you have internal decision rules that helped you decide what was appropriate to wear today. We develop heuristics for a diverse array of interpersonal processes, including deciding what to wear, but also how to greet someone, or what we think we like in a potential romantic partner. Once heuristics are developed, they are resistant to change (Van Overwalle & Siebler, 2005). Quickly changing heuristics would be maladaptive in an evolutionary sense. Consider an ancient ancestor who had determined that tigers are likely to eat people; it would be unwise to quickly change their mind that tigers are not likely to eat people on the basis of encountering one full and lazy tiger. Similarly, we may become uncomfortable when someone in our social circle acts in unpredictable ways. Many of the heuristics we use to understand both our self and others' selves are based on this concept of cognitive consistency.

Cognitive Dissonance

We also strive for cognitive consistency in the way that we view both our self and others. The concept of **cognitive dissonance** suggests that people are uncomfortable holding two opinions or ideas that are in contrast to each other (Festinger, 1957). To overcome this discomfort, when confronted with oppositional ideas, we strive to reconcile these discrepancies—often in self-serving ways. To explain cognitive dissonance, Wicklund and Brehm (1976) use an example of purchasing a house (i.e., making a commitment to the house and then later finding out that several things were wrong with the house). This creates dissonance between the idea that the house was worth purchasing and the idea that the house has problems. For many people, to resolve this dissonance, they would begin to convince themselves that they truly loved something about the house or the neighborhood to justify their commitment to the house despite the problems. We can apply the elements of this example to interpersonal relationships as well. Imagine that you have spent several years with your romantic partner and consider yourself committed to the relationship. Then you find out some troubling information about your romantic partner. Perhaps your partner lied about something important or even committed an act of infidelity. Certainly, some people break up in such circumstances. For those who choose to stay together though, partners often convince themselves that there is something particularly amazing and unique about their partner and their relationship to justify staying. Essentially, partners mentally adjust for the dissonance between the idea that they have invested in the relationship and that the relationship has problems.

Self-Serving Bias

The **self-serving bias** considers the valence or direction of the information behaviors provide about the self. Due to the self-serving bias, people attribute their own failures and negative behaviors to situational factors (Malle, 2006; Zuckerman, 1979). A review of hundreds of studies on this effect found that people avoid attributing their own negative behaviors (such as relapses in drinking, being aggressive, or problems in school) to their internal selves (Malle, 2006). For example, if Kara (from the opening scenario in this chapter) fails to get the internship, she might attribute this to her school not properly preparing her or perhaps the interviewer was rushed. However, when considering successes, the self-serving bias leads us to consider those to be the result of internal traits. If Kara lands the internship, she may congratulate herself on her hard work and polished interview performance.

On the other hand, people tend to either not be concerned enough with the behavior of others to make an attribution about their behavior or they may find other's negative attributions to be the result of personal characteristics. In Kara's case, if the interviewer was late to the meeting, Kara might simply evaluate the interviewer as an unreliable person rather than considering that another interview might have run late or that the interviewer was held up in a meeting with a superior. (Read more about the fundamental attribution bias in Chapter 3.)

According to the self-serving bias, if you land a job you want, you are likely to attribute your success to personal characteristics such as being intelligent and personable. If you fail to land a job, you are likely to attribute it to external factors, such as the interview being rushed or the company not hiring the best people.

iStock/MangoStar_Studio

The internal and external attributions made under the self-serving bias are *both* likely based on seeking consistency in the world around us (Malle, 2006). For example, if Kara has been generally successful in the past, earned good grades in school, was accepted into the university of her choice, and was hired for previous jobs, then an unsuccessful interview would contradict information Kara already has about herself. Thus, in Kara's mind, the external attributions for failure are the most consistent. However, when it comes to considering the behavior of other people, we have much less information on which to base our attributions. Thus, when we see someone fail or behave badly, it makes sense to attribute that to the most salient cue we have—that person. This attribution leads us to consider something inherent to that person, an internal attribution, to be the most likely cause of their behavior. For example, if we see a woman in the supermarket snap at her son, we might automatically assume she is impatient—and worse yet, a bad mother— instead of considering that she is tired and her son may have been testing her patience all day.

The self-serving bias can make it difficult for us to empathize with people who experience difficulty. If we consider their failures to be related to some internal shortcoming, it can be challenging to consider systemic problems that create problems in others' lives. Our heuristics may also give rise to false attributions and stereotypes. Stereotypes are mental models we hold about what we think the "typical" member of a social group is like (Allport, 1954; Lippmann, 1922; see Chapter 3 for more on stereotypes). Stereotypes often contain a substantial number of attributes, including perceptions of typical social roles, shared qualities, and anticipated behaviors (Dovidio et al., 2010). Competent and empathetic communication in interpersonal contexts often involves making a concerted mental effort to attempt to override these processes.

Competence Biases

Two other cognitive errors that affect our self-concept, albeit in different ways, are imposter syndrome and the Dunning-Krueger effect. People with **imposter syndrome** have objective evidence that they are talented, such as admissions to quality universities, high grades, or jobs in a highly skilled career field, yet still believe that they do not belong and will soon be discovered as an inept fraud (Clance, 1985; French et al., 2008). People with imposter syndrome may be more anxious and expect to perform poorly on tasks (Cozzarelli & Major, 1990; Kolligian & Sternberg, 1991). They may also self-handicap, for example, by studying less for an exam, as a mechanism of providing themselves with external reasons for failure. Imposters may be more likely to feel they have failed when they have actually been reasonably successful (Cozzarelli & Major, 1990). Women have been found to have slightly higher scores on imposter syndrome scales than men (Cozzarelli & Major, 1990). Some scholars worry that young people raised in high-pressure scholastic environments with an emphasis on grades and test scores may also experience higher levels of imposter syndrome. Although these students may be academically qualified, they may also experience anxiety in regard to academic risk-taking to avoid any hint of failure (McAllum, 2016; Pedler, 2011).

Whereas those with imposter syndrome are qualified yet perceive they are inadequate, those who experience the **Dunning-Kruger effect** are inadequate in regard to some skill or cognitive ability yet think of themselves as quite highly qualified (Kruger & Dunning, 1999). For example, people who experience the Dunning-Kruger effect might perceive themselves as highly analytical yet have difficulties with a test of higher-level reasoning (Pennycook et al., 2017), or they may consider themselves a grammar expert and yet fail to recognize grammatical errors (Kruger & Dunning, 1999). Simply having difficulty in these areas might be frustrating for an individual but wouldn't bias their sense of self. However, the twist with the Dunning-Kruger effect is that the lack of competence in a particular area makes it difficult for that person to understand that they actually lack competence. These individuals are incredibly confident in a particular ability yet are lacking both in the area and their ability to recognize their deficiency. Essentially, they don't know what they don't know.

Anecdotally, we sometimes specifically encounter the Dunning-Kruger effect in the field of interpersonal communication when someone tells us that they are an excellent communicator, yet they have little understanding of mindfulness, tact, self-monitoring, or a myriad of other elements of communication that increase perceptions of being an appropriate communicator. Yet these individuals are not aware that these are elements of competent communication, so they are also unaware that there are better ways to encode their messages (also anecdotally, we find these communicators often mean that they are blunt, which is sometimes but not often the best communicative strategy).

I DIDN'T KNOW THAT
IS FUNDAMENTAL ATTRIBUTION A FUNDAMENTAL ERROR?

Even if you are not familiar with the cognitive bias known as fundamental attribution error (FAE; also called the actor-observer hypothesis), you've probably heard the premise that we attribute our own behavior to external causes and others' behavior to internal causes. For example, if an acquaintance says something hurtful to you, you may assume that they are simply a mean or uncaring person. Yet if you say something hurtful to someone else, well, you may feel that you were misunderstood or that you were affected by having a bad day or being hungry. However, some research suggests that this cognitive bias may not be as strong as scholars once thought—and in some cases, it may not exist at all.

The fundamental attribution bias is rooted in the idea that "actors tend to attribute the causes of their behavior to stimuli inherent in the situation, while observers tend to attribute behavior to stable dispositions of the actor" (Jones & Nisbett, 1971, p. 93) This statement means that when considering our own behavior, we often think of contextual reasons for why we behave a certain way. For example, you get up early because you have an early class. You missed that traffic signal because you were tired after having to get up for that early class. You remembered your friend's birthday because you got a notification from Facebook. You went to your friend's party because other people you knew were going to be there. However, we often attribute other people's behavior to internal causes. They get up early because they are early risers. They missed the traffic signal because they are a bad driver. They remember their friend's birthday because they are conscientious. They go to parties because they are an extrovert.

Many scholars assert the existence of fundamental attribution error (e.g., Robins, Spranca & Mendelsohn, 1996; Watson, 1982) and many authors of communication textbooks assert that fundamental attribution error is an important perceptual bias that influences interaction. However, a 2006 meta-analysis found that fundamental attribution error may not be as prevalent as scholars thought. A meta-analysis is a statistical review of studies. Meta-analysts look at the results of many studies to determine the existence of effects across all of these studies. Malle (2006) examined 173 studies that had tested actor-observer hypotheses to see what the results were across all of these studies. Given how *fundamental* the fundamental attribution error has been to the way we understand cognitive biases, Malle was surprised to find that across all of the studies the effect of fundamental attribution error seems to be very small. Sixty-eight of the studies he included found no effect at all for fundamental attribution error. As Malle argued, "The actor-observer hypothesis appears to be a widely held yet false belief" (p. 907). People come up with internal and external attributions for both their own and others' behaviors.

Why would it take so long to realize this psychological effect is not nearly as fundamental as first thought? One explanation is that many of the studies have participants think about hypothetical scenarios. The effect seems to appear when people are thinking about hypotheticals but not when they are trying to explain actual events. Another explanation is that studies that asked people for their explanations were more likely to find the effect than those that used rating scales. It may be that these attribution errors are part of a system of perceptions that people use to explain their own and others' behavior but do not appear when internal or external attributions are presented as the only choice of explanation for behavior.

Malle (2006) did, however, find some evidence of the self-serving bias. When people are explaining behavior that they view negatively, they seem more likely to attribute this to situational influences. You were short with your friend because you are hungry. You can't find your textbook because your roommates are messy. In contrast, people are more likely to attribute others' negative behavior to internal causes. They are snappy because they are impatient. They can't find their textbook because they don't take care of their things.

Malle's meta-analysis provides an important summary of studies examining fundamental attribution error. More research is likely needed to understand the way that people make attributions about their own and others' behavior. However, it seems that fundamental attribution error may not be as fundamental as we once assumed.

THE SELF IN RELATIONSHIPS

In keeping with the symbolic interactionist perspective, neither the self nor our identity performances occur in a social vacuum. Our selves and identities are intertwined with a network of others, including parents, siblings, friends, co-workers, and romantic partners. One way of considering how people view their self as overlapping with various network ties is **self-expansion theory**. Self-expansion theory is the idea that as we build relationships with others, we come to see these others as becoming an interdependent part of our own self (Aron & Aron, 1996; Aron et al., 2013). Furthermore, we are motivated to expand our selves in order to increase our available resources and opportunities (Aron & Aron, 1996). Being in relationships also exposes us to new experiences that can lead us to grow and change, similar to the idea of the crystalized self that was presented earlier in this chapter.

Going new places and trying new things with someone are two of many ways that relationships can promote self-expansion.

iStock/Rawpixel

As our relationships develop, we take on similar interests, common friends, and even some of the characteristics of our relational partner (Agnew et al., 2004). People might also be willing to put more work into maintaining relationships with partners that they see as included in the self, although this finding holds more strongly for men than women (Ledbetter et al., 2013). Self-expansion occurs in different types of relationships, including romantic relationships and friendships (Ledbetter et al., 2011; McEwan & Guerrero, 2012).

Self-expansion theory may also help explain some nuances in how people conduct social comparisons. When you view a relational partner or a close friend as an extension of yourself, you are more likely to gain esteem when they outperform you (whereas generally, we might lose esteem when someone outperforms us). This likely occurs because we take on the successes and failures of those with whom we are interdependent as if they are our own. In the case of close friendships, we may even avoid engaging in the self-serving bias and come to view our friends' failures as due to external causes and help shoulder responsibility for both their successes and failures (Campbell et al., 2000). This effect may be because self-expansion allows us to feel that our friend is a greater part of our self. In addition, the knowledge we gain through the self-expansion process allows us to have a greater amount of information regarding potential external causes for our friend's behavior.

PRINCIPLES FOR UNDERSTANDING THE SELF AND IDENTITY

Understanding how you see yourself and how others see you is important for many reasons, including personal growth and self-expansion. Knowing yourself and being self-reflective also help you be a better communicator in your personal and professional relationships. Next, we present four principles that tie together some of the main ideas from this chapter in ways that we hope will give you further insight into the many facets that make up the unique person you are.

Principle 1. The self and communicative processes are tightly intertwined.

The self is formed, reified, and reproduced through communicative processes. In many ways, you are who you surround yourself with. At least, you take on a role for that particular group. For this reason, it is important to consider the social groups that you join and the relationships that you form. Positive, affirming relationships will have a positive effect on your sense of self. People who provide invalidating messages, lead you into difficult situations, or pigeonhole you into negative roles can lead you to become a very different person.

Principle 2. The self changes.

"Be yourself" and "Be true to yourself" are common sentiments. Yet the self can change and is constantly changing. It can be helpful to understand that the self is a complex set of beliefs regarding who you think you are and who you wish to be. Furthermore, these beliefs are constantly changing. You may have an aspirational self that you hope to become someday. If you have just recently started college, you may feel you are a very different person than you were just months ago due to the new array of social and intellectual choices and experiences you have recently had. Even just finding yourself in a new social group can make you feel as though you have changed. While this may feel confusing, it is also normal. Such changes are related to the concepts of the crystallized self and self-expansion. Take time to remember what is important to you but also enjoy seeking out new opportunities for growth and personal development.

Principle 3. Different contexts require different faces.

When choosing how we are going to communicate, it's important to remember the context of the communicative situation (office, social event, family gathering) as well as the people who will be the audience of our identity performances. Considering the situation, audience, and social norms helps us choose which facets of our self will be viewed as the most competent to perform in that moment. It is also important to remember that those around us may choose different communication strategies based on the different contexts they operate in. You might consider carefully whether to share a message with a friend privately or post something to their public social media account.

Principle 4. Be mindful of your biases.

Self-serving bias makes it easy to think that our successes are due to our innate abilities and our failures are due to factors out of our control. In reality, neither of these are true all the time. It is important to remember that we all have support and a bit of luck on our side when we succeed and that we should take responsibility for our failures. We are not just a collection of successes and failures but considering these mindfully can help us have a better understanding of our strengths, weaknesses, and how to accomplish goals. It is also important to remember that although we know our self better than others, other people also experience success and failure partially due to internal traits and partially due to external causes. Keeping this in mind can help us have the compassion and empathy needed to form strong interpersonal and societal bonds.

CONCLUSION

Our internal self-concept and identity performances rely on a variety of communication processes that help us understand our self and others. Building this understanding is a key skill for developing interpersonal relationships, as truly interpersonal communication relies on building knowledge regarding each other. Like Kara in the opening vignette, we constantly move through different social contexts and adjust our identity performances accordingly. Our ability to do so in ways that are seen as consistent and coherent to our various social audiences helps us to be viewed as more appropriate communicators, which can lead to a variety of positive outcomes in our personal and professional lives.

CHAPTER 2 STUDY GUIDE

KEY TERMS

Identify and explain the meaning of each of the following key terms.

agreeableness	face
bald-on-record	face threats
cognitive consistency	fixed network space
cognitive dissonance	flexible network space
conscientiousness	generalized other
context collapse	heartless
crystallized self	identity
dramaturgical perspective	imposter syndrome
Dunning-Kruger effect	looking-glass self
extraversion	negative face

neuroticism

off-record

online disinhibition

openness

performances given

performances given off

politeness strategies

positive face

racial identity

redressive action

self-concept

self-expansion theory

self-monitor

self-serving bias

shameless

social steganography

symbolic interactionism

theory of mind

REFLECTION QUESTIONS

1. What are the facets of your identity? How do you know that these facets are a part of you? How do you perform these facets for different audiences? What facets do you share with other members of the class? Do you perform these in the same way or different ways?

2. In the age of social media, where people can edit and carefully consider the identity artifacts they place online, what does it mean to be "authentic"? Is authentic a useful term given what you now know about identity presentation? Can someone be more or less authentic? What types of identity presentation would you consider to be authentic or inauthentic?

3. It can be difficult to recognize our own cognitive biases; however, knowing that you have these biases, can you think of a time when the inclination for cognitive consistency may have clouded your perception of someone else? What was the context of that situation? What was the outcome? What might you try to do differently in the future?

3 FIRST IMPRESSIONS AND INITIAL ATTRACTION

About three months ago, Maddie went through a difficult breakup with a long-term boyfriend. She has been slow to want to start meeting other guys, but lately, Maddie has started to feel like it is time to put herself out there again. Her friend, Haley, from chemistry class, has been wanting to set her up with one of her best guy friends, Elijah. Maddie checks Elijah out on social media and he is her type physically, with nice eyes and a big contagious smile. She gives Haley the okay to share her number with him, and he starts snapping her. After a couple of weeks, Elijah suggests picking her up and taking her out for dinner and a movie. Maddie is nervous about committing to spending that much time together. She doesn't know much about him except what Haley has told her plus the little bits of information they have exchanged on Snapchat. She worries that Haley has exaggerated his good qualities. Worse yet, maybe Haley has hyped her up to him, and she might not meet his expectations. Maddie suggests meeting for coffee instead. When she sees him, she is relieved that he looks even better in person. As they begin to talk, she remembers what Haley said they have in common and brings those things up. Not too long into the conversation, they are laughing together comfortably. Maddie thinks he seems fun and genuine—two qualities that are important to her. About 20 minutes into their hangout, Haley texts her a question mark. She answers with the thumbs-up emoji, puts her phone away, and concentrates on getting to know Elijah.

Have you ever found yourself in a situation like Maddie's—where you were not sure if someone would live up to your expectations or if you would live up to theirs? Or perhaps you knew you were attracted to someone but were nervous about whether they would find you attractive as well? The process of meeting and getting to know someone can be fraught with ambiguity and uncertainty, which is why people tend to form impressions to size people up during initial interactions.

This chapter takes a closer look at the processes of impression formation and attraction. **Impression formation** occurs when people develop perceptions about an individual based on that individual's appearance or behavior. Forming impressions involves *decoding* information and interpreting it to make a judgment about someone. As you learned in Chapter 2, people present themselves in certain ways to try to influence the impressions people have of them. This process, which is called self-presentation or **impression management**, is the encoding side of the equation. In Maddie's case, she engaged in impression management when she decided what to wear and how to fix her hair and makeup before meeting Elijah face-to-face for the first time. How Elijah perceives and decodes her appearance and behavior will determine the impression that she makes on him. Of course, Maddie is also forming impressions of Elijah, and their impressions of each other will influence not only their current interaction but whether they decide to interact again in the future.

WHY PEOPLE FORM IMPRESSIONS

People tend to want to size others up and form impressions of them fairly quickly, especially if they think that they will interact with someone again in the future. Think about this. When you meet a new person, what runs through your mind? The research suggests that you might access their physical appearance, estimate their age and other demographic characteristics, and make judgments about their personality. Two communication theories help explain why people do this: uncertainty reduction theory and predicted outcome value theory.

Uncertainty Reduction

Communication researchers have been studying **uncertainty** since the 1970s when Berger and Calabrese (1975) first developed **uncertainty reduction theory**. When people feel uncertainty, they do not feel confident about their ability to predict or explain someone's attitudes or behaviors (Berger & Calabrese, 1975; Brashers, 2001). According to this theory, people dislike uncertainty when it makes them uncomfortable. There is then a natural tendency to want to reduce it. This desire to reduce uncertainty is especially relevant when people are meeting for the first time and getting to know one another. Think about Maddie when Elijah asked her to hang out for the first time. Even though they had been snapping and Haley had told her many great things about him, Maddie still feels a lot of uncertainty, to the point that she suggests meeting for a short coffee date rather than dinner and a movie. As they are getting to know each other, both Maddie and Elijah are taking in information and making judgments about each other to reduce uncertainty.

Another idea central to uncertainty reduction theory is that people actively seek out information to try and reduce uncertainty. This was the case for Maddie when she went on Elijah's social media to see what he looks like and get a basic idea about his life from the types of things he posts. During their conversation at the coffeehouse, Maddie and Elijah asked each other basic questions about themselves and engaged in small talk. This type of communication is somewhat superficial, but it helps people feel comfortable and reduces uncertainty. Small talk allows people to discover things about each other and make judgments about the kind of people they are and the type of relationship they might have.

Because of social media, it is easier than ever before to find out information about people. Sometimes people prejudge others based on this information.

iStock/AntonioGuillem

The theory also specifies that the more we get to know someone, the more we can predict that person's attitudes and behaviors. Research has supported this idea by showing that during an initial interaction, uncertainty reduction occurs quickly. In one study, college students who had never interacted before talked for two, four, or six minutes (Douglas, 1990). In another, they interacted for up to 16 minutes (Redmond & Virchota, 1994). Together these studies suggest that uncertainty decreases the most over the first six minutes of initial interaction when people are exchanging basic information. The more people ask each other questions during this time, the more confident they are about the judgments they make about one another (Douglas, 1990). Reducing uncertainty usually also leads people to like one another more. There are exceptions though. Sometimes after talking to someone and reducing uncertainty, you decide you dislike them. Perhaps the conversation was awkward or they said or did something you found annoying or offensive. However, because people are typically on their best behavior to try and make a good impression when you first meet them, you are more likely to like them than dislike them after reducing uncertainty.

So how do people seek information to reduce uncertainty? There are three general strategies that people use (Berger & Calabrese, 1975; Fox & Anderegg, 2014; Tong, 2013): passive, active, and interactive. These strategies can be enacted in face-to-face or mediated situations.

Passive uncertainty reduction strategies rely on unobtrusive observation of an individual. This includes a range of activities such as watching someone at a party to see how they interact with people, paying attention to how someone dresses, looking at someone's Instagram pictures, seeing what someone has liked on Twitter, and checking for a wedding ring. All these behaviors can be engaged in privately without the other person's knowledge, and all can give you some basic information about the person's appearance, their popularity (for example, by seeing how many likes they get on their pictures), social network, and activities as well as possible glimpses into their personality. Maddie engaged in passive strategies when she looked Elijah up on his social media.

Active uncertainty reduction strategies go beyond passive observation but stop short of directly interacting with the person. There are two types of active strategies. The first involves finding information out from someone's friends. This can happen directly, such as Maddie asking Haley questions about Elijah, or indirectly, such as reading the comments on someone's Instagram pictures to see what people think of someone. The second type of active strategy involves setting up a situation and seeing how a person responds. The prototypical example of this is sending over a drink to someone at a bar to see if the person reacts favorably.

Interactive uncertainty reduction strategies involve direct communication between people. Maddie and Elijah engaged in this strategy when they snapped one another and then later when they met at the coffeehouse. They asked each other questions, encouraged the other to disclose information, and noticed one another's nonverbal behaviors. Maddie liked how Elijah smiled in his snaps; it made him seem open and friendly. Elijah liked the way Maddie leaned forward and nodded when she listened to his story about something that had happened to him the weekend before. He thought she seemed genuinely interested in what he had to say. These types of exchanges provide especially important information not only about one person but about how two people connect when together.

Places like coffeehouses and restaurants provide people with casual environments to sit and get to know one another.
iStock/powerofforever

So far, we have only discussed situations where people want to reduce uncertainty. But is this always the case? The research suggests not. There are times when people actually prefer uncertainty over certainty. The **theory of motivated information management** is based on the idea that people are only motivated to reduce uncertainty when there is a discrepancy between the amount of uncertainty they want and the amount of uncertainty they have (Afifi & Morse, 2009; Afifi & Weiner, 2004; Kuang & Wilson, 2021). Think about this.

Are there times when you would rather live with uncertainty than find out more information? Perhaps you are uncertain about why someone broke up with you, but you would rather not know all the hurtful details. You might wonder if a friend is attracted to you but decide you would rather not know because it could complicate your friendship. In Maddie's case, imagine that her coffee date with Elijah was just okay. She might walk away feeling uncertain about how he feels about her, but she might not care if he likes her or not. In all of these cases, the motivation to reduce uncertainty is low. And in some cases, uncertainty is even preferable to certainty.

The theory of motivated information management suggests that when people experience uncertainty, they go through an evaluation process that helps them decide whether or not to try to reduce uncertainty. There are two parts to this evaluation process. One part of the process involves making a judgment about whether the information you would uncover would be positive or negative. This part of the evaluation process is called **outcome expectancy** in the theory. Think about how you might feel if someone ghosted you. As you probably know, ghosting occurs when someone ends a relationship (or a potential relationship) by withdrawing from communication abruptly and without explanation. There you are, thinking everything is going fine, and then the communication stops and you do not understand why. Should you confront the person and try to reduce your uncertainty? If you suspect the person will say hurtful things about you, maybe not.

In the other part of the process, people make judgments about how well they could gather and cope with the information they might uncover, which is called **efficacy assessment** in the theory. With the ghosting scenario, you might decide that the person is unlikely to give you a straight answer and that engaging in contact will only make you feel worse (and perhaps even make the person who ghosted you see you in a more negative light). If this is the case, you would probably rather just cope with the uncertainty rather than seek information to reduce it.

Thus, uncertainty reduction is more likely in certain situations. These include wanting to get to know someone, anticipating that you will interact with someone again in the future, believing the information you would uncover will be positive, and being confident that you can gather and cope with the information you seek in an effective way. In initial interactions, the information we gather to reduce uncertainty helps us form important first impressions that can influence whether we want to get to know someone better or not. This idea is central to the next theory we will discuss, **predicted outcome value theory** (Sunnafrank, 1986, 1990).

Predicted Outcome Value Theory

According to this theory, rather than being driven simply by uncertainty, people seek information in initial interactions because they want to determine whether people are rewarding or not. Uncertainty is reduced as a way of making this judgment. The degree to which someone is regarded as rewarding or unrewarding once uncertainty is reduced is called the **outcome value**. Outcome values can range from highly positive to highly negative. If a person is judged as fun, exciting, and kind, that person would have a much more positive outcome value than would a person who is judged as boring, unintelligent, or mean. The outcome value is also grounded in predictions about the future. For example, Maddie might ask herself: Would Elijah fit in with my friends? Is he someone I would consider being in a serious relationship with or would I only want something casual with a guy like him? The more Maddie sees Elijah as someone rewarding who she would want in her life, the higher his reward value. Elijah would also be compared to other alternatives. Therefore, if Maddie has also been snapping another man who she thinks might be even more fun and interesting, then Elijah's reward value would go down.

Predicted outcome value theory is based on two main ideas. First, people are motivated to maximize rewards and minimize costs. Second, people make judgments about future outcomes to guide their current behavior. When applied to initial interactions, this means that we invest in getting to know people who we think will be rewarding to have in our lives. So if we judge a potential friend as someone who would be loyal and great to hang out with, or a potential romantic partner as someone who could make us happy, we will be motivated to put continued time and effort into getting to know them. In contrast, we will not invest in those who we think will be unrewarding. Perhaps we believe they will be too needy, are too different from us, will not fit in with our friends, or will end up hurting us. Whatever the judgment, the idea is that we predict these outcomes when we first meet people and these judgments then direct our decisions about how much or little to develop the relationship from there.

Predicted outcomes influence communication in a variety of contexts. Students who talk at the beginning of the semester are more likely to be friends at the end of the semester if they had predicted positive outcomes during their initial interaction (Sunnafrank & Ramirez, 2004). Roommates who predict positive outcomes after first talking live together longer (Marek et al., 2004). In the classroom, students who judge instructors as rewarding at the beginning of the semester later report being more responsive during class than do students who judged instructors as less rewarding (Horan & Houser, 2012). Clearly, predicting outcomes is an important reason why people seek to form impressions of others during initial interactions.

TYPES OF IMPRESSIONS

To reduce uncertainty and predict future outcomes, people form impressions of others. Impressions are the judgments people make about one another. These impressions are sometimes called **person perceptions.** If you surveyed your friends, family, and acquaintances, what type of person would they perceive you to be? They might perceive you as loyal, intelligent, tall, short, attractive, clumsy, successful, lazy, religious, athletic, self-centered, or any one of a myriad of other qualities. Impressions such as these occur on at least three levels—physical, sociocultural, and psychological (Burgoon et al., 2022).

Levels of Impressions

The **physical level of impressions** involves making judgments about a person based on what you can see externally. Such judgments include age, gender, height, weight, and level of attractiveness. When you read the short description of Elijah at the beginning of this chapter, did you picture him as young or old, as attractive or unattractive? Although there were some clues in the description (and you know that Maddie finds him attractive), it would still be easier to make these judgments if you could actually see him.

The **sociocultural level of impressions** involves judgments of a person's socioeconomic status and cultural background, including occupation, level of education, cultural identity, political attitudes, and religious affiliation. When Maddie checked out Elijah on social media, she saw that he was wearing a university sweatshirt in a few pictures, frequently goes to concerts, seems to hang out a lot with the same group of guys, and posts family pictures from vacations all over the world. He also retweets posts from the engineering department at his university. If you were Maddie, what would these pieces of information tell you about Elijah at a sociocultural level?

Finally, the **psychological level of impressions** refers to judgments about personal characteristics, such as how friendly, intelligent, ill-tempered, selfish, or caring a person is. Look back at the list of things Maddie noticed on Elijah's social media. Do they also provide some glimpses into his personality? Perhaps, but Maddie will get an even better idea of what type of person Elijah is when they interact and share their thoughts and feelings. Of the three levels of impressions, those at the psychological level are the most difficult to make based on limited information.

Physical judgments tend to be based on what people can directly observe, whereas sociocultural and psychological judgments usually involve making an inference (or assumption) about the meaning of a person's behavior, appearance, or possessions. For instance, people might infer that a person who smiles a lot is friendly, that a person who is tall is confident and powerful, or that a person who drives a Mercedes is rich. Although sociocultural and psychological judgments are often accurate, sometimes they are not: the person who smiles a lot might be hiding something, the tall person might feel awkward and out of place, and the person driving the Mercedes might be in debt.

Impressions based on how a person looks and where a person is from (or assumed to be from) can lead to cultural stereotypes. **Cultural stereotypes** are "shared beliefs about the typical attributes of members of a social category" (Ghavami & Peplau, 2013, p. 113). In one study, university students in Southern California were asked to indicate what stereotypes they believe people hold of various cultural groups (Ghavami & Peplau, 2013). Each participant was randomly assigned to think about one of the following groups: Asian, Black, Latinx, Middle Eastern, or white. Some students referenced the cultural group in general, whereas others were asked to reference women or men within one of those cultural groups. In addition, students were told to think about cultural stereotypes they have observed in general rather than their own opinions. They then wrote down 10 attributes they saw as stereotypes for the group to which they were assigned.

The cultural stereotypes that emerged are consistent with problematic biases that can unfairly influence people's impressions of others. Asians, whether female or male, were stereotyped as intelligent, short, and quiet. Black people, in general, were stereotyped as unrefined, as criminals, as loud, and as athletic. Black women were also seen as having an attitude and Black men as quick to anger. As a general group, Latinx were stereotyped as poor, as having a lot of children, as being illegal immigrants, as dark-skinned, and as uneducated. Latina women were as perceived as feisty, curvy, loud, and attractive, whereas Latino men were perceived as macho, day laborers, and promiscuous. Whites, as a group, were stereotyped as high status, rich, intelligent, arrogant, and privileged; with white men also stereotyped as assertive and tall, and white women as blond and attractive. Cultural stereotypes such as these can lead to biased expectations and discrimination as well as reinforce prejudice and white privilege (Dovidio & Gaertner, 2010). Part of being a competent communicator, therefore, involves recognizing and rejecting cultural stereotypes. When trying to make a good first impression, negative cultural stereotypes put some groups at an unfair disadvantage and give other groups an unfair advantage. Competent communicators base perceptions of people on what they learn about them rather than what they assume about them.

What physical, sociocultural, and psychological impressions do you think people would make if they saw this individual in the context shown in this photo?

iStock/globalmoments

What about the individual in this photo? How would impressions differ?

iStock/Sean_Gao

Thin-Slice Impressions

How fast do people form impressions of others? The research on "thin-slice" impressions suggests that lasting and sometimes accurate impressions can be formed very quickly. A **thin slice** is any sampling of behavior less than 5 minutes long and can include cues from "the face, the body, speech, [and] the voice" (Ambady et al., 2006, p. 5). Behavior only qualifies as a thin slice if it is dynamic and changes during the interaction. Therefore, physical appearance, which stays fairly consistent during an interaction, does not qualify as a thin slice of behavior, but body movement, vocal qualities, and facial expressions do—either separately or in combination. Recent research has found that observing 2 to 5 minutes of interaction can lead to just as much accuracy as observing 15 minutes (Murphy et al., 2019).

Thin-slice impressions are often related to enduring judgments about people. In one study, thin slices of teacher behavior at the beginning of the semester predicted student and principal evaluations of instructors at the end of the semester, even though those thin slices were only 30 seconds long (Ambady, 2010; Ambady & Rosenthal, 1993). Thin slices of behavior at the beginning of mock job interviews, which typically included the interviewee entering the room, shaking the interviewer's hand, and then sitting down for the first 10 seconds of the interview, predicted how favorably an interviewee was rated (Prickett et al., 2000). Brief thin-slice interactions at the beginning of an interview also influence an interviewer's overall impression of a candidate (Carnes et al., 2019). Even socioeconomic status can be inferred from thin slices of nonverbal behavior with a moderate degree of accuracy (Kraus & Keltner, 2009).

Research on thin-slice impressions suggests that even judgments of teachers based on observations as short as 30 seconds can predict teaching evaluations later in the semester. Do you think you can size up your professors that quickly?

iStock/SDI Productions

The voice alone can make a powerful impression and even influence job performance. For example, telephone operators who sound confident, enthusiastic, friendly, professional, and sympathetic deal more efficiently with phone calls, as indicated by the shortness of calls (Hecht & LaFrance, 1995). In another study, people listened to 10-second thin slices of news-publishing company managers' voices. When people had positive impressions of the managers based on their voices, the managers were more likely to receive favorable job performance evaluations from their supervisors (DeGroot & Motowidlo, 1999). Finally, in another set of studies, people made judgments of salespersons based on 20-second audio clips of the salespersons' voices. When the voices were rated more positively, the salespeople were not only evaluated more highly by their supervisors, but they also produced more sales (Ambady et al., 2006).

Primacy Versus Recency Effects

Whether based on appearance, behavior, or both, the perceptions people have of you (and the perceptions you have of others) can come from first impressions or from more recent revisions of those first impressions. A **primacy effect** occurs when people continue to believe the first impressions they had of you (Forgas, 2011). The preliminary judgments people make are strong because they are based on the first available cues that people process. People tend to process these early cues more carefully than they process later cues. However, if new information is consistent or convincing enough, a recency effect may emerge. A **recency effect** occurs when people put more stock into how you acted during your most recent encounters with them compared to when you first met (Forgas, 2011). If you engage in behavior that contradicts the earlier impression (such as acting flirtatious when previously you were shy), people might revise their perceptions of you.

You might be wondering which prevails—a primacy effect or recency effect? The answer is: It depends. Often people do pay more attention to the information they get from first impressions, which favors a primacy effect. However, if people pay equal attention to information from early and recent interactions, the information from the more recent interaction is remembered more clearly, producing a recency effect. This is good news for anyone who has ever made a bad first impression—although that impression might stick for a while, there are often opportunities to change impressions through further interaction.

ACCURACY OF FIRST IMPRESSIONS

In addition to realizing that first impressions can change, it is also essential to understand that first impressions vary in accuracy. As the research on thin-slice impressions demonstrates, sometimes the initial judgments we make of people hold a lot of truth. Other times, as the research on stereotypes based on appearance shows, they may not. In general, stereotypes may leave us with erroneous impressions of others if we overgeneralize impressions of group characteristics to individuals, even when stereotypes are positive. For example, Hughes and Baldwin (2002) found that white participants held perceptions of Black people as friendly and talkative, whereas Black participants rated white people as organized. Although these stereotypes are positive, they are not likely to help us deepen our interpersonal relationships with specific individuals who may or may not possess those traits. Even positive stereotypes can feel demeaning or alienating when thoughtlessly used to direct our communication choices (Kawai, 2006). Overcoming stereotypical thinking requires mindfully learning about our co-communicators as individuals (Hughes & Baldwin, 2002). Gray (2008) noted that one thing is clear about our perceptions of others: "with increasing acquaintance comes increasing accuracy" (p. 110).

This means that even though first impressions set the stage for future interaction and help us decide whether we want to get to know someone better, our most accurate perceptions of people come from communicating and getting to know them over time. However, as shown in the following Skill Builder , there are at least five aspects of first impressions that can be helpful when trying to determine how accurate your initial judgments of others are (Burgoon et al., 2022; Gray, 2008).

SKILL BUILDER
MAKING A POSITIVE FIRST IMPRESSION

These five aspects of first impressions are important to keep in mind. Think back to the last time you met someone new. How did these aspects influence your perception of them? Or take time to meet someone you haven't interacted with yet in class. How did these aspects influence your interaction with them?

- **Type of Judgment Being Made:** People's first impressions are usually most accurate when the trait being judged is related to the information on which they are basing their judgment. For example, perceiving someone as extraverted or friendly based on behavior (such as smiling and speaking in a warm tone) tends to be more accurate than perceiving someone as trustworthy and responsible based on looks or as athletic or smart because of their cultural group.

- **Access to Consistent Information:** The more verbal and nonverbal cues you can decode, the better, especially if they paint a consistent picture. Making judgments based on single cues or cues that contradict can lead to inaccurate conclusions. For example, it is easier to make a judgment about confidence level if someone smiles, gives you direct eye contact, and speaks without hesitation, compared to if someone has a neutral face, gives you direct eye contact, and speaks with a lot of hesitations.

- **Perceiver's Motivation:** When individuals are motivated to make judgments, they tend to be more accurate. For example, during initial interactions, people might want to reduce uncertainty about the other person, especially if they expect to see them again or like them. This can lead to a more engaged interaction and more careful decoding and interpretation (but be careful not to overanalyze).

- **Perceiver's Communication Skill:** Some people are better at recognizing and interpreting behavior than others (Riggio, 1986). Good decoders go with their gut intuition rather than overanalyzing. They also make people feel comfortable, which leads them to display more natural behavior that will provide better clues about the type of person they are.

- **Unbiased Interpretation:** First impressions are more accurate when they are not clouded by biased judgments. Common biases include *stereotypes* (basing a judgment on a generalization about a group), such as the cultural stereotypes discussed previously in this chapter; *fundamental attribution bias* (attributing the behavior of others to personality rather than the situation); *self-serving bias* (thinking people we like are similar to us and those we dislike are dissimilar to us); and *confirmation bias* (noticing behaviors that confirm what we already think rather than looking for additional information). Avoiding these biases leads to more accurate first impressions.

The context in which people form impressions of others also makes a difference. In particular, when perceptions are formed based solely on communication via technology, they can be skewed positively. The **hyperpersonal perspective** helps explain why this happens (Walther, 1996, 2007; see also Chapter 5). According to this perspective, communicating via technology can create more personal and positive perceptions of others than communicating face-to-face.

One reason for this is that people fill in information gaps by creating idealized images of people in their minds. In addition, when people communicate via mediums such as texting and Snapchatting, they are able to carefully control their messages. For example, they have time to think before they respond, they can send selfies that make themselves look especially good, write messages that are crafted particularly well, and choose emojis rather than showing spontaneous facial expressions. Because of this, the impressions people form when communicating using technology can be overly positive. Perhaps because people feel less vulnerable when communicating over technology compared to face-to-face, they also tend to disclose more when texting or chatting online (Wang & Chang, 2010; Wang & Lu, 2007). This all makes it easy for people to develop overly idealized images of others when they are forming impressions based on communication over technology.

It is important, then, to engage in face-to-face communication before idealized impressions can set in. Once people develop impressions that are unrealistically positive, it is difficult for the other person to meet the high expectations set by those impressions. Maddie was worried about this before meeting Elijah in person. She realized their communication had been limited to Snapchatting, and on top of that, Haley had hyped them both up to each other. Maddie was smart to be cautious and to worry that their first face-to-face encounter might not go as smoothly as either of them hoped. Maddie and Elijah were also smart to meet after only a week of talking through technology. The longer people wait to communicate face-to-face, the more likely idealized images will develop and people will be disappointed after interacting in person, with some research suggesting that it is best to meet within about 3 weeks of beginning communication through technology (Ramirez & Zhang, 2007; Ramirez et al., 2015). Waiting longer can be problematic since unrealistic expectations are more likely at that point.

ATTRACTION

The first impressions we have of people help determine whether we are initially attracted to them and want to get to know them better. **Attraction** is a force that draws people together (Guerrero et al., 20211). There are three major types of attraction: physical, social, and task (McCroskey & McCain, 1974). **Physical attraction** involves liking how someone looks, **social attraction** involves liking someone's personality and wanting to be around them, and **task attraction** involves the desire to work with someone who can help you get things done. Different types of attraction may be more important in different contexts. Houser et al. (2007) reported that speed daters overwhelmingly identified their most important date-selection behaviors as those indicative of social and physical attraction. Social attractiveness is also very important in friendships. Task attractiveness is central in the workplace and other situations that involve people working together to accomplish a common goal.

Physical Attractiveness

Physical attractiveness is primarily determined by genetics. However, as we shall see, how we communicate also influences people's impressions of our physical attractiveness. Good-looking faces tend to have three features: (1) symmetry, (2) averageness, and (3) a moderate level of femininity or masculinity depending on a person's sex (Jones et al., 2007; Little, 2014; Rhodes, 2006).

Symmetry

Symmetry is a key attribute of attractive faces (Grammer & Thornhill, 1994; Rhodes et al., 1998). If you divide a face into two halves, and one side of the face is a perfect mirror image of the other, then the face is perfectly symmetrical. No one, however, has a perfectly symmetrical face. For example, one eye might be ever so slightly farther away from the midpoint of the face than the other eye, or one cheek might be a tiny bit fuller than the other cheek. These specific differences may not even be noticeable to the naked eye, yet they can still affect the overall perception of a face. The larger asymmetries are, the less attractive faces are generally judged.

Do you think one of these faces is more attractive than the others? One is natural and the other two are symmetrical.

Courtesy of Laura Guerrero

Just as people prefer symmetrical faces, people prefer symmetrical bodies. There may be a biological basis for this. People with symmetrical bodies are not only perceived as more physically attractive, but they also tend to be more coordinated. Star athletes tend to have more symmetrical bodies than the average population, which accounts for some of their talents in running faster, jumping higher, and so forth (Manning & Pickup, 1998; Trivers et al., 2014).

Averageness

Take a careful look at the three photos of the pretty young woman. The photo to the left is her left-side symmetrical face, the one in the middle is her natural face, and the one to the right is her right-side symmetrical face. Which face do you find most attractive? Are the two symmetrical faces equally attractive? Or do you prefer one over the other? If all symmetrical faces were equally attractive, then you would not find one more attractive than the other. However, research suggests that symmetry alone does not tell the whole story when it comes to facial beauty. Indeed, there is something that is just as important, and perhaps even more important, than symmetry—averageness (Rhodes, 2006). If a face is symmetrical, but the features on that face are a lot bigger, smaller, farther apart, and so forth than you would see on an "average" face, then the face is less likely perceived as attractive (see "I Didn't Know That! Attractive Faces Are Average Faces"). This also explains why two symmetrical versions of the same face are not rated as equally attractive. A face usually looks best when the side of the face that has the most ideal (often average) proportions is used to make the face symmetrical. When the other side of the face is used, it is often not as attractive as the natural face.

One study showed that both averageness and symmetry predicted how attractive men's faces were rated, but only averageness predicted how attractive women's faces were rated (Komori et al., 2009). A later study showed that men's faces were rated as more attractive when they had features that were average, symmetrical, and masculine (Rhodes et al., 2011). Finally, a review of the research showed that overall, averageness has a larger influence on how attractive a face is rated than does symmetry (Rhodes, 2006). Rhodes (2006) concluded by saying: "Clearly, average faces are attractive" but that does not "mean that all attractive faces are average... or that average faces are optimally attractive" (p. 205). What it does mean is that faces with average configurations are more attractive than most faces.

I DIDN'T KNOW THAT!
ATTRACTIVE FACES ARE AVERAGE FACES

Most people think of attractive faces as "above average," but from a mathematical and proportional standpoint, the most attractive faces are sometimes the most average faces of all. Think about your own face. When people evaluate themselves, they often think about what they would like to change. You might wish your lips were fuller, your cheekbones were higher, your eyes were farther apart (or closer together), or your nose was smaller. In most cases, you are comparing your own features to the "average" from which you believe your face deviates.

Researchers have tested and supported the idea that average faces are beautiful (for a review, see Rhodes, 2006). In the first of these studies, researchers started with photographs of 96 college-aged men and 96 college-aged women (Langlois & Roggman, 1990). Then, using a computer program, they combined various photos to create facial composites for women and men. The composites represented the mathematical average across various facial features. So if six photographs were combined, the lips, nose, and chin in the composite picture would represent the average size and shape of those features across the six individual photos making up the composite. The researchers created composites that contained 4, 6, 8, 16, or 32 different faces, with the composites containing 32 faces being the most "average."

In this study as well as future studies, the composite faces are rated as more attractive than individual faces. In addition, composites that represent the average of more faces (e.g., 32 vs. 16) are rated as more beautiful or handsome. Average facial features are perceived as attractive for both men and women, although composites that contain both men's and women's faces are not rated as attractive. In other words, if 10 women's and 10 men's faces are combined, the resulting composite would not be as attractive as composites containing all male or all female faces.

The large photo is of a face created by morphing the faces around it. How attractive do you think this composite face is?

Courtesy of Laura Guerrero

Femininity and Masculinity

Facial attractiveness is influenced by the degree to which a face is characterized by feminine versus masculine features. This explains why combining features from male and female faces into composites does not produce particularly attractive faces. Feminine facial features include full lips, big eyes, and smooth, young-looking skin. Masculine facial features include a strong jawline, chiseled chin, heavy eyebrows, and facial hair. Consistent with the idea that average faces are beautiful, however, the optimally attractive woman possesses moderately strong (but not extreme) feminine features, while the optimally attractive man possesses moderately masculine features. An extremely feminine face is perceived as too babyish, whereas an extremely masculine face is perceived as too harsh (Cunningham et al., 1990; Langlois et al., 1994). However, the ceiling for how feminine an attractive woman's face can be is higher than the ceiling for how masculine an attractive man's face can be. In other words, women's faces must be extremely feminine to be seen as babyish. Men's faces, on the other hand, may be judged as most attractive when they are moderately masculine with some androgynous features (Rhodes, 2006).

Attractiveness Stereotypes

Physical attractiveness plays a key role in first impressions. Fair or not, research suggests that first impressions are often formed largely based on physical appearance. According to the **what-is-beautiful-is-good hypothesis**, people tend to perceive good-looking individuals as possessing an array of positive internal characteristics such as friendliness, likeability, and intelligence (Dion et al., 1972; Furnham et al., 2001; Zebrowitz & Franklin, 2014). This beauty bias starts in early childhood and persists throughout adulthood (Larose & Standing, 1998), although it may be strongest in childhood and adolescence (Zuckerman & Hodgins, 1993). Research testing the what-is-beautiful-is-good hypothesis has shown that this effect is strongest for judgments about social attributes, such as how extraverted, confident, and friendly a person is (Eagly et al., 1991; Feingold, 1992). It is weaker for judgments related to cognitive abilities, such as how intelligent and well adjusted a person is.

Of course, the what-is-beautiful-is-good hypothesis is more stereotype than fact. Better-looking people are not, on average, any nicer or more trustworthy than average-looking people. They likely gain confidence and are more extraverted as a response to how others treat them. Think about this. If Sophie is especially beautiful, people who expect her to be fun, friendly, and smart will be more likely to approach her and want to get to know her. The positive responses and attitudes of others are then likely to make Sophie more confident, and the extra opportunities for interpersonal interaction are likely to make her more socially skilled.

Despite these advantages, there are also some disadvantages to being especially good-looking. According to the **what-is-beautiful-is-conceited hypothesis,** attractive people are also perceived as materialistic, self-centered, snobbish, and vain (Ashmore et al., 1996; Dermer & Thiel, 1975). Especially attractive people may also be held to different standards than average-looking people, which makes it harder for them to live up to expectations (Andreoni & Petrie, 2008). For example, a physically attractive person may be expected to also be smart, confident, and outgoing based on stereotypes. If the beautiful person is instead seen as anything less than that, people can become disenchanted and disappointed. Women who are especially attractive and have hourglass-shaped bodies also deal with unfair stereotypes in terms of being judged as more promiscuous and more likely to be unfaithful than less attractive people (Ashmore et al., 1996; Pollock, 2012; Singh, 2004).

Being attractive is also a double-edged sword in terms of perceptions related to the type of dating partner a person would be. On the one hand, people perceive that having a relationship with an especially attractive person would be highly rewarding, but on the other hand, they believe an especially attractive person is more likely to be unfaithful or break up with them (Singh, 2004). This may be because attractive people are perceived as having more options in the dating world, so they can afford to be choosier. They are also seen as more likely to be rejected during initial interaction (Albada et al., 2002). Table 3.1 summarizes some of the perks and penalties associated with being attractive as discussed above and by Anderson et al. (2010).

TABLE 3.1 ■ The Perks and Penalties of Physical Attractiveness	
Perks	**Penalties**
perceived as having high social value	difficult to meet people's high expectations
perceived as having higher self-esteem and being more confident in social situations	perceived as vain and self-focused; too focused on appearance
social desirability as a friend or romantic partner	can be a target of jealousy and resentment
perceived as more believable and authentic	perceived as more manipulative
perceived as (and actually) healthier	perceived as more promiscuous and more likely to be unfaithful
perceived to have more power and influence	perceived to have unfair advantages in the dating world and the workplace
perceived to have more opportunities for long-term relationships	viewed as less approachable and perceived to be less committed to long-term relationships
better employment opportunities	more difficult adjustment to aging, especially if self-concept is tied to looks

Although stereotypes based on physical attractiveness are prevalent, they only provide a starting point for first impressions. The way you communicate also has a strong impact on the impressions you make on others, both when you first meet someone and later when you are getting to know someone better. By engaging in behaviors that make you more likeable, you can increase your social attractiveness, and perhaps surprisingly, your physical attractiveness as well.

Social Attractiveness

What behaviors promote social attraction and perhaps also perceptions of physical attractiveness? A classic study by Bell and Daly (1984) addressed this question by identifying **affinity-seeking strategies**, which are behaviors people use when they want someone to evaluate them favorably and like them. Of the 25 strategies these researchers uncovered, nine appear to be especially important for fostering impressions of likability, as listed next.

1. **Conversational Rule-Keeping:** adhering to the rules of polite conversation. For example, not interrupting when someone else is speaking. By following the rules, people appear polite and socially appropriate.

2. **Self-Concept Confirmation:** showing respect and trying to make the other person feel good about themself. Compliments are a prime example of this, both in person and on social media. Liking someone's pictures on social media can also act as a form of self-concept confirmation.

3. **Disclosure Elicitation:** encouraging the other person to talk and share personal information. Maddie did this during her coffee date when she brought up topics she thought Elijah would be comfortable talking about, given what Haley had told her about him.

4. **Nonverbal Immediacy:** displaying behaviors that show involvement in an interaction and communicate warmth and liking (Andersen, 1985). Maddie and Elijah engaged in immediate communication when they were sitting close to one another at the table and laughing together.

5. **Self-Inclusion:** arranging the environment to facilitate contact with someone. Elijah and Maddie did this when they set up a time to get coffee. Posting a picture on Snapchat or Instagram and hoping a particular person will see it is a 21st-century example of this strategy.

6. **Shows of Active Listening:** being attentive and focusing on what the other person is saying. Behaviors such as asking for clarification and repeating what someone says are good examples of this strategy.

7. **Enjoyment Facilitation:** trying to make the interaction fun and enjoyable. For example, during their coffee date, Elijah might tell Maddie a funny story that gets her laughing. They both might also act cheerful and friendly to set a positive mood.

8. **Openness:** sharing personal information. As you will learn in Chapter 8, openness, or self-disclosure, is a key way people develop relationships. In initial interactions, people typically limit the amount of highly personal information they reveal, yet they share enough to reduce uncertainty and determine if they want to get to know each other better.

9. **Altruism:** presenting oneself as helpful. For example, Maddie might offer to help Elijah with his science homework since she is good at chemistry and biology. He might offer to help her with brief calculus since he is a math whiz. People might also present themselves as unselfish, kind, and generally "good" people.

These affinity-seeking strategies fit within the larger literature on liking and social attraction. People are more likely to want to form and maintain relationships with others who are socially attractive. For example, people are more likely to mute or unfriend people on Facebook who they perceive as less socially attractive (Pena & Brody, 2014). Two of the most important qualities people look for when getting to know someone are that (1) the person is warm and kind and (2) the person likes them (Sprecher, 1998). Affinity-seeking strategies convey these qualities. Two of these strategies, **nonverbal immediacy** and openness (aka self-disclosure), have received the most attention in communication research. Self-disclosure is discussed in detail later in Chapter 8. Here we describe some of the main behaviors associated with nonverbal immediacy.

Nonverbal immediacy occurs when people enact behaviors that give an impression of warmth and closeness. Immediacy is often processed holistically (Andersen, 1985). In other words, rather than focusing on a single behavior, people get an overall impression of how immediate a person is. Various behaviors contribute to this impression. These include giving someone eye contact and nodding, especially while listening, and angling or leaning your body toward someone. Smiling is another key immediacy behavior. In fact, of all the nonverbal behaviors people can display, smiling is the one that reflects the most liking and warmth (e.g., Argyle, 1972; Ray &

Floyd, 2006). People also evaluate others as friendlier and as more empathetic when they speak in a soft warm voice and sound excited or animated.

The adults in this picture are practicing nonverbal immediacy by getting on the same level as the boy, therefore closing the physical distance among them.

iStock/Hispanolistic

Close distancing and touch also communicate immediacy. In his classic book on interpersonal space, Hall (1968) showed that people in the United States tend to sit or stand with a space of about 18 inches to 4 feet between them when they are engaged in social interaction. Spacing closer than this indicates that an interaction is especially intimate. Therefore, such close spacing may be inappropriate for many initial interactions. Yet sitting or standing farther away from someone than this could send a message that one is not very involved in a conversation. Similarly, while not all touch is appropriate when you first meet someone, certain forms of touch, such as handshakes and a light touch on the arm while sharing a laugh, can increase immediacy and social attractiveness.

The timing of communication is also related to immediacy. The more time people interact and the less time it takes them to respond when communicating via technology, the more immediate the communication. Think of Elijah and Maddie. If she had delayed responding every time he snapped her, Elijah probably would have seen this as a sign of disinterest and never asked her to hang out. Time also represents investment, and we do not tend to invest in people unless we value them.

In addition to affinity-seeking strategies, people can increase their social attractiveness by being confident and assertive. This may be especially important when first dating someone. In an innovative study, researchers had people imagine a situation where they believed they were an ideal partner for someone. Then they asked them what they would do to initiate a relationship with that person (Wildermuth et al., 2006). The most common strategies revolved around being confident and assertive. Specifically, people said they would take charge of initiating contact and planning dates. They also said they would let the person know they liked them and would make direct inquiries about what the other person was looking for in a partner and a relationship.

Other studies have also shown that women, in particular, are socially and romantically attracted to men who display a combination of behaviors that show dominance and altruism (Jensen-Campbell et al., 1995; Sadalla et al., 1987).

The Link Between Social and Physical Attractiveness

There are several reasons people are naturally attracted to beautiful faces in babies, friends, potential mates, and even leaders. As discussed earlier, attractive people have social advantages, including being perceived as friendlier, healthier, sexier, and more socially skilled (Furnham et al., 2001; Zebrowitz & Rhodes, 2002). People naturally want individuals with those types of attributes to be their friends, lovers, and co-workers. What, however, links physical attractiveness to perceptions of these types of internal characteristics? One explanation is that attractive people find it easier to send messages of liking and positive emotion in part because attractive faces are perceived as more pleasant and friendly than unattractive faces (Larrance & Zuckerman, 1981). This helps explain why even babies are attracted to good-looking faces—the most attractive facial expression on the human face is a smile and it would be adaptive for babies to be drawn to people who are friendly and nurturing. This link between liking and attractiveness goes in both directions, with liking also influencing how physically attractive people judge you to be.

Communication researchers studying **interaction appearance theory** have found something similar (Albada et al., 2002). The idea of this theory is that engaging in positive communication with someone increases perceptions of physical attractiveness, whereas engaging in negative communication decreases perceptions of physical attractiveness. Why does this happen? According to the theory, people believe that good relational partners are physically and socially attractive. Sometimes a person is socially attractive, but initially, they are not perceived as physically attractive enough to date. However, if an interaction is positive and makes them more desirable, they will adjust their initial perceptions and see the person as more physically attractive than they originally did. A set of studies showed that people do indeed rate others as more physically attractive after having positive interactions with them. Finding people to be socially attractive and fun increases perceptions of attraction (Hall & Compton, 2017). The effect of negative interaction was even stronger—people rated others as less physically attractive after engaging in unpleasant communication with them. This effect shows that managing impressions by communicating in a positive, warm fashion increases both social and physical attractiveness. On the flip side, people can ruin positive first impressions that were based on physical appearance by communicating in ways that make a bad impression.

Other studies have also shown that when it comes to long-term attraction, communication trumps appearance (Sunnafrank, 1991, 1992). In one of these studies, Reyes et al. (1999) had students rate people's level of attractiveness based on a photo. Then they watched a video of the person either engaging in positive or negative communication. Although physical attractiveness affected impressions of people in the beginning before they watched the video, those perceptions were revised after seeing the interaction.

WHAT WOULD YOU DO?
ETHICS OF ATTRACTIVENESS

Although we can engage in some behaviors that might make us appear more attractive such as dressing well or wearing makeup, generally we think of physical attractiveness as something we have little direct control over. In addition, our perceptions of what is physically attractive can be influenced by stereotypes and ableism.

Yet, as the **halo effect** reminds us, physical attractiveness can influence our perceptions of social attraction. In turn, social attractiveness drives decisions about social relationships, employment, and career success. How important is it for employers to try to make sure that they are not influenced by physical attractiveness? Are there some instances where candidates should be rated on physical attractiveness? How can decision-makers attempt to avoid bias in decisions regarding hiring and promotion?

Task Attractiveness

Confidence, assertiveness, and competence are also key ingredients in the recipe for task attractiveness. Although perceptions of physical and social characteristics are most important for predicting attraction in social and personal relationships, there are situations where task attraction is the primary consideration. Some examples are deciding who to include in a group project for school as well as who to hire for a job. Of course, physical and social attractiveness still play a role here. Because of the what-is-beautiful-is good effect, people may perceive that better-looking people are competent. And people who are likeable and foster social attraction are good leaders who people want to follow. Nonetheless, competence is determined mostly by one's level of composure and knowledge. People are often evaluated as competent when they communicate without showing signs of nervousness and make verbal statements to show they are knowledgeable. If people look like they are going out of their way to seem knowledgeable, however, they are often rated as unattractive (Vangelisti et al., 1990).

Nonverbal communication plays a key role in promoting task attractiveness during job interviews. For example, Parsons and Liden (1984) showed that sounding fluent and being articulate were better predictors of success in job interviews than were clothing and cleanliness. Yet not everyone possesses the communication skill necessary to excel in job interviews. In one study, only 60 percent of personnel interviewers believed that people generally show high levels of interpersonal skill during employment interviews (Peterson, 1997). Communication that reflects confidence, friendliness, and knowledge can give an interviewee an edge in the competitive employment marketplace.

To make a positive first impression during an employment interview, applicants need to consider both nonverbal and verbal communication. In two classic studies, McGovern and colleagues (McGovern & Ideus, 1978; McGovern & Tinsley, 1978) manipulated a set of nonverbal behaviors so that some interviewees for jobs appeared more expressive, friendly, and confident than others. Half the interviewees were trained to use steady eye contact, smiling, animated voices, expressive gestures, and speech fluency. The other half were trained to be nonexpressive, avoid eye contact, and use nonfluent speech. Not surprisingly, the expressive interviewees made a better first impression. The interviewers rated them higher on attributes such as self-confidence and motivation. Other studies have also shown that interviewees make better impressions and are more likely to be offered positions when they smile, use direct eye contact, are enthusiastic, nod their heads to show agreement, speak in a smooth confident voice, and use animated gestures (e.g., Burgoon & Le Poire, 1999; Peterson, 1997; Wright & Multon, 1995).

Eye contact and voice may be especially important for predicting task attractiveness. A study that examined the interviews of 101 prospective interns for an engineering firm in Great Britain found that those who were accepted used the most eye contact, whereas those who were rejected used the most gaze avoidance (Forbes & Jackson, 1980). In a study of over 500 actual interviews conducted for seasonal amusement park jobs, speech characteristics such as fluency and clear articulation emerged as much better predictors of interviewer perceptions than personal appearance (Parsons & Liden, 1984).

In situations such as job interviews, handshakes are a common form of greeting that can make a strong first impression (Chaplin et al., 2000). In the US, people are generally evaluated most favorably when they shake hands with a steady and firm (but not hard) grip while giving eye contact (Chaplin et al., 2000). Handshakes are associated with being sociable and confident. Indeed, Chaplin and colleagues found that extraverted people tend to give firmer handshakes than introverted people. Men also had firmer handshakes than women. Handshakes, and other forms of greetings, are fundamentally a way to signal cooperativeness and friendliness. In times when handshakes are not advisable, such as during the COVID-19 pandemic that began in 2020, people find other ways to signal cooperativeness, such as through smiling, facing each other directly (either from a physical distance or online), and giving eye contact upon meeting.

Using immediate and expressive behaviors such as smiling, eye contact, and touch can increase perceptions of social, physical, and task attractiveness and can therefore help someone make a positive impression during an interview.

iStock/SDI Productions

Of course, verbal communication is also key for promoting impressions of task attractiveness. Regardless of the quality of communication, applicants who are the most qualified (in terms of résumé credentials) tend to be evaluated most favorably in job interviews. When interviewees give good answers to questions, expressive nonverbal communication makes a difference; interviewees who use more eye contact, smiling, gesturing, and nodding are rated more favorably. However, when interviewees give poor answers to questions, more expressive nonverbal communication can actually lead to less favorable ratings, perhaps because judges perceived the interviewees to be trying to compensate for a lack of knowledge by being nonverbally expressive. Thus, the key for promoting perceptions of task attractiveness is to display verbal communication that shows knowledge and confidence as well as nonverbal communication that also shows confidence, friendliness, and extraversion.

PRINCIPLES OF FIRST IMPRESSIONS AND INITIAL ATTRACTION

The literature on first impressions and attraction tells us a lot about how people make judgments about others based on both verbal and nonverbal communication. Next, we summarize some of the key takeaway ideas from this literature by discussing five general principles.

Principle 1. People have a basic need to form impressions of others quickly.

The need to form impressions of others is innate. In some situations, uncertainty can make people uncomfortable. To avoid this, people seek information to try to reduce uncertainty so they can predict and explain how others will act. During initial interactions, people also make judgments about "outcome values" such as how rewarding (or unrewarding) it would be to develop a relationship with someone. As research on thin-slice impressions has shown, people make impressions after exposure to even very limited information.

Principle 2. Impressions vary in accuracy.

Although first impressions can be accurate, sometimes they are not. Because of the primacy effect, people sometimes hold on to inaccurate impressions longer than they should. Recency effects come into play and cause people to revise their initial perceptions when all information, past and present, is considered. Impressions are also more accurate under certain circumstances, including (1) making judgments that are related to what is observed, (2) having access to consistent information, (3) being motivated to make an accurate judgment, (4) going with one's intuition instead of overanalyzing, and (5) avoiding biases such as stereotypes and egocentrism. In addition, when forming impressions about people while communicating only via technology, it is wise to avoid idealizing them.

Principle 3. Initial impressions are often influenced by physical appearance, but communication can modify or override these impressions.

When we meet people, the first thing we often notice is appearance. Fair or not, people often stereotype others based on how they look. Being especially good-looking comes with perks and penalties. However, once we start interacting with people, our impressions can quickly change. The attractive man who we think might be a confident player could reveal himself to be introverted and sensitive. The woman we initially judge as plain might seem more attractive after having an interesting conversation and noticing how natural her smile is. As interaction appearance theory suggests, communication is powerful in shaping perceptions of others.

Principle 4. Affinity-seeking strategies promote social attraction.

People like to be around those who are friendly, kind, and other-focused. Therefore, it is no surprise that affinity-seeking strategies, which are designed to make positive impressions on people we want to like us, would emphasize these qualities. Key strategies involve being polite and socially appropriate, acting warm and friendly, and focusing on the other person by listening, eliciting self-disclosure, and giving compliments. Using nonverbal immediacy behaviors, such as smiling, giving eye contact, and leaning forward convey involvement in the interaction, as does self-disclosure. People are also socially attracted to those who are confident and assertive without being pushy. Finally, it is important to keep in mind that even though these behaviors are called affinity-seeking *strategies* because people sometimes use them intentionally to try to create positive impressions, they often occur naturally in interactions when we like someone.

Principle 5. Displays of knowledge and confidence promote task attraction.

In situations involving tasks, such as work relationships and employment interviews, the key is to be perceived in line with the three Cs—competent, composed, and confident. Verbal communication should show that you have the knowledge to be competent in performing relevant tasks. Nonverbal communication should show that you are composed and calm, rather than anxious. And both verbal and nonverbal communication should reflect confidence. Asserting one's opinion when appropriate, speaking fluently, and giving eye contact are some ways that people communicate confidence.

CONCLUSION

Maddie and Elijah are at the very beginning of what could be a short or long journey together. At this point, they are still getting to know one another and determining if they want to pursue some type of relationship with each other. Both are likely on their best behavior, aware that they need to make a good impression if they want things to continue. So far everything is off to a good start. Maddie thought Elijah was physically attractive when she looked him up on social media, which led her to tell Haley to give him her number. Perhaps even more importantly, when they met at the coffeehouse, they communicated in a way that showed liking and interest, bringing social attraction into the equation. Whether this attraction fades or strengthens as they communicate more is something only time will tell.

CHAPTER 3 STUDY GUIDE

KEY TERMS

Identify and explain the meaning of each of the following key terms.

active uncertainty reduction

affinity-seeking strategies

attraction

cultural stereotypes

efficacy assessment

halo effect

hyperpersonal perspective

impression formation

impression management

interaction appearance theory

interactive uncertainty reduction

nonverbal immediacy

outcome expectancy

outcome value

passive uncertainty reduction

person perceptions

physical attraction

physical level of impressions

predicted outcome value theory

primacy effect

psychological level of impressions

recency effect

social attraction

sociocultural level of impression

task attraction

theory of motivated information management

thin slice

uncertainty

uncertainty reduction theory

what-is-beautiful-is-conceited hypothesis

what-is-beautiful-is-good hypothesis

REFLECTION QUESTIONS

1. One of the problems with first impressions is that they can be inaccurate. Based on this chapter and your own experiences, what specific biases, including stereotypes, do you think lead to inaccurate first impressions of others? How can these biases be altered so that people can make more accurate judgments of others?

2. This chapter includes three ways that people reduce uncertainty—passive, active, and interactive. Think about examples for each of these that are different from those in the chapter. How have social media and technology changed the way people reduce uncertainty? Do you think some strategies are generally more effective than others? If so, why?

3. From your experiences, how true do you think the what-is-beautiful-is-good hypothesis is? Have you observed any "perks" or "penalties" associated with physical attractiveness beyond those discussed in this chapter? Do you think the prevalence of social media has affected the ways that people might stereotype others based on appearance? If so, how?

4. As discussed in this chapter, the three types of attraction are all related to one another. For example, social attraction can influence how physically attractive you rate someone, and people who are physically attractive can be perceived to be more competent than they actually are. Describe some specific ways that you think the types of attraction are related in everyday life, both when forming initial impressions and later after relationships have developed.

4

COMMUNICATING ACROSS CULTURES

WHAT YOU'LL LEARN...

When you have finished the chapter, you should be able to do the following:

4.1 Define culture and co-cultures.

4.2 Identify cultural dimensions.

4.3 Explain dialectical tensions in intercultural interactions.

4.4 Analyze intercultural communication competence from multiple theoretical perspectives.

During his first-year experience course at his university, Clarence is assigned to choose from a selection of campus activities. Clarence decides to go to the study-abroad fair. He's a communication major and thinks international experience will likely help him in the global workplace. Plus, he's always had an interest in travel even though most of his travels thus far have been closer to home. In fact, his first trip to visit this university, several states away from his home, was the farthest he had ever traveled. As a first-generation student, Clarence already feels that the culture of the college he chose is vastly different than life at home. People seem to have very different motivations, his accent attracts attention, and he struggles to explain what he's learning at college to people back at home. Upon entering the study-abroad fair, Clarence is overwhelmed with the booths and choices, from quick trips (Spring Break in Brazil!) to semester experiences (Gambian Culture and Agriculture!) to even being an exchange student with another university overseas for a year. What would it be like, Clarence wonders, to spend a year in South Korea? Would it be as difficult as it's been to figure out his place in the university culture? Or would it be easier because he expects everything to be so different? How would people interact with him? Who would he be friends with? What would they be like?

Our understanding of messages within interpersonal encounters is heavily influenced by the context in which those messages are exchanged. An important component of that context is culture. Culture forms the underlying web of meaning that allows messages to be understood and shared. These contextual underpinnings can help facilitate understanding between people and groups. At other times, when people are grounded in different cultures, it can make it more difficult to understand the motivations and goals of our fellow communicators. Yet engaging in intercultural encounters can provide incredible opportunities to learn about each other and create enduring relationships that transcend and celebrate cultural differences. Developing relationships that embrace cultural differences through interpersonal encounters can inspire us and broaden our world views. Understanding co-cultural differences can help us be more mindful and thoughtful in how we engage with the broader world. Effective communication across cultures ultimately can help us build a better world.

WHAT IS CULTURE?

There are likely as many scholarly definitions for the term *culture* as there are cultures. We note that language and meaning are the shifting and contextualized groundwork that allows for understanding across communicators. Indeed, capturing the understanding of terms and phenomena is a cultural process. Scholarship of cultural understanding and critique and the ways that this scholarship intersects with understanding interpersonal communication are constantly changing as the language and terms are consistently critiqued and contested. Similarly, the act of writing down a particular example risks essentializing cultural differences and flattening culture richness. Clarence, for example, is so much more than a Black American student considering a trip to South Korea. He experiences both marginalization and privileges in complex, negotiated ways. His experience and enactment of interpersonal encounters reflects these rich complexities. And yet, to help you, the interpersonal communication student, understand how culture influences interpersonal communication encounters and processes, we will need to choose specific terms and articulate specific, albeit limited, examples. We ask that you bring your own rich, complex, cultural lens to the reading and classroom interactions.

Students broaden their horizons by experiencing the college culture. Some students like Clarence, in the opening scenario, hope to expand their experiences even further by participating in a study-abroad program.

iStock/PeopleImages

   For our purposes in considering how culture is influenced by and influences interpersonal communication, we consider **culture** as a learned system of meaning that provides a frame of reference for understanding symbolic interaction. Cultural meanings are often grounded in cultural artifacts such as rituals, symbols, and values. Culture represents a foundation of shared meaning that provides the framework through which other messages—including those in interpersonal interactions—are interpreted and understood (Ting-Toomey & Dorjee, 2018).

On a global level, there is an increase in interactions and interdependence among people across national borders (Beck & Sznaider, 2010). People may find themselves traveling far and wide for pleasure, business, or necessity. Success in the global marketplace requires understanding cultural differences (Bovee & Thill, 2010). Modern business practices often require international travel and interaction with culturally differentiated partners (Washington et al., 2012). Managers may find themselves needing to be competent in managing intercultural relationships in order to oversee diverse sets of employees. These employees can be on distributed teams, each living in their country of origin and connected through technology.

In addition, communication technologies allow people to be in contact with culturally diverse co-communicators on a regular basis either through virtual work or purely social interaction (McEwan & Sobré-Denton, 2011). No longer is it necessary for people to undergo expensive travel to interact with people from different cultures. Such encounters may be sought out by people through specific message boards, or cross-cultural encounters may be incidental contact, as when one comes into contact with people from different cultures through social media. Other technologically mediated encounters may be required by one's workplace as corporations increasingly engage in a global, networked workplace.

Culture as a Learned System of Meaning

Max Weber wrote that "man is an animal suspended in webs of significance that he himself has spun" (see Geertz, 1973, p. 5). Weber's metaphor of the web can help us begin to grasp the influence and effects of the culture(s) that we live within. Cultures are **social constructions**—shared, co-created, and co-supported understandings of how the social world functions—that are built over time to create a shared system of meaning. Culture is ultimately the way we make sense of our shared social reality (Pacanowsky & O'Donnel-Trujillo, 1982). Because social constructions are malleable, culture and cultural meanings can change over time. Yet it would be extremely difficult for a single individual to change a cultural thread. In part, if we remember our web, this is because other threads of the cultural web depend on each other—to change one is to change them all. Like a web being spun, new threads and formations develop over time. These new cultural understandings are built from the foundation within the older web.

Similar to these dreamcatchers, culture can be seen as a web constructed of many different threads of meaning, all of which are dependent on each other.

Kerrick via Getty Images

Our choices and interpretations of behavior are then dependent on our cultural web to make sense. For example, depending on what your culture believes about the formation of romantic relationships, asking someone for a kiss could be seen as completely normal or completely scandalous. In one cultural viewpoint, the act of asking for a kiss might communicate that you admire and respect the person you are asking. From a different cultural lens, it might communicate that you do not think highly of the person because you think they would just give away these kisses. The context in which the kiss is received, the culture, provides the framework for how the kiss will be received.

We learn our culture through living within these systems of shared meaning. Indeed, messages and events mean what they mean *because* of the culture that is the context for these messages. Culture is a learned *system* of meaning. Each message depends on the cultural web of context to make sense to others with whom we are communicating. However, in our daily lives, we generally do not spend time considering the cultural underpinnings of every message we send. To do so would be cognitively exhausting. Indeed, often our own culture can appear to us "normal" or "natural" when, in fact, all cultural systems of meaning are constructed artifices of human organization. When people who have differing cultural backgrounds interact, they can experience interactional incongruity—or feel that their interaction is "out of sync" (Kim, 2014). Taking the time to mindfully interrogate our own culture can help us understand the deeper reasons for why we behave in certain ways, how messages will be received, and how we might appear to communicators who are outside of our own culture.

Cultural Artifacts

Within the learned systems of meanings that make up cultures are social constructions that represent symbolic touchstones for a particular culture. In concert with the symbolic interactionist perspective described in Chapter 2, culture both shapes and is formed through social interaction. These social constructions or cultural artifacts might include language, gestures, social relationships, religions, values, customs, food, and more (see Jandt, 2010). However, surface-level cultural artifacts, such as fashion or popular media, often change at a much faster pace than more ingrained artifacts such as symbols, rituals, and values.

Cultural symbols including the language(s) that are spoken within a particular culture provide an important building block for meaning in that culture. Word meanings, for example, may be perceived differently in cultures with gendered suffixes (e.g., *Latina/Latino*) and/or prefixes (*lia chassure, le gant*). In addition, languages take on different dialects or grammars as they are dispersed in different cultures. **Colloquialisms**, or sayings that make sense within particular cultural frameworks but can be difficult to translate directly, are a useful example of how culture shapes language use. Often the connection to a literal meaning is lost over time but the cultural meaning is retained. For example, did you know that the term "three sheets to the wind" (often used to describe someone who is very inebriated) was initially a sailing term? A ship that had lost control of all three sheets or sails would be sailing in an erratic manner with very little control. Similarly, saying something did or didn't "pan out" is believed to have originated during the California

Colloquialisms sometimes originate in historical or cultural events, such as the term "pan out" or phrases like "I hope it pans out for you" being reminiscent of the California Gold Rush.

iStock/LeeTorrens

Gold Rush when prospectors hoped to see gold at the bottom of the pan after the gravel and sand washed away.

I DIDN'T KNOW THAT!
WORLD ENGLISHES

Despite not having an official language, many Americans speak English. Indeed, many people throughout the world speak English as a first or secondary language. But did you know that not all of these "Englishes" are the same?

There are many different Englishes throughout the world. Scholars use the term "Englishes" to articulate the wide variation and cultural pluralism that exists for English-language users around the world (Pennycook, 2006; Rose & Galloway, 2019). Some countries, such as the United States, Great Britain, or Canada, speak English as a national language. In some multilingual countries, such as India or Nigeria, Englishes are used as an additional language for intranational communication. In still other countries, some citizens learn English for the purpose of international communication (Kachru & Smith, 2008). Many of these differentiated Englishes around the world are remnants of colonization by Great Britain and the United States and in some cases reflect overlaying grammar from other languages onto English. However, even across primarily English-speaking countries, differences emerge (Vaux & Golder, 2003). For example, in the wintertime, an average Canadian might put on a toque to head out to grab a double double, whereas an American might find themselves donning a hat to get a coffee with extra cream and sugar. Within-nation differences emerge as well. For example, a Michigander might grab a pop, while a Californian orders a soda, and someone in Georgia asks what kinds of coke are available. No one English is more "correct" than another; they simply emerged, exist, and are understood within different cultural frameworks.

What phrases are common to your family or the community you are from that are not common across your native language? How might these different versions of a language emerge? What can this process tell us about how cultural inferences might be different even between people who speak the "same" language?

Is this couple sharing a pop, soda, or coke? Your answer is likely to at least partially depend on where you live.

JGI/Daniel Grill via Getty Images

Wedding ceremonies are an example of an event that often reflects cultural customs and traditions.

Kevin Winter/Getty Images; iStock/rvimages; iStock/chameleons-eye; iStock/Bogdan Kurylo

Cultural rituals are collective activities that occur within a culture. These rituals help anchor cultural events and interpretations (Hofstede, 1994; Katriel & Shenhar, 1989). Cultural rituals or traditions are passed on from one generation to another (Ting-Toomey & Dorjee, 2015). In the United States, weddings are a good example of rituals that symbolize elements of American culture. Technically, to be married, you simply need a license, an officiant, and two people who wish to be married. However, other cultural rituals are often included in US culture. For example, brides often wear white, groomsmen wear tuxedos, bouquets are tossed, cakes are cut, and speeches are made. The pluralistic nature of US. culture often means that other traditions are woven through the ceremonies. You may have attended a Jewish ceremony where the groom crushes a glass, watched a Greek Orthodox bride be crowned seven times, or cheered as an African American couple jumped over a broom. At some receptions, paying a dollar to dance with the bride or groom is traditional. At others, gifts of salt and bread are provided. Each of these rituals connects the newlyweds to a broader culture and cocultures within which the marriage ceremony is performed and understood.

Cultural values help us to understand what behaviors are perceived as good or bad or normal or abnormal within a particular culture (Hofstede, 2001). Our values are our preferences for particular scenarios, behaviors, or attitudes. Cultural values affect interpersonal communication behavior by influencing our relational rules regarding relationships, attitudes toward work, and how we perform identity. For example, your culture might influence whether or not you feel it is appropriate to live with a romantic partner before marriage, or how willing you are to work overtime.

WHAT WOULD YOU DO?
CULTURAL APPROPRIATION

We live in an increasingly globalized world, where our wide-ranging cultural influences abound. One indication of this is the food that is readily available. For example, within a few minutes of one of the author's houses in the United States is a German bakery, a Polish bakery, an Italian bakery, and a Mexican bakery. This is very useful when one needs to pick up decadent pączki or a tasty concha. However, while at times experiencing the food and customs of other cultures comes from a place of appreciation, at other times people appropriate cultural artifacts. Cultural appropriation is broadly defined as when members of one culture use the symbols, artifacts, genres, and rituals of another culture (Rogers, 2006). Cultural appropriation is an active process—the member or members of one culture are actively making elements of another culture something of their own. There are elements of power, privilege, and colonization at play as well. Often the culture is appropriated to commodify elements of that culture for profit (Appiah, 2018). An example is when members of a dominant group borrow the heritage of the people they colonized to name sports teams, summer camps, and other products.

One example of cultural appropriation is when people portray stereotypical versions of people from other cultures as Halloween costumes. Another type of cultural appropriation is using an artifact that has specific cultural significance as a piece of fashion, such as a non-Hindu wearing a bindi to a music festival. Some who engage in these practices argue that they are merely appreciating the culture as a type of cultural exchange. Cultural exchange happens between cultures with roughly equal levels of power, whereas appropriation is typically the use of elements from less privileged cultures and co-cultures by members of a dominant group (Rogers, 2006). In these cases, there is little reciprocity between cultures and a lack of permission from the appropriated group. In addition, the use of aspects of the dominant culture by a subordinated culture isn't quite the same phenomenon (Rogers, 2006). Power structure matters when considering cultural appropriation and nondominant cultures may feel that they must adopt these elements to assimilate into the dominant culture.

What do you choose when faced with issues of possible cultural appropriation? Consider the following examples. Which of these seem like appropriation versus cultural exchange?

Would you send your kids to summer camps named after indigenous tribes or that use indigenous-sounding words?

Your friend, who is part Indian, has started a Bollywood dance class and the clientele is composed of mostly white suburban moms. Do you go?

Your roommate has thought of a Halloween costume that is a partial stereotype of an Asian culture (neither you nor your roommate in this scenario is Asian). What do you say?

Would you post a meme or gif of a person of a different race or culture on Twitter or Instagram to represent your thoughts?

Is engaging in a TikTok dance challenge that was started in a community that is a different race than yours a form of cultural appropriation? Or is this reaching out across differences?

Culture as the Foundation for Shared Meaning

Interpersonal messages are interpreted through the lens of our cultural knowledge. Communication interactions and messages make sense to us within the context in which they are delivered. When communicators share a cultural understanding, it may be easier for them to interpret specific messages because the underlying framework or web of significance that provides much of the meaning of a specific utterance is already mutually understood. Messages have both content and relational functions (Watzlawick et al., 1967). The **content function of a message** is the actual words that are spoken—the denotative, dictionary definition. The **relational function of a message** is the contextual elements including culture, shared past, and relational understandings. Our ability to understand the relational function of messages is why the words "I love you" could mean very different things in various interactions. "I love you" spoken to a spouse on the way out the door signals affection. "I love you" shouted to a friend who has just surprised you with concert tickets signals appreciation. "I love you" spoken for the very first time to a new romantic partner can signal an important moment and turning point in that relationship.

Often culture is a key part of understanding the relational function of a message. For example, consider one of the colloquialisms we mentioned before—"three sheets to the wind." In US. culture, most of us recognize this phrase as signaling someone has overly imbibed on alcohol. A direct translation of that phrase would make little sense to someone from another culture. Interestingly, this particular phrase is one that reflects what can happen when the residue of a particular cultural meaning exists beyond the memory of the origination of the term. We would hazard a guess that most readers of this textbook recognize the current cultural meaning of the phrase but not as a reference to sailing—where if you have lost control of three sails/sheets, you have lost control of your ship. As another example, where do you think the phrase "a flash in the pan" originated? Many people from the United States would assume that it, like "panned out," started during the California Gold Rush. However, most scholars believe its origins go further back to 17th century Europe, referring to gunpowder sparking in a musket without the ball being released.

These examples, and other language considerations such as slang, help illustrate how culture creates the contextual foundation upon which so much other meaning within interpersonal interactions rests. Indeed, people who struggle with understanding nuance and cultural norms can often struggle with effectively interpreting messages (Bennett, 2004). We say they "misread" a situation. Often in these cases, the linguistic content of messages has been perfectly understood, but the relational and cultural implications were not properly decoded.

CULTURE AND CULTURES

In considering how culture influences communication, we examine broad frameworks that help us determine and understand meaning. Some scholars of cultural and intercultural communication attempt to categorize cultures associated with nation-states into cultural dimensions as a starting point for understanding our differences. Other scholars take the position that while these broad dimensions can be a useful starting point, they have limitations. For instance, members of specific cultures all experience that culture differently depending on their position within the culture and the co-cultures with which they identify. **Co-cultures** are groups characterized by values, beliefs, and behaviors that distinguish them from the larger culture. Co-cultures often establish cultural understandings that diverge from the dominant group. Clarence, from the opening scenario, is now part of a university culture that he shares with other college students. There are numerous co-cultures, including those defined by region, ethnic background, generation, sex, and sexual orientation, among others. Another important concept is **intersectionality**, which is the idea that categorizations such as race, gender, and class are interconnected in ways that create interdependent systems of privilege, discrimination, or disadvantage for any given group or individual. All of these concepts, plus the idea of organizational culture, are discussed next.

Cultural Dimensions of Nation-States

Learning about cultural dimensions can be useful to begin to build our understanding of different ways of making meaning within different broad cultures (Ting-Toomey & Dorjee, 2015). Hofstede and colleagues outlined six cultural dimensions that have been used to measure cultural perceptions across nation-states (Hofstede, 2011; Hofstede et al., 2010). These dimensions should not be indiscriminately applied to individual communication episodes. Within cultures, there are considerable within-group differences across individuals. However, learning about the different dimensions can give communicators a sense of the possible differences in the ways in which people construct meaning. These six dimensions include individualism/collectivism, power distance, uncertainty–avoidance, long-term/short-term orientation, masculinity/femininity, and indulgence.

Individualism/collectivism is likely the most commonly known of the cultural dimensions. This dimension refers to how people within a culture see themselves as interdependent with other members. Cultures that are highly individualistic are more likely to concern themselves with "I" and perhaps their immediate family. Cultures that are highly collectivist see themselves as part of a greater "we" to which they bear responsibility. The United States, for example, ranks as a highly individualistic culture where people are expected to look after themselves. South Korea is an example of a more **collectivist** where people form strong group relationships and loyalty to the group is considered extremely important. Our US student, Clarence, might struggle to adapt between the two cultural systems if he does take a year abroad to study in South Korea. As an outsider, Clarence might have a hard time breaking into an in-group that would provide social interaction and other social resources. Studying in South Korea could be an amazing experience for Clarence, but it will be helpful for him to consider the possible cultural differences that might create challenges or misunderstandings.

Power distance refers to how cultures perceive inequality. Cultures high in power distance are more accepting of inequality as a part of how society functions. They may be more likely to appreciate hierarchies, accept unequal rights as part of the social norms, and create organizations with centralized top-down structures. Members of cultures with low power distance prefer egalitarianism, expect that all members will have access to equal rights, and may be more likely to create decentralized organizations with more informal communication chains. India, for example, is a country that is rated high on power distance. One of your authors recently went on a tour in India. Both she and her travel partner (both from the United States and used to low power distance) had to adjust to the cultural expectation that they were not really supposed to talk to their car driver, as the tour guide was considered a higher-status position. This preference by both the guides and the driver, Pradeep, occurred despite spending far more time with Pradeep over the course of the week and talking to him regularly in English when the tour guides were not around. When they did have a guide, the guide and Pradeep would converse in Hindu and then the guide would "translate" Pradeep's contributions to the trip into English.

The **uncertainty–avoidance** dimension relates to how much stress people in a culture feel when things are unknown or uncertain. In cultures that are uncertainty avoidant, cultural members feel uncomfortable when they are unsure of what the future will bring. Members of these cultures may prefer more structure and predictability. In cultures that are low in uncertainty–avoidance, members feel more comfortable with ambiguity. Countries that are rated higher on the uncertainty–avoidance scale, like Mexico or Japan, tend to have rigid rules and are less tolerant of deviations from the norm. A study of online auctions found that Japanese auctions were much more likely to draw wide participation if the auction included all of the potential sale information, including pictures, whereas the German and the US. auctions drew similar levels of participation across both high and low sale information contexts (Vishwanath, 2003). The United States has a moderate score on the uncertainty–avoidance scale. Of course, within the United States there are co-cultures and individuals who prefer greater control and those who accept greater ambiguity. This variation is true within other countries as well.

Long-term/short-term orientation refers to the role that cultural members see themselves as having in the future of a culture. When members of a culture see themselves as having an important role in the long-term plans of a culture, they have a long-term orientation. Members of these cultures find it important to prepare for the future. For example, long-term cultures may prioritize investments in education or policies that may cause short-term pain but are designed to improve life for future generations. Japan, for example, tends to invest in education and research to be better prepared for the future. More short-term cultures may be more focused on the here-and-now with less concern for the future. The United States has a more short-term orientation, so projects with quick results may be favored over long-term planning.

Hofstede and colleagues also have classified countries as to how masculine or feminine their cultures are. The Hofstede classification of **masculinity/femininity** adopts a fairly Western, and somewhat dated, social construction of how masculinity and femininity are expressed. Within this categorization, cultures that are deemed highly masculine are thought to value assertiveness and competition. Masculine cultures may be more hierarchical in nature and value stereotypical masculinity. Japan is also an example of a highly masculine culture. However, because Japan is also collectivistic, the competition tends to be between groups. Finland, on the other hand, scores quite low on masculinity. Cultures like Finland's value high quality of life outside of work, balance between work and life, and caring for others. Feminine cultures may be more horizontally structured and egalitarian.

A higher percentage of women are likely to be in leadership positions in feminine cultures. Here, the Prime Minister of Finland, Sanna Marin, is surrounded by her Ministers of Education, Interior, and Finance during a press conference.

Antti Yrjonen/NurPhoto via Getty Images

The category of **indulgence** refers to how much people in a given culture attempt to control their desires and impulses. Cultures that are ranked higher on indulgence value enjoying life and having fun and may be more optimistic. Cultures that are lower in indulgence may be more restrained, pessimistic, and less inclined to enjoy leisure. Russia, for example, rates low on indulgence. Mexicans, on the other hand, place a higher value on leisure time and fun.

Co-Cultures and Intersectionality

Although Hofstede's cultural dimensions can be a useful starting point for considering different cultures, these dimensions are a fairly rough estimate and tend to gloss over cultural differences that occur within countries. Another limitation of cultural dimensions is that focusing on nation-states as cultures can miss cultural similarities between countries as well as the existence of different co-cultures within a broader cultural system of meaning.

Indeed, most communication scholars think about culture as shared systems of meaning that do not start and stop at the borders of nations. Rather cultures tend to "overlap and mingle" with each other (Hannerz, 1990, p. 239). In addition, cultural systems are often nested within broader cultures. For example, Clarence in our opening vignette is a member of his hometown, is a Black man, and is becoming a member of the university culture. Orbe's co-cultural theory considers how different cultural frameworks may exist with a broader, dominant culture (Orbe & Roberts, 2012). The concept of co-cultures helps us understand how people within a culture may be situated within different fields of experience and different understandings and abilities to engage across co-cultures and within the dominant frame (Orbe, 1998).

Through a series of studies based on the lived experience of co-cultural group members, Orbe developed co-cultural theory to explain how members of underrepresented groups communicate within the social and cultural framework developed by the dominant group. Co-cultural groups diverge from the dominant group in their cultural understandings but also must exist and communicate within the dominant cultural frame (Orbe & Spellers, 2005). In the United States, for example, there are examples of many vibrant co-cultures. Co-cultures might occur when people bring elements of a place of origin to the community: for example, Cubans in Miami or Puerto Ricans in Humboldt Park. Other co-cultures might grow from meaning derived from cultural religious practices such as Jewish or Muslim communities. Another example of a co-cultural group might be LGBTQIA communities who have created spaces and media where they can engage with each other outside of the view of the dominant group.

Black Twitter is an example of a co-cultural online space (Brock, 2012). Black Twitter carves out space on a social medium that is often driven by the communication norms of the dominant, white, masculine culture. Yet Black Twitter users are able to perform communication patterns and constructs formed in Black American culture to network with the broader Black Twitter audience. Some of these cultural communication patterns include Black Vernacular English or *signifyin'* (Florini, 2014). Signifyin' has roots in "playing the dozens" (see Garner, 1983), a ritualized, dissing game that requires verbal dexterity and wit to trade lightning-fast put-downs. Although cultural outsiders might see a mean-spirited game, signifyin' is "a deeply collaborative practice" that "traditionally fostered group solidarity in Black American communities" (Florini, 2014, p. 226). Although Black Twitter's meaning may be lost by audience members who do not share understandings of the cultural web that provides context for the message interpretation by co-cultural members, mediated spaces provide a window into how co-cultural members construct shared understanding (Appiah, 2018).

Co-cultural spaces create systems of meaning and communication that are developed outside of the dominant group and help marginalized members negotiate with and about dominant communication structures. Although groups may be delineated by categories such as race, class, sexuality, gender, or geography, individual people are often combinations of these categories. Membership within various co-cultures provides us with different lenses with which we make sense of the world. People often experience different groups and co-cultures in intersectional ways.

Intersectionality is a concept developed by critical theorist Kimberlé Crenshaw . Class, race, gender, and other elements of our identity can lead us to experience and contribute to culture in ways that are different from people who differ from us on these factors (Crenshaw, 1994). Peoples' experiences and ways of making meaning are informed by the ways in which a variety of cultural factors intersect and the power and privilege embedded within those factors (Crenshaw, 1994). Crenshaw was particularly interested in how feminist critiques often did not give voice to the experiences of racism while Black critiques of racism did not take into account the experiences of women. Considering experiences through the lens of the concept of intersectionality can give voice to people living *at the intersection* of different social identities (Collins, 2019). The metaphor of intersectionality can help communicators, analysts, and activists think about how the social constructs of our identity might intertwine. People's experiences, perspectives, cultural understandings, and communication are all shaped by their intersectional social location (Collins, 2019). Failure to recognize the multiple facets of someone's identity within a culture can erase understanding of their experience and/or make it difficult for people to articulate experiences related to their intersectional identity.

Kimberlé Crenshaw's idea of intersectionality was first introduced as a legal concept in 1989. It is now a key concept in many disciplines, including communication.

Monica Schipper/Getty Images for The New York Women's Foundation

It is also important for interpersonal communication students to remember the developmental perspective—culture serves as an important level of information to *begin* knowing how to communicate with others, yet we find a wide array of group and individual differences within any given cultural framework. Interpersonal communication is communication that is premised on a unique, idiosyncratic understanding of your fellow communicator(s). However, the influence of culture and groups has important impacts on the way people construct and understand their own and others' personal identities (Gangi & Soliz, 2016). For example, imagine a married couple where the spouses come from different cultural backgrounds. To successfully make predictions about how to best communicate with your spouse, it would be important to understand your spouse's personal preferences. Yet understanding those personal preferences would involve being aware of =your spouse's cultural framework for understanding relationships and the concept of marriage. One could consider this type of example within the context of friendships or co-workers. As people grow closer in these relationships, they grow to communicate with each other more as specific individuals rather than members of some group. However, the way we understand each other's messages, behaviors, and roles is grounded in our cultural understandings. Indeed, the way we understand each other as individuals may be based in our perception of the unique intersectionality of our communication partner (Stewart, 2012).

Organizational Cultures

Cultural meaning and understanding can also emerge within the context of organizations. Organizations develop, over time, their own learned systems of meaning that help organizational members interpret messages within that culture. For example, American Airlines and Southwest Airlines are both consumer market aviation companies. However, they are known to have very different internal cultures. Southwest is broadly known for having a more laid-back, employee-focused environment.

Organizations can be broadly defined as "the interlocked actions of a collectivity" (Pacanowsky & O'Donnel-Trujillo, 1982, p. 122). We can think of large organizations such as multinational Fortune 500 companies, or small organizations such as a local volunteer firefighting organization. Organizations can serve a multitude of purposes. It is likely that you personally belong to many organizations such as the university or college you are attending, your place of employment, and perhaps student groups, religious congregations, service organizations, and more. Organizations are created through communication and organizational cultures and norms create the social practices and ways of thinking of organizational members (Putnam & Fairhurst, 2015). In a way, organizations resemble the webs of significance created by the residue of the communication process discussed by Weber. The entities that we think of as organizations are simply the result of or residue of the continuous communication of humans who are organizing.

Communication creates and sustains organizational culture (Putnam & Fairhurst, 2015). Through communication, organizations develop cultural stories, rituals, artifacts, and values that help organizational members create and understand meanings within that organization (Pacanowsky & O'Donnel-Trujillo, 1982; Schein, 2004). Organizational culture both creates the context within which people choose their behaviors and messages and informs how those behaviors and messages are interpreted (Keyton, 2011). Organizational culture is constantly in a state of dynamic flux because it is constantly created and re-created through "social and discursive practices" (Fairhurst & Putnam, 2015).

Organizational cultures emerge through **sensemaking** (Weick et al., 2005). Sensemaking is how we create meanings that inform how we interpret ourselves, our behavior, and others' selves and behavior (Mills, 2003). Sensemaking helps members of organizations understand what actions mean within an organization (Weick et al., 2005). The concept of sensemaking provides an important linkage between interpersonal communication and understanding communication through cultural contexts. People make sense of the interpersonal interactions that they experience through the culture(s) that provide the framework for how they make sense of their world. Interpersonal interactions provide continuing contributions to cultural frameworks (Taylor & Van Every, 2000). While interpersonal communication is ultimately about understanding people as individuals, our ability to make sense of the behavior of our interpersonal interactants depends in part on the cultures through which those individuals make sense of themselves and others.

THEORIES OF INTERCULTURAL INTERPERSONAL INTERACTIONS

Within this section, we offer different theoretical perspectives that provide insight into how we approach and manage intercultural interactions. Although cultural dimensions provided one perspective in considering the influence of culture on intercultural interactions, interpersonal communication processes tend to focus on learning about people as individuals. Treating people from a specific nation-state as having a monolithic culture can lead to misunderstanding and less than ideal communicative interactions. Often, intercultural theorists take a more nuanced view in discussing how people come to understand each other in intercultural interactions.

Cultural Dialectics

Given the interplay between interpersonal and intergroup understandings of each other within communication encounters, it may be more useful to consider intercultural interactions through the lens of process rather than categorizing them into specific cultural categories or dimensions (Martin & Nakayama, 2010). Although, as noted earlier, (Hofstede, 2011) approach to categorizing cultures does provide an easy entrée to beginning to understand global cultural differences, the approach may also oversimplify cultures and essentialize differences in cross-cultural interpersonal interactions . Indeed, culture does not stop at the arbitrary borders of nations. In addition, Hofstede's dimensional analyses regularly conflate countries with culture, and countries may contain multiple co-cultures that intersect in unique ways. Individuals within a given culture may or may not internalize the values associated with each of the dimensions. Indeed, approaching a given individual as if they represent the values of their assigned cultural dimensions may encourage stereotypical thinking and cause misattributions in interpersonal interactions. Also, many countries score in the mid-range of cultural dimensions, suggesting that within many cultures individuals seek to manage approaches to cultural values rather than find their behavior dictated by adherence to one side of a dimension or another.

Thus, although dimensions are a useful starting point, in practice it may be more appropriate to consider cultural encounters and intercultural communication through a dialectical lens. The dialectical approach to communication emphasizes that culture is continually created and re-created through communication practices. The context of culture is a dynamic, shifting process, not a stable factor influencing communication encounters. Martin and Nakayama (1999, 2010) identified six dialectical tensions inherent in intercultural communication interactions: individual/cultural, personal/social-contextual, differences/similarities, static/dynamic, present-future/history-past, and privilege/disadvantage.

Individual/Cultural

People are both unique individuals and members of broader cultures that shape their understanding of the world. This is the **individual/cultural dialectic**. When considering our communication choices and interactions with members of other cultures, it is important to remember for both ourselves and our co-interactants that our behavior may be guided by our cultural interpretations, but we are individuals within that culture. The individual/cultural dialectic illuminates the tension people feel between wanting to belong to cultural groups while also wanting to be seen as individuals. The workplace provides a good example of this tension. An employee will likely want to fit in with the organizational culture and be regarded as a team player, but that same employee will also want to be seen as an individual who makes a unique contribution to the organization.

Personal/Social-Contextual

The **personal/social-contextual dialectic** refers to how communication is grounded in both the understanding of the individual and the context in which communication is taking place. Martin and Nakayama (2006) provide an example of a professor and student. In some ways, the understanding of messages is understood through the lens of what is normal in a classroom, yet each professor and each student brings their own self to the interaction. An encounter with one of your professors is different from other professors based on the personality and unique aspects of that professor. When professors travel, for example, a Singaporean professor coming to teach students in the United States or a British professor finding herself in a classroom in India, they often find themselves needing to adjust to the classroom norms of that culture. Yet each professor likely does so in their own way.

Difference/Similarity

When considering intercultural communication, often we think of the differences between cultures and how we must adapt for those differences. Indeed, the dimensions perspective discussed earlier is predicated on identifying and understanding key cultural differences. However, a focus on the **difference/similarities dialectic** reminds us how important it is to recognizing that there are many similarities in the ways that human beings from different cultures communicate. Overemphasizing cultural differences can encourage an "us versus them" mentality. Overemphasizing cultural universals can lead people to elide important cultural differences. Attempts to engage in intercultural interaction with the "we're really all the same" approach can at best lead to losing the benefits of diversity and intercultural encounters. At worst, it might offend your fellow interactant, as such a sentiment may be read as an erasure of their culture. Levitt (2019) provided an example where a US company toured Libya and proposed American-style casinos and hotels. The Libyans, however, while interested in business propositions (similarity), wanted people to come experience Libyan culture, which would not include alcohol or casinos. Approaching intercultural communication with the understanding that we are both similar and different can help us co-create understandings with our fellow intercultural communicators.

Static/Dynamic

The **static/dynamic dialectic** articulates that cultural practices are both consistent and ever-changing. Some cultural dimensions may have long-lasting consistent effects on the interpretation of messages and events within a culture. At the same time, the application of these dimensions may vary over time or when applied to a particular social phenomenon. Intercultural communicators need to seek to understand both historical underpinnings of cultural communication and the dynamic processes and interpretations that produce any given communication moment. Nonverbal behaviors provide a good example of the static/dynamic dialectic. Some gestures and movements have meanings within cultures that have been consistent for hundreds of years, such as nodding to say "yes" in some places, whereas other gestures, such as the "hang loose" gesture that originated in Hawaii, are much newer. Some new gestures are fads that do not stand the test of time, whereas others become embedded with a culture.

Present-Future/History-Past

Similarly, the **present-future/history-past dialectic** reminds us that intercultural communication requires both an understanding of the historical forces at work within a particular culture and the current cultural understandings and hopes for the future. Our history shapes our present, but it is not deterministic of our present or future. In addition, understanding intercultural communication processes requires an understanding that our perception of our history is always shaped by the narratives and discourses of our present. Take the Black Lives Matter movement that caught the attention of so many people in 2020 during the COVID-19 pandemic, first in the United States and then around the world. In 2020, truly understanding this movement would have entailed having knowledge of the present situation (the George Floyd case, the political atmosphere, the pandemic, and so forth) as well as the past (the history of slavery, civil rights, and past cases such as Rodney King, Michael Brown, Trayvon Martin, and others, just to name a few).

Privilege/Disadvantage

The **privilege/disadvantage dialectic** helps us to see that within and between cultures there exist positions of both privilege and disadvantage. These may come in the form of political power, social position, economic wealth, or status. Both privilege and disadvantage are intersectional positions, meaning that both may be imbued within an individual at once. One might experience privileges and disadvantages based on meanings ascribed to race, skin tone, language ability, gender, wealth, education, the relative global position of one's home country, and more. An accent might disadvantage an individual within one culture, but the ability to speak multiple languages may allow for privilege across different cultures. We can also consider that a particular culture may have more political power on the world stage, but a given individual within that culture may have less political power than an individual who is very privileged within a culture with less global political power.

Communication Accommodation Theory

Another theory that helps us understand how culturally different others behave in interpersonal interactions is Howard Giles's **communication accommodation theory (CAT)**. "Accommodation" refers to the way that we adapt to others' communication styles within interactions (Giles et al., 1991). These adaptations may include convergence, divergence, or maintenance.

Convergence occurs when speakers move toward the communication styles of others. For example, some people pick up a drawl while visiting the southern states in the United States. A visitor to Ontario might begin to ask for the "washroom" rather than the "bathroom." People may converge to gain the approval of their co-communicator (Coupland, 2010). Convergence may signal increased similarity between communicators. Receivers generally think positively of speakers who begin to converge toward them (Giles et al., 1973). Convergence can occur on multiple levels of conversation. One might converge through avoiding divisive topics (Nelson et al., 2003). Other types of convergence might include beginning to pick up your co-communicator's accent or patterns of speech. Convergence might also be nonverbal mimicry. Word choices such as using "y'all" in the South or "eh" in Canada may also reflect an attempt at convergence. The more people accommodate toward each other, the higher they tend to rate the quality of their contact with diverse others and experience feelings of relational solidarity (Soliz & Giles, 2014).

Although convergence generally indicates a desire for closeness or similarity that is positively received, care must be taken to be sure that you are not feeding into stereotypes about your co-communicator or appropriating their culture. At times, people may hyperconverge or overaccommodate and express exaggerated versions of their co-communicators (Bradac et al., 1988). At other times, people may underaccommodate by not adjusting their communication patterns enough. Both over- and underaccommodation tend to be perceived negatively (Giles & Gasiorek, 2013).

Divergence, on the other hand, occurs when speakers emphasize how different their communication is from someone else's.. People may engage in divergence to highlight their own group identity or as a reaction to the denigration of their speech patterns (Bourhis & Giles, 1977). **Maintenance** occurs when people actively maintain their communication style and resist adjustments toward their co-communicator (Bourhis et al., 1979). People may also engage in reluctant accommodation where they converge to others' speaking styles out of a sense of obligation. Some speakers may also simply attempt to avoid interactions with diverse others or end such interactions quickly in order to not have to worry about accommodating others (Soliz & Giles, 2014). These divergent strategies may occur when a speaker feels that their own identity and communication style is threatened (Bourhis & Giles, 1977). Divergence and maintenance are often viewed as insulting, impolite, or even hostile. Thus, divergent accommodation is often linked to negative relational outcomes (Soliz & Giles, 2014).

Both convergence and divergence can be symmetrical or asymmetrical. In symmetrical accommodation, both parties shift their speech patterns equally toward (or away from, in the case of divergence) each other. In asymmetrical accommodation, one party makes a much stronger shift toward (or away from) the other. Asymmetrical accommodation might occur when one party is in a position of power. For example, subordinates may emulate the speech habits of a supervisor, while the supervisor does not move toward the speech habits of subordinates. Asymmetrical accommodation might also occur when one party is attempting to fit in with a particular group. For example, while traveling you may find yourself accommodating accents, language, and the nonverbal style of those surrounding you. However, it is less likely that those surrounding you will make a strong accommodation toward your style. Indeed, dominant cultures often expect that minority co-cultural groups will accommodate their communication style and choices (Ting-Toomey & Dorjee, 2015).

Tourists often need to converge to the communication patterns of the country they are visiting. Who do you think should converge more in a case like this—the tourist or the shop owner selling her something? Why?

iStock/PeopleImages

Face-Negotiation Theory

Like any human interaction, intercultural interactions can contain conflicts between the interactants. These conflicts may arise because of deep-seated differences regarding beliefs and values, or conflicts can occur because the cultural differences between the interactants lead them to interpret situations differently. **Face-negotiation theory** has been used to explain the processes that occur in interpersonal conflict in intercultural contexts (Ting-Toomey, 1988). The theory builds from Goffman's concept of face (see Chapter 2) and considers that intercultural interactions may at times involve face threats. These face threats may occur because the interactants have different ways of interpreting actions within their cultures. For example, what is considered affirming in one culture may be viewed as patronizing in another. Face becomes particularly important in situations where one or more of the communicators may feel emotionally vulnerable (Ting-Toomey & Kurogi, 1998). For example, feeling out-of-place while visiting or living in a different culture may make someone feel emotionally vulnerable. Another example might be when a request involves an aspect of identity quite close to the person, such as religion. A student needing to make a request for time off for Rosh Hashanah or Eid al-Adha might feel emotionally vulnerable because the request is both important and not already accommodated in the typical Western university schedule.

According to face-negotiation theory, people may have cultural differences regarding their face orientation. **Face orientation** refers to how people direct their attention regarding face-threatening conflict messages. There are three types of face orientations: self, other, and mutual. **Self-face orientation** refers to concern for one's own face and image. **Other-face orientation** is concern for the co-communicator's face. **Mutual-face orientation** is concern for both one's own face and the conflict partner's face. Those from cultures who are more individualistic may be more concerned with self-face, while people from collectivist cultures may have more concern for other- or mutual-face (Ting-Toomey, 2017).

However, face-negotiation theory also considers the effect of self-construal on communication choices. **Self-construal** is the way one perceives one's self in context with others. People with an independent self-construal tend to consider the self more as a unique individual with specific personal feelings and motivations. Those with an interdependent self-construal are more likely to consider how their self emerges in connection to relationships and groups (Markus & Kitayama, 1991).

Self-construal and face orientation can predict how people from different cultures approach conflict interaction (Ting-Toomey, 2017). People with a more independent self-construal typically have more self-face orientation. They engage in more competition in conflict, as they consider themselves independent entities who must reach their own goals. People with an interdependent self-construal tend to have greater other-face orientation. They also engage in more integration or avoidance of conflict in order to not upset the group. While these patterns are not universal, these differences are important to keep in mind when engaging in conflict communication with conflict partners from different cultures. Integration or avoidance from cultural members with other-face orientation can be read as not caring or being unconcerned about the conflict goals by those with an independent self-construal when, in fact, the conflict partner cares very much but places value on the relationship. Competitive strategies from those with an independent self-construal can be viewed as selfish or uncaring, while that partner doesn't understand why the other wouldn't be more assertive about their needs.

As you might guess, people within individualistic cultures are more influenced by their independent rather than interdependent self-construal, whereas people's behavior within collectivistic cultures is more influenced by their interdependent self-construal. However, the dialectical perspective might suggest that both dimensions of self, independent and interdependent, exist within everyone. It is possible for a particular individual to score high on both independent and interdependent self-construal (Ting-Toomey et al., 2001).

Culture also influences the communication choices people make to negotiate their communication strategies. Although all cultures use verbal, nonverbal, and contextual cues to create meaning, cultures can vary on how much emphasis they place on the verbal versus contextual or nonverbal components of the message. **Low-context communication** typically relies on explicit, verbal messages to carry the meaning of the interaction. **High-context communication** is more subtle, with communicators expected to pick up on meaning stemming from the history, social norms, situation, relationship, and nonverbal cues to draw out the full meaning of the message (Hall, 1976).

Similar to cultural dimensions, some cultures have been classified as engaging in greater high-context or low-context communication. The United States, for example, is generally a low-context culture. People are expected to explain themselves through verbal messages. "No" in an interaction generally means "no" and "yes" means "yes." India, on the other hand, is an example of a high-context culture. Understanding the meaning of a specific message requires knowing the context of the message, particularly the power relationships at play. As an example, Indians have a head gesture not commonly found in the United States—a shaking of the head that is halfway between a nod (yes) and a shake (no.). The meaning of the wobble is extremely dependent on the context in which it is given.

CULTURAL COMPETENCE

To develop and sustain social relationships with others from differing cultural viewpoints, people must manage their communication and their perception of others' communication choices (Gangi & Soliz, 2016). Developing competence for intercultural communication encounters requires knowledge of other cultures, motivations to be mindful and empathetic, and the skills to be flexible and adaptable within intercultural interaction (Hecht & Lu, 2015). Engaging in intercultural interactions can make people feel anxious, uncertain, and vulnerable (Gudykunst & Nashida, 2001; Ting-Toomey, 2005). However, approaching such interactions with an open mind and a desire for honest understanding of people and cultures can go a long way.

The perspectives and techniques that help us to develop understanding and co-create meaning with people from different cultures are applicable across a wide range of human communication events. Certainly, the researchers who developed these concepts considered navigating vastly different cultural backgrounds, but these concepts are also useful when considering interactions between co-cultures, or any instance where people may be approaching the interaction from different cultural frameworks. The following are key skills for interpersonal communication competence.

Key Skills for Cultural Competence

One key skill for intercultural competence is **mindfulness**. To be mindful in intercultural interactions means taking into account the many influences affecting our communication and cultural understandings (Ting-Toomey & Dorjee, 2015). These influences include our self, our own culture, our perceptions of the world, cultural systems of meaning-making, and our attitudes and behaviors. In addition, mindful communicators strive to be open about understanding others' behavior from multiple perspectives and learn about the influence of co-communicators' cultural frameworks on their behavior, attitudes, and values. Keeping in mind all of these influences can take considerable cognitive effort! To help communicators begin to develop the cognitive flexibility and skill to be mindful within intercultural and co-cultural encounters, Ting-Toomey (2009) developed three facets of mindfulness: being present, meta-cognition awareness, and affective attunement.

SKILL BUILDER
ENACTING MINDFULNESS

The first facet of enacting mindfulness is the *being present* orientation. This facet involves sustaining awareness of the present moment. To do so, communicators must be aware of their own physical and emotional reactions to an intercultural encounter. In addition, to be present, communicators should be mindful of their own ethnocentrism (see the following definition of ethnocentrism) and resist enacting judgment within the interaction. Remember, judgments one may have are developed from one's own cultural viewpoints. To be mindful, it is important to remember that co-communicators may not share those views.

The second facet is *meta-cognition awareness*. Meta-cognition means thinking about thinking. For this facet, intercultural communicators need to think about the way that they think about intercultural interaction by being aware, planning, and checking. *Awareness* is being conscious of how cultural influences affect both your own and others' mental processes and behavior. *Planning* is being able to understand and anticipate the short- and long-term consequences of particular behaviors enacted in intercultural settings. *Checking* is one's internal process throughout the interaction, where the communicators review their understanding of the interaction and adjust as novel information becomes available.

The third facet is *affective attunement*. Intercultural interactions involve emotional activation. Emotions that arise during intercultural interactions might include surprise, fear, and anger, but also joy, affection, and curiosity. It is helpful for interactants to tune into their emotional state so they can consider how those emotions might be affecting their communication choices.

Try the following activity to consider these mindfulness facets. With a partner or small group consider the following scenario:

Kailey, a first-year, first-generation college student from a working-class family in a small rural midwestern town has just moved into the dorms and met her new roommate. Her roommate, Olivia, is from an upper-middle-class family in Puerto Rico. The two first-year students come from very different cultural backgrounds. Kailey feels nervous about attending a university that is larger than her hometown. Olivia is apprehensive about being so far from her family. How might mindfulness help Kailey and Olivia develop an interpersonal relationship? Answer the following questions, then share with the class:

What might Kailey and Olivia's physical and emotional reactions to having a new roommate be? In what ways might these reactions be positive? In what ways might they be negative?

How could Kailey and Olivia be aware of their own cultural influences?

What are some possible short-term and long-term outcomes that Kailey and Olivia might be interested in?

What emotions might Kailey and Olivia experience during their initial interactions? How might those emotions affect their communication?

How might culture affect their interactions throughout the year? What questions should Kailey and Olivia ask each other about their expectations for their shared space?

Another important skill is **communication adaptability**. In addition to general communication appropriateness and effectiveness, communicators must also have communication adaptability to be competent in intercultural communication situations. Communication adaptability means that we can adjust our behavior and goals to fulfill the needs of specific communicative encounters (Ting-Toomey, 2009). Enacting this adaptability or flexibility requires a sense of mindfulness regarding intercultural contexts as well as developing sets of cognitive constructs that allow one to make appropriate communication choices. Communicators who can be open-minded regarding both cultural and individual differences and adapt appropriately are more likely to successfully navigate intercultural interactions.

Empathy is a key component of adaptability (Ting-Toomey & Dorjee, 2015). An empathetic approach to intercultural communication requires communicators to have knowledge about cultural differences, attempt to understand how those cultural differences may influence how our co-communicators understand the world, including our communication, and work to adjust behavior and our perceptions as new information provided by context and our fellow communicators becomes available to us.

A barrier to having enjoyable and productive cross-cultural interactions is ethnocentrism. Thus, overcoming ethnocentrism is a key skill for intercultural communication competence. **Ethnocentrism** is considering the culture(s) that you belong to as superior to other cultures. Ethnocentric thinking can result in people using the standards of their own culture to negatively judge the behaviors and values of other cultures simply for being different. Ethnocentric tendencies have three factors. First, we tend to perceive what happens in our own culture as *natural*. Second, we think that our own cultural values can be applied universally. Third, people try to distance themselves from other groups, particularly when they feel their own cultural identity is under attack (Ting-Toomey & Dorjee, 2015). Examples of ethnocentrism abound. Imagine Clarence in South Korea for his study-abroad program. South Korea is a high-context culture, so Clarence might be bothered that communication is not always as direct as he is used to. If Clarence is ethnocentric, he will evaluate South Koreans as "not direct enough," seeing his culture's level of directness as superior. Instead, Clarence should recognize that cultures differ in directness and that no culture is better or worse—just different. Ethnocentric thinking can also lead to **xenophobia**, a fear of cultural difference. Thus, if Clarence continually judges aspects of South Korean culture to be inferior to what he is accustomed to, he is likely to be fearful, which could ruin his study-abroad experience. Overcoming ethnocentrism is a key for effective intercultural communication as well as for being able to embrace and learn about different cultures.

Developing Intercultural Sensitivity

People are not simply ethnocentric or not ethnocentric. Rather, there are variations in the ways that people perceive cultural differences. Understanding these variations can be useful for understanding our own behavior as well as for teaching and socializing others in understanding intercultural differences. To grow in their ability to accept and engage with cultural differences, people may need to encounter messages and materials that engage their current level of ethnocentric thinking. More advanced messages may be met with confusion and reactance. **Reactance** occurs when people are presented with a message or piece of information and it causes them to behave in the opposite way as intended. To increase intercultural sensitivity while avoiding counterproductive reactions, Bennett and colleagues (1993, 2004) created a developmental model that outlines different ways people approach intercultural differences. Bennett's model is a developmental model, meaning people can progress through the levels toward greater intercultural sensitivity. The first three levels are ethnocentric. The second three levels are ethnorelative. **Ethnorelativity** refers to the ability to understand that cultures are different, but not in a hierarchical way.

Level 1: Denial

This first level is denial of difference. People at this level have difficulty understanding how culture impacts their own lives because they do not recognize culture as an entity that influences meaning-making. For them, culture is simply the way things are. Through either unintentional or intentional separation from culturally different others, they have very little experience with people from cultures that are not their own. When they do consider other cultures, they may assume that different behavior is some sort of deficiency. Their understanding of tolerance can be very superficial. If they do travel, they may assume that others will or should accommodate to their cultural preferences.

Level 2: Defense

The next level, defense against difference, describes experiencing culture from a polarized perspective. Individuals at this level stereotype others in simplistic and negative ways and have a hierarchical view of cultures. Given that they perceive their culture at the top of this hierarchy, they may feel that attempts to understand or incorporate other cultures are attacks on their own. This developmental level may manifest in three different ways: denigration, superiority, and reversal. Denigration involves negative evaluations of different cultures in order to protect one's own worldview. Those engaging in superiority exaggerate the positive aspects of their own culture. Further positive or even neutral statements about other cultures may be viewed as an attack on the culture viewed as superior. Reversal is an interesting twist on the dualistic nature of the defense-against-difference level. In reversal, cultural members may see another culture as superior and denigrate their own. They may perceive themselves as being more culturally sensitive but this way of thinking still reflects cultural differences as simplistic and hierarchical.

Level 3: Minimization

The third level is the minimization of difference. People with this level of understanding believe that worldwide, we are all fundamentally the same. However, this minimization is typically adopted in an ethnocentric manner. If everyone is alike, then there is no need to adapt to or understand real cultural differences. Those who understand cultural differences by minimizing them may really feel that they have intercultural sensitivity. After all, they aren't dehumanizing or denigrating others. However, by minimizing cultural differences, communicators at this level also aren't fully embracing the rich differences between cultures.

Level 4: Acceptance

The next level, acceptance of difference, begins to make a turn away from ethnocentric thinking toward ethnorelativity. In the framework of acceptance, people understand that behaviors and values exist within distinctive cultural contexts and that different cultures are viable and interesting systems of existence. Those in the acceptance framework move beyond preferring one cultural system over another and into a type of cultural relativism where it is understood that negative and positive evaluations of behavior, values, and perceptions not only exist within but are derived from cultural contexts.

Level 5: Adaptation

Adaptation to difference represents the next level of intercultural sensitivity. Those who approach intercultural communication from this perspective have the ability to emphasize with other worldviews. These individuals not only understand that others hold different, valid worldviews, but they can shift their perspective to adapt to others from their cultural perspective. These individuals might also be adept at authentic code-switching, where they can adjust their behavior based on a deep and rich understanding of the perspectives of other cultures.

Level 6: Integration

Finally, some individuals may experience integration of difference. Integration occurs when people intentionally make a sustained effort to become competent in one or more new cultures. These individuals may base their identity as being multicultural and engage in meaningful contact within multiple cultures. People who have integrative experiences generally have a wide repertoire of cultural perspectives to draw on, as they truly belong to both cultures rather than simply being empathetic to one. Integration may be the experience of immigrants, those who have to adapt to a dominant or colonial culture, those who live in other cultures for an extended period of time, or those who move between parents' cultures as children.

The US population is more diverse today than ever before, which might lead more people to embrace ethnorelativity and cosmopolitanism.

iStock/FatCamera

A Cosmopolitan Perspective

One approach to ethical intercultural interaction is the stance of cosmopolitanism. **Cosmopolitanism** is a willingness to engage with different cultures and people who communicate in cultural frameworks that are different than our own. A cosmopolitan stance requires being mindful, empathetic, and open to divergent cultural experiences (Appiah, 2006; Hannerz, 1990). Cosmopolitanism requires learning and understanding divergent cultural systems (Kurasawa, 2011) but goes beyond just knowledge of other cultures. The ethics of cosmopolitanism include an openness to cultural differences and taking the perspective that we belong to a world that is larger than our own local culture (Sobré-Denton & Bardhan, 2013).

Cosmopolitans are members of multiple cultural groups and make meaning and construct identity through multiple cultural contexts. A cosmopolitan way of life creates meaningful connections with people across and between cultures through everyday interactions (Sobré-Denton & Bardhan, 2013). Cosmopolitans are appreciative of both their own cultures as well as the cultures of others. They seek to engage with and enjoy the differences and diversity of the human experience. Cosmopolitanism also requires that people go beyond a surface-level understanding of different cultures. This drive for understanding requires a level of depth and learning that is simply not possible to acquire for every culture on the globe. However, despite these potential drawbacks, the key components of this ethical stance, or openness and empathy to cultural difference, will become increasingly important as friend, family, and work relationships span the globe.

PRINCIPLES OF THE INFLUENCE OF CULTURE ON INTERPERSONAL COMMUNICATION

As people increasingly have interactions with diverse people and groups, it is important to look outside our own perspectives and endeavor to engage in effective communication with people outside our own cultures and co-cultures. Such communication can also bring about positive changes that benefit individuals and society. Next, we present five general principles to keep in mind as you communicate in everyday life with the many people who have different systems of meaning than your own.

Principle 1. "Culture" refers to systems of meanings not differences between nation-states.

Often when people think of culture, they think of travel to different countries or interacting with immigrants. Culture, however, is a broad term that encompasses a wide variety of systems of meanings. Culture can refer to systems of meaning that are tied to geographic location. Culture can also refer to the internal contexts that are constructed within a particular organization (Keyton, 2011; Schein, 2004). Within a larger culture, many co-cultures might coexist and people might move fluidly within and between these cultures and systems of meaning (Orbe, 1998).

Principle 2. Cross-cultural interactions can be rewarding and enjoyable.

Communicating with others who share different perspectives than ourselves can help us develop empathy, learn new things, and create new constructs for how we understand the world. The benefits of diversity go beyond simply knowing people from a particular culture. Communicating with each other can help us identify social constructions within our own cultures and others. Understanding how culture is constructed can help societies enact change toward a more just and equitable world.

Principle 3. Cultures are socially constructed but real in their meaning and effects.

Crenshaw (1994) stated: "To say that a category such as race or gender is socially constructed is not to say that the category has no significance in our world" (p. 1296). It is true that cultures are social constructions. However, our cultural constructions are the foundation of the very way that we make meaning in the world. Often, it is difficult to see the effects of our own culture, as it may appear to be "natural" or simply "the way things are." Thus, culture is central to several processes in interpersonal communication. First, culture helps co-communicators understand each other through shared contexts. Culture defines what is perceived as appropriate behavior in particular contexts and relationships. Culture helps determine what rules and norms guide interpersonal and relational behavior. Deviations from cultural norms can be met with social sanctions or cause misunderstandings.

Principle 4. Culture is important, but in interpersonal intercultural interactions, people are central.

One could memorize all of Hofstede's intercultural dimensions and use them to direct their expectations and interactions with others from different cultures. Such an individual might consider themself extremely knowledgeable about culture. However, this knowledge is likely to translate into a rigid and nonadaptive way of interacting with others. Interactions may reflect stereotypical thinking or hyperaccommodation. Worse, rigid adherence to an external view of a culture may lead to racist or ethnocentric ways of engaging with others. Rather, our understanding of different cultures should inform our cultural interactions, but as communicators, it is important to engage with each other as people. Open-mindedness and flexibility are key as we work to understand each other and build intercultural relationships.

Principle 5. Learning about cultures and communicating cross-culturally can start small. Thinking about intercultural interactions can be intimidating and anxiety-provoking. Thinking about being mindful, open, and empathetic can feel overwhelming. To truly take a cosmopolitan stance or become ethnorelative requires fairly extensive knowledge about another culture. However, communicators have to start somewhere. Listening to the perspectives of people who come from different cultural backgrounds is an excellent way to begin learning about cultures. Technology can provide us with the means to learn about the experiences of others without impugning our own cultural values on their experiences. When we begin to learn about each other and truly value the differences of our varied perspectives, we can start to build rewarding and meaningful social relationships across cultures.

CONCLUSION

The way that we come to understand the world around us is deeply entrenched in our culture, as are our values and beliefs. Understanding our own cultural values, rituals, and artifacts can help us make sense of our own interpersonal communication choices. Understanding cultural differences can help us begin to make sense of how others engage with the world and be appreciative of diverse ways of engaging in social life. Clarence, in the opening scenario, is taking a great first step by considering studying abroad. Being immersed in another culture can help him move toward greater intercultural sensitivity, as can being mindful and shedding any ethnocentric biases. By striving for an ethnorelative lens, communicators can open up possibilities for greater engagement in interpersonal communication and relationships in an adaptive and flexible manner.

CHAPTER 4 STUDY GUIDE

KEY TERMS

Identify and explain the meaning of each of the following key terms.

co-cultures	divergence
collectivist	ethnocentrism
colloquialisms	ethnorelativity
communication accommodation theory (CAT)	face orientation
communication adaptability	face-negotiation theory
content function of a message	femininity, as a cultural dimension
convergence	high-context communication
cosmopolitanism	individual/cultural dialectic
cultural rituals	individualism
cultural symbols	indulgence
cultural values	intersectionality
culture	long-term orientation
differences/similarities dialectic	low-context communication

maintenance

masculinity, as a cultural dimension

mindfulness

mutual-face orientation

other-face orientation

person/social-contextual dialectic

power distance

present-future/history-past dialectic

privilege/disadvantage dialectic

reactance

relational function of a message

self-construal

self-face orientation

sensemaking

short-term orientation

social construction

static/dynamic dialectic

uncertainty–avoidance

xenophobia

REFLECTION QUESTIONS

1.   We increasingly interact with others from different cultures and co-cultures. What intercultural interactions have you experienced? What have you learned from those interactions? What were the opportunities and challenges?

2.   Many business trainings use Hofstede's cultural dimensions as a starting point for understanding cultural differences. How might understanding these dimensions influence how we interact with people from cultures different than our own? How might starting from a dialectical perspective change how we train people for intercultural encounters?

3.   What co-cultures or organizational cultures are you a part of? How do these co-cultures help you make meaning of the world? Can you think of things that seem "normal" to you that are different in other cultures?

4.   How might one engage in a conflict differently depending on face orientation? Would holding a different face orientation than your partner make conflict communication more difficult? Why?

5.   Bennett's developmental model helps us understand the perspectives that people bring when beginning to understand other cultures. What level do you recognize yourself in? What types of messages and training might help people move from level 2 to 3? From level 3 to 4?

5 MAKING AND MANAGING CONVERSATION

WHAT YOU'LL LEARN...

When you have finished the chapter, you should be able to do the following:

5.1 Define the features of conversation.

5.2 Explain how people manage conversation through verbal and nonverbal communication.

5.3 Articulate the goals of different conversational contexts.

5.4 Describe ways to overcome conversation challenges.

Michael waited nervously in the lounge of his university's intercultural center. He had signed up for a program called "Cultured Conversations" for extra credit for his communication class. The idea was that he would spend time having weekly conversations with an English as a Second Language (ESL) student. Signing up had seemed like a good idea at the time but now that he was sitting in the lobby, Michael wondered what he and this stranger would talk about for 30 minutes a week all semester.

> *"Hello?" a guy approaching Michael said shyly. "Are you Michael? I'm Wei."*
> *"Oh, hi!" said Michael. "Yes, I'm him!"*
> *"Hi," said Wei, and sat down in a nearby chair.*
> *"So," said Michael, once Wei had gotten settled and was looking at him again. "Why did you decide to come to this university?"*
> *"Oh," said Wei. "They have a very good archeology program and I have always been very interested in archeology."*
> *"I like archeology, too!" said Michael. "Have you had Professor Ramos for a class?"*
> *"Yes," said Wei. "He's very smart and helpful, although sometimes it's hard to pay attention because..." he trailed off.*
> *"I know!" said Michael. "Those crazy eyebrows!"*

Michael and Wei laughed and continued talking about various classes they had taken at the university.

Just like Michael and Wei, people have conversations every day. Sometimes, as Michael and Wei experienced, these conversations are the potential starting points of interpersonal relationships. In these cases, we may, like Michael, be nervous about what the right thing to say to this new person might be. When meeting new people, we may need to rely on communication norms about the underlying structure of conversation to help us to build an engaging and successful encounter. In other cases, conversations may be part of the ongoing communication of a longer-term relationship. We may look forward to conversing with friends, family, and romantic partners and enjoy the time spent discussing the world around us. In any case, conversations between people are the building blocks of interpersonal relationships.

Recently, there seems to be much concern that due to social media, texting, and other screen-based forms of communication, young people may not be developing adequate conversational skills. There have been public calls to reclaim the art of conversation (BBC News, 2014; CBS News, 2007; Sapolin, 2013; Turkle, 2015). The ability to interact competently in a face-to-face conversation is an important interpersonal skill. However, we would note that the ability to skillfully hold a conversation has been a concern of young people for quite some time. In their groundbreaking interpersonal textbook, *Between People,* Miller and Steinberg (1975) noted that the college undergraduates' most frequent request for information regarding interpersonal communication was on how to hold a conversation. *Between People* was published in 1975, long before people started using social media. This suggests that conversational skill has always been a concern, with or without the use of mediated communication channels.

DEFINING CONVERSATION

The basic features of **conversation** are communication between at least two people where one person speaks at a time and the people trade speaking turns (Schegloff & Sacks, 1973). Much of our overall language use occurs within the context of interpersonal conversations (Clarks & Wilkes-Gibbs, 1986). However, conversations are about more than just the words that are spoken. Conversations involve communication management, the production and interpretation of nonverbal communication, and the ability to understand and interpret messages produced within the particular context of the conversation.

Engaging in conversations is a useful tool for communicators to achieve a variety of communicative goals. These goals include attempts to meet instrumental, relational, and self-presentational needs (Tracy & Coupland, 1990). Examples of instrumental conversation goals include attempts to convince someone to adopt a viewpoint or provide a favor. Relational conversation goals include using conversation as a way to maintain a friendship or engaging in self-disclosure as a way to deepen a relationship. Self-presentational goals might be attempting to portray oneself as a competent and credible co-communicator. Michael and Wei are likely trying to fulfill self-presentational goals when they first meet, especially since they know they will be communicating over the course of the semester. It is natural that they would want to make a good first impression. As they get to know each other, if they want to develop a friendship, their conversations could then start revolving around relational goals as well.

Conversations are interactive and locally managed (Nofsinger, 1991). By interactive we

Conversations help people develop friendships and other close relationships. Whether Wei and Michael, from the opening scenario, become friends depends in part on how enjoyable their conversations are.

iStock/santypan

mean that conversations require at least two people who are exchanging messages in an attempt to share and create meaning. Local management means that participants themselves control the interaction. There are no specific rules for who gets to talk when, how long participants hold the floor, or how conversational turns are determined. Rather, in face-to-face conversation, all of these important communication tasks are determined in real time by the participants engaged in the conversation. To be skilled conversationalists, communicators need to quickly interpret and respond to the messages of others (Bavelas & Coates, 1992).

The meaning exchanged within conversations goes beyond just the actual words used by the conversationalists. The context surrounding the message also carries information regarding how to interpret the verbal message. For example, saying "I love you!" to your sister at breakfast when she has just agreed to loan you her favorite skirt can carry a very different meaning than saying "I love you" for the first time during a romantic moment to someone you've been dating for a short while. Messages have both content and relational meanings (Watzlawick et al., 1967). The **content meaning** of a message helps us to determine a speaker's intentions ("I" meaning the speaker, "love" meaning I wish to convey a positive emotion, "you" meaning the hearer). The **relational meaning** refers to the full meaning of the message that is only understood within the context of the environment (family breakfast vs. romantic moment) and the relationship between the two conversationalists (sister vs. romantic partner). In this example, we can see that the exchange between sisters is likely a simple expression of affection and possibly appreciation for the loan of a skirt. In contrast, the exchange between the newly dating couple can be fraught with additional meaning related to the nature and state of the relationship.

CONVERSATION MANAGEMENT

Often conversation seems effortless (McLaughlin, 1984). After all, we converse with multiple people through our everyday interactions. At the same time, the multiple skills and components of conversation can appear difficult to master (Miller & Steinberg, 1975; Turkle 2015). In part, the difficulty of understanding the components of conversations may be precisely because we have conversations fairly regularly. The conversational process can become overlearned and automatic (Bavelas & Coates, 1992). Thus, it can be difficult to break down the components of conversational management into understandable concepts. Yet the ability to hold a conversation skillfully requires not only knowledge of the topics that come up in the course of a conversation but also a variety of communication rules and norms about grammar, syntax, paired utterances, and nonverbal behaviors related to conversational management (McLaughlin, 1984).

Conversational Patterns

The communication we engage in within conversations occurs in conjunction with the communication of our conversational partners (Nofsinger, 1991). What we say and do when conversing with others depends very much on what our conversational partner is saying and doing. The messages we use in conversation vary widely from conversation to conversation and can even be difficult to predict within a conversation. If you've ever had a conversation where you stopped and said, "How did we get this on this topic?" you intuitively understand the unpredictable nature of a specific conversation. Scholars have identified a few conversational patterns that emerge within communication encounters. These standard conversational patterns form the connective tissue that the rest of an interaction uses as a framework to grow upon.

Cooperative Principles

One pragmatic structure that helps us know how to interpret messages in conversations is Grice (1975) idea of the conversational implicature. The **conversational implicature** is what people mean, or are implying, when they make a statement. The **locutions** people make are the actual words that they say. However, what people say is not always what they mean. Hearers often understand the implications of statements based on context and other cues. An example of when people say something they do not mean is how we often form requests. For example, at the dinner table, someone might say, "Is that the salt?" Taken literally, this utterance is questioning whether that white crystallized substance in the shaker is in fact salt. However, hearers do not typically take this utterance or locution literally. Rather, through contextual cues, we understand the **illocutionary force**, or what is meant rather than what is said (Searle, 1969). For most of us, our response to "Is that the salt?" is likely to say, "Oh! Yes," and hand the salt to the person who asked if that was the salt. We understand that the question was not an actual inquiry but rather a request to pass the salt. The popular children's series *Amelia Bedelia* plays with this concept as Amelia bumbles through her day taking statements and instructions literally (i.e., the locutionary force) rather than how they were meant (i.e., the illocutionary force).

Illocutionary force tells us to pass the salt to someone who asks "Is that the salt?" instead of just saying "Yes, it is" and doing nothing.

iStock/artisteer

One might wonder how people make sense of each other at all if they constantly engage in conversations saying things they don't mean. Why aren't we all as confused as Amelia Bedelia? Well, if human communication relies on listeners inferring the speaker's meaning, there must be an assumption that we are all playing by similar rules. Grice's **cooperative principle** helps explain some of the tenants that conversationalists use when they attempt to create meaning from conversational implicatures. When conversing, people generally expect that their co-conversationalists are behaving in a cooperative manner and will "make [their] conversational contribution such as is required, at the stage at which it occurs, by the accepted purpose or the direction of the talk exchange in which you are engaged" (Grice, 1975, p. 45). He proposed four maxims that conversationalists use to determine the meaning of the messages people send: quantity, quality, relevance, and manner.

The **maxim of quantity** means to "make your contribution as informative as required" and "do not make your contribution more informative than is required" (Grice, 1975, p. 45). According to this maxim, conversationalists should provide as much information as needed for their listeners to understand what they mean, but no more. Rambling on in a conversation may simply make one a bore, and providing extra information where none is needed may have additional ramifications for how the listener makes sense of what is being said. For example, an acquaintance might attempt to convince you to vote one way on a specific issue and then go on and on with different reasons. You, as the listener, could potentially perceive that the speaker is not fully convinced of the strength of their initial argument. The speaker could also offer you "one too many reasons" if you disagree with one of them.

The **maxim of quality** refers to the truthfulness of implicatures (Grice, 1975). To adhere to the maxim of quality is to avoid saying things that are false or for which the speaker lacks evidence. Engaging in deception is a violation of the maxim. Certainly, speakers are not always truthful. Yet listeners generally assume that what they are hearing is intended to be the truth, a phenomenon called **truth bias** (McCornack & Parks, 1986; Zuckerman et al., 1981; see also Chapter 11). Attempting to determine the veracity or truthfulness of every conversational statement would demand so many cognitive resources that people would be unable to keep up with the rest of the mental demands of conversation (Gilbert et al., 1990; see also Spinoza, 1982).

The **maxim of relevance** notes that speakers should make conversational contributions that are appropriate to the current needs of the interaction. Relevance can be an important aspect of making sense of conversations. However, it may also be that listeners simply assume that the speaker *is* being relevant. For example, say you ask how a co-worker knew the correct answer to a problem at work and your boss says, "Even a broken clock is right twice a day." As the hearer, you understand that the boss is not suddenly switching the conversation to a discussion on the inner workings of watches. Rather, the statement implies that the colleague got lucky coming up with the right answer and generally fails in this task. You can make meaning out of what linguistically does not appear to make sense because you anticipate your boss's conversational cooperation and apply the statement about a broken clock to the question you asked.

Just like the gearwheels in an old watch, conversation requires cooperation (with all the parts moving together) as well as good timing.

iStock/bruev

The **maxim of manner** is different from the other three maxims in that it does not involve *what* is said but rather *how* something is said. Manner includes ideas such as being brief and orderly and avoiding obscurity and ambiguity. For example, a doctor considering the maxim of manner might make sure to avoid jargon that their patient might not understand. Jargon, even when defined, can make it difficult for communicators to process and understand messages. Jargon can also heighten feelings between communicators that they belong to different social groups (Shulman et al., 2020). Within a personal conversation, someone might try to avoid being vague so that their meaning is explicitly understood. Both jargon and ambiguity or vagueness can keep communicators from an important conversational goal—learning to understand each other better.

Adjacency Pairs

As people begin to construct their actual utterances within conversations, the connective tissue between messages often comes in the form of **adjacency pairs**. Adjacency pairs are two communicative actions produced by different speakers that occur adjacent, or next, to each other (Schegloff & Sacks, 1973). They consist of two pairs (a first pair part and a second pair part) that are commonly thought of as being connected. Adjacency pairs are the smallest functional unit in a conversation (Owen, 1981).

Many types of adjacency pairs occur within conversations (McLaughlin, 1984; Nofsinger, 1991; Schegloff & Sacks, 1973). Some examples are greeting pairs and goodbye pairs. At times, greeting pairs contain the same semantic content ("Hello," "Hello"); at other times, the semantic content differs but the function of the expression remains the same ("Hey, what's up?" "Oh, hi!"). Goodbyes also typically exist in functionally similar double pairs ("Well, goodbye," "See you later"). Other types of adjacency pairs are utterances that differ both semantically and functionally. For example, questions beget answers ("Did you get the review guide?" "I did"). Invitations and offers are typically followed by acceptances or rejections ("Would you like to go to lunch?" "No"). Congratulations on the part of one speaker typically produce thanks on the part of the other speaker. Compliments correspond with acceptances or rejections of the praise and accusations are often followed by denials or confessions.

Although not all conversation is composed of adjacency pairs, adjacency pairs do have a strong influence on how we interpret the utterances of our co-conversationalists. Consider the following exchange:

Alicia: Come with us to that new Brazilian restaurant.
Devin: I'm a vegetarian.

In a purely semantic read of this exchange, Devin's response may seem to open a new topic of conversation—vegetarianism. However, opening a new topic here would be a *non sequitur*, which is communication that does not follow logically from the previous utterance. Alicia has issued an invitation; Devin should respond with a yes or no. Alicia likely does understand that Devin has responded no. We use the contextual cues (Brazilian restaurants are often heavy on the meat), our understanding of adjacency pairs (invitations are followed by acceptances or refusals), and Grice's maxim of relevance (Devin's response should address Alicia's question), to understand that Devin has told Alicia he would not like to go to the Brazilian restaurant.

Another common type of adjacency pair is related to the closing of a conversation. Instead of just ceasing to talk about a topic, people often negotiate within the conversation that they will be closing a topic (Schegloff & Sacks, 1973). First, as they recognize that the topic may be coming to a close, they engage in a preclosing utterance. Here is an example:

Jason: So that's what happened.
Heather: Well, then, okay.

The speaker can accept this preclosing utterance:

Jason: Yeah.

Or the speaker can opt not to accept it:,

Jason: But you should also know that she called him on Tuesday.
Heather: Really?

If the preclosing utterance is accepted, then the speakers generally move onto another topic.

Jason: Did you hear what Ian did?
Heather: No, what?

Or they move to close the whole conversation:

Jason: Well, I gotta get going.
Heather: Thanks for letting me know.
Jason: Bye.
Heather: Yeah, bye.

Nonverbal Management

Within conversations, speakers seem to be able to precisely time the transition between turns such that awkward pauses or speaker overlaps are usually avoided (McLaughlin & Cody, 1982). Although competent turn-taking seems normal to most of us, the phenomenon represents a sophis-tication in human communication. Neither the length nor order of conversational turns is formally determined in advance (Sacks et al., 1978). Our ability to manage pauses and turn-taking within conversations is a product of a variety of nonverbal conversational management tactics. Think about Wei and Michael at the beginning of this chapter. Even though they are just meeting, they likely have a sophisticated enough understanding of nonverbal communication to be able to manage their first conversation effectively. As they get to know each other, their interaction management will become even smoother.

Many important nonverbal cues are related to turn-taking in conversation. For example, variations in the rate of speech are vital cues for smooth conversational

Conversation requires a sophisticated set of skills that most humans take for granted. These skills include coordination, turn-taking, and the ability to hold the floor as the man in this picture is doing.

iStock/pixelfit

management. One such variation is delayed completion (Lerner, 1989). Delayed completion means that people start their turn, they say enough for the other conversation participants to start to formulate their own turn, and then the original speaker engages in pauses, lengthened words, and slower rates of speech so that by the time the original speaker is ready to give up their turn, the next speaker is ready to go. Another vocalic cue that signals turn-taking is using either a rising or falling intonation on the last word of a turn (Duncan, 1972, 1974).

Eye contact is an important conversational regulator. The ability to give and gain turns through eye contact is an important component of successful conversation. In order, to make our points, give our opinions, and answer our co-communicators we must be able to "hold the floor." As people reach the end of a sentence or a natural breakpoint, if they wish to hold on to their speaking turn, they often look away from co-conversationalists. Conversely, they may look directly at the person that they wish to take the next turn (Eder, 1982).

Relaxing one's hand gestures can also signal one is done or about to be done speaking (Duncan, 1972, 1974). On the other hand, increased hand gestures, intakes of breath, increasing volume, and, as we just noted, turning one's gaze or head away from the conversational partner can all indicate a desire to keep the conversational floor (Duncan, 1974; Kendon, 1990). Similarly, using **backchannels** such as "oh" and "uh-uh" can signal that the hearer desires the speaker to continue to hold the floor (Nofsinger, 1991).

Other nonverbal cues that are important for conversational management are those related to interpersonal coordination. **Interpersonal coordination** is the "degree to which the behaviors in an interaction are nonrandom, patterned, or synchronized in both timing and form" (Bernieri & Rosenthal, 1991, p. 403). Interpersonal coordination can refer to either **interactional synchrony**, which is the rhythm or flow of the conversation (Bernieri et al., 1994), or **mirroring**, which is the typically unintentional mirroring of conversationalists' postures, gestures, and mannerisms (Chartrand & Bargh, 1999).

Interactional synchrony and mirroring have positive effects on conversational outcomes. These behaviors may increase feelings of affiliation, rapport, and liking between co-conversationalists (Lakin et al., 2003). However, mirroring is typically a nonconscious behavior, meaning that people may have little to no control over whether or not they nonverbally mimic their speaking partner.

When people are feeling in sync with each other, they often mirror some of each other's nonverbal behaviors, including body movements, positioning, and facial expressions.

iStock/VioletaStoimenova

Conversational Coherence

To bring all of these utterances and cues together into a meaningful pattern requires communicators to create **conversational coherence**. Conversational coherence means co-conversationalists are able to understand and make meaning out of the exchanges between partners (Kellerman & Sleight, 1988; McLaughlin, 1984). People use a variety of cohesion strategies such as repetition, providing topic cues (e.g., "Oh, I meant to tell you what happened the other day"), and using grammatical rules appropriate to the situation. Invoking coherence does depend somewhat on the words being spoken, and senders need to be aware of the knowledge and beliefs held by the speaker in order to compose potentially coherent messages (Planalp & Tracy, 1980). However, ultimately coherence resides in the mind of the receiver—can they make sense of the interaction (Kellerman & Sleight, 1988)? This is why some conversations that seem to make very little sense to observers, such as those based on inside jokes, can be perfectly coherent to the interactants. Other conversations, perhaps a doctor explaining a procedure to a patient using extensive medical jargon, might make pragmatic sense to the doctor or a similarly educated observer, but can seem incomprehensible to the patient. Similarly, because English is Wei's second language, he might not understand some of the colloquialisms Michael uses. If Wei looks confused, Michael is likely to recognize this and explain what he means. All conversations require participants to make inferences based on knowledge of the speaker, context, and content. People are motivated to be coherent so that they can be understood and also have an expectation that other people are attempting to be coherent (Kellerman & Sleight, 1988).

CONVERSATIONS IN CONTEXT

Conversations occur in a variety of contexts and we engage in conversations to meet many different goals. Often our conversations are held within social relationships where our goals might be to entertain ourselves, spend time with our co-conversationalist, and/or share information about others in our social circle. At other times our conversations may be more formal and directed toward instrumental goals. These types of conversations might include negotiations and various types of interviews. It is also important to recognize that conversations are not limited to face-to-face interactions. We might interview for a job over the phone, conduct a negotiation over email, or connect with a friend via social media.

Small Talk

Much conversation relies on "small talk," also called **phatic communication**. Phatic communication is communication that appears to have very little functional content (Malinowski, 1923). For example, we share observations about the weather or affirmations of something obvious. These utterances do not convey new information (both conversational partners can see that it is raining), rather phatic communication serves a social purpose. Phatic communication simply allows us to express a desire for companionship and highlight the social connection between communicators. These conversations do not typically contain any content that is new or informational, but they can let communicators recognize that they are sharing a social space and that they are connected in this moment. Moreover, phatic communication and other low-level disclosures can be important communication for starting and maintaining conversation. Topics that are too heavy or too personal break social communication norms and can put a strain on developing relationships (Petronio, 2002). For Wei and Michael, phatic communication is a good place to start their first conversation. Exchanging basic information about the classes they are taking will help them get comfortable with each other and pave the way for more personal communication.

Gossip

While some conversations revolve around self-disclosure, often our topics include discussing other people in our social networks. Instead of self-disclosure, these conversations might be thought of as "other disclosure" or **gossip** (Turner et al., 2003, p. 131). Gossip has four characteristics (McEwan, 2006b). The primary characteristic of gossip is that it is about someone who is not present. Second, gossip is embedded in social and personal relationships. We gossip with our social connections about other people in our social network. Third, gossip is typically thought of as being negative but gossip conversations may also encompass positive information. Finally, and perhaps most importantly, gossip communication has evaluative content. Gossip is not just talk about others; it is talk that also makes some sort of social judgment about the behavior of others within our social network. Gossip makes up a significant portion of our everyday conversations. Dunbar (2004) found about 65 percent of conversational speaking time is concerned with social topics.

Although gossip has a negative reputation, sharing gossip may actually have useful relational functions. Indeed, people tend to like others who gossip at a moderate rate (Jaeger et al., 1998). People tend to share gossip with individuals they know and trust. Sharing gossip may let co-gossipers recognize their similarities and feel closer to each other, which helps people maintain friendships (McEwan, 2006a). Immigrant communities may use gossip as a way of developing group connections and passing down cultural values (Lu, 2015). There is, of course, a difference between benign gossip that is not designed to hurt anyone and malicious gossip that is focused on bringing another person down. Gossiping too much or with malicious intent can backfire, leading people not to trust the person doing the gossiping (Farley, 2011).

Gossip has a bad reputation and can, indeed, sometimes be a hurtful or disloyal act. However, benign gossip can actually help bond people together in ways that strengthen relationships.

iStock/jacoblund

Negotiations

Another specific type of conversation is a **negotiation,** a strategic conversation where participants engage in communication tactics to accomplish specific goals (Wilson & Putnam, 1990). Typically, negotiation participants have goals that are at least in partial opposition to the other party's goal. A negotiation may be formal, such as negotiating a job offer or the price of a high-ticket item.

Negotiations may also be informal, such as deciding with your roommates how the household chores will be accomplished or discussing with your romantic partner where you will live as a couple.

Negotiations require that communicators pursue multiple conversational goals (Wilson & Putnam, 1990, p. 374). First, negotiators must handle all of the regular discursive work of conversations as discussed previously in this chapter. Negotiators must produce relevant utterances, handle turn changes, and introduce and change topics. Negotiators must also develop new tactics as needed throughout the interaction. Communicators in negotiations must also use messages that minimize any potential threats to the other's face (see Chapter 2 for an explanation of face needs and threats) and avoid unnecessarily antagonizing their opponent (Wilson & Putnam, 1990). Negotiators must also be able to reach the more instrumental goals within the negotiation. These could include convincing the other person to collaborate, compromise, or accommodate on the issues at stake. (See Chapter 10 for more on these strategies.) Negotiators also have to manage any internal conflicts about their own goals.

Negotiations are competitive. Negotiation partners are each trying to meet potentially incompatible and sometimes zero-sum goals. Yet the negotiation partners must also cooperate or else neither negotiating party will be able to achieve any portion of their goal. In this way, negotiation conversations require at least a minimal level of trust between parties even though each party is potentially attempting to thwart the plans of the other (Wilson & Putnam, 1990).

WHAT WOULD YOU DO?
ETHICAL NEGOTIATIONS

Negotiations involve two or more people trying to come to an equitable solution. While we hope that our co-negotiators are acting in good faith, there are several "questionable tactics" that negotiators might rely on. The following is a table of questionable tactics.

Tactic	Description
Lies	Statements made in contradiction to the negotiator's knowledge or belief about something material to the negotiation
Puffery	Exaggerating the value of something in the negotiation
Deception	An act or statement intended to mislead the opponent about the negotiator's intent or future actions relevant to the negotiations
Weakening the opponent	Actions or statements designed to improve the negotiator's relative strength by directly undermining that of the opponent
Strengthening one's own position	Actions or statements designed to improve the negotiator's position without directly weakening that of the opponent
Nondisclosure	Keeping back knowledge that would benefit the opponent
Information Exploitation	Using information provided by the opponent to weaken them, either in direct exchange or by sharing it with others
Change of mind	Engaging in behaviors contrary to previous statements or positions
Distraction	Acts or statements that lure the opponent into ignoring information or alternatives that might benefit them
Maximization	The negotiator's single-minded pursuit of payoffs at the cost of the opponent's payoffs

There are, of course, times when negotiators use one or some of these tactics. Are there times when you think some of these tactics might be justified? Do you find some of these tactics to be more or less justifiable than others? When considering these tactics, does it matter what the potential outcome of the negotiation will be? For example, if you were in a custody case for your child, would you keep information to yourself that might benefit your ex-spouse (nondisclosure)? Would you be okay with using information on the car history report to try to get a dealership to lower their price (information exploitation)? How would you feel if you found out a co-negotiator used these tactics with you?

Source: Reitz et al., 1998.

Interviews

Interviews are structured conversations with the specific purpose of gathering information. Interviews allow people to "gather information about things or processes that cannot be observed effectively by other means" (Lindlof & Taylor, 2011, p. 175). Interviewing techniques can be used for a variety of interview types. Different types of interviews include psychological, therapeutic, appraisal, research, and selection interviews. In psychological interviews, psychologists attempt to assess personality traits (Ryan & Sackett, 1989). Therapeutic interviews focus on helping clients develop deeper insights regarding themselves and their behaviors (Millar et al., 2017). Appraisal interviews help managers evaluate employees (Cederblom, 1982). Research interviews are part of the collection of qualitative data for research projects (Lindlof & Taylor, 2011). In this section, we focus on one of the most common types of interview scenarios people encounter—selection interviews. Selection interviews are designed to select a new employee from a pool of job candidates (McDaniel et al., 1994).

Interviews may be structured or unstructured (McDaniel et al., 1994). **Unstructured interviews** do not use a standardized set of questions, typically do not specify questions in advance, and are usually not formally scored. Interviewers may use unstructured interviews for preplanned purposes such as setting an informal tone, having different goals for different interviewees, or desiring to let the interviewee drive the topics of conversation. However, at times, relying on a completely unstructured interview is the result of the interviewer's lack of forethought and limited interviewing skills.

Structured interviews typically have a preset list of questions and a planned interview schedule, and they may include a formal scoring rubric (McDaniel et al., 1994). Structured interviews allow for a more homogeneous experience across interviewees, allowing for easier comparisons between interviewees. Often interviewers rely on a mix of structured and unstructured components. Introducing structure into the interview schedule has been shown to increase the accuracy and reliability of the interview process (Campion et al., 1997). Using a structured interview can reduce the cognitive demands placed on the interviewer, which may help them avoid relying on faulty heuristics (Posthuma et al., 2002). For example, structured interviews can help interviewers focus on candidate qualifications rather than attributes such as attractiveness (Weirsma, 2016).

Interviews, whether structured or unstructured, typically occur in four stages (Weirsma, 2016). The greeting stage, the small-talk stage, the information-gathering stage, and the closing stage in which interviewees are given an opportunity to ask questions. The greeting and small-talk phases serve the purpose of establishing rapport with the interviewee (Millar et al., 2017). The information-gathering portion of interviews uses several types of questions to help the interviewer and interviewee learn from each other (Campion et al., 1997).

Some questions are designed to assess a candidate's background or knowledge. **Background questions** explore a candidate's qualifications such as previous experience and education (Campion et al., 1997). **Job knowledge questions** ask candidates to describe or demonstrate expertise relevant to the position.

Interviews typically have four stages: greeting, small talk, information-gathering, and closing stage.

iStock/fizkes

More sophisticated questions are situational and behavioral questions. **Situational questions** (Latham & Skarlicki, 1995) provide interviewees with a hypothetical scenario and ask them to explain how they think they would react in that situation. For example, an interviewer may ask a receptionist candidate how he would communicate to a client who insisted on seeing his boss that the boss was unavailable. **Behavioral questions** ask participants how they have performed in the past and explain how this behavior relates to the job at hand (Pulakos & Schmitt, 1995). Interviewees might be asked about a time when they had to resolve a conflict or to explain their decision-making process when they had to make a difficult choice. Both behavioral and situational questions have been shown to help interviewers gauge honesty and reduce selection biases surrounding, gender, race, weight, and pregnancy (Bragger et al., 2002; Kutcher & Bragge, 2006; Weirsma, 2016).

The interviewer is not the only one who should be asking questions. Interviewees should also think carefully about the questions they ask within interviews. . People who tailor their questions to the specific job and use their questions as a way to link their personal backgrounds to the job and organization may be perceived as better candidates (Weirsma, 2016).

Beyond the information exchanged in verbal questions and answers, nonverbal cues also contribute to the perceived competence of job interviewees. Vocal cues such as variability in pitch and volume and visual cues such as physical attractiveness, smiling, and orienting one's body toward the interviewer had a small effect on interview performance ratings (DeGroot & Motowidlo, 1999). Factors related to attractiveness that are perceived as controllable by the applicant, such as choices related to grooming, clothing, and jewelry, may also affect interviewer perceptions (Posthuma et al., 2002). Other behaviors such as handshake quality and solid eye contact have been shown to affect hiring decisions (Stewart et al., 2008). Although these non-verbal behaviors may affect interviewer decisions, they are not good predictors of overall job performance (Chiaburu et al., 2011). (See Chapter 3 for more on the role nonverbal communication plays in making impressions during interviews.)

The interviewer's nonverbal behavior also matters. Interviewers who appear cold or intimidating may make candidates less interested in the job (Liden et al., 1993; Turban & Dougherty, 1994). When applicants like an interviewer's communication style, they are more attracted to the job and more likely to continue with the hiring process (Ralston & Brady, 1994).

Mediated Conversations

Some conversations may occur entirely through a mediated channel such as text messaging, email, or an online messenger application. Although gossip, negotiations, and/or interviews may occur through mediated channels in any of the conversational contexts discussed here, mediated channels may introduce variations into conversational processes.

Mediated conversations may differ in how simultaneously messages can be exchanged via a particular mediated channel. Some systems such as email are nonsimultaneous or asynchronous. Others are nearly simultaneous or synchronous, such as instant messages or texts. Channels such as the phone or systems where communicators can view the typing of each other are considered highly synchronous (Anderson et al., 2010). Both conversational gaps and overlaps between communicators may occur more frequently in computer-mediated communication than in face-to-face conversations (Anderson et al., 2010). This likely occurs because the nonverbal cues that regulate turn-taking during face-to-face conversation are missing in primarily text-based mediated channels. On the other hand, communicators generally adapt to the communication medium.

At times, mediated conversations may even be more efficient than face-to-face conversations. Some studies have found that decision-making over synchronous computer-mediated communication can be completed using about half of the number of words as face-to-face communication (Condon & Čech, 2001). Of course, it is also possible that face-to-face communicators are accomplishing other more relational communicative tasks while engaging in decision-making.

I DIDN'T KNOW THAT!
IS TECHNOLOGY A "CONVERSATION KILLER"?

There are many claims that social media is somehow diminishing our ability to hold face-to-face conversations (Chan, 2019; Iqbal, 2018; Turkle, 2015). Conversational skill is an important component of interpersonal communication (Tracy, 2020). As noted throughout this chapter, conversations provide the means to accomplish many of our interpersonal communication goals. The concerns surrounding mediated channels and conversational skill are generally of two variations. The first concern is that social media usage may degrade communication skills needed for conversations. The second is that social media and smartphone use may lead us to not communicate with those around us in favor of keeping up with connections.

There is little evidence that the use of social media and other mediated channels diminishes conversational skill. Rather, studies have found that engaging in online interactions can improve offline communication skills (Valkenburg & Peter, 2009). Spending time interacting with others through mediated channels can promote intimate self-disclosure, the very kind of communication that those promoting the primacy of face-to-face interactions worry might be abandoned due to the use of mediated channels (Bazarova & Choi, 2014; Taylor & Bazarova, 2018). In addition, channel selection is in-and-of-itself a modern conversational skill. At times, people may choose a text-based channel *precisely* because the affordances of that channel meet their conversational needs at the moment (Walther, 2011).

The evidence also does not support that social media and smartphone use limits communication with those around us. Burke and colleagues (2011) found that people with higher social communication skills generally engage in more communication all around, more social media, more texting, *and* more face-to-face communication. Indeed, people who are outgoing and gregarious likely engage in communication across many channels. The Pew Research Center has found that heavy internet users tended to have *more* offline friends than others (Hampton et al., 2009).

In addition, there is a connection between social skill and mediated communication. Some research (e.g., Ruppel & Burke, 2015) suggests that people who have lower social skills might choose mediated channels over face-to-face options. Asynchronous and editable channels might be particularly appealing ways to construct messages more thoughtfully for those who struggle with conversational control in face-to-face settings.

In any case, human-to-human connection is an important part of our daily lives and well-being. However, many of our interpersonal goals and needs can be met across a variety of different channels.

In what ways do you use technology to communicate with friends, family members, and romantic partners? Are there types of conversations that you think are more appropriate for face-to-face contexts than mediated contexts? Are there times when you find a mediated channel to be more appropriate? Do you think video apps like Zoom or FaceTime are similar to face-to-face communication? Why or why not?

During the COVID-19 pandemic, many people turned to Zoom as a way to communicate while practicing social distancing, especially for school and business meetings. How do you think communicating via Zoom differs from face-to-face communication in these contexts?

iStock/LeoPatrizi

CONVERSATION CHALLENGES

Although conversation makes up the majority of our daily communication, communicators still face challenges when it comes to competently managing a conversation. Some of these challenges are related to the coordination concepts discussed earlier. In addition, competent communication requires carefully listening to our co-communicators. Further, some communicators may face additional challenges, such as experiencing communication apprehension, that may make it more difficult to successfully carry out a conversation. Finally, some conversations are difficult because they revolve around issues that make people feel uncomfortable and vulnerable. Topics that are related to our identities, such as discussing race, sexual orientation, gender, and class, can be especially difficult to discuss.

Listening

When conversations go well, people aren't just speaking—they are also listening (Turkle, 2015). Listening goes beyond the physical process of hearing. **Listening** involves the selection of stimuli, interpretation of that stimuli, as well as how we store and recall that information (Bodie et al., 2008). Listening is a complex process. Good listeners need to hear, perceive, interpret, and store messages. In addition, good listeners use nonverbal behaviors and appropriate responses to show they are engaged in the processes of quality listening (Bodie et al., 2008; Weger et al., 2010). The stakes for quality listening are high. Outcomes of competent listening include increasing understanding through knowledge acquisition, increasing relationship quality, increasing empathy, and motivation (Bodie et al., 2008). Fortunately, there is evidence that people can be trained to be better listeners (Weger et al., 2010).

Knowing how and when to listen is every bit as important of a communication skill as speaking ability is.

iStock/SDI Productions

Many communication training programs focus on **active listening**. Active listening contains three components (Weger et al., 2010). First is using nonverbal immediacy cues such as eye contact or orienting one's body toward the speaker to convey attention giving. Second is paraphrasing the speaker's message to check that what the listener has heard is what the speaker meant to convey. Third, active listening requires listeners to ask speakers questions as a means of conveying interests and continuing the conversation.

However, research has found that some of the main tenets of active listening, such as constantly paraphrasing the sender's message, have little effect on conversational satisfaction (Weger et al., 2010). It is likely that it is sometimes useful to paraphrase speakers, particularly when the conversational content is complex or a misunderstanding may cause future problems. Other times it is unnecessary. Paraphrasing may also be useful in specific communication contexts, such as counseling, where the focus is primarily on one speaker (the patient) (Weger et al., 2010). However, in everyday conversation, constant paraphrasing may interrupt the flow of the conversation, leading to stilted and less enjoyable interactions.

The mixed effects regarding paraphrasing draw attention to the complexity and contextual nature of listening. Listening researchers such as Graham Bodie have expressed concerns that many listening training programs oversimplify the listening process (Bodie et al., 2008). These researchers proposed that there are four stages of listening: attention, decoding, working memory, and long-term memory.

First, to listen, we must pay **attention**. Attending to certain sounds and cues is a fundamental part of what separates intentionally listening from the mere physical act of hearing (Bodie et al., 2008). For example, as Wei sits at his desk, he can hear a variety of sounds throughout the day—traffic on the street, birds in trees, people walking by outside. He "tunes out" most of these sounds to focus on the task at hand. However, at times there will be sounds that catch Wei's attention, such as the local tornado siren or someone calling his name. Attention is an important part of listening in conversations as well. When we are distracted, we may physically hear the words that someone is saying to us but realize that we haven't actually been attending to the words and aren't sure what was said.

After message information is attended to, people must cognitively interpret or **decode** the meaning of the message (Bodie et al., 2008). People generally decode messages immediately. Later, however, they might remember an interaction and wonder if they had processed it accurately the first time. Decoding messages accurately is a complex process that requires having a shared understanding of the words and language used in the interaction, an accurate interpretation of accompanying nonverbal messages, and knowledge of the associated contextual information. For example, imagine that one day Michael arrives for their conversation and Wei is finishing a phone call in Cantonese. Michael doesn't speak Cantonese, so won't be able to listen to the message even if he hears it perfectly because he has no shared understanding of the symbols/language Wei is speaking. In another example, Michael might use a common colloquialism such as telling Wei he's reading to "shoot the breeze." This colloquialism may confuse Wei because he's not used to the American context of expressions like this.

Listeners should also be aware that they are biased information processors because they must rely on prior knowledge, preconceived judgments, and relational history to make sense of the new message that they are receiving (Bodie et al., 2008). Although these heuristics are a vital part of the process of making meaning from new messages, communicators need to be wary of how stereotypes and biased framing might influence how they interpret messages.(See Chapter 3 for more on these types of biases.)

Listening and responding in conversation requires accessing memory systems, including both working memory and long-term memory (Bodie et al., 2008). **Working memory** allows us to actively hold a certain amount of information in our minds as we participate in a conversation. Conversational turns usually adhere to the limits of our working memory, although there are times when people extend their turns beyond these limits. For example, have you ever thought of something to say while a friend was speaking, only to forget it by the time your friend completed their turn? This is an example of you running up against the limits of working memory.

People also use **long-term memory** to participate in conversations. Listeners process speech faster than people speak. To process speech, people transfer information from long-term memory into working memory (Bodie et al., 2008). For instance, we might use our knowledge of common phrases to understand what communicators are likely to say. We also likely use our knowledge of the person who is speaking, the situation, and the setting to appropriately interpret the conversation. In addition, we are pulling information from our long-term memory to prepare our own conversational turns (Baddeley, 1990).

SKILL BUILDER
THE ACTIVE–EMPATHETIC LISTENING SCALE

Active and empathetic listening (AEL) are listening choices made by the receiver that are also performative, meaning that listeners engaging in active and empathic listening are not only engaging in a cognitive process but also showing the speaker they are engaged. Engaging in active-empathic listening is useful because it may lead to emotional improvement (Burleson & Goldsmith, 1996) and increased satisfaction between salespersons and customers (Drollinger et al., 2006).

Drollinger et al. (2006) developed a scale to measure a listener's level of active-empathic listening in sales contexts. Bodie (2011) later examined the scale in the context of interpersonal interactions . Individuals higher on AEL were more involved in conversations and rated as more effective, appropriate, and immediate. The scale measures three factors related to active-empathic listening: sensing, processing, and responding. Complete the following scale to gauge your skill at active-empathic listening.

	Strongly Disagree				Strongly Agree
1. I am sensitive to what people are not saying.	1	2	3	4	5
2. I am aware of what people imply but do not say.	1	2	3	4	5
3. I understand how my communication partner feels.	1	2	3	4	5
4. I assure people that I will remember what they say by taking notes when appropriate.	1	2	3	4	5
5. I summarize points of agreement and disagreement when appropriate.	1	2	3	4	5
6. I keep track of points people make.	1	2	3	4	5
7. I assure people I am listening by using verbal acknowledgments.	1	2	3	4	5
8. I assure people that I am receptive to their ideas.	1	2	3	4	5
9. I ask questions that show I am understanding of people's positions.	1	2	3	4	5
10. I show people I am listening through my body language (e.g., head nods).	1	2	3	4	5

Take an average of all items to find your score on the AEL. To find scores for the separate subfactors, take separate averages for items 1–3 (sensing), 4–6 (processing), or 7–10 (responding). The closer to 5 your average is, the more you perceive yourself to possess that skill. Are you surprised by your results? What are some areas you might work on to be a more effective listener?

Communication Apprehension

Some individuals may find themselves dreading conversations due to high levels of communication apprehension in interpersonal settings. **Communication apprehension** refers to people who experience reticence about communication situations. They may be nervous, anxious, or even fearful about communicating. People with communication apprehension feel that the risks of participating in interpersonal encounters outweigh whatever might be gained through the interaction (McCroskey, 1970).

The idea of communication apprehension was first developed to explain apprehension and performance in relation to public speaking (McCroskey, 1978). However, McCroskey and colleagues expanded the concept to include apprehension people may feel when conversing in dyads (McCroskey et al., 1985). When people have **dyadic communication apprehension**, they feel nervous about participating in conversations with new acquaintances and experience fear and nervousness about speaking up in any conversation (McCroskey et al., 1985). People who have high levels of communication apprehension may avoid communication encounters or only participate in conversations at a minimal level (McCroskey & Richmond, 1976). Unfortunately, avoidance of conversation may mean that those who have communication apprehension do not take advantage of opportunities to practice conversational skills. In turn, this lack of practice may lead them to feel increasingly apprehensive about future conversational encounters. In addition, people with high communication apprehension tend to have a low level of conversational involvement that may lead other communicators to perceive them as less credible, attractive, and influential (McCroskey & Richmond, 1976).

Communication apprehension can affect our ability to listen. In part, this is because people who are highly communication apprehensive may focus so strongly on their own communicative performance that they have difficulties concentrating on the messages their co-communicators are sending (McCroskey et al., 1998). People may also experience **receiver apprehension,** where they have difficulty concentrating because they think that the information will be overly complex or so new that they will have difficulty understanding the message (Bodie et al., 2008). In these cases, receiver apprehension becomes a self-fulfilling prophecy as the apprehension itself increases the difficulty of comprehension.

Difficult Conversations

Some individuals find themselves dreading conversations because of the topic at hand. Some conversations are difficult because of their topic or purpose. For example, discussing topics such as race, sexuality, sexism, and politics can be difficult, as can conversations aimed at firing an employee, ending a relationship, or confronting someone about offensive behavior. **Difficult conversations** involve discussing a topic that is hard for someone to talk about (Stone et al., 2010). These conversations often cause feelings of discomfort, are emotionally charged, and create or exacerbate uncertainty (Chen & Lawless, 2018).

Conversations that tap into identity issues can be especially difficult, especially in interactions among people from different social, cultural, and racial groups. As Miller et al. (2004) explained, conversations around issues such as class, gender, race, and sexuality are difficult in part because "differences in social identity do not only involve 'difference,' but also represent societal inequities of power, privilege, and oppressions" (p. 377). Differences are also complex. Miller and colleagues gave the example of a white middle-class lesbian, who may feel underprivileged and discriminated against for her gender and sexuality but privileged due to her class and race. People bring these complex identities with them into difficult conversations.

Sometimes people avoid difficult conversations. This is true across a variety of situations. For example, a person might ghost someone to avoid having a breakup conversation, or they might avoid someone with whom they recently had a disagreement. In U.S. society, conversation about issues such as sexuality and race is often discouraged and avoided. Sue (2013) explained some of the reasons for this, including the politeness and color-blind protocols. The **politeness protocol** is the idea that people want to be perceived as friendly and polite, so they avoid difficult conversations, such as those about race, which they consider to be potentially contentious and uncomfortable. The **color-blind protocol** is based on the ideal that race and skin color should not matter; people should be judged based on their character, personality, and accomplishments, rather than race. White people, therefore, sometimes think that talking about race will make them seem racist, since they should see people as individuals rather than as belonging to a racial group. The color-blind protocol, however, leads white individuals to avoid conversations about race and to minimizes differences. This can feel invalidating to people of color who have experienced discrimination and believe that race does indeed matter. Some research has shown that a multicultural view, which recognizes and celebrates diversity rather than ignoring it, promotes more understanding and reduces bias and discrimination compared to the color-blind protocol (Sue, 2013).

When difficult conversations revolve around identity issues, Stone et al. (2010) suggest that people need to shift their focus from protecting their self-image to having a learning conversation. This is an important shift. During difficult conversations, people often feel threatened and vulnerable. They might recoil to protect themselves and worry about how others might judge them. Having a **learning conversation** is instead focused on inviting others to express their opinions and feelings and trying to understand their perspective. A learning perspective is fueled by curiosity. It also involves sharing stories, actively listening and empathizing, and understanding that all parties in the conversation have complex identity issues at stake. Having a learning conversation requires patience and effort, but the effort can be well worth it if people ultimately understand one another better.

PRINCIPLES OF MAKING AND MANAGING CONVERSATION

Although you might not always think about how you make and manage conversation, doing so is an art form that requires considerable skill and knowledge. We all go into conversations with certain motivations and expectations. Enjoyable and productive conversations are the product of a number of coordinated skills. Next, we outline four general principles that further highlight some of the key features of conversations.

Principle 1. Multiple communication phenomena happen within the structure of conversation.

While today there are many exhortations to return to interpersonal conversation and learn conversational skills (e.g., Turkle, 2015), these appeals often fail to mention that there are many different types of conversations. Conversations can occur across multiple types of channels such as texting, messenger apps, social networking sites, and face-to-face communication. Conversations can be sought to achieve multiple interpersonal goals. Conversations encompass a variety of contexts, including those outlined in this chapter—small talk, gossip, negotiations, interviewing—as well as a plethora of others such as self-disclosure, seeking and providing social support, engaging in conflict, and more. Conversations also involve sophisticated coordination of verbal and nonverbal information exchanged between two or more speakers that relies on knowledge or context, social norms, and the individual idiosyncrasies of the co-conversationalists (Spitzberg, 2014). Yet, we accomplish these communication tasks multiple times every day. Despite the multiple phenomena involved, communicators can comprehend what is happening on global and immediate levels. Bavelas and Coates (1992) elegantly compare this process to looking at an Impressionist painting where we intuit the meaning of the design prior to examining every tiny detail.

Principle 2. Conversations are structured yet spontaneous.

Communicators rely on a variety of norms, such as Grice's cooperative principle, and standard features of conversation, such as adjacency pairs, to understand what is being communicated in conversations. Yet no matter how finely communication scholars, linguists, and pragmatics parse the process of communication, any given conversation has an element of spontaneity. You may have experienced stopping in the middle of a conversation and asking your co-conversationalist how you got there, going off on a tangent, or realizing a topic has veered "off the rails" into a humorous exchange. Understanding the structure of conversation may help us to be better conversationalists but any given conversation is the unique creation of the communicators.

Principle 3. Conversations help us to reduce uncertainty.

Brenner (1985) noted that interviews "quite literally … develop a *view* of something between (*inter*) people." While interviews are most certainly designed to reduce our uncertainty about other communicators, many different types of conversations also help with uncertainty reduction. Berger and Calabrese (1975) found that sharing information within the context of a conversation helped people reduce uncertainty within the first 5 minutes of meeting each other. Gossip may help us reduce uncertainty about how our fellow gossipers perceive our shared social world. Other types of conversations such as patient-doctor interactions or annual reviews can be important sites of information sharing and assessment for future interactions.

Principle 4. Conversations are skilled activities.

Conversations require multiple skills to be successful. First, conversationalists must be able to provide verbal contributions to the conversations. They must also be able to manage nonverbal cues that provide information regarding feedback, conversational flow, and the interpretation of messages. Good conversationalists must be able to consider the possibilities of their next contribution while remaining engaged in listening to their co-conversationalists. Traits such as communication apprehension can make it more difficult to master these skills. Further, due to the spontaneous nature of conversation, people cannot just master a set of rote instructions to make them better conversationalists. Similar to many communication phenomena, flexibility is a key part of performing skillfully. People may benefit from practicing high-stakes conversations such as interviews or negotiations but must balance this practice with the ability to come across as relaxed and fluid. Similarly, it takes skill to engage in difficult conversations, especially when the topic is related to our social identities and makes us feel vulnerable or threatened. Approaching such conversations with curiosity and inviting others to share their opinions, feelings, and stories can help turn a difficult conversation into a learning conversation.

CONCLUSION

Michael and Wei are right to be concerned about the potential difficulties of their conversation. Although conversations are part of our everyday communication, successful conversations require employing a variety of verbal and nonverbal skills. In addition, communicators need to be competent listeners and overcome concerns such as communication apprehension. In face-to-face conversations, all of this work to be cooperative, cognitively craft one's message, and manage nonverbal signals appropriately happens very quickly and leaves little room for error. Mediated conversations may help assuage some of these challenges through asynchronous messages and the potential for editability. Yet mediated conversation brings additional challenges, including appropriately managing tone and being able to access the receiver's feedback. All in all, although conversation is part of our everyday communication repertoire, being a competent conversationalist requires multiple skills.

CHAPTER 5 STUDY GUIDE

KEY TERMS

Identify and explain the meaning of each of the following key terms.

active and empathetic listening

active listening

adjacency pairs

attention

backchannels

background questions

behavioral questions

color-blind protocol

communication apprehension

content meaning

conversation

conversational coherence

conversational implicature

cooperative principle

decode

difficult conversations

dyadic communication apprehension

gossip

illocutionary force

interactional synchrony

interpersonal coordination

interviews

job knowledge questions

learning conversation

listening

locutions

long-term memory

maxim of manner

maxim of quality

maxim of quantity

maxim of relevance

mirroring

negotiation

phatic communication

politeness protocol

receiver apprehension

relational meaning

situational questions

structured interviews

truth bias

unstructured interviews

working memory

REFLECTION QUESTIONS

1. Conversation requires many different types of skills. How might you practice improving these skills for future conversations? How can improved conversation skills lead to positive outcomes in different aspects of your life, such as relationships and the workplace?

2. How do human beings make meaning out of conversational choices? How do our verbal and nonverbal choices influence what we mean and how we are interpreted in conversation? How does conversation help us to understand our fellow human beings?

3. Within the chapter, we discussed that our communication within interpersonal conversations can become routinized and automatic. In what ways can we become more mindful when we engage in conversation? How might this mindfulness improve our communication outcomes? Are there situations where it is more important to be mindful than others?

6 EXPRESSING AND MANAGING EMOTION

WHAT YOU'LL LEARN...

When you have finished the chapter, you should be able to do the following:

6.1 Define emotions and what components are part of experiencing and expressing emotion.

6.2 Describe various skills related to expressing, managing, and decoding emotions.

6.3 Understand various types of emotions, including basic emotions and the research supporting and modifying the universal thesis.

After a long night of studying for an exam, Ryan feels tired and groggy when the alarm on his phone wakes him in the morning. He hits snooze a couple of times and then with great determination forces himself to get up, shower, and throw some clothes on before heading out for his first class. Although Ryan expects his first class to be boring as usual, he is pleasantly surprised when a guest speaker engages everyone in a thought-provoking activity. On his way to his second class, Ryan runs into an old friend from high school, Kai, who he hasn't seen for a while. She looks more mature and beautiful than he remembers, and he feels an instant attraction mingled with excitement. He engages her in conversation for a few minutes and then feels regret that he has to get to his next class to take an exam. They add each other's numbers to their cell phones and he runs to class. As Ryan sits quietly with the other students waiting for the professor to pass out the exam, he begins to feel nervous. The professor has a reputation for giving difficult exams, and although Ryan studied hard, he can't help but feel a sense of dread. Upon receiving the exam, he quickly scans the first few questions and realizes that he knows the answers. Feeling a sense of relief, Ryan calms down and concentrates on the task at hand.

Ryan's day is only a few hours old, yet he has already experienced several different emotions—determination, surprise, excitement, nervousness, dread, and finally, relief. As his day progresses, Ryan will undoubtedly experience other emotions, and these emotions will influence how he communicates with others. Emotional expression plays a critical role in our lives. It is no accident that the word "motion" is in the word emotion. Emotions move us, and they often propel us to action, including communication.

In this chapter, we discuss the role emotion plays in the process of interpersonal communication. After defining concepts related to emotion, we describe skills related to encoding and decoding emotion and then summarize some of the key ways that specific emotions are associated with communication. The chapter ends with five principles that illuminate the relationships between communication and emotion.

WHAT ARE EMOTIONS?

Emotions are the feelings you have in response to precipitating events. For example, Kai might be happily surprised when Ryan sends her a snap later that day, or you might be angry if your best friend starts hanging out with someone who always talks behind your back. Emotions are experienced internally and expressed externally. However, people's expressions of emotion do not always match what they are feeling inside. A jealous person might appear indifferent, an angry person might seem calm, and a disappointed person might try to look happy. Because of this distinction, it is valuable to distinguish between emotional experience and emotional expression. **Emotional experience** is an internal, intrapersonal reaction that occurs inside a person's mind and body. **Emotional expression**, in contrast, is an external, interpersonal reaction that is manifest in a person's behavior. We examine each of these concepts in more detail next.

Components of Emotional Experience

Emotional experiences are powerful because they often affect people at three levels—the feeling level, the physical level, and the cognitive (thought) level. For instance, when Ryan discovered that the material on the test was familiar to him, he experienced pleasant feelings, his body relaxed, and he immediately became more confident about his ability to do well on the exam. Had he looked over the test and found the questions unfamiliar, his emotional experience would have been very different. His feelings would likely have been more unpleasant, his body tenser, and his confidence lower. As this example illustrates, feelings, physical changes, and cognition are all essential components of emotional experience. To really understand your feelings, you need to consider all three of these levels.

The Feeling Level: Affect

Affect refers to the positive or negative feelings people have when experiencing an emotion. Some emotions, such as anger, guilt, and sadness, are inherently unpleasant. Other emotions, such as happiness, contentment, and reciprocated love, are inherently pleasant. Emotions such as surprise, anticipation, and pride vary depending on the situation. For instance, you might be pleasantly or unpleasantly surprised when you run into an ex-boyfriend or girlfriend, depending on your feelings for that person. Many scholars regard affect as the most fundamental component of emotional experience (Frijda, 1986). When people are feeling "affectively neutral," they are not experiencing emotion.

The Physical Level: Physiological Changes

In addition to having positive or negative feelings, people tend to experience physiological changes when they feel emotion. **Physiological changes** refer to internal changes in one's body, such as increased or decreased arousal or blood pressure, warmer or cooler body temperature, and tenser or more relaxed muscles. Although some physiological changes are shown externally through sweating, blushing, shallow breathing, and the like, people cannot control these behaviors. Therefore, these types of physiological reactions can betray people's true feelings. Some researchers have referred to these physiological reactions as **leakage** for precisely this reason—physiological reactions leak emotion despite people's best efforts

Because physiological cues such as blushing are difficult, if not impossible, to control, they can provide good clues about what someone is feeling.

Design Pics/Radius Images/Alamy Stock Photo

to hide emotion. For instance, if you become embarrassed and blush, you may become even more embarrassed when everyone notices your red face. Yet there is nothing you can do to make the redness in your cheeks disappear. Some researchers suggest that if you want to know how another person is feeling, physiological reactions such as these provide excellent clues precisely because people cannot control them.

The Cognitive Level: Appraisals

People interpret the feelings and physiological changes they experience. A **cognitive appraisal** refers to how people evaluate and make sense of an event (Lazarus, 1991; Omdahl, 1995). Expectations and goals shape how people appraise situations and experience emotions (Berscheid, 1983; Burgoon, 1993). When something falls short of expectations or fails to meet our goals, we tend to experience negative emotion. For example, imagine that Zahira receives a gift card for a massage and facial from her daughters for her 50th birthday. If Zahira is used to getting flowers and cards from her daughters, she would likely feel happiness and surprise upon receiving the gift card. On the other hand, if Zahira was expecting her daughters to do something extra special for her 50th birthday and they always get her a spa package, she would likely be disappointed. Notice that in both cases the precipitating event is receiving a gift certificate for a massage and facial. The event would be interpreted differently, however, based on expectations. Expectations and how we evaluate stimuli also vary based on culture. For example, in the United States, people are likely to feel happy and surprised when they receive an unexpected gift from someone they like. In another culture, people might have emotional responses more rooted in gratitude or may even feel humbled upon receiving such a gift.

Components of Emotional Expression

When people encounter events that either block or enhance their chances of reaching a personal goal, they are likely to experience emotion. However, the emotion they experience may or may not be expressed. This is because people learn how to manage their emotional expressions to show what they want others to see rather than what they actually feel. Emotional expression is the result of two forces: (1) the tendency to spontaneously display an emotion a particular way and (2) the desire to manage emotional expression to communicate a certain message.

Sometimes these two forces complement one another. For example, you might be excited and happy to receive an especially nice gift from a good friend. In this situation, spontaneously showing your feelings by clapping your hands and smiling reflects exactly what you want to communicate— happiness and appreciation—so you are not likely to curb your expression. Imagine instead that your good friend gives you a hideous gift—perhaps a green sweater with purple and red polka dots on it. Your spontaneous reaction may be to grimace and push the sweater away, but you quickly decide to manage your emotional expression by putting on a polite smile and saying "thank you." As this example illustrates, emotional expression is influenced by the push and pull of two forces: spontaneity and the need to regulate expression to communicate in a competent manner. As you will learn later, regulating emotional expressions is often tied to social motives that also reflect emotion. In the case of the hideous sweater, you might hate the gift but love your friend, so the smile you put on your face reflects your positive feelings for your friend.

People often simulate or exaggerate emotions to try and be polite and likeable, as can be the case when opening gifts.

blickwinkel/McPHOTO/ADR/Alamy Stock Photo

Expressing Emotions Spontaneously Through Action Tendencies

Spontaneous emotional expressions are guided by **action tendencies**, which are biologically based behavioral impulses that help people cope with emotion in adaptive ways (Lazarus, 1991). At a basic level, action tendencies direct people to approach, attack, or flee from someone or something that caused them to experience emotion. For example, if you are about to drive north through an intersection and you see a speeding car approaching from the east, you are likely to slow down and prepare to stop even if the light is green. Action tendencies such as this are thought to be hard-wired in people's brains as a mechanism to help people cope with their emotions and the environment effectively (Frijda, 1993).

Various emotions are related to different action tendencies (Lazarus, 1991; Smith & Lazarus, 1990). For example, the action tendency for fear is to escape or move away from harm. (See Table 6.1 for more action tendencies.) This tendency helps people react quickly to dangerous situations such as speeding cars, violent people, and rattlesnakes. Some people even dream about being unable to get away from something scary. You may have had one of these dreams—where you are trying to escape from a monster or get out of your house when a burglar breaks in, but your feet won't move or you can't get out of bed. Such dreams are especially frightening because they portray a situation in which you have lost the ability to perform the action tendency that protects you from harm.

TABLE 6.1 ■ Selected Emotions and Action Tendencies	
Emotion	**Action Tendency**
Anger	Approach and attack
Fear	Escape and move away from harm (flight)
Happiness, love	Approach and get close to
Sadness	Withdraw or distract oneself from problems
Guilt	Make amends/repair damage
Embarrassment	Save face
Romantic jealousy	Engage in behavior to try and keep your partner

Some action tendencies help people develop, maintain, or repair relationships. If Ryan and Kia, from the beginning of this chapter, start to develop feelings for one another, they will want to spend more time together. If Kia's friends get upset that she is ignoring them to spend time with Ryan, that could prompt Kia to experience guilt and the associated action tendency of wanting to fix things with her friends. Kia might even try to reconcile these two action tendencies. One tendency pulls her to spend time with her new love and the other pulls her toward trying to make amends with her friends. To solve this, Kia could try to integrate Ryan into her broader social network.

In addition to understanding action tendencies, it is important to recognize that people communicate emotions using many different channels. In one study, researchers asked people to watch a person they knew (usually someone they lived with) for signs that the person was experiencing an emotion and to record what they observed (Planalp et al., 1996). The researchers uncovered the following seven categories of behavior that are used to express emotions.

- **Vocal cues:** the sound of the voice, such as how fast, loud, or nervous it sounds

- **Facial cues:** face and eye movements, such as smiling, frowning, rolling one's eyes, and arching one's eyebrows

- **Body cues:** movements of the body (other than the face), such as stomping one's foot, clenching one's fist, and throwing one's arms up in the air

- **Activity cues:** behaviors that involve taking actions, such as going for a walk or slamming a door, as well as tactile behavior such as hugging, kissing, and hitting

- **Physiological cues:** biologically based reactions such as crying, blushing, and breathing more rapidly

- **Direct verbal cues:** disclosure of feelings by making statements such as "I'm really mad at you," "I'm so happy," and "I feel really proud of myself"

- **Indirect verbal cues:** words that convey emotions without identifying the emotion being experienced, such as calling someone a name to show anger, or apologizing as a way to admit guilt

As this list suggests, most of the time emotions are encoded and decoded through nonverbal cues. Vocal and facial cues are the most frequent means of communicating emotion to others. Direct verbal expressions of emotion are infrequent by comparison (Planalp et al., 1996).

Managing Emotion Through Display Rules

While action tendencies represent innate and impulsive reactions to emotion, **display rules** represent ways people manage the communication of emotion to be socially appropriate within a given situation or culture (Ekman & Friesen, 2003; Koopmann-Holm & Matsumoto, 2011; Moran et al., 2013). People manage emotions for a variety of reasons. To make a good impression on someone, you might smile and laugh even though you are feeling ill. Despite being in a bad mood, you might act cheerful at work as a way to maintain good relationships with your co-workers. Importantly, these display rules vary based on context, including the situation you find yourself in and your culture. For example, in some cultures, people learn to inhibit negative emotions more than in other cultures. In the United States, people tend to more readily express negative emotions to people they have close relationships with than to strangers. There are at least five specific types of display rules that help people manage their emotions: simulation, inhibition, intensification, deintensification, and masking (see Table 6.2). Each of these is discussed next.

TABLE 6.2 ■ Display Rules		
Rule	**Do You Feel an Emotion?**	**How Do You Manage the Emotion?**
Simulation	No	Pretend to feel something
Inhibition	Yes	Pretend not to feel anything
Intensification	Yes	Pretend to feel more than you actually feel
Deintensification	Yes	Pretend to feel less than you actually feel
Masking	Yes	Pretend to feel a different emotion

Masking is the most difficult display rule to master since it involves covering up one expression with another.

iStock/TatyanaGl

Simulation and inhibition are opposite processes. **Simulation** involves acting like you feel an emotion when you actually feel nothing. For example, you might act happy when an acquaintance tells you he is getting married, but you might not really feel any emotion because you barely know him. You act happy because it is the socially polite thing to do. **Inhibition**, on the other hand, involves acting like you do not feel any emotion when you actually feel something. When a professor announces that someone got a perfect score on an exam, the high-achieving student might keep her face neutral so no one knows it was her. Or a man might act like it does not faze him when he sees his girlfriend in a corner talking to an attractive co-worker at a company party.

Intensification and deintensification are also opposites. When people use **intensification**, they act like they feel more of an emotion than they actually feel. Children learn how to exaggerate (or intensify) their emotions at a young age. A 2-year-old boy might feel pain when he skins his knee; if his mom is nearby, he might cry especially loud so she will come over and cuddle him. Adults also exaggerate their emotions quite frequently. Think about all the times you act happier than you really are when receiving gifts or hearing about a friend's good news. When people use **deintensification,** they downplay rather than exaggerate their emotion. You might be bitterly disappointed when you hear that you didn't get into the school of your choice, but you might curb your expression so that you only seem mildly disappointed.

The key to understanding intensification and deintensification is to recognize that in each of these cases, people communicate emotional states that are *similar* to what they feel. They simply modify the expression to show more or less of that emotion. A person might act elated when mildly happy (intensification) or annoyed when angry (deintensification), but the basic type of emotion expressed is similar to the emotion being experienced. By contrast, the final type of display rule, **masking**, involves covering up a felt emotion by expressing a different type of emotion. You might act happy when you find out your friend got the promotion you wanted when actually you feel anger and resentment, or you might act shocked and angry when your 3-year-old uses a four-letter word even though secretly you are amused.

Emotional Labor

Being able to manage emotions appropriately is an important skill in many professions, especially within the service industry. The term **emotional labor** was introduced by Hochschild (1979, 1983). Emotional labor is the effort involved in expressing emotions in appropriate ways based on job expectations. Consistent with the idea of display rules, people manage emotional expressions to fit the needs of the context. For example, cruise ship personnel, Disney ride operators, and salespeople often put on a pleasant face even when they feel bored or frustrated (e.g., Tracy, 2000; Van Maanen & Kunda, 1989). Firefighters (Scott & Myers, 2005) and 911 operators (Tracy & Tracy, 1998) learn to appear calm and composed even when they are not. Correctional officers engage in many different types of emotional labor, such as appearing pleasant and understanding when in a nurturing role, hiding feelings of fear and disgust, and acting angry and tough to control inmates (Tracy, 2005; Waldron & Krone, 1991).

Researchers have identified three specific types of emotional labor (Ashforth & Humphrey, 1993). **Surface acting** involves simulation or masking or, in other words, displaying emotions that you do not have. For example, a flight attendant might smile even when frustrated with a fussy customer. **Deep acting** occurs when people try to feel the emotions that are appropriate to express. This is common in the health care field. Think about how stressed many health care providers must feel during situations like the COVID-19 pandemic, yet most hide those feelings and act calm, sensitive, and empathetic to provide effective care for their patients. Through those efforts, health care professionals may even begin to feel more empathy. This is because, as we discuss later in this chapter, when people simulate emotions, they sometimes actually start to feel them. Finally, **genuine expression** can be emotional labor when people need to put effort into showing others that they are feeling the appropriate emotion. The idea here is that we can feel an emotion without expressing it outwardly in meaningful ways that people will notice. Perhaps a customer service representative feels badly that a customer's flight was canceled. Putting in effort to communicate those feelings to the customer would involve some emotional labor. Part of a good performance, then, is showing people when you are experiencing the proper emotion.

Many service-oriented jobs require a lot of emotional labor.

iStock/andresr

Sometimes, emotional labor is related to positive outcomes such as good performance and customer satisfaction. Other times, is it related to stress and burnout. The following Skill Builder provides more information on how emotional labor can lead to either positive or negative consequences.

SKILL BUILDER
USING EMOTIONAL LABOR TO OPTIMIZE PERFORMANCE

Individuals skilled in emotional labor are able to manage their communication to display the appropriate emotion for a given situation. In some cases, emotional labor leads to exhaustion and stress. In other cases, it leads people to perform better at work, be more attached to their company, and feel a sense of personal accomplishment (Humphrey et al., 2015). What can you do, then, to increase the benefits of emotional labor while reducing possible negative consequences?

- **Try to avoid using surface acting and instead focus on deep acting and genuine expression.** Surface acting can lead to negative outcomes such as stress and burnout because faking emotions requires a lot of effort and can be exhausting (Humphrey et al., 2015). In addition, when people use surface acting, they experience **emotive dissonance**, or discomfort about the clash between what they really feel versus what they are pretending to feel (Hochschild, 1983). Because deep acting and genuine expression involve internalizing emotion, there is less emotive dissonance.

- **As much as possible, keep emotional labor consistent with how you see yourself.** People feel more emotive dissonance when emotional labor clashes with how they see themselves. For example, a correction officer who believes she is a fair and cooperative person may become distressed if she has to repeatedly administer harsh punishments. That same correction officer may be more comfortable trying to muster up expressions of empathy toward a troubled teen because the officer sees herself as a caring person.

- **Keep in mind that you are likely to be more stressed when directing emotional labor to people you think are undeserving of it.** Having to direct emotional labor toward an individual you perceive to be undeserving of your efforts makes emotional labor stressful (Tracy, 2005). This means a correction officer might feel better about acting nurturing toward a petty thief than a murderer, and a Disney operator might enjoy acting friendly with most people, but not with visitors complaining about long lines or heat. Of course, there are times when your job may require you to exert emotional labor toward someone who is undeserving. Recognizing that your stress in this situation is understandable can be helpful, as can the self-satisfaction that comes from knowing you handled a difficult situation well.

- **Consider how important emotional labor is to your job.** People are less likely to feel emotional dissonance if they believe emotional labor is an important part of their job. In this case, strategically managing one's emotional expression can be enjoyable and fun (Shuler & Sypher, 2000). People feel good if they sell a product, help make someone's vacation more memorable, or give a patient comfort and hope. Remembering what you are accomplishing by engaging in emotional labor can also give you a sense of self-satisfaction.

With emotional labor, people experience less stress when they internalize the emotion. The less authentic the expression is, the more stress people feel. The same is true for emotion management in social interaction. This is why it is important to keep in mind that using a display rule does not necessarily mean that you are being phony or insincere (see "What Would You Do? The Ethical Dimension of Managing Emotional Expression"). In fact, the idea of display rules has been criticized as too simplistic (e.g., Fridlund & Duchaine, 1996). Rather than seeing display rules as ways of hiding or modifying one's true emotions, some researchers believe display rules help people manage multiple emotions at once. Think again about what would happen if a good friend gave you a hideous polka-dotted sweater for your birthday. Aside from feeling repulsion and disappointment, you might feel both badly that your friend wasted their money as well as happy that your friend remembered your birthday. When you smile and thank your friend, it reflects your appreciation rather than inauthenticity.

WHAT WOULD YOU DO?
THE ETHICAL DIMENSION OF MANAGING EMOTIONAL EXPRESSION

People manage emotional expressions for different reasons. Some people believe certain types of emotion management are deceptive. Whether it's the actress who acts surprised when she wins an award she expected to get, the boyfriend who pretends not to feel jealous, the teenager who feigns amazement that her parents think she might be having sex (when she is), or the friend who smiles and says your new hair cut looks fine when it actually looks horrible, all acts of emotional management involve creating an image that differs to at least some extent from what a person is feeling internally.

Whether such actions are unethical hinges on the motives that guide a person's attempt to manage emotional expression. Which of the four examples from above would you classify as most and least ethical? Most students in our classes consider the friend who smiles and says "your haircut looks fine" as the most ethical. This is because the friend's motive is probably to protect you by not hurting your feelings. Most students in our classes regard the "amazed teenager" as the most unethical because emotion is being feigned as a manipulative strategy to deceive the parent about something important. What do you think? When, if ever, does managing emotion become an unethical behavior? Can you think of situations where it would be ethical to use display rules and others where it would be unethical?

SKILL IN ENCODING AND DECODING EMOTION

As the research on emotional labor suggests, being able to communicate emotions appropriately and effectively is an important social skill. In relationships and on the job, having the so-called soft skills necessary to recognize and empathize with the emotional states of others is critical for success. Such skills build understanding and allow you to think outside of your own perspective.

Emotional Intelligence

Emotional intelligence is the ability to understand, manage, and utilize emotions to meet your goals and to understand the emotions of others (Goleman, 2006; Salovey & Mayer, 1990). People high in emotional intelligence analyze their emotions rationally. They also use emotions to facilitate thought and problem-solving. For example, imagine that Jamal is feeling angry at work because he is overlooked and underappreciated. If Jamal is high in emotional intelligence, he will analyze why he is feeling this way. Rather than putting the blame on his supervisors or co-workers, Jamal might determine that he needs to be more assertive in showing his abilities. Jamal might then speak up and take on more leadership roles. In this case, emotional intelligence helped Jamal meet his goals. People high in emotional intelligence also tend to be rated as open, agreeable, and cooperative and to be drawn to careers that involve social interaction and problem-solving, such as teaching, counseling, or sales (Mayer et al., 2004). There are five specific areas related to emotional intelligence, as shown in the Skill Builder box.

SKILL BUILDER
BECOMING MORE EMOTIONALLY INTELLIGENT

According to work on emotional intelligence (see Goleman, 1995, 2006), you are likely to be successful in your personal and professional relationships if you have the following five skills.

1. **Recognize and understand your own emotions.** Are you able to fully appreciate the role emotions play in your life? Analyzing your feelings can help you understand their depth and intensity. What caused you to feel this way? How are your emotions related to your goals? Listen to your body and your mind. Are your emotions stressing you out or interfering with your ability to get things done?

2. **Manage your emotions.** Are you able to control impulses so you display emotions in constructive rather than destructive ways? Can you regulate your mood to prevent negative emotions from flooding your mind and interfering with your ability to think? Can you redirect emotions so you remain optimistic? Try taking some time to calm down if you are overly stressed or upset. Think positive thoughts or visualize success when you are feeling angry or frustrated.

3. **Motivate yourself.** Are you able to put your emotions to work for you? Positive emotions can be energizing. Negative emotions are more challenging, but they can push us to overcome obstacles and improve ourselves. Learn to persist in the face of setbacks and frustration and to keep your goals in sight.

4. **Recognize and understand other people's emotions.** Are you sensitive to what the people around you are feeling? Do you have empathy for others? Being an active observer and listener can be helpful. Also, try to put yourself in the other person's place, but be careful not to jump to conclusions about what other people are thinking or feeling.

5. **Manage the emotions in your relationships.** Are you able to keep the emotional tone of your relationships positive? Can you influence the emotions of others? Remember that the people around you are affected by the emotions you experience and express. If an interaction takes a negative emotional turn, try expressing positive emotions to get the interaction on a better track. If your partner is feeling badly, let her or him talk through the problem while you listen empathetically.

To pull these skills together in your mind, think about a time when you were challenged to act in an emotionally intelligent way. Perhaps you were frustrated or too wrapped up in your own thoughts to communicate your emotions effectively. Now that you have learned about some of the concepts related to emotional intelligence, what might you do differently if you find yourself in a similar situation in the future?

Other work on emotional skill has focused on three areas: emotional expressivity, emotional control, and emotional sensitivity (Riggio, 1986, 2006). These three areas of emotional skill are related to how good you are at encoding your own emotions and decoding the emotions of others, as discussed next.

Emotional Expressivity

The concept of **emotional expressivity** refers to skill in communicating how you feel to others (Riggio, 2006, 2010). Being able to express your emotions so others know what you are feeling has many benefits. A fearful face or loud scream can signal that you need help, a loving glance can telegraph affection, and a sad voice can elicit comfort. Individuals high in emotional expressivity are typically extraverted and self-confident. They can liven up a dull party or bring people down with them when depressed. People who are good at expressing positive emotions also tend to be more popular, have better relationships, and be physically and mentally healthier (e.g., Burgoon & Bacue, 2003).

People skilled in emotional expressivity are also good at simulating and exaggerating emotions. They are able to pretend they are happy when they are not, and they can act more empathetic toward a friend than they actually feel. Dozens of studies have shown that when people simulate or exaggerate emotion, they may end up feeling the very emotion that at first they only pretended to feel (Laird & Apostoleris, 1996; Noah et al., 2018). This idea has been called the **facial feedback hypothesis** (Dimberg & Söderkvist, 2011; Ekman, 1973). Overall, research suggests that if you are good at expressing emotions, you have two advantages. First, you are able to telegraph your feelings to others so that people understand you better. Second, your ability to feign emotions may help pump you up if you want to feel happy or excited and calm you down if you want to feel less anger or anxiety.

Emotional Control

Of course, sometimes people who are skilled in expressing emotions run into trouble when they spontaneously communicate emotions that they would rather not, or should not, share. They might scare a potential romantic partner off by acting too interested too soon, or betray their frustration at work when people disagree with their idea. People skilled in **emotional control** are able to manage their emotional expression to show the appropriate emotion and avoid these kinds of problems (Riggio, 2006, 2010). Classic examples include men stifling tears to avoid looking weak and women curbing displays of anger to avoid appearing too aggressive.

Emotional control can also help people develop and maintain relationships. In the beginning stages of relationships, people are likely to inhibit strong expressions of negative emotion to make a good impression and appear likeable. Once relationships are established, people in happy relationships still sometimes curb their expressions of negative emotion to avoid initiating or escalating conflict (Aune et al., 1996). However, it is important not to suppress emotion too often. When people continually keep emotions bottled inside without expressing them, they usually feel stressed and frustrated and their relationships suffer (English et al., 2013; Velotti et al., 2016). The most skilled individuals know not only when it is helpful to control their emotional expressions but also when it is important to express rather than suppress how they are feeling.

Emotional Sensitivity

Being able to determine when your partner is sad, mad, or feeling any other emotion is also important. **Emotional sensitivity** refers to the skill in interpreting emotional information to accurately determine how other people feel (Riggio, 2006). People with this skill generally have happier relationships (Burleson & Denton 1997; Gottman & Porterfield, 1981). It is especially important to be able to recognize other people's expressions of positive emotions. In good relationships, people decode positive emotions more accurately (Fitness, 2006). Sometimes they even overattribute positivity to their partner, seeing them through the proverbial rose-colored glasses. This can be healthy to some extent, but it is also important to notice when someone is feeling bad or is unhappy so you can offer support and try to fix problems in your relationships.

When people lack decoding skills, one of the biggest potential problems is overestimating negativity. In general, people pay more attention to expressions of negative emotion than positive emotions. There is also a tendency to interpret some neutral expressions as negative. For example, a classic study showed that husbands sometimes hear a negative tone in their wives' voices, even when they are not feeling any negative emotion (Noller, 1980). This is in part because men expect women to sound friendly and happy most of the time. There are similar stereotypes about smiling, with women's lack of smiling interpreted more negatively than men's lack of smiling. A good decoder is able to make accurate judgments of people's emotional expressions without relying on stereotypes or overestimating negativity. Of course, as with the other skills we have discussed, there are limits to the positive effects of emotional sensitivity. Being too emotionally sensitive can lead you to be so tuned into people that you take what others say and do too personally.

A good decoder can pick up subtle differences in emotional expressions, such as the difference between a posed smile and a genuine smile.

mihailomilovanovic/E+ via Getty Images

Does the woman in this picture look more genuinely happy here than in the other picture? If so, what makes you think so?

mihailomilovanovic/E+ via Getty Images

BASIC EMOTIONS AND BEYOND

So far you have learned that emotional expression is influenced by innate action tendencies as well as culture and display rules, but we have not yet discussed how specific emotions are encoded or decoded. To that end, we move into a discussion about how people communicate various emotions, starting with the so-called basic emotions.

Basic Emotions

Considerable research has focused on what scholars call the **basic or primary emotions**. The concept of basic emotions is akin to the idea of primary colors. Just as blue, red, and yellow provide the foundation for other colors such as orange (yellow and red) or purple (red and blue), aspects of primary emotions combine to produce secondary or blended emotions. Basic emotions fit two requirements (Ekman & Cordaro, 2011). First, they must be discrete, which means they are distinguishable from one another in terms of nonverbal expression and feeling states. Second, they must have evolved as adaptations that provide a useful way to respond to something, such as moving toward people who keep us safe and moving away from anything or anyone dangerous. Researchers have advanced different lists of primary emotions. Based on the criteria discussed earlier, Ekman and Cordaro (2011) listed seven basic emotions: happiness, sadness, anger, fear, surprise, contempt, and disgust. Examples of secondary or blended emotions include disappointment (a blend of surprise and sadness), frustration (a blend of surprise and anger), and hurt (a blend of anger and sadness).

A key area of debate related to basic emotions revolves around the issue of universality. According to the **universal thesis**, basic emotions are encoded and decoded similarly across cultures. Early research supported this thesis. In many of these studies, researchers had people from different countries look at photos of faces of individuals posing expressions of basic emotions such as anger, happiness, and fear. The participants then matched the faces with the emotions they thought people were expressing. People from all around the globe expressed these emotions fairly similarly. Moreover, people from different cultures decoded the expressions of the basic emotions at above chance levels (Boucher & Carlson, 1980; Ekman, 1993; Ekman & Friesen, 1986; Ekman et al., 1972; Izard, 1971; Russell, 1994; Scherer & Wallbott, 1994; Shimoda et al., 1978). The emotion easiest to recognize across cultures is happiness, probably because it is the only basic emotion consistently associated with smiling and pleasant feelings. A more recent study using MRI imaging showed that each basic emotion even has a "discrete neural signature" in the brain (Saarimäki et al., 2016, p. 2563).

The universal thesis has been challenged by researchers who believe emotions are, at least to a large extent, socially and culturally constructed (e.g., Barrett, 2006; Elfenbein & Ambady, 2002a, 2002b; Jack et al., 2009, 2012). According to this perspective, the universal thesis overestimates the degree to which people from different cultures decode and encode emotions similarly. Studies have shown, for example, that when people from East Asia decode emotions from faces or emoticons, they focus mostly on the eyes, whereas people from Western cultures focus more on the mouth or the whole face (Jack et al., 2009; Yuki et al., 2007). Another study compared children from a Western culture (Spain) with children from two indigenous cultures (the Trobriand Islands in the South Pacific and Matemo Island in Africa). The children were shown photographs of faces and asked to indicate which person they thought was experiencing happiness, sadness, fear, anger, or disgust (Crivelli et al., 2016). Spanish children were better at identifying most of the emotions, although the children from the Trobriand Islands and Matemo Island did identify some emotions (such as happiness) at above chance levels.

Dialect theory provides an explanation for these findings (Elfenbein, 2013). The theory rests on two main ideas—that individuals from different cultures vary in their styles of nonverbal expression, and that people evaluate others' nonverbal expressions based on their own culture's style (Elfenbein, 2013). This can lead to people from different cultures misinterpreting each other's expressions. Two important concepts in the theory are nonverbal accents and nonverbal dialects. **Nonverbal accents** are any subtle and culturally distinct differences "across cultures in the appearance of an emotional expression" (Marsh et al., 2007, p. 91). A **nonverbal dialect** is a specific type of accent that impedes accurate decoding. Elfenbein (2013) compares accents and dialects to their counterparts in language. If you listen hard, you can understand what someone is saying despite their accent, but differences in dialect can make it even more challenging to understand what someone is saying.

Smiling is a universally recognized facial expression, yet people smile in ways that reflect cultural nonverbal accents as well as individual personality.

adamkaz/E+ via Getty Images

When nonverbal accents and dialects are present, so is an **in-group advantage**. This means people are better able to decode the emotion of someone from their own culture compared to another culture when the nonverbal expression of that emotion is marked by differences in dialect (Elfenbein & Ambady, 2002a, 2002b). In one study, people from two French-speaking areas—Quebec and Gabon—were compared (Elfenbein et al., 2007). In the study, there were noticeable differences in the ways that people from these two areas expressed anger, happiness, sadness, and especially contempt, based on nonverbal dialectics. For other emotions, such as fear, the differences were less noticeable. The stronger the nonverbal dialects were, the stronger the in-group advantage (Elfenbein et al., 2007). For the emotions like contempt, where a stronger dialect was present, people from Quebec could decode other Quebecois' emotions more accurately than Gabonese emotions, and vice versa for people from Gabon.

Other studies have supported the presence of nonverbal accents and in-group advantages (e.g., Marsh et al., 2007; Yan et al., 2016). For example, when people from the United States were asked to choose who was American versus Australian, their accuracy rates went up if the individuals they were judging had an emotional expression on their faces compared to a neutral expression. Something about the nonverbal expression—likely an accent or dialect—tipped them off (Marsh et al., 2007).

Expressions of secondary emotions, such as hurt or disappointment, are more difficult to recognize both across and within cultures. There are at least three reasons for this. First, secondary emotions are usually not associated with a particular type of expression. A smile is associated with happiness and a furrowed brow and clenched jaw with anger, but specific behaviors such as these are not associated with secondary emotions such as jealousy or hurt. Second, because secondary emotions blend aspects of basic emotions, it can be difficult to differentiate the secondary emotion from the basic emotions that comprise it. Relief might be interpreted as expressing happiness, and showing jealousy might be interpreted as expressing anger. Third, some secondary emotions are experienced and expressed more in some cultures than others. In German, for example, the word *schadenfroh* describes feeling pleasure when someone experiences misfortune. Although people from the United States might feel this type of emotion, they will process it differently because they do not have a specific word for it.

With a recognition that secondary emotions are more challenging to decode, we now move to discussing several clusters of emotion that are common in social interactions. As you will see, some of these clusters include basic and secondary emotions that are related to each other, whereas others include only secondary emotions.

Hostile Emotions

People experience hostile emotions when something or someone interferes with their goals. Hostile emotions include anger, frustration, hatred, and contempt. You might be angry because your roommate ate something you put in the refrigerator, frustrated that you are always picking up after someone, or hate someone who talks behind your back and is fake to your face. In all these cases, a goal (eating a snack, doing a fair amount of household work, being well thought of by others) is threatened. Refraining from personal attacks and instead concentrating on the issue causing hostile feelings is a good strategy in these situations. One of the hostile emotions, contempt, may be especially toxic in relationships (Lisitsa, 2013b). As you will learn in Chapter 10, contempt involves attacking a person by directly or indirectly casting that person as inferior. People communicate contempt through behaviors such as name-calling, eye-rolling, sighing, sneering, and sarcasm.

In interpersonal interactions, regularly experiencing hostile emotions can be stressful, as can being on the receiving end of angry outbursts and contemptuous looks or comments. One key for coping with hostile emotions is to use a nonthreatening approach to communicate about the issues causing them . This can be difficult since the action tendency for anger and other hostile emotions is to attack (Lazarus, 1991). When people experience hostile emotions, their faces and bodies tend to tense up, voices get loud, and blood pressure and heart rate go up. When people's bodies become flooded with these emotions, it is best to take a break from interaction to calm down (Gottman, 1994; Lisitsa, 2013a).

Aggression is often a natural reaction to feeling hostile emotions, but not all aggression involves direct communication. Psychologists have identified two very different types of aggression related to hostility: physical aggression and relational aggression. When most people think about aggression, physical aggression comes to mind. Some people use violence as a means of controlling someone, but the most common incidences of physical aggression are linked to experiencing hostile emotion. One fairly common form of physical aggression is common couple violence (Johnson, 1995; McEwan & Johnson, 2008). This type of physical aggression is called "common" couple violence because partners usually engage in aggressive behavior in a reciprocal manner. Common couple violence typically occurs within the context of a heated conflict interaction, where two people are overloaded with emotion.

Whereas common couple violence usually occurs in the heat of the moment, relational aggression tends to be strategic. **Relational aggression** involves using indirect and manipulative behaviors that cause someone social harm. Relational aggression includes tactics such as spreading rumors, talking behind someone's back, excluding or sabotaging someone, and even bullying and cyberbullying (Crick & Grotpeter, 1995; Grimaldi et al., 2014; South Richardson, 2014). The movie *Mean Girls* provides an example of relational aggression, with both Regina and Cady engaging in manipulative tactics such as these to try to take each other down. Relational aggression, like physical aggression, can have lasting harmful effects on people and relationships.

The movie *Mean Girls* is filled with examples of relational aggression, with Cady and Regina covertly trying to manipulate and sabotage each other.

CBS via Getty Images

Positive Emotions

When people experience positive emotions, the action tendency is to approach. We want to be close to people and things that make us feel good. This explains why Ryan, in the opening scenario in this chapter, stopped to talk to Kai even though afterward he had to run to make it to class on time. He felt attraction and excitement, which caused him to linger longer than he otherwise would have. Positive emotions include joy, love, affection, and excitement. These emotions bond people together.

Smiling is one of the key behaviors used to express positive emotion. Smiling is used not only to show internal feelings of happiness but also to share emotions and communicate friendliness. For example, a classic study by Kraut and Johnston (1979) examined smiling at bowling alleys. Bowlers rarely smiled when alone or when looking at the pins, and they smiled more after scoring a spare or strike once they turned to face their friends. In addition to communicating happiness and friendliness, smiling may also make people seem more familiar to us. Research on the **smiling familiarity bias** (see the "I Didn't Know That: A Smiling Face Is a More Familiar Face") shows that we are drawn to and recognize smiling faces more than nonsmiling faces.

Positive emotions are also communicated through a variety of nonverbal behaviors that show energy as well as positive affect. When people feel joy or excitement, their behavior is described as bouncy and bubbly, their faces are described as bright and glowing, and their voices are described as expressive and enthusiastic with a quick tempo and laughter (Guerrero & Floyd, 2006). These types of positive expressions help people create an exciting positive atmosphere that makes interpersonal interaction more enjoyable.

Experiencing and expressing these emotions can even have positive consequences for mental and physical health. Feeling love and sharing positive emotion is associated with elevated levels of oxytocin—a hormone that makes us feel good (Lane et al., 2013). Giving and receiving affection promotes both physical and mental health (e.g., Floyd, 2006; Floyd et al., 2007). Studies by Floyd and colleagues have shown that individuals who give and receive more affectionate communication tend to experience less depression, less social anxiety, and more overall well-being. Affection can also lower cholesterol, blood pressure, and blood sugar while promoting healthy cortisol levels. Communicating positive emotions clearly has benefits for people's relationships and personal well-being.

I DIDN'T KNOW THAT!
A SMILING FACE IS A MORE FAMILIAR FACE

You would probably guess that people are perceived as nicer, friendlier, and more extraverted when they are smiling versus frowning. However, you might not know that people also rate smiling faces as more familiar than either neutral or unhappy faces. This smiling familiarity bias has been tested in several studies (e.g., Baudouin et al., 2000; Lander & Metcalfe, 2007). These studies have shown that people recognize famous people more quickly when they are smiling. Moreover, both strangers and famous people are judged as more familiar when they are smiling versus frowning or showing a neutral expression. Strangers and famous people were judged as least familiar when their faces displayed negative emotion. Researchers provided three explanations for the smiling familiarity bias. First, according to the **warm glow heuristic**, people associate positive things with familiarity (Monin, 2003). Second, smiling may be associated with familiarity because we tend to acknowledge friends and acquaintances with a smile (Garcia-Marques et al., 2004). Finally, faces may be more distorted when displaying negative versus positive emotion, leading them to be less recognizable and look less familiar (Lander & Metcalfe, 2007). In any case, the smiling familiarity bias has implications for interpersonal communication. If you want someone from your past to recognize you—smile! And if someone approaches you and asks, "Don't I know you from somewhere?" it may be because you smiled.

Vulnerable Emotions

Vulnerable emotions surface when we feel abandoned, rejected, unloved, or devalued. Common vulnerable emotions are hurt, sadness, hopelessness, and loneliness. These emotions cause people to draw inward and become self-reflective. **Hurt** has been defined as an unpleasant emotion that occurs when people are psychologically injured by another person (Folkes, 1982; Vangelisti & Sprague, 1998). Hurt feelings often arise when people believe others do not value them (Feeney, 2005; Leary et al., 1998). For example, you are likely to feel hurt in the following types of situations: someone you ask out turns you down; someone says you are not very coordinated, good-looking, nice, or intelligent; or someone breaks up with you because they found someone new. Words can be hurtful. In Chapter 11, you will learn about things people say to each other that are particularly hurtful. You will also learn about actions that are hurtful, such as criticism and cheating. Hurtful messages and actions can create interpersonal distancing and reduce relational closeness, especially when they are used frequently and perceived to be intentionally hurtful (Vangelisti, 1994; Vangelisti & Young, 2000).

On the other hand, feelings of sadness can, in some cases, draw people together. In one set of experiments, people imagined someone close to them dying or watched a movie scene depicting a social loss. The sad mood induced by these activities led participants to be more attuned to other people's nonverbal communication and to desire more social interaction with others (Gray et al., 2011). Communicating sadness can also signal that someone needs social support. Sadness is generally displayed through behaviors such as frowns, looking down, slumping over, and speaking slower and in a more subdued tone. Interestingly, tears appear to be decoded as an especially significant indicator of sadness. In one study, people looked at faces with sad and neutral expressions (Balsters et al., 2013). These faces were shown either with or without tears. Regardless of whether the face looked sad or neutral, the addition of tears made people more likely to think the individual needed social support.

Competitive Emotions

Some emotions, such as jealousy and envy, stem from wanting to keep or get something or someone. When most people think of jealousy, they imagine a love triangle, with someone trying to steal another person's partner. This type of jealousy is called romantic jealousy. It occurs when people believe their relationship is threatened by a third party (White & Mullen, 1989). However, jealousy can occur in various situations (Bevan & Samter, 2004). For example, you might be jealous when your best friend starts spending time with a new friend. Or you might be jealous when a new employee starts to take your place as "the bright young star" in the company. The key is that you are worried something you value is in danger of being taken away. Envy, on the other hand, occurs when you want something that you desire but do not have. You might want the type of marriage a friend has or envy someone who is successful and well regarded by others because that is what you wish you had.

Sometimes emotions like jealousy and envy are associated with hostility, such as using relational aggression against someone you envy, but other times they are associated with more positive emotions, such as love and admiration. You might not realize how much you value your significant other until you feel threatened by a third party. Instead of hating your successful friend, you might admire her. Jealousy is a normal human emotion. However, some people cope with jealousy in healthier ways than others. Discussing jealous feelings in a calm manner and using jealousy as an impetus to improve yourself and your relationship are both very positive ways to cope with jealousy. Less healthy ways to deal with jealousy include making accusations, becoming violent, and engaging in counter-jealousy inductions (Guerrero et al., 2011). A **counter-jealousy induction** involves responding to jealousy by trying to make your partner jealous too. This can be accomplished in a number of ways, such as flirting with someone else, or mentioning an ex-girlfriend or boyfriend.

Another common way people deal with jealousy is through surveillance. This is when you act like an investigator and gather information about your partner's activities and about the rival (or potential rival). Some surveillance is normal and can help people reduce uncertainty and feel less jealous, but it can be easy to get caught in a surveillance trap. If you find yourself continually doing things like creeping on your partner's social media or Snapchatting your partner to see who he or she is with, this can turn into a vicious cycle. The more you engage in these types of surveillance, the more you might imagine you have a reason to be worried even if you don't (Elphinston et al., 2013; Muise et al., 2009).

Self-Conscious Emotions

Self-conscious emotions include embarrassment, guilt, regret, and pride (Fischer & Tangney, 1995). These emotions are tied together because they focus on internal feelings in relation to real or imagined judgment by oneself or other people. We feel embarrassed when we make an unfavorable impression. Situations as diverse as accidentally walking into a wall while looking at someone, performing poorly on an exam that was supposed to be easy, and having a significant other make inappropriate comments in front of your family or friends can be embarrassing. When people are embarrassed, they often use communication to try to save face. For example, if you get a low grade on an exam that your friends all aced, you might say you didn't study hard. If your significant other makes embarrassing comments in front of your friends, you might say that they are "not usually like that."

People feel guilt when they have done something they consider wrong and pride when they have done something that they consider special. In interpersonal contexts, guilt-inducing situations include hurting or not helping someone (Vangelisti & Sprague, 1998). We can also regret these behaviors, which means that we wish we had done something differently. Regret can stem from actions that are embedded in interpersonal interaction, such as breaking up with someone prematurely or wishing you had not said something. As mentioned earlier in this chapter, the action tendency associated with guilt is to try to make amends. Guilt can also be used as a tool, sometimes in manipulative ways, within interactions. You might guilt someone into doing something for you or give someone a "guilt trip" for not doing something. Using these behaviors can sometimes get you what you want, but they can also impact relationships negatively (Overall et al., 2009).

Finally, pride is a highly social emotion (Barrett, 1995). Sharing our accomplishments with one another actually increases feelings of pride, although there is a limit on how much pride we should communicate. People who can celebrate accomplishments with others while appearing grateful and humble make the best impressions. Pride can also be a freeing and unifying emotion. It is no accident that groups of people who experience prejudice get together for parades and other events to display their pride in who they are.

Individuals from groups that have historically been discriminated against sometimes come together to express their pride and solidarity.

iStock/SoumenNath

Fearful Emotions

Finally, fear is not reserved only for situations such as encountering a rattlesnake or a threatening person. There are many social situations that involve fear or its sister emotions, social anxiety and communication apprehension. Socially anxious people worry that others will not accept or like them. Consequently, they avoid opening up to people in ways that could make them vulnerable. This has been termed a **self-protective strategy**, by which people avoid communication that could make them vulnerable. Research has shown that socially anxious individuals not only engage in this self-protective strategy with strangers but also with friends and romantic partners (Cuming & Rapee, 2010). Some individuals even have what is called a *fearful attachment style*, which means that they have low self-esteem and expect to be hurt or rejected in relationships (Bartholomew, 1990). People with a fearful attachment style tend to avoid expressing emotions or putting themselves in situations that could make them vulnerable.

Communication apprehension is a personality characteristic that involves feeling anxious about communicating with another person or persons in a social or public setting (McCroskey & Beatty, 1986; McCroskey et al., 1986; see also Chapter 5). The root of communication apprehension is feelings of anxiety. People with high communication apprehension tend not to see themselves as competent communicators, which likely fuels their communication apprehension (Teven et al., 2010). They are also more inhibited and self-conscious during social interactions and less likely to express opinions. Having communication apprehension also affects people's motives for using social networking sites. In one study, college students high in communication apprehension tended not to use Facebook for motives such as engaging in interpersonal communication or expressing themselves (Hunt et al., 2012).

Social anxiety, fearful attachment, and communication apprehension all prevent people from communicating openly, which ironically can stymie communication in ways that make someone seem less approachable and likeable. This can create a self-fulfilling prophecy: People who are afraid of being rejected or judged negatively act in ways that keep them isolated and prevent them from pursuing personal and professional relationships.

PRINCIPLES OF EMOTIONAL COMMUNICATION

So far, this chapter has focused on defining concepts related to emotion, describing skills related to encoding and decoding emotion, and summarizing some of the key ways specific emotions are associated with communication. Next, we advance five principles that further describe the relationship between communication and emotion.

Principle 1. Most emotion occurs within the context of interpersonal interaction.
Andersen and Guerrero (1998) made the following claim: "Certainly, emotions can exist apart from interpersonal interaction. Viewing a sunset may produce joy. Hitting one's thumb with a hammer may prompt anger… However… most typically, emotions result from social interaction and interpersonal communication" (p. 57). A friend breaks a promise, which makes you angry; a new romantic interest holds your hand during a movie, which makes you feel warm and affectionate; or a co-worker mentions that your work on a particular project is sloppy, which hurts your feelings. People also tend to express more emotion when with others than when alone (Chovil, 1991). For instance, people express more emotions when viewing a happy, scary, or sad film if with others versus alone (e.g., Matsumoto, 2006).

Principle 2. Emotional expression is influenced by biology and social learning.

Studies examining emotional expressions in movies have also shown that people display different facial expressions when alone versus with others. The facial expressions that occur when people are with others appear to be affected by rules of social appropriateness. For example, people from the United States and Japan display similar facial expressions when they sit alone and watch highly stressful films; however, when other people are present, the Japanese are likely to cover up their negative emotions with a smile, whereas people from the United States are likely to express more negative affect (Matsumoto, 2006). One interpretation of these findings is that there is more similarity across cultures when emotional expressions occur in private. When people are interacting with others, expressions are tempered by display rules. The research reviewed in this chapter on the universal thesis also shows that although there is similarity in how people across cultures encode and decode emotion, there are also in-group advantages based on nonverbal accents and dialects. Together, the research shows the complex interplay that biology and social learning share in shaping emotional communication.

Principle 3. Emotions are contagious.

People sometimes "catch" the emotions of others. You may have experienced this. A friend of yours laughs and you start laughing too. When you sense students in your class are worried and confused about an upcoming test, you start to feel a sense of dread. The process of catching another person's emotions has been called **emotional contagion** (Hatfield et al., 1994). A sad individual may be lifted up by the presence of a cheerful friend, but the cheerful friend may also feel a little down after listening to the sad friend's problems. Emotional contagion is related to other communication processes: motor mimicry and the interpersonal facial feedback hypothesis. **Motor mimicry** occurs when a person's emotional expression reflects what someone else is feeling (Bavelas et al., 1986). For instance, you may wince when you watch a child fall and scrape her knee or nervously wring your hands together when you watch your favorite athlete getting ready to compete in the Olympics. The **interpersonal facial feedback hypothesis** is based on the idea that matching someone's emotional expression leads you to experience the emotion that the other person is feeling (Cappella, 1993). You mimic their expression and then start to feel what they are feeling because your expression sends signals to your brain telling you to feel that way

When people mirror the emotions expressed by others, they start to feel the emotions they are mirroring, which contributes to emotional contagion.

iStock/vm

Principle 4. Sharing positive emotions helps develop and maintain relationships.

One of the key characteristics that differentiates happy relationships from unhappy relationships is how much positive emotion partners express. Compared to people in dissatisfying relationships, people in satisfying relationships smile at, laugh with, and touch each other more (Kelly et al., 2003). Being cheerful and positive, expressing emotional support, and showing affection contribute to relationship satisfaction and help people maintain healthy relationships (Stafford, 2003; Stafford & Canary, 1991). Positive expressions of emotion can even counterbalance negativity in relationships. In one study, researchers compared couples who used similarly high levels of negative behavior (Fincham et al., 1997). Couples who expressed both positive and negative emotions were happier than those who expressed mostly negative emotions.

Principle 5. In general, it is best to express hostile and competitive emotions in a direct but nonthreatening manner.

It probably does not surprise you that unhappy couples display more hostile emotion, as well as more sadness and fear, than do happy couples (e.g., Kelly et al., 2003; Weiss & Heyman, 1997). However, it is important to recognize that even happy couples sometimes experience negative emotions in their relationships. Emotions such as anger, jealousy, and hurt are fairly common within relationships. The key is how people *express* these emotions. Keeping emotions bottled inside can be detrimental to your relationships and your health; problems go unresolved and partners become increasingly dissatisfied. Therefore, it is important to talk about your negative feelings, but not when you are emotionally flooded and feeling aggressive. In addition, if someone you know is expressing emotions in an aggressive way, practice empathy and try not to get defensive.

CONCLUSION

The next day, after snapping back and forth a few times, Ryan decides to FaceTime Kai and invite her to meet at Starbucks on campus between classes. When he FaceTimes, he tries to look and sound casual even though his heart is beating rapidly in his chest. When they meet up, they reminisce for a few minutes about their high school days. Kai, for her part, went into the conversation trying to be warm and friendly. She had been in a really bad mood before they met up, but she soon starts to feel the stress of the day melt away as she silently contemplates the new possibilities that her chance encounter with Ryan might bring. She wouldn't tell him this now—but she had a crush on him during their junior year of high school—something she will eventually tell him if things really start to progress.

Both Ryan and Kai show that they have mastered some of the skills necessary to communicate their emotions effectively. For example, they realize it might not be wise to communicate all their emotions to each other too openly in the beginning, lest they scare one another away. If they continue talking, hopefully they will be open to expressing their emotions and allowing themselves to be vulnerable. During their meeting at Starbucks, Kai probably did not even realize that Ryan's good mood had rubbed off on her. You, however, might have recognized the process of emotional contagion in action since you had read this chapter. Hopefully, this chapter has given you some fresh insight into how you communicate your emotions and decode the emotions of others so you can create a positive emotional climate within your interpersonal interactions.

CHAPTER 6 STUDY GUIDE

KEY TERMS

Identify and explain the meaning of each of the following key terms.

action tendencies

affect

basic or primary emotions

cognitive appraisal

counter-jealousy induction

deep acting

deintensification

dialect theory

display rules

emotional contagion

emotional control

emotional experience

emotional expression

emotional expressivity

emotional intelligence

emotional labor

emotional sensitivity

emotive dissonance

facial feedback hypothesis

genuine expression

hurt

in-group advantage

inhibition

intensification

interpersonal facial feedback hypothesis

leakage

masking

motor mimicry

nonverbal accents

nonverbal dialect

physiological changes

relational aggression

self-protective strategy

simulation

smiling familiarity bias

surface acting

universal thesis

warm glow heuristic

REFLECTION QUESTIONS

1. Table 6.2 ("Display Rules") asks about the line between display rules and deception. What do you think? Are there situations where using a display rule is inherently deceptive? Are there other situations where using a display rule reflects the range of emotions people are experiencing? If so, provide examples for each and explain why you believe they fit these descriptions.

2. This chapter provided a lot of information about various skills related to expressing, managing, and decoding emotion. The Skill Builder on "Using Emotional Labor to Optimize Performance" discussed how you can maximize the benefits associated with engaging in emotional labor while minimizing stress. Describe the skills you have, those you wish you had, and how you might work on developing and enhancing those skills.

3. You learned that people have "nonverbal accents" when it comes to expressing emotion. What stereotypes do you think people have about the ways people from different cultures communicate emotion? How can people avoid the trap of generalizing others based on those stereotypes?

4. Think about one of your important relationships. Which of the emotions (or emotion clusters) discussed in this chapter characterize that relationship? What could you do to enhance emotional communication in that relationship?

7 INFLUENCING OTHERS

WHAT YOU'LL LEARN...

When you have finished the chapter, you should be able to do the following:

7.1 Define social influence and persuasion.

7.2 Identify different influences on individual behavior, including power, social norms, and social pressure.

7.3 Recognize interpersonal influence strategies and messages.

7.4 Articulate compliance-gaining strategies.

7.5 Identify different ways to resist influence attempts.

Calvin was walking down the street when someone handed him a flyer. He took a look at it while he was waiting for the light to change. "Be Your Own Person," stated the flyer, "Unlock the Inner You! Come to our consciousness-expanding retreat. A once-in-a-lifetime experience in a secret salt cave only accessible to our members. Visit our website for more information." Huh, thought Calvin, who was skeptical of such experiences. Did they really expect him to be persuaded that he could find his individuality by joining a crowd at a retreat? And how secret could that salt cave be if they were handing out flyers about it? Calvin shoved the flyer in his back pocket. Later in the day, he remembered his girlfriend's birthday was approaching. Brandy was training to teach yoga classes and had recently recommended a meditation app to him. Perhaps tickets to this retreat would make a good gift for her. She'd think he was a great boyfriend if he got her something unique that she would like and took a whole weekend to spend time on a retreat. And perhaps it would be cool to see that salt cave after all. Calvin found himself typing in the website address to find out more information.

The study of social influence and persuasion is broad and covers multiple contexts, from the sponsored posts in your Twitter feed, the influencer accounts on Instagram, large national advertising campaigns, organizations influencing their employees' behavior, political messaging, and more. In the opening story, we can see the many instances of influence. The flyer advertising the salt cave is the most overt form of influence, but Calvin is also influenced by Brandy's behavior to consider activities like yoga, meditation, and visiting salt caves. Calvin is also, at least subtly, considering how his actions (getting Brandy a gift related to her interests) will influence her attitude toward him (she'll think he's a good boyfriend). For our purposes regarding interpersonal communication, we are going to consider the ways that influence manifests in interpersonal interactions in our everyday lives.

DEFINITIONS AND COMPONENTS OF INFLUENCE

Social influence refers to processes that change or adjust the thoughts, feelings, and behavior of other people (Pratkanis, 2007). Social influence processes might involve a desire to conform to the way that people around you are behaving, to construct a belief system that is similar to your families, to respond favorably to similar or attractive others, or adjust the way that you dress when you attend a formal versus informal event. Almost any communication interaction has the ability to shape the attitudes and behavior of others (Stiff & Mongeau, 2003). All of these are ways that we are influenced to think and act in certain ways.

At times social influence involves messages directly intended to influence others. These specific messages are persuasive communication.

Persuasive communication is "any message that is intended to shape, reinforce, or change the responses of another or others" (Miller, 1980, p. 11). *Response shaping* is a change from no response to some response, *response changing* involves changing from one position to another, and *response reinforcement* involves strengthening an already held position (Stiff & Mongeau, 2003). Although social psychologists tend to focus on cognitive responses such as belief adoption or attitude change, Miller's (1980) broader categorization of response allows interpersonal communicologists to focus on a wider range of outcomes, including attitudes and beliefs but also emotions and behaviors (Stiff & Mongeau, 2003).

An extreme form of persuasion is coercion. **Coercion** generally means forcing someone to engage in some behavior. Most of the forms of influence and persuasion we will discuss in this chapter are not usually considered coercive. However, we also (like other scholars, such as Gass & Seiter, 2016; Miller, 1980; Powers, 2007; Stiff & Mongeau, 2003) consider coercion to be an extreme form of persuasive behavior. In addition, while some behaviors are obviously coercive, such as threatening someone with violence if they do not comply, others occupy a gray area. If a persuasive message works well but the person targeted doesn't realize they are being influenced by a compliance-gaining strategy, are they being coerced? If refusing a social request comes with a social punishment—upsetting a friend or causing problems within your family—that could be considered somewhat coercive. Many social influence interactions are not fully coercive but at the same time are also not fully noncoercive either. Thus, when we discuss persuasion and influence, there are different ways in which people may "change their minds." People can be influenced in regard to their attitudes, beliefs, and behaviors (Fishbein & Azjen, 2010).

Influence Outcomes

Behavior refers to the way that we outwardly act. For example, we may wish to inspire a new roommate to do their share of the dishes or encourage a romantic partner to be more proactive about planning something for a birthday. In these cases, we wish for our relational partner's behavior to change. We may or may not care about our roommate's feelings about the dishes as long as they get done.

Attitudes are our tendency to respond favorably or unfavorably to some idea, plan, or action (Fishbein & Azjen, 2010). Fishbein and Ajzen's **theory of reasoned action** argues that the more favorable one's attitude is toward a behavior, the stronger one's intention to perform that behavior will be. Of course, the actual behavior depends also on how one perceives other people will react to the behavior and one's perceived self-efficacy. **Self-efficacy** refers to a person's perception that he or she can competently execute a behavior (Bandura, 1993). For example, perhaps you find yourself at a karaoke bar. You may feel that you hold a positive attitude toward karaoke—you think that it is fun, you enjoy the typical pop music. However, you may be more or less likely to sign up to sing depending on (a) how you perceive the people you're with think about karaoke singers and (b) your own perceptions about your ability to deliver a song that people will like.

Would you readily sing in front of others at a karaoke bar or would you need to be persuaded by your friends to do so? What might make you (and others you know) more or less likely to do it?

iStock/BraunS

Self-efficacy is a type of belief—a belief that you can competently perform some action. **Beliefs** provide the foundation for intentions and actions and provide expectations for positive or negative consequences that may occur if people perform a particular behavior (Fishbein & Azjen, 2010). Behavioral beliefs influence attitudes about that behavior or set of behaviors (Fishbein & Azjen, 2010). For example, if you hold a strong belief that everyone has an equal opportunity in their ability to participate in the labor force, you would be unlikely to vote for policies that seek to ameliorate structural imbalances.

FIGURE 7.1 ■ The Theory of Reasoned Action

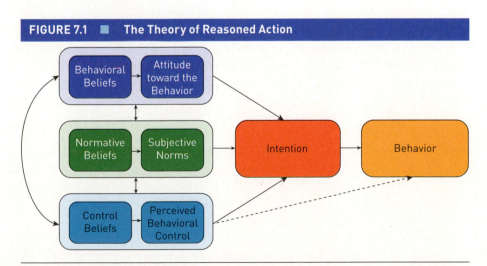

Source: Kan M. P. H., & Fabrigar L. R. (2017). Theory of planned behavior. In V. Zeigler-Hill & T. Shackelford (Eds.), *Encyclopedia of personality and individual differences*. Springer. https://doi.org/10.1007/978-3-319-28099-8_1191-1

People's beliefs, attitudes, and behaviors change all the time, although with perhaps different frequencies (Figure 7.1). Our behavior changes constantly, although within consistent patterns. For example, people may believe they need to eat a healthy breakfast every morning and have a positive attitude toward some breakfast foods. The general behavior of eating breakfast may be consistent but perhaps one day's breakfast is yogurt and granola, the next day poached eggs and toast, and the following day a smoothie. These may seem like small variations, but many a marketer gets paid to change behaviors about which brand of yogurt is best and what gets put in that smoothie. This example illustrates that throughout our day, we are subject to a myriad of influence and persuasion attempts. Other courses and texts focus on persuasion in sales and campaigns. Our goal in this chapter is to consider the everyday influence that occurs in the context of interpersonal interactions.

Power and Interpersonal Dominance

We may be influenced by others because of different types of social power those others have over us. However, not all social power comes from the same foundation. Raven and colleagues have identified multiple types of interpersonal power (Elias, 2008; French & Raven, 1959; Raven et al., 1998).

One type of power is the ability to reward or coerce someone to make them behave a certain way. **Reward power** refers to being able to provide some type of compensation for compliant behavior. **Coercive power** relies on the threat of punishment to influence someone. Although these forms of power have some conceptual differences, some studies (e.g., Raven et al., 1998; see also Elias, 2008) have found that people who hold reward power are generally seen to hold coercive power and vice versa.

Both coercion and rewards can be personal or impersonal. The parent–child relationship can be a good example of parents using both personal rewards/coercion and impersonal rewards/coercion. For example, a parent may influence a child to contribute to the household chores by increasing their respect and appreciation for the child's abilities or they may require some household contributions in exchange for an allowance. The former would be a personal reward, whereas the latter would be an impersonal reward. Parents might also express disappointment with the child if a task is not completed as asked (personal coercion) or may take away electronics or assign a time-out if chores are not completed (impersonal coercion).

Power derived from **credibility** comes from expert power or informational power (Raven, 1965; Raven et al., 1998). For example, a friend who is a known "foodie" may have more influence than others over where the group selects for a dinner out since everyone views that individual as having greater knowledge of the potential choices. The foodie may have **expert power** if they are generally seen as having superior knowledge about restaurants. However, that friend may also invoke **informational power** where they provide specific information regarding why a restaurant is the best choice.

Another type of power derives from norms of reciprocity and equity (see Chapter 9 for definitions of equity and norms of reciprocity). **Reciprocity power** occurs when persuaders influence the target to do as they ask because they note that the target owes them some favor based on past exchanges. For example, a cohabiting romantic partner might influence the other partner to do the dishes by saying, "I cooked dinner so please do the dishes." **Equity power** refers to attempts to restore equity by noting that the target has done something that leaves the relationship somewhat inequitable. For our cohabiting couple, the persuader might influence the target to do the dishes this night by noting that "you've left me to the do the dishes all week so it's your turn to pick up the slack."

Power may also come from the more powerful person having **legitimate position power**. A police officer is perceived to have the legitimate power to influence you to pull over your car and accept a ticket. A resident assistant in the dorms may be recognized as an authority able to impose various rules, and a judge has legitimate power to make rulings in a courtroom.

Judges hold legitimate position power in their courtrooms. Because they are well educated in the law, they also have expert and informational power.

iStock/DarrenMower

People may also be able to influence others by holding **legitimate dependence power**. In this case, the influence target feels obliged to help another person who is dependent on their assistance (Berkowitz & Daniels, 1963). This type of power is the "power of the powerless" (Raven et al., 1998, p. 311). Elderly parents who require the assistance of their children for maintaining their home or accomplishing other tasks may be thought of as having power derived from legitimate dependence.

Referent power relies on the relationship between the influencer and the target. Liking, respect, and affection for the influencer can cause the target to adapt their behavior. For example, you may be willing to take on extra tasks for a co-worker who you genuinely like even though that person cannot reward you and has no legitimate power over you. You might adapt your behavior for a new romantic partner—not because you fear punishment or think of your partner as an expert—but because you enjoy their company and wish to please.

Of course, people do not hold just one type of power. Managers with reward power may be more effective at influencing employees if they also have referent power. Similarly, the "foodie" friend may have less influence over the group if they are not also well-liked (referent power). A parent may have coercive power but try to rely on their expert power in a particular situation. In addition, power only works if the target believes that the influencer (a) has that type of power and (b) will actually use it (Raven et al., 1998). An employee may work for a supervisor who is known for not providing raises and thus that supervisor's reward power may be severely diminished. A child whose parent consistently does not follow through with punishments soon learns to ignore the parent's commands.

In addition, people may comply with various types of power for different motivations. Being influenced by soft power strategies such as referent or personal reward may be related to intrinsic motivations, whereas compliance with hard power strategies such as legitimate position may be related to extrinsic motivations (Pierro et al., 2008). When motivation is *intrinsic*, we do something because we find it enjoyable and/or personally rewarding. For example, Calvin was motivated to plan something special for Brandy's birthday in part because he enjoys spending time with her and it makes him feel good to make her happy, both of which are related to her referent power. On the other hand, when motivation is *extrinsic*, we do something because of the expected external consequences—such as getting a reward or avoiding being punished.

Power and Privilege

So far, we have been discussing power as if it only resides in a person. Power, however, can also come from societal and institutional structures that impact the way people are perceived, the biases they face, and the resources they have. The concept of privilege has been used to help better understand the power that is embedded in and conferred by these kinds of structures. **Privilege** refers to having more unearned social status, resources, and access to resources in comparison to others. There are many types of privilege. For example, *male privilege* refers to the unearned advantages that men in a society have in comparison to women, and *white privilege* refers to the unearned advantages that white individuals have over people of color. Other types of privilege include, but are not limited to, heterosexual, cisgender, and able-bodied privilege as well as privilege stemming from socioeconomic status or religious affiliation (Anderson & Middleton, 2017).

One way to think of privilege was famously expressed by McIntosh (1997), who likened privilege to an invisible knapsack that contains unearned benefits that people accrue based on qualities such as gender, race, sexual orientation, and social class. Privilege is often invisible to those who have it because they do not understand the struggles people in other social groups face. It is also uncomfortable for people to believe they have any unearned advantages over others. People want to believe they have earned everything they have fairly. The concept of privilege, however, does not mean that people from certain groups do not work hard and do not deserve what they have accomplished; instead, it means that some groups of people have advantages that others do not have. Kimmel (2018) explained that the difference between being privileged or not is like the difference between having the breeze at your back versus running into a strong headwind: "Being white, or male, or heterosexual in this [US] culture is like running with the wind at your back. It feels like just plain running, and we rarely if ever get a chance to see how we are sustained, supported, and even propelled by that wind" (p. 1). Those without privilege, on the other hand, feel like they have to run harder and be stronger to push against the headwind.

People also tend to compare everything to the status quo for the privileged. Kimmel (2018) gives the example of the wage difference between men and women being expressed as women making about 79 cents for every dollar a man earns (and yes, this ratio has been about the same for decades). This highlights discrimination against female workers. However, if you turn this around and say that men earn $1.29 for every dollar a woman earns, privilege is emphasized. People also show privilege in the words they chose. For example, you rarely hear anyone with privilege say "my straight friend" or "a male doctor" but you do hear people with privilege say "my gay friend" or "a female doctor" quite often.

What does privilege have to do with power? Some scholars believe privilege confers power because it comes with unearned advantages and resources that create power inequities. Collins (2018) described three types of power related to white privilege that also apply to other types of privilege. First, there is what Collins (2018) calls the power of normal. A great example of this is in the movie *On the Basis of Sex* about Supreme Court Justice Ruth Bader Ginsberg. At the beginning of the movie, Ginsberg's character walks to her classes at Harvard Law School surrounded by men. Being a lawyer was only considered a men's profession then. Second, Collins (2018) argues that privilege gives people the power of a benefit of the doubt. He gives examples of white people being regarded with less suspicion than people of color or being approved for a house loan even if their credit is just okay. Finally, Collins (2018) cast privilege as the power of accumulated power, which means that the unearned and earned benefits people have create resources that build over time. So, if one person has only earned benefits and another has earned and unearned benefits, resources accumulate faster for the second person. Collins (2018) gives the example of wealth, reporting that in 2014 the Pew Research Center estimated that the median net worth of white households in the United States was more than 10 times the median net worth of Black and Hispanic households. Why? The reason was not education or occupation as much as inheritance and having parents with accumulated resources who could help their children achieve their educational and financial goals.

SOCIAL NORMS, PROOF, AND PRESSURE

Just as society and institutional structures affect power and influence, so too do the people around us. Indeed, our behavior is influenced by those around us in some way every day. Parents teach their children how to behave, sometimes using punishments and rewards but more often by modeling behavior (Bandura, 1977). People choose the type of clothing they wear to work partially based on dress code policy but also on the styles and level of formality their co-workers have chosen. People choose what restaurant to eat at based somewhat on their own tastes but also by reading or hearing about the recommendations of others. Often people defer to the consensus of the majority around them when they form an opinion (Erb et al., 1998). The deference to others when forming our own attitudes is part of how we respond to social norms, social proof, and social pressure.

Social Norms

Social norms help shape our understanding of how to respond to the world around us. **Social norms** are a type of social construction that emerges through repeated, collective communication about different types of behavior (Kincaid, 2004). Norms are standards for behavior that guide social behavior through sanctions from members of our social group or network (Cialdini & Trost, 1998). Communication is central to both norm formation (our perception of norms is influenced by the behaviors and messages about behavior we perceive from others) and the social sanctions related to norms (people communicate their approval or disapproval of particular behaviors) (Lapinski & Rimal, 2005). For example, a teenager may avoid swearing at home because he knows his mother will disapprove and admonish him, but he may swear copiously around his peers because they model and reward swearing. Both the disapproval of his mother and the reward of fitting in are social sanctions enacted by members of the teenager's social network. This particular teenager has learned that different social norms are in place within different groups and is able to adapt accordingly.

People perceive different types of norms that influence their understanding of their social world and their own attitudes and behaviors. **Subjective norms** are "an individual's perception that most people who are important to [them] think [they] should or should not perform a particular behavior" (Fishbein & Azjen, 2010, p. 131). **Descriptive norms** are perceptions/beliefs about what most people are actually doing (Fishbein & Azjen, 2010). These norms may or may not line up with actual behavior but descriptive norms do influence our own behavior. **Injunctive norms** are norms about what is typically approved or disapproved by our social group (Cialdini et al., 1991; Fishbein & Azjen, 2010). People may modify their behavior based on injunctive norms to avoid social sanctions (Lapinski & Rimal, 2005).

Norms influence our behavior because we are often driven by a desire to conform to others around us (Asch, 1955; Cialdini & Trost, 1998). One of the most famous conformity studies is Asch's (1955, 1956) "short line" study. Participants were shown a line and then asked which line out of a set of three the first line matched (Figure 7.2). They were asked to do this 18 times. Some participants completed the task alone, whereas others completed it sitting at a table with a group. What the participants did not know was that the other group members were actually helping the experimenter by all giving the same wrong answers 12 out of the 18 times they were asked to make a judgment. The participant heard these incorrect answers and then was asked to make a judgment. What do you think you would do in this situation? Would you choose the line that you thought was the obvious match or would you conform and choose the line your group members chose? Asch found that participants gave the correct answer over 99 percent of the time when they were in the nongroup condition and when their group members identified the correct line. However, when their group chose the wrong line, they conformed around 37 percent of the time; across all 12 times that the group chose the wrong line, about three-quarters of the participants conformed to the group at least once. This study showed the powerful pull of conformity—even when the correct answer was obvious, some participants felt compelled to choose the line that the rest of the group chose.

FIGURE 7.2 ■ The Asch Line Study

Some participants in Asch's famous line study were influenced by confederates even though their eyes told them the truth. For example, even though it is obvious that the third line in the second card matches the target line, if everyone in the group said the middle line was a match, about a third of participants agreed.

Target Line

Which Line Matches the Target Line?

Often acting according to social norms provides us with an appropriate and effective course of action (Lapinski & Rimal, 2005). However, there are times when social norms can lead us to behavior that is detrimental to ourselves and others (Lapinski & Rimal, 2005). One such example is the **bystander effect**. The bystander effect explains a social phenomenon where people who are alone are more likely to help someone in distress than people in a group (Latané & Nida, 1981). The theory behind the bystander effect is that we take our cues about what is an appropriate way to behave or respond from nearby others. When people are the lone potential helper, they take on the responsibility. However, when they are in a group, they may take their cues from others who are also not helping and conclude either that help is not needed or that someone else will take responsibility for helping. CPR and first aid training often try to combat the bystander effect by training potential helpers to point to a specific person and give instructions. However, the bystander effect may be weaker in true emergencies (i.e., people are more willing to help, even in a group) than in more ambiguous situations (Fischer et al., 2011). The ambiguity may lead bystanders to look to the group for social cues as to how to proceed. The bystander effect is also less pronounced when we are familiar with the other members of the group (Fischer et al., 2011). Again, this may be because we have previous knowledge suggesting that people we know will be helpful, but with strangers, we can only look to the group's immediate behavior to seek out relevant social cues.

The bystander effect can also occur in online settings. Over 70 percent of Americans report having witnessed online bullying, known as **cyberbullying** (Duggan, 2014). Although many people notice cyberbullying, a much smaller number of witnesses are willing to directly intervene (Dillon & Bushman, 2015). If people perceive that there are many other witnesses to the cyberbullying, they may be less likely to try and intervene (Brody & Vangelisti, 2016). Cyberbullying witnesses who perceived their online behavior to be anonymous were also less likely to intervene (Brody & Vangelisti, 2016). However, bystanders who witness multiple bullies targeting a victim may be more likely to say that they would intervene. In addition, we may be more likely to intervene on behalf of close others (Brody & Vangelisti, 2016).

Another example of norms leading to potentially detrimental behavior is when our perception of norms becomes misaligned with the actual behavior in our social group. For example, cultivation theory suggests that overrepresentation of certain behaviors in the media can lead people to assume those behaviors occur more often in the world than they actually do (Gerbner et al., 1994). In regard to interpersonal communication, people who discuss a particular issue frequently may overestimate the occurrence of behaviors related to that issue (Real & Rimal, 2007).

I DIDN'T KNOW THAT!
COLLEGE STUDENTS' (MIS)PERCEPTIONS OF HIGH-RISK ALCOHOL USE

Several scholars have examined communication regarding alcohol use on campus and found that often students' perception of the campus norm is that alcohol use is higher than it actually is. In these cases, students' descriptive norm (the behavior that they perceive is occurring) is mismatched with the actual behavior of their fellow students. The misperception can come about for a couple of reasons. One, pop culture about college often portrays wild parties and constant drinking (e.g., *Van Wilder, Old School, Pitch Perfect*). Two, because the student culture may expect and celebrate drinking behaviors, students who do engage in risky behaviors may be more vocal and visible than students who drink more responsibly or do not drink at all. This can lead other students to engage in more risky behavior or exaggerate the stories of their risky behavior.

A desire to fit in within the new social environment can lead to pluralistic ignorance. Pluralistic ignorance occurs when people overestimate the occurrence of a false norm but underestimate the occurrence of the actual behavior (Miller & McFarland, 1987). In the case of college drinking, students may overestimate risky behavior and underestimate the number of students drinking responsibly or not at all. These misperceptions can lead college students to engage in risky behaviors if they perceive that a majority of the peer group is also behaving this way (Glazer et al., 2010; Lederman & Stewart, 2005; Park et al., 2011).

Thus, it is important for college students to carefully consider the risks and consequences of heavy (and illegal if you are under legal drinking age) drinking. While making your own choices, it might be useful to remember that the stories you hear of how "wasted" someone got or how "crazy" things got last weekend may not reflect the actual behaviors around you. Consider carefully how much you let these norms influence your own choices.

Despite narratives around party culture, many, if not most, college students find ways to engage in fun and social activities with no or limited alcohol use.

iStock/Prostock-Studio

One specific type of norm is relational or interaction rules. **Relational rules** are norms related to behavior within particular types of relationships. People have a variety of relational rules in both formal and informal relationships (Argyle & Henderson, 1984; Argyle et al., 1985). Adherence to relational rules can lead to greater relational quality (Kline & Stafford, 2004). Rules can be specific in that they apply only to a specific relationship. For example, a romantic couple may come to an agreement that they will call each other if they are going to be out later than a certain hour. Rules can also be general in that they are applied to a certain relationship type by a broad swath of a particular group. For example, in Western societies, many romantic couples consider infidelity to be breaking a general relational rule for romantic relationships. Rules can also be implicit or explicit. Implicit rules are held by one or both members of a relationship but are never specifically spoken. One might assume that one's cohabiting partner will call to check in if they are out late. Explicit rules are specifically discussed and agreed upon by relational partners. For example, partners may have a specific discussion about whether they should call and at what time. If you have ever had a conflict where someone said "I shouldn't have to tell you that!" they are lamenting the fact that a previously implicit rule was apparently not held by both parties and needed to be made explicit. As discussed in Chapter 11, when implicit or explicit relational rules are violated, these violations are called relational transgressions.

Friendship rules, in particular, may be difficult to navigate because rules are often less general—various friendships may have very different rules that are more implicit than explicit.

Yet the violation of friendship rules can lead to dissatisfaction and ultimately dissolution of the relationship (Argyle & Henderson, 1984). Rules about friendship include rules about sustaining intimacy (such as the degree of self-disclosure and the appropriateness of expressing emotion), rules about social exchange (such as the repayment of debts and the provision of social support), rules about potential conflicts (such as privacy norms and levels of teasing), and rules about engaging with the greater social network (such as rules related to conflict or time spent with other network members). Obviously, people do not always follow relational rules, but the rules help determine impressions of other people's behavior and influence our own behavioral choices.

Recent studies have also investigated communication rules in the way people use technology. For example, college students can identify multiple rules regarding Facebook use (Bryant & Marmo, 2012). The most important rules were as follows:

1. People expect responses to posts on a wall [timeline],

2. You should avoid saying disrespectful things publicly,

3. Consider if a post might negatively affect someone else, and

4. Close friends should be communicated with in other channels besides Facebook.

Similarly, in studies by Miller-Ott and colleagues, couples identified relational rules regarding using the phone to contact others while in the company of the romantic partner, using texting and voice calls to handle relational conflict, determining how often they contact each other during the day, and if and when they are allowed to monitor each other's phone activity (Miller-Ott et al., 2012).

As more technologies emerge, new rules influencing people's use of and interactions on these platforms also solidify. Thus, the influence of technology on behavior is not simply the design and function of the actual technological tool but also how that tool is adopted and adapted into a culture of users. For example, email and text messaging are now actually incredibly similar in terms of functionally (text-based messaging, potentially synchronous but often asynchronous, accessible through handheld devices), but users are likely to perceive different social affordances for those two channels because different interaction rules developed around those technologies at different times (Fox & McEwan, 2017). In addition, different age cohorts may have different relational rules regarding email. Older adults might be more likely to use email for relational purposes, having first experienced email as a potential relational tool (Stafford et al., 1999). Younger adults, by contrast, choose different channels for relational purposes and see email primarily as a professional channel (McEwan, 2013, 2015).

Social Proof

People tend to engage in similar behaviors and hold similar attitudes as those around them. People view behaviors as more appropriate when we see many similar others engaging in such behaviors. This phenomenon is called **social proof** (Cialdini, 2009; Lun et al., 2007). Consider this example: Have you ever been at a crosswalk where a few people decided to walk against the light? Did other people then follow those people? Did you? Generally, the principle of social proof works well for us. If our friends are all interested in a particular band, then we might like that band too. If a restaurant looks empty and has few reviews, we might decide it isn't very good before we've even sampled the food. The more uncertain we are about a situation, the more likely we are to follow the crowd (Cialdini, 2009). In these cases, the "wisdom" of the crowd becomes our primary clue for how to behave.

We make everyday choices based on how others around us behave but we can also be influenced specifically by messages invoking social proof. For example, in one study, researchers increased the number of people taking the stairs by 64 percent when they posted a sign that said, "More than 90 percent of the time, people in this building use the stairs instead of the elevator" (Burger & Shelton, 2011). A sign suggesting stairs are a healthy choice did not work nearly as well. Think about the flyer advertising the salt cave that Calvin initially dismissed. What if the flyer had called the cave "The Most Popular Attraction in the Area!" and suggested getting tickets early because they frequently sell out. Do you think this type of appeal using social proof would be more successful than casting the cave as "only accessible to our members?"

Do you think you would be more likely to take the stairs instead of the elevator if you thought most of your colleagues did?

iStock/mixetto

Social Pressure

Social pressure encourages people "to engage or not engage in the behavior based on the possible rewards or punishments they feel they may endure from important others" (Fishbein & Azjen, 2010, p. 20). Peer pressure is a type of social pressure where people perceive that they are being explicitly pressured by members of their peer group to act or think in certain ways (Brown et al., 1986; Santor et al., 2000). Peer pressure is "a subjective experience of feeling pressured, urged, or dared by others to do certain things" (Santor et al., 2000).

Peer pressure and peer conformity may peak in early or middle adolescence as teens work to fulfill their need for affiliation (Newman & Newman, 1976). Becoming a member of a peer group is an important part of developing as an adolescent, but this process may leave adolescents susceptible to pressure from the group because they want to fit in (Santor et al., 2000). In later adolescence, a stronger sense of self may begin to emerge and group conformity may lessen (Brown et al. 1986). For college women, peer pressure predicts low body esteem and weight concerns (Sheldon, 2010), whereas college men may experience peer pressure in regard to body size and sport performance (Ricciardelli et al., 2006). Studies on voting-age adults have also found evidence of influence via social pressure. Yale researchers found that mailing people postcards that stated an intention to let their neighbors know whether they voted or not increased voting behavior by 8.1 percentage points (Gerber et al., 2008).

INFLUENCE IN CLOSE RELATIONSHIPS

Often when we think of persuasion and influence, our thoughts turn to marketing campaigns, advertisements, or perhaps Instagram or TikTok influencers. However, considerable communication within close relationships is also designed to influence your relational partners so you can achieve a variety of relational goals. While this could be manipulative, particularly if influence attempts are using deception or coercion, it generally is not. Consider Calvin in our opening vignette; he's influencing Brandy because he wants her to be happy so they can have a satisfying relationship. We might also persuade our friends to join us in activities or influence them to like the same shows or books that we do. We might persuade family members to join us in healthy activities or to make us a favorite meal. A variety of influence behaviors, both negative and positive, are enacted between close relational partners.

Ingratiation

Ingratiation involves engaging in behaviors with the goal of getting someone to like you more so they will do things for you (Gordon, 1996; Jones, 1964). Those wishing to influence us may offer flattery and compliments. Even just learning and remembering our name can subtly sway us toward submitting to a request from another individual. The more we like someone, the more likely it is that we want to form a close relationship with that person, and the more likely we are to agree to their request (Cialdini & Goldstein, 2004).

Additionally, we like people who are similar to us. When we perceive greater similarity between ourselves and the compliance-seeker, we are more likely to comply with their requests (Burger et al., 2003). While perceived similarity may indicate that we are already somewhat close to an individual and thus likely to agree to requests (e.g., from friends or family members), similarity can be manipulated as well. For example, studies have found that people are more likely to agree to small requests from someone who is dressed similarly to them (Emswiller et al., 1971; Suedfeld et al., 1971).

Another way people might manipulate feelings of similarity is through behavioral mimicry. People naturally begin to subtly mimic or converge toward the communication style of others whom they like (Giles et al., 1991). The reverse appears to also work—people feel a greater affinity for interaction partners who subtly mimic their behaviors (Chartrand & Bargh, 1999). Matching body posture, mood, and verbal style can help a compliance-seeker be a bit more successful (Lakin & Chartrand, 2003; van Baaren et al., 2003).

The Norm of Reciprocity

The norm of reciprocity, which is the social norm or expectation that we should return favors and other acts of kindness, is a strong force on human behavior (Gouldner, 1960). This social norm drives everyday behavior as we return favors from friends, engage in sharing behaviors, and feel obligated to be nice to those who are kind to us. Sometimes those seeking to use this norm to gain compliance offer up a small favor or token gift so the target will feel obligated to respond positively to the compliance request. For example, the real estate agent who sold you your house might send you a bimonthly letter, sometimes accompanied by a small gift such as coupons for free food or decorative magnets for your refrigerator as token gifts. If you ever sell your house, those small gifts may make you feel just indebted enough to choose that agent again, even though the cost of the gifts would be nowhere near the commission the agent would make on the sale of your house. On a smaller scale, candy placed near the restaurant till or helpful messages written on the back of sales receipts have been shown to help servers increase the size of their tips (Rind & Strohmetz, 1999; Strohmetz et al., 2002).

There is a strong expectation, called the norm of reciprocity, that people should return favors and other acts of kindness.

iStock/Hafiez Razali

Confirming/Disconfirming Messages

Within relationships, people engage in both confirming and disconfirming messages to influence their relational partners' attitudes, behaviors, and approaches to the relationship (Cissna & Sieberg, 1981). **Confirming messages** validate the receivers' sense of self. These messages can include supportive and validating behaviors. These messages endorse the partner and their positions, thoughts, and feelings (Cissna & Sieberg, 1981). For example, a relational partner might communicate respect and show that they accept the other's position as reasonable (Fisher, 1987). They might say things like this: "I understand where you're coming from," "You have a valid point," or "If I was you, I might feel the same way." **Disconfirming messages** are those that attempt to invalidate the other person's position and experiences (Bavelas, 1985). Disconfirming tactics include blame, criticism, and threats. Examples of these messages might be "I can't believe you actually think that," "Well, you have only yourself to blame," or "You don't actually believe that, do you?"

Newton and Burgoon (1990b) divided verbal interpersonal influence measures into a categorical scheme serving three relational objectives – achieving goals, managing the relationship, and identity management. Each of these categories includes confirming and disconfirming messages. Prosocial strategies are likely more persuasive in relationships than antisocial strategies (Miller et al., 1977) because they allow the influence target to feel competent and happy about their behavior choices (Hecht, 1984). (See Table 7.1 for examples of each message.)

TABLE 7.1 ■ Newton and Burgoon's Strategies and Tactics of Relational Influence			
Strategy	**Tactic**	**Definition**	**Example Message***
Instrumental			
Content Validation	Agreement on an issue	Statements that indicate harmony in opinion or feeling, or acceptance of the other's position	"I think you are right that we should do something unique on vacation."
	Description/ explanation of an issue	Nonevaluative statements that describe observable events or behavior	"We need to choose a vacation spot that both of us will enjoy."
	Summarizing the issue	Statements that focus communicators on relevant issues	"So, what have we agreed upon so far?"
	Problem-solving	Statements that provide possible solutions to the situation	"What if we try to find somewhere that has interesting museums for me but also has beaches for you?"
	Positive information-seeking	Soliciting information from the other, trying to understand the other's thoughts, feelings, or position on the issue	"What have you researched so far?"
Content Invalidation	Disagreement on an Issue	Statements that indicate lack of harmony in opinion or feeling and/ or reject the other's claim, warrant, evidence, or conclusions	"I just don't want to go there."
	Correcting other	Typically, short statements designed to correct the other's perceptions of their relaying of information about the issue	"No, I did tell you that my boss won't give me that week off."
	Exaggeration	Statements that reframe or redefine the other's comment so that one's comment provides an exaggerated version of what the other said	"So, you're telling me you just don't even care if I have a good time on the trip."
	Pseudo-accommodation	Statements where one pretends to go along with the other's interpretation of the problem or solution to the problem, but it is obvious from nonverbal behaviors that they do not agree	"Sure, (shrugs), we'll go wherever you want (sigh)."
	Abstraction	Attempts to support one's argument by invoking abstract principles	"But vacation is about enjoyment and experiencing something new."
Relationship Management			
Other-Support	Reinforcement/support of other	Statements that express empathy, sympathy, understanding, or positive regard for the other	"I know it's really important to you to experience the culture where we travel."
	Emphasis on commonalities	Statements that comment on shared interests, goals, and compatibilities with the partner	"We both like trying new cuisines, maybe we should go somewhere with really interesting food."

(Continued)

TABLE 7.1 ■ Newton and Burgoon's Strategies and Tactics of Relational Influence (*Continued*)			
Strategy	**Tactic**	**Definition**	**Example Message***
	Accepting responsibility	Statements that show acceptance of responsibility for the problem	"It's my fault that we can't go exactly where you want to."
	Concessions to the other	Statements providing concessions of responsibility for negative events or behavior. May involve apologies or offers to repair the situation	"I should have told you earlier that I wouldn't be able to contribute as much money to the trip."
	Compliments	Statements that are intended to make the other feel good	"You're really good at finding great hotel deals."
Other-Accusations	Accusations/blaming	Statements that attack the other's behavior, thoughts, or feelings about something or attribute responsibility for the problem to the other	"Your last choice for a vacation spot was terrible."
	Implied accusations	Statements of disclosure or justification that imply that the other has behaved wrongly	"It hurts me when you don't take my feelings into account."
	Criticism of other	Statements that criticize the other's personal characteristics, beliefs, attitudes, or values	"You're boring, so how are you going to pick something fun?"
	Superiority over the other	Procedural statements criticizing the other's ability to understand or grasp one's point or to deal with the issue effectively	"You're not thinking that through…"
	Poking fun at other	Statements that are made in jest but are really intended to put the other person down	"You're such a hick, I bet you'd love that."
	Advice giving to other	Specific requests, demands, or prescriptive statements that seek a specified change in the partner's behavior	"If you would look at the hotel sites that I gave you, this process would be a lot easier."
	Threats	Intimidating statements meant to induce fear in the other	"If you insist on going there, I'm just not going."
	Negative information-seeking	Statements that seem like one is soliciting information from the other but are really trying to make a point and/or put the other down	"Isn't it interesting that you want to go to the same city as where your ex lives?"
Identity Management			
Self-Assertions	Assertions	Straightforward statements that set forth one person's position	"I think we should go somewhere closer to home this year."
	Self-promotion	Statements designed to influence the other by elaborating on personal achievements	"I'm really good at finding unique and quirky things to do in places that seem familiar."

Strategy	Tactic	Definition	Example Message*
	Exemplification	Statements that suggest the actor is morally worthy or behaves in an exemplary fashion that should be imitated	"I'm just more cautious with money than the average person, but it pays off in the end."
	Stubbornness	Statements that suggest the actor will not be persuaded	"I'm just not going to change my mind about this."
	Disclosure	Statements about thoughts, feelings, intentions, motivations, and perceptions	"I'm really worried that we won't be able to come to an agreement."
	Wish statements	Statements expressing how one wishes things would be or the other would behave. These statements simply express one's desires and are not accusatory	"I wish I had more time to travel."
	Wants/needs Statements	Statements expressing what a person wants or needs	"I want to be able to experience something new."
Self-Defense	Justifications	Statements providing reasons for considering negative behavior as legitimate, justified, moral, and/or good	"I know I'm getting overly upset about this, but when you only get one vacation a year it is important to get it right."
	Excuses	Statements designed to excuse failure or poor performance	"My boss is watching my computer usage—I couldn't log on to the airfare sale in time."
	Denials	Statements that unequivocally deny responsibility for the problem	"It's not my fault we can't afford that."
	Self-inquiry	Soliciting information from the other that specifically deals with complaints about oneself	"Do you think it's my fault that we can't go overseas?"

TABLE 7.1 ■ Newton and Burgoon's Strategies and Tactics of Relational Influence (*Continued*)

*Message descriptions are direct quotes from Newton and Burgoon (1990b).

Inconsistent Nurturing as Control

Sometimes within relationships, people experience a relational partner with extremely dysfunctional behaviors such as alcoholism or severe eating disorders. In such cases, the nonafflicted partner, be it a romantic partner or parent, may work to control the behavior of the afflicted partner. This control may come out of a desire to help the afflicted person, but also to regain some level of control of their own life within the relationship.

Inconsistent nurturing as control theory (INC) argues that sometimes romantic partners or parents who are attempting to manage their relationship and their partner's undesirable behavior may alternate between nurturing and controlling strategies (Le Poire, 1995). This inconsistency in their attempts to manage the relational partner's behavior may lead to increasing or reinforcing the very undesirable behavior that the parent or nonafflicted romantic partner is attempting to control.

INC assumes that the functional or nonafflicted partner is in some way dependent on the relationship with the afflicted partner. This dependence could be economic, such as a spouse who has limited financial resources to leave, but more likely is, at least in part, socioemotional, such as one's self-image as a good mother being dependent on caring for one's children . Nonafflicted partners' cycle through reinforcing and punishing communication strategies (Le Poire et al., 2000). The nonafflicted partner attempts to control the afflicted partners' undesirable behavior but also nurtures the afflicted partner through undesirable behavior episodes. For example, the partner of an alcoholic may attempt to control the undesirable behavior by removing alcohol from the house or cutting off the alcoholic. Other times, they may provide support for the drinking behavior by being a designated driver or keeping the house quiet when the alcoholic is hungover. The control may be seen as rewarding or unrewarding. But the nurturance is generally perceived by the afflicted partner as rewarding.

Another case where INC can be seen in action is in the relationship between anorexic teens and their mothers. One study found mothers of anorexics to be *both* more nurturing *and* more neglectful than other mothers (Humphrey, 1989). Mothers may nurture eating disorder behavior by comforting the child when she has symptoms but then being controlling and using punishment when the child's behavior gets frustrating. Imagine how this might happen: A mother has a bulimic teenager who is going through spells of binging and purging. The mother provides foods that she knows her child likes (and will binge on), quietly cleans the bathroom, or perhaps provides additional affection during these periods as she worries about her child. Yet because that same mother is frustrated by her child's actions, one week she refuses to buy favorite foods for the child, she closely monitors the child's eating, and begins barging into the bathroom when she suspects purging. Soon, the mother feels guilty that she is punishing an illness and reverts to increased affection.

The key idea in INC is that inconsistency in nurturing behavior strengthens the undesirable behavior (Le Poire, 1992). Think about how this cycle can work. First, the nonafflicted partner nurtures the afflicted partner, which can be perceived as a reward for engaging in negative behavior. Eventually, the nonafflicted partner may begin to resent the demand for this nurturing and withdraw the nurturing. Later, perhaps due to feelings of guilt or responsibility, they resume their nurturing, leading to a cycle of inconsistent reinforcement. Unfortunately, inconsistent rewards are actually more effective than continuous rewards in strengthening undesirable behavior (Burgoon et al., 1981). Specifically, intermittent reinforcement and punishment by the nonafflicted partner may strengthen substance-abuse behaviors by the afflicted partner. Nurturing mixed with punishment is less effective relational persuasion than reinforcement of alternative behaviors or punishment alone (Duggan et al., 2008). For example, the more consistent a mother is with punishing disordered eating behaviors and reinforcing alternative behaviors, the more effective her efforts are perceived to be by the daughter (Prescott & La Poire, 2002). Some of the key ideas of INC are shown in the Figure 7.3 depicting this cycle. Both nurturing and controlling behaviors may be intended as functional behaviors designed to end or reduce an undesirable behavior; if they become hard to sustain and intermittent, they actually lead to a strengthening of the undesirable behavior. Consistency then is key.

If consistency is more effective, then why do nonafflicted partners engage in inconsistent influence strategies? Well, both the afflicted and nonafflicted partners may have an interest (whether they are cognizant of this interest or not) in *not* succeeding in curtailing the undesired behavior (Le Poire, 1995). If the afflicted partner succeeds in successfully controlling their undesired behavior, they risk losing rewarding nurturing behavior. For the functional partner, although they may desire a reduction in the undesired behavior, they may also fear that when the undesirable behavior stops, the afflicted partner will no longer be dependent on them. Successfully influencing the partner to stop the behavior will certainly result in changed relational dynamics and could potentially lead to relational termination.

FIGURE 7.3 ■ **The Cycle of Inconsistent Nurturing as Control**

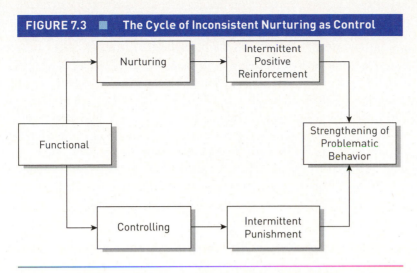

Source: Le Poire, B. A. (2006). Nurturing and controlling communication surrounding unde-sirable behavior in the family. In *Family communication: Nurturing and control in a changing world* (pp. 217–240). Sage. https://www.doi.org/10.4135/9781452233048.n9

COMPLIANCE-GAINING

At times people may make particular requests of others, hoping the other will comply with the request (Cialdini & Goldstein, 2004). Sometimes close others will engage in **compliance-gaining** tactics with us, but often compliance-gaining involves people invoking features of close relationships to convince others to do something from them. Other times compliance-gaining relies on specific message types that may make people more likely to comply with a request. Compliance-gaining techniques are often more impersonal, as the use and success of the technique does not rest on understanding the unique characteristics of the other person. Rather, these techniques are more often used in sales and campaigns where compliance-seekers use the techniques across many targets in the hopes of persuading people to make a purchase, sign a petition, or join a movement.

Getting people to comply with requests, such as signing a petition or registering to vote, often entails considerable interpersonal skill.

Ariel Skelley/DigitalVision via Getty Images

Door-In-The-Face

The **door-in-the-face** (DITF) technique involves asking for an extremely large request that the target is sure to say no to and then following up with a secondary request that is related but much smaller (Cialdini et al., 1975). Research has found that use of the door-in-the-face technique increases compliance with the second request (O'Keefe & Hale, 1998). It is likely that the norm of reciprocity is also at work in the door-in-the-face technique, this time in the form of reciprocal concessions. In DITF, the requester has made a concession by giving up the initial request, thus the target may be influenced by the norm of reciprocity to also provide a concession, by responding positively to the second request (Cialdini & Goldstein, 2004). Other combinations of factors such as engaging in dialogue (Dolinski et al., 2001), a sense of social responsibility, and a desire to reduce guilt (Millar, 2002; Tusing & Dillard, 2000) may also influence the success of the DITF technique.

Foot-In-The-Door

The flip side of the DITF technique is the **foot-in-the-door** (FITD) technique. The FITD technique first asks someone to comply with a small request. Once this compliance is secured, the requester follows up with a larger request (Burger, 1999). The FITD technique works on the principle that people will want to feel consistent in their actions (Freedman & Fraser, 1966). For example, say you are asked to sign a petition (a small request) on a particular social issue. Once you signed the petition, you essentially told the requester that this issue is important to you. This then makes it more likely that you will agree that you should also donate money or volunteer because, of course, you want to be consistent in your support for the issue. FITD techniques have a greater chance of working when the requester has the target perform the initial request, the initial request requires a small amount of effort, the second request is a continuation of the first request, and the requester tells the target that he or she is a helpful supporter (Burger, 1999). In addition, people who have a greater preference for appearing consistent may be more likely to acquiesce to FITD techniques (Cialdini et al., 1995).

That's-Not-All

Salespeople using the **that's-not-all** technique first offer the buyer the initial product and price. After letting the buyer consider the initial offer, the seller then adds an additional product or service to sweeten the deal (Burger, 1986). For example, at a car dealership, the dealer might offer to throw in an extended warranty or service plan. The "that's-not-all" technique may work for a couple of reasons. One, buyers actually are getting a slightly better deal that they may be more likely to accept. Two, when the seller adds in the extra item, buyers may feel they are a superior negotiator—even though the seller always intended to offer the additional item. Another factor may be the size of the request. People are more likely to be influenced by the "that's-not-all" technique when the difference between the initial and final request is smaller rather than larger (Burger et al., 1999).

But-You-Are-Free-to-Say-No

The **but-you-are-free-to-say-no** technique (BYAF) involves making a request and then adding the statement that "but you are free to accept or to refuse" (Guéguen & Pascual, 2000). This phrasing, and variants of it, works by showing that the requester recognizes the target's individual autonomy. Adding the language "but you are free" after an initial request has been shown to increase compliance in a variety of contexts, including requesting disaster relief donations (Pascual et al., 2009), street survey taking (Guéguen & Pascual, 2005), and participating in activities with other nursing home residents (Marchand et al., 2009). In addition, users of the BYAF technique may be liked more than compliance-gainers using direct requests. The technique appears to work better when the phrase is used in a face-to-face context rather than a mediated one, such as email (Carpenter, 2013).

For each of these message-based compliance techniques, it is important to note that they have been found to increase compliance, but the effect sizes are generally small (Carpenter, 2013; Dillard et al., 1984; O'Keefe & Hale, 1998). For practical purposes, this means that perhaps a few more people say yes to a request than would have otherwise.

SKILL BUILDER
CONDOM NEGOTIATION STRATEGIES

The rate of transmission of sexually transmitted infections (STIs) is climbing in the United States (Centers for Disease Control and Prevention, 2018). Almost 2.3 million cases of chlamydia, gonorrhea, and syphilis were diagnosed in 2017, marking yet another year of increases in STI rates since 2013. Although there are multiple avenues individuals can take to prevent acquiring and spreading STIs, including regular testing as well as regular checkups with both primary care doctors and gynecologists, one avenue of STI prevention is the regular use of condoms. Asking a partner to wear a condom is a specific instance of compliance-gaining (Chatterjee & Stafford, 2008).

Although many safe-sex programs and public service announcements advocate talking to your partner, asking one's partner about their sexual history may not produce truthful results—not necessarily because your partner intends to hurt you, but because your partner may be embarrassed. For example, many people lie about the number of prior partners they have had (Horan, 2016). In romantic relationships, one study found 25 percent of the conversations about safe sex occurred after the couple had already engaged in sexual activity (Chatterjee & Stafford, 2008).

Luckily, the research on how people convince their partners to wear a condom suggests that gaining compliance regarding condom use is not overly difficult. Horan and Cafferty (2017) conducted a study asking college undergraduates how they negotiate condom use. Simply asking "Do you have a condom?" was fairly effective. Of 13 participants who used this strategy, in all but one case a condom was used. Earlier research suggests that, for men, direct nonverbal strategies such as putting on a condom or opening the package and putting the condom on your partner is all the negotiation that is required (Debro et al., 1994; Lam et al., 2004).

In Horan and Cafferty's study, people also reported asking, "Should we use a condom?" This question helps open up communication about safe-sex expectations. On the other hand, the question of "should we use a condom?" may seem more like the opening of a negotiation leading a partner to bring up justifications for nonuse. Another strategy is demanding a partner wear a condom. Participants using this strategy indicated they would not participate in sexual activity without one.

Participants also reported discussing health concerns including pregnancy and STIs. Some participants noted that if their partner said they were "clean," this became a reason to not use a condom. Yet people often misunderstand the risks of unprotected sex. For example, a participant might say that because of hormonal birth control a condom isn't necessary. Of course, birth control does nothing to prevent STIs. In the heat of the moment, partners may feel embarrassed to admit they have an STI or they simply may not know they have one. Horan and Cafferty (2017) found that 40 percent of their sample had never been tested for an STI despite having an average of six sexual partners.

Participants also reported not using a condom because of the spontaneity of the moment. So, if you're sexually active or might like to be, consider carrying a condom with you. And then when the moment is right, use it.

RESISTING SOCIAL INFLUENCE

Learning about different influence techniques can help improve resistance to persuasion. People may be less likely to acquiesce to a compliance-gaining technique when they suspect that the requester is using a "sales device" (Mowen & Cialdini, 1980). Another potential way to resist social influence is to check your perceptions against someone else's. For example, research has found that targets of ingratiation—attempts to demonstrate liking and offer praise—are less likely to consider this flattery critically than observers (Gordon, 1996). Thus, taking a friend along for a major purchase may be useful because your friend may be better able to see when a salesperson is simply buttering you up.

Being able to resist persuasive attempts is as much of a skill as is the ability to gain someone's compliance.
iStock/JackF

It may also be useful to try to be aware when your internal motivations are leading you astray. For example, people have a desire to behave in a way that is consistent with their internal views of themselves as well as the way they have presented themselves to various social audiences (Baumeister, 1982; Goffman, 1967). The strength of our need to feel consistent may be a function of personality traits and cultural contexts. People who score lower on openness and higher on conscientiousness may be more likely to desire to appear consistent (Cialdini et al., 1995). People from individualistic cultures, such as the United States, may feel this need to be consistent more strongly than people from collectivist cultures (Cialdini, et al., 1999). However, the need to be consistent may lead to being influenced by the sunk-cost bias (also called the sunk-cost fallacy).

The **sunk-cost bias** is the "tendency to continue an endeavor once an investment in money, effort, or time has been made" (Arkes & Blumer, 1985, p. 124). Once people have made an investment, including the social investment of performing a particular action, it may be difficult for them to change their behavior in the future. For example, someone who has spent a lifetime voting for a particular political party may find it difficult to vote for a candidate from a different party even if that candidate's views align more closely with their own than the candidate from "their" party.

It is, however, possible to resist the sunk-cost bias. Older adults may be able to resist the sunk-cost bias more than younger adults (Strough et al., 2008), perhaps because they have more experiences to pull from in regard to consistency or remember times when previous changes away from consistency were fruitful. Additionally, mindfulness training in the form of focusing on the present has been shown to help people resist sunk-cost decisions (Hafenbrack et al., 2014).

WHAT WOULD YOU DO?
INFLUENCING OTHERS

We influence and are influenced by people every day. Some of the influence that we have on others is simply through living out our daily lives. Other times we make specific attempts to influence others, perhaps in negotiating a new job, making purchasing decisions, or negotiating the rent on a new apartment. Often some attempt at influence and persuasion is expected when it comes to financial decisions. But what about matters of the heart? What types of influence attempts are ethical when you are trying to get someone to like you, to date you, or to have sex with you? Behavioral mimicry is a natural reaction when people like each other. Is it ethical to try to actively mimic someone's behavior on a date? Is it ethical to use compliance-gaining strategies (Would you sleep with me? You are free to say no!) in romantic contexts? Why or why not?

PRINCIPLES OF SOCIAL INFLUENCE WITHIN INTERPERSONAL CONTEXTS

Your daily choices and behaviors influence others and, in turn, their behaviors influence you. Although we often think of professional advertising campaigns or slick salespeople when we consider persuasion, many influence attempts come through interpersonal interactions. These principles can help you understand how both overt and subtle forms of persuasion influence your attitudes, beliefs, and behaviors.

Principle 1. Influence is not coercion.
Although we discuss the idea of being susceptible to influence and resisting influence, generally influencing and being influenced is a normal and natural part of human relationships. Couples who are able to discuss issues and influence each other's responses are engaging in the healthy relational work of negotiating their relationship together. Family influence can keep people grounded in their values. Adhering to group norms can help people organize and accomplish a variety of goals. Coercion, on the other hand, is not a healthy component of human relationships. Feeling coerced into certain behaviors likely indicates a power imbalance between relational partners.

Principle 2. Persuading others is complicated.

Although Asch's line study is held up as evidence of people's submission to peer influence, it's worth noting that participants trusted their own eyes 71 percent of the time rather than the 12 people before them (Asch, 1955). Although we are influenced in many ways by various people throughout our daily lives, there is no one influence type that convinces all people all of the time. Often, the effects found in persuasion studies are small and researchers have to control for other aspects of daily life that might affect the study. In addition, people incorporate new messages into their existing belief systems. When thinking about the ways people are persuaded, it can be difficult to determine what specific messages cause which behaviors.

Principle 3. We influence each other through interpersonal interactions.

Our choices and behaviors throughout the day are a function of many different types of influence, such as the values our parents instilled in us as children, our desire to make friends, mediated messages and advertising, requests from romantic partners, and more. Influence attempts from interpersonal connections are often more persuasive than expensive advertising campaigns. In addition, we may not even consider interpersonal influence *as* a persuasive interaction. You might adopt a style of dress because your fashionable roommate influences your taste. You may make relationship decisions based on your perception of your parents' opinions. It's likely you don't think of these as "persuasion" but the influence of your relationships does affect your attitudes, beliefs, and behaviors.

Principle 4. Individual/cultural differences may affect our susceptibility to being influenced by others.

Individual and cultural differences may affect how and why we are influenced. Certainly, the culture that we live in is foundational to the attitudes we hold, the social norms we perceive, and the social proof that exists around us. Some dimensions of culture may also affect how we are influenced. For example, people from collectivist cultures may be more likely to be influenced because of social proof (Cialdini et al., 1999). For example, one study found that people in collectivist cultures are more likely to conform to the Asch line judgment task than people from individualistic cultures (Bond & Smith, 1996). On the other hand, people from individualistic cultures may feel more strongly the desire to be consistent (Cialdini et al., 1995). Thus, they may be more likely to be persuaded by influence attempts that manipulate that desire.

CONCLUSION

Like Calvin in our opening vignette, we are subject to influence from multiple sources throughout our day. Some of these influences are apparent to us as influence attempts. For example, when you see advertisements before your Netflix show, see a billboard, or are handed a flyer on the street, most people recognize these as attempts to change our behavior or convince us to take some action. At other times, the influence of close others can have a meaningful effect on our behaviors and choices but might not seem as salient to us as an advertisement. For example, Calvin probably didn't think of his girlfriend as influencing him to purchase retreat tickets—after all, she didn't even know about it! But indeed, her interests and his desire for her to perceive him as a good boyfriend drove a series of decisions he made about how to spend money and allocate his time. We could even consider that Calvin is attempting to influence her by making himself seem more likable and similar by choosing a high-quality present. Humans are undeniably social animals. As we communicate in our interpersonal relationships, it is to be expected that we are constantly influencing and being influenced.

CHAPTER 7 STUDY GUIDE

KEY TERMS

Identify and explain the meaning of each of the following key terms.

attitude

behavior

beliefs

but-you-are-free-to-say-no

bystander effect

coercion

coercive power

compliance-gaining

confirming messages

credibility

cyberbullying

descriptive norms

disconfirming messages

door-in-the-face

equity power

expert power

foot-in-the-door

inconsistent nurturing as control theory

informational power

ingratiation

injunctive norms

legitimate dependence power

legitimate position power

norm of reciprocity

persuasive communication

privilege

reciprocity power

referent power

relational rules

reward power

self-efficacy

social influence

social norms

social pressure

social proof

subjective norms

sunk-cost bias

that's-not-all

theory of reasoned action

REFLECTION QUESTIONS

1. In the chapter, we discuss a variety of compliance-gaining techniques. Is it ethical to use these techniques to try to influence others? How would you feel if you knew someone was trying to obtain your compliance using one of these techniques?

2. Much of our communication influences the ways that we interact and engage with the social world around us. Is there any communication that is not influenced? What are the more subtle influence messages that you've encountered?

3. Often, persuaders are attempting to change people's behavior, but behavior is tightly linked to our attitudes and beliefs. In what ways do your beliefs influence your behavior? Can you think of a time when you changed your attitude about an issue?

8 INITIATING AND DEVELOPING RELATIONSHIPS

WHAT YOU'LL LEARN...

When you have finished this chapter, you should be able to do the following:

8.1 Explain how interpersonal relationships vary in terms of voluntariness, closeness, satisfaction, and length.

8.2 Identify interpersonal needs that are met through interpersonal relationships.

8.3 Recognize different stages and dialectical tensions within interpersonal relationships.

8.4 Explain how relationships experience turning points.

8.5 Describe how relationships are initiated in mediated spaces.

Last summer at a music festival, Jordan met Taylor. They hit it off quickly, started talking through texts and snaps, and later decided to date. Jordan felt instantly that Taylor might be a long-term partner, whereas Taylor had just gotten out of a serious relationship and wanted to take things slowly. Although their relationship keeps progressing in terms of telling each other more about themselves, becoming more physically intimate, and meeting each other's friends, Jordan worries about how bumpy the road has been. Taylor broke up with Jordan shortly after they decided to date and then later asked to rekindle the relationship. They've had light-hearted arguments about their different tastes in Netflix shows and serious arguments about how much partying Jordan does on the weekends. They made plans to spend Thanksgiving together and then canceled because each of their moms was upset that they wouldn't be at their own home. "Is this normal?" Jordan wonders. "Shouldn't a relationship get easier over time?"

Much of our interpersonal communication occurs within the context of interpersonal relationships. Within Taylor and Jordan's story, we can see the concerns they have as they go about building a romantic relationship, but we also see the many other types of relationships that Taylor and Jordan navigate. Their behavior in their relationship has been influenced by ex-romantic partners, their friends, and their mothers. People generally have networks of relationships composed of family, friends, acquaintances, and romantic partners.

This chapter examines the different types of relationships that people have, with a specific focus on interpersonal relationships. Relationships vary on different dimensions and stages. We also experience tensions and turning points in our relationships. The way that we manage and understand these tensions helps us to build the stories of our relationships.

WHAT IS AN INTERPERSONAL RELATIONSHIP?

Relationships are interdependent dyadic connections. This simple statement contains three important elements of relationships. First, relationships are **dyadic**, meaning they are formed between two people. These dyads may be connected to others within a larger social network, but the fundamental building block of social networks and groups is the dyadic ties people form with each other. Second, relationships require some level of **interdependence** (Berscheid, 1988). For a relationship to be a relationship, at some level relational partners' thoughts and actions are influenced by the other. On a simple level, interdependence might surface when choosing a restaurant for dinner. Friends, family, and romantic partners who want to spend time together often find themselves negotiating these types of choices. As relationships deepen, the interdependence may become more complex. For example, married couples often have to negotiate very impactful choices related to each other's careers, where they will live, and what choices they will make about children. Finally, relational partners are *connected* through communication. Communication helps us create, develop, and maintain our relationships (Burleson et al., 2000).

Relationships vary greatly on several dimensions. Some important dimensions include the **voluntariness** of the relationship, whether the relationship is platonic or romantic, how satisfying the relationship is, whether the relationship is long term or short term, and the level of "interpersonalness."

Voluntary Versus Involuntary

The voluntariness of a relationship refers to both an individual's ability to choose the relationship and how easily they could exit the relationship. Almost no relationship is completely voluntary or completely involuntary, but relationships range on this dimension. An example of a very involuntary relationship would be a sibling. Children are typically born or adopted into a family without input from the existing siblings. In addition, although people do sometimes become estranged from their siblings, it is very difficult to cut a sibling tie. An example of a more voluntary relationship is friendship. Friends typically choose to be in a relationship with each other and people can and do leave friendships (McEwan et al., 2008). However, not all friendships are completely voluntary. Perhaps you are friends with someone simply because they

Family relationships fall closer to the involuntary side of the voluntary to involuntary continuum.

Flashpop/Stone via Getty Images

are friends with other people you know. It would be difficult to end that friendship without affecting other relationships in your social network. In other cases, friendships may become so close the relationship begins to feel involuntary. Black Americans often perceive close friendships to be more like family relationships with a network of brothers and sisters (Jackson et al., 2020). Romantic relationships also vary on voluntariness. When we are first talking to people we might be interested in dating, the relationship can seem very voluntary. Yet, as we become more committed, although we voluntarily chose our partner, it can seem harder to exit the relationship. Indeed, getting married is entering into a legal agreement regarding your relationship, which increases the difficulty to exit and makes the relationship more (but not completely) involuntary.

Romantic Versus Platonic

Relationships can also vary in terms of whether they are romantic or platonic. Romantic relationships are thought to involve concepts of being in love, commitment, and possibly sexual interaction or desire (Aron et al., 2008). However, romantic relationships can vary greatly on these factors as well. In addition, platonic, or nonromantic, relationships can include elements of these factors. For example, some friends-with-benefits relationships are considered platonic but include sexual interaction (Levine & Mongeau, 2010). Conversely, some romantic relationships do not include sex. Ultimately, a romantic relationship is romantic because the individuals involved have mutually decided to label themselves as a couple (Guerrero & Mongeau, 2008).

I DIDN'T KNOW THAT!
FRIENDS-WITH-BENEFITS

The term "friends-with-benefits" is common in the "hook-up culture" of college campuses (Levine & Mongeau, 2010; Perlman & Sprecher, 2012). Although many college students think they know the meaning of friends-with-benefits, people actually use the term to refer to several different relational types. Mongeau and colleagues (2013) conducted a study where they asked people to describe their own experiences with platonic relationships that included some degree of sexual intimacy. The authors found five different types of friends-with-benefits relationships (FWBRs).

True Friends

This relationship type reflects the meaning of the term "friends-with-benefits." These dyads have an actual friendly, platonic relationship and sometimes engage in sexual activity.

Just Sex

These partners reflect the benefits of the FWBR, but they aren't really friends. The relationship does not reflect the trust, respect, and affection that emerges in friendships. A popular label for this type of relationship is "hook-up buddies."

Network Opportunism

These FWBRs engage in sexual activity after being at the same social event. They may be connected in their social network as friends of friends but are not close themselves. After they start hooking up, they label themselves "friends-with-benefits" to avoid other relational labels.

Transition In

This type of FWBR represents an attempt by one or both members of the dyad to initiate a romantic relationship. The FWBR label is applied to keep things less intense while exploring the possibility of entering a romantic relationship. The transition may be desired by one or more partners at the beginning of a FWBR. Sometimes the FWBR develops a more romantic tone and is eventually labeled a romantic relationship by the couple. Other times, one member wishes the FWBR was a *transition in* to a romantic relationship, yet is unsuccessful at persuading the other party.

Transition Out

When couples decide to end a romantic relationship, they do not always also end their sexual relationship. This type of FWBR involves couples who used to be in a romantic relationship but still engage in sexual activity. Sometimes, this relationship involves a desire to maintain a real friendship. At other times, one or more parties may find it a way to ease the ending of the romantic relationship.

When you've heard or used the term friends-with-benefits, what type of FWBR was being referred to? What could be considered a successful FWBR? Maintaining a nonromantic relationship? Becoming a romantic relationship? What are relational communication challenges specific to FWBR relationships?

Satisfying Versus Dissatisfying

Satisfaction refers to general positive feelings about one's relational partner and the relationship (Rusbult, 1983). One way to think of relational satisfaction is how well a relationship meets your needs and expectations (Hendricks, 1988). A relationship is generally considered satisfying if the relationship provides more rewards than costs, and dissatisfying if it provides more costs than rewards. Rewards and costs are often idiosyncratic perceptions, meaning they are unique to the individual. For example, Taylor and Jordan may find it rewarding to attend music festivals together. Yet perhaps Taylor's previous relational partner did not enjoy music festivals. In that relationship, Taylor's partner may have perceived time spent on festivals as a relational cost.

Although relationships are more satisfying when rewards outweigh costs, there is a catch. People have different expectations for what types of rewards and costs they anticipate in different types of relationships. These expectations are our comparison level (CL) (Thibaut & Kelley, 1959). Social exchange theory predicts that if a particular relationship is more rewarding overall than your comparison level, you will be satisfied with the relationship. So Jordan and Taylor may have similar levels of rewards versus costs in their relationship, but if Taylor has a higher comparison level than Jordan, Taylor will be less satisfied. In addition, some relationships have high rewards *and* high costs, but we still find them satisfying. For example, people experience the most conflict in the relationships where they experience the most closeness. Closeness drives interdependence and interdependence provides more opportunities for relational partners to have conflicting goals. Yet if the relationship provides substantial rewards, relational partners will likely feel generally satisfied.

WHAT WOULD YOU DO?
RELATIONAL REWARDS

Alondra and Grayson have been a couple since their junior year of high school. While they were in high school, Alondra thought she was incredibly lucky to have Grayson as a boyfriend. He was thoughtful and always made sure to get her a gift for special occasions. Plus, Grayson was popular and a great lacrosse player. Alondra enjoyed not having to worry about getting a date for high school dances and it was fun to cheer on Grayson at lacrosse and have him cheer her on at soccer

Now Alondra and Grayson are sophomores at different colleges. While they were proud of themselves for surviving the distance during the first year, it was not easy. There were fights over how they spent their free time away from each other and missed visits due to social plans and obligations at their respective schools. In addition, Alondra missed having a boyfriend she could hang out with on a regular basis. Lately, and a little guiltily, Alondra's engaged in a flirtation with Brendon, a guy from her political science class. Brendon is cute, tells funny stories, and has read some of the same books she likes. Brendon asked her to go to a party with him this weekend and she said yes. Alondra doesn't want to tell Grayson about the party; she doesn't want to have yet another fight. And this thing with Brendon might go nowhere, and then she wouldn't have either Grayson or Brendon. What would you do in Alondra's situation? Do you accept Brendon's invitation? Do you tell Grayson about the party?

Social exchange theory argues that not only do people compare their partners to an internal comparison level, but they also consider their partners in light of other potential alternatives for relationships (CLalt). While the CL drives satisfaction, the CLalt drives commitment. So one might be satisfied in their current relationship (as Alondra is with Grayson) and yet still think an alternative might provide a better option (as Brendan might). Of course, how we communicate our changing desires to our partners is up to us.

Long Term Versus Short Term

We expect some relationships will continue for a very long time. For example, siblings are often the longest relationship a person will have—from birth until death. In general, people expect family relationships to be fairly long term. We may have long-term expectations about some romantic relationships, whereas with other romantic relationships we may expect the relationship to be short term (for example, a summer fling, or a relationship during a study-abroad trip). Similarly, some friendships last for decades, while others may only last for the length of a shared activity.

Interpersonal Level of the Relationship

Relationships vary in how interpersonal they are. Relationships where people feel closer, know more about one another, and make predictions about one another's communication based on personal and idiosyncratic knowledge of the other are more interpersonal than other relationships (Miller & Steinberg, 1975). These are our closest and most interpersonal relationships. Less interpersonal relationships may be considered role relationships.

Role relationships are functional, casual, and often temporary (Guerrero et al., 2021). Examples of a role relationship might include the coffeeshop barista, the security guard who lets you into your building in the morning, or your teaching assistant in a large class. Much of the communication occurring within role relationships does not meet the definition of interpersonal communication we set forth in Chapter 1. Although there is an exchange of messages, the messages are not unique nor do they affect the thoughts, emotions, or behaviors of the communicators in a meaningful way. People can have polite, social interactions in role relationships, such as saying hello to your building's security guard or making small talk with your TA, but the communication is typically rote and perfunctory.

As relationships develop, the communication becomes more unique and meaningful (Knapp et al., 2014). Thus, the communication becomes interpersonal rather than impersonal (Miller, 1978; Miller & Steinberg, 1975). Sharing messages that are unique and meaningful communication is a marker of interpersonal relationships (Guerrero et al., 2021). The more we make our choices regarding *how* and *what* we communicate with other people based on our understanding of that person as a unique individual, the more likely it is the relationship is *interpersonal* rather than *impersonal* (Miller & Steinberg, 1975). In addition, interpersonal relationships go beyond the simple exchanges of role relationships and involve some level of mutual influence (Guerrero et al., 2021). In other words, the thoughts, behaviors, and perceptions of each partner have an effect on the thoughts, behaviors, and perceptions of the other partner. People in interpersonal relationships may engage in the exchange of tangible objects, but also share time with each other, provide messages of support, and make emotional connections.

Role relationships, such as the interaction that occurs between a barista and a customer, are functional and often revolve around a task.

iStock/jacoblund

Relationships can be *more* or *less* interpersonal (Miller, 1978). Very interpersonal relationships might be labeled **intimate relationships** such as a best friend, a romantic partner, or a sibling. Relationships that are less intimate but still interpersonal might include family members with whom you are moderately close, friends, casual dating partners, or co-workers.

RELATIONAL NEEDS

To thrive in the social world, people have to find ways to fulfill several interpersonal needs. In the *fundamental interpersonal relations orientation* (FIRO), Schutz (1966) outlined three basic interpersonal needs: the need for inclusion, the need for control, and the need for affection.

The Need for Inclusion

Human beings have a need to form and maintain social bonds with other people in order to be included in interactions and maintain a sense of belongingness (Baumeister & Leary, 1995). This is known as the **need for inclusion**. People use communication to build connections with others and feel greater social inclusion. Through interpersonal relationships, people can access a variety of social resources (Foa & Foa, 1980; McEwan & Guerrero, 2012).

The perception that one can access resources through one's social network can help people feel stable and connected to their social environment. For example, first-year college students who perceive they have built a rewarding social network were more likely to want to stay at their current university (McEwan, 2013). People who feel a sense of community at work may also have a greater sense of well-being (Boyd & Nowell, 2017). Developing relationships and perceiving support in the workplace may lead employees to have more positive perceptions of their organizations and avoid burnout (Brown & Roloff, 2015). For millennials, in particular, feeling engaged at work may lead to increased organizational commitment (Walden et al., 2017).

Conversely, feelings of loneliness can lead to negative outcomes such as depression, lack of social support, and negative health effects (Hawkley & Cacioppo, 2010; Hawkley et al., 2003). People's perceptions of their social relationships drive their experience of loneliness. When people feel there is some discrepancy between the quantity and/or quality of what they want versus what they have, they feel lonely (Ernst & Cacioppo, 1999). Yet lonely and nonlonely people tend to engage in similar numbers of activities and spend similar amounts of time by themselves (Hawkley et al., 2003). A person might have several friends and even some high-quality interpersonal relationships and still feel lonely because they feel that they should have an even greater number of relational outlets. Another person might have one or two close relationships and feel perfectly satisfied with their social situation. First-year residential college students often report feelings of loneliness despite being surrounded by dorms full of people because they perceive everyone else is having an easier time building a social network and making close friends (Giannini et al., 2007). Elderly individuals are another population who often experience loneliness as their social networks change due to relocations and the deaths of their peers (Beller & Wagner, 2017).

The Need for Control

People have a desire to feel that the world is a predictable and controllable place (Heider, 1958; Schutz, 1966). The **need for control** may vary from person to person. People with a very high need for control may attempt to control others either through persuasive or coercive means. Another way people may address their need for control is to gather information and knowledge to manage and reduce uncertainty (review Chapter 3 for uncertainty principles in initial interactions) (Afifi & Weiner, 2004; Berger & Bradac, 1982).

Beyond initial interactions, reducing and managing uncertainty plays an important role in close relationships. **Relational uncertainty** refers to how confident people are in their perceptions of themselves and their partners in their interpersonal relationships (Knobloch & Solomon, 2002). There are three sources of uncertainty related to relational uncertainty: self, partner, and relationship (Knobloch & Solomon, 1999). **Self-uncertainty** is the concerns you have about your own participation in the relationship. For example, in a dating relationship, you might be unsure if you want to continue the relationship past graduation or how much affection you want to show your partner in public. **Partner uncertainty** refers to concerns you might have about your partner. You might worry how committed your partner is to the relationship, if they really meant it when they said, "I love you," or if they are interested in another potential relationship. **Relationship uncertainty** refers to uncertainty about the relationship itself. For example, you may wonder how you should behave toward each other as relational partners, how to define your relationship (Talking? Dating? Exclusive? Serious?), and what the future holds for your relationship.

Communication with your relational partner can help reduce uncertainty and increase your confidence in how they will behave (Berger & Bradac, 1982; Clatterbuck, 1979). People embarking on relationships with greater initial uncertainty, such as interracial or intercultural relationships, may use more direct communication early on (Harris & Kalbfleisch, 2000). However sustained uncertainty or sudden increases in uncertainty have been linked to negative emotions such as jealousy and can lead people to terminate their relationships (Knobloch et al., 2001; Planalp et al., 1988). Overall, reducing uncertainty can help people feel more in control of their social environment.

Humans have an innate need for affection that begins at birth and continues throughout their lifespan.

iStock/jacoblund

The Need for Affection

The communication of affection contributes to necessary human goals of survival and procreation (Floyd, 2006). **Affection** refers to the positive internal feelings one person has for another (Floyd & Morman, 1998). The phenomenon of affection occurs across relational contexts including romantic relationships, siblings, platonic friendships, grandparents-grandchildren, and even in-laws.

To satisfy the **need for affection**, people need others to communicate positive feelings toward them, often through friendly and warm interactions. Affection can be communicated through a variety of different verbal and nonverbal behaviors (Floyd & Morman, 1998). Nonverbal expressions of affection include holding hands, kissing, putting an arm around someone's shoulder, hugging, eye gazing, giving massages, winking, and sitting close to one another. Verbal expressions of affection include saying "I love you," saying how important the relationship is, and giving compliments and praise (Floyd & Morman, 1998). Often feeling affection and expressing affection are linked. However, people can certainly feel affection and not express it. Conversely, people can also express **deceptive affection**. In cases of deceptive affection, people may not be feeling affectionate but perform affectionate behaviors anyway (Horan & Booth-Butterfield, 2010, 2011, 2013). People might engage in deceptive affection to save face or maintain their relationships.

Affection has been shown to be associated with a variety of relational outcomes. In romantic relationships receiving affection is associated with increased relational satisfaction, while expressing affection is related to increased relational commitment (Horan & Booth-Butterfield, 2010). Expressed affection is also associated with increased closeness and satisfaction in friendships and family relationships (Floyd & Morman, 2003). In contrast, people who feel deprived of affection in their romantic relationships may experience less satisfaction and relational closeness with their romantic partner (Hesse & Mikkelson, 2017).

RELATIONSHIP TRAJECTORIES

Relational trajectories tell us about the path of a particular relationship. For example, Taylor and Jordan's trajectory was characterized by increasing closeness at the beginning, but then a breakup and reconciliation later. Think about your relationships. Do you have friendships where you hit it off immediately and become close quickly, and others where it took longer to develop a close bond? What about your romantic relationships or those of your friends? Was the road rocky or smooth as you moved toward becoming a couple? Research on relational trajectories helps people understand the different ways relationships develop and change.

Social Penetration Theory

A common way of thinking about relationship development is as a series of stages. Communication is processual and developmental (Miller, 1978), so it can be useful to consider the phases of development in relationships. **Social penetration theory** provides one way of thinking about stage models (Altman & Taylor, 1973). Social penetration theory posits that relationships develop slowly over time as relational partners engage in gradually increasing amounts of disclosure. To illustrate this point, the theorists proposed an onion model of the self, where individuals reveal layers of themselves over time (Figure 8.1).

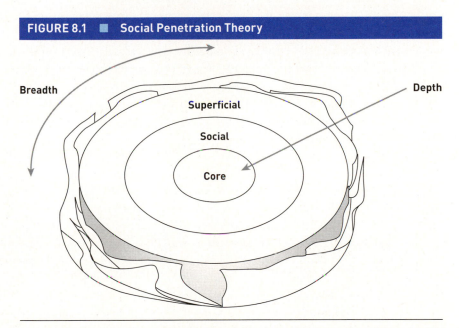

FIGURE 8.1 ■ Social Penetration Theory

Altman and Taylor's (1973) model of self-disclosure is often referred to as the onion model. The idea is that self-disclosure peels away layers of ourselves, revealing the deeper, more tightly held information.

The outer layer is the surface. This layer contains things others can learn just by looking at you. For example, your approximate age, your race, your performed gender, or your taste in clothes. The next layer is the superficial or peripheral layer. This layer contains information you feel comfortable sharing with just about anyone. For example, your name, where you work, or your favorite sports teams. This is typically the level of information we share when we make small talk or meet someone for the first time. Perhaps you have had a class where the instructor asks you on the first day to "share three things" about yourself. You likely shared peripheral-level information during that first meeting—just enough to give people a sense of who you might be, but nothing too personal.

Superficial-level information can then provide a starting point to develop greater depth and breadth of disclosure. **Breadth** refers to how many different topics people discuss with each other. You might talk about everything and anything with a very close friend, whereas with co-workers perhaps you keep your discussions centered on work with some light commentary about current events or the weather. On one hand, you and your close friend engage in greater amounts of breadth. On the other hand, you and your co-worker may discuss in detail industry trends, the performance of your co-workers, and solutions for work-related problems. Thus, your co-worker may have more **depth** of information than your best friend regarding aspects of your work life.

Increases in depth lead communicators to the social or intermediate layer. This layer contains information people do not necessarily think of as secret but that they also might not bring up in every conversation. For example, at the superficial level, you might tell people you work as a nurse in a pediatrician's office. At the social level, you could get into a discussion regarding the science behind vaccinations and your feelings about parents who choose not to vaccinate their kids. At the superficial level, you may tell a co-worker you are engaged. If you progress to the social level, you may describe the story of how you and your fiancé met or concerns you have regarding merging your household pets. People may also use social media as an indirect method of gathering information at both the superficial and social layers (Fox et al., 2013; Trottier, 2012)

Further increases in depth lead to the core or central layer. Core-layer information is considered very personal and reveals the core aspects of who you are as a person. Typically, this information is only disclosed in developed and close relationships where the discloser trusts the message receiver. Examples of core-level information might be revealing to your best friend you are afraid you will be fired from your job. Another example might be telling your family about your ongoing relational conflict with your fiancé and that you are considering calling off the wedding. Core-level information is often information you might keep secret. **Secrets** are intentionally concealed private information (Bok, 1989).

While the onion analogy is helpful for understanding how social penetration theory proposes that disclosure typically unfolds, a staircase analogy represents the type of overall trajectory that the theory predicts. As people share more disclosure, they move up a proverbial staircase toward a more intimate and stable relationship. In social penetration theory, there are four relational stages based on the breadth and depth of information that relational partners share. The first is the *orientation* stage. The orientation phase describes people who are meeting for the first time or do not know each other very well. Typical orientation phase interactions involve low levels of breadth and depth.

The second stage is *exploratory affective exchange*. In the exploratory affective exchange stage, relational partners are beginning to get to know each other better. They may start to explore a wider range of topics. For example, a newly dating couple may begin sharing more of their interests. Work colleagues might move beyond purely work topics and mention their families or a hobby they engage in on the weekend. Much of the communication in the exploratory affective exchange phase is at the peripheral level, but occasionally, relational partners disclose something more intermediate.

The next stage is *affective exchange*. In this phase, relational partners still engage in peripheral and intermediate levels of disclosure, but they also begin to reveal central-level information as well. Trust may be an important factor for engaging in the deeper disclosures of the affective exchange stage. For example, Black friends may disclose more to each other than they do to white friends, whereas white friends disclose fairly equally to their Black and white friends. Shelton et al. argued that Black friends likely need more time and evidence to trust their white friends with deeper disclosures, as they may have experienced prejudice and discrimination from supposed white friends in other contexts. However, interracial friendships can become close if people perceive that their friend will be responsive to their disclosures and concerned about their needs (Shelton et al., 2010). Regardless of relationship context, many close relationships, friends, romantic partners, and familial relationships stay at the affective exchange stage.

The final stage proposed is the *stable exchange*. At this level, relational partners have disclosed nearly everything about themselves. However, stable exchange is rare for several reasons. First, people may never disclose absolutely everything to a partner. There may be stories that they keep to themselves or memories they simply don't think to bring up. Second, people are constantly growing and changing. As they grow and change, they learn new things about themselves and engage in new experiences that they have yet to disclose to their relational partner. Finally, openness at this extreme level is likely to lead to constant conflict (Altman & Taylor, 1973).

Stage models provide a framework to understand relational trajectories. There is a fairly strong relationship between how much people self-disclose and reduce uncertainty and how much people like one another over time (Aron et al., 1991; Berger & Bradac, 1982; Berger & Calabrese, 1975). However, actual relationships seldom follow neat linear paths (Altman et al., 1981). Although the onion model is useful for thinking about levels of disclosure, many scholars have rejected the idea that people slowly peel back layers to reach some ultimately honest and stable perception of each other and the relationship. Rather people constantly negotiate intimacy within their relationships (Riegel, 1979), and relationships often ebb and flow at their own pace (Mongeau & Henningsen, 2015). Even within very intimate relationships, people primarily discuss superficial topics and cycle between superficial and intimate information (Altman et al., 1981).

Relational Dialectics

Rather than seeing relationships as progressing stage by stage to some end goal, Montgomery and Baxter (1998) argued that relationships begin when people start to co-construct social interaction and end when the partners no longer engage in dialogue (p. 160). To account for the nonlinear development of intimate relationships, many scholars have turned to another way of thinking about relational development—**relational dialectics** (Baxter & Montgomery, 1996). Whereas stage models attempt to track the development of relationships in a step-by-step linear fashion, dialectical theorists argue that relational partners, relationships, and the meaning people create about and of their relationships is constantly in a state of unresolvable flux (Baxter & Montgomery, 1998). People manage this flux by coming together through communication to briefly create moments of shared reality (Baxter, 2004b). Relationships become closer not because the self is revealed but because the self and the relationship are co-authored through the relational partners' interactions (Baxter, 2004a).

The dialectical approach understands competing discourses are inherent in relationships (Baxter, 2010). Relational partners often struggle with relational goals and narratives that are perceived to be opposites but yet are also interdependent (Baxter, 1990). For example, as noted above, people disclose personal information to each other to create close relationships. These disclosures result in decreased privacy between the relational partners. However, some level of privacy is important for people to maintain a sense of self and personal agency. Thus, relational partners are continually negotiating the amount they share and conceal within a relationship.

One way to think about a dialectical contradiction is to consider a faucet that runs both hot and cold. As you turn the faucet from hot to cold, you experience opposite temperatures. Yet the concept of hot is dependent on cold as the heat in the water is an absence of cold water. Similarly, the cold water reflects the absence of heat. One cannot understand cold without knowing the concept of warmth and vice versa. This is the **unity** of the dialectical forces. However, hot and cold also **negate** each other. If something is hot, it is not cold. The metaphor of the faucet also helps us understand how people negotiate dialectical tensions differently at different times. You could run the water as "warm" all of the time, but this would be unsatisfying when what you desire is a cold drink or a hot bath. Throughout your day you desire *both* hot *and* cold water. Baxter and Montgomery (1996) term these seemingly competing needs as the "both/and"-ness of dialectics in relationships.

When relational partners communicate with each other, their communication is informed by multiple discourses (Baxter, 2010). Consider Jordan and Taylor's canceled Thanksgiving plans. Wrapped within the communication that Jordan and Taylor share about the event are discourses about what it means to be a romantic couple, the ways that Jordan and Taylor negotiate their relationship, family discourses about sharing the holidays, broader societal narratives regarding Thanksgiving, and perhaps even organizational discourses related to the amount of time that can be spent experiencing Thanksgiving. Each of these discourses influence the way that Jordan and Taylor negotiate the event.

Rather than seeing relationship development as analogous to a staircase, dialectic theory envisions relationship development as fluid, with dialectical tensions representing competing systems of meaning that, like the ends of this ribbon, are interconnected to one another.

iStock/SDI Productions

People experience dialectical tensions throughout different types of relationships and different relational stages (Baxter, 1990). Relational dialectics can be both internal and external to the relationship. *Internal dialectics* are the dialectical desires both people have about their relationship. *External dialectics* are those tensions managed between the relational partners and the external social network (Montgomery & Baxter, 1998). While there are likely as many different types of dialectical tensions as there are perspectives regarding relationships, three are of particular importance in close relationships: integration–separation, expression–privacy, and stability–change (Altman et al., 1981; Baxter, 1990, 2004a; Montgomery & Baxter, 1998).

These three types of tension provide a road map for exploring tensions within relationships as well as the systems of meaning connected to them. For example, what meaning do people connect to seemingly contradictory ideas such as stability (security, boredom, etc.) and change (e.g., excitement, growth) based on how people talk about these concepts? Understanding these dialectical tensions can help us understand and manage our own and our partner's varying relational needs, as well as better understand the competing sets of meanings associated with these tensions

Integration–Separation

The tension of **integration–separation** refers to how people wish to be close to others yet also wish to be independent (Baxter, 1990). The internal aspect of this tension is often referred to as *autonomy-connection*. For example, Taylor wants to be an autonomous individual but also wants to be close to Jordan. The external aspect of the integration–separation tension has been called *seclusion-inclusion*. Jordan and Taylor might want to spend time with their common friends (inclusion) or alone together (seclusion). As noted earlier in the chapter, people need to connect to others for companionship, affection, and access to social resources. At the same time, people have a desire to be autonomous individuals who make their own decisions about their life and behavior (Brown & Levinson, 1987). Researchers have identified the experience of the integration–separation dialectic in a variety of relationships, including friendships (Allen & Loeb, 2015), romantic relationships (Baxter & Ebert, 1999; Sahlstein & Dun, 2008), and families (Golish, 2000), particularly in step-family relationships (Afifi, 2003; Speer & Trees, 2007).

Expression–Privacy

The dialectic of **expression–privacy** addresses similar concepts of **self-disclosure** and privacy as social penetration theory (Altman et al., 1981). The expression side of the dialectic addresses our need to be known by others, to create affiliations, to self-disclose, and to create relationships (Altman et al., 1981; Baxter, 1990). The internal aspect of this dialectic has been called **openness–closedness**. For example, Taylor might want to share a lot of things with Jordan, but not everything. The external aspect of the dialectic has been called *revelation-concealment*. Taylor and Jordan are likely to tell members of their social networks some information about their relationship, but they will keep other information private. People have an expectation for a certain level of openness in close friendships and romantic relationships (Baxter et al., 2001). As Altman et al. (1981) argued, a dyad completely closed to each other is not experiencing a relationship. On the other hand, disclosure involves interpersonal risks (Rawlins, 1983). To mitigate these risks, people choose to keep some information private (Petronio, 2002). In addition, a completely open dyad would result in a loss of personal identity and control.

The dialectical perspective is different than the idea of slowly pulling back layers of the onion model as proposed by social penetration theory (Altman & Taylor, 1973). Rather people experience disclosure as a dialectical tension. In romantic relationships, people report relational rules and norms about being open and honest with one's partner *and* also about not telling your partner everything (Baxter et al., 2001). Within personal relationships, people wish to have *both* disclosure *and* privacy. People also frequently share details about their relationships with others, but there are some details that most people agree are best kept private between partners.

Managing the openness–closedness dialectic is a part of every social relationship. One example is in blended families. Children in blended families may experience tensions as they desire to be open with their nonresidential parent and yet avoid or limit discussion about certain topics regarding their step-family to avoid conflict or inflicting pain on their nonresidential parent (Braithwaite & Baxter, 2006). There is also a delicate balance between disclosing information about your relationship to others while respecting your partner's right to keep some of that information private.

Stability–Change

A third important relational dialectic is **stability–change**. The internal aspect of this dialectic is called *predictability–novelty*. Taylor and Jordan may fall into a predictable pattern of behaviors that makes them comfortable, such as texting every night they are not together and engaging in certain activities together on a regular basis. But they may also mix things up by surprising each other or trying new things once in a while. The external aspect of this dialectic is called *conventionality-uniqueness*. This is the idea that Taylor and Jordan want to be like most couples in some ways—perhaps they value monogamy and believe they should be more loyal to each other than to anyone else. At the same time, they want their relationship to be different, unique, and special.

People desire some level of predictability regarding their interpersonal relationships (Berger & Bradac, 1982). Many theories of human behavior argue that humans seek consistency in their lives and relationships (Altman et al., 1981). However, we also enjoy spontaneity and novelty. There are times people seek out new experiences and desire change (Altman et al., 1981). New experiences help people grow as individuals and as a dyad. Too much predictability can also lead to boredom. Within relationships, people have been known to end relationships due to both the unpredictability of a partner *and* for experiencing boredom (Montgomery & Baxter, 1998).

We don't want to constantly be on a relational rollercoaster, yet we do enjoy some novelty and spontaneity.

iStock/Philartphace

Competing Discourses

A revised version of the theory, relational dialectics theory 2.0, shifts the focus away from tensions reflecting individual needs and toward competing discourses that create meaning (Baxter, 2010). Baxter et al. (2021) give the example of competing themes in discourse about family, noting that the dominant discourse of heteronormativity positions families as based on marriage between a woman and a man. However, other discourses about family contradict this, suggesting that two committed adults, regardless of gender (or a single person, for that matter) can anchor a family. A key idea in relational dialectics theory 2.0 is that *"meaning making emerges in the interplay of competing discourses"* (Baxter et al., 2021, p. 9). This means that people derive meaning by making sense of different, and sometimes opposing, perspectives as expressed within cultures and groups. One study looked at competing discourses in relationships between parents and their LGBTQIA children (Tyler & Abetz, 2019). Parents expressed tension between discourses of expectations and support. Specifically, they had to reconcile the old expectations they had, which might include things like having biological grandchildren, with wanting to supportive their child. Both of these discourses were reflected in the parent's identity.

Relational dialectics theory 2.0 also includes the idea of **aesthetic moments**, which occur when competing discourses merge in a transformative way. An example of this was found in a study by Ritter et al. (2020): A woman transformed her thinking about her hearing loss into something positive and life-changing, rather than simply a "disability" as the dominant discourse would suggest. Aesthetic moments like these change individual identities, but relational identities can also be transformed. A couple that begins to think about time apart as a way to grow and have more to share and learn from one another, for example, has transformed their relational identity.

SKILL BUILDER
MANAGING DIALECTICAL TENSIONS

Montgomery and Baxter (1998) outlined patterns of managing dialectical tensions. However, from the dialectical perspective, relational partners are not choosing from these as if from a restaurant menu. Rather these choices may be mixed, merged, and rotated through to constantly create the current state of the relationship. Nevertheless, we will make some attempt at illustrating the basic patterns outlined by Montgomery and Baxter.

- *Denial* occurs when relational partners attempt to exclude the need to engage in one side of the dialectical tension. For example, a couple may set a goal of not keeping secrets from one another and being completely open. These goals deny the need to also have some secrets and privacy.

- *Disorientation* is when relational partners take the perspective that the contradictions in their relationship are inherent and cannot be negotiated or changed. Relational partners engaging in this perspective on dialectical tensions may feel there is simply no way to manage the tensions or the related conflicts.

- *Reaffirmation* is similar to disorientation in that couples accept the inevitability of dialectical contradictions. However, they view the challenge of dialectical tensions as a positive allowing for growth, change, and new possibilities in the relationship.

- *Spiraling inversion* is when couples engage one side of the dialectic at certain times and the other side of the dialectic at other times. For example, in addressing the internal manifestation of autonomy–connectedness, when a couple might decide to have a "date night" to get a sense of connectedness back when they feel they have been spending a lot of time addressing autonomy by doing things on their own. That same "date night" may also represent the experience of seclusion as a couple, which relates to the external side of the dialectic. Similarly, if they have been spending a lot of time alone, they may choose to go out with groups of friends or to an event with extended family to address the need for inclusion as a couple.

- *Segmentation* is similar to spiraling inversion in that couples choose to engage in one side of the dialectic or the other, but in this case, the engagement is related to the activity rather than simply fluctuations over time. For example, one partner may have a weekly sports match on the schedule with friends while the other attends a game night with family. Or they might choose to always spend Saturdays together but to hang out with separate friends on Sunday.

- *Balance* is when relational partners do not fully engage in either end of the dialectic but rather try to stay within some middle point. For example, friends might never be 100 percent open with each other and may never be completely closed off from one another. Rather, they negotiate the tension of openness–closedness through steady but strategic disclosures within an acceptable range for the friendship.

- *Integration* occurs when partners are responding to the opposing forces at once. A wedding can be an interesting example of the novelty-predictability dialectic. Couples often attempt to integrate unique aspects of their "special day" while still maintaining the predictable framing of a wedding.

A truly dialectical approach to relationships goes beyond the naming of particular dialectical tensions and management patterns. Dialectics provide a way for approaching and thinking about relationships from multiple perspectives in a deep and thoughtful manner. Yet students must start somewhere to understand a dialectical perspective. In what ways have you used communication to manage dialectical tensions in relationships?

RELATIONAL TURNING POINTS

Even a cursory understanding of relational dialectics illuminates that relationships are constantly in flux. Research on relational turning points and relational turbulence can help us understand and negotiate the ever-changing nature of close relationships. **Relational turning points** (RTPs) are remembered events in relationships that relational partners pinpoint as transforming the relationship in either a positive or negative way (Baxter & Bullis, 1986; Surra & Hughes, 1997).

Turning points have a dual significance for close relationships (Baxter, 2004a). First, they are a common experience the relational partners shared. Second, relational turning points become a key part of the story about the relationship. RTPs will be remembered over and over and become part of the narrative couples jointly created about their relationship (Baxter & Pittman, 2001). RTPs vary in whether they have a positive or negative impact on the relationship. RTPs can lead to increased commitment to the relationship but also can increase uncertainty about the relationship (Solomon & Knobloch, 2004; Solomon & Theiss, 2008). Of course, it is also possible that some turning points in relationships do both. For example, if friends share an unexpected first kiss, it might increase uncertainty about the state of the relationship initially, but eventually contribute to commitment not only to maintaining the relationship, but also toward becoming a couple. Later, this RTP can become part of the narrative of the relationship as the couple remembers the experience of their first kiss and how it was confusing at first but ended up being the turning point that lead them to start transitioning from being friends to a couple.

Turning Points in Romantic Relationships

Romantic couples report a variety of different types of RTPs. Some are perceived to have a positive impact on the relationship, while others are negative. For romantic couples, spending increased time together can represent a turning point. Romantic couples report both *get to know* time and *quality time* as turning points. Get to know time involves the deepening self-disclosure and knowledge acquisition that occurs within developing relationships (Baxter & Bullis, 1986). Quality time is time a couple reserves to spend specifically with each other (Baxter & Pittman 2001). Couples typically report a moment where they chose to take a vacation together or specifically spend time with each other as having a positive impact on the relationship. Similarly, making decisions to be *exclusive* was also perceived as positive (Baxter & Pittman, 2001). Memories of experiencing *passion* in the relationship, such as the first time couples kiss, have sex, or say "I love you," are also generally remembered positively (Baxter & Pittman, 2001; Theiss & Solomon, 2007).

Another RTP is *network interaction* (Baxter & Pittman, 2001). This RTP might involve introducing a new romantic partner to one's friends or bringing a partner home to meet one's parents. These interactions are usually but not always remembered in a positive light. *Serious commitment events* such as becoming engaged or cohabiting are also viewed positively some but not all of the time.

Another RTP that is sometimes positive and sometimes negative is *external competition* (Baxter & Pittman, 2001). These external demands on the relationship include the emergence of old and new rivals (perhaps an ex resurfacing or witnessing some flirtation with a third party) or the nonromantic demands on one or both partners' time, such as a stressful time at work or dealing with a close family member's illness. One might remember the time when a partner disclosed an ex contacted them and the couple then worked through the appropriateness of such contact, bringing the couple closer together. For another couple, that same contact by an ex-partner might lead to conflict and distrust and be remembered in a negative light. Another turning point with about an equal chance of being a positive or negative influence on a relationship is *physical separation*. For some couples, times where they were separated due to the demands of school or work are viewed positively as something the couple overcame together. For other couples, the strain of distance was remembered as having a negative effect on the relationship. In addition, some couples in long-distance romantic relationships break up after they reunite geographically. Breaking up after reuniting may be due to partners feeling a loss of the autonomy they enjoyed while being long-distance or gaining more knowledge about the partner that seems incompatible with continuing the relationship (Stafford et al., 2006). Similarly, experiencing *conflict* was sometimes remembered as leading to increased commitment and sometimes remembered as leading to decreased commitment. The first big fight couples have typically either results in couples feeling closer to each other than before the fight or leads to a breakup (Siegert & Stamp, 1994). The RTP primarily viewed as having a negative impact on the relationship was *disengagement events,* such as breakups or "taking a break."

People remember the turning points of their relationship in different ways. One way is by reminiscing together about different events in their relationship (Baxter & Pittman, 2001). For example, a couple may talk together about a trip they took or a hobby they share. Another common way is through telling the "story" of the couple's relationship to others. This storytelling not only creates and confirms the narrative of the relationship for the couple but also legitimizes the relationship to other social network members (Baxter & Pittman, 2001). Beyond story creation, communication may play another important role, with regard to turning points. The way couples communicate during and about a relational turning point may predict whether the turning point has a positive or negative effect on the relationship. For example, those who communicate directly about sex prior to their first sexual encounter may experience more positive relational outcomes than couples who do not (Theiss & Solomon, 2007).

Turning Points in Friendships

Friendships differ from romantic relationships in that they are flexible and may experience more changes in commitment over time (Becker et al., 2009). Friendships may be more resilient to changes in commitment over time than romantic relationships. Friends may expect that commitment and engagement with the friendship will change over the life course (Johnson et al., 2009; Rawlins, 1994). The most common turning point for friends is beginning to share an activity together (Johnson et al., 2003). The increased time spent together and mutual experience of activities such as joining a sport, starting a band, or playing an ongoing game together can lead to positive outcomes for friends. Other turning points in friendship include taking a trip together, providing or receiving social support, engaging in self-disclosure, and experiencing changes in the friendship due to increased or decreased geographical distances (Becker et al., 2009; Johnson et al., 2003). Friends may also experience different turning points based on the closeness level of the friendship. Best friends and close friends report *living together* as a turning point in their relationship more than casual friends (Becker et al., 2009).

Turning Points in Family Relationships

Although people think of family relationships as somewhat static, family members also experience turning points in their relationships. For example, siblings can experience multiple turning points over the course of their relationships (Corti, 2009). Some of these turning points include co-experiencing turbulent moments for the family, such as a parent losing their job.. Other turning points are related to rites of passage such as the siblings graduating from school or moving to different areas. Siblings also report spending quality time together as an important aspect of their relationship as well as giving and receiving social support and advice about major life decisions.

The relationship between emerging adults and their parents is inherently turbulent (Nelson et al., 2007; Troll & Fingerman, 1996). Parents and children alike are trying to figure out their new roles and new patterns for their relationships (Arnett, 2000). Increased physical distance due to moving away to college or moving out of the home is one common turning point experienced by emerging adults and their parents. Another turning point is experiencing crises such as the parents or the adult child getting a divorce or a death in the family. A third turning point is directly related to the shifting nature of the parent–adult child relationship. Adult children reported engaging in open communication by involving parents in their decision-making and communicating honesty and respect for differences as an important turning point in the adult child–parent relationship. As the adult child grows older, other important turning points include the child's marriage and bringing new children/grandchildren into the family (Golish, 2000). Families including an LGBTQIA child often see the child's coming out to parents, as well as the child's first romantic relationship, as significant turning points (Tyler & Abetz, 2021). Similarly, lesbian parents often regard coming out to their children, having conversations about people's comments and judgments about their family, and announcing commitment ceremonies or weddings as important turning points that affect family identity (Breshears, 2011). Turning points also occur in blended families, with family members reporting changes in the household composition, conflict, holidays and special celebrations, quality time, and family crises representing important moments in the development of a blended family (Baxter et al., 1999).

Overall, turning points research demonstrates that people do not experience relationships as static entities. Rather, relationships are constantly developing throughout the life cycle of the relationship.

INITIATING RELATIONSHIPS IN MEDIATED CONTEXTS

The proliferation of social media, including online communities and social network sites, has provided new spaces for people to meet potential friends and lovers that they might not have otherwise. In many ways, online relationship trajectories and processes are fairly similar to the processes and trajectories humans generally followed in initiating relationships before the internet. Gradual disclosure still leads to relational development; people have needs for inclusion, affection, and control; and relational partners experience and manage dialectical tensions. Indeed, people do not generally experience relationships as "offline" and "online." Rather people weave together a variety of channels throughout their daily lives to initiate, manage, and maintain relationships. For example, you might meet someone new at a campus social event and add them to Snapchat or follow them on Instagram. You may learn more about them through these channels and use that information to fuel your conversation the next time you meet in person.

However, mediated communication spaces have introduced some changes. The audience for interpersonal messages may be much greater than in in-person settings. People may be able to find others with shared interests at a much greater scale than previously available. In flexible network spaces, as defined in Chapter 2, people may be able to have greater identity experimentation, which influences the relationships they form with fellow communicators.

The lines between mediated and in-person communication can be blurred when people switch seamlessly from one channel to another. This family is simultaneously communicating to each other in person but also to someone else through a phone.

iStock/skynesher

Electronic Propinquity

An early theoretical concept that helped us understand why people have the opportunity to form certain network connections but not others is propinquity. **Propinquity** refers to how physically close people are to each other. We tend to form friendships with those who we are in close proximity to at a greater rate than with those who are farther away. A classic study examined friendships in a housing community for young married veterans. In this study, the researchers found that couples who lived closer together were more likely to form friendships (Festinger et al., 1950). As you think about your own friendship network, you may notice that those with whom you've formed close relationships are the people who live near you in your dorm, share a class with you, or belong to the same organization or workplace. Propinquity gives people a chance to meet, communicate, and form relationships.

Prior to the advent of the internet, it was practically necessary for people to first meet in a face-to-face encounter before forming a relationship. There were a few exceptions such as pen pals or video dating services, but primarily people met because they shared some physical space. Third spaces such as coffeehouses and bars served as community locations where people could come into close proximity with others not in their current social network (Oldenburg, 1989).

Social media allows for electronic propinquity **electronic propinquity**. Online social spaces, including social network sites like Facebook, Instagram, and Twitter as well as message board communities such as Reddit, allow for people to come into contact with each other without being in the same physical space (Korzenny, 1978). Electronic propinquity allows for the same opportunity to meet, communicate, and form relationships in online spaces that previously was only available in physical spaces (Walther & Bazarova, 2008). Electronic propinquity may function differently in different types of online spaces. For example, a Twitter feed brings you into contact with a variety of messages that are generally connected to the social network you have created on Twitter. On the other hand, you may join a Reddit board or an online support community because you are seeking out information on a specific topic. In either case, mediated channels allow us to expand our networks by creating an opportunity to come into proximity with people we might not have met otherwise.

Online communities like Reddit facilitate perceptions of electronic propinquity.

Photo Illustration by Rafael Henrique/SOPA Images/LightRocket via Getty Images

Masspersonal Communication

Online communication is often persistent, meaning that the messages exist on the internet much longer than our memory of spoken face-to-face encounters. In addition, messages can be searchable and replicable. These affordances of online communication spaces allow a great number of receivers to view our messages—even if the intent of the message is for interpersonal purposes. The viewing of interpersonal messages by a wider audience is one type of masspersonal communication. **Masspersonal communication** refers to instances where the uses and goals of mass and interpersonal communication overlap (Figure 8.2) (O'Sullivan & Carr, 2018). One type of masspersonal communication is when people use mass communication channels for interpersonal communication, such as proposing to someone on the jumbotron or having a children's television show wish your child a happy birthday. Another type is when people use channels that are typically interpersonal to reach mass audiences. A third type is when people engage in interpersonal and mass communication at the same time. This third type is often facilitated by the use of social media. For example, Facebook posts might carry the type of self-disclosure we would use to further interpersonal relationship development (e.g., announcements about life events, political opinions, stories about our daily life) but transmit this information to hundreds of people at once. Instagram photos may help us perform particular identities to a mass audience. These communication options can change the way that we think about the effects of our messages, our social network, and our presentation of self.

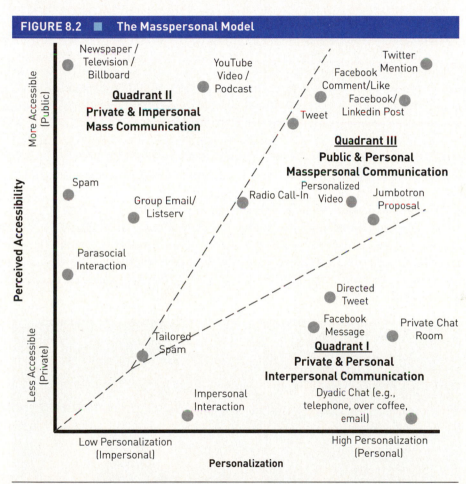

FIGURE 8.2 ■ The Masspersonal Model

Source: O'Sullivan, P. B., & Carr, C. T. (2018). Masspersonal communication: A model bridging the mass-interpersonal divide. *New Media & Society, 20*(3), 1161–1180. https://doi.org/10.1177/1461444816686104

Social Capital and Social Resources

One of the outcomes of electronic propinquity and masspersonal communication is that social media users can maintain much larger social networks than they could previously. In particular, social network sites may help us stay in touch with a wider variety of weak ties and can help people maintain their social network connections throughout life changes (Ellison et al., 2007). The ability to form and maintain larger networks may help people have greater access to social capital. **Social capital** can be defined as the resources found within the network of relationships one has with other people (Coleman, 1988). Having a wide and varied social network allows people to perceive that there are wide and varied social resources available to them from their social network. Developing social networks that we perceive will provide us with resources and support is connected with being satisfied with the social network (McEwan & Guerrero, 2012). Using social media to develop satisfying social networks may be connected to our overall subjective well-being (Taylor & Bazarova, 2018). Thus, using social media to facilitate the initiation of new relationships as well as the maintenance of ties (as will be covered in Chapter 9) can help people feel more satisfied overall with their social network.

Online Dating

When it comes to romantic relationships, many mediated options have proliferated to help people find potential romantic partners. Online dating can refer to profile-browsing-style websites as well as "micro-dating" sites such as Tinder, Grindr, and Bumble. Online dating sites such as Match.com or eHarmony allow people to move beyond their social network and proximal neighbors to meet people who may be potential romantic partners. In addition, online dating allows people to filter by characteristics in a way that would be considered fairly inappropriate if you tried to do that in a face-to-face setting (Baker, 2008). The ability to edit and select specific identity presentations online also allows people the potential to present their best, most ideal selves to potential partners. Of course, striving to present a best version of self has long been common in daters (Tooke & Camire, 1991), and research suggests deception in online dating is minor and often adjusted for by savvy online daters (Toma et al., 2008). For example, when evaluating others' profiles, online daters might adjust height downward for men and weight slightly upward for women. Experienced online daters also report avoiding profiles that use concealment strategies such as limited or fuzzy photographs (Ellison et al., 2006). Although some deception may be expected in profiles, if upon meeting online daters perceive that their partner was deceptive when communicating with them via email before a first date, that date tends not to be successful (Sharabi & Caughlin, 2019).

Dating apps give people the opportunity to meet people they never would have otherwise.

d3sign/Moment via Getty Images

Dating sites may change the number and type of available potential romantic or sexual partners. A study showed that in 2010, nearly 70 percent of same-sex couples and almost 35 percent of opposite-sex couples met online (Rosenfeld & Thomas, 2010). However, even in the most modern micro-dating site, the relational processes may not be that different. Tinder users have reported using the app primarily for entertainment goals, followed by relational goals, and then for sexual goals (Carpenter & McEwan, 2016). These findings pretty closely follow pre-Tinder research on first date goals, suggesting people in the pre-Tinder age dated primarily to "have fun," then to potentially pursue a relationship, and finally to pursue sexual goals (Mongeau et al., 2004).

In addition, to pursue a relationship formed online, people need to meet in person at some point. Certainly, safety concerns such as meeting up in public and telling friends where you will be should be addressed. The timing of the first offline meeting may also have an effect on the overall relationship. Meeting in person 17–23 days after first connecting online may be the ideal time frame (Ramirez et al., 2015). This time frame allows early daters to begin to learn about each other prior to meeting but has daters meet before they begin to form hyperpersonal perceptions such as those discussed in Chapter 3. Keeping the relationship online long enough to form a hyperpersonal perspective may lead to expectancy violations and disappointment when the daters finally do meet in person.

PRINCIPLES OF RELATIONSHIPS AND COMMUNICATION

As social beings, we form many different relationships throughout our lifetime. Our connections to friends, family, acquaintances, and romantic partners can serve different goals and purposes in our lives. The relationships that you initiate with others also grow and change through communication. The following principles help articulate how communication influences relationship initiation and development.

Principle 1. People use communication to form and develop relationships to meet basic human needs.

Although phase models and dialectical models take different approaches to the ways people experience relational change and growth, both models agree that people use communication to form and develop relationships. Human beings are an incredibly social species and depend on networked social relationships to survive and thrive. Communication is the tool we use to initiate and grow a variety of relationships to help us meet our needs for inclusion, control, and affection.

Principle 2. Relationships vary in their levels of closeness. Not every relationship is intended to be close.

It is sometimes assumed that the better a relationship is, the closer it will become over time. However, not every relationship is destined to become our closest relationship. People need a wide variety of relationships of varying levels of closeness. Indeed, less close relationships, or weak ties, may be particularly useful for bringing us different information and opportunities than our close relationships can provide (Granovetter, 1973). We may use different communication strategies to keep relationships at our desired level of closeness.

Principle 3. Social groups develop norms and rules about relational trajectories.

Although every relationship is a unique constellation between the parties forming the relationship, people do apply social norms to their relationships. These interaction rules are generally unspoken but provide shared knowledge for expectations regarding how a specific relationship is to be conducted. Some common relational rules in the United States include not pursuing your friends' romantic partners or exes, being appropriate about public displays of affection, and being respectful of one's partner (Baxter et al., 2001). Rules for friendship might include not dropping a friend due to a new romantic relationship and being supportive and respectful of friends (Argyle & Henderson, 1984; Baxter et al., 2001). Other research has found that people have developed rules for the use of social media (Bryant & Marmo, 2012). For example, people expect a response if they post directly on someone's profile and if someone deletes a post it should not be reposted (Bryant & Marmo, 2012). As these Facebook "rules" illustrate, people do not always follow the rules or norms in relationships, but these social expectations do help provide a framework for determining appropriate and inappropriate behavior.

Principle 4. Close relationships develop greater idiosyncrasies in the relationship over time.
Reduced uncertainty may be marked by the introduction of the use of idiomatic communication. Idiomatic communication is communication unique to the communicative partners (Bell et al., 1987). Idiomatic communication might include having an endearing unique nickname for a romantic partner. For example, in the show, *How I Met Your Mother*, the characters Lily and Marshall called each other "Lilypad" and "Marshmallow." Other forms of idiomatic communication include inside jokes, phrases, and slang that mark the communicators as in-group members. These idioms are layered in shared past experiences and memories of other iterations of the joke, which signals closeness between the communicative partners (see Bell & Healey, 1992).

Principle 5. We create linear narratives to help us make sense of our relationships, but relationship development is not necessarily a linear process.
We often think of relationships, particularly romantic ones, as following a linear trajectory of becoming increasingly close and committed. The narratives that we co-construct with partners and network members about our relationships are often organized linearly. However, real relationships do not always follow the pattern of meeting, then becoming closer, and then becoming publicly committed. Also, even very close and committed relational partners have to negotiate different tensions as well as increases and decreases in relational quality throughout the relationship. Through their communication choices, people continually are creating and re-creating their relationships. This process involves managing increases and decreases in commitment, closeness, and satisfaction throughout the lifespan of the relationship.

CONCLUSION

People are social creatures. The primary way that we fulfill our social needs is through relationships. We engage in many different types of relationships—role relationships, family, friends, romantic partners—in order to fulfill our various social needs. These relationships may vary on factors such as how voluntary the relationship feels or whether it is a satisfying relationship. Communication, particularly self-disclosure, helps us deepen and develop these relationships and become closer over time. Yet relationships experience change, growth, and decay over their lifespan. Thus, it is not surprising that Jordan and Taylor's relationship has not followed a smooth linear path toward increasing intimacy, and has been characterized by turning points such as meeting each other friends, breaking up, and getting back together again. Communication also helps us manage the dialectical tensions that exist in relationships and plays a vital role in helping us initiate, define, and navigate the multitude of relationships that we experience throughout our lives. Where Taylor and Jordan's relationship goes next is largely dependent on how they communicate with and about each other.

CHAPTER 8 STUDY GUIDE

KEY TERMS

Identify and explain the meaning of each of the following key terms.

aesthetic moments	openness–closedness
affection	partner uncertainty
breadth	propinquity
deceptive affection	relational dialectics
depth	relational turning points
dyadic	relational uncertainty
electronic propinquity	relationship uncertainty
expression–privacy	relationships
integration–separation	role relationships
interdependence	satisfaction
interpersonal relationships	secrets
intimate relationships	self-disclosure
masspersonal communication	self-uncertainty
mutual influence	social capital
need for affection	social penetration theory
need for control	stability–change
need for inclusion	unity
negation	voluntariness

REFLECTION QUESTIONS

1. What types of different relationships do you have in your life? How do these relationships fulfill different needs?

2. Often when we think about improving our relationships, we think about making a relationship closer or more satisfying. Are there relationships in your life where you deliberately tried to keep the relationship and a specific level of closeness and quality? Perhaps you had a dating partner with whom you did not want to become more serious (but did not want to break off the relationship) or a friendship that had reached your desired level of closeness. How did you manage these relationships?

3. The relational dialectics perspective suggests that we are constantly managing competing tensions in our relationships. Can you provide a description of a time when you've experienced the both/and-ness of dialectical tensions? In what ways did you and your relational partners manage that tension? Can you recognize conflicts or difficulties you may have had in the past that were dialectical in nature?

4. What are the benefits and drawbacks of initiating relationships in mediated spaces? In what ways do we weave together both nonmediated and mediated communication to help us form new relationships? How does mediated communication influence the way that we self-disclose to new romantic and platonic connections?

9 MAINTAINING QUALITY RELATIONSHIPS

As Candace nears graduation, she and her long-term partner, Peyton, are experiencing the stress typical of major life transitions. Candace feels like everything is up in the air, she doesn't have a job lined up, she doesn't know where she'll be living, she's not sure where Peyton will be living, and she's worried that her relationship with Peyton may not make it through this stressful transition. On a trip home, Candace asks, "Mom, how do you and Dad make it work through all of these years and changes?" "Hmmm," says Candace's mom, Dena, "It's really the little things that make a relationship work over time. Your dad and I make sure to help each other out with the things we need to get done, remind each other that we're important to each other, and we make each other laugh and try to make each other's day more pleasant." "Oh," continues Candace, "but what about the big things? Like weddings, and kids, and trips, and new homes? All the milestones, you know?" "The milestones are fun," replies Dena, "and it can be good to be focused on a goal together, but when a relationship lasts, you'll spend far more time living in the day-to-day than having big milestone celebrations. How you communicate with each other every day is what makes a life."

"The little things" that are our day-to-day behaviors in our relationships can be thought of as **relational maintenance**. Much of our time in interpersonal relationships is spent in the maintenance phase (Duck, 1988). Just as a car needs a tune-up or a roof needs to be re-shingled from time to time, relationships require constant communication in order to keep them running smoothly.

There are many different strategies and tactics that people use to maintain various relationships. To stay in existence, all relationships require continued communication.. The type and level of relational maintenance that people engage in vary depending on relational type. In addition, the way that we engage in relational maintenance can affect the quality of our relationships and our perceptions of equity within the relationship.

WHAT IS RELATIONAL MAINTENANCE?

Relational maintenance behaviors are the actions relational partners take to sustain their relationships in a desired way (Canary & Stafford, 1994). Much of this relational maintenance activity occurs through communication between relational partners (Dindia, 2003). In Chapter 8, we discussed different types of relationships people initiate. Each of these relationships requires some level of maintenance (Dindia, 2003; Stafford & Canary, 1991), and relational maintenance communication occurs across romantic partners (Haas, 2003; Ogolsky & Bowers, 2013; Stafford & Canary, 1991), friendships (Guerrero & Chavez, 2005; McEwan & Guerrero, 2012; Oswald & Clark, 2003; Oswald et al., 2004), family relationships (Mansson et al., 2010; Mikkelson et al., 2011; Serewicz et al., 2007), and work relationships (Waldron, 1991). Indeed, any type of relationship that you can think of requires some type of communication to sustain it. For our purposes in this chapter, we will often use the term "relational partners." We mean relational partners as a general term that could encompass any type of relationship: friendships, superior–subordinate, acquaintanceships, familial, and romantic relationships. We clarify this at this point in the chapter because "relational partner" is often taken to mean simply romantic relationships. We will specifically state when we mean romantic relationships or romantic partners.

Dindia and Canary (1993) proposed four levels of relational definitions in sustaining desired relational definitions. At a very basic level, relational maintenance serves to keep a relationship in existence (Dindia and Canary, 1993). Once relational partners stop communicating, the relationship is over (Dindia, 2003). A common way to end an acquaintance or friendship is to simply stop communicating with that individual, letting the relationship slowly fade away (McEwan et al., 2008). We might also think of times where an estrangement between family members is facilitated by one or both members giving each other the cold shoulder or where the breakup of romantic relationship is accomplished through ghosting.. These cases of relationship termination illustrate that communication serves the important function of keeping relationships in existence.

The second level of relational definition is to keep a relationship in "a specified state or condition" (Dindia & Canary, 1993, p. 5). Relationships exist at many stages (Knapp & Vangelisti, 2000), and romantic partners may wish to maintain their relationship at various stages. For example, a dating couple may wish to enjoy their time dating, so they neither escalate the relationship to an engagement nor de-escalate their relationship by breaking up (Chapter 12 will discuss relational termination). We could also think of friends who might wish to maintain their friendship and not escalate to a romantic relationship. Such friends might develop careful boundaries regarding topics of conversation and physical touch in order to maintain their friendship. Heterosexual cross-sex friends often maintain the friendship by specifically avoiding flirtatious interactions (Messman et al., 2000).

The third definition expands beyond the idea of a specified condition and notes that many relational partners want to keep their relationship in a satisfactory state (Dindia, 2003). People generally don't just want a relationship to exist. They would prefer a relationship that is enjoyable and fulfilling. In addition to satisfaction, relational partners may also desire other related relational qualities such as commitment, liking, and trust. But relationships differ in terms of desired qualities. For example, when in the talking stage, a potential couple may feel more satisfied if they see how things unfold before committing to something serious, and co-workers may prefer keeping their relationship professional.

Experiencing high-quality, satisfying relationships can have positive effects on other areas of one's life and health.

iStock/Prostock-Studio

The fourth definition of relational maintenance is to repair a relationship (Dindia, 2003). Relationships experience a wide range of stressors, from internal conflict and hurtful messages to external stressors such as balancing other activities and relationships. Romantic relationships may experience jealousy or even infidelity. Relational partners must communicate in order to repair the relationship back to an acceptable desired state. Relationship maintenance related to repair might be both preventative and corrective (Dindia, 2003). For example, friends who make sure to engage in joint activities together might be preventing themselves from drifting away and needing to restore closeness. Romantic couples who experience infidelity might engage in corrective maintenance by assuring each other that they value their relationship and want it to continue.

Why Maintain Relationships?

According to **Social exchange theory**, people wish to maximize rewards and minimize costs in their relationships (Thibaut & Kelley, 1959). Explanations of the reasons people engage in relational maintenance behaviors and the effects of those behaviors have been connected to social exchange theory (Canary & Stafford, 1993, 1994, 2007). Costs within a relationship might include the time you invest that cannot be spent with others, gifts that you purchase for your partner, or stress that you experience when a partner is ill or when you are experiencing conflict in the relationship. Rewards in relationships might include gifts that you receive, the enjoyable companionship of your partner, having a partner for a variety of activities you enjoy together, and having someone to look out for you. Maintenance behaviors can reduce costs and maximize rewards within a relationship (Braiker & Kelley, 1979).

The concept of **equity** is related to the idea of exchange. People want their ratio of rewards and costs to be similar to what their partner is receiving in the relationship; they want an equitable amount of rewards and costs. People likely consider their balance of costs and rewards when they consider if they want to maintain their relationships (Duck, 1994). In addition, some maintenance behaviors on the part of one partner may serve as rewarding outcomes for the other partner (Canary & Stafford, 2007). People are more likely to be motivated to maintain relationships that are fair and equitable (Canary & Stafford, 1994, 2007). Maintenance inputs are also likely to serve as investments into relationships. These investments pay off when people are able to develop network connections that can potentially provide important interpersonal resources (McEwan & Guerrero, 2012).

People prefer to have equitable relationships, where rewards and costs are balanced between partners.

iStock/artisteer

RELATIONAL MAINTENANCE BEHAVIORS

Relational maintenance consists of both communication strategies and behavioral tactics. **Communication strategies** are general approaches for accomplishing a particular relational goal. **Behavioral tactics** are the specific behaviors people use to enact a communication goal strategy (Canary & Stafford, 1994).

Individuals use both strategic and routine maintenance behaviors for relationship maintenance (Canary & Stafford, 1994; Dainton & Stafford, 1993; Duck, 1994). **Strategic maintenance behaviors** are those that relational partners use mindfully for the specific purpose of maintaining the relationship (Dainton & Stafford, 1993). **Routine maintenance behaviors** are those communicative behaviors that relational partners engage in throughout their daily activities that serve to maintain the relationship but that the partners are not specifically considering as maintenance (Dindia, 2003; Duck 1988). For example, a couple may greet each other upon arriving home in a friendly manner but not really consider the maintenance element of that enactment of positivity. Thus, most relational maintenance behaviors are routine (Dainton, 1995). Our routine everyday behaviors create the glue that maintains our relationships (Berger & Kellner, 1964).

We should note that the same behavior could be routine or strategic—what matters is the intent of the communicator. Engaging in that same friendly greeting could become an extremely strategic behavior if the relational partners are actively remembering to perform it after having had an intense conflict the night before. In addition, relational maintenance behaviors are **multiphasic**—people can use similar behaviors to accomplish different relational goals throughout the lifespan of a relationship (Dindia, 1994, 2003; Guerrero & Chavez, 2005). For example, the first time that a couple exchanges the words "I love you" holds a very different meaning and effect than the exchange of these words as a daily good-bye by an established romantic couple. Researchers have identified many different strategies that people use to maintain their relationships.

Maintenance Strategies

Researchers have examined a variety of different relational **maintenance strategies**. Within each of these strategies are different tactics that can be deployed in either a routine or strategic fashion.

Stafford (2011) developed a typology of seven common maintenance strategies (see Relational Maintenance Tactics in the Skill Builder).

Positivity consists of behaviors that reflect cheerfulness and optimism (Stafford & Canary, 1991). Specific tactics within the strategy of positivity might include trying to be upbeat, acting positively, being cheerful, and acting optimistic (Stafford, 2011).

Openness is having direct conversations about the state of the relationship. As discussed in Chapter 8, self-disclosure is an important part of relationship development. Specific tactics within the strategy of openness include telling your relational partner how you feel about the relationship, having periodic talks about the relationship, and encouraging your partner to disclose their thoughts and feelings (Canary & Stafford, 1992). Openness might also include **meta-communication** or communication that is specifically about the status and functioning of the relationship and communication within the relationship (Braiker & Kelley, 1979; Canary et al., 1993; Dindia, 2003). Openness can also include self-disclosure, advice, and engagement in conflict (Canary et al., 1993).

It may be that the original idea of openness might actually comprise multiple maintenance strategies. Stafford (2011) relabeled the strategy of openness as three separate strategies: self-disclosure, understanding, and relationships talks. The tactics of self-disclosure as maintenance include talking about fears and feelings and encouraging their partner to also share their thoughts and feelings.

While keeping lines of communication open is important for relational partners, what couples are communicating about can have differing impacts on the relationship.

iStock/Stephanie Verhart

Understanding involves behaviors that help to communicate understanding one's partner or a desire to try to understand one's partner better. This strategy includes tactics such as forgiving one's relational partner and apologizing when in the wrong (other ways to address relational transgressions are discussed in Chapter 12). Another understanding of maintenance behavior is to withhold judgment regarding a relational partners' behavior until you and your partner can discuss it.

Relationship talks are a specific type of openness. The relationship-talks strategy is when relational partners have discussions that are specifically about the quality of the relationship. Partners can use relationship talks to share their feelings about their relationship.

Relational assurances are another maintenance strategy related to openness. Whereas openness is more general talk about the relationship, assurances is more specifically related to confirming the importance of the relationship to the relational partners and affirming a commitment to maintaining the relationship in the future. Tactics that might support this relational strategy include making future plans, telling your partner how important they are to you, or buying an engagement ring. Talking with your partner about the future of the relationship helps create the "rhetorical vision" of what the relationship is and might be (Duck, 1994). The occurrence of conversation can be more important than the topics discussed (Duck et al., 1991).

Social networks involve connecting with each other's broader social networks. One specific tactic in the social networks strategy might include spending time with each other's friends and family (Canary & Stafford, 1992). Keeping in contact with the social network may also allow relational partners to use another tactic related to social networks—accessing social support. For example, romantic partners may rely on assistance and advice from their families (Stafford, 2011). Network support may be uniquely important for interracial couples. Women in interracial relationships with good network support may be more committed to their relationships (Brooks & Ogolsky, 2017). Low levels of family network support in interracial relationships can lead to strain and stress within a couple, but also mistrust and estrangement between family members (Brummett & Afifi, 2019). Conversely, when parents were supportive of the relationship, both the family and romantic couple experienced more positive outcomes.

Task-sharing occurs when relational partners help each other with daily tasks and share responsibilities. Specific tactics within the strategy of task-sharing might include spending time with a friend while they run their laundry at the laundromat, trading carpooling one's kids with a friend, or texting your romantic partner to coordinate the weekly grocery list. Task-sharing may look very different depending on the relationship context and phase. Dating couples might go to the laundromat together, while spouses could spend an evening together folding shirts while watching Netflix. Although task-sharing is clearly important for cohabitating relational partners (including platonic roommates), the tactics are useful for maintaining platonic relationships as well. Helping each other with tasks has been shown to be related to increased liking, closeness, and satisfaction in close friendships (McEwan & Guerrero, 2012).

SKILL BUILDER
RELATIONSHIP MAINTENANCE TACTICS

There are many different tactics that a relational partner can use to enact particular relational maintenance strategies. Consider the following tactics assembled by Stafford (2011). (See also Canary et al., 1993.) Which of these do you use with your romantic partner? Your friends? Also, consider—would your partner agree that you use these tactics? Relational maintenance behaviors that are enacted by one partner but not perceived by the other may not contribute to relational quality.

Positivity

____Acts positively with my partner.

____Am upbeat when we are together.

____Act cheerfully with my partner.

____Act optimistically when they are with me.

Understanding

____Am understanding.

____Am forgiving of my partner.

____Apologize when I am wrong.

____Do not judge my partner.

Self-Disclosure

____Talk about my fears with my partner.

____Am open about my feelings with my partner.

____Encourage my partner to share their thoughts with me.

____Encourage my partner to share their feelings with me.

Relationship Talks

____Discuss the quality of our relationship.

____Tell my partner how I feel about the relationship.

____Have talks about our relationship.

Assurances

____Talk about future events.

____Talk about our plans for the future.

____Tell them how much they mean to me.

____Show them how much they mean to me.

Tasks

____Share in the joint responsibilities that face us.

____Perform my household responsibilities.

____Help with the tasks that need to be done.

____Do not shirk from my duties.

Social Networks

____Include our friends in our activities.

____Do things with our friends.

____Spend time with our families.

____Ask a family member for help.

____Turn to a family member for advice.

Scholars have identified other behaviors beyond the main seven (positivity, understanding, self-disclosure, relationship talks, assurances, tasks, and social networks) that may help relational partners maintain their relationship. Some of these expansions are due to refining the way relational maintenance is measured or conceptualized (Dainton & Gross, 2008; Stafford, 2011). Other expansions are due to considering different types of relationships (McEwan & Guerrero, 2012; Oswald et al., 2004). Other additions to maintenance behaviors occurred as computer-mediated communication allowed for new possibilities in relational maintenance (Tong & Walther, 2011; Walther & Ramirez, 2010).

Humor refers to communicating with jokes and sarcasm (Canary et al., 1993) This type of banter might also include inside jokes, small talk, and light gossip (McEwan & Guerrero, 2012). **Routine contact** means making sure you stay in contact with a relational partner through both face-to-face visits and mediated channels (McEwan & Guerrero, 2012). **Joint activities** involve spending time with one another and engaging in social events and activities together (Canary et al., 1993). Co-workers might engage in joint activities by going to lunch with one another. A married couple might set aside time to binge-watch the latest Hulu release. Friends might sign up for a race together to connect over training and ensure that they will hang out together on race day. Communicating while playing video games online might also help friends maintain their relationships (Ledbetter & Kuzenkoff, 2012).

All relationships require maintenance. However, different types of relationships may be better served by different kinds of maintenance. For example, friendships are often maintained through shared interests and activities.

Gregory Costanzo/Photodisc via Getty Images

Not all maintenance strategies are positive behaviors. *Antisocial maintenance behaviors* are those which seem unfriendly or coercive (Canary et al., 1993). These antisocial behaviors have also been called **negative maintenance strategies** (Dainton & Gross, 2008). Negative maintenance strategies have been shown to be related to lower relational satisfaction, commitment, control mutuality, liking, and respect in romantic relationships (Dainton & Gross, 2008;

Goodboy et al., 2010). An example of a negative maintenance strategy is **jealousy induction,** which is an intentional strategy to make partners jealous. Jealousy induction may serve as a relational **secret test**, where partners attempt to determine the other partner's commitment to the relationship through indirect means (Baxter & Wilmot, 1984). Tactics might include flirting with others or commenting on the attractiveness of other potential partners (with the specific intention of making their romantic relational partner jealous) (Dainton & Gross, 2008). People may also express jealousy as a way of maintaining the relationship (Guerrero & Andersen, 1998). Jealousy induction may be perceived by those who use it as a maintenance strategy as a way to get their partner to see that they love them. Of course, jealousy induction may backfire if the induction doesn't make the partner jealous, perhaps indicating a lack of investment in the primary relationship, or if the strategy causes stress, conflict, or an increased perception of distrust within the relationship. Jealousy induction may be more likely to backfire than work as it has been shown to be negatively correlated with relational satisfaction (Dainton & Gross, 2008).

Going beyond the attempted induction of jealousy, some partners may also engage in **infidelity** as a way to maintain their current relationships. These relational partners may state that they have affairs or flirt with others as a way to stay satisfied or keep from getting bored with their current relationship (Dainton & Gross, 2008). Relational partners who use infidelity as a maintenance strategy report lower relational satisfaction (Dainton & Gross, 2008). However, it is unclear if the partners were unsatisfied before they engaged in infidelity or if the infidelity itself leads to lower satisfaction (see Chapter 12 for a broader discussion of infidelity).

Using **avoidance** as a relational maintenance strategy refers to avoiding bringing up topics that may cause stress or conflict within a relationship (Canary et al., 1993). People may try to use avoidance to maintain their relationships in order to prevent conversations and interactions that could be upsetting or lead to increased arguments (Dainton & Gross, 2008). Another example comes from research on cross-sex friendships. Heterosexual cross-sex friends may sometimes avoid discussing the state of their relationship in order to not introduce complications related to potential romance (Afifi & Burgoon, 1998).

Avoidance can also refer to avoiding the individual themselves. While this may sound like a strange way to maintain a relationship, remember that maintenance can be about keeping a relationship at a desired state. Perhaps you need to maintain a polite acquaintance with an aunt whose politics you disagree with for the sake of family peace. You might avoid situations where you would need to be alone with this aunt. When you must interact with her, then you avoid bringing up any political issues.

Another negative maintenance strategy is **surveillance** (Dainton & Gross, 2008). Tactics included in this strategy involve spying to make sure you know who is in contact with your partner, keeping tabs on their daily activity, or even engaging in interpersonal electronic surveillance where you check their phone messages or social media accounts (Dainton & Gross, 2008).

The final two negative maintenance strategies are related to control within a relationship (Dainton & Gross, 2008). **Destructive conflict** occurs when a relational partner engages in fights and arguments with their partner to try and control their partner's behavior (other types of conflict will be discussed in Chapter 10). **Allow control** is when someone breaks plans with friends and families or ceases engaging with other activities or responsibilities in order to spend more time with the partner and allow the partner more control over their daily life. Both destructive conflict and allowing control may technically maintain the relationship but these behaviors are associated with less relational satisfaction and can be markers of abusive relationships.

Snooping through a partner's cellphone might seem necessary in the moment, but it is indicative of low levels of trust and can cause harm to the overall relationship. Plus, the more you snoop, the more suspicious you are likely to get even if your suspicions are unwarranted.

iStock/urbazon

Negative maintenance strategies may be related to relational uncertainty. If partners are uncertain about the definition of their relationship (i.e., Are we dating? Is this an exclusive relationship? Do we have similar relational goals?), they were more likely to engage in maintenance tactics related to jealousy induction, spying, and destructive conflict (Dainton et al., 2017). Negative maintenance may be the result of romantic partners "mutually influencing each other to engage in questionable relational behavior because they had doubts about the relationship itself" (Dainton et al., 2017, p. 179).

Mediated Maintenance

In earlier research, relational maintenance researchers identified a maintenance strategy labeled *Cards, Letters, and Calls* (Canary et al., 1993). This strategy included tactics such as writing letters to friends or keeping in touch with family members via frequent phone calls. As time has progressed and the number of mediated channels has bloomed, people may use a variety of new media channels to communicate. In the late 1990s, Stafford and colleagues found that people used the newly emerging channel of email to help them maintain relationships with far-flung connections (Stafford et al., 1999). As new channels emerge, people integrate these channels into the way that they communicate relational maintenance.

Many maintenance behaviors are communicated through a variety of channels. For example, people can send positive, cheerful messages through Snapchat. Spouses can check in with each other about what to pick up at the grocery store (task-sharing) via text messages. Even communicating while playing online video games has been shown to increase friendship closeness (Ledbetter & Kuzenkoff, 2012). The number of channels that we use with a relational partner has been shown to be correlated with relational closeness (Ledbetter, 2009). This phenomenon is called **media multiplexity** (Haythornthwaite, 2005). We tend to use multiple, or a multiplex of, channels to communicate with close ties. Consider how you communicate with your best friend.

Perhaps you send them a quick text in the morning to ask their opinion on an outfit. While you wait for a class to start, you send your friend several silly Snapchats to maintain your streak. You send another text after class to confirm that you're meeting up later. You meet face-to-face for dinner. After you go home, you like your friend's Instagram post from the restaurant and put the picture they tagged you in on your Snapchat story. While this is a hypothetical scenario, it illustrates the way that we weave communication through multiple channels into our day. The communication through channels itself may help maintain the relationship, as it shows our friends that we care enough about them to think of them even when we are not physically present. However, the messages we share also carry other maintenance messages. Our silly snaps may serve as a form of positivity, and text messaging helps us coordinate dinner—a joint activity. Taking pictures together and posting them to Instagram helps us perform our relationship for the rest of our network.

Friends and other relational partners use many channels, including social media, to keep in touch with each other.

d3sign/Moment via Getty Images

Facebook and other social network sites have emerged as important sites for relational maintenance. Indeed, Walther and Ramirez (2010) argued that the "greatest social utility" of social network sites may be their function as ways to maintain relationships with large numbers of network ties. People use Facebook for relational assurances as well as two unique relational maintenance strategies: social contact and response-seeking (McEwan et al., 2014, 2018). **Social contact** maintenance behaviors involve using Facebook to reach out and interact with a friend or acquaintance. Specific behaviors might be posting on a friend's Facebook timeline, liking a status update, or coordinating future interactions. These behaviors generally are related to positive relational outcomes. The other Facebook relational maintenance strategy, **response-seeking**, involves posting updates hoping that network ties will respond or offer social support. Response-seeking behaviors may not lead to favorable outcomes. This may be because people may not respond to a response-seeking behavior, or it may be that using a social network site in hopes that a specific friend will respond may indicate a lower-quality friendship to begin with.

In some ways, Facebook and other social network sites can serve as a noninteractive way to maintain relationships. We can develop lists of "friends" or connections who simply remain present in the list until we find it useful to activate the connection. Some channels such as social network sites like Instagram and Facebook also make it more likely that friendships and acquaintanceships will be maintained indefinitely. Dindia (2003) argued that "once two people stop communicating (and do not anticipate future interaction) the relationship is over" (p. 1). If people then continue to be connected through a social network site like Twitter or LinkedIn, does the relationship continue indefinitely? In the past, relationships with friends with whom we did not actively maintain our friendship might have become dormant (Rawlins, 1992). Today, these connections may exist in perpetuity.

WHAT WOULD YOU DO?
IS CREEPING CREEPY?

Technology today provides relational partners with the means to perpetually keep in touch and maintain hundreds if not thousands of relationships that otherwise would have been difficult if not impossible to maintain. Social network sites are particularly useful for maintaining weak ties (Ellison et al., 2007). However, people use social network sites and other forms of social media as a way to maintain close relational ties as well (McEwan et al., 2018). One strategy that people use is surveillance or "creeping" (Fox et al., 2013).

Electronic surveillance can be functional. We can learn about a new dating partner's interests and preferences. We could see if a friend will be coming to our city soon. We can view photographs of adorable new family members. Social surveillance can be quite common among acquaintances and long-distance friends (Koban & Krüger, 2018). However, electronic interpersonal surveillance can also be much, much darker. Jealous ex-partners could follow their partner's weekend activities. New acquaintances could learn more about us than we would like to reveal. People can struggle to make sure that their online identity performances are appropriate for everyone who might view a particular post. It can be difficult to consider the full audience for our online communication.

Where do you draw the line? When does creeping someone's social media go too far? Is it okay to Google a potential partner before a date? If you learn information through electronic surveillance, do you tell your relational partner? Or do you wait for them to reveal that information through more interpersonal means? Would you feel the same if you were the target of the surveillance?

OUTCOMES OF RELATIONAL MAINTENANCE

People use relational maintenance behaviors to keep their relationships in existence. Many people would prefer to have an enjoyable, high-quality relationship. Maintenance behaviors can also help relational partners meet this goal. Engaging in relational maintenance behaviors has been associated with a variety of relational quality outcomes, including relational satisfaction, commitment, liking, control mutuality, and closeness (Canary & Stafford, 1994; McEwan et al., 2018).

Satisfaction

People experience **satisfaction** in relationships when the outcome of their relationship is equal to or exceeds what they perceive that they should be getting out of a relationship (Kelly & Thibaut, 1978; Thibaut & Kelley, 1959; see also Chapter 8). Consider Amy's relationship with her girlfriend, Stephanie. Stephanie treats Amy really well, is reasonably attractive, and is quite intelligent. If Amy expects that these qualities are what she can get out of a relationship, then she should be satisfied. However, let's say Stephanie is a freelance worker who experiences extended periods of unemployment. If Amy expects that she should have a partner with a steady job, she will be dissatisfied no matter how well Stephanie treats her. Low expectations can also influence satisfaction. If Amy comes to the relationship feeling that she's lucky just to have a relationship and can't believe that Stephanie would date her, then Amy might continue to feel satisfied even if Stephanie is careless of Amy's feelings.

Relational maintenance has been shown to be correlated with relational satisfaction in romantic relationships (Ogolsky & Bowers, 2013). In particular, positivity and relational assurances are strongly correlated with relational satisfaction. Openness, social networks, and task-sharing are moderately correlated with relational satisfaction. Interestingly, these correlations are stronger when study participants are reporting on their partner's perceived behavior rather than their own behavior. We may at times engage in maintenance behaviors that our partner simply does not notice or consider as maintenance. This result suggests that what we perceive is happening in our relationships may have a bigger effect than what is actually happening.

Commitment

Commitment reflects how much people wish to remain in their relationship in the future and how much energy they would expend to maintain the relationship (Parks, 2007; Parks & Adelman, 1983; Rusbult et al., 1998). Thus, commitment and maintenance behaviors are tightly intertwined, given that the choice to maintain a relationship implies a commitment to that relationship. In the investment model, commitment is a combination of how satisfied partners are, how invested they are, and the quality of alternatives they have (Rusbult 1980, 1983). The investment model draws from the social exchange perspective, which argues that how committed we are to a relationship may depend on our perception of relational alternatives (Thibaut & Kelley, 1959). Let's consider our example of Amy and Stephanie again. Amy may find her relationship to be very satisfying, but if she thinks that she can have a relationship with Courtney that will be even more satisfying, she may very well leave Stephanie for Courtney. Of course, our investments also matter to commitment. If Amy and Stephanie have invested several years into their relationship, own a home together, and started a family, Amy may be unwilling to leave these investments behind, as a relationship with Courtney would be unable to include these co-investments.

In relationships where there is little expectation of exclusivity, such as friendships, the quality of alternatives may not be related to commitment (Allen et al., 2012). People wouldn't become less committed to a casual friend because they also had other casual friends. However, people do experience some tension in managing multiple relationships even without the expectation of exclusivity. For example, someone might engage in less maintenance with their best friend when they are beginning a new romantic relationship. Ignore your best friend for long enough, and they might get the message that you are no longer interested in maintaining the friendship.

For romantic couples, assurances are strongly correlated with commitment (Ogolsky & Bowers, 2013). The connection between assurances and commitment makes sense given that relational assurances include discussions of how committed you are to your partner. In romantic couples, positivity, openness, social networks, and task-sharing are moderately correlated with commitment in romantic couples (Ogolsky & Bowers, 2013). Performing these relational maintenance behaviors may be how people show their relational partners that they are committed to the relationship. There is also evidence that people reduce their efforts at relational maintenance when they begin to disengage from a relationship (Guerrero et al., 1993).

In addition to the investment model variables, researchers have also used the relational maintenance framework to predict other relational quality indicators such as liking, control mutuality, and trust.

I DIDN'T KNOW THAT!
WE NEED TO TALK

In almost any relational advice article you'll find admonitions to just "talk to your partner" and "improve your communication." Sometimes it seems that simply communicating is a panacea for almost every relational woe. We agree that keeping the lines of communication open is important for maintaining relational quality. In addition, research on relational decline has found that *circumscribing* or declaring certain communication topics off-limits can signal the beginning of the end of a relationship (Gottman, 1994). And yet, the phrase "We need to talk" has struck dread in the heart of many a relational partner. Just being "open" with one's partner may not have the universally positive effect that pop psychologists might have us believe.

The original category of openness measured how much one talks and listens to one's partner. This category has been shown to be negatively associated with how much spouses want to be committed to the relationship (personal commitment) and how much they think they should be committed to the relationship (moral commitment) (Ramirez, 2008). In terms of mediated communication, McEwan and Horn (2016) found that engaging in maintenance via text messaging was generally associated with increased relational satisfaction but when people used text messaging to keep tabs on their partner and keep the lines of communication open throughout the day, this behavior was associated with decreased relational satisfaction.

More communication isn't always better. Couples who are extremely "open" may be engaging in copious amounts of communication due to conflict, trust issues, or other relational concerns. Instead of just being open, the type and quality of communication may matter. Discussing the relationship (relational talk), relational assurances, and seeking to understand the partner may be behaviors that involve openness directed toward specific relational goals (Stafford, 2011). Behaviors designed to meet these specific goals may be more likely to have a positive impact on relational quality than simply making time to talk with one's partner.

Liking

Liking someone means experiencing positive affect or feeling when thinking of that person (Veksler & Eden, 2017). In addition, to like someone usually means that we are receptive to having potential future interactions with that person . We can experience liking in many different types of relationships and scholars have generally differentiated between feelings of love and liking (Rubin, 1970; Sternberg, 1987). In romantic relationships, the relational maintenance behaviors of positivity, openness, assurances, social networks, and task-sharing are strongly correlated with liking (Dainton et al., 1994; Ogolsky & Bowers, 2013). The connection between liking and maintenance may be particularly important in friendships (Fehr, 2000). The use of positivity and liking is correlated in friendships (McEwan & Guerrero, 2012). In casual friendships, engaging in banter and hanging out with a common social network is associated with greater liking (McEwan & Guerrero, 2012). Using social media to maintain one's friendship may also be associated with greater liking (McEwan, 2013; McEwan et al., 2018).

Sharing even simple tasks, like making dinner together, can foster a sense of teamwork and control mutuality.

iStock/Ridofranz

Control Mutuality

Control mutuality refers to how much relational partners share in relational decision-making (Canary et al., 1991). Control mutuality does not necessarily mean that partners have equal influence regarding decisions but instead that they agree on who does make the decisions (Stafford & Canary, 1991). For example, if Gianni and Natasha agree that Natasha will choose what is for dinner because she makes most of the meals, this would be high-control mutuality. Or if Gianni and Natasha decide together to rotate who makes dinner each night and agree that whoever is cooking decides on the meal choice, this would also represent high-control mutuality. On the other hand, if Gianni always makes the decision about what is for dinner and Natasha is frustrated because she would like to choose what is for dinner sometimes, then this would be a low level of control mutuality. Romantic relationships where couples make decisions together and share agreement on relational goals are more satisfying than those that experience unilateral influence where one partner controls more of the relational outcomes (Canary & Stafford, 1994).

Control mutuality is strongly correlated with positivity, openness, task-sharing, and assurances and moderately correlated with social networks (Ogolsky & Bowers, 2013). Maintenance researchers have predicted that relational partners with high levels of control mutuality are more likely to engage in relational maintenance because they are generally more attuned to the need to communicate within and about the relationship (Canary & Stafford, 1992, 1993; Canary et al., 2002; Stafford & Canary, 1991).

Closeness

Aron and colleagues have argued that our perception of how close we are to another person is a function of feeling that aspects of another person are partially our own (Aron & Aron, 1996; Aron et al., 1992). Thus, **closeness** requires both having knowledge about another person and perceiving similarities in our lives and interests. For example, friends might become closer through sharing a hobby. Members of a romantic couple may take on each other's interests as they grow closer or find themselves sharing similar goals as they move through life together. Relational partners may learn about each other through self-disclosure, as discussed in Chapter 8. This conceptualization of closeness is called self-expansion theory. The idea is that as we meet others, our self expands to take on aspects of their selves and we grow closer as this happens. Indeed, breaking up with a romantic partner can feel particularly difficult because people often feel as if a part of their self has been lost after the breakup—the part that they had expanded due to the relationship in the first place (Lewandowski et al., 2006).

Relational maintenance strategies do appear to be related to increased feelings of closeness, or inclusion of others into the self. Ledbetter et al. (2013) found moderate relationships between maintenance strategies (positivity, openness, assurances, networks, and task-sharing) and closeness. The use of electronic tie-signs as maintenance, such as tagging a romantic partner in Facebook photos, has also been shown to be related to greater inclusion of the other into the self (Carpenter & Spottswood, 2013). Positivity and closeness are also linked in friendships, and people generally report using more maintenance strategies with close versus casual friends (McEwan & Guerrero, 2012).

DIFFERENT MAINTENANCE STRATEGIES IN DIFFERENT RELATIONSHIPS

Up until this point in the chapter, we have been discussing the maintenance of romantic relationships with some consideration of friendship. However, all relationships require some type of maintenance (Canary & Stafford, 1993, 1994). Indeed, people maintain a wide variety of relationships (Burleson & Samter, 1994; Dindia et al., 2003). However, maintenance may vary by relational context. People may use different maintenance strategies in different contexts (Canary et al., 1993). The effects of maintenance within a relationship may also vary by relational type.

Friendship Maintenance

Some scholars have defined friendship as a self-maintaining relationship (Fehr, 1996; Rose, 1985; Rose & Serafica, 1986). While friendships may require less active maintenance than romantic relationships like all relationships, friendships require some level of maintenance (Canary et al., 1993; Duck, 1994). Friendships may use different amounts of maintenance communication depending on the level of closeness of the relationship (McEwan & Guerrero, 2012; Oswald et al., 2004).

With your best friends, you may share tasks and social networks and more frequently engage in positivity and talks about the importance of your friendship (McEwan & Guerrero, 2012). With a very weak tie such as a casual acquaintance, simply having them linked to you on a social network site may be enough communication to maintain that relationship at the desired level (Bryant & Marmo, 2010). Using social network tactics is linked to greater liking, closeness, and satisfaction in casual friendships (McEwan & Guerrero, 2012). Regardless, maintenance is important for both new and established friendships (Blieszner & Adams, 1992;McEwan & Guerrero, 2012; Oswald & Clark, 2006).

Friends may also use different maintenance strategies than romantic partners. For example, the strategy of routine contact may not provide much maintenance for cohabiting romantic partners. For friends though, routine contact is correlated with increased liking, closeness, and satisfaction in both close and casual friendships (McEwan & Guerrero, 2012). Routine contact is also associated with perceiving greater rewards and investments in friendship (Oswald et al., 2004). Banter is also important for friendships (McEwan & Guerrero, 2012). Another important strategy for friendships may be keeping in touch with the broader social network. The maintenance of the overall network may allow for broader connections with casual friends and acquaintances.

Other friendships that might experience relational maintenance differently include cross-sex friendships and long-distance friendships. Over 80 percent of adults have had a close cross-sex friend (Halatsis & Christakis, 2009). However, cross-sex friends may manage the closeness of their friendships in order to avoid various challenges to the cross-sex friendship, such as the audience challenge where cross-sex friends are viewed by others as potential romantic partners (Monsour et al., 1997). Cross-sex friends who are uncertain about whether they want their friendship to turn romantic (especially if they think their partner does) are less likely to use positive maintenance strategies (Guerrero & Chavez, 2005). In addition, cross-sex friends may increase their use of relational maintenance if they are attempting to transition their friendship to a romantic relationship (Guerrero & Chavez, 2005).

Geographically close friends may use more maintenance behaviors, particularly joint activity and social networks, than long-distance friends (Johnson, 2001). However, long-distance friendships also require maintenance. Research has shown that long-distance friends that engage in openness and relational assurances have friendships that are similar in satisfaction and closeness to geographically close friends (Johnson, 2001). Maintenance through mediated channels such as social network sites, messaging apps, and texting may be particularly useful for long-distance friends. Indeed, social network sites allow us to maintain more friendships and acquaintanceships than ever before (McEwan, 2015).

Familial Relational Maintenance

Family relationships are typically thought of as the most involuntary relationship. After all, you can't pick your family, right? For those of you with siblings, how many times were you told, "You don't have to like them, but you do have to love them"? But family relationships also require maintenance behaviors in order to maintain the quality of the relationship and access to social support. Relatives use assurances, sharing tasks, and mediated forms of communication to maintain the status of their relationships (Canary et al., 1993). Once family members reach adulthood, maintaining the relationship requires a choice (albeit sometimes a fairly passive choice) to do so (Goodboy et al., 2009). Generally, engaging in relational maintenance behaviors is positively associated with family satisfaction (Serewicz et al., 2007), but some differences may be evident in different types of family relationships.

Young adults engage in maintenance to sustain their adult sibling relationships. In the case of siblings, people may also use maintenance strategies to complement the involuntary nature of the relationship. Mikkelson et al. (2011) found that genetically related siblings (twins, full siblings, and half-siblings) use more maintenance strategies as adults than stepsiblings and adopted siblings. Siblings report a variety of reasons for maintaining the sibling relationship (Myers, 2011; Myers et al. 2008). These reasons can be structural (we are family, we live close to each other), instrumental (we provide each other with support, we share similar or common interests and experiences), and relational (we are friends, I love my sibling, we are relationally close).

Like other relationships, siblings use positivity, openness, networks, task-sharing, and assurances to maintain their relationships. Siblings may use the task-sharing maintenance behavior most frequently (Myers et al., 2001). Affectionate communication can also serve as an important way to maintain sibling relationships (Myers et al., 2011). Relational maintenance between siblings has been connected to higher relational quality outcomes. For example, liking between siblings is related to the use of positivity, networks, and tasks (Myers et al., 2001).

Emerging adults use a variety of relational maintenance strategies with their parents, including networks, assurances, positivity, and task-sharing (Myers & Glover, 2007). Use of maintenance strategies with parents has been shown to be related to perceived commitment, trust, and control mutuality (Myers & Glover, 2007). For college students, engaging in regular communication and assurances with their parents may help lessen daily stress and feelings of loneliness (Burke et al., 2016).

The amount of emotional support grandchildren perceive as available from their grandparents is correlated with grandchildren's use of relational maintenance behaviors. Openness, networks, and assurances are positively associated with grandparents providing emotional support. Openness and networks are also related to communication satisfaction between grandparents and grandchildren (Mansson et al., 2010).

Affection may also be important in maintaining grandparent relationships, as greater affection on the part of grandparents may lead to greater trust and engagement in relational maintenance on the part of young adult grandchildren. Grandparents from different cultures may express their affection differently. In the United States, white grandparents might engage in more celebratory affection specifically focusing on birthdays and holidays and Latinx grandparents might engage in more memories and humor. However, grandparents are likely making the choices that fit best for their culture. For example, while celebratory affection was related to more closeness between white grandparent/child dyads, it was not related to closeness for Latinx or Asian American grandparent/child dyads (Bernhold & Giles, 2018).

In some cultures, sharing memories is an especially important maintenance behavior for families.

Jose Luis Pelaez Inc/DigitalVision via Getty Images

Grandchildren report feeling stronger emotional ties to grandparents who live geographically closer than those who live farther away (Folwell & Grant, 2006). This effect of proximity may be due to geographically close grandparent/grandchild dyads having more opportunity to engage in relational maintenance behaviors, as grandchildren also report feeling closer to grandparents who are regularly involved in their lives (Holladay et al., 1998).

LGBTQIA Relational Maintenance

Fundamentally, relational maintenance is about co-constructing and maintaining a shared definition of the relationship between the relationship partners. In many ways, romantic relationships function in similar ways regardless of the makeup of the gender identity or sexual orientation of the relational partners. Thus, many couples with one or more partners who identify as LGBTQIA use relational maintenance strategies that are found across romantic relationships (Haas & Stafford, 2005). For example, positivity is a relational maintenance strategy that is identified as important in gay, lesbian, and straight couples, romantic couples with transgender or cisgender partners, and even platonic friendships (Alegría, 2010;Canary et al., 1993; Haas & Stafford, 2005).

And yet, LGBTQIA relationships may experience additional challenges due to the need to negotiate gender roles within their relationship (Goldberg, 2013; Kurdek, 1993) as well as perceived stress and stigma due to historic marginalization of their identity and relationships. **Minority stress theory** articulates that couples in marginalized relationships may experience additional stress and stigma (Meyer, 2003). This experience has been linked to suboptimal relational outcomes such as decreased intimacy, passion, and satisfaction (Doyle & Molix, 2015). Relational maintenance strategies then take on an important role in helping LGBTQIA couples maintain satisfying and committed relationships (Ogolsky et al., 2017). For transgender individuals, in particular, higher levels of commitment can be associated with reduced anxiety and depression (Gamarel et al., 2019).

Relational talk is one maintenance behavior that is important for all romantic relationships but may be especially significant for LGBTQIA couples. Same-sex couples may engage in more relational talk than heterosexual couples (Haas & Stafford, 2005; Riggle et al., 2016). The need for additional relational talk may be necessary in same-sex couples as they negotiate their own norms and relational rules. (Meir et al., 2013).

Couples where one member is transgender also report the importance of relational talk as they renegotiate their gendered and relational identities (Alegría, 2010). In many cases, couples experiencing a transitioning partner may choose not to maintain the relationship. For couples with a transitioning or transitioned partner that do intend to maintain their romantic relationship, communication surrounding both partners' feelings, experiences, and desires is key to maintaining the relationship (Platt & Bolland, 2018).

Similarly, social network support is associated with increased commitment and relational quality across romantic relationships (Ogolsky & Bowers, 2013). However, LGBTQIA couples may find themselves not just drawing on support for their relationship from their network but also needing to engage in behaviors that help them *develop* a supportive network. Choosing to interact in LGBTQIA supportive environments is an important maintenance strategy for gay and lesbian couples (Haas & Stafford, 1998). Couples with at least one transgender partner also report the importance of building supportive networks, particularly if they experience rejection from pre-transition network members (Alegría, 2010). Queer families, although sometimes modeled as nuclear two-parent families, are configured in far more heterogeneous ways than most heterosexual-headed families (Moore & Stambolis-Ruhstorfer, 2013; Vacarro, 2010). For heterosexual couples, some of the work of relational maintenance is simplified by following societal norms and relational rules not necessarily accessible to or chosen by LGBTQIA relational partners. Access to a supportive environment could help families negotiate and navigate creative relational and familial constructions.

Same-sex couples tend to share tasks equitably and to engage in household chores and childcare together.

iStock/xavierarnau

Finally, sharing tasks is an important part of relational maintenance for many couples, but it may look different in LGBTQIA relationships compared to heterosexual relationships. Studies have shown that gay and lesbian couples tend to share household tasks and childcare more equitably than straight couples (Goldberg et al., 2012; Patterson et al., 2004). One reason for this might be that same-sex couples do not feel tied to gender roles about which tasks are feminine or masculine, so they create what works best for them and their families. Same-sex couples are also more likely to do tasks together. For example, some research indicates that a lesbian couple is likely to cook and do the dishes together, whereas in a heterosexual couple one partner is likely to cook and the other partner is likely to do the dishes. Working together as a team to share tasks and childcare may then be an especially important form of bonding for same-sex couples. When household and childcare tasks are compartmentalized, same-sex couples feel freer to divide labor based on who is better at a particular task or likes it more instead of relying on gender norms to dictate who does which task (Goldberg, 2013). In many ways, same-sex couples provide a model of how to share tasks in collaborative and creative ways.

PRINCIPLES FOR MAINTAINING QUALITY RELATIONSHIPS

To keep the people who are important to us in our lives, we have to maintain those relationships. As described in this chapter, communication scholars have identified several behaviors that help people maintain their interpersonal relationships. These behaviors can also help strengthen relationships or even increase the quality of our relationships. The following principles outline how relational maintenance functions across a variety of interpersonal relationships.

Principle 1. All relationships require maintenance.

Stafford and Canary (1991) specifically state that "all relationships require maintenance or else they deteriorate" (p. 7; see also Canary & Stafford, 1993, 1994; Dindia, 2003). First, if relational partners do not engage in behaviors that maintain the relationship, the relationship will likely experience a reduction in quality and eventually cease to be. Second, scholars have shown the existence of relational maintenance behaviors in many different types of relationships. Dating couples in escalating and stable relationships use more maintenance behaviors than those in de-escalating relationships (Guerrero et al., 1993). Other scholars have shown that friendships also require relational maintenance (McEwan & Guerrero, 2012; Oswald et al., 2004; Rose, 1985) Relationships in the workplace also need and are improved by the use of maintenance behavior (Waldron, 1991). Even family relationships, despite often being perceived as involuntary relationships, require maintenance (Canary et al., 1993; Myers et al., 2001).

Principle 2. Maintenance activities may vary according to the development and type of the relationship.

Maintenance strategies may vary depending on how developed and close the relationship becomes. In romantic relationships, people may use more maintenance strategies in more developed relationships (Stafford & Canary, 1991). Close friends report using more maintenance strategies than casual friends (McEwan & Guerrero, 2012).

Maintenance strategies also vary between relational types (Canary et al., 1993). Family members may invoke different strategies than do friends who use different strategies than married couples. In addition, specific tactics within the general strategies may vary from relationship to relationship. For example, both a dating couple and a married couple may rate themselves highly on task-sharing, yet the dating couple may be considering helping each other with building IKEA furniture and the married couple may be considering sharing their children's nighttime routine. Assurances for friends may consist of telling a friend you value their friendship, whereas assurances for an engaged couple may be related to planning their future wedding.

Principle 3. Prosocial maintenance behaviors both keep relationships in existence and generally increase the quality of the relationship.

As noted at the beginning of the chapter, one function of maintenance strategies is to keep a relationship in existence. However, we generally wouldn't be satisfied with having relationships that exist but are low quality or latent. Many maintenance researchers have studied not only how maintenance behaviors keep relationships continuing, but the effect that perceived and actual maintenance behaviors have on the quality of relationships. In general, prosocial relational maintenance choices such as positivity, joint activities, and assurances have positive effects on relational satisfaction, liking, trust, control mutuality, and other important qualities of relationships (Ogolsky & Bowers, 2013). Negative maintenance strategies, on the other hand, are related to low levels of satisfaction and trust, perhaps because they are used when people are feeling uncertain about their relationships or their partner's feelings for them.

CONCLUSION

Together Candace and her mom make a very good point: it is both our everyday routine behaviors and strategic communication choices that help us to maintain our relationships. We spend more of our interpersonal communication maintaining relationships than we do starting or ending them. In addition, maintenance is important to all of our relationships—romantic, familial, friendships, and even acquaintanceships. The choices we make regarding how we maintain our relationships can help us keep our relationships at desired levels of satisfaction, closeness, and commitment that are specific to each relationship.

CHAPTER 9 STUDY GUIDE

KEY TERMS

Identify and explain the meaning of each of the following key terms.

allow control
avoidance
behavioral tactics
closeness
commitment
communication strategies
control mutuality
destructive conflict
equity
humor
infidelity as maintenance
jealousy induction
joint activities
liking
maintenance strategies
media multiplexity
metacommunication
minority stress theory
multiphasic

negative maintenance strategies
openness
positivity
relational assurances
relational maintenance
relationship talks
response-seeking
routine contact
routine maintenance behaviors
satisfaction
secret tests
social contact
social exchange theory
social networks
strategic maintenance behaviors
surveillance
task-sharing
understanding

REFLECTION QUESTIONS

1. Although there are many maintenance strategies and associated behaviors listed in this chapter, there are certainly many more behaviors that might help people maintain their relationships. Can you think of behaviors not listed in the chapter? Do these behaviors fall under one of the listed strategies or constitute an entirely different strategy? What is the goal of that behavior?

2. The advent of social media has brought about new channels that people can use to maintain their social relationships. In what ways has social media helped people improve the quality of their social relationships? In what ways has social media harmed social relationships? Does social media have a different effect on relational maintenance depending on the type of relationships?

3. The chapter covers several negative relational maintenance behaviors. Are these behaviors ever appropriate? What relational goals might these behaviors help people achieve? What might be some reasons that people wish to keep certain connections at a desired distance?

4. Sometimes maintenance strategies are described as doing the work of the relationship. Yet some strategies like positivity, humor, and joint activities appear to be their own reward. Do you find maintenance strategies to be a chore of your relationships or are they part of the joy of connecting with others? Why?

10 MANAGING CONFLICT COMMUNICATION

WHAT YOU'LL LEARN...

When you have finished the chapter, you should be able to do the following:

10.1 Describe what conflict is and is not.

10.2 Describe and distinguish among the different styles of conflict.

10.3 Discuss common patterns of conflict communication that are destructive.

10.4 Explain the behaviors people can use to manage conflict constructively, as well as why it can be challenging to engage in constructive communication during conflict.

Ethan and Leo have known each other since high school. They both ran track and hung out with the same close group of guy friends. When they both got scholarship offers to the same university, they were excited about being roommates and continuing as teammates during their collegiate careers. However, the first semester of college did not go as smoothly as either of them had hoped. Previously, Ethan and Leo never fought. But now it seems like they are always at each other's throats about something, whether it is Ethan complaining that Leo never picks up after himself or Leo upset that Ethan's girlfriend, Adelyn, is always "in his way" in their small dorm room. To make matters worse, since track season has begun, the two young men have started to find themselves competing against each other on the field. They once ran together on their high school relay team, but now they are both vying for a position on their talented college squad. If one of them secures a position and the other does not, both Ethan and Leo worry that it will make it even harder to live with each other.

Conflict is an inevitable part of close relationships. Being emotionally close and spending a lot of time together make it particularly likely that conflicts will arise between people. Having conflict is not necessarily problematic. Conflict can help people solve issues and improve their interactions with each other. Think about being upset with a co-worker who always takes sole credit for work you did together. If you never confronted the co-worker, the situation would probably never change. You would likely harbor continued frustration that could eventually affect your performance and satisfaction at work. The same is true for Leo and Ethan. They have issues that must be managed if they want to be happy being roommates, teammates, and, most importantly, best friends.

This chapter examines how people engage in conflict. We start by defining what conflict is and is not, followed by a discussion of common conflict styles people use when they disagree or have a problem to solve. Next, we discuss several common patterns of conflict interaction that can make the situation either worse or better. As you read through this chapter, keep in mind that having conflict is normal and even healthy. How people handle conflict is what matters more.

WHAT CONFLICT IS AND IS NOT

If you stopped people on the street and asked them to define the term "conflict," you would likely receive many different responses. Some people would equate conflict with fighting, aggression, arguing, or yelling. Others would think of countries that are in conflict or at war with each other, or people who are locked in some type of battle or holding grudges against one another. According to scholars, however, these definitions of conflict are on the extreme end since not all conflict involves aggression or even protracted engagement. Instead, communication researchers commonly describe **interpersonal conflict** as "an expressed struggle between at least two interdependent parties who perceive incompatible goals, scarce resources, and interference from others in achieving their goals" (Hocker & Wilmot, 2018, p. 9).

Conflict as an Expressed Struggle

Let's take a closer look at each part of this definition. First, interpersonal conflict involves an expressed struggle. This means that interpersonal conflict requires some level of joint communication between the people involved. Some conflict stays at the intrapersonal or perceptual level. For example, Leo might do little things that bother Ethan, but Ethan might decide they are not worth bringing up and arguing about. However, once Ethan starts to express those feelings—either directly or indirectly—and Leo notices, conflict has been expressed. Ethan might confront Leo or perhaps just act a little differently than usual around him. He could get quiet around Leo or look unhappy. In any case, the idea is that conflict requires some level of communication.

In their book on interpersonal conflict, Hocker and Wilmot (2018) describe three key ways communication and interpersonal conflict are related. First, *communication can create conflict*. This can range from everyday behaviors, such as letting the dirty dishes stack up in the sink, to more purposeful communication, such as saying something critical to hurt someone's feelings. In fact, words or behaviors are usually what trigger conflict. Second, *communication reflects conflict*. When people are dealing with conflict, the struggle they are experiencing is often either subtly or obviously evident in their communication. They might appear annoyed, agitated, or avoidant, among many other possibilities. Finally, *communication is the means by which people manage conflict productively or destructively*. This is a key point emphasized by many communication researchers. Indeed, what is most important is usually not the conflict itself, but how the conflict is handled. Some conflicts go unresolved and fester within relationships. Others lead to breakups. Yet sometimes conflict is managed constructively so that relationships not only survive but even improve and thrive. In fact, in various countries, including the Netherlands, Turkey, and Portugal, engaging in interpersonal arguments is perceived as useful, enjoyable, and even playful (Hample & Demir, 2019; Labrie et al., 2020; Lewiński et al., 2018). Later in this chapter, you will learn about different styles and patterns of conflict communication that tend to be more productive or destructive.

Conflict Is Between Interdependent People

Interdependence is the degree to which people are connected to each other in meaningful ways. When people have a high degree of interdependence, their thoughts, feelings, and actions influence and are influenced by each other. Some level of interdependence is necessary for conflict to occur. Interdependence can occur between strangers, such as a customer who wishes to return an item to a store and a manager who decides whether to issue a refund. However, most conflict occurs between people who are interdependent in more significant ways. For example, because Leo and Ethan have a close bond, it is uncomfortable for them to be put in a position where they are rivals. In addition, Ethan might feel caught between Leo and Adelyn when Adelyn wants to relax at his place but Leo needs his space. These circumstances set the stage for conflict. When people are independent from one another rather than interdependent, they usually do not care if they disagree about something.

Goals and Resources

The last part of the definition of interpersonal conflict focuses on how conflict is linked to goals and resources. Conflict occurs when two or more people perceive their goals to be incompatible. In other words, the goals they have are in opposition to one another. This incompatibility can lead to the perception that other people are interfering with one's goals. Ethan and Leo provide an example of this. Ethan likes to keep his room clean and wants to be able to have Adelyn over whenever he wants. Leo, on the other hand, wants the freedom to clean up after himself on his timetable; a little mess does not bother him so he'd rather clean in spurts. He also wants time alone and gets annoyed when Adelyn is over too much. Notice that their goals are incompatible—keeping the room clean versus cleaning periodically and Adelyn being present or not. They are also both interfering in the other's goals. The room will not stay clean the way Ethan likes it if Leo does not pick up after himself, and Leo will not have the privacy he needs if Adelyn is in their room all the time. Incompatibility and interference are also key features of the competitiveness they are experiencing as new members of their university's track team. There is only one spot on the relay team; they both want it, but only one of them can get it.

Even conflict between children is around resources, ranging from concrete resources such as toys to abstract resources such as love and attention from parents.

iStock/stefanamer

Notice that these conflicts all revolve around resources that the two roommates consider scarce and valuable—feeling pride about the appearance of one's room, having the freedom to clean when one wants, having enough privacy and personal space, being able to spend time with one's girlfriend, and securing a spot on the relay team. Within relationships, **resources** can include a wide range of tangible or intangible things, including money, time, effort, love, and status. Valued resources are usually at the core of even seemingly mundane conflicts. If Leo gets upset that Ethan ate the candy he left on top of the microwave, the conflict is not just about candy but also about ownership and having control of one's possessions.

CONFLICT STYLES

For decades, communication researchers have worked to develop a list of common conflict styles. A **conflict style** represents the predominant or most likely way a person communicates during conflict (Thomas, 2006). As such, conflict styles reflect a person's baseline tendency to act and react in a certain manner during conflict situations in general. However, conflict styles can change based on both the interaction and the person or people involved. For example, Ethan may engage in a calmer conflict style with Leo than Adelyn because his disagreements with her are more emotionally charged. People can also shift conflict styles during an interaction. One person may try to compromise but end up frustrated and withdraw, or a person might start out angry and aggressive but then mellow out after venting. As you will learn later in this chapter, in close relationships, conflict styles sometimes become habitual, especially if the same conflicts are repeated and partners start to fall into patterns.

Psychologists, business scholars, and communication researchers have all tried to identify the most common conflict styles (e.g., Pruitt, 1983; Putnam & Wilson, 1982; Rahim, 1983; Sillars et al., 2004; Van de Vliert, 1997). Although the number of conflict styles in these various systems ranges from three to six, two dimensions are at the heart of every system: how *cooperative* versus *competitive*, and how direct versus indirect, each style is. When people are cooperative, they focus on meeting the needs of both people; when they are competitive, they focus on fulfilling their own needs. When people are direct, they engage in the conflict in a straightforward manner that can be either assertive or aggressive. When people are indirect, they avoid direct verbal confrontation and communicate in a passive or passive-aggressive manner, if they communicate at all.

When these two dimensions are crossed, six distinct conflict styles emerge (Guerrero, 2020; La Valley & Guerrero, 2012; Van de Vliert, 1997). As shown in Figure 10.1, three styles are direct and three are indirect, two styles are competitive, two are cooperative, and two are in the middle.

FIGURE 10.1 ■ Conflict Styles		
Direct	Competitive Fighting	Compromising	Collaborating
Indirect	Indirect Fighting	Avoiding	Yielding

Uncooperative ←————————————————————→ Cooperative

Competitive Fighting

Almost all systems include a style that is competitive and direct. This style, labeled **competitive fighting** in Figure 10.1, has also been called competing, dominating, and direct fighting, among other names. As these names suggest, this style is all about winning. It has been called a "win-lose" strategy because the person wants to win, even if it is at the expense of the other person. Competitive fighting is very common, especially in cultures like the United States where people are taught to value their individuality, personal rights, and goals. People strive to be "winners" and prove they are right. It can be easy to be drawn into competitive fighting.

The competitive fighting style usually leads to negative outcomes, especially in the long term. People who use this style tend to be viewed as incompetent communicators and are more likely to have unhappy relationships than are people who use more cooperative conflict styles (Canary & Spitzberg, 1987, 1989, 1990; Gross & Guerrero, 2000; Sillars, 1980). Sometimes competitive fighting appears to work in the short term. People might feel intimidated and give in to the competitive person, or some legitimate points may be embedded within the attacks, leading the competitive person to "win" the argument. The problem, of course, is that the other person will feel mistreated, setting up either an adversarial relationship or one with an unequal balance of power. Although some of the behaviors used with this style, such as personal insults and name-calling, are almost always inappropriate, some level of competitive fighting is necessary in some situations. For example, an attorney may need to get aggressive with a witness or a mom might need to use accusations and threats to manage a rebellious son. But even in these situations, there is a fine line. Too much aggressiveness could backfire by making the witness or the teen look sympathetic. Ethan and Leo provide another good example. Leo might pick his dirty socks off the floor and put his dishes in the sink after Ethan yells and calls him a slob, but Leo would likely resent being talked to that way.

Indirect Fighting

The other style that is highly competitive is **indirect fighting**, which has also been called passive aggression. This style communicates hostility in an indirect fashion (Guerrero, 2020). Rather than using words to insult the partner or communicate negative emotion, people using the indirect fighting style will engage in behaviors such as rolling their eyes, giving someone the silent treatment, or pulling away. As with competitive fighting, indirect fighting is usually intended as a "win-lose" strategy, but instead of directly confronting the partner to win the argument, the person resorts to passive-aggressive means such as giving the cold shoulder or withholding affection. Such strategies are typically used to show a person's displeasure or anger and to try and punish the partner. However, as with competitive fighting, the indirect fighting style usually produces a lose-lose situation in the end.

In fact, in some ways, the indirect fighting style is even more uncooperative than competitive fighting. At least with competitive fighting the two parties are talking and expressing feelings directly. With indirect fighting, communication is indirect and sometimes ambiguous but also hostile, leaving people with fewer options for talking through the problem and feeling good about the situation. Imagine that instead of talking about their grievances with each other, Ethan and Leo communicate their displeasure through passive-aggressive means. When Leo leaves his dirty clothes around their dorm room, perhaps Ethan picks them up and hides them so Leo cannot find them. And perhaps Leo gives both Adelyn and Ethan the cold shoulder when he feels that they are invading his space. These types of strategies vent frustration, but only in indirect ways that do not work toward solving the underlying issues causing the conflict.

Indirect fighting, which includes behaviors such as rolling your eyes or giving someone the silent treatment, tends to escalate negativity during conflict.

iStock/izusek

Compromising

The **compromising** style is moderately cooperative and moderately direct. This style occurs when people make concessions to each other so both parties give up something to get some of what they want. The style is only moderately cooperative because of the give and take involved. Both parties are looking out for their own interests but giving in when they believe they either have to or would gain something from doing so. That is why the compromising style is sometimes thought of as a part-win, part-lose strategy. This style is moderately direct because when people compromise, they are usually selective in what they express so as to try and gain the upper hand in the situation. For example, you might not tell the other party everything you would be willing to give up, just like a good poker player does not reveal their hand too early.

Trading off, meeting the partner halfway, and exchanging resources are three common ways to compromise. Trading off involves taking turns. For example, one way that Ethan and Leo could manage the problem of Adelyn being in their dorm room so much would be to trade off nights. Some nights could be specified as Adelyn free, whereas Leo would welcome her other nights. Similarly, if two people disagree about what movie to go see, they might decide that one person gets to choose this time, but the other person gets to choose next time. Meeting the partner halfway involves reaching a position that is somewhere in the middle from where they started. So, they might strike a cleaning agreement that involves Leo picking up after himself a little more often and Ethan trying not to stress out about clutter as much. Another negotiation tactic involves exchanging resources or the "I'll do this for you if you do this for me" type of strategy. For example, Ethan might promise to spend a couple of extra nights out with Adelyn if Leo keeps their room cleaner. The compromising style can be helpful in these types of situations and is often the best option available when choices for managing a conflict are limited. However, as discussed later, the collaborating style is an even better way to manage conflict.

Compromising is common during negotiations. When buying a car or a home, for example, the salesperson and the buyer often meet in the middle.

pixelfit/E+ via Getty Images

Avoiding

The **avoiding** style is indirect and varies in terms of how cooperative it is. When people employ the avoiding style, they stop communicating. They might change the topic, refuse to talk about something, or even leave the situation. Sometimes avoiding is beneficial and even cooperative. As Roloff and Ifert (2000) explained, it can be better to simply "agree to disagree" and stop talking about something when two people have reached a stalemate. Similarly, it is advisable to take a break during a conflict when one or both people become emotionally heated. Avoidance can also be preferable to aggression. If someone knows they are likely to get aggressive toward someone, deciding to disengage may be the better option.

Other times, avoiding either makes matters worse or is part of a larger problem. For instance, if people continually put off talking about an important issue, or deny there is a problem, inaction will maintain the status quo, and nothing will be solved. Another potential problem connected to avoiding is the **chilling effect**, which occurs when one person is afraid to disagree with the other (Roloff & Cloven, 1990; Solomon & Samp, 1998) Sometimes people do not talk about important conflict issues because they worry about angering their partner or harming the relationship. Other times people may be afraid they will not be properly heard. For example, Black women may use more passive metaphors regarding workplace conflict, such as describing conflict as "waiting for a time bomb to go off" than do white women (Turner & Shuter, 2004). Black women were also less optimistic about how conflict would be managed in the workplace than were white women, which could lead to Black women to avoid discussing issues because they think nothing will change. When the chilling event stops important issues from being discussed, it usually indicates an unhealthy power balance in a relationship or a workplace. Another potential problem is **gunnysacking**, which occurs when people silently store up all their grievances until they finally explode and unload everything on another person all at once. The analogy here is that once the sack gets too full, it bursts, so it is better to talk about important issues before it gets to this point.

The timing of avoiding may also may a difference. For example, if Leo makes the relay team over Ethan, they both might feel awkward talking about it. What would be better in this case—talking about it or not? It depends. If bringing it up makes Ethan feel worse, perhaps not talking about it, at least for a while, is a good option. However, if it is causing resentment, then it might be necessary to talk about it and lay down some ground rules. Ethan might feel better if he can express his feelings, say he is happy for Leo, but also say that he would appreciate it if Leo did not talk about the relay team for a while in front of him. This mix of avoiding when appropriate but talking about an issue when it is important to do so can be a winning combination in some cases.

Collaborating

Collaborating is cooperative and direct, and therefore considered the most effective and appropriate way to handle conflict (Gross & Guerrero, 2000; Guerrero, 2020). Compared to the other styles, when people use collaborating during conflict, they are more likely to meet both parties' needs. Therefore, collaborating has been dubbed the "win-win" style. Collaborating has also been called problem-solving and integrative communication because of its focus on finding solutions that integrate the goals and needs of all parties involved. Some of the key strategies used by those employing the collaborating style are active listening, brainstorming, sharing information openly, making supportive and validating comments, identifying common goals, and working together as a team (Carnevale & Pruitt, 1992; Sillars et al., 2004). People who are good at using the collaborating style find creative ways to manage conflict, often by thinking "outside the box." This is a huge advantage of the collaborating style; it is not a cookie-cutter, one-size-fits-all approach. Instead of looking only at conventional solutions or considering options that are already obvious, the best collaborators search for new and creative ways to manage conflict that fit the unique needs of a particular situation.

Collaborating is a more creative process than compromising. It involves brainstorming and thinking outside of the box.

iStock/PeopleImages

People often confuse collaborating and compromising because both styles involve negotiation and working together. The difference is that the more innovative strategies employed by collaborators tend to satisfy everyone's needs more fully and, in some cases, exceed original expectations. With compromising, on the other hand, people start with a negotiating position and then make modifications based on what they are willing to give up and what is most important for them to get. Think about Leo and Ethan's situation with Adelyn. They could compromise by designating time for each man to have the dorm room to use how he pleases. However, this type of compromising would be hard to live with when unexpected things come up. It would also fail to address the underlying causes of the conflict. Therefore, they might sit down to talk about other potential ways to ease the tension. Suppose they decide that Ethan and Adelyn should find a regular activity to do outside of the dorm and that when Adelyn is in their room, they should try to do things Leo likes to do sometimes. As a result, Ethan and Adelyn join a fun club they both like and the three of them start watching a series on Hulu that piques all their interests. Not only do these activities help solve some of their issues, but they also bring everyone closer together, which eases the tension.

Yielding

The **yielding** style has also been called accommodating or conceding. This style involves giving in and making concessions to meet the other partner's needs (Carnevale & Pruitt, 1992). In some ways, this can be thought of as a peace-making style. Such a style is highly cooperative. People using the yielding style put the needs of the partner and, in some cases, the good of the relationship over their own personal goals. Such a style has been cast as a "lose-win" orientation. The person who yields loses to let the other person win. However, it is important to keep in mind that sometimes giving in and doing what is best for the partner and the relationship is a winning strategy in the long run.

Several factors are at play. If one person is always yielding, as with the chilling effect, this could indicate a problem in terms of power imbalance in a relationship. This might be okay if the relationship is between a subordinate and a superior in the workplace, or a young child and parent, but it is usually not okay if it is between peers or romantic partners. When people continually yield, their needs are unlikely to be met so frustration and dissatisfaction could eventually permeate the relationship.

Culture plays a role here, too. In the United States, people generally think of approaching and avoiding conflict as opposites; however, this isn't the case across the world. For example, in studies in Cameroon, India, Malaysia, Korea, and the United Arab Emirates, communication behaviors that were viewed as approaching conflict, such as defending one's point of view, are not perceived as opposite to behaviors viewed as avoiding conflict, such as preferring to be with people who rarely disagree with one's self (Hample & Njweipi-Kongo, 2020; Kim et al., 2020;Rapanata & Hample, 2015; Waheed & Hample, 2019). People who have a collectivist orientation, where people put the group and relationships over their individual goals, may be more likely to engage in yielding conflict tactics (Cai & Fink, 2002). Yet, even in individualistic cultures, yielding is practical in many situations. As noted above, conceding to someone in a power position can be a smart move, as long as doing so does not go against one's morals. Also, sometimes something means more to one person than another. In this case, yielding is usually a smart strategy that strengthens a relationship.

DESTRUCTIVE CONFLICT PATTERNS

So far, we have discussed conflict styles as ways individuals tend to approach conflict. However, conflict involves at least two people. The way one person handles conflict is influenced by and influences how the other person handles conflict as well as how they both react to one another. Researchers have uncovered several common conflict patterns that reflect how people's conflict styles interact. Three patterns that tend to be destructive are negative reciprocity, demand-withdrawal sequences, and the four horsemen of the apocalypse. Constructive patterns have also been identified, including accommodation and the antidotes for the four horsemen of the apocalypse. All of these patterns are discussed next.

Negative Reciprocity

Most people have been in a situation where conflict has spiraled out of control. If this has happened to you, you might have found yourself wondering how things could get out of control so quickly. The truth is that **negative reciprocity**, which occurs when a person responds to aggressive communication with more aggressive communication, is a very common pattern. There are several reasons why aggression begets more aggression. One of the most fundamental reasons is that humans have a natural fight-or-flight instinct. When people feel attacked, they tend to respond by either attacking back (fight) or by getting away from and avoiding the person who attacked them (flight). In the case of negative reciprocity, the fight instinct has been activated.

People also fall into patterns of negative reciprocity for several other reasons. Research has shown that during conflict, people remember and react to their partner's negative comments more than any positive comments they make (Gaelick et al., 1985; Sillars & Canary, 2013). This negativity bias then predisposes people to be in attack mode during conflict situations. If you expect your partner to be negative because that is what you remember most, then you are on guard. It can be a self-fulfilling prophecy. This may help explain why it is critical to engage in at least five positive behaviors for every one negative behavior during conflict interaction. Researchers at the Gottman Institute call this the **magic ratio** (Benson, 2017). Studies by Gottman and his colleagues have shown that happy couples tend to have this ratio, whereas unhappy couples have a ratio closer to one positive behavior for every negative behavior (Benson, 2017; Gottman, 1994).

The **fundamental attribution bias** can also lead to negative spirals. During conflict, people tend to attribute their partner's negative behavior to stable personality traits, whereas they attribute their own negative behavior to the situation (Bradbury & Fincham, 1990). So, if Leo gets cranky when he feels his privacy is being encroached upon, he is likely to attribute his bad mood to the situation. He might think, "I feel trapped in this small, crowded space and that puts me in a bad mood." Ethan, on the other hand, is likely to attribute Leo's crankiness to his personality, making comments such as "you're too impatient" or "you need to chill." Notice that attributing the problem to Leo's personality comes off as a personal attack, which can then foster an aggressive or defensive response, leading to a negative spiral.

In addition to these biases, people are more likely to fall into a pattern of negative reciprocity, and in some cases even get violent, when they lack communication skills (Christopher & Lloyd, 2000). Being able to engage in constructive communication about contentious issues is a skill that many people do not possess. Indeed, even good communicators can struggle to express themselves appropriately in such situations. People with limited social skills are therefore especially likely to get frustrated and react negatively or even violently, especially when frustrated.

Finally, emotions can prompt a host of negative behaviors during conflict, including negative reciprocity. **Emotional flooding** occurs when people become "surprised, overwhelmed, and disorganized" in response to their partner's negative behavior (Gottman, 1994, p. 21). When people feel attacked, criticized, or discarded, they become aroused and filled with emotion, often to the point where logic is replaced by an unstoppable urge to either fight or flee. The emotion is so strong that it circumvents thinking and talking through issues. Instead, people are absorbed in their own emotions. In such cases, little understanding or meaningful exchange can occur between people. In all types of relationships, including those between friends, lovers, family members, and co-workers, patterns of negative reciprocity are related to a host of negative outcomes, including less relational satisfaction, trust, and liking (Canary et al., 1995). See the "I Didn't Know That! What's Worse for Children: Fighting or Divorce?" feature for information on how reoccurring cycles of negative reciprocity between parents impact children.

I DIDN'T KNOW THAT!
WHAT'S WORSE FOR CHILDREN: FIGHTING OR DIVORCE?

Couples sometimes stay together for the sake of the children, but is this always the best move for a family? Research has uncovered two somewhat surprising findings: First, sometimes divorce has fewer negative effects on children than continual parental fighting. Second, sometimes openly engaging in conflict in front of children is better in the long run than always keeping conflict behind closed doors. What this means is that children usually fare the worst when their parents stay together and continually act aggressively toward one another. In contrast, children fare the best when they see their parents engage in cooperative forms of conflict management.

Children are fairly resilient. Most children witness their parents engaging in conflict and suffer little to no ill effects, even if the conflict gets personal or aggressive. However, when conflict is reoccurring, is hostile, and involves the kinds of negative spirals discussed in this chapter, children can be negatively affected in a number of ways. Kids who frequently see and hear their parents battling it out in a destructive manner tend to internalize conflict (sometimes by blaming themselves), act aggressively in their own interactions, and even have short attention spans or trouble sleeping (El-Sheikh et al., 2006; Jouriles et al., 2016). For children who witness considerable hostility between their parents, sometimes divorce is actually the better option (Booth & Edwards, 1989; Emery, 2004). If parents can get along better after divorcing and maintain positive relationships with their children as co-parents, this can bring children a sense of relief. The key is that the stress from the fighting is eliminated and replaced with a more peaceful co-existence between the parents. This will not be the case if the child feels "caught between" the parents after a divorce, so parents need to refrain from any communication that would make their children feel like they are being disloyal to one parent in favor of another (Afifi & Schrodt, 2004).

Living in a household where the parents are continually fighting can also lead children to develop unhealthy conflict patterns in their own relationships. Children learn how to engage in conflict in part by modeling what they grow up seeing and hearing (Koerner & Fitzpatrick, 2002). After interviewing several conflict researchers, Dotinga (2006) noted that the experts recommend keeping particularly negative conflict behind closed doors; however, they also recommend that parents sometimes let their children see them disagreeing. Why? Because if children never see conflict, they will not realize it is a normal part of relationships. This may lead them to see conflict as a danger signal and try to avoid it instead of recognizing that it is okay to argue sometimes. The experts also suggest that parents make it a point to resolve conflict and make up in front of their children. Gottman's golden rule likely applies here—if children see their parents engaging in five positive behaviors for every negative behavior, this models what a productive conflict interaction should look like. Think about the conflict (or perhaps the lack of conflict) you witnessed in your own family. How did those experiences shape you and your conflict style as an adult? What did you learn to do and not to do during conflict based on those experiences?

Demand-Withdraw

With negative reciprocity, aggression is met with a flight response. With the **demand-withdraw** pattern, aggression is met with withdrawal, or withdrawing is met with aggression (Christensen & Shenk, 1991; Heavey et al., 1995). Thus, the demand-withdraw pattern is based in part on the "flight" response. One person wants to talk about issues; the other person does not so he or she withdraws. Many of the same problems that prompt a fight response also trigger the flight response. For example, if you think that someone has negative personality characteristics, you might disengage with that person, believing that nothing can be solved because they will always stay the same. If you are not a skilled communicator, you may feel especially awkward about trying to discuss conflict issues and therefore try to avoid such discussion altogether. And if you are emotionally flooded, you might shut down as a way to guard yourself against feeling further emotion.

Another more unique reason for the demand-withdraw pattern occurs when one person wants to change something but the other person is happy with things the way they are. In such cases, the person who wants change is usually in the "demand" position, and the person who wants to keep the status quo is in the "withdraw" position (Kluwer et al., 1998; Sagrestano et al., 2006). Take Leo and Ethan. Leo does not care at all if their dorm room is cluttered. Ethan is the one who hates the mess and wishes Leo was neater. Given the situation, it would make no sense for Leo to initiate discussion about the issue; he likes things the way they are. Ethan, on the other hand, wants things to change so he is likely to bring the issue up and complain about it.

Demand-withdraw patterns can be further complicated by **punctuation problems** that occur when partners make different attributions about who is causing the conflict. From Ethan's perspective, it is Leo's fault. If Leo were a considerate roommate, he would try to keep the place clean, and then Ethan would not have to keep telling him to pick up after himself. From Leo's perspective, the place is not that messy and Ethan keeps nagging him for next to nothing. It is also easy to blame each other for their conflict behavior. Leo thinks he withdraws because Ethan is demanding; Ethan thinks he gets demanding because Leo withdraws.

Interestingly, early research on demand-withdraw patterns showed that women are more likely to be in the demanding position and men are more likely to be in the withdrawing position (e.g., Christensen & Shenk, 1991; Heavey et al., 1993; Wheeler et al., 2010). This feeds into stereotypes that women want to talk things out more than men. However, later research showed that the biggest reason women are more likely than men to be in the demanding position is that they tend to have more they want to change in their relationships. When men have things they want to change, they are just as demanding as women.

The Four Horsemen of the Apocalypse

Both negative reciprocity and demand-withdraw are destructive conflict patterns that, unfortunately, often become routine, especially between people in close relationships. Gottman and his colleagues developed a broader framework for studying conflict patterns that includes both fight and flight responses (Gottman, 1994; Lisitsa, 2013b). His research showed that couples who exhibit four behaviors that he termed the **four horsemen of the apocalypse** are more likely to be unhappy and divorce. These behaviors are criticism, defensiveness, contempt, and stonewalling. Even though the horsemen have been studied primarily in married couples, these types of behavior can surface in any type of conflict interaction. They are especially likely to occur in relationships and interactions that are emotionally intense.

Criticism is communication that includes personal attacks. As such, criticisms are different than complaints. When people are unhappy about something, they might need to complain, especially if they want things to change. For example, if Ethan never told Leo it bothers him when he leaves his dirty clothes lying around their dorm room, Leo would assume that Ethan was fine with it. However, there is a fine line between complaints and criticisms. A comment that is clearly a complaint but not a criticism focuses on describing behavior without blaming, making accusations, or insulting someone.

To be particularly effective, complaints should center on describing a behavior and explaining how you feel about it in a nonthreatening way. For example, it is much more constructive to say, "I'm kind of a neat freak so it bothers me when dirty clothes are on the floor instead of in the laundry basket" than "You are such a slob. How hard is it to put your dirty clothes in the hamper instead of leaving them on the floor?" Of course, these are two ends of an extreme. Statements such as "I hate it when you leave your dirty clothes on the floor. Why can't you just put them in the hamper where they belong?" or "It's hard living with someone who is as messy as you are" are not as critical, but if Ethan said these types of things, Leo might still feel attacked. Feeling attacked can then trigger negative emotions, defensiveness, and other destructive behaviors.

Contempt goes beyond criticism. **Contemptuous communication** attacks a person's core sense of self and casts a person as inferior. According to the Gottman Institute:

> When we communicate with contempt, we are truly mean. Treating others with disrespect and mocking them with sarcasm and condescension are forms of contempt. So are hostile humor, name-calling, mimicking, talking down to someone, and body language such as eye-rolling and sneering. In whatever form, contempt is poisonous to a relationship because it conveys disgust and superiority (Lisitsa, 2013b).

Indeed, of the four horsemen, contempt is the most destructive, having long-lasting negative effects on people's relationships as well as their health. Common statements that communicate contempt include "You're crazy," "You can't do anything right," and "You just don't get it." These statements imply that the individual being attacked is deeply flawed. As Lisitsa put it, "Contempt, simply put, says, 'I'm better than you. And you are lesser than me.'"

Contemptuous communication is the most destructive of the four horsemen of the apocalypse.

iStock/AntonioGuillem

Contempt can also include **mindreading**, which occurs when one person assumes that she or he knows what another person is feeling or thinking, which, again, implies superiority. Saying things like "I *know* you took that wrong," "You always need to be in control," "I can tell that you're angry," and "You are just trying to make me feel guilty" are examples of mindreading. People dislike being told what they are thinking or feeling and they do not like their motives questioned. It is also presumptuous for someone to think they know how someone else is feeling or thinking. Imagine that at the end of their freshman year, Ethan tells Leo he is considering moving in with Adelyn for sophomore year instead of living with him as they had originally planned. Leo might mindread by saying, "I know you don't want to live with me anymore because I made the relay team over you and you resent me for it." This may or may not be true. Ethan may be over his initial disappointment and his decision may have everything to do with his positive feelings for Adelyn and nothing at all to do with having any negative feelings toward Leo. Leo's mindreading could escalate the argument. Ethan might respond by saying something like, "Wow. You really have a big ego if you think that. And stop acting like you know my reasons when you don't." It is okay to try and understand how someone might be feeling during an argument, but it is not okay to assume you know with any certainty how they actually feel.

Defensiveness is communication aimed at deflecting responsibility or blame onto someone or something else. When people get defensive, they are usually trying to save face and make themselves look better. They are, in a way, trying to shield themselves from attack, but they are going about it in a way that undermines their own success. According to Gottman (1994), defensive behaviors encompass denying responsibility for a problem, making excuses, whining, accusing others to deflect blame, and issuing counter-complaints or criticisms.

A major problem with defensiveness is that it gets people off topic. If you are busy thinking about how to defend yourself, it is hard to focus on problem-solving. Instead of listening to your partner, you are concentrating on yourself and all the things you can say to make yourself look better. Sometimes people get off topic by engaging in a tactic called kitchen-sinking. **Kitchen-sinking** occurs when people throw everything they can think of into an attack on their partner (i.e., they bring up everything but the "kitchen sink"). This strategy is a little different than gunnysacking, which you learned about earlier in this chapter. With gunnysacking, you hold back when conflict issues first come up until you get to a point where you have had enough and explode. With kitchen-sinking, you bring up everything you can, whether you have been holding it back or not, and whether the issues are old or new, to overwhelm and ambush your partner. Kitchen-sinking is used to try to make oneself look good and the other person look bad. Ambushing through kitchen-sinking may prevent people from attacking you because they are overwhelmed, but it also prevents people from discussing and managing problems.

A more insidious tactic that some people use as a defensiveness maneuver is **gaslighting**, which occurs when someone manipulates you in a way that makes you question your own reality.

Gaslighting happens within and outside of conflict situations. Common statements indicative of potential gaslighting include someone saying, "I never did that," when you both know they did; "I'm sorry that you are taking this all wrong," when you are actually taking it the right way; and "It's all in your head," when it really did happen. Masters of gaslighting are able to turn the tables during conflict by making their partners question their perception of things. Why do they do this? Gaslighting makes it seem like the gaslighter is blameless and their partner is crazy, or at least misinterpreting things, when that actually is not the case. As such, it is a manipulative strategy used by the gaslighter to make themselves look good and their partners look bad, which is exactly what people hope to accomplish when they are defending themselves. Gaslighting can also communicate contempt, since using this strategy implies that the person doing the gaslighting is superior to the person being gaslighted.

Stonewalling is perhaps the ultimate expression of defensiveness. Stonewalling occurs when people withdraw "from the interaction, shutting down and closing themselves off … because they are feeling overwhelmed or physiologically flooded. Metaphorically speaking, they build a wall between them and their partner" (Lisitsa, 2013c). Stonewalling can become the go-to reaction in conflict interactions when people believe that engaging in conflict will be hurtful and fail to solve anything. Often stonewalling emerges after a climate of negativity has built up over time. If the other three horsemen—criticism, contempt, and defensiveness—have become a pervasive part of the conflict interaction between two people, stonewalling gives people the ultimate "out" whereby they can detach from someone both physically and psychologically during conflict. Attempts to confront issues and solve problems are abandoned. Instead, people engage in behaviors such as focusing on something else (like looking at their phone or the TV), becoming completely unresponsive, tuning out, and walking away. When one or both people start stonewalling habitually, it is an indication that there are deep problems in a relationship. Indeed, when stonewalling is routine in a marriage, it is a harbinger of divorce in many, if not most, cases (Gottman, 1994). Stonewalling can also extend beyond conflict, permeating the relationship in a more general way as people separate themselves from each other.

Stonewalling is the ultimate expression of defensiveness, with people shutting down and closing themselves off to communication.

iStock/fizkes

CONSTRUCTIVE CONFLICT PATTERNS

So far, we have focused on patterns of negative conflict behavior. There are, however, some patterns of conflict communication that are positive. As noted earlier, these include accommodation and using a specific set of behaviors (called antidotes) in place of the four horsemen of the apocalypse.

Accommodation

Accommodation has been defined as the willingness to "inhibit impulses to react destructively and instead react constructively" in response to a partner's aggression (Rusbult et al., 1991, p. 53). The process of accommodation is grounded in the idea that natural fight and flight tendencies must be curbed for people to act cooperatively and circumvent the escalation of conflict. Being able to accommodate helps distinguish couples who are happy and committed from those who are having problems in their relationships (e.g., Campbell & Foster, 2002; Wieselquist et al., 1999). There is, however, a dark side to accommodation that is similar to the drawbacks of overusing the yielding style. If one person in the relationship frequently engages in accommodation but the other does not, this may be indicative of a power imbalance (Rusbult et al., 2001). Accommodation should be used by both partners as a way to halt conflict escalation and build patterns of positive rather than negative reciprocity. As discussed earlier, having a five-to-one ratio of positive to negative behaviors during conflict is the key to a successful relationship. When the ratio starts to tip closer to a two-to-one or a one-to-one ratio, accommodation is needed to get the interaction back on a satisfying trajectory.

The Antidotes to the Four Horsemen of the Apocalypse

Another way to prevent conflict escalation and promote positivity is to practice using the **antidotes to the four horsemen** of the apocalypse (Lisitsa, 2013a). There is an antidote to help neutralize each of the four horsemen and promote more positive interaction during conflict and in general. They can be used reactively when conflict is starting to take a negative turn, or proactively to keep conflict interaction positive and healthy.

The antidote for criticism is **complaints**. The Gottman Institute has published a three-step formula for how to complain effectively (Beaty, 2017). First, express your feelings in a straightforward and nonthreatening manner using an "I" statement. Gottman has referred to this as a soft start-up. Second, talk about a very specific behavior or situation to ground the discussion. Third, state something positive that the other person can do. For example, Leo might say, "I'm really tired [step 1] and just want to relax and unwind in peace tonight [step 2], so can you and Adelyn go out tonight instead of hanging out here [step 3]?" Contrast this to harsh start-ups like "Oh, no. Please don't tell me Adelyn is coming over *again* tonight?" or "Can't you see I'm tired and just want to relax? Can't you ever give me my space?" Obviously, using the three-step formula is a more effective way to get the discussion going.

Now the proverbial ball is in Ethan's court. Hopefully, he will respect Leo's feelings and respond in a positive manner. His response could also follow the three-step formula: "I've had a hard day [step 1], and I really want to see Adelyn [step 2]. Can she just come over for an hour [step 3]?" Leo could agree or perhaps propose that Ethan and Adelyn hang out somewhere else. Of course, conflict is usually not this scripted. The idea, however, is that using some or all of these steps can help get the discussion started in a way that increases the chances of a constructive solution.

The Gottman Institute also mentions two other ingredients in successful complaining: using repairs (Beaty, 2017) and expressing one's wishes (Benson, 2017; Brittle, 2014). **Repairs** are attempts to defuse the tension in the situation. Unless Ethan and Adelyn break up, the problems related to her coming over are not going away. But the two roommates may be able to talk about the situation in a way that reframes it as less threatening. They might even find a way to joke about it. Expressing one's wishes is also key. This is related to the third step of the complaint formula, but people can take this further by allowing themselves to be vulnerable. Benson (2017) makes a good point by saying, "Blaming our partner or hiding our feelings by criticizing is easy. Speaking our feelings and fears requires a willingness to be vulnerable." Rather than being a sign of weakness, Benson casts vulnerability as courageous. Opening ourselves up can be scary, but it can also help us understand each other on a deeper level. Perhaps at some point, Leo realizes that while yes, he does value his space and wants quiet time, part of what bothers him about Adelyn being over all the time is that he envies Ethan for finding someone he loves and genuinely enjoys spending time with since Leo has not found that yet. Opening up about these feelings could go a long way in Ethan respecting Leo's wish for space.

The antidote for defensiveness is **accepting responsibility**. Conflicts are a two-way street. It is rare that only one party is responsible for any negativity that occurs. Yet as you have learned, when people are criticized or feel attacked, their natural impulse is to become defensive, usually by fighting back or avoiding conflict. On the surface, accepting responsibility seems to be the exact opposite of what a person should do to defend themself. In fact, many people are hesitant to accept responsibility because they have had it backfire on them. Imagine Ethan accepting responsibility by saying, "Yeah, I probably should ask you before I invite Adelyn over so late. I'm sorry about that." If such a statement is made in the heat of an argument, Leo could jump on it and say something like, "Yeah, you should. It's about time you figured that out." Seeing this type of exchange in black and white on this page makes Leo's response seem rude and unreasonable, but people sometimes jump on admissions of responsibility this way when they are flooded with emotion and want to defend themselves and win the argument. This is why it is critical to try not to let the conflict escalate in the first place. Within a less heated discussion, accepting responsibility is usually seen as a mature and positive move. Moreover, when one person accepts responsibility, the other person should reciprocate. Leo might say something like, "Thanks. I also need to be more patient. I know Adelyn is important to you."

The antidote for contempt is **showing respect**. Notice that Leo's hypothetical response not only accepts responsibility ("I also need to be more patient") but also shows respect by expressing gratitude and acknowledging that Ethan's relationship with Adelyn is important to him. This type of respect goes a long way in helping people manage conflict. Showing respect is the antidote to contempt. In fact, these two concepts are opposites. When you engage in contemptuous communication, you are telling people you are more important than them, know more than them, or are somehow a better person than them. Contempt invalidates the other person and their concerns. When you communicate respect, on the other hand, you are telling people that their thoughts and feelings are valid and that you hold them and their needs in high regard. As discussed earlier in this chapter, there are often deeper issues lurking behind conflicts than first meet the eye. On the surface, it may seem like the conflicts between Ethan and Leo are about Adelyn, the track team, and the desired cleanliness of their dorm room. However, respect is a deeper issue running through their conflicts. Ethan wants Leo to respect his relationship; Leo wants Ethan to respect his space. Ethan wants Leo to respect that he feels badly about not making the relay team; Leo wants Ethan to acknowledge and respect his accomplishments on the team. Ethan wants Leo to respect his wish that their dorm room stays clean; Leo wants Ethan to respect his freedom to clean when he wants to. Although their needs and desires are incompatible, they can still try to respect each other.

An important ingredient in the respect equation is to be able to put yourself in the other person's place. Gottman (1994) recommended making mental maps to try to understand your partner's position better. **Mental maps** are an attempt at understanding the other person's psychology—their thoughts, feelings, and needs—without mindreading and without any negative biases or attributions. It involves trying to understand where someone is coming from without making assumptions. It also involves imagining how you would feel in their place, again without assuming that they will feel the same way. Oftentimes, when people either attack or avoid during conflict, they are hurt and upset that their needs are not being met. They might not feel respected. They may feel like you do not care about them or value their opinions. Understanding this can help people empathize with each other instead of taking things said during the heat of conflict personally.

Finally, the antidote for stonewalling is **physiological self-soothing**, which is a method that involves taking a break from the conflict to calm down, reduce arousal, and feel refreshed before re-engaging in conflict. It is helpful to know when to self-soothe, as well as when to release your partner from the conflict to let themself-soothe. When partners are stonewalling, pushing them to discuss issues will only make matters worse. Remember the demand-withdrawal cycle discussed earlier? If you keep demanding, your partner will pull even farther away. So instead give your partner space. Similarly, if you feel emotionally flooded or feel yourself starting to stonewall, let your partner know you need to take a break to cool down. The Gottman Institute suggests taking a break that is at least 20 minutes long but no longer than 24 hours (Brittle, 2015; Lisitsa, 2014). That way you have time to calm down and practice physiological self-soothing, but you do not stew over the problem for too long before addressing it.

If you feel emotionally flooded during conflict, practice physiological soothing by taking a break for at least 20 minutes to do something pleasant and relaxing.

iStock/Delmaine Donson

The Gottman Institute also suggests a four-step process for self-soothing. First, you and your partner should think of an innocuous signal that you can use to let each other know that you are feeling flooded with emotion and need a break. It could be something simple like signaling time out or saying a funny phrase like "whoopsy woo," which could also help break the tension. Both partners should agree to respect this signal and take a break. Second, when you distance yourself to take a break, do something that will relax you. You might envision yourself walking on the beach or listen to a favorite music track sitting on a cozy chair—whatever makes you feel safe and calm. Third, pay attention to how you are breathing. Try to inhale and exhale naturally to calm your body down. Finally, tense and then relax different parts of your body. Some people find it helpful to start in the center of their body (such as the stomach muscles) and then move out toward the fingers and toes. After completing these steps, you should feel much less stressed, and therefore more able to think clearly about the conflict. (Self-soothing and other keys to managing conflict effectively are further discussed in the following Skill Builder feature.)

SKILL BUILDER
THE GOTTMAN INSTITUTE'S SIX SKILLS FOR MANAGING CONFLICT

John Gottman has made a career researching how couples engage in conflict in helpful versus harmful ways. According to the Gottman Institute, six skills are especially important for healthy conflict management: self-soothing, the soft start-up, repair, listening, accepting influence, and compromise. Here are some of the communication practices associated with each of these skills.

Self-Soothing

- Use a neutral signal that you and your partner will understand means you need to take a "time out."
- Close your eyes and imagine yourself in a place that makes you feel happy and relaxed.
- Take deep, regular breaths.
- Tense up the parts of your body that carry your stress and then relax them.

Soft Start-Up

- When appropriate, use "I" statements instead of "you" statements (e.g., "I feel frustrated" versus "You frustrate me.").
- Give a simple description of what is happening without any blame or judgment.
- Describe what you need and want in a positive way.
- Let your partner know you respect and appreciate them.

Repair and De-Escalate

- Ask your partner about their needs and desires.
- Apologize, ask for forgiveness, and accept responsibility if appropriate.
- Use positive forms of nonverbal communication to show you care.

Actively Listen to Your Partner

- Ask about and listen to your partner's feelings and wishes.
- Try to put yourself in your partner's place to understand their perspective.
- Show that you are concerned about your partner.

Accept Your Partner's Influence

- Be open to what your partner is saying instead of getting defensive and shutting down or attacking.
- Take a "we" position instead of a "me" position by focusing on winning as a team instead of as an individual.
- Be okay with letting your partner change your mind or changing your mind because of something the partner says.

Compromise (or Collaborate!)

- Determine what you are flexible about (will change) and inflexible about (will not change) as a starting point. (To increase understanding, Gottman recommends that each person make a list and then talk about what is flexible and inflexible.)

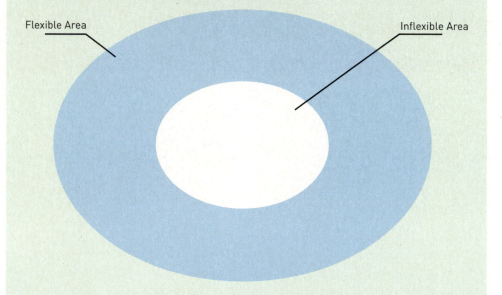

Flexible Area

Inflexible Area

- Find common ground. In the figure above, the shaded area represents the areas where both people are flexible. This is where the common ground lies. Finding that common ground is key.
- Find ways to help each other meet both individual and common goals.

Think about the last few conflicts you have had. Which of these techniques, if any, did you use? Which do you think would be easiest for you to adopt the next time you have a conflict? Choosing a few strategies to try and then building on those is a good way to move toward being a more effective communicator during conflict.

PRINCIPLES FOR MANAGING CONFLICT COMPETENTLY

Principle 1. Conflict communication is not inherently good or bad.

Conflict arises in all kinds of relationships, ranging from co-workers and superiors–subordinates to friends and family and also to lovers. People are never going to agree on everything, and sometimes one person's needs and goals are incompatible with those of another. The key is to manage conflict is a way that helps people solve problems and improve their relationships. Some people avoid conflict because it makes them feel uncomfortable or awkward, or because they are worried it will harm their relationship with someone. However, avoiding conflict rarely solves anything.

Principle 2. Conflict styles that are cooperative and direct tend to be perceived as especially appropriate and effective.

Although there are exceptions, a general rule is that people are perceived to be more competent communicators when they are cooperative and direct. This is why the collaborating style is rated as the most competent and satisfying way to manage conflict (e.g., Gross & Guerrero, 2000). The indirect fighting style is especially destructive because it is neither cooperative nor direct. The more neutral styles of avoiding and compromising are competent ways of communicating in certain situations but not others. Yielding is an indirect cooperative style that can be effective at times, especially when the issue is mundane or more important to one person than another.

Principle 3. It takes two people to manage conflict in a competent manner.

The interaction between people's communication plays a critical role in how a conflict interaction unfolds. If one person tries to be cooperative but the other stubbornly withdraws or pushes a competitive agenda, it can be difficult to stay the course and collaborate or compromise with someone. This is why people tend to fall into patterns of negative reciprocity and demand-withdraw. It also helps explain why the four horsemen of the apocalypse make regular appearances in many people's conflict interactions. The basic flight and fight tendencies humans have, combined with emotional flooding, can make it difficult to keep conflict that gets heated on a positive track. Conflict disputants must work together to try and overcome these problems, stick to the issues at hand, and consider both their own needs and their partner's needs.

Principle 4. Aim for a five-(or more)-to-one ratio of positive to negative interactions in conflicts.

Gottman's (1994) magic ratio is a major predictor of happiness in marriages. It is a good rule to follow in other relationships as well. This is why accommodation and the antidotes to the four horsemen of the apocalypse are so important. The antidotes, which include accepting responsibility, showing respect, and self-soothing, are all positive forms of communication that can help offset any negativity that arises during conflict. The six related skills in the earlier Skill Builder feature also help create healthy five-to-one ratios. It is especially important to remember the magic ratio because "negativity holds a great deal of emotional power, which is why it takes five positive interactions to overcome any one negative interaction" (Benson, 2017). Conflicts are likely to include negative communication, even in healthy relationships. The key is to counterbalance negativity with communication that validates your partner and shows appreciation, respect, and empathy.

CONCLUSION

Like most people who are highly interdependent, Ethan and Leo are having their share of conflict as new roommates. How they manage the conflict will affect how the rest of their story unfolds. In some ways, their situation is especially precarious because they live together and because a third party is part of some of their conflicts. For Leo's part, it is important that he not cause Ethan to feel caught between him and Adelyn. Both men also need to be careful to keep their complaints descriptive rather than critical and to attribute one another's bad behavior to the situation rather than their personalities. Using many of the strategies discussed in this chapter, including accommodation, self-soothing, the soft start-up, repair, and active listening, among others, would be beneficial for their friendship.

CHAPTER 10 STUDY GUIDE

KEY TERMS

Identify and explain the meaning of each of the following key terms.

accepting responsibility	gaslighting
accommodation	gunnysacking
antidotes to the four horsemen	indirect fighting
avoiding	interdependence
chilling effect	interpersonal conflict
collaborating	kitchen-sinking
competitive fighting	magic ratio
complaints	mental maps
compromising	mindreading
conflict styles	negative reciprocity
contempt	physiological self-soothing
contemptuous communication	punctuation problems
criticism	repairs
defensiveness	resources
demand-withdraw	showing respect
emotional flooding	stonewalling
four horsemen of the apocalypse	yielding
fundamental attribution bias	

REFLECTION QUESTIONS

1. Based on your observations, which conflict styles do you think are most common in various types of relationships? Do you think people's conflict styles stay relatively stable across relationships—such as those between co-workers versus friends or family members? If you think conflict styles change based on the relationship, how do you think they change and why?

2. As mentioned in this chapter, the conflict patterns within a family can influence how children engage (or don't engage) in conflict when they grow up. What do you think families, and especially parents, can do to encourage children to develop healthy ways of dealing with conflict? What specific behaviors should parents model?

3. During conflict, we can know in our minds how we need to behave to be a competent communicator. But when a conflict gets going, sometimes we seem to ignore all that knowledge and resort to unhealthy patterns of conflict communication. What are some reasons the chapter gives for us falling into those unhealthy patterns? Are there any other reasons you can think of that were not mentioned in the chapter?

4. The end of this chapter lists the antidotes for the four horsemen of the apocalypse and also includes a Skill Builder feature that expands on some of these antidotes. Which of these positive communication behaviors do you think would be easiest and most challenging to enact in the heat of conflict? What are your specific weaknesses in terms of conflict communication, and how might the tips in this chapter best help you turn those weaknesses into strengths?

11 COPING WITH TRANSGRESSIONS

WHAT YOU'LL LEARN…

When you have finished the chapter, you should be able to do the following:

11.1   Describe what a relational transgression is.

11.2   Describe different events that are considered relational transgressions.

11.3   Better understand how to seek and provide effective social support.

11.4   Understand what forgiveness is and what it is not, as well as how people seek and grant forgiveness using communication.

Maritza considers Chloe to be her closest friend. Recently, however, they have started having issues. Their problems started when Maritza met Carter, a man she met through a co-worker. Maritza and Carter immediately hit it off and started spending all their time together. At first, Chloe was excited for Maritza and understood she needed time to develop things with Carter. After a while, however, Chloe started to feel neglected, especially when she constantly saw Snapchat stories showing Maritza with Carter and a group of new friends that included the co-worker who introduced them. Chloe felt she was no longer a priority in Maritza's life, so when she ran into some old acquaintances from college who invited her to a get-together, she was happy to accept. This caused even more problems since two of Chloe's new friends treated Maritza badly during college and caused all kinds of problems for her. When Chloe starts posting pictures with those two women on Instagram and Snapchat, Maritza feels angry and betrayed. Both women wonder if their friendship will survive.

One of the ironies about relationships is that the people who can make us feel happiest also have the power to hurt us the most. Chloe feels bad about Maritza spending all her time with Carter because she misses her company. Maritza feels betrayed and angry because she expects Chloe to be loyal. If they did not care about each other, neither of them would feel hurt. Most people in relationships—including those between friends, family members, and romantic partners—hurt each other at some point. In fact, one study found that 20 percent of people reported that they get their feelings hurt at least once a week, and 60 percent reported having their feelings hurt more than once over the course of a month (Leary & Springer, 2001). How people communicate during these times helps determine whether the relationship will strengthen or deteriorate, and continue or end.

This chapter focuses on hurtful actions and words, which are also called relational transgressions. We begin by defining relational transgressions and explaining why they cause problems in relationships. This is followed by a discussion of common transgressions. Next, we focus on the communication following relational transgressions, which can include seeking social support, engaging in forgiveness, and trying to repair the relationship. Of course, not all transgressions are forgivable. Sometimes transgressions mark the sudden or gradual de-escalation or end of a relationship. Other times, people communicate about the transgression in ways that actually strengthen their relationships.

WHAT ARE RELATIONAL TRANSGRESSIONS?

Take a moment and think about the times someone hurt you. Who hurt you and what did those people do or say to cause you to feel that way? Chances are the person who hurt you was someone you knew well or at least someone you liked and respected. Of course, you can feel bad when strangers or acquaintances make rude remarks or treat you disrespectfully, but the same remarks or mistreatment would feel even worse if they came from someone who you truly care about. When people are asked to think about situations where their feelings were hurt, over 90 percent of the time they think about an issue involving someone they have a close relationship with, such as a good friend, romantic partner, or family member (Leary et al., 1998).

The most intense hurt feelings usually occur in the context of our closest relationships or with people we like and admire.

iStock/martin-dm

When you thought about the times people have hurt you, what did you remember them doing or saying that made you feel that way? Communication researchers and psychologists study two main types of hurtful events—relational transgressions and hurtful messages. **Relational transgressions** are actions that are perceived as violating implicit or explicit relational rules (Metts, 1994). For example, to Chloe, Maritza's continued lack of attention goes against the unspoken rule that best friends should make time for each other. On the other hand, to Maritza, Chloe's budding friendship with her two worst enemies from college suggests a level of disloyalty that is unexpected between best friends. As we shall see later, transgressions range from fairly mild to severe and can include major betrayals such as infidelity or lying about something important as well as more minor offenses such as forgetting to call someone back.

Relational transgressions focus broadly on actions and include what people do or what they say. Hurtful messages focus on what people say and are also considered a type of relational transgression. Specifically, **hurtful messages** are words that cause people to feel psychological or emotional pain (Vangelisti, 1994). Common examples include personal attacks ("You are the most selfish and spoiled person I know"), disclosing unwanted information ("I never saw you as someone I would date"), and directives that go against what you want ("I don't want to work with you"). Of course, these are only a few types of hurtful messages; there are numerous ways people can hurt each other with words. Next, we discuss a few key features of relational transgressions, including hurtful messages.

Explicit Versus Implicit Rules

A defining feature of relational transgressions is that they violate relational rules. These rules can be explicit or implicit. An **explicit rule** has been openly discussed, or at least mentioned, and agreed upon. Someone might ask a friend to keep certain information secret. Co-workers may agree to give each other credit if they have collaborated on a project, and lovers might define their relationship as monogamous. When explicit rules such as these are broken, both people likely concur that a transgression has occurred.

Implicit rules are usually more ambiguous and subject to a wider range of interpretations than explicit rules. An **implicit rule** is something people assume based on general norms within society or a relationship. Implicit rules are not discussed but instead are thought to be understood. The problem, of course, is that sometimes they are not. What if you never told your friend to keep certain information secret and the friend told people? Is that a transgression or not? You may have assumed your friend would know that the information you shared was highly personal and therefore confidential. You may also have thought that your friend knows anything personal you talk about should stay between the two of you. If this is the case, you would regard your friend's behavior as a transgression. However, your friend could deny knowing that you would care if the information was shared, thereby claiming that no transgression occurred.

Although you would not want to spend a lot of time discussing the rules of your relationship with someone all the time, when an issue is important to you, it is often best to have a direct conversation with someone about your expectations. For example, co-workers who discuss the rules for working together and giving each other credit for collaboration are less likely to have misunderstandings revolving around perceived transgressions. Similarly, couples who define their relationships as monogamous (or nonmonogamous) create parameters for what behavior is considered acceptable and unacceptable in their relationships.

Degree of Expectancy Violation

Explicit and implicit rules set up expectations for what types of behavior are out of bounds within a given interaction or relationship. For this reason, relational transgressions can be thought of as a type of expectancy violation (Bachman & Guerrero, 2006). **Expectancy violations** are behaviors that deviate from what people think will or should happen. Some expectancy violations are positive. This occurs when the actual behavior is better than the expected behavior. Someone might be kinder or more generous than you expected or react less harshly to something than you thought they would. This could have happened when Chloe started talking to Maritza's enemies. She might have expected them to be catty and conceited and then been surprised when they were sweet to her.

Something as simple as a birthday post on your Instagram story can be either a positive or negative expectancy violation. Think about who you would expect to post on your birthday and what you would expect different people to say. How would that affect your reaction to a post?

Courtesy of Laura Guerrero

In the case of relational transgressions, however, expectancy violations are negative. In other words, the actual behavior is worse than the expected behavior. You might expect your co-worker to acknowledge your contributions to a project when presenting her findings at a meeting, and then be disappointed and even angry when she does not. Or you might expect your significant other to do something really special for you on your birthday, and then be upset when all they do is post a picture of the two of you with a "Happy Birthday, babe" caption on Instagram. Of course, if you had not expected your significant other to do anything for your birthday, posting something on Instagram could be perceived as a positive expectancy violation.

As the example of a birthday post on Instagram illustrates, both expectancy violations and relational transgressions are relative to the situation and to the implicit or explicit rules that are operative in that situation. The same behavior might be considered a negative expectancy violation in one case, a positive expectancy violation in another case, or an expected behavior in yet another case. But it would only have the potential to be considered a relational transgression if it was a negative expectancy violation. One way to think of this is that not all expectancy violations are relational transgressions, but relational transgressions are usually negative expectancy violations. Similarly, not all negative behaviors are relational transgressions—to be a relational transgression, a behavior must violate the implicit or explicit rules governing a relationship or interaction between people.

The extent to which a relational transgression deviates from relational rules and violates expectancies makes a difference (Bachman & Guerrero, 2006). When violations are especially negative, people feel more hurt, forgiveness is less likely, and the relationship suffers the most damage. An even bigger problem occurs when negative behaviors stop being seen as expectancy violations or transgressions. People in toxic relationships start to expect the other person to engage in hurtful or negative behavior, so these behaviors become normative rather than being negative expectancy violations. The problem, of course, is that if people do not see negative behaviors as transgressions, they are less likely to stand up for themselves or leave the relationship. Thus, relational transgressions can serve the function of helping people to set limits for the types of behaviors that are acceptable within a relationship.

Degree of Cost

In addition to being conceptualized as negative expectancy violations, relational transgressions can be thought of as costs. There is a long tradition of research in social psychology showing that people gravitate to those who provide them with more rewards than costs (Figure 11.1). According to social exchange theory, people develop and maintain relationships with people they perceive as rewarding (Thibaut & Kelley, 1959). People also avoid relationships they see as costly. **Rewards** include any exchanged resources that make you happy and/or give you wanted opportunities, whereas **costs** include any relationship outcomes that give you pain and/or result in a loss (Sprecher, 1998). Relational transgressions are costs. The more intense the hurt they cause, the higher the cost.

From a social exchange perspective, people will distance themselves from those who they see as costly. This helps explain why people break up after a hurtful event like infidelity, quit a job if a manager is always yelling at them, or stop being friends with someone who talks behind their back. Sometimes, however, people stay in these situations despite the costs. A husband who has been happily married to his wife for 10 years and is devoted to his three young sons might try to make things work after his wife admits to a meaningless hookup. An employee might decide to stay at a well-paying job with colleagues she likes even though she cannot stand her manager. And friends like Chloe and Maritza might try to work things out after transgressions occur because they have a long history and genuinely care about each other.

As these examples show, when people provide us with rewards, those rewards can sometimes (although not always) help counterbalance the cost of relational transgressions (see Figure 11.1 for an illustration). For example, one study showed that people who reported receiving more affection in their relationships said that they engaged in less rumination and were less hurt following transgressions (Horan, 2012). Not surprisingly, people are also more likely to forgive their partners and see transgressions as less serious if they were happy in the relationship prior to the transgression occurring (Bachman & Guerrero, 2006; Menzies-Toman & Lydon, 2005). The more rewarding the partner and the relationship, the more there is to counterbalance the cost of a transgression. However, there are limits. If a transgression is especially serious or hurtful, or if a transgression repeatedly occurs, no amount of rewards may be able to save the relationship. Think about Chloe and Maritza. Imagine them having a frank discussion about the things that are bothering them. They decide on boundaries, including spending more time together and prioritizing their friendship, but one of them continually breaks those agreed-upon boundaries. Their friendship would be unlikely to survive that type of repeated cost.

FIGURE 11.1 ■ The Cost of Relational Transgressions

Relational Transgressions Can Be Conceptualized as Costs That Need to Be Outweighed by Rewards If a Relationship Is to Survive

costs

rewards

Devaluation and Negative Emotion

Another key feature of relational transgressions is that they make people feel devalued (Feeney, 2005). **Devaluation** revolves around feeling that someone sees you as unimportant, unwanted, unappreciated, and easily discarded. People want to feel valued and respected by others. They also want to be included in people's lives in ways that make them feel others like them and want to be around them. It is difficult to think about a relational transgression that does not involve some degree of devaluation. One study found that being rejected, criticized, or betrayed or having your character attacked were all described as key activities that hurt people's feelings (Vangelisti et al., 2005). Another study showed that online behaviors such as having a friend request declined, having a tag deleted, or not appearing on someone's "top friend list" were hurtful and often considered relational transgressions (Tokunaga, 2011a, 2014). Such behaviors likely violate implicit rules about how to treat friends online (Walther et al., 2008). They could also make people feel devalued.

Think also about the scenario with Maritza and Chloe. Devaluation is a main theme. Chloe feels she is no longer a priority in Maritza's life—their friendship has been devalued in comparison to Maritza's new relationship with Carter. Maritza feels like Chloe stabbed her in the back by becoming friends with her enemies. She thinks that if Chloe really cared about her and how she felt, she would not become friends with women who treated her badly in the past.

Devaluation helps explain why people experience a lot of negative emotions in response to transgressions. No one wants to feel devalued. And being devalued by someone you care about is especially hurtful. Mild forms of devaluation are often linked to inconsiderate behavior or thoughtless negative comments. If someone is uncharacteristically slow in responding to your messages, and this continues for a couple of days, you might be annoyed and feel slightly devalued but not enough to consider their behavior a transgression. On the other hand, if someone deletes you from their social media and unlikes a bunch of your pictures, you are likely to feel much more offended and to consider such behavior a transgression. The most severe forms of devaluation are also connected to feeling angry and betrayed. This is what Maritza is experiencing—she can understand that Chloe would want new friends since she is so busy with work and Carter, but what she is having trouble understanding is why Chloe would be friends with women who made her life miserable in the past. It feels like an act of disloyalty and betrayal. Chloe, on the other hand, may feel that Maritza has no right to tell her who to be friends with since she is spending all her time with Carter and virtually ignoring her.

Feeling devalued is at the root of hurt feelings.

iStock/AntonioGuillem

A person's intentions also make a difference. In general, the more intentional a transgression is perceived to be, the more hurtful it is (McLaren & Solomon, 2008; Mills et al., 2002; Vangelisti & Young, 2000). Think about how Maritza would feel if instead of randomly running into her old enemies, Chloe had sought them out and initiated friendships with them as a way of getting back at Maritza for spending so much time with Carter. The fact that Chloe would go out of her way to try and hurt her would make the betrayal much worse. Similarly, there is a big difference between being slow to respond to someone's messages because you are busy or tired, compared to going on someone's social media and intentionally doing things like unfollowing them and taking your likes off their pictures. The latter behavior is obviously much more hurtful.

In sum, relational transgressions have the following characteristics—they violate explicit or implicit relational rules, negatively violate expectations, are considered costs in relationships, and communicate devaluation in ways that typically lead people to feel negative emotions. But what types of specific actions and words are typically considered to be relational transgressions?

TYPES OF RELATIONAL TRANSGRESSIONS

No single list could cover all the possible ways people can implicitly or explicitly break relational rules and hurt each other. Researchers have, however, uncovered some behaviors that are commonly thought of as relational transgressions (Bachman & Guerrero, 2006; Feeney, 2004, 2005; Jones & Burdette, 1993; Metts, 1991; Vangelisti, 1994). These include acts of disloyalty, acts of disassociation and exclusion, deceptive words or actions, personal criticism, relationship-devaluing communication, inconsiderate acts and false promises, and violent or threatening acts.

Acts of Disloyalty

Many people consider acts of disloyalty to be one of the worst types of relational transgressions. Although a range of actions falls under this category, all acts of disloyalty tend to be viewed as betrayals, often producing deep feelings of hurt, anger, and jealousy. In monogamous romantic relationships, most people view sexual infidelity as the ultimate form of betrayal. Sexual exclusivity is highly valued in most serious romantic relationships, so having sex with someone else is considered one of the most hurtful and least forgivable actions that could occur (Bachman & Guerrero, 2006; Feeney, 2004; Malachowski & Frisby, 2015). Kissing, flirting, dating, or wanting to date someone else are also commonly mentioned as transgressions in romantic relationships (Metts, 1991). Of course, acts of disloyalty are not limited to romantic relationships. When people choose one friend over another, associate with someone's enemies, or establish a stronger emotional connection with a new friend than an old one, these can be considered acts of disloyalty. For example, if Chloe complains about Maritza to her old enemies, this could be viewed as an additional act of disloyalty.

WHAT WOULD YOU DO?
WITNESS TO BETRAYAL

Sometimes people find themselves in the unenviable position of being a third-party witness to a transgression. For example, you might discover your friend's significant other is cheating, hear someone talking badly about a good friend of yours, or know someone is lying to a friend. If you are mutual friends with the transgressor and the person being transgressed against, this can be complicated. To whom do you owe your loyalty? Will you be committing a transgression if you tell—or don't tell—what you know?

These are ethical questions that do not have easy answers. Some people believe the best course of action is to side with the person with whom you are closest. Therefore, if your best friend is the person who committed the transgression, you should not tell; but if your best friend was being transgressed against, you should. Others would argue that it depends on how serious the transgression is. If the transgression included violence or was a long-term issue, then, according to this perspective, you have a moral obligation to reveal the transgression. Another common strategy is to talk to the person who committed the transgression and urge them to confess. Sometimes a deadline is even given—if they don't tell your friend by a certain time, you say you will tell. Which of these strategies is closest to what you would do? How might your response as a third party differ based on the situation? And finally, can you think of any other ways to manage being a third-party witness to a transgression?

Acts of Disassociation and Exclusion

Acts of disassociation involve distancing oneself from someone. As with acts of disloyalty, a wide range of actions fall under this category. Maritza's choice to spend all her free time with Carter and only check in with Chloe once in a while is an example of an act of disassociation, as is the example involving unfollowing someone on social media. Many other forms of communication (or lack of communication) on social media can function as acts of disassociation, including ending a Snapchat streak, no longer liking or commenting on someone's pictures, or removing someone (or yourself) from group chats on either social media platforms or texts. Other acts of disassociation include making excuses not to spend time with someone, avoiding someone, leaving someone on "read" more frequently than usual, and not inviting someone places. Most people can recall a time when *not* being invited to something made them feel bad, especially in cases where they expected to be invited and were left out. In romantic relationships, breakups are often considered relational transgressions. In one study, being broken up with was one of the top three relational transgressions reported by college students (Bachman & Guerrero, 2006). Ghosting, or suddenly cutting off all communication with someone, is an extreme act of dissociation that many people find particularly hurtful and disrespectful (LeFebvre, 2017; Truscelli & Guerrero, 2019; Vihauer, 2015).

Another form of acts of disassociation and exclusion is racialized or gendered **microaggressions**. Microaggressions are more covert acts of racism or misogyny that occur within everyday communication exchanges (Sue et al., 2007). These might include asking someone where they are from or complimenting someone on being "so articulate." Another type of microaggression might be relying on heteronormative assumptions, such as using language that only references opposite-sex romantic partners (Munro et al., 2019). These types of messages may not register as aggressive to the sender but can produce anger and frustration in the receiver, and over time may negatively affect self-esteem and subjective well-being (Sue & Spanierman, 2020). Engaging in these types of microaggressions can hinder the formation of interpersonal relationships between diverse individuals. Awareness and prevention of microaggressions may be particularly important for college students who are exposed to greater diversity on their college campuses than they have previously experienced, especially since microaggressions in school environments have been shown to harm self-esteem (Midgette & Mulvey, 2021).

Deceptive Words or Actions

Deception is also one of the most frequently mentioned relational transgressions. Not all deceptions, however, are transgressions. Sometimes deception is expected and even appreciated, as is discussed in the following "I Didn't Know That!" box. Ongoing deception about serious issues is especially likely to be damaging to a relationship. Lying to your significant other about an affair and spreading false rumors about a co-worker to get ahead at work are examples of types of deception that are seen as severe relational transgressions. Less significant deception, such as telling a "white lie" to protect someone's feelings, is typically expected and therefore not seen as a relational transgression. In online situations, such as dating apps, people commonly engage in mild forms of deception (such as exaggerating one's good qualities) to attract others (Toma et al., 2008). However, this strategy can backfire. When you meet in person for a first date, if you believe your date was deceptive in how they presented themselves online, you are more likely to downgrade your date's social and physical attractiveness and less likely to want to go on a second date (Sharabi & Caughlin, 2019).

I DIDN'T KNOW THAT!
MYTHS ABOUT DECEPTION

Myth 1. Deception is lying. One myth is that deception is all about lying. In actuality, **deception** *includes various types of behavior that intentionally misrepresent the truth*. Five types of deception are common: lies, equivocation, concealment, exaggeration, and understatement. **Lying** is saying something opposite or very different from what you know is true. **Equivocation** involves being strategically ambiguous by communicating in an indirect or confusing way that skirts the truth. **Concealment** occurs when people intentionally hide or omit relevant information. **Exaggeration** entails stretching the truth by embellishing details or making something sound better or worse than it really was, whereas **understatement** is defined as downplaying aspects of the truth. For example, when Maritza asks Chloe what she did the night before, instead of being truthful and saying she hung out with Maritza's enemies, Chloe could lie ("I stayed home all night") or equivocate ("Nothing exciting. What about you?"). Chloe might also decide not to tell Maritza that she has been spending a lot of time with them (concealment), to downplay how much fun she has with them, or to exaggerate how much she would prefer to hang out with Maritza compared to them.

Myth 2. Deception is always "bad" and is never justified. Many children grow up hearing that "honesty is the best policy," lies are hurtful, and only bad people lie. In many cases, honesty is the best path to take, but is it always? You can probably think of situations when it would be unnecessarily hurtful to be completely truthful with someone. Telling someone you hate a gift they gave you, sharing intimate details about your ex with your new partner, being brutally honest about someone's flaws, and revealing information that you promised to keep secret are just four of many examples of times when being deceptive might actually be preferred. In general, deception is more acceptable if it is being used for unselfish reasons, such as protecting someone, than for selfish reasons. Therefore, *deception ranges in terms of how acceptable versus unacceptable, as well as how cruel versus kind, it is.*

Myth 3. It is easy to tell when someone is being deceptive, especially if you know someone well. Both parts of this statement are incorrect. First, it is very challenging to detect deception and no perfectly reliable set of clues to deception have been identified. This is because people try to control their behavior to appear truthful. Some nervousness might leak out, but most people are able to control at least some of their behaviors. Think about eye contact. Most people believe a lack of eye contact signals deception, but because most people know that, they look others straight in the eye when deceiving them. Most people also believe it is easier to tell when a friend or loved one is deceiving compared to a more casual friend or acquaintance. Yet people have **truth biases**; they expect people they like to be honest (Kam, 2004; McCornack & Parks, 1986). This can cause you to overlook inconsistencies in a friend's story or to believe something your significant other says without putting much thought into what they are saying. We *want* to believe the people we care about are being honest, so we assume that they are. Overall then, *deception is challenging to detect, even with people we know and like.*

Does the information presented here challenge any long-standing beliefs you have about deception? How might this knowledge change the way you approach potentially deceptive situations?

Personal Criticism

As discussed in Chapter 10, personal criticism is an especially destructive behavior. Being personally attacked floods people with negative emotions and leads to defensive reactions. Personal criticism can also be a relational transgression. This is because we expect people who care about us to support us rather than tear us down. In contrast to a constructive complaint that focuses on specific behaviors or issues, personal criticism attacks a person's character. Calling someone lazy, crazy, insecure, or incompetent is just one of many examples. Bringing up hurtful events from the past and casting them as someone's fault ("This is the third time this has happened to you so it's obviously your problem") or using third parties to make broader criticisms ("Everyone knows how irresponsible and flaky you are") are particularly hurtful. Personal criticism is also more hurtful to the extent that it touches on characteristics we value and see as a central part of our identity.

Relationship–Devaluing Communication

Whereas personal criticism involves attacking someone's personality or character, relationship-devaluing communication involves making statements that show disregard for the relationship. When people make relationship-devaluing statements, they communicate that a relationship is unimportant to them. Here are some examples: "This relationship has been a waste of my time," "I only dated you because I was on the rebound," and "We really aren't good friends anymore" (Bachman & Guerrero, 2006; Vangelisti, 1994). Such comments constitute a relational transgression when they violate expectations that a particular relationship is valued and considered important.

Inconsiderate Acts and False Promises

Some transgressions revolve around feeling unappreciated, taken for granted, or taken advantage of by someone. Common transgressions in this category include canceling on someone last minute, showing up late without a good reason, and forgetting someone's birthday or another special occasion. These behaviors can make people feel that they are a low priority. Similarly, when people make "false promises" that they do not keep or "lead someone on" by acting like they care more than they do, people feel that taken advantage of. All of these behaviors can also make people question whether they will be treated well in the future.

Violent or Threatening Actions

Violence has no place in any relationship. Therefore, it is not surprising that people often consider threats or acts of violence to be relational transgressions. Violence and threats of violence produce considerable uncertainty and are also among the most unforgivable of transgressions (Davidson et al., 2015; Emmers & Canary, 1996). In relationships, violent behavior ranges from spontaneous to intentional and controlling. Violence can also be enacted by both people or by one person toward the other (Table 11.1). The following characteristics help define four types of interpersonal violence identified by Johnson (2008):

- **Intimate terrorism**: the use of physical violence as one of many tactics designed to maintain control over a relational partner

- **Violent resistance**: the use of violence in response to violent and controlling behavior

- **Common couple violence**: an isolated pattern where people engage in reciprocal violence during conflict

- **Mutual violent control**: a continuing violent struggle between two people who are both violent and controlling

TABLE 11.1 ■ Types of Violent Behavior				
Do You Get Violent?	**Are You Controlling?**	**Does Your Partner Get Violent?**	**Is Your Partner Controlling?**	**You Are Engaged in**
Yes	Yes	No	No	Intimate terrorism
Yes	No	Yes	Yes	Violent resistance
Yes	No	Yes	No	Common (situational) couple violence
Yes	Yes	Yes	Yes	Mutual violent resistance

Note: The information presented in this table is based on descriptions of these four types of violence as reported in: Johnson, M. P. (2008). *A typology of domestic violence: Intimate terrorism, violent resistance, and situational couple violence.* Lebanon, NH: University Press of New England.

Of these types of violence, common couple violence occurs the most often. This form of violence tends to occur in the midst of a heated conflict when people are experiencing negative emotions such as hurt, frustration, and anger (Hamel, 2009; Johnson, 1995; McEwan & Johnson, 2008). Common couple violence also tends to be reciprocal, meaning that both people engage in it. Some couples show a pattern of **repeated common couple violence** in which arguments tend to escalate into violence on a regular basis, but instances of common couple violence are rare for most couples (Johnson & Leone, 2005). Violence that is intentional rather than spontaneous, and enduring rather than situational, sometimes falls under the category of intimate terrorism (Johnson & Ferraro, 2000). This type of violence is one-sided, with one partner using violence or threats of violence to try to control the other partner, but also showering the partner with love, affection, and gifts at times so they stay. This is also an example of someone trying to counterbalance a cost (violence) with rewards (love and gifts). If you find yourself in a violent relationship, get help from someone you trust.

SOCIAL SUPPORT

If you are having a difficult time coping with a relational transgression, seeking social support can be helpful. Similarly, if you know someone who has been hurt, you can be a source of support for that person. Some forms of social support, however, are better than others.

Seeking Social Support

People report feeling better if they discuss relational transgressions with someone who provides them with emotional support. Receiving such support can reduce feelings of hurt, stress, anger, and dejection (Pederson & McLaren, 2017). A word of caution is in order, however. There are two general ways to communicate about relational transgressions with your social network: transgression-maximizing versus transgression-minimizing messages (Vallade & Dillow, 2014). Transgression-maximizing messages can make you feel better, but they can also have negative consequences if you maintain a relationship with the person who transgressed against you.

When people use **transgression-maximizing messages**, they focus on telling others about the negative aspects of the transgression and their partners. For example, Maritza might tell people Chloe is a horrible best friend who purposively tried to hurt her by becoming friends with two women who hate her. She might also downplay, or not mention at all, her role in the issues between the two of them. The problem here is that Maritza has painted Chloe in such a negative light that it could be difficult for the rest of her social network to continue to see Chloe positively. This could later cause tension between Maritza's friends and Chloe.

If Maritza had instead used **transgression-minimizing messages**, she could have received support without jeopardizing the degree to which her social network will continue to accept Chloe. Transgression-minimizing messages focus on putting the transgression in context and mentioning some of the mitigating factors. Maritza could say that she is hurt because she and Chloe have been friends for such a long time and she cares about her. She could say that she thinks Chloe did not intentionally seek out her enemies as friends, but that she nonetheless feels betrayed. She could also admit that she had not been spending as much time as she should with Chloe because she is so involved with Carter. Transgression-minimizing messages like this are likely to elicit more helpful and objective responses than transgression-maximizing messages. Instead of taking sides with Maritza against Chloe, people might help Maritza talk through her feelings and think about ways to fix the situation.

Instead of directly going to people for support, people sometimes turn to social media. One option is to post status updates to express emotions or complain (Carpenter, 2012). These can also be used to gain attention, with the hope that friends will ask them what is wrong and give them either private or public support. Sometimes status updates are subtweets intended to communicate a message to the transgressor. Some studies have shown that people who have narcissistic and manipulative personalities are most likely to engage in some of these behaviors on social media (Carpenter, 2012).

Providing Social Support

If you know someone who is feeling hurt, you can sometimes help that person by offering comfort and support. This extends beyond hurt feelings and transgressions—you can also offer support to those who have experienced a loss, disappointment, or some other type of distress. However, despite your best intentions, sometimes providing effective support can be challenging. Think about how might you feel if you were hurt because your significant other broke up with you. Would you want everyone telling you how bad they felt for you? Probably not. Research has shown that people often get uncomfortable when others give them unwanted sympathy or advice. You might feel like everyone feels sorry for you, sees you as weak, and thinks you cannot handle the situation on your own. This is why it is often best to use **invisible support** as a way to make someone feel better (Bolger & Amarel, 2007; Bolger et al., 2000).

Invisible support is indirect and is not interpreted as "help" by the recipient (Zee & Bolger, 2019). This type of support may be especially effective when people are giving instrumental support rather than emotional support. **Instrumental support** involves giving someone information or advice, whereas **emotional support** involves expressing care, empathy, and comfort. Think about how you would feel if a friend told you this: "You are just making yourself sick thinking about this. You need to block your ex from everything, take all traces of your ex off your social media, and start talking to other people right away." Compare that statement to this one: "When I was going through my last break up, it really helped me to block my ex, take my ex off my social media, and start talking to other people." The first statement is more visible in terms of offering direct advice; the second is more indirect. A benefit to using less visible forms of support is that it does not sound like you are telling the person what to do. Instead, you are giving them information and letting them decide what to do with it.

Invisible or implicit forms of social support are preferred in collectivist compared to individualistic cultures. Although there are critiques of these dimensions (see Chapter 4), some research suggests that Asians and Asian Americans who identify with collectivism are less likely to ask others for social support than are Americans identifying with individualism (Kim et al., 2008). People with a collectivist focus may worry more about disrupting group harmony and being perceived negatively if they disclose personal information about their feelings of distress (Kim et al., 2008). This finding helps explain why people from Asian cultures may prefer implicit support, which involves receiving emotional comfort from one's social network without disclosing personal feelings and problems. People with a more individualistic outlook were found to be more comfortable receiving explicit support, which involves talking about stressful events with others (Kim et al., 2008). Another study investigated differences in social support between Jewish and Arab individuals living in the same area (Pines & Zaidman, 2003). Arab individuals tend to have a more collectivist cultural orientation. Similarly to the Asian sample, Arab individuals reported being more likely *not* to turn to anyone when they were distressed, and to instead handle it themselves (Pines & Zaidman, 2003).

There are, of course, times when support is necessarily explicit. If someone breaks down and cries, for example, it is difficult to comfort them without making your support explicit. There are also times when people need emotional support rather than informational support. They want to feel validated and comforted. Behaviors such as active listening, empathetic expressions, and giving someone a hug can help provide emotional support. One study showed that when college students were asked how they would comfort someone who was going through a breakup, the most common response (given by nearly 42 percent of respondents) was to give them a hug (Dolin & Booth-Butterfield, 1993).

One study found that giving someone a hug was the most common way people said they would comfort someone.

Josh Edelson/AFP via Getty Images

Verbally, using **person-centered messages** can be effective in supporting someone. Person-centered messages acknowledge, elaborate on, and validate the feelings of a distressed person (Burleson, 1982; High & Dillard, 2012; MacGeorge et al., 2019). These types of messages also help someone gain perspective. Going back to the breakup example, imagine someone saying, "It's about time you broke up. You two were never right for each other." This message is very low in person-centeredness. It does little to validate the hurt person's feelings and actually implies that the person should be happy or should have known the breakup was imminent. In contrast, say that a friend told you, "I understand why you feel bad. Let me know if you want to talk." This statement would validate your feelings and encourage you to disclose them. Your friend could even help you elaborate on and gain more perspective by listening and then making statements such as this: "It seems like you realize you weren't right for each other, but I'm sure that doesn't make it hurt any less. You deserve to end up with someone who is better for you." Notice that this group of statements would validate your feelings while also helping you put things in perspective, without sounding preachy or passing judgment on you.

Person-centered messages have been shown to be an effective way to provide social support (High & Dillard, 2012). In addition, when support seekers and providers share a social identity, the ability to reference that identity and use humor and other idiomatic messages shared by the group can also be a useful way to provide social support. Davis (2019) found that Black women providing support about experiencing microaggressions often contextualized the support seekers' experience by discussing their shared experiences as Black women in the United States, ultimately making them feel more supported.

FORGIVENESS

Seeking social support is only one of many forms of communication that occur following a relational transgression. Most relationships, regardless of whether they are between friends, lovers, family members, or co-workers, have high and low points. People make mistakes and hurt each other. When a transgression occurs, it is up to the people involved to decide if it is worth trying to work things out or if they should simply move on. The person who was transgressed against also needs to decide whether to be forgiving or not. Sometimes this is a very difficult decision. As Waldron and Kelley (2008) put it,

> Nearly everyone has struggled to find the right response to the hurtful actions of a friend, co-worker, family member, or romantic partner. Should I seek revenge? Hold a grudge? Try to "get over it?" Can I really forgive someone whose behavior caused me so much emotional pain? (pp. 3–4)

In some cases, people are able to forgive easily; in other cases, trust is broken irrevocably and people have difficulty forgiving someone. Even what people do forgive, they may not want to continue having a relationship with the person who hurt them. You can forgive but still want to move on.

What exactly is forgiveness then? **Forgiveness** is a process that involves letting go of the negativity you feel toward someone who has wronged you. According to Waldron and Kelley (2008), this process typically has four parts:

- Acknowledging the transgression,

- Extending undeserved mercy,

- Letting go of negative emotion, and

- Renegotiating the relationship.

Two key aspects of the process of forgiveness are the change in emotions and the renegotiation of the relationship. For forgiveness to take place, there must be an emotional transformation (Boon & Sulsky, 1997; McCullough et al., 1997; Waldron & Kelley, 2008). When people are hurt, they usually have a fight-or-flight instinct; they either want to get back at the person who hurt them (fight) or get away from that person (flight). Letting go of the negative emotions connected to fight-or-flight impulses allows people to reconnect and engage in more positive forms of communication. This does not mean, however, that the relationship will be the same. The last part of the forgiveness process, relationship negotiation, could mean you decide to fix things, but it could also mean that you decide to de-escalate or end your relationship. Even in family relationships, where you cannot "quit" the relationship easily, forgiveness can be a complex process. After family members decide to forgive each other, they often have to work on focusing on the positive rather than the negative in their relationships to move on from the transgression (Carr & Wang, 2012). Table 11.2 shows some of the different outcomes following transgressions and forgiveness.

TABLE 11.2 ■ Outcomes Following Relational Transgressions	
Outcome	**Sample Descriptions**
New relationship type	"We are friends now but not dating." "We are still co-workers but not close friends anymore."
Rule change	"We don't call each other names anymore when we fight." "Now I always call if I'm going to be late."
Strengthening	"It was a hard time, but we talk more now than ever before." "If we can survive that, we know we can get through anything."
Weakening	"He did forgive me, but we aren't as close as we used to be." "I'm not sure I will ever trust her the way I used to."
Normalizing	"I could tell he forgave me when things felt normal between us again." "We eventually went back to the way things used to be."
Terminating	"After that, we drifted apart and eventually stopped talking altogether." "We broke up."
Short-term consequences	"Immediate shock. Confusion about what to do. Anger." "We couldn't talk about it for days."
Long-term consequences	"I forgave him but I will never forget how much he hurt me." "Twenty years later, we are just now really dealing with it."

Source: This is a slightly modified version of a table from Waldron, V. R., & Kelley, D. L. (2008). *Communicating forgiveness*. Los Angeles, CA: Sage.

As the outcomes in Table 11.2 suggest, forgiveness does not always mean reconciliation. Sometimes we repair the relationship; other times we do not. Forgiveness is also not pardoning, forgetting, condoning, excusing, or denying (Waldron & Kelley, 2008). In fact, it can be part of a process that is the opposite of all of these things. Chloe does not have to say it is okay for

Maritza to spend all her time with Carter. She also does not have to excuse Maritza's behavior by thinking that she is only neglecting their friendship because she is in love. She can be forgiving and understanding without doing either of those things. She can believe that Maritza should still make time for her despite her new relationship with Carter—in fact, this is a point she might want to emphasize when they talk about the situation and renegotiate what is expected (and not expected) in their friendship.

It is also important to consider that forgiveness can have different meanings depending on the culture (Hook et al., 2009, 2012; Zhang et al., 2015). In collectivist cultures, forgiveness is an interpersonal construct and a cultural obligation; people are motivated to forgive because they desire social harmony and relational repair. Forgiveness is also associated with concepts such as harmony, grace, and benevolence. In individualistic cultures, forgiveness is more of an intrapersonal construct and a personal choice, with people motivated to forgive for personal healing and to be the bigger person. In line with these ideas, Chinese people, who are more likely to identify with collectivism, are more likely than individuals from the United States to say they granting forgiveness to heal their relationship (Zhang et al., 2015). People from the United States, who are more likely to identify with individualism, also see forgiveness as more intentional and as requiring more effort than do people from China (Zhang et al., 2019).

Seeking Forgiveness Through Communication

Communication plays an essential role in helping to determine whether and how forgiveness is granted. Table 11.3 lists (a) the three primary ways people respond when they want to fix things following a transgression and (b) five common ways people communicate when granting forgiveness. Of course, sometimes people do not want to repair the relationship. In some cases, people even engage in transgressions hoping that doing so will prompt the other person to stop talking to them or break up with them. (You will learn more about this in Chapter 12.) Assuming the person who engaged in the transgression is sorry and wants to continue the relationship, they will likely engage in forgiveness-seeking behaviors such as apologies, compensation, and explanation.

TABLE 11.3 ■ Communication Used to Seek and Grant Forgiveness	
Forgiveness-Seeking Communication	**Forgiveness-Granting Communication**
Apology	Explicit forgiveness
Compensation	Conditional forgiveness
Explanation	Nonverbal displays
	Discussion
	Minimization

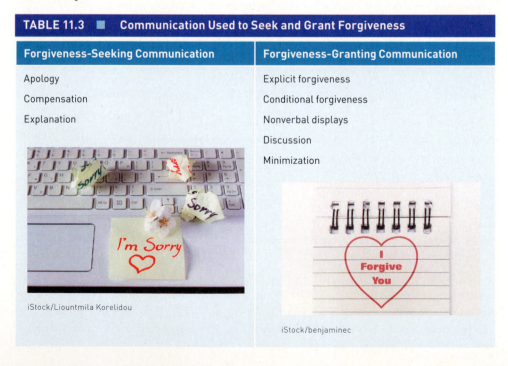

iStock/Liountmila Korelidou

iStock/benjaminec

Apologies

The most common way to seek forgiveness is to offer an **apology**, which involves saying you are sorry. But not all apologies are equal. Apologies are most effective when they are offered freely, include an admission of wrongdoing, contain a promise to be better in the future, and elicit empathy (McCullough et al., 1997; Morse & Metts, 2011). If you have to ask someone to apologize, the effect is not the same because the apology seems forced rather than sincere. Apologies also seem hollow if the person apologizing does not admit wrongdoing. This is especially true if the offense was serious. If someone says something like, "I'm sorry but I didn't mean to upset you," this is usually less effective than simply saying "I'm sorry I did that and upset you." This does not mean you should take sole responsibility for everything all the time, but you should think about what you did and admit responsibility for any mistakes you made. Another important part of an effective apology is giving assurances that you will not engage in similar behavior in the future—or at least that you will make a sincere effort not to.

Finally, the best apologies elicit empathy. This might seem odd to you at first—why should people feel empathy for the person who is apologizing rather than the person who is hurt? In some cases, the person who engaged in wrongdoing truly feels bad and wishes they could fix things. If you think someone is wracked with guilt or other negative feelings because of something they said or did that hurt you, in some cases you might feel badly for them. If you do, then you are more likely to see their apology as sincere and less likely to think they will hurt you again, making the apology particularly effective.

Compensation

Compensation, which is also called appeasement, goes beyond apologies by taking action to try to correct or make up for wrongdoing (Waldron & Kelley, 2008). Recall that hurtful behavior can be thought of as a "cost" in a relationship. Compensation involves using "rewards" to compensate for that cost. Common compensation strategies include being extra attentive or affectionate, buying someone gifts, and showing more commitment or loyalty. For example, Chloe might take a picture she posted with Maritza's enemies off her Instagram and post a new picture with Maritza, captioning it "me and my BFF." Maritza, for her part, might start asking Chloe to go to lunch or shopping at least twice a week to compensate for all the time she was spending with Carter. Compensation can be an effective strategy because it shows that you care enough to try and make things right. You can overdo compensation, though, which sometimes makes you appear desperate. Perhaps, for this reason, apologies are even more important than compensation when seeking forgiveness, although both can be effective (Waldron & Kelley, 2008).

When people want to make things right after a transgression, they often do special things for the person they hurt.

iStock/PeopleImages

Explanations

People have a natural pull toward wanting to explain why they engaged in hurtful behavior. No one wants to be seen as a "bad person," so instead of, or in addition to, admitting wrongdoing, people often offer explanations for their bad behavior. Sometimes explanations can make things better, but others can actually make things worse. There are two main types of explanations—excuses and justifications (Aune et al., 1998; Mongeau & Schulz, 1997). **Excuses** involve trying to minimize responsibility for one's actions by blaming someone or something else. Chloe could do this by blaming Maritza for having to make new friends and say, "Well, I wouldn't be hanging out with those girls if you weren't spending every waking moment of every day and night with Carter." Other common excuses include saying someone else made you do it, you were drunk or sick, or you "had no choice." **Justifications**, on the other hand, involve saying your behavior was not that bad. Maritza, for example, could say, "I really wasn't ignoring you; I was just excited to be with Carter and that's normal at the beginning of a new relationship." Both excuses and justifications can be effective if they are perceived to be valid, but oftentimes, making excuses or trying to justify one's behavior just makes matters worse. People want the person to admit wrongdoing and promise not to do it again, not to make excuses for bad behavior.

Granting Forgiveness Through Communication

People have at least five options for communicating forgiveness: minimizing, conditional forgiveness, nonverbal displays, explicit forgiveness, and discussion (Waldron & Kelley, 2005). The likelihood of using each type of forgiving communication varies based on how serious the transgression was, how happy people were with their relationship before the transgression, and whether they will continue their relationship or not.

Minimizing

Minimizing occurs when the hurt person downplays the transgression by saying things like, "It wasn't a big deal" or "Don't worry about it" (Waldron & Kelley, 2005). This type of forgiving communication is likely when a person receives a sincere apology, values the relationship, has few better alternatives, and decides the transgression was not very serious (Guerrero & Bachman, 2010; Sheldon et al., 2014; Waldron & Kelley, 2005). Minimizing can help people move past a transgression, but it can be problematic if the person who engaged in the transgression thinks the other person is condoning their behavior. Perhaps this is why minimizing is the least frequently used of the five common ways people communicate forgiveness (Waldron & Kelley, 2005). People may worry the person will do something similar in the future since they said it was "no big deal." And of course, many transgressions are "a big deal," so it is unlikely that people will say they are not. Minimizing is best used when a transgression is mild and not too hurtful.

Conditional Forgiveness

Conditional forgiveness occurs when forgiveness is granted but with strings attached. For example, Chloe might tell Maritza, "It's okay as long as you start making time for me now." r Maritza might say, "I forgive you but only if you promise to stop hanging out with people who hate me." In cases like these, forgiveness is "conditional" on the person fulfilling a promise to behave better in the future. If those promises are broken, the hurt person will feel free to take forgiveness back. Conditional forgiveness is a common response to a severe transgression, especially if the relationship had been good before the transgression occurred (Guerrero & Bachman, 2010). If someone does something really hurtful, you would probably want assurances that it would not happen again. Conditional forgiveness is not complete forgiveness; it is either not fully given until conditions are met, or it can be rescinded if conditions are not met. Therefore, it is not surprising that people who use conditional forgiveness tend to be less happy in their relationships and more likely to go their separate ways than people who communicate forgiveness a different way (Merolla, 2014; Sheldon et al., 2014).

Nonverbal Displays

People can communicate forgiveness through **nonverbal displays of forgiveness** such as acting like everything is normal, hugging the person who hurt you, and not acting mad anymore (Waldron & Kelley, 2005). These types of displays show that people have let go of some of the negative emotions they felt when they were hurt. When people forgive using nonverbal displays there are positive effects on relationships. Communicating forgiveness nonverbally provides reassurance to both people that things can go back to normal or at least get better. One study showed that using nonverbal displays like hugging and being affectionate again can actually strengthen the relationship after a transgression (Waldron & Kelley, 2005). Another study showed that people are especially likely to use nonverbal displays when the relationship was highly satisfying prior to the transgression (Guerrero & Bachman, 2010). Of all the ways of communicating forgiveness, nonverbal displays seem to best reflect a transformation from feeling negative emotions such as hurt, anger, and betrayal to moving on and feeling better about oneself and possibly the relationship (Waldron & Kelley, 2008).

Explicit Forgiveness

Explicit forgiveness involves making a straightforward statement such as "I forgive you." People who have a more forgiving nature tend to use explicit forgiveness (Sheldon et al., 2014). Explicit forgiveness can also be a response to a direct apology. Although this is a clear way to extend forgiveness, sometimes people never say "I forgive you" and instead show their forgiveness through actions. For example, one study showed that family members are more likely to use minimizing or nonverbal displays rather than explicit forgiveness (Carr & Wang, 2012). Verbally forgiving someone often marks a clear transition point between withholding and granting forgiveness (Waldron & Kelley, 2008). This can give the people involved a sense of closure so they can move on from the situation more easily with fewer doubts about where the relationship stands. Waldron and Kelley (2005) found that people's relationships sometimes got stronger after victims communicated forgiveness explicitly. People also say they are happier in their relationship if this type of forgiveness was offered and that positive emotions such as relief can accompany explicit forgiveness (Merolla, 2014).

Forgiveness Through Discussion

The final type of forgiving communication, **forgiveness through discussion**, is when people talk through what happened and forgiveness is granted based on that discussion. Discussion is the most common way that forgiveness is offered (Waldron & Kelley, 2005). An example from Waldron and Kelley (2005) is when one of their participants said, "I felt like we could move past this if we understood why it happened" (p. 109). It makes sense that people would need to talk about the hurtful event before deciding whether or not to grant forgiveness. The need to talk is especially strong when people are feeling a disconnect between the hurt they feel and their desire to stay in the relationship. For example, as angry and hurt as Maritza is that Chloe is hanging out with her enemies, she still sees Chloe as her best friend and as someone she has a history of positive interactions with, so she is willing to try and work through things rather than walk away. Discussion can also be a tool to resolve any doubts people have about whether the transgressor is genuinely sorry and will not hurt them, or at least try not to hurt them, in the future. As this suggests, discussion can be an avenue toward possible forgiveness when people are looking for reassurance. Other times, discussion is used as a way to clarify rules. Waldron and Kelley (2008) gave the example of a woman saying she was upset because one of her best friends told a mutual friend something she had wanted to stay private. She used discussion to see what the friend's intentions were and found out her friend had not understood how much she had wanted the information kept secret. They then made a rule to tell each other when to keep things private, after which she forgave her.

PRINCIPLES FOR COPING WITH RELATIONAL TRANSGRESSIONS

You might think that in an ideal world everyone would get along and no one would ever get hurt. The reality, of course, is very different. Even when our intentions are good, sometimes we cannot help hurting someone. When we are hurt by what others do and say, it can be difficult to cope with the situation. We might feel rejected, devalued, and even hopeless or defeated. The principles advanced here may help you contextualize these situations so you can cope with your feelings in a more constructive way.

Principle 1. The people we care about most have the most power to hurt us.

Relational transgressions can occur in any relationship. A co-worker can sabotage you, your boss can pass you over for a promotion you were led to expect, a friend can talk behind your back, and a romantic partner can break up with you. These and other events often qualify as relational transgressions. The most hurtful events, however, occur within close (or previously close) relationships. When we care about people, we are more interdependent and have more at stake when they betray us. We expect people we know and trust to be kind and loyal to us, so it can be particularly hurtful when they are not. Sometimes, after being hurt, people are afraid to get involved with new people because they do not want to be hurt again and may have trouble trusting others. Being closed off and not allowing yourself to be vulnerable, however, can stop you from developing new connections that would enrich your life.

Principle 2. Relational transgressions are costs that are weighed against rewards.

Relational transgressions are events that negatively violate relational rules and expectations, communicate devaluation, and trigger aversive emotions. At the heart of this definition is the idea that a relational transgression is a *cost*. As mentioned earlier in this chapter, all relationships are characterized by costs and rewards. A cost might be that you have to put up with a co-worker's perfectionism, but a reward might be that working with someone who is a perfectionist pushes you to do your best work. In close relationships, we typically gain many rewards, including receiving social support, feeling liked and respected, and having fun with someone. We also experience costs, such as having to deal with someone's moodiness or giving up some of our independence. Relational transgressions are a special kind of cost that is particularly hurtful and harmful to relationships. We often feel betrayed and devalued following a transgression. The question then becomes, are there enough rewards to compensate for the cost of the transgression? This is why people tend to be more forgiving and to communicate more constructively when they are in relationships that were previously rewarding. If you are in an unrewarding relationship or work situation, you are much less likely to be forgiving. This is also why people who caused the hurt try to make it up to the other person by engaging in compensatory behaviors and promising to act better in the future.

Principle 3. Communication helps determine the path a relationship takes following a transgression.

When people experience a relational transgression, the immediate reaction is usually to either fight by retaliating or to flee by distancing oneself. Being able to talk about the transgression calmly and constructively can be difficult. The onus to try to make things right is often on the person who committed the transgression. Three key ways of seeking forgiveness include apologizing, engaging in compensation, and providing an explanation. Enacting each of these forgiveness-seeking strategies requires communication skill. An apology can backfire if it comes across as insincere, so it is critical to offer an apology voluntarily and to mean what you say. If the transgression you committed was serious, you should also be prepared to own up to your mistake and promise to engage in better behavior in the future. Compensation can help counter the negative effects of a transgression, but too much compensation can appear desperate, so there is a fine line. Similarly, some explanations can be helpful, but others make matters worse. If you have hurt someone, try to put yourself in that person's position. Would the explanation make you feel better, or would you rather just have the person who hurt you apologize than try to justify their actions? Sometimes people get caught up in trying to explain and defend themselves instead of admitting wrongdoing and apologizing. The latter can pave the way for constructive communication about the transgression.

Principle 4. Communication cannot fix everything.

Even if you do everything right—apologize sincerely, let someone know how badly you feel, and try to repair the damage—it might not be enough. Some transgressions are just too severe. They break the trust between people and change the dynamics of the relationship. In other cases, there were already problems in the relationship, so the transgression just reinforces that it is time to move on. Even when a relationship is not fixable, people can still be forgiving. Indeed, forgiveness helps free people of the negative emotions surrounding the transgression, allowing them to heal and move on. Forgiveness does not always mean that everything goes back to normal or that you stay friends or in a relationship with someone, but it does give you a sense of closure.

CONCLUSION

Transgressions can rock the foundations of even the most stable relationships. Such was the case for our fictional best friends, Maritza and Chloe, who had no issues with each other until Carter came along and Chloe started hanging out with Maritza's worst enemies. You could argue that both women have the right to spend time with whomever they want, but that does not change how hurt either of them feels. Both women feel devalued, which is a key part of relational transgressions. Chloe feels like she is not a priority anymore. Maritza feels that Chloe betrayed her. If they want to preserve and possibly even strengthen their relationship, they need to forgive one another and redefine the rules in their friendship. Both women might apologize sincerely and listen to how the other feels. They might then compensate in ways that confirm that Maritza still sees Chloe as a priority and that Chloe is still a loyal friend. They might also communicate forgiveness to one another through the various strategies discussed here so they can close this rough chapter in their friendship and trust one another again.

CHAPTER 11 STUDY GUIDE

KEY TERMS

Identify and explain the meaning of each of the following key terms.

apology

common couple violence

compensation

concealment

conditional forgiveness

costs

deception

devaluation

emotional support

equivocation

exaggeration

excuses

expectancy violations

explicit forgiveness

explicit rule

forgiveness

forgiveness through discussion

hurtful message

implicit rule

instrumental support

intimate terrorism

invisible support

justifications

lying

microaggressions

minimizing

mutual violent control

nonverbal displays of forgiveness

person-centered messages

relational transgressions

repeated common couple violence

rewards

transgression-maximizing messages

transgression-minimizing messages

truth biases

understatement

violent resistance

REFLECTION QUESTIONS

1. Based on your observations, what are common transgressions in different types of relationships? How might transgressions differ in friendships, workplace relationships, and romantic relationships?

2. What types of deception do you believe are acceptable and even expected, and what types do you believe are the clearest examples of transgressions? Can you think of guidelines that might help people know when deception is okay versus when it is not?

3. Some transgressions are so severe that people decide to walk away from a relationship. Others lead to increased understanding through communication and strengthen the relationship over time. Think about some of the most serious transgressions that you have encountered in your life. What was the outcome in terms of if and how the relationship changed? Do you see any patterns that might predict which relationships survive transgressions versus which do not?

4. Imagine that a friend comes to you extremely upset. This friend committed a transgression that could threaten their romantic relationship. Your friend does not know what to do. Your friend's significant other is unaware of what has happened and your friend is not sure if confessing is a good idea. Just as importantly, your friend does not want the relationship to end. What advice would you give your friend?

12 ENDING RELATIONSHIPS

Keiko and McKenna were close friends throughout college. They were even roommates their sophomore year. The two women were confidants who disclosed everything to each other. After graduating, however, they gradually started spending less and less time together. Keiko tried to keep in touch by Facetiming McKenna at least a couple of times a week and extending invitations to go to lunch or shopping together. At first, McKenna accepted Keiko's invitations, but then she became immersed in a demanding new job and started declining a lot of Keiko's invitations, saying she was too busy to go out. Since Keiko had also started her career, she was understanding. They continued their Snapchat streak, sent each other direct messages on Twitter to share funny or relatable Tweets, and texted once in a while. But over time the texting and direct messages stopped and their communication was limited to a few Snapchats each day. Then Keiko found a romantic partner, fell in love, and was so caught up in her new relationship and career that without even realizing it, she stopped communicating with McKenna altogether. When their Snapchat streak ended, McKenna Facetimed Keiko and asked her if everything was alright. The two women talked and decided they needed to put more effort into their friendship. They planned to go to lunch, get their nails done, and catch up on everything happening in each other's lives the next weekend.

Do you think Keiko and McKenna will get their friendship back on track, or will their friendship continue to become distant until eventually, they stop talking again? Getting together for lunch could be a major step toward restoring their friendship to its previous level of closeness, or it could represent a genuine last effort to rejuvenate a friendship that is heading toward demise. A lot will depend on the communication that occurs during and after their meeting.

In today's busy world, it is not uncommon for friendships and other relationships to fade out despite the ease with which people can stay connected at some level via social media. This chapter focuses on understanding relational de-escalation and termination. **Relational de-escalation** refers to the process of reducing the closeness of a relationship. In this case, the relationship does not end, but people are no longer as close as they once were. Some relationships that de-escalate never end, but instead are permanently or temporarily "downgraded." **Relational termination** refers to the process of ending a relationship altogether. To better understand both de-escalation and termination, this chapter examines general characteristics of relationships that influence their longevity, different pathways relationships take when they decline, and specific types of communication people engage in to end relationships.

RELATIONSHIP CHARACTERISTICS THAT PREDICT STABILITY

Some relationships are more resilient than others. Think about various relationships you have with friends, family members, and possibly co-workers and romantic partners. Why do some of those relationships survive through hard times and others fall apart? Research suggests that the likelihood of staying in relationships depends on a number of factors, including how voluntary the relationship is, how many investments and barriers characterize the relationship, the alternatives we have, and how rewarding a relationship is. Of course, positive communication is also a key ingredient in preventing relationships from declining or ending.

Voluntary Versus Involuntary Relationships

As you learned in Chapter 8, some relationships are voluntary. In other words, you had a choice regarding whether to be in the relationship or not. Other relationships are involuntary because you had no choice. It is best to think of this as a continuum, with some relationships being more voluntary or involuntary than others. Friendships and romantic relationships tend to be more voluntary. Family and work relationships tend to be more involuntary. It can be difficult to end some involuntary relationships completely. For example, you cannot stop being a member of your family (although you can act like you are not) and you cannot stop being co-workers with someone unless one of you quits.

Investments and Barriers

The extent to which there are investments and barriers preventing dissolution also affects how resilient relationships are. **Investments** are all the "resources that become attached to a relationship and would decline in value or be lost if the relationship were to end" (Rusbult et al., 1994, p. 119). Investments include time, energy, love, shared possessions, enmeshment in a joint social network, and building an identity as a couple, among others. **Breakup barriers** are all the forces that stop people from ending a relationship (Attridge, 1994). These can include obligation, public commitment, religious or moral beliefs, the legal process, concerns about children, and financial or emotional dependence.

When times get tough or feelings start to fade, investments and barriers provide people with reasons to put effort into trying to make a relationship work. For example, when you get married, you put barriers against breaking up in place. Instead of just being able to walk away, you would need to go through the process of a divorce. You might also need to navigate issues related to children and a shared home and possessions after investing time and effort into building a life together. Romantic partners, friends, and family members are often part of larger interconnected social networks. If you end your relationship with someone in this broader social network, it can alter your other relationships within the network. Your friends and family might take sides, and you may be excluded from certain group activities and deleted from group chats. After a breakup, people sometimes even unfollow their ex's friends on social media, so breakups can have a domino effect; ending a relationship with one person can lead you to lose relationships with other people as well. The more embedded we are into other people's lives, the more difficult it is to end a relationship without these types of consequences.

When you end a friendship or break up with someone, your shared social network can be affected. If a couple in this group broke up, how might it affect their standing in the group as well as their relationships with common friends?

iStock/g-stockstudio

Rewards and Costs

As you learned in Chapter 11, many social psychologists believe that the ratio of rewards versus costs plays a key role in predicting whether a relationship continues or falls into decline. Recall that rewards are all the positive consequences people get from being in a relationship (Sprecher, 1998). These include material resources like shared possessions, but more importantly, rewards include more abstract resources such as feeling loved, being comfortable around someone, and having fun together. Positive communication is essential for creating a rewarding climate in a relationship. In Chapter 9, you learned about various positive forms of communication that help people maintain healthy and happy relationships, including self-disclosing positive information, spending time together having fun, complimenting one another, and showing affection. The more people engage in these behaviors, the more rewarding their relationship is and the more resilient it is to problems. Indeed, the Gottman Institute uses the term **positive sentiment override** to describe how developing a constructive and caring communication climate helps couples better handle disagreements (Werrbach, 2016). When people experience positive sentiment override, they are optimistic about their relationship and see problems as relatively minor and easily managed. The positive emotion they feel in the relationship acts as a buffer against misinterpreting their partner's actions or taking things overly personally.

Costs, on the other hand, are all the negative consequences people get from being in a relationship (Sprecher, 1998). These can include the time, effort, and lost opportunities associated with being in a relationship. As discussed in Chapter 11, relationships are also home to a lot of the most intense negative emotions we experience. When people engage in transgressions like cheating, or when conflict patterns become destructive, the costs within a relationship go up. The concept of **negative sentiment override** helps explain what happens when the negativity during conflict spills into other aspects of the relationship (Werrbach, 2016). People expect negativity, so they take things personally and are always on the defensive or the attack. This kind of communication climate makes a relationship costly rather than rewarding. According to social exchange theory, , people are much more likely to end a relationship if costs outweigh rewards than if rewards outweigh costs (Stafford, 2008; Thibaut & Kelley, 1959). This idea can be extended to other kinds of relationships and situations as well. For example, if the costs at your workplace outweigh the rewards, you are likely to look for another job. If your roommate is inconsiderate and always in a bad mood, a new roommate may be in order.

Alternatives

Social exchange theory also suggests that the quality of alternatives influences whether people continue or end relationships (Rusbult et al., 2011; Thibaut & Kelley, 1959). The **quality of alternatives** refers to the various options people have outside of a current relationship. For example, Keiko has a new boyfriend, so spending time with him is a better alternative to her than spending most of her time with McKenna. In romantic relationships, people assess their alternatives by thinking about new potential partners or what it would be like to be single. If those alternatives are more appealing than staying in the current relationship, a breakup is likely. You might also stick with a friend group you are somewhat unhappy with until you have new friends to hang out with.

Alternative relationships can play a role in ending relationships in other ways. When people move into separate friend groups, start spending time with a new significant other, or start hanging out with people from work, the time and effort they put into these new relationships detracts from the investment they can make into old relationships. Indeed, studies have shown that when people transition from being single to being in a serious relationship, the number of close friends they have decreases (Fehr, 2000). Thus, the more positive alternatives you have, the harder it is to maintain all your relationships, and the more likely it is that some of your relationships will de-escalate or end. Conversely, when you see your current relationships as your best alternatives, you are likely to stay in those relationships. Some research even shows that when we are in happy relationships, we derogate our alternatives even if they are attractive (Rusbult et al., 1994). Therefore, if a man Keiko had a crush on in college texts her and confesses that he still thinks about her all the time, Keiko might think "he's not all that anymore" if she is happy with her new boyfriend.

GENERAL TYPES OF DE-ESCALATION AND RELATIONSHIP ENDINGS

When relationships become too costly, there are better alternatives, or there is simply not enough affection and positive communication to sustain them, they are likely to de-escalate or end. The way this happens, though, can vary greatly. Some patterns of de-escalation or termination are more likely in some relationships than others, as discussed next.

Drifting Away

Drifting away involves a gradual decrease in contact that marks the de-escalation of a relationship. Drifting away is common, especially in friendships and former work relationships. A classic study by Rose and Serafica (1986) showed that casual friends are especially likely to fade out when they are no longer in proximity to each other. Common reasons for drifting away include changing jobs, moving away, and spending time with other people. The most common reasons precollege and college friendships end is that people grow apart, start to lack common experiences, and have fewer opportunities to spend time with each other (Owens, 2003). Sometimes friends do not even realize they are drifting apart at first (Rose, 1984), as was the case for Keiko and McKenna. People get absorbed in their lives and decrease communication with certain people without meaning to. Even married couples can drift apart. In fact, about 10 percent of divorced couples believe that there was no major reason that their marriage failed other than they simply grew apart (Amato & Previti, 2003).

When drifting apart is a mutual process, a friendship, or even a potential romantic relationship, can end without negativity. This leaves the door open for resuming the relationship in the future (Rawlins, 1994). Indeed, friends who drift away are better able to restore their friendships at a later date than those who end their relationships because of betrayals or competition (Fehr, 2000).

In today's high-tech society, drifting away rarely leads to completely ending a friendship. Even though the friendship may not be as close as it once was, former close friends usually stay in contact through social media. Staying connected on sites like Twitter, Facebook, and Instagram is an easy way to maintain "weak ties" with someone (e.g., Burke et al., 2011; Ellison et al., 2007). **Weak ties** are acquaintances within our social networks. Studies have shown that most people want to maintain weak ties with a lot of people to keep their social network broad and diverse. Social media allows people to do that without expending a lot of energy. Therefore, two formerly close friends can easily de-escalate their relationship so that it functions more as an acquaintanceship by keeping in touch via social networking sites but not having much other contact.

Social media makes keeping in touch with a lot of people easy, but if that is the only communication occurring, a relationship will usually de-escalate or remain a weak tie.

Vladimir Vladimirov/E+ via Getty Images

Ending on Bad Terms

Instead of drifting apart peacefully, some relationships de-escalate or end after turmoil. Betrayal, hostility, criticism, and violence are all reasons people give for ending friendships (Rose, 1984). We expect our friends to be loyal and supportive, not disloyal and critical. Despite this, betrayals by friends are fairly common (Davis & Todd, 1985; Jones & Burdette, 1994; Shackelford & Buss, 1996). The worst betrayals involve a friend becoming involved with a current, potential, or former romantic partner. Other especially hurtful betrayals by friends include having a friend talk behind your back, fail to stand up for you, or betray a confidence.

These same issues lead to breakups in romantic relationships. The top reason for divorce in the United States is infidelity (Amato & Previti, 2003), which most people consider to be one of the worst acts of betrayal. When a major event like cheating occurs, even the closest relationships can end suddenly. Davis (1973) explained this phenomenon as **catastrophe theory**. This idea has been supported by research showing that about 25 percent of romantic relationship breakups are caused by a critical event that leads to rapid disengagement (Baxter, 1984; Bullis et al., 1993; Lampard, 2014). Some of these events are extremely hurtful, such as cheating, having an especially nasty argument, being subjected to physical violence, or having someone spread untrue rumors about you. Close friends are more likely than casual friends to say that critical events ended their relationships (Rose & Serafica, 1986). Other research shows that pervasive conflict patterns that include criticism, contempt, defensiveness, and stonewalling predict divorce (Gottman, 1994: see also Chapter 10). These costly behaviors can drain the warmth and fun out of a relationship, creating a toxic environment that eventually leads to a messy breakup.

When relationships end on bad terms, they can turn antipathetic. **Antipathetic relationships** are characterized by mutual dislike (Card, 2007). A sizeable proportion of antipathetic relationships started out as friendships. Researchers have investigated the reasons why some friendships turn antipathetic (Card, 2007; Casper & Card, 2010). The most common reasons have to do with jealousy and competition. The worst of these is one friend stealing another friend's partner or love interest. But jealousy and competition also include situations such as feeling a friend is becoming close to another person and excluding you.

Incompatibility was the second most common reason friendships turned antipathetic. People can become incompatible in ways that do not cause conflict, such as developing different interests. This type of incompatibility is more likely to lead to drifting apart than an antipathetic relationship. However, when incompatibility is based on perceiving another person's negative personality characteristics, the possibility that the friendship will turn into an antipathetic relationship rises. Behaviors perceived as annoying, fake, and controlling are just some of many possible examples.

Finally, the third most common reason friendships turn antipathetic is that the friend violated the implicit or explicit rules about how friends should act. In other words, they broke the "friend code" by engaging in behaviors such as lying, proving to be untrustworthy or unreliable, or not keeping promises. Behaviors involving competition and jealousy also break the friend code, but in a different way because they involve third parties.

Although research on antipathetic relationships has focused on friendships gone wrong, the same principles can be extended to other types of relationships. Couples who endure betrayals, jealousy, and destructive patterns of conflict are more likely to end on bad terms than partners who maintained loyalty and positive communication despite their problems.

Family Estrangement

Some people think family relationships can never really end because a person cannot stop being someone's daughter, brother, or aunt. While that may be true, family members can cut ties from one another so that they have no real relationship. Researchers have described two types of family estrangement (Agllias, 2016). **Physical estrangement** occurs when family members no longer have any contact with one another. **Emotional estrangement**, on the other hand, is a situation where family members have infrequent contact with one another but usually only when they feel obligated to do so. When they are in contact, communication is often awkward and uncomfortable.

A defining feature of family estrangement is that it is intentional. Losing contact with a cousin or not knowing where your Great Aunt lives anymore do not necessarily qualify as estrangement. For lack of contact to qualify as physical estrangement, communication must be cut off intentionally (Scharp, 2006). Another feature of family estrangement is that other family members are aware of it. Oftentimes, other family members act as intermediaries, not to try to fix things between the estranged family members but to convey general information. For example, if Gary and his sister, Brianna, are estranged, their other sibling, Jordan, might talk to them both about who should go where for the holidays. Significant unresolved conflict also defines estrangement. Typically, family members had some type of significant conflict that damaged their relationship so much that they no longer want to communicate with each other. Most of the time, grudges are held and one or both of the family members feels fully justified in stopping all communication.

The specific reasons cited for family estrangement are similar to those mentioned as causing the demise of friendships and romantic relationships. These include having unresolvable disagreements, including those related to issues such as money, divorce, and substance abuse (Agllias, 2016). But family estrangement is almost always the result of a series of problems rather than one major conflict or transgression (Sichel, 2007), with a particular event sometimes thought of as the "straw that breaks the camel's back" (Scharp et al., 2015, p. 330). Family estrangements can be described as falling on various points along a continuum that ranges from no communication at all, called **continuous estrangement**, to a chaotic pattern where family members fluctuate between trying to connect but then acting distant (Scharp et al., 2015). Part of this fluctuation may be due to societal pressure to maintain relationships with family members.

On-Again–Off-Again Relationships

Family estrangements are not the only type of relationship characterized by cycling through patterns of closeness (the "on-again" side) and distance (the off-again side). On-again–off-again relationships are also especially common between romantic partners (Bevan & Cameron, 2001). In one study, two-thirds of college students reported that they had been in at least one on-again–off-again relationship (Dailey et al., 2009). These relationships may be more prevalent today than ever before, in part because social media keeps some ex-partners connected after breakups (Blight et al., 2019; Halperin, 2012). It used to be easy to avoid seeing an ex, but now unless you unfollow or block your exes, you may be subjected to seeing unexpected images of them on your social media. This may cause you to miss an ex, or to feel jealous if the ex is out with someone new. For more about how people deal with social media following a breakup, see the I Didn't Know That! feature.

I DIDN'T KNOW THAT!
BLOCKING, PRUNING, AND UNFOLLOWING ON SOCIAL MEDIA

People have very different opinions about what to do about their ex when it comes to social media. Some people strongly believe you should remove all traces of the person from your life, including your phone and social networking sites. Others believe doing so is petty and vengeful. What do you think? It might surprise you to know that the two main reasons people purge someone from their phones and social media are almost direct opposites—to either hurt the partner or to avoid being hurt oneself.

In a study of teens (who arguably are the savviest when it comes to cell phone communication), nearly half reported that they removed their exes from the contacts in their phones, and just under one-third said they blocked them (Lenhart et al., 2015). Almost half of the girls and one-third of the boys said that they took couple pictures off their social media (a process sometimes referred to as **scrubbing**; see Child et al., 2011) and pruned their ex from their account by unfriending and/or blocking. And it's not just teens who engage in scrubbing and **pruning** behaviors. A study on post-breakup behavior on Facebook showed that young adults engaged in actions such as blocking or unfollowing an ex, changing passwords so their ex could no longer get on their accounts, and even changing privacy settings from public to private so their exes could not monitor their behavior (Quan-Haase et al., 2018).

The reasons teens and young adults engage in these behaviors is more often to protect themselves than to hurt the ex. Seeing an ex on social media can stir up lingering feelings, create jealousy, or make someone miss their ex more. People also have the urge to "creep" on their exes and see what they are doing, which can also make it more difficult to get over someone. Unfollowing and blocking someone can help reduce the temptation to stalk someone's page. By changing privacy settings, people can also prevent exes from creeping on their pages. Pruning, by removing stories and comments, can be helpful in the healing process as well. You no longer have a reminder on your page of some of the good times you shared, and when people look at your page they will not mistakenly assume that you are still together. After some time, when people have sufficient closure, they might follow their ex again, and even repost some of the archived pictures. There are, of course, times when people block, unfollow, remove likes and comments, and so forth to try to hurt an ex by showing they no longer care. It can, indeed, be hurtful to have someone delete you from their social media as well as their lives as if you were never there. But instead of assuming that these actions were done in spite or out of pettiness, consider that maybe it is a normal part of the healing process for your ex.

What do you think? Based on your own experiences and those of your friends, what are some of the most common reasons people prune, unfollow, or block their exes? How do people feel when their ex engages in these types of behaviors? Do people engage in similar behaviors when their friendships end?

On-again–off-relationships are defined as breaking up and getting back together at least once, with the majority of couples going through this cycle between two and five times before either breaking up for good or staying together (Dailey et al., 2009;Halperin, 2012). As you might have guessed, most of these relationships end in a final breakup rather than a stable continuing relationship. As they run their course, on-again–off-again relationships appear to be characterized by a mix of highs and lows. These relationships have enough rewards that people go back to them, but enough costs that they do not usually last. A lot of times these relationships are also plagued by uncertainty (Blight et al., 2019). During the "on" times, people are not sure the relationship will last, and during the "off" times the possibility of a renewal seems possible, especially if it has happened before.

There are different types of on-again–off-again relationships (Dailey et al., 2013). One of the most common is a *habitual relationship* in which people gravitate back to each other because it is comfortable and convenient. In these relationships, it is easy to fall back into old communication patterns, including those that were destructive to the relationship. Unless couples address the issues that caused them to break up, they are likely to repeat the same cycle and break up again. Another type of on-again–off-again relationship involves *gradual separation*. In this case, partners may not be ready to let one another go, but with each on-again–off-again cycle they feel less connected until the relationship finally ends. In other situations, *one person is in control* of the on-again–off-again relationship. This is usually the person who is less attached to the relationship. This person can dictate the terms of any renewals and decides when to break up and when to get together again. Ultimately the person in control is likely to end the relationship for good at some point. None of these types of on-again–off-again relationships have particularly good prospects for lasting.

Some couples, however, are able to capitalize on transitions in a way that helps them be more successful if they get back together. **Capitalizing on transitions** means the couple uses the "off" time in the cycle to reflect on the relationship, improve themselves, sort out their feelings, and decide what they want and don't want as individuals and in the relationship. If they then come back together, they are more prepared to make the significant kind of changes necessary to improve the relationship. Couples who spend the transition time this way have less conflict, more positive feelings, and more relational improvement if they decide to try again (Dailey et al., 2013).

Both romantic partners and friends have other communication strategies at their disposal that can help them reconnect with someone after a relationship ends. In a classic study, Wilmot and Stevens (1994) described ways people were able to rejuvenate friendships that had declined or were in the process of declining. The top three rejuvenation strategies involved changing behaviors, having a relationship talk, and making gestures of reconciliation. Keiko and McKenna are on the path to doing all of these things. Meeting for lunch is a good start. This is a gesture of reconciliation—an activity signaling that they want their friendship to get back on track. During lunch, the women may have a relationship talk where they decide to put more effort into their friendship so it does not slip away. They agree to set time aside each week to catch up Facetiming or hanging out.

It's easy for friends to get busy and drift apart. Making time to talk is a key way to prevent friendships from de-escalating.

SDI Productions/E+ via Getty Images

FEATURES OF BREAKUP BEHAVIOR

Sometimes rejuvenation strategies work, but other times, people do not put the effort in to keep a relationship going, or one or both people decide it is better to part ways. Some relationships end without hurt feelings; the decision to end the relationship is mutual and both parties agree it is time to move on. Oftentimes, however, the ending of a relationship is painful. As the old song lyrics say, breaking up can be hard to do. This can be true for many types of relationships, ranging from the former best friend who betrayed you to the significant other you thought was "the one." Although relationship endings can be as unique as relationships themselves, certain strategies for ending or de-escalating relationships are fairly common. These strategies vary in important ways, including how direct versus indirect they are, how much information they provide, and how kind or hurtful they are.

Direct Versus Indirect Strategies

A critical feature of breakup strategies is how direct versus indirect they are. There are advantages to using direct communication to end a relationship. Intentions are clearer, so there is less room for someone to hang on and hope the relationship will continue. Direct strategies are expected when relationships were long term and serious. In these cases, there is more of a need for a formal "breakup." While this is truer in romantic relationships than in friendships, even close friends sometimes engage in direct communication to end their friendship. For friends, direct communication is most likely when a major event or problem precipitated a desire to end the friendship. By contrast, people tend to use indirect strategies when the relationship has a shorter history or when there were no major problems or issues. Keiko and McKenna had a long history as close friends, but because they were not experiencing any specific issues they just started to drift away, which is common in many friendships. People also use indirect strategies to avoid the pain and drama that can accompany some direct breakups (LeFebvre et al., 2019).

Level of Information Provided

With some exceptions, direct breakup strategies also provide people with more information about the reasons behind the breakup, whether there is a possibility of restoring the relationship in the future, and how people are expected to treat each other now that the relationship is over. For example, do you unfollow each other on social media? If you have common friends, do you avoid hanging out in a group with them at the same time? The more enmeshed two people were in each other's lives, the more necessary this type of information exchange is. Information is also important for helping people achieve closure. The **need for closure** is based on wanting to know the answers to questions as a way to alleviate confusion and ambiguity (Roets et al., 2015). When applied to breakups, the need for closure suggests that people have a natural desire to know why the relationship did not work out. This is normal. If you have invested a lot of time and effort into something, you want to understand what went wrong and learn from it. You also want to be able to move on rather than feeling as if you still have unfinished business with someone. Without getting answers, it can be difficult to gain closure and move on. Having a coherent explanation of the breakup in your head helps you learn and grow, which makes you more likely to have satisfying relationships in the future (Kansky & Allen, 2018).

WHAT WOULD YOU DO?
IS HONESTY THE BEST POLICY WHEN ENDING A RELATIONSHIP?

Ending a relationship is difficult. Most people want to make sense of the breakup and understand what went wrong. Without this understanding, it can be challenging to achieve closure and move on. However, the reasons people end relationships are often messy and complex, and understanding those reasons can lead to more hurt. Indeed, needing closure and wanting to prevent further hurt are often two goals that are at odds with one another during breakups. These are ethical issues as well. How much closure should you feel obligated to give someone or compelled to ask someone to give you? And should you be completely honest about the reasons you are breaking up with someone? What is more ethical—to be truthful even though it hurts someone, or to be ambiguous or untruthful so as not to hurt someone's feelings more than you have to? And is it true that you sometimes need to be "cruel to be kind" so that someone understands that the breakup is final and moves on? Consider the following scenarios and think about (a) what you would do if you were in Sebastian or Audra's positions as well as (b) how you would feel if you were Jaycee or Dylan.

At first, Sebastian thinks Jaycee is the perfect woman—beautiful, smart, and outgoing. But after they go on a few dates, the glow starts to wear off. Sebastian still thinks Jaycee is great, but he realizes she isn't the fantasy girl he made her out to be in his head. He expected to have great chemistry and stimulating conversations with her, but things have fallen a little short in both those areas. Jaycee has told him that she really cares for him and sees a lot of potential in their budding relationship. He's not sure how to tell her that he does not feel the same, especially since she has not done anything wrong.

Audra thought she was in love with Dylan but now that they have started to settle into a relationship, she realizes that she latched on to him for all the wrong reasons. She had been feeling insecure and having trouble getting over her ex-boyfriend, and Dylan had been there for her. He was completely different than her ex, and at first that made him appealing. Now Audra always finds herself comparing Dylan to her ex in her head and wishing Dylan was more like him. Sometimes when she looks at Dylan she even wonders why she once found him attractive. He really isn't her type at all. She knows she needs to break up with him, but she dreads hurting him, especially since he had been there for her when she needed someone.

If you were in Sebastian's place, what would you say to Jaycee that could give her the closure she needs without hurting her feelings unnecessarily? Would you tell her the whole truth—that you had put her on a pedestal and then been disappointed? Or that the chemistry wasn't there and conversations with her were boring? These would be honest responses, but they would be hurtful.

Audra faces similar choices. Should she tell Dylan she now realizes that she used him to try to get over her ex? If he pushes her to try to work it out, should she tell him that he's not her type and she doesn't find him attractive anymore? Such words would certainly be difficult for Dylan, or anyone else, to hear.

On the other hand, giving vague or cliché reasons for breaking up does not seem authentic and may not provide people closure. For example, Sebastian may say, "I'm sorry. You're great, but it's just not there for me." Or Audra might tell Dylan, "My feelings have changed." These types of cliché breakup lines are often meant to save people from the hurt of hearing more specific reasons for the breakup, but they also seem impersonal and can leave people frustrated and wondering what the deeper causes of the breakup were. Knowing this, what would you advise Sebastian and Audra to say and do?

Level of Hurtfulness

Ending a relationship can make people feel uncomfortable, awkward, and vulnerable. People's identity is at stake during breakups. We want others to see us as possessing an array of positive characteristics, such as kindness, competence, friendliness, and intelligence. Yet if you initiate a breakup, people might see you as cold and unkind for hurting someone you once cared about. If you are the person being left, you may question if you have the good qualities necessary to attract and keep people close to you. So how then do you end a relationship without being unkind and hurting someone? In some cases, it is impossible to avoid deeply hurting another person during a breakup, but the strategies you use can make a big difference. As you will learn, breakup strategies vary in terms of how kind versus cruel they are.

COMMON BREAKUP BEHAVIORS

People can break up using a single strategy, such as texting someone and saying "I want to break up" (not a particularly kind strategy), ghosting or ignoring someone completely (also not a particularly kind strategy), or having a face-to-face conversation with someone to try and show respect while still letting them know the relationship is not working (a better strategy). As you read about the various ways people end relationships, keep in mind that more than one strategy can be used to break off a relationship. A common pattern, for example, is gradually decreasing communication for a while but then meeting with the person to communicate directly that the relationship is over.

The Direct Dump

The most common direct strategy for ending a relationship is the **direct dump,** which involves simply stating that the relationship or friendship is over (Baxter, 1984; Dailey et al., 2009; Thieme & Rouse, 1991). This strategy can be used by itself. More often, though, it is used along with other strategies. For example, you could receive a text message saying "It's over" without any other discussion, or you could receive the same message after a week of limited contact that signaled something was wrong. Most people agree that the most respectful way to tell someone a relationship is over is to deliver the message face-to-face. Even among teens, breaking up with someone in person is perceived to be more than twice as acceptable as breaking up with someone via text (Lenhart et al., 2015). Among adults, sending a breakup message through text is regarded as disrespectful and lacking in compassion (Sprecher et al., 2010). If the relationship was at all important, people feel they deserve to have the person take the time to break up with them in person. Using the direct dump without any discussion can also fail to give the receiver of the breakup message closure. People usually want to know the reasons why someone is ending a relationship with them. Sometimes those reasons are obvious. Perhaps two friends have been struggling with issues of competitiveness for a while or someone in a dating relationship cheated. In these cases, using the direct dump can provide an unambiguous way to mark the end of a relationship. Other times, however, people are surprised that the other person wants to end things and need more discussion than the direct dump alone supplies.

The Relationship-Talk Trick

Another strategy people use to end relationships, the **relationship-talk trick**, involves at least some discussion of what went wrong in the relationship. This strategy is called the relationship-talk trick because the person who wants to break up says they want to talk about the relationship when, in actuality, people using this strategy have no intention of working things out; their intention is to break up. The relationship talk is structured in a way that a breakup will be a logical conclusion. This strategy is fairly common (Baxter, 1984). It provides a way for people to talk before breaking up, which can give both people more closure. The relationship-talk trick also gives people who are thinking about initiating a breakup a way out if they change their mind.

Sometimes people need to talk to fix things or because they have something important to share; other times this can be a harbinger of the relationship-talk trick.

iStock/dannikonov

During the "relationship talk," the person initiating the breakup often provides justifications for why the relationship should end. There is a fine line, however, between providing justifications that help give someone closure and hurting someone more than necessary. Some justifications, such as "It's just not working anymore," can be too vague to be helpful. More specific justifications, however, can be hurtful. Saying someone is annoying, unintelligent, or boring or making statements such as "I never really loved you" might be honest, but they can also cause additional hurt at a vulnerable moment. The What Would You Do? feature ponders the issue of whether honesty is always the best policy when ending relationships.

Positive Tone Strategy

Although it may be true that sometimes there is no good way to end a relationship, one of the best strategies is to use the **positive tone strategy**. This strategy focuses on breaking up in a direct and unambiguous manner, while also trying to reduce the degree of hurt experienced (Banks et al., 1987; Baxter, 1982; Cody, 1982; Perras & Lustig, 1982). People view the positive tone strategy as a compassionate way to break up with someone (Collins & Gillath, 2012). While ideal in many ways, this strategy can be difficult to implement effectively. The key is to focus on the specific positives of the person and the relationship rather than using cliché lines.

Referring back to the examples in the What Would You Do? feature, instead of saying "I'm sorry. You're great, but it's just not there for me," Sebastian might instead point out some of Jaycee's positive qualities and even say that he is surprised that his feelings aren't stronger given how great she is. Rather than tell Dylan that her feelings have changed, Audra might emphasize that he helped her through a difficult time when she was confused about a lot of things, that he is a truly wonderful person, and that he deserves someone who is 100 percent into him. Are these statements better than clichés? They are, but they would still be hurtful. Positive tone can help make a breakup a little easier and provide needed closure (Collins & Gillath, 2012). Yet even with the best of intentions, feelings are going to be hurt. Another challenge for someone using positive tone is not to sound condescending. Communicating in a sincere manner that shows genuine regret about having to end a relationship is critical.

The Negotiated Farewell

Another breakup strategy that aims for kindness is the **negotiated farewell**. With positive tone, one person is clearly in the position of initiating the breakup, as was the case in the scenarios involving Sebastian and Audra. The negotiated farewell, in contrast, represents an amicable and mutual breakup process that involves negotiating how to best end or de-escalate a relationship that both people agree is in decline (Dailey et al., 2009; Emmers & Hart, 1996; Metts, 1997; Sprecher et al., 2010). In this case, two people have agreed that ending the relationship is either the best thing to do or is necessary.

One example is a couple who falls out of love but wants to be good parents to their children. Another is business partners who worked together for years, had projects and patents together, but are now going their separate ways. In these cases, it is important to negotiate the terms of the change in relationships status. For example, the couple might end their marriage but maintain a relationship as co-parents. They also have to decide how to equitably split up their possessions and how to deal with their former in-laws. The former business partners might end their professional relationship but agree to continue to give each other credit for work they did together and to bolster each other's reputations when possible. Fairness and being open-minded are key ingredients for a successfully negotiated farewell.

The process of determining how to split up possessions after a divorce is smoother and more amiable if a couple uses the negotiated farewell strategy.

iStock/AndreyPopov

The Blame Game

In contrast to the kinder strategies of positive tone and the negotiated farewell, the **blame game** describes a situation where ending a relationship becomes a competitive struggle between two people. Some friendships that turn into antipathetic relationships follow this path. Two people who were once best friends become enemies, with each trying to make the case that the other is more to blame for the demise of the friendship.

The blame game is often the "end game" in a relationship where negative cycles of conflict or demand-withdraw started to pervade the relationship (see Chapter 10). Both people know the relationship is deteriorating, both blame the other for their problems, and sometimes they give different reasons for why the relationship is ending (Cody, 1982; Dailey et al., 2009). This type of relationship ending can be messy. Ex-friends and ex-partners might block each other on social media and try to get people on their sides. Although the blame game is clearly a hurtful way to end a relationship, it can give people closure because both individuals usually feel justified in ending the relationship and are glad to get out of a toxic situation.

Genuine and Pseudo De-Escalation

Sometimes people do not completely end a relationship. Instead, the relationship either de-escalates or changes. For example, the divorced couple mentioned above will continue to be co-parents, and the former business partners will maintain a cordial professional relationship. Sometimes de-escalating a relationship is want we want. Maybe we still want to be friends with a former best friend or be on good terms with an ex-boyfriend or girlfriend.

The **genuine de-escalation** strategy allows people to reduce the closeness of a relationship without completely ending it. This strategy can involve taking a break to give each other space, deciding to be friends instead of dating, or acknowledging that even though you are not best friends anymore, you still want to stay in contact and consider each other friends. The key for genuine de-escalation is that it represents an honest attempt to maintain a relationship with the person, either by taking a break to improve it or by reducing closeness but staying on good terms (Banks et al., 1987; Cody, 1982).

In contrast to genuine de-escalation, **pseudo de-escalation** involves a false declaration about wanting to decrease the closeness of the relationship either temporarily or permanently (Baxter, 1985). In this case, the person requesting to "take a break" or "still be friends" has no intention of doing either; the intention is to end the relationship altogether but to let the person down easily or not have to face hurting them. A major problem with this strategy, however, is that it can give people false hope. One study showed that less than 10 percent of people who received a pseudo de-escalation message understood that the relationship was really over (Baxter, 1984). The rest hung on to hope that the relationship would resume or get back to normal sometime in the future.

Ghosting

Avoidance can be used to end any relationship, but it is an especially common way to end relatively new relationships or to stop progress toward developing a close relationship with someone (Baxter, 1982; Cody, 1982; Emmers & Hart, 1996;Perras & Lustig, 1982). Avoiding can take different forms, the most extreme of which is ghosting. **Ghosting** is the process of shutting down all communication with someone, usually abruptly and with no explanation, so that someone disappears from your life as if they were a ghost who had never really been there at all (LeFebvre,

iMessage
Yesterday 11:44 PM

Fun night, huh? 😉   11:44 PM

Yeah! We should do it
again soon 😘   11:45 PM

Definitely ❤️   11:45 PM

How about Friday? ❤️   11:45 PM

Today 10:16 AM

Did u fall asleep? 😂   10:16 AM

Today 11:45 AM

Is Friday not good?   11:45 AM

Today 2:33 PM

I guess not...   2:33 PM

iMessage

Ghosting has become so common that it is a frequent subject of memes and was even a Halloween costume. Ghosting strikes a chord in people; it may be a convenient and easy way to break things off with someone, but it is often seen as disrespectful.

Courtesy of Laura Guerrero

2017; Truscelli & Guerrero, 2019; Vilhauer, 2015). A study of college students identified three especially common ways that people ghost (Truscelli & Guerrero, 2019). First, cell phone communication stops. People are left on "read," Snapchat streaks are broken, and no likes or comments are left on your social media. Second, ghosting involves stopping all face-to-face communication, including actively avoiding talking to the person or being places they might be. Third, sometimes social media is purged. This involves removing the person and any traces of the former relationship from one's social media. Specific tactics include unfollowing or blocking someone and removing pictures or comments from social media.

Ghosting is viewed by many as an especially disrespectful way of ending a relationship. People often feel that they at least deserve an explanation. Ghosting provides little if any closure, although some people believe that if someone ghosts them, then that person does not deserve to have them in their life, which can give some closure. If ghosting is perceived so negatively, why do people do it? The most common reason is that it is easier and less emotionally stressful to ghost someone than to engage in a discussion about breaking up (LeFebvre et al., 2019). People are also more likely to ghost if they fear the person they are ending things with will get emotional or try to hang on to them. Finally, for relationships in the early stages of development, some people believe ghosting is an acceptable alternative to going through the emotional labor of ending things that never got serious. In contrast, ghosting is rarely seen as acceptable in relationships that were highly committed (Freedman et al., 2019).

Fading Out

A less extreme form of avoidance involves fading out. Fade-outs generally happen two ways. One is the **one-way fade,** which occurs when one person gradually reduces communication and the other person is left trying to figure out how to respond to the reduced contact. Unlike ghosting, the drop in communication is gradual rather than sudden. College students describe fading out as a weak form of ghosting that is more acceptable than decreasing communication completely (Truscelli & Guerrero, 2019). Strategies involve maintaining some forms of contact while relinquishing others, while also decreasing the overall amount of communication. For example, someone trying to fade out might send someone fewer Snapchats every day while still maintaining a Snapchat streak. When they do answer Snapchats, they might send just their face when in the past they included words or emojis. Another strategy is to increasingly leave messages unanswered for longer stretches of time. As these examples show, with the mutual fade out, both the quantity and quality of communication decreases, providing a signal to the receiver that the initiator no longer cares as much about the relationship.

The second way of fading out is the **mutual fade out**, which is also referred to as "drifting away." This is what happened with Keiko and McKenna. They simply got busy with their lives after graduating and slowly started communicating less with one another. Mutual fade-outs can be intentional, with both people trying to fade out a friendship or romantic relationship that they both know is no longer working, but more often mutual fade-outs are unintentional. This type of drifting apart is common in friendships and long-distance relationships where proximity is the main reason for relationship decline. Lack of shared interests can also lead people to mutually fade out.

The one-way fade is characterized by strategic decreases in communication, such as increasingly long intervals between replies to texts and shorter or "drier" responses when they finally do reply.

iStock/MangoStar_Studio

In some cases, fading out makes it easier to re-establish a relationship in the future (Truscelli & Guerrero, 2019). While strategies such as the blame game or ghosting leave people angry and confused, fading out can be gradual enough that is less hurtful. In addition, the relationship often ends without either person having to say hurtful things about why the relationship is not working. If people change their minds and want to try again, they do not have as much baggage from their old relationship as do people who used more direct negative strategies. However, this is much truer when people fade out in the early stages of relationships. When people fade out from committed relationships, and especially if it is a one-way fade, it can feel almost as disrespectful as ghosting (Truscelli & Guerrero, 2019). All avoidant strategies, but especially the one-way fade and ghosting, are seen as providing less closure and producing more uncertainty than more direct strategies for ending relationships (Collins & Gillath, 2012).

Manipulation

Finally, people can end relationships in indirect ways that are manipulative. These strategies are indirect because the person initiating the breakup does not communicate directly to the partner. Two common manipulative strategies are cost escalation and third-party manipulation. **Cost escalation** involves making yourself appear less attractive and rewarding to your partner so your partner breaks up with you (Baxter, 1984; Emmers & Hart, 1996; Thieme & Rouse, 1991). Think back to the discussion about rewards and costs in relationships. People tend to stay in relationships where rewards outweigh costs. Therefore, if you want someone to break up with you, it follows that you might decrease how rewarding your presence in their life is. People who use cost escalation purposefully engage in strategies such as being obnoxious, disloyal, or selfish as a way to make the partner like them less, in the hope that they will initiate the breakup (Baxter, 1985). While this strategy is certainly manipulative, people report feeling better about breaking up with someone whom they started disliking. Overall though, cost escalation is viewed as a less-than-ideal way of ending a relationship because it shows low concern for the partner's feelings (Collins & Gillath, 2012).

A second manipulative way to end a relationship involves using third parties. **Third-party manipulation** can be accomplished in two general ways. First, people can use their social network to either leak news of the impending breakup to their partner or ask someone in the social network to talk to their partner and tell them they want to break up. This, of course, has a ring of "middle school" to it, but it still happens in adult relationships, just more subtly. For example, Audra might talk to Dylan's best friend about how she feels, asking him to help her soften the blow by talking to Dylan for her. Although her intentions are good, she is still manipulating the situation by hoping she will not have to do as much emotional labor during the breakup after getting Dylan's friend involved. For friends, third-party manipulation is a more common way of either de-escalating or ending a friendship. Imagine that you have not been getting along with a certain friend who we will call Kyler. You discover, through mutual friends, that Kyler hosted a hang-out over the weekend and did not invite you. Moreover, Kyler intentionally decided not to invite you, knowing that you would find out about the party and interpret it as a sign that you are no longer close friends. In this case, Kyler's third-party manipulation worked as a way of communicating a lack of closeness.

A second way of manipulating third parties is to engage in activity that lets someone know that they are being replaced. In romantic relationships, this could involve telling your partner that you should both feel free to date other people (Baxter, 1982; Collins & Gillath, 2012). In friendships, this includes actions such as deciding to go on a Spring Break trip with a new group of friends instead of the old group you always went with previously. These types of strategies are indirect, but the message is still usually clear.

BREAKUP RECOVERY

Although the end of a relationship can be one of the most heartbreaking events humans face, ending a relationship is not always a negative experience. Getting out of a relationship that is not working can open the door to new experiences. There is more time to devote to developing oneself and to making new connections. People can also experience personal growth after breakups, feeling stronger and more confident because they were able to get through a difficult time (Tashiro & Frazier, 2003; Tuval-Mashiach et al., 2015). See the following Skill Builder for suggestions of positive ways to cope with a breakup.

SKILL BUILDER
COPING WITH BREAKUPS

Breakups are difficult, especially if your partner broke up with you. Breakups are also harder the more attached you were, the more time you spent together, the longer the relationship, and the more enmeshed you were in each other's lives. Although most of the research on breakups has focused on divorce or dating relationships, the ending of a friendship can also be painful. The literature on breakups and recovery gives some helpful information on how to cope when you are having trouble dealing with any kind of breakup (Brenner & Vogel, 2015; Fisher & Alberti, 2016; Kansky & Allen, 2018;Tashiro & Frazier, 2003; Yıldırım & Demir, 2015). Here are some key suggestions.

1. **Give yourself time.** It takes time to recover after a breakup, and the longer and more serious the relationship was, the longer the recovery time is likely to be. Think of recovery as

a process. It will not happen overnight. Just as it takes a while for a new relationship to develop, it takes a while to get over one.

2. **Do things that make you feel good about yourself.** After a breakup, your self-esteem can take a hit. You might wonder what you did wrong and why your partner did not love you enough to treat you right or stay with you. These thoughts are natural. However, breakups are usually about two people, not just one; even if you do everything right, the relationship can still end. Realizing this, engaging in activities that make you feel good about yourself, and spending time with people who support you can all help you feel better about yourself. Getting over a breakup also shows you are a strong person, which is something to feel good about.

3. **Get your mind off your partner.** If you find yourself thinking about your ex, try distracting yourself by reading a good book, watching a good movie, hanging out with friends, or doing whatever you find entertaining. Resist the temptation to creep on their social media, keep tabs on them, or contact them. In some cases, unfriending or blocking them may be helpful, at least while you are trying to move on. Try not to think about the possibility of getting back together, and instead focus on being the best person you can be.

4. **Embrace and capitalize on your new freedom.** Relationships take time away from other activities. Think about things you enjoy doing but did not have time to do while you were in the relationship and do them now. Start a new hobby, attend a class, and reconnect with old friends. Focus on yourself and what makes you happy personally. The extra time you have can also give you an opportunity for personal growth and exploration.

5. **Focus on what you learned.** Regardless of the level of closure you got, you can learn from your relationship experience. Ask yourself what you liked and disliked about your past relationship. Are there certain things you now know you need in a relationship and a partner? Think about what you could have done differently. Could you have communicated better or put in more effort? Or perhaps you put in too much effort or become too dependent on the relationship. Don't blame yourself, and do not dwell on the past, but do learn from your experience. Create a narrative that helps you make sense of what happened so you can learn from it.

6. **Stay open to new relationships.** It can be tempting to shut yourself off after a breakup to avoid further hurt. When the time is right, however, you should be ready to drop your guard and be open to new relationships. The research is mixed on how quickly you should get into a new relationship following a breakup. It is important not to rush into something for the wrong reasons, but it is also important to be open to exploring something new if it seems right.

Which of these ways of coping do you think would be particularly helpful in promoting healing after a relationship ends? Can you think of other strategies that might be beneficial in working through the aftermath of a breakup, either with a romantic partner or a good friend?

A repeated theme in the breakup recovery literature is the importance of being able to learn from your experience. In a study of 18- to 24-year-old gay and bisexual men, those who were able to positively appraise their breakups as helping them better understand what they want in future relationships reported low levels of anxiety and depression, along with high levels of self-esteem (Ceglarek et al., 2017). Studies of both same-sex and opposite-sex couples have shown that people can actually experience positive emotions such as happiness and relief after breakups (Hebert & Popadiuk, 2008;Kurdek, 1993; Lewandowski & Bizzoco, 2007). In one study, college students were interviewed and asked about their breakups. These students mentioned many more positive than negative outcomes associated with their breakups, the most common of which were learning things that would be helpful for future relationships, being a stronger person, "feeling more independent or free," being more self-aware and mature, and reprioritizing things in their lives (p. 5). Thus, even though breakups can be extremely hurtful and upsetting, they can eventually lead to increased growth and new opportunities.

PRINCIPLES FOR DE-ESCALATING OR ENDING RELATIONSHIPS

Principle 1. Breakups are usually hard.

This first principle may seem obvious, but it frames everything else about ending relationships. Being broken up with and losing a friendship are considered particularly hurtful events. A person who you cared about is basically saying they do not want to continue having a relationship with you. Breakups cause people to feel rejected and abandoned. The person doing the breaking up also usually feels bad. Most people do not want to hurt anyone, especially someone they care about. Because breakups can be emotionally traumatic, it is especially important to try to communicate in constructive ways when ending or de-escalating a relationship.

Principle 2. Relationship decline can occur naturally or be precipitated by critical events.

Some relationships decline naturally and gradually due to factors such as moving apart from each other, having different friend groups, or having less opportunity to spend time together. When people drift away from each other, like Keiko and McKenna did, the breakup is usually less painful and people can easily take steps to rejuvenate the relationship in the future. On the other hand, some relationships end suddenly after a catastrophic event such as a romantic partner cheating or a friend being disloyal. In these cases, more repair would need to be done to try to restore the relationship. Still other times, people fall into destructive communication patterns that spread negative affect through a relationship, eventually leading to its end. For these relationships to be revived, real change must take place, as is the case for those who learn how to capitalize on transitions to improve themselves and their relationships.

Principle 3. The directness and information level of a breakup strategy affects closure.

This chapter included several strategies that are indirect, including ghosting and the one-way fade. In general, strategies such as these do not provide the receiver of the breakup message with much information about the reasons why the relationship is ending. Sometimes the reasons are obvious, but when they are not, indirect strategies can lead people to experience uncertainty and prevent people from getting closure and moving on. Some indirect strategies, such as pseudo de-escalation, can even lead people to harbor false hope that a relationship will resume after a short break. Although it can be difficult to be direct when breaking up with someone, such strategies, when delivered in a positive tone, can help both people cope more effectively with a breakup.

Principle 4. Some ways of ending relationships are kinder than others.

Strategies such as ghosting and the one-way fade can be viewed as disrespectful because people believe they deserve someone to take the time to break up with them in a considerate manner. Therefore, in-person communication is generally preferable to being broken up with by text or other electronic means. But in-person communication can be difficult. Facing someone whom you are breaking up with, or who is breaking up with you, can make you feel vulnerable and uncomfortable. Sometimes there is no right thing to say. However, remembering to stay clear of clichés, and instead focus on showing the other person respect and giving details about why you appreciate them and valued your time with them, can often help make a breakup easier. It is important to be clear about your intentions, but also to let the other person know they are valued.

Principle 5. There are benefits to ending relationships.

Although the end of an important relationship can sadden people, ending relationships can also open the door to many new experiences and opportunities (Hebert & Popadiuk, 2008; Tashiro

& Frazier, 2003). People sometimes feel relief and happiness when ending a relationship that was toxic or filled with unpredictable ups and downs. After ending or de-escalating a relationship, people also have more time and energy to spend on improving themselves and developing other relationships. Even the process of getting through a hard breakup can end up giving a person a newfound sense of strength and confidence. Another bright spot in breakups is that they can be a learning process. After ending any type of relationship, lessons can be learned about the type of relationship you want, the mistakes you made and will try not to repeat, and the type of friend or relational partner you want to be.

CONCLUSION

Not all relationships are meant to last forever. Some relationships run their course and end amicably or de-escalate into a relationship that is less close. Others end in turmoil, leaving former friends, romantic partners, and even family members confused or angry. The key is not to dwell on these feelings but to move on and make good decisions about relationships in the future. For friends like Keiko and McKenna, some relational de-escalation can be beneficial because it triggers people to assess where they are in a relationship and decide if they want to rejuvenate it. At the beginning of this chapter, we asked whether you thought Keiko and McKenna would be able to revive their friendship, or whether getting together for lunch could mark a last attempt to save a failing friendship. A lot depends on how they communicate. If they are honest about their feelings, talk about their friendship, and negotiate guidelines for expected behavior, their friendship has a good shot of not only surviving but flourishing.

CHAPTER 12 STUDY GUIDE

KEY TERMS

Identify and explain the meaning of each of the following key terms.

antipathetic relationships	negotiated farewell
blame game	on-again–off-again relationships
breakup barriers	one-way fade
capitalizing on transitions	physical estrangement
catastrophe theory	positive sentiment override
continuous estrangement	positive tone strategy
cost escalation	pruning
direct dump	pseudo de-escalation
emotional estrangement	quality of alternatives
genuine de-escalation	relational de-escalation
ghosting	relational termination
investments	relationship-talk trick
mutual fade out	scrubbing
need for closure	third-party manipulation
negative sentiment override	weak ties

REFLECTION QUESTIONS

1. Based on your experiences and observations, what are some differences in how various types of relationships—such as romantic relationships, friendships, work relationships, and family relationships—de-escalate? Do you think the communication that accompanies de-escalation varies in these relationships? If so, how? What do you think the success rate of on-again–off-again relationships is? Based on what you learned in this chapter, what are some telltale signs that suggest a couple might be better off ending an on-again–off-again relationship instead of cycling back in? What are some signs that it might be worthwhile to give the relationship another try?

2. What role do you think social media plays in preventing and/or helping people get closure after ending a dating relationship or friendship? Do you think people should sever ties on social media by unfollowing or blocking each other after ending a relationship? Why or why not? Should they remove all relationship pictures or leave some up? What other behaviors related to social media do you think people engage in after breakups, and how healthy are those behaviors?

3. In this chapter, you learned about various ways that people can end relationships. Thinking about your own experiences, the experiences of people you know, and the information you learned in this chapter, what breakup messages do you think are the most hurtful and why? If someone came to you asking for advice on how to break up with someone in the kindest but clearest way possible, what communication strategies would you recommend?

13 CAPSTONE

Connections and Conclusions

WHAT YOU'LL LEARN...

When you have finished the chapter, you should be able to do the following:

13.1 Explain how interpersonal communication enables us to build relationships with other people in our social world.

13.2 Identify goals essential to interpersonal communication.

13.3 Identify key skills for competent interpersonal communication.

13.4 Explain how interpersonal networks facilitate social support and resources.

13.5 Contextualize interpersonal communication concepts within cultural understandings.

13.6 Describe how considering another's perspective leads to more effective communication.

13.7 Engage in cognitive flexibility and responsiveness in interpersonal encounters.

13.8 Demonstrate how differences in communication choices lead to various interpersonal outcomes.

As she travels home from her first semester, Sydney scrolls through her Instagram looking at the new connections she's made over the past few months. Some of the photos and memories make Sydney smile, like a photo of a large group of her new friends at the Dance Marathon fundraiser. She remembers how nervous she was during the first days of school and is happy that she has been able to start these new relationships. Other accounts give her pause though; for example, she's still connected with another first-year student, Akilah, who she met the first week of school. Sydney thought she and Akilah would end up being best friends based on their first interaction. They lived on the same floor and had some similar interests. However, after a few weeks, Akilah stopped coming by Sydney's room and started choosing another table in the dining hall. Sydney isn't sure what happened, but she and Akilah clearly are not going to be best friends and she is wondering what went wrong.

Throughout this book, we have discussed various ways people connect with each other through different types of interpersonal encounters. Some first interactions, like the ones between Sydney and Akilah, seem promising at first but are not enough to lead to a closer relationship. Other interactions are the start of something special, and still others are among the countless encounters we have with people with whom we either have casual relationships or never talk to again.

Regardless of whether our interactions with a particular person are brief, casual, or within a close relationship, it is important to communicate in a competent manner. Hopefully, this book has given you some tools to do just that.

In this capstone chapter, we offer some broad underlying principles that tie some of the literature on interpersonal communication together. Understanding these principles will help you think about communication differently and, ultimately, be a more competent communicator. There is no set formula for how to best engage in an interpersonal interaction and we do not offer prescriptions in the form of "Say this, not that." However, we do offer an understanding of how to engage with others, consider their perspectives, and work toward having more competent interpersonal interactions in daily life. Our hope is that this capstone chapter will help you take away some of the larger messages about interpersonal communication that cut across many of the previous chapters.

Before launching into these principles, it is important to review what we mean by communication competence. Recall from Chapter 1 that **communication competence** refers to a family of concepts that include having the knowledge, motivation, and skills to adapt to a changing social environment (Spitzberg & Cupach, 1989). Recall also that when scholars and professional practitioners of interpersonal communication use the term *competence*, they are generally referring to two outcomes of interpersonal interactions: effectiveness and appropriateness. *Effectiveness* entails achieving one's communication goals. *Appropriateness* involves engaging in communication that meets social norms and helps maintain relationships.

Sometimes it is easy to achieve both of these outcomes. You act friendly and professional during a job interview, which makes you likable and helps secure an offer. Other times, however, one outcome is met at the expense of the other. Think about a boss who gets her employees to work late a couple of times every week by hinting that not doing so could adversely affect their likelihood of getting a pay raise or promotion. Such a strategy may be effective, but not appropriate. A teacher who does not call out his students when they are on their phones rather than paying attention has the opposite issue—his behavior may make him more likable but not more effective.

Of course, being communicatively competent does not only revolve around the messages you send; it also involves being a good listener and being adaptable to the receiver and the context. How you interpret messages is just as important as what you say and do within the communication process. These and other issues will be touched on in the following principles.

PRINCIPLE 1. OUR SOCIAL WORLD IS BUILT THROUGH INTERPERSONAL COMMUNICATION

A good communicator has a strong sense of self, and our understanding of ourselves is built through interpersonal communication. Throughout our lifespan, we understand our self and our place in the broader social sphere based on how others communicate with us. At times, this communication can be detrimental, such as when people perpetuate stereotypes or other aggressions.. Yet, as noted in Chapter 2, generally communication about ourselves and responses to our identity performances are integrated into our broader conception about the self. Our sense of self is tied to others through our interactions. We know we are funny when others laugh at our attempts at humor. We feel loved when someone is affectionate toward us. We are hurt when others do not take our opinions and perceptions into account. And like Sydney, we may wonder if there is something about us that caused a potential relationship to stop developing. The connection between self and others also means that we have a responsibility to others in how we engage with them. Unkind words and thoughtless actions can deeply influence how those we are communicating with view themselves. Indeed, as you learned from Chapter 11, our interactions with others can give us great joy, but also great pain and sorrow.

Interpersonal communication is what allows us to build relationships with others. Some relationships, such as those between dating partners or friends, may rely almost exclusively on communication, whereas other relationships may have biological (e.g., family) or legal (e.g., marriage) underpinnings. Still, in these cases, the relationship *as a relationship* exists because the two people involved engage in some type of communication and likely have some expectation of future communication. Relationships begin when communication begins and end when the parties involved no longer communicate. In addition, the quality of a relationship depends on the type of communication that occurs within and about the relationship. For example, consider the relationship between a parent and an emerging adult. Although different parent–child pairs are all structurally tied in a similar way, the actual relationship may look very different. One pair may have a warm relationship where they share many topics of conversation, whereas another pair might have a relationship fraught with passive-aggressive communication and continuous conflict episodes. Many other variations also exist within this relational type. The difference between one parent–child relationship and another is the choices individuals within the relationship make about how they communicate with each other.

PRINCIPLE 2. INTERPERSONAL COMMUNICATION IS A MULTIGOAL SITUATION

Understanding our own goals and other people's goals is critical for being an effective communicator. It is also essential to recognize that our goals can be consistent with, or in opposition to, other people's goals and that more than one goal can guide any given interaction. In Chapter 1, we outlined three categories of goals that arise in interpersonal situations: instrumental, self-presentational, and relational. **Self-presentational goals** involve displaying positive aspects of ourselves to others. For example, Sydney's friends will likely post pictures of their Dance Marathon; although it is a fun event, they may primarily have the goal of wanting to be seen as altruistic, charitable people. During a job interview, you might attend to self-presentational goals by choosing an outfit that suggests you are professional. **Instrumental goals** focus on trying to accomplish a task. You might attempt to convince your roommate to clean more or persuade a professor to recommend you for an internship. Instrumental goals may also be related to achieving tangible outcomes, such as borrowing money or having someone give you a ride. People also have **relational goals** that revolve around maintaining positive relationships with others. When you like someone's Instagram picture, keep a Snapchat streak going, or have dinner with a friend to catch up, you are likely attending to relational goals.

Self-presentational goals drive us to try to make good impressions on others.
iStock/XiXinXing

Throughout this book, we have explored specific examples of goals such as attempting to reduce uncertainty, initiate a relationship, persuade someone, and manage a conflict. Think back to what you learned in Chapter 10 on conflict. The ways people communicate during conflict reflect their consideration of both their own goals and (at least sometimes) the goals of others. How we act following a relational transgression depends largely on whether or not we have the goal of repairing and continuing the relationship. And when we express emotions, we may be attending to not only what we are feeling internally but also to what we want to present to other people. In every interpersonal encounter, the communicators involved are trying to manage multiple communication goals at once (Caughlin, 2010).

As communicators, sometimes we are mindful of these goals, whereas other times we may work toward communication goals in ways that feel automatic (Kellerman, 1992). For example, when you first meet someone, you may be very conscious that you want to learn more about that person and share information about yourself in a reciprocal fashion. You may also use verbal politeness strategies and nonverbal immediacy behaviors as discussed in Chapter 2 that help further communication goals (building a new acquaintanceship, being perceived as a friendly and warm person) without really consciously thinking, "Okay, now I will smile. Okay, now I will nod my head." When Sydney and Akilah met, they were first-year students who did not know anyone, so they were both conscious that they wanted to make a good impression on everyone they met. At some point, however, Akilah stopped reaching out to Sydney. This could have been a mindful choice on Akilah's part, which reflected a goal to distance herself from Sydney, or it could have been an automatic process that Akilah did not think much about but now regrets. Learning to be mindful of our goals in interpersonal encounters may help us enact behaviors that are more closely aligned with the messages we wish to send (Burgoon et al., 2000). If Akilah wanted to develop a stronger friendship with Sydney, her behaviors did not reflect that goal.

In some scenarios, we may find it difficult to achieve our goals in tandem with each other. For example, as noted in Chapter 10, in conflict scenarios we often want to achieve an instrumental goal that is in opposition to our conflict partner's goal, while maintaining the relationship *and* being seen as a good person. Thus, to skillfully manage conflict situations, people must be able to assert their instrumental goal, while also learning and caring about the position of their conflict partner. This can be quite challenging when emotions become heated or when one is heavily invested in the conflict issue and/or the relationship. Yet, being effective in reaching one's conflict goals while also being seen as appropriate by one's relational partner is a key component of having a satisfying relationship (Cupach et al., 2009).

Despite the potential difficulties, it is useful to remember that both ourselves and others are striving to achieve multiple goals within interpersonal encounters. Understanding both sets of goals can help communicators craft messages and enact strategies that allow them to achieve more of their goals. Using communication skills such as empathetic listening and perspective-taking allows interactants to work toward understanding their fellow communicators' goals and help everyone have more successful interactions.

WHAT WOULD YOU DO?
MANAGING MULTIPLE GOALS IN ETHICAL INTERACTIONS

As discussed in Principle 2, communication is a multigoal event. Many of the functions and goals outlined in previous chapters represent communication outcomes that we are trying to achieve simultaneously. When we are attempting to communicate with others, we are often attempting to manage our self-presentation and the presentation or face of those with whom we are communicating, in addition to achieving relational or instrumental goals.

Imagine a scenario where your romantic partner shows up with a new and terrible haircut. You, of course, want to further your relational goals by not insulting them, but you also wonder if they realize the haircut is terrible. Should someone tell them? Should it be you?

Consider being on a job interview and noticing that the interviewer has something stuck in their teeth. If it was your friend, perhaps you would feel comfortable discreetly letting them know; but in this case, you want to get the job. Will the interviewer feel embarrassed if you point out the spinach stuck between their cuspids? Will that reflect poorly on you as an interviewee? Would they notice later and realize you hadn't told them?

In the grand scheme of our intertwined relational environment, these are low-stakes multigoal interactions, but other situations can be far more difficult. People are constantly weighing their own goals against their perception of their co-communicators goals and making choices about the messages they exchange.

Think about the following questions regarding how you approach communication situations where some of your goals may be at odds with each other.

- Do you consider it acceptable to tell a "white lie" to avoid hurting someone's feelings?

- Is withholding information the same thing as telling a lie? Why or why not?

- Are some communicative goals more important than others? If you had to choose, would you rather save your face or someone else's? Does your answer depend on the relationship you have with that person?

- If you are in a group situation and someone says something offensive, should you speak up and threaten their face by letting everyone know you think what they said is inappropriate? Or, instead, should you either keep your thoughts to yourself or talk to them privately?

- Is it more important to get your way in a conflict? Or is it more important to maintain the relationship with your conflict partner?

- What other situations can you think of where communication goals might be at odds?

PRINCIPLE 3. INTERPERSONAL COMMUNICATION IS A SKILLED ACTIVITY

This principle is drawn in part from Spitzberg and Cupach's (1989) contention that becoming competent at interpersonal communication is a matter of knowledge, motivation, and *skill*. We hope you find yourself motivated to become a more competent interpersonal communicator. Certainly, you have made choices (taking this course, reading this book) that are in line with such a motivation. Throughout the book, our goal has been to describe and explain human communication processes in ways that can help you better understand your daily interpersonal communication encounters. In addition, we note that although we cannot say each of the following behaviors is appropriate in every situation, there is a set of skills that can be useful across many interpersonal communication interactions. These skills have to do with both developing messages that accurately impart meaning to your communication partner as well as learning how to have a deeper understanding of the perspectives, motivations, and goals of your fellow interactant. Some of these skills can be found in the Skill Builder on the Social Skills Inventory.

SKILL BUILDER
THE SOCIAL SKILLS INVENTORY

The following chart includes six key interpersonal communication skills related to competence. You might be more skilled in some of these areas than in others. As you read through the chart, assess which areas are your strengths and weaknesses and devise a plan for practicing building your skills in the areas you would like to improve.

	Social Intelligence	Emotional Intelligence
How well do you express yourself?	*Social Expressivity* • Skill in verbal communication • Ability to engage in social interaction and get along with others • Tend to be extraverted and sociable	*Emotional Expressivity* • Skill in nonverbal communication • Ability to express emotions easily • Often able to affect other people's emotions
How well can you control your communication?	*Social Control* • Ability to role-play • Able to monitor situations and adjust behavior accordingly • Makes a good first impression and feels comfortable leading discussions	*Emotional Control* • Ability to hide, downplay, or exaggerate emotions • Good at regulating one's emotions • Knows how to manage emotional expressions appropriately
How well do you decode others' communication?	*Social Sensitivity* • Skill in decoding verbal communication • Sensitivity and understanding of norms related to social appropriateness • Can read social situations	*Emotional Sensitivity* • Skill in decoding nonverbal communication • Empathetic and understanding toward others • Good at focusing on emotional and nonverbal information

Source: Adapted from the Social Skills Inventory in Riggio, R. E. (1986). Assessment of basic social skills. *Journal of Personality and Social Psychology, 51*, 649–660.

Some skills are necessary for the effective and appropriate sending of messages. These can include being articulate, being able to use different phrasings to help your communication partner understand, and making language choices that are appropriate for your message and the receiver. Other skills are required for decoding messages effectively. In Chapter 5 we discussed that skilled communicators are not only able to listen carefully, but they also show they are listening carefully by engaging in behaviors such as nodding to indicate understanding and giving their partner eye contact. Understanding the messages being sent is an important skill but so is the ability to ask for clarification when it is needed. It is also important to realize that sometimes we decode people's communication incorrectly. You may be able to recall a time when you were sure someone would call you after a first date or you would get a job after an interview but did not. It would be a mistake to go into every interaction thinking that you will read the other person's communication the wrong way, but it is also a mistake to assume that your interpretations are always accurate. In Sydney and Akilah's case, Sydney may have assumed that Akilah felt the same way she did, when in actuality, Akilah did not see much potential beyond a casual friendship.

Other communication skills important for interpersonal communication include being aware of the context and the relationship within which the messages are being sent. As you learned in Chapter 8, the depth and breadth of communication typically reflect the type of relationship (or nonrelationship) people share. Too much disclosure too fast may be inappropriate and ineffective. New technologies also require new skills. For example, a well-chosen emoji can help a receiver interpret your message and intentions correctly, and the lack of emojis can communicate a message in and of itself. Understanding the norms regarding a given channel can help communicators choose messages that will be viewed as appropriate within those channels.

PRINCIPLE 4. BUILDING INTERPERSONAL NETWORKS BENEFITS OUR EVERYDAY LIVES

Engaging in competent interpersonal interactions helps us build our social networks (Fehr, 2008; McEwan & Guerrero, 2010). In our fast-paced, technologically connected, modern world, it may be especially important for individuals to be able to use interpersonal communication to build rewarding social networks (McEwan, 2015). Think about the COVID-19 pandemic. When people were isolated from others, being able to communicate skillfully with one's social network via technology became especially important.

Through social network connections, people can access a variety of resources (McEwan & Guerrero, 2010). Some of these may be instrumental resources such as when a classmate shares their notes for a missed day of class or when a sibling provides you with a ride home at Thanksgiving. Other resources might be less tangible but are nonetheless extremely important for our quality of life. For example, people might provide emotional resources such as a listening ear, general companionship, or validation of our self and choices. In addition, we all can use a variety of social resources such as having people to hang out with to share activities, hobbies, and interests. Various people and different relationships can help fulfill these

Social networks give people access to tangible, social, and emotional resources.

Dimitri Otis/Stone via Getty Images

resource needs in different ways. Thus, it is likely beneficial to be able to build a broad social network with ties of varying strength and relational type.

Communication is also the vehicle by which people build healthy and fulfilling relationships. In Chapter 6 you learned that giving and receiving affection is related to better physical and mental health. You also learned that experiencing and sharing positive emotions helps people develop and maintain good relationships. Much communication in interpersonal interaction is routine, but there also needs to be effort on both sides. Think about the various maintenance behaviors you learned about in Chapter 9, such as positivity and social networking. Some of these behaviors occur naturally and routinely in relationships, but other times maintenance is intentional. For example, if you are happy around someone, then you will likely be cheerful and optimistic, which helps maintain a relationship. When you are in a bad mood, however, you may need to work to *not* take your negativity out on the people you are around and instead try to be in a better mood. Similarly, there may be times when you and a friend are invited to the same party, so social networking happens naturally. There may be other times when you ensure that your friend is included. Whether these maintenance behaviors occur naturally or with effort, the point is that they benefit us and our relationships. If we act positively around our friends after being in a bad mood all day, we will probably feel better. If a friend includes us in a fun social gathering that we would not otherwise have been invited to, we may make new friends and connections. The key idea here is that having a social network of people with whom we have fun and by whom we feel loved and accepted enhances our well-being and enriches our lives.

The social network also plays a key role in providing us with social support. In Chapter 11, you learned about some of the ways people provide support and comfort to someone who is hurt or distressed. The provision of resources is often called **social support**, while the verbal and nonverbal behaviors that convey a desire to help another person are called **supportive communication** (Burleson & MacGeorge, 2002). Social support can serve a variety of needs. Emotional support helps others cope with emotional distress by providing love, care, and affection (Burleson, 2003). Esteem support helps others feel better about themselves through compliments and validation (Holmstrom, 2012). Informational support includes giving suggestions, offering advice, or providing needed facts or referrals (Cohen, 2004). Finally, people can provide tangible instrumental support. Instrumental support might include giving or loaning money, providing labor such as helping a friend move, or other tangible goods, like setting up a meal service when a friend is experiencing a time of stress (Cutrona & Suhr, 1992). Receiving the right support, at the right time, from the right person can help alleviate stress and enhance well-being.

I DIDN'T KNOW THAT!
SOCIAL RESOURCES THROUGH SOCIAL MEDIA

People maintain interpersonal connections for a variety of reasons. One important reason is that social connections allow us to both survive and thrive. Although there are often stories in the media deriding social media use as a potential drawback for building interpersonal relationships and skills, the research paints a different picture.

Social media, particularly social network sites, can be very useful in helping us build social capital through developing both strong and weak tie connections (Ellison et al., 2007; Rykov et al., 2020). In turn, these networked connections may help provide support and resources when needed. People perceive they have a greater amount of social support available to them if they have a larger network through social networking sites (Nabi et al., 2013). However, the connections that are the most likely to actually fulfill support requests are people who actively engage with each other through the site (Ellison et al., 2014). The type of support requested may matter as well. Social networking sites might be more helpful for informational and emotional support than other types, such as providing tangible aid like cash or items (Mikal et al., 2013).

Of course, it is important not to over-rely on those channels for support. Facebook messages posted in hopes of receiving responses may have a negative effect on friendship quality (McEwan, 2015). Research has also shown that requesting support following a breakup in multiple ways on social media may demand too much emotional bandwidth from the support network (High et al., 2014).

PRINCIPLE 5. UNDERSTANDING IS GROUNDED IN CONTEXT

Communication does not occur in a vacuum. Instead, the way we understand each other is deeply grounded in culture, the situation, and the relationship. In addition, as discussed in Chapters 4 and 6, determining the meaning of specific messages requires understanding the culture in which those messages were shared. When it comes to decoding emotions accurately, we know people have in-group advantages. In other words, we are able to decode emotions better when someone is from the same culture as we are. This type of in-group advantage extends to other groups and situations as well. Think about the slang you use in your text messages. Would your grandparents understand all of what you are saying when you are hanging out with your friends? Probably not because they are from a different generation. As noted in Chapter 4, even within cultures, knowing the context in which a message was shared influences how we understand each other. For example, in conflict situations, it is common for people to say something like, "Well, you said this!" Yet the exact words that are spoken, even if we could remember them precisely, are only one part of the message that communicators intend to impart. We cannot get in each other's heads to fully understand what was meant.

Communication goes beyond the specific meaning of words and nonverbal behaviors. Each word, each symbolic message, is chosen with the idea that our interactional partner will share some contextual understanding with us that will enable our symbolic exchanges to make sense. When people are able to share messages with each other based on shared culture, context, and relationships, then communication truly becomes interpersonal. Ultimately, interpersonal communication is about finding a way for one communicator to understand another. Think back to the different types of information exchange we discussed in Chapter 1. Successful communication, where a receiver encodes a message that a receiver decodes accurately, is the goal. However, it is challenging for any two people to reach this level of understanding, and it is even more challenging for people to do so when they have different perspectives. Thus, the context in which messages are shared plays a key role in determining the desired and received meaning of messages.

Another important issue is that people's biases and stereotypes can interfere with the ability to truly understand and communicate effectively with others. Think about the Black Lives Matter movement. One of the key messages within this movement is that many people have unconscious biases based on stereotypes. In particular, some people have a bias that causes them to believe that Black men are more violent or dangerous than other people. Think about some of the other unfair biases individuals have about people of color and women. For example, women are sometimes judged more harshly than men if they refuse to take on a task at work because women are expected to be cooperative. Different ethnic groups are unfairly stereotyped in terms of all sorts of talents and personality traits, and these biases influence our expectations and communication. Of course, as you have learned, stereotypes are more complex than putting people into a single category. The concept of intersectionality shows us that social identities, such as gender, race, and sexual orientation, do not simply sum together to affect people's experiences and perceptions, but instead interact in complex ways that represent more than just their summed parts. Stereotypes and biases can cause misunderstanding and discrimination. The next principle suggests you can improve communication and fight such biases by engaging in perspective-taking.

Do you think some people's perceptions of Asian Americans changed during the COVID-19 pandemic? If so, why? How do you think intersectionality plays a role in the way these two Asian American protesters are perceived?

Lev Radin/Pacific Press/LightRocket via Getty Images

PRINCIPLE 6. COMPETENT COMMUNICATION REQUIRES PERSPECTIVE-TAKING

To communicate effectively, you need to try to understand your interactional partner. This often involves **perspective-taking**, which is the process of looking beyond your own perspective and trying to determine what another person needs. This process is related to the concept of uncertainty reduction. As you learned in this book, the reduction or management of uncertainty is an important concept for interpersonal communication. When we discussed uncertainty in Chapter 3, we considered how we use communication to help us reduce or manage our uncertainty. However, reducing uncertainty has another benefit in some situations—it can help us to become more effective and appropriate communicators. The more we learn about our fellow communicators, the more we can craft messages that are developed specifically for that communicator.

Indeed, the importance of learning about our fellow communicators is highlighted across scholarship that informs all interpersonal communication research. Recall our fictional potential couple, Maddie and Elijah, from Chapter 3. Maddie used social media to uncover basic information about Elijah that made her feel more comfortable talking with him. As she learned more about his likes and dislikes, she was better able to bring up topics she knew they would both enjoy talking about. Beyond initial interactions, perspective-taking can help us craft appropriate messages based on the situation and what another communicator needs. Imagine that your friend is upset about a recent breakup. He is trying to act like it does not bother him, but you can tell by his demeanor that it does. You try and put yourself in his position. He is obviously putting up a brave front by acting like it does not bother him, so you decide the last thing he needs is you telling him "I know you are all broken up about this" and then giving him advice on how to get over his ex. Instead, you suggest going out and doing something fun without ever mentioning anything about the breakup. In another situation, you might be able to tell that a friend needs self-esteem support. Perhaps she did poorly on an exam she studied hard for and also missed out on getting an internship opportunity she really wanted. Reminding her about her all of her other accomplishments may be the best form of support in this case.

Of course, there is a danger in presuming to know more about someone than you actually do. In Chapter 10, you learned that people dislike it when someone engages in mindreading—which involves making assumptions about how a person is thinking and feeling—during conflict and that sometimes those assumptions are wrong. Chapter 3 included a discussion of the various person–perceptions, or judgments, we make about people when forming first impressions. These include making judgments at the physical level (based on how a person looks), the sociocultural level (based on a person's background), and the psychological level (based on a person's inferred personality). As you learned, these first impressions can be biased, so a good communicator refrains from making quick judgments and sees interacting with someone as an opportunity to get to know that person as a unique individual. There is a fine line between uncertainty reduction that is easy and feeds into stereotypes and uncertainty reduction that is rooted in effortful perspective-taking. There is also a fine line between trying to understand where someone is coming from and assuming that your "understanding" is right. This is why it is essential to listen to be responsive during interpersonal interactions.

PRINCIPLE 7. COMPETENT COMMUNICATION REQUIRES FLEXIBILITY AND RESPONSIVENESS

Often students come to an interpersonal communication course hoping that we will teach them the "right" way to communicate. Both authors of this book have read papers where students hope that by pointing out everything that their communication partner did wrong, the student will somehow "win." But communication is not a competition with winners and losers. People can communicate exactly as they might have imagined or role-played and still have their attempts fall flat. Interpersonal communication is a cooperative activity that requires negotiation with one or more other people.

The concepts that we have covered in the previous chapters—from culture to listening, to self-disclosure, to social influence—are all concepts that either are part of how we begin to understand our fellow communicators or are how we can apply that understanding. To meet communication goals in an appropriate manner, communicators need to be flexible in how they respond to others. **Cognitive flexibility** involves knowing there are options and alternatives in the communication process as well as being willing and able to be flexible and adapt to situations (Martin & Rubin, 1995). **Responsiveness** requires paying attention to our fellow communicators, listening and learning about them, and tailoring our messages to reflect our understanding of them. Both of these skills are also related to perspective-taking. Basing our messages on the constraints and opportunities of the moment while considering the needs and desires of our fellow interactants can help us reach mutually beneficial and appropriate outcomes within interpersonal communication contexts. Clinging to a static "right" or "winning" strategy can prevent people from being optimally adaptive to the needs of communicative encounters.

Flexibility isn't just an asset for dancers; it's also an asset anytime people are communicating.

Copyright Christopher Peddecord 2009/Moment via Getty Images

Part of being flexible and responsive involves knowing how to craft unique messages for different people at various times. As we learned in Chapter 3, being mindful of context and culture can help people craft messages that help build relationships and connections with people who may be very different from ourselves. People who are skilled in adapting their communication to a particular person or audience are not only perceived as more socially appropriate but are also more effective. For example, the behaviors you might engage in during a job interview can be very different from how you might act when hanging out with friends. As discussed in Chapter 2, Snyder (2002) called this ability to shift performances for specific audiences **self-monitoring**. High self-monitors can "read the room" and adjust interpersonal communication behaviors to be appropriate for a particular audience. High self-monitors tend to have better overall communication outcomes than low self-monitors. Low self-monitors may find it difficult to competently manage communication because they do not have the knowledge needed for perspective-taking or for making appropriate adjustments based on what their interactional partners need.

Online communication can throw a wrench into the self-monitoring process. Messages communicated through online channels tend to have persistence—they exist long after they are posted, and a wide variety of potential audiences might be able to view these messages. Online communicators, particularly on social media, can experience a phenomenon called **context collapse** (Marwick & boyd, 2012). Context collapse happens when people fail to differentiate the various audiences their social media reaches and instead treat everyone as a singular audience. The consequences of context collapse might include a boss seeing a message intended for friends about "enjoying the sun" on a day when an employee called in sick or a parent commenting with embarrassing information on a message meant for friends. Some people address context collapse by only posting things that are appropriate for the least common denominator in their potential audience (Hogan, 2010), which means they only post things that they would be comfortable having anyone who is on their social media audience see. Others manage context collapse by setting up separate channels for different audiences (boyd, 2014).

PRINCIPLE 8. COMMUNICATION IS NOT A PANACEA

As this book has hopefully shown you, communication is immensely important. It is what connects us to other human beings. However, contrary to a lot of advice you hear, communication does not and cannot solve everything. In fact, sometimes communication can make a situation worse. For example, in Chapter 12, you learned that the ways people break up with someone range on a continuum from kind to cruel. During a breakup, it may not be appropriate to disclose all your negative feelings toward someone. You want to be clear about your intentions to break up, but at the same time, you do not need to communicate hurtful details (e.g., "I don't think I ever really loved you") that would hurt the other person unnecessarily. This situation exemplifies the importance of both appropriateness and effectiveness. Being respectful and sensitive to the other person's feelings (appropriateness) while also being clear about your intentions (effectiveness) is the best recipe for breaking up with someone in an ethical way. Similarly, Sydney and Akilah may or may not want to talk about why their budding friendship fizzled out. Sydney might be curious about what went wrong or she could prefer to remain uncertain. In her mind, uncertainty may be preferable to learning that Akilah disliked something about her. For her part, Akilah could simply have met other friends she liked better. Explaining this to Sydney could be an awkward conversation she would rather avoid. If they did talk, communication could bring them closer or make the situation between them more uncomfortable.

Just as there are times when it is better not to communicate than to communicate, there are also times when ineffective or inappropriate communication can make a situation worse rather than better. Engaging in destructive patterns of conflict and expressing negative emotions in an unproductive manner are two cases in point. In Chapter 10, you read about some common destructive patterns of conflict communication. These include demand-withdraw patterns and the four horsemen of the apocalypse—criticism, contempt, defensiveness, and stonewalling. These forms of communication can destroy rather than fortify relationships. Similarly, in Chapter 6, you learned it is best to express negative emotions in a direct but non-threatening manner. Doing so can be challenging, however. When people are embroiled in conflict and are feeling negative emotions it can be almost impossible to refrain from engaging in negative behavior. Indeed, the Gottman Institute recommends that couples take a timeout from communicating when destructive behavior and intense negativity start to surface.

The final principle in Chapter 11 also tells us that communication does not always provide a cure for everything. Recall that Chapter 11 focused on relational transgressions—those actions people take that violate implicit or explicit relationship rules. Transgressions include acts of disloyalty (such as cheating or betraying a friend), deception, exclusion, and violence, among other actions. The last principle in Chapter 11 was: Communication cannot fix everything. When relational transgressions occur, sometimes it does not matter if someone asks for forgiveness and says and does all the right things; the transgression was simply too severe for the relationship to survive. No matter how competent the communication, it is not enough to save the relationship. Thus, knowing when to communicate, and when not to communicate, is a key part of communication competence. Sometimes it is best not to talk about something at all; other times postponing communication is a positive move.

CONCLUSION

Communication matters. Although there are times when it is better not to communicate, or when communication makes matters worse, engaging in competent communication is beneficial. Communicating in an effective and appropriate manner improves people's personal and professional lives, and having happy relationships is related to being mentally and physically healthy. Even though her friendship with Akilah did not blossom the way she expected it to, Sydney still made several good friends during her first semester of college, and there is little doubt those new friendships were developed through communication. Learning how to be a competent communicator is a life-long process. We hope this book has given you information that will help you develop the skills needed to build happy and healthy social connections now and later in your life.

CAPSTONE STUDY GUIDE

KEY TERMS

Identify and explain the meaning of each of the following key terms.

cognitive flexibility

communication competence

context collapse

instrumental goals

perspective-taking

relational goals

responsiveness

self-monitoring

self-presentational goals

social support

supportive communication

CAPSTONE QUESTIONS

1. Think of times when it is challenging to engage in communication that is both effective (it gets the job done) and appropriate. How might you balance those two goals in such situations?

2. This chapter focuses on tying some of the ideas in this book together in a way that supports eight principles of communication competence. Based on your reading of the book, are there any principles you would add? Which of the principles do you think is most important in terms of communication competence and why?

3. This chapter also mentions numerous skills that are related to being a competent communicator. Which of these skills do you think you are closest to mastering and which do you think you need to work on the most? What can you do to build your skills in the areas you would like to strengthen?

4. The last principle is that communication is not a panacea. This goes against common folk wisdom that suggests communication always makes things better and that everything would be alright if people only communicated more. Imagine that you are a communication expert and someone is interviewing you. They say, "Don't you think that if people just communicated more, everyone would get along a lot better?" What would you say in response to this question?

GLOSSARY

accepting responsibility: the antidote for defensiveness; involves admitting your mistakes and faults

accidental communication: a type of communication that occurs when a sender does not intend to send a message, yet a receiver still notices and correctly interprets the sender's behavior

accommodation: the willingness to inhibit impulses to react destructively and instead react constructively in response to a partner's aggression

action tendencies: biologically based behavioral impulses that help people cope with emotion

active and empathetic listening: listening choices that convey sensing, processing, and responding to speakers in an engaged manner

active listening: engaging in listening while using nonverbal immediacy cues to express attention, paraphrasing the speaker's message, and asking questions to convey interest and continue the conversation

active uncertainty reduction: gathering information regarding a target person's attitudes and behavior through interacting with others who can provide information about the target or seeing how they react to a specific scenario

adaptors: idiosyncratic behaviors that people engage in, often by habit, when they are nervous or restless

adjacency pairs: conversational utterances consisting of a first pair part and a second pair part that are commonly considered to be connected, such as question/answer or greeting/greeting

aesthetic moments: moments when competing discourses merge in a transformative way

affect: the positive or negative feelings that underlie an emotion

affect displays: kinesic behaviors, such as facial expressions or posture, that show emotion

affection: positive internal feelings one person has for another

affective empathy: feeling what others feel

affinity-seeking strategies: behaviors people use when they want someone to evaluate them favorably and like them

agreeableness: a personality trait of being good-natured, cooperative, and trustworthy

allow control: a negative maintenance strategy that involves letting the partner make decisions about activities and plans

antidotes to the four horsemen: behaviors that neutralize negativity during conflict; the antidotes include making noncritical complaints, accepting responsibility, showing respect, and physiological soothing

antipathetic relationships: relationships characterized by mutual dislike

apology: saying you are sorry for committing wrongdoing

attempted communication: a message that is sent with intent, but is not received by anyone

attention: focusing on stimuli within the environment

attitude: the tendency to respond favorably or unfavorably to some idea, plan, or action

attraction: a force that draws people together

avoidance: a maintenance strategy that involves avoiding topics that may cause stress or conflict

avoiding: an indirect conflict style that varies in its level of cooperativeness; involves avoiding communication about the conflict issue

backchannels: verbal and vocal cues that convey that a hearer is listening and engaged with the speaker but are not extensive enough to be an interruption to the speaker

background questions: interview questions that explore a candidate's qualifications and previous experience

bald-on-record: communicative messages that simply state a face-threatening act without attempting to soften the message or make it more polite

basic or primary emotions: emotions that are distinguishable from one another in terms of characteristics such as nonverbal expression and feeling states and have evolved as adaptations that provide a useful way to respond to something (also called primary emotions)

behavior: outward actions

behavioral questions: interview questions that ask participants to reflect on past related performances

behavioral tactics: specific behaviors that people use to enact a communication goal strategy

beliefs: an acceptance that something is true or exists

blame game: a situation where a breakup becomes a competitive struggle between two people

breadth: a concept from social penetration theory indicating the range of topics involved in self-disclosure

breakup barriers: forces that stop people from ending a relationship

but-you-are-free-to-say-no: a compliance-gaining technique that involves making a request and then adding a variant of the statement "but you are free to say no"

bystander effect: the effect that people who are alone rather than in a group are more likely to help someone in distress because each group member takes their cues for socially appropriate behavior from the other nonhelping group members

capitalizing on transitions: when couples in on-again–off-again relationships use the "off" time in the cycle to reflect on the relationship, improve themselves, sort out their feelings, and decide what they want and don't want as individuals and in the relationship

catastrophe theory: the concept that sometimes breakups occur rapidly due to a critical event that ends the relationship

channel: the means by which a message is sent from sender to receiver, including face-to-face, writing, talking, texting, Facetiming, and so on

chilling effect: an effect that occurs when a person does not bring up conflict issues because they are afraid to disagree with someone

chronemics: the use of time to communicate messages

closeness: feelings that aspects of another person are ourself overlap so that we are interconnected

co-cultures: groups characterized by values, beliefs, and behaviors that distinguish them from the larger culture

code: a set of signals that is transmitted through a particular medium or channel

coercion: making someone engage in some behavior through force

coercive power: reliance on the threat of punishment to influence someone

cognitive appraisal: the process by which people evaluate and make sense of an event

cognitive consistency: a desire for the social world to be understandable and predictable

cognitive dissonance: the concept that people are uncomfortable holding two opinions or ideas that are in contrast to each other

cognitive empathy: being able to put oneself in another person's place to understand that person's perspective

cognitive flexibility: a mindset that involves knowing there are options and alternatives in the communication process as well as being willing and able to be flexible and adapt to situations

collaborating: a direct and cooperative conflict style that involves engaging in problem-solving, brainstorming, and other innovative strategies to find creative ways to meet both individuals' goals

collectivist: a cultural dimension where people are more likely to be concerned about the good of the greater group than themselves as an individual

colloquialisms: sayings that make sense within particular cultural frameworks

color-blind protocol: when the ideal that race and skin color should not matter leads people (especially white individuals) to minimize differences and avoid talking about race

commitment: a feeling of wishing to remain in a relationship in the future

common couple violence: an isolated pattern where people engage in reciprocal violence during an emotional conflict

communication accommodation theory: a communication theory explaining how culturally different others' communication patterns may converge or diverge within an interaction

communication adaptability: the ability to adjust behaviors and goals to the needs of a specific communicative encounter

communication apprehension: the experience of nervousness, anxiousness, or fear regarding communication situations

communication competence: the degree to which a person successfully uses communication to meet goals in a manner that is effective and appropriate

communication strategies: general approaches for accomplishing a particular interpersonal goal

communicators: people who are senders (and usually also receivers) in the communication process

compensation: also called appeasement, this remedial strategy involves taking action to try to correct or make up for wrongdoing

competitive fighting: a direct and uncooperative conflict style that involves trying to win an argument and/or achieve one's own goals, often at the expense of others' goals

complaints: as an antidote to criticism, complaints describe and voice concerns without blaming, making accusations, insulting, or acting superior to someone

compliance-gaining: the use of persuasive message strategies to convince a target to do something for the compliance-seeker

compromising: a moderately cooperative and moderately direct conflict style that involves individuals giving up something to get some of what they want

concealment: a behavior focused on intentionally hiding or omitting relevant information from someone

conditional forgiveness: when forgiveness is granted but with strings attached

confirming messages: messages that confirm the receiver's sense of self

conflict styles: ways individuals tend to communicate during conflict

connotative meaning: the subjective meaning of a word based on context and the feelings we associate with the word

conscientiousness: a personality trait of being orderly, responsible, and dependable

constitutive rules: rules that tell us what words represent

contempt: one of Gottman's four horsemen of the Apocalypse; involves acting superior to someone

contemptuous communication: personal attacks on a person's core sense of self that cast that person as inferior, such as mocking, sneering, and being condescending

content function of a message: the literal meaning of a message

content meaning: the meaning of a message based on the understanding of the words used by the speaker

context collapse: a phenomenon that occurs when audiences from different contexts of a person's social world are all able to see the same messages on a social media platform

continuous estrangement: a chaotic pattern where family members fluctuate between trying to connect but then acting distant

control mutuality: agreement between relational partners regarding how relational decisions are made

convergence: a communication pattern that occurs when speakers with a different communication style may begin to move toward their co-communicator's style

conversation: communication between at least two people where turn-taking among communicators occurs

conversational coherence: conversations that communicators are able to understand due to the meaningful co-created pattern of utterances and cues

conversational implicature: the intended or implied meaning of statements within conversations

cooperative principle: Grice's conversational rules regarding how speakers should form their conversational contributions in order to have a cooperatively constructed conversation

cosmopolitanism: an ethical stance encouraging openness to cultural differences and appreciation of one's own and other cultures

cost escalation: a breakup strategy that involves making yourself appear less attractive and rewarding to your partner so your partner breaks up with you

costs: any relationship outcomes that give you pain and/or result in a loss

counter-jealousy induction: a communicative response to jealousy that involves trying to make your partner jealous too

credibility: being trusted, convincing, or believed

criticism: communication that personally attacks someone; can include blaming, making accusations, or insulting someone.

crystallized self: a metaphorical view of the self that considers various identity performances as different facets of the self that can grow and change

cultural rituals: collective activities within a culture that occur within social contexts and help anchor cultural events and interpretations

cultural stereotypes: shared beliefs about the typical attributes of members of a social category

cultural symbols: an arbitrary sign whose meaning is derived from a particular culture

cultural values: perceptions of what behaviors are good/normal or bad/abnormal within a particular culture

culture: a learned system of meaning that provides a frame of reference for understanding symbolic interaction

cyberbullying: bullying behavior that occurs via electronic or digital media

deception: various types of behavior that intentionally misrepresent the truth

deceptive affection: instances when people do not feel affectionate but perform affectionate behaviors anyway

decode: cognitive interpretation of verbal and nonverbal messages

decoding: the process of making sense and attaching meaning to the messages produced by someone

deep acting: a type of emotional labor that involves trying to feel the appropriate emotions that you want to express

defensiveness: one of Gottman's four horsemen of the Apocalypse; involves communication aimed at deflecting responsibility or blame onto someone or something else

deintensification: a display rule that involves downplaying an emotion that you feel

demand-withdraw: a common conflict pattern in which one person's aggression is met with the other person's withdrawal, and vice versa

denotative meaning: the meaning of a word based on its basic dictionary definition

depth: a concept from social penetration theory indicating the degree of intimacy in self-disclosure

descriptive norms: norms that develop from perceptions about how most other people behave

destructive conflict: attempting to use arguments in order to control a partner's behavior

devaluation: feeling that someone sees you as unimportant, unwanted, unappreciated, and easily discarded

dialect theory: a theory based on the ideas that individuals from different cultures vary in their styles of nonverbal expression, and that people evaluate others' nonverbal expressions based on their own culture's style

differences/similarities dialectic: a cultural dialectic articulating that people from different cultures experience both differences and similarities

difficult conversations: conversations that involve discussing topics that are hard for someone to talk about; often cause feelings of discomfort, are emotionally charged, and create or exacerbate uncertainty

direct dump: a breakup strategy that involves simply stating that the relationship is over

disconfirming messages: messages that attempt to invalidate the other person's position and experiences

display rules: ways people manage the communication of emotion to be socially appropriate within a given situation or culture

divergence: a communication pattern that occurs when speakers with different communication styles emphasize those differences in their communication

door-in-the-face: a compliance-gaining strategy where the compliance-seeker first makes a large request and then follows up with a smaller secondary request

dramaturgical perspective: Goffman's theory that identities are performed for specific social audiences

Dunning-Krueger effect: a cognitive effect where people are inadequate at some skill but are not able to recognize their inadequacy and instead consider themselves highly qualified

dyadic: an interaction between two people

dyadic communication apprehension: the experience of nervousness, anxiousness, or fear regarding conversational interactions

efficacy assessment: a judgment about how well you could gather and cope with information you might uncover when reducing uncertainty

electronic propinquity: the psychological feeling of nearness facilitated by sharing the same online spaces

emblems: behaviors that substitute for words

emotional contagion: the process of catching another person's emotions

emotional control: skill in managing or regulating emotional expression to show the appropriate level and type of emotion

emotional estrangement: in families, when family members have infrequent contact with one another but usually only when they feel obligated to do so

emotional experience: an internal, intrapersonal emotional reaction that occurs inside a person's mind and body

emotional expression: an external, interpersonal emotional reaction that is manifest in a person's behavior

emotional expressivity: skill in being able to communicate how you are feeling to others

emotional flooding: a reaction that occurs when people become overwhelmed and confused in response to their partner's negative behavior, making it difficult to respond in a constructive manner

emotional intelligence: the ability to understand, manage, and utilize emotions to meet your goals and to understand the emotions of others

emotional labor: the effort involved in expressing emotions in appropriate ways based on the expectations of one's job

emotional sensitivity: skill in interpreting emotional information to accurately determine how other people feel

emotional support: support that revolves around expressing care, empathy, and comfort

emotions: feelings people have in response to precipitating events

emotive dissonance: discomfort about the clash between what one really feels versus what one is pretending to feel

encoding: taking an idea or information and translating it into a code that you can use to communicate that message

equity: the state of two partners having an equivalent balance of rewards and costs in their relationship

equity power: power that occurs in relational persuasion attempts because the persuasion target has created some inequity in the relationship

equivocation: strategically ambiguous, indirect communication that skirts the truth

ethnocentrism: a bias that leads people to consider the culture they belong to as superior to other cultures

ethnorelativity: the ability to understand that cultures are different but not in a hierarchical way

exaggeration: stretching the truth by embellishing details or making something sound better or worse than it really was

exchange: a process that includes a sender and a receiver, with, at minimum, a sender directing a message toward a receiver, or a receiver attending to something a sender said or did and interpreting that message

excuses: a remedial strategy aimed at trying to minimize responsibility for one's actions by blaming someone or something else

expectancy violations: behaviors that deviate (in positive or negative ways) from what people think will or should happen

expert power: power =based on other people perceiving someone to have a high level of needed knowledge or skill

explicit forgiveness: making a straightforward statement such as "I forgive you" to communicate forgiveness in a direct manner

explicit rule: a rule that has been openly discussed, or at least mentioned, and agreed upon

expression–privacy: a dialectical tension where relational partners desire both the ability to engage in self-disclosure and to have privacy regarding personal information

extraversion: the personality trait of being talkative, assertive, and energetic

face: identity performances formed from our own understanding of our internal self, our perception of our social audience, and support from external sources of information

face-negotiation theory: a communication theory explaining the process related to face threats that influence interpersonal conflicts in intercultural contexts

face orientation: the orientation a communicator has toward self, others, or both self and others face while experiencing face-threatening messages

face threats: communicative actions that harm positive or negative face

facial feedback hypothesis: the hypothesis that pretending to feel an emotion while posing an expression makes you start to feel that emotion

feedback: messages you receive from others in response to your own communication, as well as messages you send to others in response to their communication

femininity, as a cultural dimension: a cultural dimension indicating that the culture values a higher quality of life and caring for others

field of experience: the unique set of perceptions, attitudes, beliefs, and experiences communicators bring to an interaction

fixed network space: online communication spaces where the audience expects an identity performance from a single consistent entity

flexible network space: online communication spaces where people communicate identities that can be created, performed, and discarded easily

foot-in-the-door: a compliance-gaining strategy where the compliance-seeker first makes a trivial request and then follows up with a larger secondary request

forgiveness: a process that involves letting go of the negativity you feel toward someone who has wronged you

forgiveness through discussion: when forgiveness is granted based on what happens when people talk through a transgression

four horsemen of the apocalypse: four behaviors—criticism, defensiveness, contempt, and stonewalling—that are especially destructive during conflict

fundamental attribution bias: the tendency to over-attribute other people's behavior to personality explanations rather than situational explanations

gaslighting: a strategy that involves someone manipulating you in a way that makes you question your reality

generalized other: an internal representation of the presumed attitudes and perceptions of how an individual's social group perceives that individual

genuine de-escalation: a strategy that provides people with a way to reduce the closeness of a relationship without completely ending it

genuine expression: a type of emotional labor that involves someone putting effort into showing that they are indeed feeling the appropriate emotion

ghosting: a breakup strategy that involves abruptly shutting down all communication with someone

gossip: communication with evaluative content about a non-present third party known to both conversational partners

gunnysacking: a phenomenon that occurs when people silently store up all their grievances until they finally explode and unload everything on another person all at once

halo effect: see the *what-is-beautiful-is-good hypothesis*

haptics: touch as a nonverbal code and form of communication

heartless: Goffman's term for when people's face is spoiled due to others' behavior

high-context communication: communication where implicit contextual and nonverbal cues carry the meaning of the interaction

humor: as a maintenance strategy, using jokes, light teasing, and laughter to maintain a relationship

hurt: an unpleasant emotion that occurs when people are psychologically injured by another person

hurtful message: words that cause people to feel psychological or emotional pain

hyperpersonal perspective: a perspective that explains why people sometimes have more personal and positive interactions with people they are getting to know online versus face-to-face

identity: performances of self for an external audience

illocutionary force: what is meant by an utterance

illustrators: kinesic behaviors that describe or emphasize something

implicit rule: a rule that is assumed based on general norms within society or a relationship, but is not explicitly discussed

imposter syndrome: when a person has objective evidence that they are talented, yet they believe that they do not belong and will be discovered as a fraud

impression formation: when people develop perceptions about an individual based on decoding that individual's appearance or behavior

impression management: when people engage in communication to try to favorably influence other people's judgments of them

in-group advantage: the advantage that people have such that they are better able to decode the emotion of someone from their own culture compared to another culture

inconsistent nurturing as control theory: a theoretical explanation that relational partners' behavior alternating between nurturing and controlling strategies may lead to increasing or reinforcing the undesirable behavior that the partner is attempting to control

indirect fighting: an indirect and uncooperative conflict style that involves using passive-aggressive behaviors

individual/cultural dialectic: a cultural dialectic considering how people are members of broader cultures as well as unique individuals

individualism: a cultural dimension where people are more likely to be concerned about themselves and close others than a greater group

indulgence: a cultural dimension referring to how much people in a given culture attempt to control their desires and impulses

infidelity as maintenance: a negative maintenance strategy where partners engage in affairs or flirting to prevent boredom in their primary relationship

informational power: power derived from having access to and control of needed information

ingratiation: engaging in behaviors with the goal of increasing liking from others

inhibition: a display rule that involves acting like you do not feel any emotion when you actually do

injunctive norms: norms that develop from perceptions regarding what a social group typically approves or disapproves

instrumental goals: goals focused on getting tasks done or trying to accomplish a task

instrumental support: support that revolves around giving someone information or advice, or helping them with tasks

integration–separation: a dialectical tension where relational partners desire both connection and closeness, as well as independence or autonomy

intensification: a display rule that involves acting like one feels more of an emotion than they actually feel

interaction appearance theory: the theory that engaging in positive communication with someone increases perceptions of physical appearance, whereas engaging in negative communication decreases perceptions of physical attractiveness

interactional synchrony: the rhythm or flow of a conversation

interactive uncertainty reduction: gathering information regarding a target person's attitudes and behavior through direct communication with the target person

interdependence: a relational state where people are connected to each other in meaningful ways such that the thoughts and actions of one partner are influenced by the other relational partner

interpersonal communication: the exchange of nonverbal and verbal messages between people who have some level of personal or social connection with one another

interpersonal conflict: an expressed struggle between at least two interdependent parties who perceive incompatible goals, scarce resources, and interference from others in achieving their goals

interpersonal coordination: the degree to which the behaviors in an interaction are nonrandom, patterned, or synchronized in both timing and form

interpersonal facial feedback hypothesis: the hypothesis that when you unconsciously mirror someone's emotional expression, you start to feel the same emotions that person is experiencing

interpersonal relationships: relationships marked by the exchange of unique and meaningful messages as well as mutual influence

intersectionality: a concept for considering how intersecting social identities, such as race, class, and gender, combine to create differing experiences of privilege and marginalization

interviews: conversations people engage in with the specific purpose of gathering information

intimate relationships: relationships marked by a high level of idiosyncratic and personal communication as well as feelings of closeness

intimate terrorism: the use of physical violence as one of many tactics designed to maintain control over a relational partner

intimate zone: the conversational distance zone that extends from 0 to 18 inches and is typically reserved for interaction between people who share a close relationship

intrapersonal communication: communication with oneself, such as through one's thoughts

investments: resources that are attached to a relationship and would lose value or be lost if the relationship ends

invisible support: indirect support that is not interpreted as "help" by the recipient

jealousy induction: attempting to maintain a relationship through making the partner jealous

job knowledge questions: interview questions that ask an interviewee to describe or demonstrate expertise relevant to the position

joint activities: a maintenance strategy involving engaging in social events and activities together

justifications: when used as a remedial strategy, this type of communication involves trying to show that your behavior was not as bad as someone thinks it is

kinesics: a nonverbal code that encompasses facial expressions, body movements, and eye behavior

kitchen-sinking: a conflict tactic that occurs when people throw everything they can think of into an attack on their partner

language: a method of spoken or written human communication consisting of the use of words

leakage: physiological reactions that leak emotion despite people's best efforts to hide them

learning conversation: a conversation that is fueled by curiosity and focused on creating understanding and empathy by inviting others to express their opinions and feelings, sharing stories, and listening actively

legitimate dependence power: when power is derived because the person is dependent on someone else for their assistance

legitimate position power: when power is derived from an individual being recognized as an authority

liking: feelings of affection, respect, and receptivity to potential future interactions

listening: a complex process involving the selection of stimuli, the interpretation of stimuli, as well as how we store and recall that information

locutions: the words in an utterance

long-term memory: memory system that stores information for an indefinite period of time

long-term orientation: a cultural dimension indicating a culture that focuses on the more distant future

looking-glass self: the idea that we come to know ourselves in a way that is mirrored back to us through the communication of others

low-context communication: communication where explicit, usually verbal messages carry the meaning of the interaction

lying: saying something that is opposite or very different from what you know is true

magic ratio: Gottman's recommended ratio of five (or more) positive behaviors for every negative behavior

maintenance: in communication accommodation theory, a communication pattern that occurs when speakers actively maintain their communication style and resist adjustments toward a co-communicator with a different style

maintenance strategies: behaviors used to keep a relationship in existence, in a specified state or condition, satisfying, and/or in repair

masculinity, as a cultural dimension: a cultural dimension indicating that the culture values assertiveness and competition

masking: a display rule that involves covering up a felt emotion by expressing a different type of emotion

masspersonal communication: a convergence of mass and interpersonal communication channels such as when people use mass communication channels for interpersonal communication, use interpersonal channels for mass communication, or engage in mass and interpersonal communication simultaneously

maxim of manner: a conversational rule that speakers should be brief and orderly

maxim of quality: a conversational rule that speakers should avoid saying things that are false

maxim of quantity: a conversational rule that speakers should provide as much information as their listener needs to understand but no more

maxim of relevance: a conversational rule that speakers' utterances should be appropriate for the current state of the conversation

media multiplexity: the use of multiple communication channels to communicate with relational partners

mediated communication: communication that involves a technology-based channel of communication

mental maps: cognitive representations of your partner's thoughts, feelings, and needs based on trying to see things from their perspective

messages: the nonverbal and verbal information being exchanged

metacommunication: communication about communication

microaggressions: covert acts of racism or misogyny that occur within the context of everyday communication exchanges

mindfulness: an understanding that multiple influences create our understandings of each other and our communication

mindreading: a phenomenon that occurs when people assume they know how their partner is thinking or feeling

minimizing: as a forgiveness-granting strategy, downplaying the importance or severity of a transgression

minority stress theory: theoretical explanation that couples in marginalized relationships may experience additional stress and stigma

mirroring: the mirroring of a communication partner's postures, gestures, and mannerisms

miscommunication: a form of communication that occurs when a message is sent with intent but is interpreted inaccurately

misinterpretation: the process that occurs when a sender does not intentionally send a message, yet something the sender says or does is interpreted incorrectly by a receiver

motor mimicry: the process that occurs when a person's emotional expression reflects what someone else is feeling

multimodal: communication through more than one nonverbal mode or channel simultaneously

multiphasic: the idea that similar behaviors might accomplish different goals at different points or phases of the lifespan of a relationship

mutual-face orientation: a face orientation where the communicator is concerned for both their own face and their fellow communicator's face

mutual fade out: a breakup strategy where people gradually drift apart from each other

mutual influence: when the thoughts, behaviors, and perceptions of each partner have an effect on the thoughts, behaviors, and perceptions of the other partner

mutual violent control: a continuing violent struggle between two people who are both violent and controlling

need for affection: the need to have others communicate warm and friendly feelings toward us

need for closure: the need to know answers to questions as a way to alleviate confusion and ambiguity to move on

need for control: a social need involving the desire to predict and manage one's social world

need for inclusion: a social need involving forming and maintaining social bonds with other people in order to maintain a sense of belongingness

negation: a concept in relational dialectics where the absence of one end of a dialectical continuum signals the presence of the other end of the dialectical continuum

negative face: the desire to make autonomous decisions regarding our behavior in the world

negative maintenance strategies: antisocial strategies used to try to maintain a relationship

negative reciprocity: a pattern that occurs when a person responds to aggressive communication with more aggressive communication, leading to an escalation of reciprocal aggression

negative sentiment override: when people expect negativity in their relationships, so they take things personally and are always on the defensive or attack

negotiated farewell: a breakup strategy that involves mutual negotiation about how to best end or de-escalate a relationship that both people agree is in decline

negotiation: strategic conversation in which participants engage in communication tactics in an attempt to accomplish specific goals

neuroticism: a personality trait of being nervous, worried, and easily upset

noise: sounds or distractions that interfere with the sending or receiving of messages

nonverbal accents: subtle cultural distinctions in how people express emotions

nonverbal communication: nonlinguistic behaviors that are sent or received during the communication process

nonverbal dialect: a specific type of accented behavior that impedes accurate decoding

nonverbal displays of forgiveness: using nonverbal communication, such as acting like everything is normal, hugging the person who hurt you, or not acting mad anymore to show forgiveness

nonverbal immediacy: behaviors that increase physical and psychological closeness and are typically related to impressions of warmth and liking

norm of reciprocity: a social norm or expectation that we should return favors and other acts of kindness

off-record: messages constructed in such a way that the sender can be evasive regarding the intended meaning of the message

on-again–off-again relationships: relationships that include a pattern of breaking up and getting back together at least once

one-way fade: a breakup strategy where one person gradually reduces communication and the other person is left trying to figure out how to respond to the reduced contact

online disinhibition: when people behave differently than they might offline due to an anonymous online context

openness: a maintenance behavior related to having direct conversations that increase understanding, involve active listening, and in some cases help define the state of your relationship

openness–closedness: a personality trait of being intellectual, imaginative, and open-minded

other-face orientation: a face orientation where the communicator primarily has concern for their fellow communicator's face

outcome expectancy: a judgment about whether information you would uncover to reduce uncertainty would be likely to be positive or negative

outcome value: the degree to which someone is perceived as rewarding or unrewarding

partner uncertainty: the degree to which people are unsure about their partner's feelings, intentions, and/or participation in a relationship

passive uncertainty reduction: gathering information regarding a target person's attitudes and behavior through unobtrusive observation of that person

performances given: the ways that people use verbal and non-verbal cues to portray their identity to others

performances given off: the way that others receive our identity performances

person perceptions: judgments people make about one another's internal characteristics

person-centered messages: messages that acknowledge, elaborate on, and validate the feelings of a distressed person

personal idioms: words that have a special meaning to people in an interpersonal relationship that is not readily deducible to those outside the relationship

personal/social-contextual dialectic: refers to how communication is grounded in both the understanding of the individual and the context in which communication is taking place

personal space bubble: an invisible, adjustable bubble of space that you carry around with you

personal zone: a conversational distance zone, ranging from 18 inches to 4 feet in the United States, within which most interactions with casual friends and acquaintances occur

perspective-taking: the process of looking beyond your own perspective and trying to determine what another person needs

persuasive communication: messages intended to shape, reinforce, or change the responses of another or others

phatic communication: communication that appears to have very little functional content

phonological rules: rules that tell people how to pronounce words within a given language

physical attraction: being drawn to someone based on how they look

physical estrangement: in families, when family members no longer have any contact with one another

physical level of impressions: judgments about a person based on what you can see externally

physiological changes: internal changes in one's body

physiological self-soothing: a method that involves taking a break from conflict to calm down, reduce arousal, and feel refreshed before re-engaging in conflict

politeness protocol: the idea that people want to be perceived as friendly and polite, so they avoid difficult conversations that they think could be contentious and uncomfortable

politeness strategies: communication choices used to minimize face threats

positive face: the socially appropriate self-image people wish to present to others

positive sentiment override: being optimistic about a relationship such that you see problems as relatively minor and easily managed

positive tone strategy: a breakup strategy that focuses on ending the relationship in a direct and unambiguous manner while also trying to reduce the degree of hurt experienced, typically by focusing on specific positives of the person and the relationship

positivity: a maintenance behavior that reflects cheerfulness and optimism

power distance: a cultural dimension describing how cultures perceive inequality and hierarchies

pragmatics: the study of how the meaning of language is affected by context, the speaker, and the relationship between communicators

predicted outcome value theory: a theoretical explanation arguing that our drive to reduce uncertainty or not about a person is based on our perception of how rewarding future interaction with that individual might be

present-future/history-past dialectic: a cultural dialectic regarding the need to understand both historical forces at work within a particular culture and the culture's understandings and hopes for the future

primacy effect: the tendency for our first impressions of others to strongly impact our feelings toward them, in part because we tend to recall information from the beginning of an interaction better than we recall later information

privilege/disadvantage dialectic: a cultural dialectic explaining that positions of privilege and disadvantage exist within and between cultures

privilege: having more unearned social status, resources, and access to resources in comparison to others

propinquity: the psychological feeling of nearness

proxemics: a nonverbal code that revolves around the use of space as communication, including conversational distance and territory

pruning: removing people from one's contacts on social media sites by unfriending or blocking

pseudo de-escalation: a breakup strategy that involves making a false declaration about wanting to decrease the closeness of the relationship either temporarily or permanently (often by suggesting taking a break or being friends) when you actually want to end the relationship altogether

psychological level of impressions: judgments about a person's personal characteristics such as personality, thoughts, and feelings

public zone: a conversational zone that is greater than 10 feet and is common for public forms of communication where one person is speaking to others

punctuation problems: a problem that occurs when partners make different attributions about who is causing the conflict, with both thinking that the other person's behavior initiated the conflict

quality of alternatives: the various options people have outside of a current relationship

racial identity: the part of a person's self-concept that is based on their racial membership and their interpretation of what it means to be a member of that race

reactance: a cognitive process where people are presented with a piece of information and react in the opposite manner from the way the presenter intended

receiver apprehension: experiencing nervousness or anxiousness regarding listening because of fear of not being able to understand the message

recency effect: the tendency for our most recent interactions with others to strongly impact our feelings toward them

reciprocity power: power that occurs because a persuasion target owes the persuader some favor based on past exchanges

redressive action: a communicative choice people use to form messages that are viewed as more appropriate or polite than simply baldly stating the request or face threat

referent power: power derived from liking, respect, and affection for the influencer

regulators: kinesic behavior that helps people manage interaction

relational aggression: indirect and manipulative behaviors that cause someone social harm

relational assurances: maintenance communication related to affirming commitment to the relationship

relational de-escalation: the process of reducing the closeness of a relationship

relational dialectics: a theoretical perspective arguing that relational partners manage seemingly contradictory relational tensions and construct meaning through competing discourses

relational function of a message: the meaning of a message derived from contextual cues

relational goals: goals that revolve around being able to successfully navigate relationships, including being able to initiate, develop, maintain, and end relationships

relational maintenance: actions and activities used to sustain desired relational definitions

relational meaning: the meaning of a message based on the understanding of the context and relationship shared by the speaker and hearer

relational rules: norms related to behavior within particular types of relationships

relational termination: the process of ending a relationship altogether

relational transgressions: actions that are perceived as violating implicit or explicit relational rules

relational turning points: remembered events in relationships that relational partners pinpoint as transforming the relationship in either a positive or negative way

relational uncertainty: the degree to which people are unsure about the accuracy of their perceptions of their own and their partner's involvement in interpersonal relationships

relationship talk trick: a breakup strategy that involves telling someone you want to talk when your intention is to break up

relationship talks: maintenance communication that specifically addresses feelings about the relationship and relationship quality

relationship uncertainty: the degree to which people are unsure about how they define a relationship and/or see the relationship in the future

relationships: interdependent connections between two people

repairs: attempts to defuse the tension in the situation during conflict

repeated common couple violence: a conflict pattern whereby arguments tend to escalate into violence on a regular basis

resources: tangible and intangible commodities, including money, time, effort, love, status, and respect, which are valued

response-seeking: a Facebook relational maintenance strategy where people post status updates in hopes that people will reach out with responses and support

responsiveness: a communication pattern that involves paying attention to our fellow communicators, listening to and learning about them, and tailoring our messages to reflect our understanding of them

reward power: the ability to provide some type of compensation for compliant behavior

rewards: any exchanged resources that make you happy and/or give you wanted opportunities

role relationships: functional, casual, and often temporary relationships that occur due to the roles that the relational partners hold, such as server-customer

routine contact: a maintenance strategy involving maintaining regular communication with a relational partner

routine maintenance behaviors: communicative behaviors that relational partners engage in throughout their daily activities that might serve to maintain relationships but are not specifically enacted to maintain the relationship

satisfaction: a feeling that the outcome of a relationship meets or exceeds expectations of what a person thinks they deserve in a relationship

scrubbing: editing a social media account to include less content by doing things such as deleting photos posts, and tags

secret tests: tactics designed to covertly assess a relational partner's commitment to the relationship

secrets: intentionally concealed private information

self-concept: internal cognitive understanding of the multiple dimensions that make up who we are

self-construal: the way one perceives one's self in terms of their individuality and group connections

self-disclosure: communication that reveals personal information about the self to others

self-efficacy: a person's perception that they can competently execute a behavior

self-expansion theory: theory explaining that, as we build relationships with others, we come to see these others as an interdependent part of our own self

self-face orientation: a face orientation where the communicator primarily has concern for their own face

self-monitor: the ability to adapt communication and emotional expressions to a particular context

self-monitoring: the ability to shift performances for specific audiences

self-presentational goals: goals that revolve around presenting yourself in a positive way so people accept and like you

self-protective strategy: a strategy that involves avoiding communicating so that you do not make yourself vulnerable

self-serving bias: a cognitive bias where people attribute their own failures and negative behaviors to situational factors, but attribute their successes and positive behaviors to their personality

self-uncertainty: the degree to which people are unsure about their feelings and involvement in a relationship

semantics: the study of how people interpret and attach meanings to words and sentences

sensemaking: the process of creating meanings that inform how we interpret the behavior and identity of ourselves and others

shameless: Goffman's term for when people spoil their face due to their own behavior

short-term orientation: a cultural dimension indicating a culture that focuses on the present and more immediate future

showing respect: the antidote to contempt; involves telling people that their thoughts and feelings are valid and that you hold them and their needs in high regard

simulation: a display rule that involves acting like you feel an emotion when you actually feel nothing

situational questions: interview questions that ask an interviewee to explain how they would react in hypothetical situations

slang: informal words and phrases that are used more in speech than in writing and are only understood by certain people

smiling familiarity bias: a bias that draws us to recognize smiling faces more than nonsmiling faces

social attraction: being drawn to someone based on their personality and having positive interactions with them

social capital: resources perceived to be available from the network of relationships one has with other people

social construction: shared understandings, created through communication, of how our social world functions

social contact: a relational maintenance strategy where people use socal media like Facebook to reach out and interact with friends and acquaintances

social exchange theory: a theoretical explanation that people wish to maximize rewards and minimize costs across interpersonal interactions

social influence: communication processes whereby one person, group, or entity can change or adjust the thoughts, feelings, and behavior of other people

social networks: maintenance behaviors that connect relational partners to their broader social networks

social norms: social constructions that serve as guides for how people should behave based on exposure to repeated, collective communication about different types of behavior

social penetration theory: a theoretical model illustrating the gradual process of how people form relationships with each other through self-disclosure

social pressure: social rewards or punishments from socially important others that encourage people to engage or not engage in a behavior

social proof: perceiving behaviors as appropriate because we see many similar others engaging in such behaviors

social steganography: engaging in privacy management by choosing words and phrases that might intentionally be vague to unintended receivers

social support: the provision of resources

social zone: a conversational zone that ranges from 4 to 10 feet wherein many impersonal conversations take place

sociocultural level of impression: judgments about a person's socioeconomic status and cultural background

stability–change: a dialectical tension where relational partners desire both predictability and spontaneity in their relationships

static/dynamic dialectic: a cultural dialectic explaining that cultural practices are both consistent and ever-changing

stonewalling: the ultimate expression of defensiveness; occurs when people withdraw from their partner, shut down communication, and close themselves off

strategic maintenance behaviors: communicative behaviors that relational partners mindfully choose for the specific purpose of maintaining relationships

structured interviews: interviews that have a planned interview schedule and may include a more formal scoring process

subjective norms: perceptions regarding how a person thinks important others consider particular behaviors

successful communication: the type of communication that occurs when a person sends a message with intent and a receiver attends to and interprets that message correctly

sunk cost bias: a cognitive heuristic leading people to continue an endeavor once an investment into that endeavor has been made

supportive communication: verbal and nonverbal behaviors that convey a desire to provide emotional or tangible support and/or comfort to another person

surface acting: a type of emotional labor that involves displaying emotions that you do not feel

surveillance: keeping tabs or spying on one's partner in an attempt to maintain the relationship, including creeping

symbolic interactionism: a theoretical stance that behavior toward objects, messages, and people is based on meanings that people develop about those objects, messages, and people through social interaction with others

syntax: the study of the way words are arranged to form sentences

task attraction: being drawn to someone because they are helpful with specific tasks

task-sharing: sharing daily tasks and responsibilities to help maintain a relationship

that's-not-all: a compliance-gaining strategy where the compliance-seeker lets the buyer consider the initial offer and then adds another product or service to sweeten the deal

theory of mind: a person or being's ability to understand that they have a mental state, others have different mental states, and a person can influence the mental states of others

theory of motivated information management: a theory based on the idea that people are only motivated to reduce uncertainty when there is a discrepancy between the amount of uncertainty they want and the amount of uncertainty they have

theory of reasoned action: a theoretical explanation predicting that a person's intention to perform a behavior determines their actions, r and that this intention is rooted in their attitude toward the behavior as well as perceived norms about the appropriateness of the behavior.

thin slice: any sampling of behavior that is less than 5 minutes long

third-party manipulation: as a breakup strategy, using your social network to leak your intention to break up with your partner, or engaging in activities with others that let someone know they are being replaced

transactional model of communication: a model that includes the following elements to explain the communication process: communicators, encoding and decoding, message, feedback, channel, field of experience, and noise; communication is seen as a series of overlapping moves and countermoves rather than as a linear process

transgression-maximizing messages: communication focused on telling people in your social network about the negative aspects of a transgression and the partner who committed the transgression

transgression-minimizing messages: communication with people in your social network that is focused on putting a transgression in context and mentioning some of the mitigating factors

truth bias: a cognitive heuristic leading us to generally believe that other communicators are telling the truth

truth biases: in relational to deception, the expectation that people we like are honest

unattended behavior: behavior that people emit unintentionally without anyone noticing or interpreting it as meaningful

uncertainty: a lack of confidence about one's ability to predict or explain others' attitudes and behaviors

uncertainty-avoidance: a cultural dimension referring to cultural members' comfort level with ambiguity

uncertainty reduction theory: an explanation of how uncertainty makes people uncomfortable in social settings and how people seek to reduce these feelings of discomfort through reducing uncertainty

understanding: behaviors that communicate understanding one's partner

understatement: a statement that downplays aspects of the truth

unity: a concept in relational dialectics where one cannot understand one end of a dialectical continuum without the comparison to the other end of the dialectical continuum

universal thesis: the hypothesis that basic emotions are encoded and decoded similarly across cultures

unstructured interviews: interviews that do not use a standardized set of questions and are typically not formally scored

violent resistance: the use of violence in response to violent and controlling behavior

vocalics: a nonverbal code that includes the way words are spoken along with pauses and silences that occur during interaction

voluntariness: a relational dimension referring to people's ability to choose a particular relationship and how easily they could exit that relationship

warm glow heuristic: the idea that people associate positive things with familiarity

weak ties: acquaintances within your social network

what-is-beautiful-is-conceited hypothesis: a cognitive bias whereby attractive people are also perceived as materialistic, self-centered, snobbish, and vain

what-is-beautiful-is-good hypothesis: a cognitive bias where people tend to perceive physically attractive people as also possessing an array of positive internal characteristics

working memory: a memory system that temporarily stores information

xenophobia: fear of cultural difference

yielding: an indirect and cooperative conflict style that involves giving in and making concessions to meet the other partner's needs

REFERENCES

Afifi, T. D. (2003). 'Feeling caught' in stepfamilies: Managing boundary turbulence through appropriate communication privacy rules. *Journal of Social and Personal Relationships*, *20*, 729–755.

Afifi, T. D., & Schrodt, P. (2004). Adolescents' and young adults' feelings of being caught between their parents in divorced and non-divorced households. *Communication Monographs*, *70*, 142–173.

Afifi, W. A., & Burgoon, J. K. (1998). 'We never talk about that': A comparison of cross-sex friendships and dating relationships on uncertainty and topic avoidance. *Personal Relationships*, *5*, 255–272.

Afifi, W. A., & Morse, C. R. (2009). Expanding the role of emotion in the theory of motivated information management. In S. W. Smith & S. R. Wilson (Eds.), *New directions in interpersonal communication research* (pp. 87–105). SAGE.

Afifi, W. A., & Weiner, J. L. (2004). Toward a theory of motivated information management. *Communication Theory*, *14*, 167–190.

Agar, M. (2012). Cultural blends. In L. Monaghan, J. E. Goodman, & J. M. Robinson (Eds.), *A cultural approach to interpersonal communication* (2nd ed., pp. 12–23). Wiley.

Agllias, K. (2013). Family estrangement. In *Encyclopedia of social work*. Oxford University Press. https://doi.org/10.1093/acrefore/9780199975839.013.919

Agllias, K. (2016). *Family estrangement: A matter of perspective*. Routledge.

Agnew, C. R., Loving, T. J., Le, B., & Goodfriend, W. (2004). Thinking close: Measuring relational closeness as perceived self-other inclusion. In D. J. Mashek & A. Aron (Eds.), *Handbook of closeness and intimacy* (pp. 103–115). Erlbaum.

Albada, K. F., Knapp, M. L., & Theune, K. E. (2002). Interaction appearance theory: Changing perceptions of physical attractiveness through social interaction. *Communication Theory*, *12*, 8–40.

Alegría, C. A. (2010). Relationship challenges and relationship maintenance activities following the disclosure of transsexualism. *Journal of Psychiatric and Mental Health Nursing*, *17*, 909–916.

Allen, J. P., & Loeb, E. L. (2015). The autonomy–connection challenge in adolescent–peer relationships. *Child Development Perspectives*, *9*, 101–105.

Allen, L. F., Babin, E. A., & McEwan, B. (2012). Emotional investment: An exploration of young adult friends' emotion experience and expression using an investment model framework. *Journal of Social and Personal Relationships*, *29*, 206–227.

Allport, G. W. (1954). *The nature of prejudice*. Harvard University Press.

Altheide, D. L. (2000). Identity and the definition of the situation in a mass-mediated context. *Symbolic Interaction*, *23*, 1–27.

Altman, I., & Taylor, D. A. (1973). *Social penetration theory: The development of interpersonal relationships*. Holt Renfrew.

Altman, I., Vinsel, A., & Brown, B. (1981). Dialectic conceptions in social psychology: An application to social penetration and privacy regulation. In L. Berkowitz (Ed.), *Advances in experimental social psychology* (Vol. 14, pp. 107–160). Academic Press.

Amato, P. R., & Previti, D. (2003). People's reasons for divorcing: Gender, social class, the life course, and adjustment. *Journal of Family Issues*, *24*, 602–626.

Ambady, N. (2010). The perils of pondering: Intuition and thin slice judgments. *Psychological Inquiry*, *21*, 271–278.

Ambady, N., Krabbenhoft, M. A., & Hogan, D. (2006). The 30-sec sale: Using thin-slice judgments to evaluate sales effectiveness. *Journal of Consumer Psychology*, *16*, 4–13.

Ambady, N., & Rosenthal, R. (1993). Half a minute: Predicting teacher evaluations from thin slices of nonverbal behavior and physical attractiveness. *Journal of Personality and Social Psychology*, *64*, 431–441.

Andersen, P. A. (1985). Nonverbal immediacy in interpersonal communication. In A. W. Siegman & S. Feldstein (Eds.), *Multichannel integrations of nonverbal behavior* (pp. 1–36). Lawrence Erlbaum.

Andersen, P. A. (1991). When one cannot communicate: A challenge to Motley's traditional communication postulates. *Communication Studies*, *42*, 309–325.

Andersen, P. A., & Guerrero, L. K. (1998). Principles of communication and emotion in social interaction. In P. A. Andersen & L. K. Guerrero (Eds.), *Handbook of communication and emotion: Research, theory, applications, and contexts* (pp. 49–96). Academic Press.

Anderson, J. F., Beard, F. K., & Walther, J. B. (2010). Turn-taking and the local management of conversation in a highly simultaneous computer-mediated communication system. *Language@Internet*, *7*, 7. http://www.languageatinternet.org/articles/2010/2804

Anderson, S. K., & Middleton, V. A. (Eds.). (2017). *Explorations in diversity: Examining the complexities of privilege, discrimination, and oppression* (3rd ed.). Oxford University Press.

Anderson, T. L., Grunert, C., Katz, A., & Lovascio, S. (2010). Aesthetic capital: A research review on beauty perks and penalties. *Sociology Compass*, *4*, 564–575.

Andreoni, J., & Petrie, R. (2008). Beauty, gender and stereotypes: Evidence from laboratory experiments. *Journal of Economic Psychology*, *29*, 73–93.

Appiah, K. A. (2006). *Cosmopolitanism: Ethics in a world of strangers*. W. W. Norton & Company.

Appiah, O. (2018). Cultural voyeurism: A new framework for understanding race, ethnicity, and mediated intergroup interaction. *Journal of Communication*, *68*, 233–242. https://doi.org/10.1093/joc/jqx021

Argyle, M. (1972). Non-verbal communication in human social interaction. In R. A. Hinde (Ed.), *Non-verbal communication* (pp. 248–268). Cambridge University Press.

Argyle, M., & Henderson, M. (1984). The rules of friendship. *Journal of Social and Personal Relationships*, *1*, 211–237.

Argyle, M., Henderson, M., & Furnham, A. (1985). The rules of social relationships. *British Journal of Social Psychology*, *24*, 125–139.

Arkes, H., & Blumer, C. (1985). The psychology of sunk cost. *Organizational Behavior and Human Decision Processes*, *35*, 124–140.

Arnett, J. J. (2000). Emerging adulthood: A theory of development from the late teens through the twenties. *American Psychologist*, *55*, 469–480. https://doi.org/10.10937/0030-066X.55.5.469

Aron, A., Aron, E. N., & Smollan, D. (1991). Inclusion of other in the self scale and the structure of interpersonal closeness. *Journal of Personality and Social Psychology*, *63*, 596–612.

Aron, A., Aron, E. N., & Smollan, D. (1992). Inclusion of other in the self scale and the structure of interpersonal closeness. *Journal of Personality and Social Psychology*, *63*, 596–612.

Aron, A., Fisher, H. E., Strong, G., Acevedo, B., Riela, S., & Tsapelas, I. (2008). Falling in love. In S. Sprecher, A. Wenzel, & J. Harvey (Eds.), *Handbook of relationship initiation* (pp. 315–336). Psychology Press.

Aron, A., Lewandowski, G. W., Mashek, D., & Aron, E. N. (2013). The self-expansion model of motivation and cognition in close relationships. In J. A. Simpson & L. Campbell (Eds.), *The Oxford handbook of close relationships* (pp. 90–115). Oxford University Press.

Aron, E. N., & Aron, A. (1996). Love and expansion of the self: The state of the model. *Personal Relationships*, *3*, 45–58. https://doi.org/10.1111/j.1475-6811.1996.tb00103.x

Asch, S. E. (1955). Opinions and social pressure. *Scientific American*, *193*, 31–35.

Asch, S. E. (1956). Studies of independence and conformity: A minority of one against a unanimous majority. *Psychological Monographs*, *70*, 1–70.

Ashforth, B. E., & Humphrey, R. H. (1993). Emotional labor in service roles: The influence of identity. *Academy of Management Review*, *18*, 88–115.

Ashmore, R. D., Solomon, M. R., & Longo, L. C. (1996). Thinking about fashion models' looks: A multidimensional approach to the structure of perceived physical attractiveness. *Personality and Social Psychology Bulletin*, *22*, 1083–1104.

Attridge, M. (1994). Barriers to dissolution of romantic relationships. In D. J. Canary & L. Stafford (Eds.), *Communication and relational maintenance* (pp. 141–164). Academic Press.

Aune, K. S., Buller, D. B., & Aune, R. K. (1996). Display rule development in romantic relationships: Emotion management and perceived appropriateness of emotions across relationship stages. *Human Communication Research*, *23*, 115–145.

Aune, R. K., Metts, S., & Hubbard, A. S. E. (1998). Managing the outcomes of discovered deception. *Journal of Social Psychology*, *138*, 677–689.

Bachman, G. F., & Guerrero, L. K. (2006). An expectancy violations analysis of relational quality and communicative responses following hurtful events in dating relationships. *Journal of Social and Personal Relationships*, *23*, 943–963.

Backlund, P. M., & Morreale, S. P. (2015). Communication competence: Historical synopsis, definitions, applications, and looking to the future. In A. Hannawa & B. Spitzberg (Eds.), *Communication competence* (pp. 11–38). De Gruyter Mounton.

Baddeley, A. D. (1990). *Human memory: Theory and practice*. Allyn & Bacon.

Baker, A. J. (2008). Down the rabbit hole: The role of place in the initiation and development of online relationships. In A. Barak (Ed.), *Psychological aspects of cyberspace: Theory, research* (pp. 163–184). Cambridge University Press.

Balsters, M. J., Krahmer, E. J., Swerts, M. G., & Vingerhoets, A. J. (2013). Emotional tears facilitate the recognition of sadness and the perceived need for social support. *Evolutionary Psychology*, *11*, 148–158.

Bandura, A. (1977). *Social learning theory*. Prentice-Hall.

Bandura, A. (1993). Perceived self-efficacy in cognitive development and functioning. *Educational Psychologist*, *28*, 117–148.

Banks, S. P., Altendorf, D. M., Greene, J. O., & Cody, M. J. (1987). An examination of relationship disengagement: Perceptions, breakup strategies and outcomes. *Western Journal of Speech Communication, 51*, 19–41.

Barnlund, D. C. (2008). A transactional model of communication. In C. D. Mortensen (Ed.), *Communication theory* (2nd ed., pp. 47–57). Transaction.

Barrett, K. C. (1995). A functionalist approach to shame and guilt. In J. P. Tangney & K. W. Fischer (Eds.), *Self-conscious emotions: The psychology of shame, guilt, embarrassment, and pride* (pp. 25–63). Guilford.

Barrett, L. F. (2006). Solving the emotion paradox: Categorization and the experience of emotion. *Personality and Social Psychology Review, 10*, 20–46.

Bartholomew, K. (1990). Avoidance of intimacy: An attachment perspective. *Journal of Social and Personal Relationships, 7*, 147–178.

Bartlett Ellis, R. J., Carmon, A. F., & Pike, C. (2016). A review of immediacy and implications for provider-patient relationships to support medication management. *Patient Preference and Adherence, 10*, 9–18.

Baudouin, J. Y., Gilibert, D., Sansone, S., & Tiberghien, G. (2000). When the smile is a cue to familiarity. *Memory, 8*, 285–292.

Baumeister, R. F. (1982). Self-esteem, self-presentation and future interaction: A dilemma of reputation. *Journal of Personality, 50*, 29–45.

Baumeister, R. F., & Leary, M. R. (1995). The need to belong: Desire for interpersonal attachments as a fundamental human motivation. *Psychological Bulletin, 117*, 497–529.

Bavelas, J. B. (1985). A situational theory of disqualification. Using language to "leave the field". In J. Forgas (Ed.), *Language and social situations* (pp. 439–499). SAGE.

Bavelas, J. B., Black, A., Chovil, N., & Mullett, J. (1990). *Equivocal communication*. SAGE.

Bavelas, J. B., Black, A., Lemery, C. R., & Mullett, J. (1986). "I show how you feel": Motor mimicry as a communicative act. *Journal of Personality and Social Psychology, 50*(2), 322–329. https://doi.org/10.1037/0022-3514.50.2.322

Bavelas, J. B., & Coates, L. (1992). How do we account for the mindfulness of face-to-face dialogue? *Communication Monographs, 59*, 301–305.

Baxter, L. A. (1982). Strategies for ending relationships: Two studies. *Western Journal of Speech Communications, 46*, 223–241.

Baxter, L. A. (1984). Trajectories of relationship disengagement. *Journal of Social and Personal Relationships, 1*, 29–48.

Baxter, L. A. (1985). Accomplishing relational disengagement. In S. Duck & D. Perlman (Eds.), *Understanding personal relationships: An interdisciplinary approach* (pp. 243–265). SAGE.

Baxter, L. A. (1990). Dialectical contradictions in relationship development. *Journal of Social and Personal Relationships, 7*, 69–88.

Baxter, L. A. (2004a). A tale of two voices: Relational dialectics theory. *The Journal of Family Communication, 4*, 181–192.

Baxter, L. A. (2004b). Relationships as dialogues. *Personal Relationships, 11*, 1–22.

Baxter, L. A. (2010). *Voicing relationships: A dialogic perspective*. SAGE.

Baxter, L. A., & Bullis, C. (1986). Turning points in developing romantic relationships. *Human Communication Research, 12*, 469–493.

Baxter, L. A., Dun, T., & Sahlstein, E. (2001). Rules for relating communicated among social network members. *Journal of Social and Personal Relationships, 18*, 173–200.

Baxter, L. A., & Ebert, L. (1999). Perceptions of dialectical contradictions in turning points of development in heterosexual romantic relationships. *Journal of Social and Personal Relationships, 16*, 547–569.

Baxter, L. A., & Montgomery, B. M. (1996). *Relating: Dialogues and dialectics*. Guilford.

Baxter, L. A., & Montgomery, B. M. (1998). A guide to dialectical approaches to studying personal relationships. In B. M. Montgomery & L. A. Baxter (Eds.), *Dialectical approaches to studying personal relationships* (pp. 1–16). Psychological Press.

Baxter, L. A., & Pittman, G. (2001). Communicatively remembering turning points of relationship development. *Communication Reports, 14*, 1–18.

Baxter, L. A., Scharp, K. M., & Thomas, L. J. (2021). Original voices: Relational dialectics theory. *Journal of Family Theory & Review, 13*, 7–20.

Baxter, L. A., & Wilmot, W. W. (1984). "Secret tests" social strategies for acquiring information about the state of the relationship. *Human Communication Research, 11*, 171–201.

Baxter, L., Braithwaite, D. O., & Nicholson, J. H. (1999). Turning points in the development of blended families. *Journal of Social and Personal Relationships, 16*, 291–314.

Bazarova, N. N., & Choi, Y. H. (2014). Self-disclosure in social media: Extending the functional approach to disclosure motivations and characteristics on social network sites. *Journal of Communication, 64*, 635–657.

BBC News. (2014, July 2). Fighting for the 'lost art of conversation'. *BBC News*. http://www.bbc.com/news/technology-28089246

Beaty, J. (2017, March 14). *A couple's guide to complaining*. https://www.gottman.com/blog/a-couples-guide-to-complaining/

Beck, U., & Sznaider, N. (2010). Unpacking cosmopolitanism for the social sciences: A research agenda. *British Journal of Sociology*, *61*, 381–403.

Becker, J. A. H., Johnson, A. J., Craig, E. A., Gilchrist, S. E., Haigh, M. M., & Lane, L. T. (2009). Friendships are flexible, not fragile: Turning points in geographically-close and long-distance friendships. *Journal of Social and Personal Relationships*, *26*, 347–369.

Bell, G. C., & Hastings, S. O. (2011). Black and white interracial couples: Managing relational disapproval through facework. *The Howard Journal of Communications*, *22*, 240–259. https://doi.org/10.1080/10646175.2011.590405

Bell, R. A., Buerkel-Rothfuss, N. L., & Gore, K. E. (1987). "Did you bring the yarmulke for the cabbage patch kid?": The idiomatic communication of young lovers. *Human Communication Research*, *14*, 474–467.

Bell, R. A., & Daly, J. A. (1984). The affinity-seeking function of communication. *Communication Monographs*, *51*, 91–115.

Bell, R. A., & Healey, J. G. (1992). Idiomatic communication and interpersonal solidarity in friends' relational cultures. *Human Communication Research*, *18*, 307–355.

Beller, J., & Wagner, A. (2017). Disentangling loneliness: Differential effects of subjective loneliness, network quality network size, and living alone on physical, mental, and cognitive health. *Journal of Aging and Health*, *30*, 521–539. https://doi.org/10.11177/0898264316685843

Bennett, M. J. (1993). Towards a developmental model of intercultural sensitivity. In R. M. Paige (Ed.), *Education for the intercultural experience*. Intercultural Press.

Bennett, M. J. (2004). J. S. Wurzel (Ed.), *From ethnocentrism to ethnorelativism. Toward multiculturalism: A reader in multicultural education*. Intercultural Resource Corporation.

Benson, K. (2017, May 17). *Transforming criticism into wishes: A recipe for successful conflict*. https://www.gottman.com/blog/transforming-criticism-into-wishes-a-recipe-for-successful-conflict/

Berger, C. R., & Bradac, J. J. (1982). *Language and social knowledge: Uncertainty in interpersonal relationships*. Edward Arnold.

Berger, C. R., & Calabrese, R. J. (1975). Some explanations in initial interaction and beyond toward a developmental theory of interpersonal communication. *Human Communication Research*, *1*, 99–112.

Berger, P., & Kellner, H. (1964). Marriage and the construction of reality: An exercise in the microsociology of knowledge. *Diogenes*, *12*(46), 1–24.

Berkowitz, L., & Daniels, L. R. (1963). Responsibility and dependency. *Journal of Abnormal and Social Psychology*, *66*, 429–436.

Berlo, D. K. (1960). *The process of communication*. Holt, Rinehart, and Winston.

Bernhold, Q. S., & Giles, H. (2018). Ethnic differences in grandparent–grandchild affectionate communication. *Communication Reports*, *31*(3), 188–202.

Bernieri, F. J., Davis, M., Rosenthal, R., & Knee, C. R. (1994). Interactional synchrony and rapport: Matching synchrony in displays devoid of sound and facial affect. *Personality and Social Psychology Bulletin*, *20*, 303–311.

Bernieri, F. J., & Rosenthal, R. (1991). Interpersonal coordination: Behavior matching and interactional synchrony. In R. S. Feldman & B. Rime (Eds.), *Fundamentals of nonverbal behavior* (pp. 401–32). Cambridge University Press.

Berscheid, E. (1983). Emotion. In H. H. Kelley, E. Berscheid, A. Christensen, J. H. Harvey, T. L. Huston, G. Levinger, E. McClintock, L. A. Peplau, & D. R. Peterson (Eds.), *Close relationships* (pp. 110–168). Freeman.

Berscheid, E. (1988). Some comments on love's anatomy: Or whatever happened to old-fashioned lust? In R. J. Sternberg & M. L. Barnes (Eds.), *The psychology of love* (pp. 359–371). Yale University Press.

Bevan, J. L., & Cameron, K. A. (2001, November). *Attempting to reconcile: The impact of the investment model* [Paper presentation]. The Annual Meeting of the National Communication Association, Atlanta, GA, United States.

Bevan, J. L., & Samter, W. (2004). Toward a broader conceptualization of jealousy in close relationships: Two exploratory studies. *Communication Studies*, *55*, 14–28.

Blake, R. R., & Mouton, J. S. (1964). *The managerial grid*. Gulf.

Blieszner, R., & Adams, R. G. (1992). *Adult friendship*. SAGE.

Blight, M. G., Ruppel, E. K., & Jagiello, K. (2019). "Using Facebook lets me know what he is doing": Relational uncertainty, breakups, and renewals in on-again/off-again relationships. *Southern Communication Journal*, *84*, 328–339.

Blum-Kulka, S. (1989). Playing it safe: The role of conventionality in indirect requests. In S. Blum-Kulka, J. House, & G. Kasper (Eds.), *Cross-cultural pragmatics*. Ablex.

Blumer, H. (1969). *Symbolic interactionism: Perspective and method*. University of California Press.

Bodie, G. D. (2011). The Active-Empathic Listening Scale (AELS): Conceptualization and evidence of validity within the interpersonal domain. *Communication Quarterly*, *59*(3), 277–295. https://doi.org/10.1080/01463373.2011.583495

Bodie, G. D., Worthington, D., Imhof, M., & Cooper, L. O. (2008). What would a unified field of listening look like? A proposal linking past perspectives and future endeavors. *The International Journal of Listening*, *22*, 102–122. https://doi.org/10.1080/10904010802174867

Bok, S. (1989). *Secrets: On the ethics of concealment and revelation*. Vintage Books.

Bolger, N., & Amarel, D. (2007). Effects of social support visibility on adjustment to stress: Experimental evidence. *Journal of Personality and Social Psychology, 92*, 458–475.

Bolger, N., Zuckerman, A., & Kessler, R. C. (2000). Invisible support and adjustment to stress. *Journal of Personality and Social Psychology, 79*, 953–961.

Bond, R., & Smith, P. B. (1996). Culture and conformity: A meta-analysis of studies using Asch's (1952b, 1956) line judgment task. *Psychological Bulletin, 119*(1), 111–137. https://doi.org/10.1037/0033-2909.119.1.111

Boon, S. D., & Sulsky, L. M. (1997). Attributions of blame and forgiveness in romantic relationships: A policy-capturing study. *Journal of Social Behavior and Personality, 12*, 19–44.

Booth, A., & Edwards, J. N. (1989). Transmission of marital and family quality over the generations. *Journal of Divorce, 13*, 41–57.

Boucher, J. D., & Carlson, G. E. (1980). Recognition of facial expression in three cultures. *Journal of Cross-Cultural Psychology, 11*, 263–280.

Bourhis, R. Y., & Giles, H. (1977). The language of intergroup distinctiveness. *Language, Ethnicity and Intergroup Relations, 13*, 119.

Bourhis, R. Y., Giles, H., Leyens, J.-P., & Tajfel, H. (1979). Psycholinguistic distinctiveness: Language divergence in Belgium. In H. Giles & R. N. St. Clair (Eds.), *Language and social psychology* (pp. 158–185). Basil Blackwell.

Bovee, C. L., & Thill, J. V. (2010). *Business communication today* (10th ed.). Pearson.

boyd, d. (2014). *It's complicated: The social lives of networked teens*. Yale University Press.

boyd, d., & Marwick, A. (2011). *Social steganography: Privacy in networked publics* [Paper presentation]. Meeting of the International Communication Association, Boston, MA, United States.

Boyd, N. M., & Nowell, B. (2017). Testing a theory of sense of community and community responsibility in organizations: An empirical assessment of predictive capacity on employee well-being and organizational citizenship. *Journal of Community Psychology, 45*, 210–229.

Bradac, J. J., Mulac, A., & House, A. (1988). Lexical diversity and magnitude of convergent versus divergent style-shifting: Perceptual and evaluative consequences. *Language and Communication, 8*, 213–228.

Bradbury, T. N., & Fincham, F. D. (1990). Attributions in marriage: Review and critique. *Psychological Bulletin, 107*, 3–33.

Bragger, J. D., Kutcher, E., Morgan, J., & Firth, P. (2002). The effects of the structured interview on reducing biases against pregnant job applicants. *Sex Roles, 46*, 215–226.

Braiker, H. B., & Kelley, H. H. (1979). Conflict in the development of closer relationships in R. In L. Burgess & T. L. Huston (Eds.), *Social exchange in developing relationships* (pp. 135–168). Academic Press.

Brashers, D. E. (2001). Communication and uncertainty management. *Journal of Communication, 51*, 477–497.

Brenner, M. (1985). Intensive interviewing. In M. Brenner, J. Brown, & D. Canter (Eds.), *The research interview* (pp. 147–162). Academic Press.

Brenner, R. E., & Vogel, D. L. (2015). Measuring thought content valence after a breakup: Development of the Positive and Negative Ex-relationship Thoughts (PANERT) scale. *Journal of Counseling Psychology, 62*, 476–487.

Breshears, D. (2011). Understanding communication between lesbian parents and their children regarding outsider discourse about family identity. *Journal of GLBT Family Studies, 7*(3), 264–284.

Brittle, Z. (2014, September 3). *R is for repair*. https://www.gottman.com/blog/r-is-for-repair/

Brittle, Z. (2015, June 4). *Managing conflict: Part 4*. https://www.gottman.com/blog/manage-conflict-part-4/

Brock, A. (2012). From the blackhand side: Twitter as a cultural conversation. *Journal of Broadcasting and Electronic Media, 56*, 529–549.

Brody, N., Mooney, C. M., Westerman, S. A., & McDonald, P. (2009). lts gt 2gthr l8r: Text messaging as a relational maintenance tool. *Kentucky Journal of Communication, 28*, 109–127.

Brody, N., & Vangelisti, A. L. (2016). Bystander intervention in cyberbullying. *Communication Monographs, 83*, 94–119.

Brooks, J. E., & Ogolsky, B. G. (2017). Effects of network approval on accounts of commitment trajectories in intraracial and interracial relationships. *Marriage & Family Review, 53*(4), 347–364.

Brown, B. B., Clasen, D. R., & Eicher, S. A. (1986). Perceptions of peer pressure, peer conformity dispositions, and self-reported behavior among adolescents. *Developmental Psychology, 22*, 521–530.

Brown, L. A., & Roloff, M. E. (2015). Organizational citizenship behavior, organizational communication, and burnout: The buffering role of perceived organizational support and psychological contracts. *Communication Quarterly, 63*, 384–404.

Brown, P., & Levinson, S. C. (1987). *Politeness: Some universals in language use*. Cambridge University Press.

Brummett, E. A., & Afifi, T. D. (2019). A grounded theory of interracial romantic partners' expectations for support and strain with family members. *Journal of Family Communication*, *19*(3), 191–212.

Bryant, E. M., & Marmo, J. (2010). Relational maintenance strategies of Facebook. *Kentucky Journal of Communication*, *28*, 129–150. http://kycommunication.com/jenniferpdf/Bryant.pdf

Bryant, E. M., & Marmo, J. (2012). The rules of Facebook friendship: A two-stage examination of interaction rules in close, casual, and acquaintance friendships. *Journal of Social and Personal Relationships*, *29*, 1013–1035.

Bucholtz, M. (2012). Word up: Social meanings of slang in California youth culture. In L. Monaghan, J. E. Goodman, & J. M. Robinson (Eds.), *A cultural approach to interpersonal communication* (2nd ed., pp. 274–297). Wiley.

Bullis, C., Clark, C., & Sline, R. (1993). From passion to commitment: Turning points in romantic relationships. In P. J. Kalbfleisch (Ed.), *Interpersonal communication: Evolving interpersonal relationships* (pp. 213–236). Lawrence Erlbaum.

Burger, J. M. (1986). Increasing compliance by improving the deal: The that's-not-all technique. *Journal of Personality and Social Psychology*, *51*, 277–283.

Burger, J. M. (1999). The foot-in-the-door compliance procedure: A multiple process analysis and review. *Personality and Social Psychology Review*, *3*, 303–325.

Burger, J. M., Messian, N., Patel, S., del Prado, A., & Anderson, C. (2003). What a coincidence! The effects of incidental similarity on compliance. *Personality and Social Psychology Bulletin*, *30*, 35–43.

Burger, J. M., Reed, M., DeCesare, K., Rauner, S., & Rozolis, J. (1999). The effects of initial request size on compliance: More about the that's-not-all technique. *Basic and Applied Social Psychology*, *21*, 243–249.

Burger, J. M., & Shelton, M. (2011). Changing everyday health behaviors through descriptive norm manipulations. *Social Influence*, *6*, 69–77.

Burgoon, J. K. (1993). Interpersonal expectations, expectancy violations, and emotional communication. *Journal of Language and Social Psychology*, *12*, 30–48.

Burgoon, J. K., & Bacue, A. (2003). Nonverbal communication skills. In B. R. Burleson & J. O. Greene (Eds.), *Handbook of communication and social interaction skills* (pp. 179–219). Lawrence Erlbaum.

Burgoon, J. K., Berger, C. R., & Waldron, V. R. (2000). Mindfulness and interpersonal communication. *Journal of Social Issues*, *65*, 105–127.

Burgoon, J. K., Burgoon, M., Miller, G. R., & Sunnafrank, M. (1981). Learning theory approaches to persuasion. *Human Communication Research*, *7*, 161–179.

Burgoon, J. K., Guerrero, L. K., & Floyd, K. (2022). *Nonverbal communication* (2nd ed.). Routledge.

Burgoon, J. K., Guerrero, L. K., & White, C. H. (2013). The codes and functions of nonverbal communication. In A. J. Cienki, E. Fricke, S. H. Ladewick, D. McNeil, C. Müller, & S. Tessendorf (Eds.), *Body – language – communication. An international handbook on multimodality in human interaction* (Vol. 1, pp. 609–626). De Gruyter Mouton.

Burgoon, J. K., & Le Poire, B. A. (1999). Nonverbal cues and interpersonal judgments: Participant and observer perceptions of intimacy, dominance, composure, and formality. *Communication Monographs*, *66*, 105–124.

Burgoon, J. K., & Newton, D. A. (1991). Applying a social meaning model to relational message interpretations of conversational involvement: Comparing observer and participant perspectives. *Southern Communication Journal*, *56*, 96–113.

Burke, M., Kraut, R., & Marlow, C. (2011). *Social capital on Facebook: Differentiating users and users* [Conference session]. The SIGCHI Conference on Human Factors in Computing Systems, Vancouver, BC, Canada.

Burke, T. J., Ruppel, E. K., & Dinsmore, D. R. (2016). Moving away and reaching out: Young adults' relational maintenance and psychosocial well-being during the transition to college. *Journal of Family Communication*, *16*, 180–187. https://doi.org/10.1070/15267431.2016.1146724

Burleson, B. R. (1982). The development of comforting communication skills in childhood and adolescence. *Child Development*, *53*, 1578–1588.

Burleson, B. R. (2003). Emotional support skill. In J. O. Greene & B. R. Burleson (Eds.), *Handbook of communication and social interaction skills* (pp. 551–594). Lawrence Erlbaum.

Burleson, B. R., & Denton, W. H. (1997). The relationship between communication skill and marital satisfaction: Some moderating effects. *Journal of Marriage and the Family*, *59*, 884–902.

Burleson, B. R., & Goldsmith, D. J. (1996). How the comforting process works: Alleviating emotional distress through conversationally induced reappraisals. In P. A. Anderson & L. K. Guerrero (Eds.), *Handbook of communication and emotion* (pp. 245–280). https://doi.org/10.1016/B978-012057770-5/50011-4

Burleson, B. R., & MacGeorge, E. L. (2002). Supportive communication. In M. L. Knapp & J. A. Daly (Eds.), *The handbook of interpersonal communication* (3rd ed., pp. 374–424). SAGE.

Burleson, B. R., Metts, S., & Kirch, M. W. (2000). Communication in close relationships. In C. Hendrick & S. S. Hendrick (Eds.), *Close relationships: A sourcebook* (pp. 244–258). SAGE.

Burleson, B. R., & Samter, W. (1994). A social skills approach to relationship maintenance: How individual differences in communication skills affect the achievement of relational functions. In D. J. Canary & L. S. Staffrod (Eds.), *Communication and relational maintenance* (pp. 62–90). Academic Press.

Cai, D., & Fink, E. (2002). Conflict style differences between individualist and collectivists. *Communication Monographs*, *69*(1), 67–87. https://doi.org/10.1080/03637750216536

Campbell, W. K., & Foster, C. A. (2002). Narcissism and commitment in romantic relationships: An investment model analysis. *Personality and Social Psychology Bulletin*, *28*, 484–495.

Campbell, W. K., Sedikides, C., Redder, G. D., & Elliot, A. J. (2000). Among friends? An examination of friendship and the self-serving bias. *British Journal of Social Psychology*, *39*, 229–239.

Campion, M. A., Palmer, D. K., & Campion, J. E. (1997). A review of structure in the selection interview. *Personnel Psychology*, *50*, 655–702.

Canary, D. J., Cupach, W. R., & Messman, S. J. (1995). *Relationship conflict*. SAGE.

Canary, D. J., & Spitzberg, B. H. (1987). Appropriateness and effectiveness perceptions of conflict strategies. *Human Communication Research*, *14*, 93–118.

Canary, D. J., & Spitzberg, B. H. (1989). A model of perceived competence of conflict strategies. *Human Communication Research*, *15*, 630–649.

Canary, D. J., & Spitzberg, B. H. (1990). Attribution biases and associations between conflicts strategies and competence outcomes. *Communication Monographs*, *57*, 139–151.

Canary, D. J., & Stafford, L. (1992). Relational maintenance strategies and equity in marriage. *Communications Monographs*, *59*(3), 243–267.

Canary, D. J., & Stafford, L. (1993). Preservation of relational characteristics: Maintenance strategies, equity, and locus of control. In P. J. Kalbfleisch (Ed.), *Interpersonal communication: Evolving interpersonal relationships* (pp. 237–259). Lawrence Erlbaum Associates.

Canary, D. J., & Stafford, L. (1994). Maintaining relationships through strategic and routine interaction. In D. J. Canary & L. Stafford (Eds.), *Communication and relational maintenance*. Academic Press.

Canary, D. J., & Stafford, L. (2007). People want – and maintain- fair marriages: Reply to Ragsdale and Brandau-Brown. *Journal of Family Communication*, *7*, 61–68.

Canary, D. J., Stafford, L., Hause, K., & Wallace, L. A. (1993). An inductive analysis of relational maintenance strategies: A comparison among lovers, relatives, friends, and others. *Communication Research Reports*, *10*, 5–14.

Canary, D. J., Stafford, L., & Semic, B. (2002). A panel study of the associations between maintenance strategies and relational characteristics. *Journal of Marriage and the Family*, *64*, 395–406.

Canary, D. J., Weger, H., & Stafford, L. (1991). Couple's argument sequences and their associations with relational characteristics. *Western Journal of Speech Communication*, *55*, 159–179.

Capella, J. N. (1994). The management of conversational interaction in adults and infants. In M. L Knapp & G. R. Miller (Eds.), *Handbook of interpersonal communication* (2nd ed., pp. 380–418). SAGE.

Cappella, J. N. (1993). The facial feedback hypothesis in human interaction: Review and speculation. *Journal of Language and Social Psychology*, *12*, 13–29.

Card, N. A. (2007). "I hated her guts!": Emerging adults' recollections of the formation, maintenance, and termination of antipathetic relationships during high school. *Journal of Adolescent Research*, *22*, 32–57.

Carnes, A. M., Knotts, K. G., Munyon, T. P., Heames, J. T., & Houghton, J. D. (2019). Think fast, the role of thin slices of behavior in employee selection decisions. *International Journal of Selection and Assessment*, *27*, 357–370.

Carnevale, P. J., & Pruitt, D. G. (1992). Negotiation and mediation. *Annual review of psychology*, *43*, 531–582.

Carpenter, C. J. (2012). Narcissism on Facebook: Self-promotional and anti-social behavior. *Personality and Individual Differences*, *52*, 482–486.

Carpenter, C. J. (2013). A meta-analysis of the effectiveness of the "but you are free" compliance-gaining technique. *Communication Studies*, *64*, 6–17.

Carpenter, C. J., & McEwan, B. (2016). The players of micro-dating: Individual and gender differences in goal orientations toward micro-dating apps. *Frist Monday*.

Carpenter, C. J., & Spottswood, E. L. (2013). Exploring romantic relationships on social networking sites using the self-expansion model. *Computers in Human Behavior*, *29*, 1531–1537.

Carr, D., & Friedman, M. A. (2005). Is obesity stigmatizing? Body weight, perceived discrimination, and psychological well-being in the United States. *Journal of Health and Social Behavior*, *46*(3), 244–259. https://doi.org/10.117700221 4650504600303

Carr, K., & Wang, T. R. (2012). "Forgiveness isn't a simple process: It's a vast undertaking": Negotiating and communicating forgiveness in nonvoluntary family relationships. *Journal of Family Communication*, *12*, 40–56.

Casper, D. M., & Card, N. A. (2010). "We were best friends, but...": Two studies of antipathetic relationships emerging from broken friendships. *Journal of Adolescent Research*, *25*, 499–526.

Caspi, A., & Herbener, E. S. (1990). Continuity and change: Assortative marriage and the consistency of personality in adulthood. *Journal of Personality and Social Psychology*, *58*, 250–258.

Caughlin, J. (2010). A multiple goals theory of personal relationships: Conceptual integration and program overview. *Journal of Social and Personal Relationships*, *27*, 824–848.

CBS News. (2007, December 12). Is the conversation dying? *Sunday Morning*. http://www.cbsnews.com/news/is-the-conversation-dying/

Cederblom, D. (1982). The performance appraisal interview: A review, implications, and suggestions. *The Academy of Management Review*, 7, 219–227.

Ceglarek, P. J. D., Darbes, L. A., Stephenson, R., & Bauermeister, J. A. (2017). Breakup-related appraisals and the psychological well-being of young adult gay and bisexual men. *Journal of Gay & Lesbian Mental Health*, 21(3), 256–274. https://doi.org/10.1080/19359705.2017.1293579

Centers for Disease Control and Prevention. (2018). New CDC analysis shows steep and sustained increases in STDs in recent years. *National Center for HIV/AIDS, Viral Hepatitis, and TB Prevention Newsroom*. https://www.cdc.gov/nchhstp/newsroom/2018/press-release-2018-std-prevention-conference.html

Chaiken, S. (1987). The heuristic model of persuasion. In M. P. Zanna, J. M. Olson, & C. P. Herman (Eds.), *Social influence: The Ontario symposium* (Vol. 5, pp. 3–40). Lawrence Erlbaum Associates.

Chan, M. (2019). The dying art of conversation – Has technology killed our ability to talk face-to-face? *The Conversation*. https://theconversation.com/the-dying-art-of-conversation-has-technology-killed-our-ability-to-talk-face-to-face-112582

Chaplin, W. F., Phillips, J. B., Brown, J. D., Clanton, N. R., & Stein, J. L. (2000). Handshaking, gender, personality, and first impressions. *Journal of Personality and Social Psychology*, 79, 110–117.

Chartrand, T. L., & Bargh, J. A. (1999). The chameleon effect: The perception-behavior link and social interaction. *Journal of Personality and Social Psychology*, 76, 893–910.

Chatterjee, K., & Stafford, L. (2008). *Self-reports of young adults' talk about safer-sex* [Paper presentation]. The Annual Meeting of the National Communication Association, San Diego, CA, United States.

Chen, Y. W., & Lawless, B. (2018). Rethinking "difficult" conversations in communication instruction from an intercultural lens: Pedagogical strategies for "SWAP-ing" the communication classroom. *Communication Studies*, 69, 372–388.

Chiaburu, D. S., Oh, I., Berry, C. M., Li, N., & Gardner, R. G. (2011). The five-factor model of personality traits and organizational citizenship behaviors: A meta-analysis. *Journal of Applied Psychology*, 96, 1140–1166.

Child, J. T., Petronio, S., Agyeman-Budu, E. A., & Westermann, D. A. (2011). Blog scrubbing: Exploring triggers that change privacy rules. *Computers in Human Behavior*, 27(5), 2017–2027. https://doi.org/10.1016/j.chb.2011.05.009

Chovil, N. (1991). Social determinants of facial displays. *Journal of Nonverbal Behavior*, 15, 141–154.

Christensen, A., & Shenk, J. L. (1991). Communication, conflict, and psychological distance in nondistressed, clinical, and divorcing couples. *Journal of Consulting and Clinical Psychology*, 59, 458–463.

Christopher, F. S., & Lloyd, S. A. (2000). Physical and sexual aggression in relationships. In C. Hendrick & S. S. Hendrick (Eds.), *Close relationships* (pp. 331–343). SAGE.

Cialdini, R. B. (2009). *Influence: Science and practice* (5th ed.). Pearson.

Cialdini, R. B., & Goldstein, N. J. (2004). Social influence: Compliance and conformity. *Annual Review of Psychology*, 55(1), 591–621. https://doi.org/10.1146/annurev.psych.55.090902.142015

Cialdini, R. B., Kallgren, C. A., & Reno, R. R. (1991). A focus theory of normative conduct: A theoretical refinement and reevaluation of the role of norms in human behavior. In M. P. Zanna (Ed.), *Advances in experimental social psychology* (Vol. 24, pp. 201–234). Academic Press.

Cialdini, R. B., & Trost, M. R. (1998). Social influence: Social norms, conformity, and compliance. In D. T. Gilbert, S. T. Fiske, & G. Lindzey (Eds.), *The handbook of social psychology* (pp. 151–192). McGraw-Hill.

Cialdini, R. B., Trost, M. R., & Newsom, J. (1995). Preference for consistency: The development of a valid measure and discovery of surprising behavioral implication. *Journal of Personality and Social Psychology*, 69, 318–328.

Cialdini, R. B., Vincent, J. E., Lewis, S. K., Catalan, J., Wheeler, D., & Darby, B. L. (1975). Reciprocal concessions procedure for inducing compliance: The door-in-the-face technique. *Journal of Personality and Social Psychology*, 31(2), 206–215. https://doi.org/10.1037/h0076284

Cialdini, R. B., Wosinska, W., Barrett, D. W., Butner, J., & Gornik-Durose, M. (1999). Compliance with a request in two cultures: The differential influence of social proof and commitment/consistency on collectivists and individualists. *Personality and Social Psychology Bulletin*, 25, 1242–1253.

Cissna, K. N. L., & Sieberg, L. (1981). Patterns of interactional confirmation and disconfirmation. In C. Wilder-Mott & J. H. Weakland (Eds.), *Rigor & imagination: Essays from the legacy of Gregory Bateson* (pp. 253–282). Praeger.

Clance, P. R. (1985). *The imposter phenomenon: When success makes you feel like a fake*. Bantam Books.

Clark, R. A., & Delia, J. G. (1979). *Topoi* and rhetorical competence. *Quarterly Journal of Speech*, 65, 187–206.

Clarks, H. H., & Wilkes-Gibbs, D. (1986). Referring as a collaborative process. *Cognition*, 22, 1–39.

Clatterbuck, G. W. (1979). Attributional confidence and uncertainty in initial interaction. *Human Communication Research*, 5, 147–157.

Cody, M. (1982). A typology of disengagement strategies and an examination of the role intimacy and relational problems play in strategy selection. *Communication Monographs*, *49*, 148–170.

Cohen, S. (2004). Social relationships and health. *American Psychologist*, *59*, 676–684.

Coker, D. A., & Burgoon, J. (1987). The nature of conversational involvement and nonverbal encoding patterns. *Human Communication Research*, *1*, 463–494.

Cole, D. A., Maxwell, S. E., Martin, J. M., Peeke, L. G., Seroczynski, A. D., Tram, J. M., Hoffman, K. B., Ruiz, M. D., Jacquez, F., & Maschman, T. (2001). The development of multiple domains of child and adolescent self-concept: A cohort sequential longitudinal design. *Child Development*, *72*, 1723–1746.

Coleman, J. S. (1988). Social capital in the creation of human capital. *American Journal of Sociology*, *94*, S95–S120.

Collins, C. (2018). What is white privilege, really? *Teaching Tolerance*, *60*, 1–11.

Collins, P. H. (2019). *Intersectionality: As critical social theory*. Duke University Press.

Collins, T. J., & Gillath, O. (2012). Attachment, breakup strategies, and associated outcomes: The effects of security enhancement on the selection of breakup strategies. *Journal of Research in Personality*, *46*, 210–222.

Condon, S. L., & Čech, C. G. (2001). *Profiling turns in interaction: Discourse structure and function* [Conference session]. Proceedings of the 35th Hawaii International Conference on System Sciences (HICSS-35), IEEE Press.

Cooley, C. H. (1902). *Human nature and the social order*. Charles Schribner's Sons.

Correa, T., Hinsley, A. W., & de Zuniga, H. G. (2010). Who interacts on the Web?: The intersection of users' personality and social media use. *Computers in Human Behavior*, *26*, 247–253. https://doi.org/10.1016/j.chb.2009.09.003

Corti, J. K. (2009). *Sibling relationships during the young adult years: An analysis of closeness, relational satisfaction, everyday talk, and turning points (Unpublished doctoral dissertation)*. https://digitalcommons.du.edu/cgi/viewcontent.cgi?referer=https://scholar.google.com/&httpsredir=1&article=1792&context=etd

Coupland, N. (2010). Accommodation theory. In J. Jaspers, J.-O. Östman, & J. Verschueren (Eds.), *Society and language use* (pp. 21–27). John Benjamins Publishing Company.

Cozzarelli, C., & Major, B. (1990). Exploring the validity of the imposter phenomenon. *Journal of Social and Clinical Psychology*, *9*, 401–417.

Crenshaw, K. W. (1994). Mapping the margins: Intersectionality, identity politics, and violence against women of color. In M. Albertson Fineman & R. Mykitiuk (Eds.), *The public nature of private violence* (pp. 93–118). Routledge.

Crick, N. R., & Grotpeter, J. K. (1995). Relational aggression, gender, and social psychological adjustment. *Child Development*, *66*, 710–722.

Crivelli, C., Jarillo, S., Russell, J. A., & Fernández-Dols, J. M. (2016). Reading emotions from faces in two indigenous societies. *Journal of Experimental Psychology: General*, *145*, 830–843.

Cuming, S., & Rapee, R. M. (2010). Social anxiety and self-protective communication style in close relationships. *Behaviour Research and Therapy*, *48*, 87–96.

Cunningham, M. R., Barbee, A. P., & Pike, C. L. (1990). What do women want? Facial metric assessment of multiple motives in the perception of male facial physical attractiveness. *Journal of Personality and Social Psychology*, *59*, 61–72.

Cupach, W. R., Canary, D. J., & Spitzberg, B. H. (2009). *Competence in interpersonal conflict* (2nd ed.). Waveland.

Cutrona, C. E., & Suhr, J. (1992). Controllability of stressful events and satisfaction with spouse support behaviors. *Communication Research*, *19*, 154–174.

Dabbs, J. M., Evans, M. S., Hopper, C. H., & Purvis, J. A. (1980). Self-monitors in conversation? What do they monitor? *Journal of Personality and Social Psychology*, *39*, 278–284.

Daft, R., Lengel, R., & Trevino, L. K. (1987). Message equivocality, media selection, and manager performance. Implications for information systems. *MIS Quarterly*, *11*, 355–366.

Dailey, R. M., McCracken, A. A., Jin, B., Rossetto, K. R., & Green, E. W. (2013). Negotiating breakups and renewals: Types of on-again/off-again dating relationships. *Western Journal of Communication*, *77*, 382–410.

Dailey, R. M., Pfiester, A., Jin, B., Beck, G., & Clark, G. (2009). On-again/off-again dating relationships: How are they different from other dating relationships? *Personal Relationships*, *16*, 23–47.

Dailey, R. M., Rossetto, K., Pfiester, A., & Surra, C. A. (2009). A qualitative analysis of on-again/off-again romantic relationships: "It's up and down, all around.". *Journal of Social and Personal Relationships*, *16*, 23–47.

Dainton, M. (1995, November). *Interaction in maintained marriages: A description of type, relative routineness, and perceived importance* [Paper presentation]. The Annual Meeting of the Speech Communication Association, San Antonio, TX, United States.

Dainton, M., Goodboy, A. K., Borzea, D., & Goldman, Z. W. (2017). The dyadic effects of relationship uncertainty on negative relational maintenance. *Communication Reports*, *30*, 170–181.

Dainton, M., & Gross, J. (2008). The use of negative behaviors to maintain relationships. *Communication Research Reports*, *25*, 179–191.

Dainton, M., & Stafford, L. (1993). Routine maintenance behaviors: A comparison of relationship type, partner similarity, and sex differences. *Journal of Social and Personal Relationships, 10,* 255–271.

Dainton, M., Stafford, L., & Canary, D. J. (1994). Maintenance strategies and physical affection as predictors of love, liking, and satisfaction in marriage. *Communication Reports, 7,* 88–98.

Davidson, M. M., Lozano, N. M., Cole, B. P., & Gervais, S. J. (2015). Relations between intimate partner violence and forgiveness among college women. *Journal of Interpersonal Violence, 30,* 3217–3243.

Davis, K. E., & Todd, M. J. (1985). Assessing friendships: Prototypes, paradigm cases, and relationship description. In S. Duck & D. Perlman (Eds.), *Understanding personal relationships: An interdisciplinary approach* (pp. 17–38). SAGE.

Davis, M. (1973). *Intimate relations.* Free Press.

Davis, S. M. (2019). When sistahs support sistahs: A process of supportive communication about racial microaggressions among Black women. *Communication Monographs, 86*(2), 133–157. https://doi.org/10.1080/03637751.2018.1548769

Dawson, G. A., Karl, K. A., & Peluchette, J. V. (2019). Hair matters: Toward understanding natural black hair bias in the workplace. *Journal of Leadership & Organizational Studies, 26*(3), 389–401. https://doi.org/10.1177/1548051819848998

Debro, S. C., Campbell, S. M., & Peplau, L. M. (1994). Influencing a partner to use a condom: A college student perspective. *Psychology of Women Quarterly, 18,* 165–182.

DeGroot, T., & Motowidlo, S. J. (1999). Why visual and vocal interview cues can affect interviewers' judgments and predict job performance. *Journal of Applied Psychology, 84,* 986–993.

Dermer, M., & Thiel, D. L. (1975). When beauty may fail. *Journal of Personality and Social Psychology, 31,* 1168–1176.

Dillard, J. P., Hunter, J. E., & Burgoon, M. (1984). Sequential-request persuasive strategies: Meta-analysis of foot-in-the-door and the door-in-the-face. *Human Communication Research, 10,* 461–188.

Dillard, J. P., Wilson, S. R., Tusing, K. J., & Kinney, T. A. (1997). Politeness judgments in personal relationships. *Journal of Language and Social Psychology, 16,* 297–325.

Dillon, K., & Bushman, B. J. (2015). Unresponsive or unnoticed?: Cyberbystander intervention in an experimental cyberbullying context. *Computers in Human Behavior, 45,* 144–150. https://doi.org/10.1016/j.chb.2014.12.009

Dimberg, U., & Söderkvist, S. (2011). The voluntary facial action technique: A method to test the facial feedback hypothesis. *Journal of Nonverbal Behavior, 35,* 17–33.

Dimmick, J., Kline, S., & Stafford, L. (2000). The gratification niches of personal email and the telephone: Competition, displacement, and complementarity. *Communication Research, 27,* 227–248.

Dindia, K. (1994). A multiphasic view of relationship maintenance strategies. In D. J. Canary & L. Stafford (Eds.), *Communication and relational maintenance* (pp. 91–112). Academic Press.

Dindia, K. (2003). Definitions and perspectives on relational maintenance communication. In D. J. Canary & M. Dainton (Eds.), *Maintaining relationships through communication: Relational, contextual, and cultural variations* (pp. 1–30). Lawrence Erlbaum Associates.

Dindia, K., & Canary, D. J. (1993). Definitions and theoretical perspectives on maintaining relationships. *Journal of Social and Personal Relationships, 10,* 163–173.

Dion, K. K., Berscheid, E., & Walster, E. (1972). What is beautiful is good. *Journal of Personality and Social Psychology, 24,* 285–290.

Dolin, D. J., & Booth-Butterfield, M. (1993). Reach out and touch someone: Analysis of nonverbal comforting responses. *Communication Quarterly, 41,* 383–393.

Dolinski, D., Nawrat, M., & Rudak, I. (2001). Dialogue involvement as a social influence technique. *Pers Soc Psychol Bull, 27*(11), 1395–1406. https://doi.org/10.1177/014616720 12711001

Dotinga, R. (2006, February 10). *Parents' fighting has long term impacts on kids.* http://news.healingwell.com/index.php?p=news1&id=530961

Douglas, W. (1990). Uncertainty, information-seeking, and liking during initial interaction. *Western Journal of Speech Communication, 54,* 66–81.

Dovidio, J. F., & Gaertner, S. L. (2010). Intergroup bias. In S. T. Fiske, D. T. Gilbert, & G. Lindzey (Eds.), *The handbook of social psychology* (4th ed.). John Wiley.

Dovidio, J. F., Hewstone, M., Glick, P., & Esses, V. M. (2010). Prejudice, stereotyping, and discrimination: Theoretical and empirical overview. In J. F. Dovidio, M. Hewstone, P. Glick, & V. M. Esses (Eds.), *Handbook of prejudice, stereotyping, and discrimination* (pp. 3–28). SAGE.

Doyle, D. M., & Molix, L. (2015). Social stigma and sexual minorities romantic relationship functioning: A meta-analytic review. *Personality and Social Psychology Bulleting, 41,* 1363–1381.

Dragovich, M., & Giles, H. (2012). Language and interpersonal communication: Their intergroup dynamics. In C. R. Berger (Ed.), *Handbook of interpersonal communication.* DeGruyter Mounton.

Dreyer, A., Dreyer, C., & Davis, J. (1987). Individuality and mutuality in the language of families of field-dependent and field-independent children. *Journal of Genetic Psychology, 148,* 105–117.

Drollinger, T., Comer, L., & B., Warrington, P. T. (2006). Development and validation of the active empathic listening scale. *Psychology & Marketing, 23,* 161–180. https://doi.org/10.1002/mar2005

Drummond, D. K., & Orbe, M. P. (2009). "Who are you trying to be?": Identity gaps within intraracial encounters. *Qualitative Research Reports in Communication*, *10*(1), 81–87. https://doi.org/10.1080/17459430903236098

Duawalder, J. P., Perrez, M., & Hobi, V (Eds.). (1988). *Annual series of European research in behavior therapy* (Vol. 2, pp. 27–59). Swets & Zeitlinger.

Duck, S. (1994). Steady as (s)he goes: Relational maintenance as a shared meaning system. In D. J. Canary & L. Stafford (Eds.), *Communication and relational maintenance*. Academic Press.

Duck, S. W. (1988). *Relating to others*. Dorsey.

Duck, S. W., Rutt, D. J., Hurst, M. H., & Strejc, H. (1991). Some evident truths about everyday conversation: All communications are not created equal. *Human Communication Research*, *18*, 228–267.

Duggan, A. P., Dailey, R. M., & LePoire, B. A. (2008). Reinforcement and punishment of substance abuse during ongoing interactions: A conversational test of inconsistent nurturing as control theory. *Journal of Health Communication*, *13*, 417–433.

Duggan, M. (2014, October 22). Online harassment. *Pew Research Center*. http://www.pewinternet.org/2014/10/22/online-harassment/

Dunbar, R. I. M. (2004). Gossip in evolutionary perspective. *Review of General Psychology*, *8*, 100–110.

Duncan, S. (1972). Some signals and rules for taking speaking turns in conversations. *Journal of Personality and Social Psychology*, *23*, 283–292.

Duncan, S. (1974). On the structure of speaker–auditor interaction during speaking turns. *Language in Society*, *3*(2), 161–180. https://doi.org/10.1017/S0047404500004322

Eagly, A. H., Ashmore, R. D., Makhijani, M. G., & Longo, L. C. (1991). What is beautiful is good, but...: A meta-analytic review of research on the physical attractiveness stereotype. *Psychological Bulletin*, *110*, 109–128.

Eccles, J. S., Midgely, C., & Adler, T. (1984). Grade-related changes in the school environment: Effects on achievement motivation. In J. G. Nicholls (Ed.), *Research on motivation in education* (Vol. 3, pp. 139–181). Academic Press.

Eder, D. (1982). The impact of management and turn-allocation activities on student performance. *Discourse Processes*, *5*, 147–160.

Ekman, P. (1973). Cross-cultural studies of facial expression. In P. Ekman (Ed.), *Darwin and facial expression: A century of research in review* (pp. 169–222). Academic Press.

Ekman, P. (1993). Facial expression and emotion. *American Psychologist*, *48*, 384–392.

Ekman, P., & Cordaro, D. (2011). What is meant by calling emotions basic. *Emotion Review*, *3*, 364–370.

Ekman, P., & Friesen, W. V. (1969). The repertoire of nonverbal behavior: Categories, origins, usage, and coding. *Semiotica*, *1*, 49–98.

Ekman, P., & Friesen, W. V. (1986). A new pancultural facial expression of emotion. *Motivation and Emotion*, *10*, 159–168.

Ekman, P., & Friesen, W. V. (2003). *Unmasking the face: A guide to recognizing emotions from facial clues*. Prentice Hall.

Ekman, P., Friesen, W. V., & Ellsworth, P. (1972). *The face of emotion*. Pergamon.

El-Sheikh, M., Buckhalt, J. A., Mize, J., & Acebo, C. (2006). Marital conflict and disruption of children's sleep. *Child Development*, *77*, 31–43.

Elfenbein, H. A. (2013). Nonverbal dialects and accents in facial expressions of emotion. *Emotion Review*, *5*, 90–96.

Elfenbein, H. A., & Ambady, N. (2002a). Is there an in-group advantage in emotion recognition? *Psychological Bulletin*, *128*, 243–249.

Elfenbein, H. A., & Ambady, N. (2002b). On the universality and cultural specificity of emotion recognition: A meta-analysis. *Psychological Bulletin*, *128*, 203–235.

Elfenbein, H. A., Beaupré, M., Lévesque, M., & Hess, U. (2007). Toward a dialect theory: Cultural differences in the expression and recognition of posed facial expressions. *Emotion*, *7*, 131–146.

Elias, S. (2008). Fifty years of influence in the workplace: The evolution of the French and Raven power taxonomy. *Journal of Management History*, *14*, 267–283.

Ellison, N. B., Steinfield, C., & Lampe, C. (2007). The benefits of Facebook "friends:" Social capital and college students' use of online social network sites. *Journal of Computer-Mediated Communication*, *12*, 1143–1168.

Ellison, N. B., Vitak, J., Gray, R., & Lampe, C. (2014). Cultivating social resources on social network sties: Facebook relationship maintenance behaviors and their role in social capital processes. *Journal of Computer-Mediated Communication*, *19*, 855–870.

Ellison, N., Heino, R., & Gibbs, J. (2006). Managing impressions online: Self-presentation processes in the online dating environment. *Journal of Computer-Mediated Communication*, *11*, 415–441.

Elphinston, R. A., Feeney, J. A., Noller, P., Connor, J. P., & Fitzgerald, J. (2013). Romantic jealousy and relationship satisfaction: The costs of rumination. *Western Journal of Communication*, *77*, 293–304.

Emery, R. (2004). *The truth about children and divorce: Dealing with emotions so you and your children can thrive*. Viking/Penguin.

Emmers, T. M., & Canary, D. J. (1996). The effect of uncertainty reducing strategies on young couples' relational repair and intimacy. *Communication Quarterly*, *44*, 166–182.

Emmers, T. M., & Hart, R. D. (1996). Romantic relationship disengagement and coping rituals. *Communication Research Reports*, *13*(1), 8–18. https://doi.org/10.1080/08824099609362065

Emmers-Sommer, T. M. (2004). The effect of communication quality and quantity indicators on intimacy and relational satisfaction. *Journal of Social and Personal Relationships*, *21*, 399–411. https://doi.org/10.1177/0265407504042839

Emswiller, T., Deaux, K., & Willits, J. E. (1971). Similarity, sex, and requests for small favors. *Journal of Applied Social Psychology*, *1*, 284–291.

English, T., John, O. P., & Gross, J. J. (2013). Emotion regulation in relationships. In J. A. Simpson & L. Campbell (Eds.), *Handbook of close relationships* (pp. 500–513). Oxford University Press.

Erb, H.-P., Bohner, G., Schmälzle, K., & Rank, S. (1998). Beyond conflict and discrepancy: Cognitive bias in minority and majority influence. *Personality and Social Psychology Bulletin*, *24*, 396–409.

Ernst, J. M., & Cacioppo, J. T. (1999). Lonely hearts: Psychological perspectives on loneliness. *Applied and Preventive Psychology*, *81*, 1–22.

Eysenck, H. J. (1946). The measurement of personality. *Proceedings of the Royal Society of Medicine*, *40*, 75–80.

Eysenck, H. J. (1947). Student selection by means of psychological tests—A critical survey. *British Journal of Educational Psychology*, *17*(1), 20–39.

Fairhurst, G., & Putnam, L. (2015). Revisiting "organizations as discursive constructions": 10 years later. *Communication Theory*, *25*, 375–392.

Farley, S. D. (2011). Is gossip power? The inverse relationships between gossip, power, and likability. *European Journal of Social Psychology*, *41*, 574–579.

Feeney, J. A. (2004). Hurt feelings in couple relationships: Toward integrative models of the negative effects of hurtful events. *Journal of Social and Personal Relationships*, *21*, 487–508.

Feeney, J. A. (2005). Hurt feelings in couple relationships: Exploring the role of attachment and perceptions of personal injury. *Personal Relationships*, *12*, 253–271.

Fehr, B. (1996). *Friendship processes*. SAGE.

Fehr, B. (2000). The life cycle of friendship. In C. Hendrick & S. Hendrick (Eds.), *Close relationships: A sourcebook* (pp. 71–82). SAGE.

Fehr, B. (2008). *Friendship formation*. In S. Sprecher, A. Wenzel, & J. Harvey (Eds.), *Handbook of relationship initiation* (pp. 29–54). Psychology Press.

Feingold, A. (1992). Good-looking people are not what we think. *Psychological Bulletin*, *111*, 304–341.

Festinger, L. (1957). *A theory of cognitive dissonance*. Stanford University Press.

Festinger, L., Schachter, S., & Back, K. (1950). *Social pressures in informal groups; A study of human factors in housing*. Harper.

Fincham, F. D., Bradbury, T. N., Arias, I., Byrne, C. A., & Karney, B. R. (1997). Marital violence, marital distress, and attributions. *Journal of Family Psychology*, *11*, 367–372.

Fischer, K. W., & Tangney, J. P. (1995). Self-conscious emotions and the affect revolution: Framework and overview. In J. P. Tangney & K. W. Fischer (Eds.), *Self-conscious emotions: Shame, guilt, embarrassment, and pride* (pp. 3–22). Guilford Press.

Fischer, P., Krueger, J. I., Greitemeyer, T., Vogrincic, C., Kastenmüller, A., Frey, D., Heene, M., Wicher, M., & Kainbacher, M. (2011). The bystander-effect: A meta-analytic review on bystander intervention in dangerous and non-dangerous emergencies. *Psychological Bulletin*, *137*, 517–437.

Fishbein, M., & Azjen, I. (2010). *Predicting and changing behavior: The reasoned action approach*. Psychology Press.

Fisher, B. A. (1987). *Interpersonal communication: Pragmatics of human relationships*. Random House.

Fisher, B., & Alberti, R. (2016). *Rebuilding: When your relationship ends*. New Harbinger Publications.

Fitness, J. (2006). Emotion and cognition in close relationships. In P. Noller & J. A. Feeney (Eds.), *Close relationships: Functions, forms and processes* (pp. 285–304). Psychology Press.

Florini, S. (2014). Tweets, tweeps, and signifyin': Communication and cultural performance on "Black Twitter". *Television and New Media*, *15*, 223–237.

Floyd, K. (2006). *Communicating affection: Interpersonal behavior and social context*. Cambridge University Press.

Floyd, K., Boren, J. P., Hannawa, A. F., Hesse, C., McEwan, B., & Veksler, A. E. (2009). Kissing in marital and cohabiting relationships: Effects on blood lipids, stress, and relationship satisfaction. *Western Journal of Communication*, *73*, 113–133.

Floyd, K., Hess, J. A., Mizco, L. A., Halone, K. K., Mikkelson, A. C., & Tusing, K. J. (2005). Human affective exchange: VIII. Further evidence of the benefits of expressed affection. *Communication Quarterly*, *53*, 285–303.

Floyd, K., Hesse, C., & Haynes, M. T. (2007). Human affection exchange: XV. Metabolic and cardiovascular correlates of trait expressed affection. *Communication Quarterly*, *55*, 79–94.

Floyd, K., & Morman, M. T. (1998). The measurement of affectionate communication. *Communication Quarterly*, *46*, 144–162.

Floyd, K., & Morman, M. T. (2003). Human affection exchange II: Affectionate communication in father-son relationships. *The Journal of Social Psychology*, *143*, 599–612.

Foa, E. B., & Foa, U. G. (1980). Resource theory. In K. G. Gergen, M. S. Greenberg, & R. H. Willis (Eds.), *Social exchange* (pp. 77–94). Springer. https://doi.org/10.1007/978-1-4613-3087-5_4

Folkes, V. S. (1982). Communicating the causes of social rejection. *Journal of Experimental Social Psychology*, *18*, 235–252.

Folwell, A. L., & Grant, J. A. (2006). Adult grandchildren's accounts of closeness and changes in their grandparent relationships. *Journal of Northwest Communication Association*, *35*, 1–21.

Forbes, R. J., & Jackson, P. R. (1980). Non-verbal behaviour and the outcome of selection interviews. *Journal of Occupational Psychology*, *53*, 65–72.

Forgas, J. P. (2011). Can negative affect eliminate the power of first impressions? Affective influences on primacy and recency effects in impression formation. *Journal of Experimental Social Psychology*, *47*, 425–429.

Fox, J., & Anderegg, C. (2014). Romantic relationship stages and social networking sites: Uncertainty reduction strategies and perceived relational norms on Facebook. *Cyberpsychology, Behavior, and Social Networking*, *17*, 685–691.

Fox, J., & McEwan, B. (2017). Distinguishing technologies for social interaction: The perceived social affordances of communication channels scale. *Communication Monographs*, *84*(3), 298–318. https://doi.org/10.1080/03637751.2017.1332418

Fox, J., Warber, K. M., & Makstaller, D. C. (2013). The role of Facebook in romantic relationship development: An exploration Knapp's relational stage model. *Journal of Social and Personal Relationships*, *30*, 771–794. https://doi.org/10.1177/0265407512468370

Freedman, G., Powell, D. N., Le, B., & Williams, K. D. (2019). Ghosting and destiny: Implicit theories of relationships predict beliefs about ghosting. *Journal of Social and Personal Relationships*, *36*, 905–924.

Freedman, J. L., & Fraser, S. C. (1966). Compliance without pressure: The foot-in-the-door technique. *Journal of Personality and Social Psychology*, *4*(2), 195–202. https://doi.org/10.1037/h0023552

French, B. F., Ullrich-French, S. C., & Follman, D. (2008). The psychometric properties of the Clance Imposter Scale. *Personality and Individual Differences*, *44*, 1270–1278.

French, E. P., & Raven, B. H. (1959). The bases of social power. In D. Cartwright (Ed.), *Studies in social power* (pp. 150–167). Institute for Social Research.

Freud, S. (1949). *The ego and the Id*. The Hogarth Press Ltd.

Fridlund, J. A., & Duchaine, B. (1996). Facial expressions of emotion' and the delusion of the hermetic self. In R. Harre & W. G. Parrott (Eds.), *The emotions: Social, cultural and biological dimensions* (pp. 259–284). SAGE.

Frijda, N. H. (1986). *The emotions*. Cambridge University Press.

Frijda, N. H. (1993). Moods, emotion episodes, and emotions. In M. Lewis & J. M. Haviland (Eds.), *Handbook of emotions* (pp. 381–403). Guilford Press.

Furnham, A., Lavancy, M., & McClelland, A. (2001). Waist to hip ratio and facial attractiveness: A pilot study. *Personality and Individual Differences*, *30*, 491–502.

Gaelick, L., Brodenshausen, G. V., & Wyer, R. S., Jr. (1985). Emotional communication in close relationships. *Journal of Personality and Social Psychology*, *49*, 1246–1265.

Gamarel, K. E., Sevelius, J. M., Reisner, S. L., Coats, C. S., Nemoto, T., & Operario, D. (2019). Commitment, interpersonal stigma, and mental health in romantic relationships between transgender women and cisgender male partners. *Journal of Social and Personal Relationships*, *36*(7), 2180–2201.

Gangestead, S., & Snyder, M. (2000). Self-monitoring: Appraisal and reappraisal. *Psychological Bulletin*, *126*, 530–555.

Gangi, K., & Soliz, J. (2016). De-dichotomizing intergroup and interpersonal dynamics: Perspectives on communication, identity, and relationships. In H. Giles & A. Maass (Eds.), *Language as social action: Advances in intergroup communication* (Vol. 21, pp. 35–50). Peter Lang.

Garcia-Marques, T., Mackie, D. M., Claypool, H. M., & Garcia-Marques, L. (2004). Positivity can cue familiarity. *Personality and Social Psychology Bulletin*, *30*, 585–593.

Garner, T. (1983). Playing the dozens: Folklore as strategies for living. *Quarterly Journal of Speech*, *69*, 47–57.

Gass, R. H., & Seiter, J. S. (2016). *Persuasion: Social influence and compliance gaining*. Routledge.

Geertz, C. (1973). *The interpretation of cultures: Selected essays*. Basic Books.

Gerber, A. S., Green, P. D., & Larimer, C. W. (2008). Social pressure and voter turnout: Evidence from a large-scale field experiment. *The American Political Science Review*, *102*, 33–48.

Gerbner, G., Gross, L., Morgan, M., & Signorielli, N. (1994). Growing up with television: The cultivation perspective. In J. Bryant & D. Zillmann (Eds.), *Media effects: Advances in theory and research* (pp. 17–41). Erlbaum.

Ghavami, N., & Peplau, L. A. (2013). An intersectional analysis of gender and ethnic stereotypes: Testing three hypotheses. *Psychology of Women Quarterly*, *37*(1), 113–127.

Giannini, G., Hamilton, K. A., & Spitzberg, B. H. (2007). *Coping with college: Exploring loneliness through coping strategies enacted by incoming college freshmen* [Paper presentation]. Meeting of the National Communication Association, Chicago, IL, United States.

Gilbert, D. T., Krull, D. S., & Malone, P. S. (1990). Unbelieving the unbelievable: Some problems in the rejection of false information. *Journal of Personality and Social Psychology, 59*, 601–613.

Giles, H. (1973). Accent mobility. *Anthropological Linguistics, 15*, 87–105.

Giles, H., Coupland, N., & Coupland, J. (1991). *Contexts of accommodation: Developments in applied sociolinguistics.* Cambridge University Press.

Giles, H., & Gasiorek, J. (2013). Parameters of non-accommodation: Refining and elaborating communication accommodation theory. In J. Forgas, J. László, & O. Vincenze (Eds.), *Social cognition and communication* (pp. 155–172). Psychology Press.

Giles, H., Taylor, D. M., & Bourhis, R. Y. (1973). Towards a theory of interpersonal accommodation through language. *Language in Society, 2*, 177–192.

Glazer, E., Smith, W. S., Atkin, C., & Hamel, L. M. (2010). The effects of sensation seeking, misperceptions of peer consumption, and believability of social norms messages on alcohol consumption. *Journal of Health Communication, 16*, 82–839.

Goffman, E. (1959). *The presentation of self in everyday life.* Doubleday.

Goffman, E. (1967). *Interaction ritual: Essays on face-to-face behavior.* Anchor/Doubleday.

Goldberg, A. E. (2013). "Doing" and "Undoing" gender: The meaning and division of housework in same-sex couples. *Journal of Family Theory & Review, 5*, 85–104.

Goldberg, A. E., Smith, J. Z., & Perry Jenkins, M. (2012). The division of labor in lesbian, gay, and heterosexual new adoptive parents. *Journal of Marriage and Family, 74*(4), 812–828.

Goldsmith, D. J., & Baxter, L. A. (1996). Constituting relationships in talk: A taxonomy of speech events in social and personal relationships. *Human Communication Research, 23*, 87–114.

Goldsmith, D. J., & MacGeorge, E. (2000). The impact of politeness and relationship on perceived quality of advice about a problem. *Human Communication Research, 26*, 234–263.

Goleman, D. (1995). *Emotional intelligence.* Bantam Books.

Goleman, D. (2006). *Emotional intelligence: Why it can matter more than IQ.* Bantam Books.

Golish, T. D. (2000). Changes in closeness between adult children and their parents: A turning points analysis. *Communication Reports, 13*, 79–97.

Goodboy, A. K., & Bolkan, S. (2011). Attachment and the use of negative relational maintenance behaviors in romantic relationships. *Communication Research Reports, 28*, 327–336.

Goodboy, A. K., & Brann, M. (2010). Flirtation rejection strategies: Toward an understanding of communicative disinterest in flirting. *The Qualitative Report, 15*, 268–278.

Goodboy, A. K., Dainton, M., Borzea, D., & Goldman, Z. W. (2017). Attachment and negative relational maintenance: Dyadic comparisons using an actor-partner interdependence model. *Western Journal of Communication, 81*, 541–559.

Goodboy, A. K., & Myers, S. A. (2010). & Members of Investigating Communication. Relational quality indicators and love styles as predictors of negative maintenance behaviors in romantic relationships. *Communication Reports, 23*, 65–78.

Goodboy, A. K., Myers, S. A., & Patterson, B. R. (2009). Investigating elderly sibling types, relational maintenance, and lifespan affect, cognition, and behavior. *Atlantic Journal of Communication, 17*(3), 140–148.

Gordon, R. A. (1996). Impact of ingratiation on judgments and evaluations: A meta-analytic investigation. *Journal of Personality and Social Psychology, 71*, 54–70.

Gore, J. S., & Cross, S. E. (2014). Who am I becoming? A theoretical framework for understanding self-concept change. *Self and Identity, 13*, 760–764.

Gottman, J. M. (1994). *What predicts divorce? The relationship between marital processes and marital outcomes.* Lawrence Erlbaum.

Gottman, J. M., & Porterfield, A. L. (1981). Communicative competence in the nonverbal behavior of married couples. *Journal of Marriage and the Family, 43*, 817–824.

Gouldner, A. W. (1960). The norm of reciprocity: A preliminary statement. *American Sociological Review, 25*, 161–178.

Grammer, K., & Thornhill, R. (1994). Human (Homo sapiens) facial attractiveness and sexual selection: The role of symmetry and averageness. *Journal of Comparative Psychology, 108*, 233–242.

Granovetter, M. S. (1973). The strength of weak ties. *American Journal of Sociology, 78*(6), 1360–1380.

Gray, H. M. (2008). To what extent, and under what conditions, are first impressions valid? In N. Ambady & J. Skowronski (Eds.), *First impressions* (pp. 106–128). Guilford.

Gray, H. M., Ishii, K., & Ambady, N. (2011). Misery loves company: When sadness increases the desire for social connectedness. *Personality and Social Psychology Bulletin, 37*, 1438–1448.

Grice, H. P. (1975). Logic and conversation. In P. Cole & J. Morgan (Eds.), *Syntax and semantics, 3, speech arts* (pp. 41–58). Academic Press.

Grimaldi, E. M., Napper, L. E., & LaBrie, J. W. (2014). Relational aggression, positive urgency and negative urgency: Predicting alcohol use and consequences among college students. *Psychology of Addictive Behaviors*, *28*, 893–898.

Gross, M. A., & Guerrero, L. K. (2000). Managing conflict appropriately and effectively: An application of the competence model to Rahim's organizational conflict styles. *International Journal of Conflict Management*, *11*, 200–226.

Gudykunst, W. B., & Nashida, T. (2001). Anxiety, uncertainty and perceived effectiveness of communication across relationships and cultures. *International Journal of Intercultural Relations*, *25*, 55–71.

Guéguen, N., & Pascual, A. (2000). Evocation of freedom and compliance: The "but you are free of..." technique. *Current Research in Social Psychology*, *5*, 264–270.

Guéguen, N., & Pascual, A. (2005). Improving the response rate to a street survey: An evaluation of the "but you are free to accept or to refuse" technique. *The Psychological Record*, *55*, 297–303.

Guerrero, L. K. (2020). Conflict style associations with cooperativeness, directness, and relational satisfaction: A case for a six-style typology. *Negotiation and Conflict Management Research*, *13*, 24–43.

Guerrero, L. K., & Andersen, P. A. (1998). Jealousy experience and expression in romantic relationships. In P. A. Andersen & L. K. Guerrero (Eds.), *Handbook of communication and emotion: Theory, research, applications, and contexts* (pp. 155–188). Academic Press.

Guerrero, L. K., Andersen, P. A., & Afifi, W. A. (2021). *Close encounters: Communication in relationships*. SAGE.

Guerrero, L. K., & Bachman, G. F. (2010). Forgiveness and forgiving communication in dating relationships: An expectancy-investment explanation. *Journal of Social and Personal Relationships*, *27*, 801–823.

Guerrero, L. K., & Chavez, A. M. (2005). Relational maintenance in cross☐sex friendships characterized by different types of romantic intent: An exploratory study. *Western Journal of Communication*, *69*(4), 339–358. https://doi.org/10.1080/10570310500305471

Guerrero, L. K., Eloy, S. V., & Wabnik, A. L. (1993). Linking maintenance strategies to relationship development and disengagement. A reconceptualization. *Journal of Social and Personal Relationships*, *10*, 273–283.

Guerrero, L. K., & Floyd, K. (2006). *Nonverbal communication in close relationships*. Lawrence Erlbaum.

Guerrero, L. K., Hannawa, A. F., & Babin, B. A. (2011). The communicative responses to jealousy scale: Revision, empirical validation, and associations with relational satisfaction. *Communication Methods and Measures*, *5*, 223–249.

Guerrero, L. K., & Mongeau, P. M. (2008). On becoming "more than friends": The transition from friendship to romantic relationship. In S. Sprecher, A. Wenzel, & J. Harvey (Eds.), *Handbook of relationship initiation* (pp. 175–195). Psychology Press.

Haas, S. (2003). Relationship maintenance in same-sex couples. In D. J. Canary & M. Dainton (Eds.), *Maintaining relationships through communication: Relational, contextual, and cultural variations* (pp. 209–230). Lawrence Erlbaum Associates.

Haas, S. M., & Stafford, L. (1998). An initial examination of maintenance behaviors in gay and lesbian relationships. *Journal of Social and Personal Relationships*, *15*, 846–855.

Haas, S. M., & Stafford, L. (2005). Maintenance behaviors in same-sex and marital relationships: A matched sample comparison. *The Journal of Family Communication*, *5*, 43–60.

Hafenbrack, A. C., Kinias, Z., & Barsade, S. G. (2014). Debiasing the mind through mediation: Mindfulness and the sunk-cost bias. *Psychological Science*, *25*, 369–376.

Halatsis, P., & Christakis, N. (2009). The challenge of sexual attraction within heterosexuals' cross-sex friendship. *Journal of Social and Personal Relationships*, *26*(6–7), 919–937.

Hall, E. T. (1968). Proxemics. *Current Anthropology*, *9*, 83–109.

Hall, E. T. (1976). *Beyond culture*. Anchor Books/Doubleday.

Hall, E. T. (1990). *The hidden dimension* (2nd ed.). Anchor Press.

Hall, J. A., Carter, S., Cody, M. J., & Albright, J. M. (2010). Individual differences in the communication of romantic interest: Development of the Flirting Styles Inventory. *Communication Quarterly*, *58*, 365–393.

Hall, J. A., & Compton, B. L. (2017). Pre- and postinteraction physical attractiveness ratings and experience-based impressions. *Communication Studies*, *68*, 260–277.

Halperin, K. (2012, May 26). On-off couples should stop recycling romance, and call it quits. *ABC News*. http://abcnews.go.com/Health/off-couples-cyclical-couples-call-quits/story?id=16000441

Hamel, J. (2009). Toward a gender-inclusive conception of intimate partner violence research and theory: Part 2—New directions. *International Journal of Men's Health*, *8*, 41–59.

Hample, D., & Demir, Y. (2019). A cross-cultural study of argument orientations in Turkish and American college students: Is silence really golden and speech silver for Turkish students? *Argumentation*, *33*, 521–540. https://doi.org/10/1007/s10503-019-09483-1

Hample, D., & Njweipi-Kongo, D. (2020). *How do people feel about arguing in Cameroon? OSSA Conference Archive*, *12*. https://scholar.uwindsor.ca/cgi/viewcontent.cgi?article=2534&context=ossaarchive

Hampton, K. N., Sessions, L. F., Her, E. J., & Rainie, L. (2009). Social isolation and new technology. *Pew Internet and American Life Project*, 4.

Hannerz, U. (1990). Cosmopolitans and locals in world culture. *Theory, Culture, & Society*, 7, 237–251.

Harris, M. A., Brett, C. E., Johnson, W., & Deary, I. J. (2016). Personality stability from age 14 to age 77 years. *Psychology and Aging*, 31, 862–874.

Harris, T. M., & Kalbfleisch, P. J. (2000). Interracial dating: The implications of race for initiating a romantic relationship. *Howard Journal of Communication*, 11, 49–64.

Harwood, J., Giles, H., & Palomares, N. A. (2005). Intergroup theory and communication processes. In J. Harwood & H. Giles (Eds.), *Intergroup communication: Multiple perspectives* (pp. 1–20). Peter Lang.

Hatfield, E., Cacioppo, J. T., & Rapson, R. L. (1994). *Emotional contagion. Studies in emotion and social interaction*. Cambridge University Press.

Hawkley, L. C., Burleson, M. H., Berntson, G. G., & Cacioppo, J. T. (2003). Loneliness in everyday life: Cardiovascular activity, psychosocial context, and health behaviors. *Journal of Personality and Social Psychology*, 85, 105–120.

Hawkley, L. C., & Cacioppo, J. T. (2010). Loneliness matters: A theoretical and empirical review of consequences and mechanisms. *Annual Behavioral Medicine*, 40, 218–227.

Haythornthwaite, C. (2005). Social networks and internet connectivity effects. *Information, Communication, and Society*, 8, 125–147.

Hazel, M., Keaten, J., & Kelly, L. (2014). The relationship between personality temperament, communication reticence, and fear of negative evaluation. *Communication Research Reports*, 31, 339–347.

Heavey, C. L., Christensen, A., & Malamuth, N. M. (1995). The longitudinal impact of demand and withdrawal during marital conflict. *Journal of Consulting and Clinical Psychology*, 63, 797–801.

Heavey, C. L., Layne, C., & Christensen, A. (1993). Gender and conflict structure in martial interaction: A replication and extension. *Journal of Consulting and Clinical Psychology*, 61, 16–27.

Hebert, S., & Popadiuk, N. (2008). University students' experiences of nonmarital breakups: A grounded theory. *Journal of College Student Development*, 49(1), 1–14. https://doi.org/10.1353/csd.2008.0008

Hecht, M. A., & LaFrance, M. (1995). How (fast) can I help you? Tone of voice and telephone operator efficiency in interactions. *Journal of Applied Social Psychology*, 25, 2086–2098.

Hecht, M. L. (1984). Persuasive efficacy: A study of the relationship among types and degrees of change, message strategies, and satisfying communication. *Western Journal of Speech Communication*, 48, 373–389.

Hecht, M., & Lu, Y. (2015). Culture and competence: Ethnicity and race. In A. F. Hannawa & B. H. Spitzberg (Eds.), *Communication competence* (pp. 289–314). DeGruyter.

Heider, F. (1958). *The psychology of interpersonal relations*. Wiley.

Heisel, A. D., La France, B. H., & Beatty, M. J. (2003). Self-reported extraversion, neuroticism, and psychoticism as predictors of peer rated verbal aggressiveness and affinity-seeking competence. *Communication Monographs*, 70, 1–15.

Hendricks, S. S. (1988). A generic measure of relational satisfaction. *Journal of Marriage and the Family*, 50, 93–98.

Hesse, C., & Mikkelson, A. C. (2017). Affection deprivation in romantic relationships. *Communication Quarterly*, 65, 20–38. https://doi.org/10.1080/01463373.2016.1176942

High, A. C., & Dillard, J. P. (2012). A review and meta-analysis of person-centered messages and social support outcomes. *Communication Studies*, 63, 99–118.

High, A. C., Oeldorf-Hirsch, A., & Bellur, S. (2014). Misery rarely gest company: The influence of emotional bandwidth on supportive communication on Facebook. *Computers in Human Behavior*, 34, 79–88.

Hochschild, A. R. (1979). Emotion work, feeling rules, and social structure. *American Journal of Sociology*, 85, 551–575.

Hochschild, A. R. (1983). *The managed heart*. University of California Press.

Hocker, J. L., & Wilmot, W. W. (2018). *Interpersonal conflict* (10th ed.). McGraw-Hill.

Hofstede, G. (1994). The business of international business is culture. *International Business Review*, 3, 1–14.

Hofstede, G. (2001). *Culture's consequences: Comparing values, behaviors, institutions, and organizations across nations*. SAGE.

Hofstede, G. (2011). Dimensionalizing cultures. The Hofstede model in context. *Online Readings in Psychology and Culture*, 2.

Hofstede, G., Hofstede, G. J., & Minkov, M. (2010). *Cultures and organizations: Software of the mind* (3rd ed.). McGraw-Hill.

Hogan, B. (2010). The presentation of self in the age of social media: Distinguishing performances and exhibitions online. *Bulletin of Science, Technology, and Society*, 30, 377–386.

Holladay, S., Lackowich, R., Lee, M., Coleman, M., Harding, D., & Denton, D. (1998). (re) constructing relationships with grandparents: A turning point analysis of granddaughters' relational development with their maternal grandmothers. *International Journal of Aging and Human Development*, 46, 287–303.

Holmstrom, A. J. (2012). What helps – and what doesn't – when self-esteem is threatened?: Retrospective reports of esteem support. *Communication Studies*, 63, 77–98.

Honeycutt, J. M. (1999). Typological differences in predicting marital happiness from oral history behaviors and imagined interactions. *Communications Monographs*, *66*, 276–291.

Hook, J. N., Worthington, E. L., Jr., & Utsey, S. O. (2009). Collectivism, forgiveness, and social harmony. *The Counseling Psychologist*, *37*(6), 821–847. https://doi.org/10.1177/0011000008326546

Hook, J. N., Worthington, E. L., Jr., Utsey, S. O., Davis, D. E., & Burnette, J. L. (2012). Collectivistic self-construal and forgiveness. *Counseling and Values*, *57*(1), 109–124. https://doi.org/10.1002/j.2161-007X.2012.00012.x

Hopper, M. L., Knapp, M. L., & Scott, L. (1981). Couples' personal idioms: Exploring intimate talk. *Journal of Communication*, *31*, 23–33.

Horan, S. M. (2012). Affection exchange theory and perceptions of relational transgressions. *Western Journal of Communication*, *76*, 109–126.

Horan, S. M. (2016). Further understanding sexual communication: Honesty, deception, safety, and risk. *Journal of Social and Personal Relationships*, *33*(4), 449–468. https://doi.org/10.1177/0265407515578821

Horan, S. M., & Booth-Butterfield, M. (2010). Investing in affection: An investigation of affection exchange theory and relational qualities. *Communication Quarterly*, *58*, 394–413.

Horan, S. M., & Booth-Butterfield, M. (2011). Is it worth lying for? Physiological and emotional implications of recalling deceptive affection. *Human Communication Research*, *37*, 78–106.

Horan, S. M., & Booth-Butterfield, M. (2013). Understanding the routine expression of deceptive affection in romantic relationships. *Communication Quarterly*, *61*, 195–216.

Horan, S. M., & Cafferty, L. A. (2017). Condom communication: Reports of sexually active young adults' recent messages with new partners. *Journal of Health Communication*, *22*, 763–771.

Horan, S. M., & Houser, M. L. (2012). Understanding the communicative implications of initial impressions: A longitudinal test of predicted outcome value theory. *Communication Education*, *61*, 234–252.

Hostetter, A. B., & Potthoff, A. L. (2012). Effects of personality and social situation on representational gesture production. *Gesture*, *12*, 62–83. https://doi.org/10.1075/gest.12.1.04hos

Houser, M. L., Horan, S. M., & Furler, L. A. (2007). Predicting relational outcomes: An investigation of thin slice judgments in speed dating. *Human Communication*, *10*, 69–81.

Hughes, P. C., & Baldwin, J. R. (2002). Communication and stereotypical impressions. *The Howard Journal of Communication*, *13*, 113–128.

Humphrey, L. L. (1989). Observed family interactions among subtypes of eating disorders using structural analysis of social behavior. *Journal of Consulting and Clinical Psychology*, *57*, 206–214.

Humphrey, R. H., Ashforth, B. E., & Diefendorff, J. M. (2015). The bright side of emotional labor. *Journal of Organizational Behavior*, *36*, 749–769.

Hunt, D., Atkin, D., & Krishnan, A. (2012). The influence of computer-mediated communication apprehension on motives for Facebook use. *Journal of Broadcasting & Electronic Media*, *56*, 187–202.

Ickes, W. J., & Barnes, R. D. (1977). The role of sex and self-monitoring in unstructured dyadic interactions. *Journal of Personality and Social Psychology*, *35*, 315–330.

Iqbal, N. (2018, August 5). Have smartphones killed the art of conversation? *The Guardian.* https://www.theguardian.com/technology/2018/aug/05/smartphones-kill-art-of-conversation-voice-calls-whatsapp-emojis

Itzchakov, G., Kluger, A. N., Emanuel-Tor, M., & Gizbar, H. K. (2014). How do you like me to listen to you? *International Journal of Listening*, *28*, 177–185.

Izard, C. E. (1971). *The face of emotion*. Appleton-Century-Crofts.

Jack, R. E., Blais, C., Scheepers, C., Schyns, P. G., & Caldara, R. (2009). Cultural confusions show that facial expressions are not universal. *Current Biology*, *19*, 1543–1548.

Jack, R. E., Garrod, O. G., Yu, H., Caldara, R., & Schyns, P. G. (2012). Facial expressions of emotion are not culturally universal. *Proceedings of the National Academy of Sciences*, *109*, 7241–7244.

Jackson, R. L. (2002). Cultural contracts theory: Toward an understanding identity negotiation. *Communication Quarterly*, *50*(3), 359–367.

Jackson, R. L., Johnson, A. L., Hecht, M. L., & Ribeau, S. A. (2020). *African-American communication: Examining the complexities of lived experiences*. Routledge.

Jaeger, M. E., Skelder, A. A., & Rosnow, R. L. (1998). Who's up on the low down: Gossip in interpersonal relations. In B. H. Spitzberg & W. R. Cupach (Eds.), *The dark side of close relationships* (pp. 103–118). Lawrence Erlbaum Associates.

James, W. (1890). *The principles of psychology*. Henry Holt and Company.

Jandt, F. (2010). *An introduction to intercultural communication* (6th ed.). SAGE.

Jenkins, M., & Dragojevic, M. (2013). Explaining the process of resistance to persuasion: A politeness theory-based approach. *Communication Research*, *40*, 559–590.

Jensen-Campbell, L. A., Graziano, W. G., & West, S. G. (1995). Dominance, prosocial orientation, and female preferences: Do nice guys really finish last? *Journal of Personality and Social Psychology*, *68*, 427–440.

John, O. P., & Srivastava, S. (1999). The big 5 trait taxonomy: History, measurement and theoretical perspectives. In L. A. Pervin & O. P. John (Eds.), *Handbook of personality: Theory and research* (2nd ed., pp. 102–138). Guilford.

Johnson, A. J. (2001). Examining the maintenance of friendships: Are there differences between geographically close and long-distance friends? *Communication Quarterly, 49,* 424–435.

Johnson, A. J., Becker, J. A. H., Craig, E. A., Gilchrist, E. S., & Haigh, M. M. (2009). Changes in friendship commitment: Comparing geographically close and long-distance young-adult friendships. *Communication Quarterly, 57,* 395–415.

Johnson, A. J., Wittenberg, E., Villagran, M. M., Mazur, M., & Villagran, P. (2003). Relational progression as a dialectic: Examining turning points in communication among friends. *Communication Monographs, 70,* 230–249.

Johnson, M. P. (1995). Patriarchal terrorism and common couple violence: Two forms of violence against women. *Journal of Marriage and the Family, 57,* 283–294.

Johnson, M. P. (2008). *A typology of domestic violence: Intimate terrorism, violent resistance, and situational couple violence.* University Press of New England.

Johnson, M. P., & Ferraro, K. J. (2000). Research on domestic violence in the 1990s: Making distinctions. *Journal of Marriage and the Family, 62,* 948–963.

Johnson, M. P., & Leone, J. M. (2005). The differential effects of intimate terrorism and situational couple violence: Findings from the National Violence against Women Survey. *Journal of Family Issues, 26,* 322–349.

Jones, B. C., DeBruine, L. M., Little, A. C., Burriss, R. P., & Feinberg, D. R. (2007). Social transmission of face preferences among humans. *Proceedings of the Royal Society B: Biological Sciences, 274,* 899–903.

Jones, E. E. (1964). *Ingratiation: A social-psychological analysis.* Appleton-Century-Crofts.

Jones, E. E., & Nisbett, R. E. (1971). *The actor and the observer: Divergent perceptions of the causes of behavior.* General Learning Press.

Jones, W. H., & Burdette, M. P. (1993). Betrayal in close relationships. In A. L. Weber & J. Harvey (Eds.), *Perspectives on close relationships* (pp. 1–14). Allyn & Bacon.

Jones, W. H., & Burdette, M. P. (1994). Betrayal in relationships. In A. L. Weber & J. H. Harvey (Eds.), *Perspectives on close relationships* (pp. 243–262). Allyn & Bacon.

Jouriles, E. N., McDonald, R., Rosenfield, D., Levy, N., Sargent, K., Caiozzo, C., & Grych, J. H. (2016). TakeCARE, a video bystander program to help prevent sexual violence on college campuses: Results of two randomized, controlled trials. *Psychology of Violence, 6*(3), 410–420.

Kachru, Y., & Smith, L. E. (2008). *Cultures, contexts, and world Englishes.* Routledge.

Kam, K. Y. (2004). *A cultural model of nonverbal deceptive communication: The independent and interdependent self-construals as predictors of deceptive communication motivations and nonverbal behaviors under deception* [Unpublished doctoral dissertation, University of Arizona].

Kansky, J., & Allen, J. P. (2018). Making sense and moving on: The potential for individual and interpersonal growth following emerging adult breakups. *Emerging Adulthood, 6*(3), 172–190. https://doi.org/10.1177/2167696817711766

Kapferer, J. (1990). *Rumors: Uses, interpretations, and images.* Transaction Publishers.

Karchru, Y., & Smith, L. E. (2008). *Cultures, contexts, and world Englishes.* Routledge.

Katriel, T., & Shenhar, A. (1989). Rituals of socialization: On performing Israeli cultural identity. *Text and Performance Quarterly, 9,* 337–341.

Kawai, Y. (2006). Stereotyping Asian Americans: The dialectic of the model minority and the yellow peril. *The Howard Journal of Communications, 16*(2), 109–131. https://doi.org/10.1080/10646170590948974

Kazerooni, F., Taylor, S. H., Bazarova, N. N., & Whitlock, J. (2018). Cyberbullying bystander intervention: The number of offenders and retweeting predict the likelihood of helping a cyberbullying victim. *Journal of Computer-Mediated Communication, 23,* 146–162.

Kellerman, K. (1992). Communication: Inherently strategic and primarily automatic. *Communication Monographs, 59,* 288–300.

Kellerman, K., & Cole, T. (1994). Classifying compliance-gaining messages: Taxonomic disorder and strategic confusion. *Communication Theory, 4,* 3–60.

Kellerman, K., & Sleight, C. (1988). Coherence: A meaningful adhesive for discourse. *Communication Yearbook, 12,* 95–129.

Kelly, A. B., Fincham, F. D., & Beach, S. R. H. (2003). Communication skills in couples: A review and discussion of emerging perspectives. In B. R. Burleson & J. O. Green (Eds.), *Handbook of communication and social interaction skills* (pp. 723–751). Erlbaum.

Kelly, H., & Thibaut, J. (1978). *Interpersonal relations: A theory of interdependence.* Wiley.

Kendon, A. (1990). *Conducting interaction: Patterns of behavior in focused encounters.* Cambridge University Press.

Keyton, J. (2011). *Communication and organizational culture: A key to understanding work experiences.* SAGE.

Kilduff, M., & Day, D. (1994). Do chameleons get ahead? The effects of self-monitoring on managerial careers. *Academy of Management Journal, 37,* 1047–1060.

Kim, H. S., Sherman, D. K., & Taylor, S. E. (2008). Culture and social support. *American Psychologist, 63,* 518–526.

Kim, J. S., So, H. S., & Ko, E. (2019). Influence of role conflict, nursing organizational culture and resilience on nursing performance in clinical nurses. *Journal of Muscle and Joint Health, 26,* 195–204.

Kim, Y., Chung, S., & Hample, D. (2020). How do culture, individual traits, and context influence Koreans' interpersonal arguing? Toward a more comprehensive analysis of interpersonal arguing. *Argumentation*, *34*(2), 117–141.

Kim, Y. Y. (2014). Interpersonal communication in intercultural encounters. In C. R. Berger (Ed.), *Interpersonal communication* (pp. 517–540). DeGruyter.

Kimmel, M. S. (2018). *Privilege: A reader*. Routledge.

Kincaid, D. L. (2004). From innovation to social norm: Bounded normative influence. *Journal of Health Communication*, *9*, 37–57.

King-To, Y., & Martin, J. L. (2003). The looking glass self: An empirical test and elaboration. *Social Forces*, *81*, 843–879.

Kline, S. L., & Stafford, L. (2004). A comparison of interaction rules and interaction frequency in relationship to marital quality. *Communication Reports*, *17*(1), 11–26. https://doi.org/10.1080/08934210409389370

Kluwer, E. S., De Dreu, C. K. W., & Buunk, B. P. (1998). Conflict in intimate vs. non-intimate relationships: When gender role stereotyping overrides biased self-other judgment. *Journal of Social and Personal Relationships*, *15*, 637–650.

Knapp, M. L., & Vangelisti, A. (2000). *Interpersonal communication and human relationships* (4th ed.). Allyn & Bacon.

Knapp, M. L., Vangelisti, A., & Caughlin, J. P. (2014). *Interpersonal communication and human relationships*. Pearson.

Knobloch, L. K., & Solomon, D. H. (1999). Measuring the sources and content of relational uncertainty. *Communication Studies*, *50*, 261–278.

Knobloch, L. K., & Solomon, D. H. (2002). Information seeking beyond initial interaction: Negotiating relational uncertainty within close relationships. *Human Communication Research*, *28*, 243–257.

Knobloch, L. K., Solomon, D. H., & Cruz, M. G. (2001). The role of relationship development and attachment in the experience of romantic jealousy. *Personal Relationships*, *8*, 205–224.

Koban, K., & Krüger, S. (2018). Out of sight, (not yet) out of mind: The impact of tie strength on direct interaction and social surveillance among geographically close and long-distance- Facebook friends. *Communication Research Reports*, *35*, 74–84.

Koerner, A. F., & Fitzpatrick, M. A. (2002). You never leave your family in a fight: The impact of family of origin on conflict behavior in romantic relationships. *Communication Studies*, *53*, 234–251.

Kolligian, J., & Sternberg, R. J. (1991). Perceived fraudulence in young adults: Is there an 'Imposter Syndrome'? *Journal of Personality Assessment*, *56*, 308–326.

Komori, M., Kawamura, S., & Ishihara, S. (2009). Averageness or symmetry: Which is more important for facial attractiveness? *Acta Psychologica*, *131*, 136–142.

Koopmann-Holm, B., & Matsumoto, D. (2011). Values and display rules for specific emotions. *Journal of Cross-Cultural Psychology*, *42*, 355–371.

Korzenny, F. (1978). A theory of electronic propinquity: Mediated communications in organizations. *Communication Research*, *5*, 3–24.

Kraus, M. W., & Keltner, D. (2009). Signs of socioeconomic status: A thin-slicing approach. *Psychological Science*, *20*, 99–106.

Kraut, R. E., & Johnston, R. E. (1979). Social and emotional messages of smiling: An ethological approach. *Journal of Personality and Social Psychology*, *37*(9), 1539–1553. https://doi.org/10.1037/0022-3514.37.9.1539

Kruger, J., & Dunning, D. (1999). Unskilled and unaware of it: How difficulties in recognizing one's own incompetence lead to inflated self-assessments. *Journal of Personality and Social Psychology*, *77*, 1121–1134.

Kuang, K., & Wilson, S. R. (2021). Theory of motivated information management: A meta-analytic review. *Communication Theory*, *31*(3), 463–490. https://doi.org/10.1093/ct/qtz025

Kurasawa, F. (2011). Critical cosmopolitanism. In M. Rovisco & M. Nowicka (Eds.), *The Ashgate research companion to cosmopolitanism* (pp. 279–292). Ashgate Publishing Company.

Kurdek, L. (1993). The allocation of household labor in gay, lesbian, and heterosexual married couples. *Journal of Social Issues*, *49*, 127–139.

Kurdek, L., & Schmitt, J. P. (1986). Relationship quality of partners in heterosexual married, heterosexual cohabiting, gay and lesbian couples. *Journal of Personality and Social Psychology*, *51*, 711–720.

Kutcher, E. J., & Bragge, J. D. (2006). Selection interviews of overweight job applicants: Can structure reduce the bias? *Journal of Applied Social Psychology*, *34*, 1993–2022.

La Valley, A. G., & Guerrero, L. K. (2012). Perceptions of conflict behavior and relational satisfaction in adult parent–child relationships: A dyadic analysis from an attachment perspective. *Communication Research*, *39*, 48–79.

Labrie, N., Akkermans, A., & Hample, D. (2020). A Dutch dose of dissent: Exploring the role of gender, education, and culture on Dutch students' argumentative predispositions. *Journal of Argumentation in Context*, *9*(2), 219–242. https://doi.org/10.1075/jaic.19009.lab

Laird, J. D., & Apostoleris, N. H. (1996). Emotional Self-control and Self-perception: Feelings are the. In R. Harre & W. G. Parrott (Eds.), *The emotions: Social, cultural and biological dimensions* (pp. 285–301). SAGE.

Lakin, J. L., & Chartrand, T. L. (2003). Using nonconscious behavioral mimicry to create affiliation and rapport. *Psychological Science*, *14*, 334–339. https://doi.org/10.1111/1467-9280.14481

Lakin, J. L., Jefferis, V. E., Cheng, C. M., & Chartrand, T. L. (2003). The chameleon effect as social glue: Evidence for the evolutionary significance of nonconscious mimicry. *Journal of Nonverbal Behavior, 27*, 145–162.

Lam, A. G., Mak, A., Lindsay, P. D., & Russell, S. T. (2004). What really works? An exploratory study of condom negotiation strategies. *AIDS Education and Prevention, 16*, 160–171.

Lampard, R. (2014). Stated reasons for relationship dissolution in Britain: Marriage and cohabitation compared. *European Sociological Review, 30*(3), 315–328. https://doi.org/10.1093/esr/jct034

Lander, K., & Metcalfe, S. (2007). The influence of positive and negative facial expressions on face familiarity. *Memory, 15*, 63–69.

Lane, A., Luminet, O., Rimé, B., Gross, J. J., de Timary, P., & Mikolajczak, M. (2013). Oxytocin increases willingness to socially share one's emotions. *International Journal of Psychology, 48*, 676–681.

Langlois, J. H., & Roggman, L. A. (1990). Attractive faces are only average. *Psychological Science, 1*, 115–121.

Langlois, J. H., Roggman, L. A., & Musselman, L. (1994). What is average and what is not average about attractive faces? *Psychological Science, 5*, 214–220.

Lapinski, M. K., & Rimal, R. N. (2005). An explication of social norms. *Communication Theory, 15*, 127–147.

Larose, H., & Standing, L. (1998). Does the halo effect occur in the elderly? *Social Behavior and Personality: An International Journal, 26*, 147–150.

Larrance, D. T., & Zuckerman, M. (1981). Facial attractiveness and vocal likeability as determinants of nonverbal sending skills 1. *Journal of Personality, 49*, 349–362.

Latané, B., & Nida, S. (1981). Ten years of research on group size and helping. *Psychological Bulletin, 89*, 308–324.

Latham, G. P., & Skarlicki, D. P. (1995). Criterion-related validity of the situational and patterned behavior description interviews with organizational citizenship behavior. *Human Performance, 8*, 67–80.

Lawrence, E. J., Shaw, P., Baker, D., Baron-Cohen, S., & David, A. S. (2004). Measuring empathy: Reliability and validity of the Empathy Quotient. *Psychological Medicine, 34*, 911–920.

Lazarus, R. S. (1991). Cognition and motivation in emotion. *American Psychologist, 46*, 352–367.

Le Poire, B. A. (1992). Does the codependent encourage substance-dependent behavior? Paradoxical injunctions in the codependent relationship. *The International Journal of Addictions, 27*, 1465–1474.

Le Poire, B. A. (1995). Inconsistent nurturing as control theory: Implications for communication-based research and treatment programs. *Journal of Applied Communication Research, 23*, 60–74.

Le Poire, B. A., Hallett, J. S., & Erlandson, K. T. (2000). An initial test of inconsistent nurturing as control theory: How partners of drug abusers assist with their partners' sobriety. *Human Communication Research, 26*, 432–457.

Leary, M. R., & Springer, C. A. (2001). *Hurt feelings: The neglected emotion.* In R. M. Kowalski (Ed.), *Behaving badly: Aversive behaviors in interpersonal relationships* (pp. 151–175). American Psychological Association.

Leary, M. R., Springer, C., Negel, L., Ansell, E., & Evans, K. (1998). The causes, phenomenology, and consequences of hurt feelings. *Journal of Personality and Social Psychology, 74*, 1225–1237.

Ledbetter, A. M. (2009). Patterns of media use and multiplexity: Associations with sex, geographic distance and friendship interdependence. *New Media & Society, 11*, 1187–1208.

Ledbetter, A. M., & Kuzenkoff, J. H. (2012). More than a game: Friendship relational maintenance and attitudes toward Xbox LIVE communication. *Communication Research, 39*, 269–290. https://doi.org/10.1177/0093650210397042

Ledbetter, A. M., Mazer, J. P., DeGroot, J. M., Meyer, K. R., Mao, Y., & Swafford, B. (2011). Attitudes toward online social connection and self-disclosure as predictors of Facebook communication and relational closeness. *Communication Research, 38*, 57–53.

Ledbetter, A. M., Stassen-Ferrara, H. M., & Dowd, M. M. (2013). Comparing equity and self-expansion theory approaches to relational maintenance. *Personal Relationships, 20*, 38–51. https://doi.org/10.1111/j.1475-6811.2012.01395.x

Lederman, L. C., & Stewart, L. (2005). *Changing the culture of college drinking: A socially situated health communication campaign.* Hampton Press.

LeFebvre, L. (2017). Ghosting as a relationship dissolution strategy in the technological age. In N. M. Punyanunt-Carter & J. S. Wrench (Eds.), *The impact of social media in modern romantic relationships* (pp. 219–235). Lexington Books.

LeFebvre, L. E., Allen, M., Rasner, R. D., Garstad, S., Wilms, A., & Parrish, C. (2019). Ghosting in emerging adults' romantic relationships: The digital dissolution disappearance strategy. *Imagination, Cognition and Personality, 39*, 125–150.

Lenhart, A., Anderson, M., & Smith, A. (2015, October 1). Technology and romantic relationships: From flirting to breaking up, social media and mobile phones are woven into teens' romantic lives. *Pew Research Center.* https://www.pewinternet.org/2015/10/01/teens-technology-and-romantic-relationships/

Lerner, G. H. (1989). Notes on overlap management in conversation: The case of delayed completion. *Western Journal of Speech Communication, 53*, 167–177.

Levine, T. R., & Mongeau, P. M. (2010). Friends with benefits: A precarious negotiation. In M. Bruce & R. M. Stewart (Eds.), *College sex.* Wiley.

Levitt, S. R. (2019). Cultural dialectics in international teamwork dynamics. *International Journal of Business Communication*, *56*(3), 326–348. https://doi.org/10.1177/2329488416629094

Lewandowski, G. W., Aron, A., Bassis, S., & Kunak, J. (2006). Losing a self-expanding relationship: Implications for the self-concept. *Personal Relationships*, *13*, 317–331.

Lewandowski, G. W. Jr., & Bizzoco, N. M. (2007). Addition through subtraction: Growth following the dissolution of a low quality relationship. *The Journal of Positive Psychology*, *2*(1), 40–54. https://doi.org/10.1080/17439760601069234

Lewiński, M., Hample, D., Sàágua, J., & Mohammed, D. (2018). Arguing in Portugal: A cross-cultural analysis. *Journal of International and Intercultural Communication*, *11*(3), 233–253. https://doi.org/10/1080/17513057.2018.1450888

Liden, R. C., Martin, C. L., & Parsons, C. K. (1993). Interviewer and applicant behaviors in employment interviews. *Academy of Management Journal*, *36*(2), 372–386. https://doi.org/10.5465/256527

Lindlof, T. R., & Taylor, B. C. (2011). *Qualitative communication research methods* (3rd ed.). SAGE.

Lippmann, W. (1922). *Public opinion*. Harcourt, Brace.

Lippmann, W. (1922). Stereotypes. In W. Lippmann (Ed.), *Public opinion* (pp. 79–94). MacMillan.

Lisitsa, E. (2013a, April 27). The four horsemen: The antidotes. *The Gottman Institute*. https://www.gottman.com/blog/the-four-horsemen-the-antidotes

Lisitsa, E. (2013b, May 13). The four horsemen: Contempt. *The Gottman Institute*. https://www.gottman.com/blog/the-four-horsemen-contempt/

Lisitsa, E. (2013c, May 20). The four horsemen: Stonewalling. *The Gottman Institute*. https://www.gottman.com/blog/the-four-horsemen-stonewalling/

Lisitsa, E. (2014, March 14). Combat stonewalling with self-care. *The Gottman Institute*. https://www.gottman.com/blog/weekend-homework-assignment-stonewalling-self-care/

Little, A. C. (2014). Facial attractiveness. *Wiley Interdisciplinary Reviews: Cognitive Science*, *5*, 621–634.

Lu, P. H. (2015). "Gossip makes us one": A qualitative analysis of the role of gossip in the process of Taiwanese immigrants' social integration in Canada. *Journal of Asian Pacific Communication*, *25*(2), 279–304. https://doi.org/10.1075/japc.25.2.10lu

Lun, J., Sinclair, S., Whitchurch, R. E., & Glenn, C. (2007). (Why) do I think what you think? Epistemic social tuning and implicit prejudice. *Journal of Personality and Social Psychology*, *93*, 957–972.

MacGeorge, E. L., Branch, S. E., Carlson-Hill, C. L., Tian, X., Caldes, E. P., Mikovsky, M. N., Beatty, S., & Brinker, D. L. (2019). Verbal person centeredness in interaction: Connecting micro- and macro-level operationalization. *Journal of Language and Social Psychology*, *38*, 149–169.

Malachowski, C. C., & Frisby, B. N. (2015). The aftermath of hurtful events: Cognitive, communicative, and relational outcomes. *Communication Quarterly*, *63*, 187–203.

Malinowski, B. (1923). The problem of meaning in primitive languages. In C. K. Ogden & I. A. Richards (Eds.), *The meaning of meaning* (pp. 296–336). Routledge & Kegan Paul.

Malle, B. F. (2006). The actor-observer asymmetry in attribution: A (surprising) meta-analysis. *Psychological Bulletin*, *132*, 895–919.

Manning, J. T., & Pickup, L. J. (1998). Symmetry and performance in middle distance runners. *International Journal of Sports Medicine*, *19*, 205–209.

Mansson, D. H., Myers, S. A., & Turner, L. H. (2010). Relational maintenance behaviors in the grandchild–grandparent relationship. *Communication Research Reports*, *27*, 68–79.

Marchand, M., Halimi-Falkowicz, S., & Joule, R.-V. (2009). How to help the residents of an old age home to freely decide to take part in a social activity? *European Review of Applied Psychology*, *59*(2), 153–161. https://doi.org/10.1016/j.erap.2008.05.001

Marek, C. I., Wanzer, M. B., & Knapp, J. L. (2004). An exploratory investigation of the relationship between roommates' first impressions and subsequent communication patterns. *Communication Research Reports*, *21*, 210–220.

Markus, H. R., & Kitayama, S. (1991). Culture and the self: Implications for cognition, emotion, and motivation. *Psychological Review*, *98*, 224–253.

Marsh, A. A., Elfenbein, H. A., & Ambady, N. (2007). Separated by a common language: Nonverbal accents and cultural stereotypes about Americans and Australians. *Journal of Cross-Cultural Psychology*, *38*, 284–301.

Martin, J. N., & Nakayama, T. K. (1999). Thinking dialectically about culture and communication. *Communication Theory*, *9*, 1–25.

Martin, J. N., & Nakayama, T. K. (2006). Thinking dialectically about culture and communication. *Communication Theory*, *9*(1), 1–25. https://doi.org/10.1111/j.1468-2885.1999.tb00160.x

Martin, J. N., & Nakayama, T. K. (2010). Intercultural communication and dialectics revisited. In R. T. Halualani & T. K. Nakayama (Eds.), *Handbook of critical intercultural communication* (pp. 51–53). Blackwell.

Martin, M. M., & Rubin, R. B. (1995). Development of a communication flexibility measure. *Psychological Reports*, *76*, 623–626.

Marwick, A., & boyd, d. (2012). I tweet honestly, I tweet passionately: Twitter users, context collapse, and the imagined audience. *New Media & Society*, *13*, 114–133.

Matsumoto, D. (2006). Are cultural differences in emotion regulation mediated by personality traits? *Journal of Cross-Cultural Psychology*, *37*, 421–437.

Mayer, J. D., Salovey, P., & Caruso, D. R. (2004). Emotional intelligence: Theory, findings, and implications. *Psychological Inquiry*, 15, 197–215.

McAllum, K. (2016). Managing imposter syndrome among the "Trophy Kids": Creating teaching practices that develop independence in millennial students. *Communication Education*, 65, 363–365.

McCornack, S. A., & Parks, M. R. (1986). Deception detection and relationship development: The other side of trust. *Annals of the International Communication Association*, 9(1), 377–389.

McCroskey, J. C. (1970). Measures of communication-bound anxiety. *Speech Monographs*, 37, 269–277.

McCroskey, J. C. (1978). Validity of the PRCA as an index of oral communication apprehension. *Communication Monographs*, 45, 192–203.

McCroskey, J. C., & Beatty, M. J. (1986). Oral communication apprehension. In W. H. Jones, J. M. Cheek, & S. R. Briggs (Eds.), *Shyness: Perspectives on research and treatment* (pp. 279–293). Springer.

McCroskey, J. C., Beatty, M. J., Kearney, P., & Plax, T. G. (1985). The content validity of the PRCA-24 as a measure of communication apprehension across communication contexts. *Communication Quarterly*, 33, 165–173.

McCroskey, J. C., Daly, J. A., Beatty, M. J., & Martin, M. M (Eds.). (1998). *Communication and personality: Trait perspectives*. Hampton Press.

McCroskey, J. C., & McCain, T. A. (1974). The measurement of interpersonal attraction. *Speech Monographs*, 41, 261–266.

McCroskey, J. C., & Richmond, V. (1976). The effects of communication apprehension on the perception of peers. *Western Speech Communication*, 40, 14–21.

McCroskey, J. C., Richmond, V. P., & Davis, L. M. (1986). Apprehension about communicating with supervisors: A test of a theoretical relationship between types of communication apprehension. *Western Journal of Speech Communication*, 50, 171–182.

McCullough, M. E., Worthington, E. L., & Rachal, K. C. (1997). Interpersonal forgiving in close relationships. *Journal of Personality and Social Psychology*, 73, 321–336.

McDaniel, M. A., Whetzel, D. L., Schmdit, F. L., & Maurer, S. D. (1994). The validity of employment interviews: A comprehensive review and meta-analysis. *Journal of Applied Psychology*, 79, 599–616.

McEwan, B. (2006a). *Between friends: Correlations between gossip, bonding, and relationship maintenance* [Paper presentation]. Meeting of the Western States Communication Association, Palm Springs, CA, United States.

McEwan, B. (2006b). *Defining gossip: An examination of reports of gossip interactions* [Paper presentation]. Meeting of the National Communication Association, San Antonio, TX, United States.

McEwan, B. (2013). *Choosing channels: Exploring multiple motivations for communication medium choice* [Paper presentation]. Meeting of the International Association of Relationship Researchers, Louisville, KY, United States.

McEwan, B. (2015). *Navigating new media networks: Understanding and managing communication challenges*. Lexington.

McEwan, B., Babin, B., & Farinelli, L. (2008). *The end of a friendship: Friendship dissolution reasons and methods* [Paper presentation]. Meeting of the National Communication Association, San Diego, CA, United States.

McEwan, B., Fletcher, J., Eden, J., & Sumner, E. (2014). Development and validation of a Facebook relational maintenance measure. *Communication Methods and Measures*, 8(4), 244–263. https://doi.org/10.1080/19312458.2014.967844

McEwan, B., & Flood, M. (2018). Passwords for jobs: Compression of identity in reaction to perceived organizational control via social media surveillance. *New Media & Society*, 20, 1715–1734.

McEwan, B., & Guerrero, L. K. (2010). Freshmen engagement through communication: Predicting friendship formation strategies and perceived availability of network resources from communication skills. *Communication Studies*, 61, 445–463.

McEwan, B., & Guerrero, L. K. (2012). Maintenance behavior and relationship quality as predictors of perceived availability of resources in newly formed college friendship networks. *Communication Studies*, 63, 421–440.

McEwan, B., & Horn, D. (2016). ILY & can u pick up some milk: Effects of relational maintenance via text messaging on relational satisfaction and closeness in dating partners. *Southern Communication Journal*, 81, 168–181.

McEwan, B., & Johnson, S. L. (2008). Relational violence: The dark side of haptic communication. In L. K. Guerrero & M. L. Hecht (Eds.), *The nonverbal communication reader* (3rd ed., pp. 232–241). Waveland Press.

McEwan, B., & Sobré-Denton, M. (2011). Virtual cosmopolitanism: Constructing third cultures and transmitting social and cultural capital through social media. *Journal of Intercultural and International Communication*, 4, 252–258.

McEwan, B., Sumner, E., Eden, J., & Fletcher, J. (2018). The effects of Facebook relational maintenance on friendship quality: An investigation of the Facebook Relational Maintenance Measure. *Communication Research Reports*, 35, 1–11.

McGovern, T. V., & Ideus, H. (1978). The impact of nonverbal behavior on the employment interview. *Journal of College Placement*, 38, 51–54.

McGovern, T. V., & Tinsley, H. E. (1978). Interviewer evaluations of interviewee nonverbal behavior. *Journal of Vocational Behavior*, 13, 163–171.

McIntosh, P. (1997). White privilege: Unpacking the invisible knapsack. In B. Schneider (Ed.), *An anthology: Race in the first person* (pp. 119–126). Crown Trade Paperbacks.

McLaren, K. (2013). *The art of empathy: A complete guide to life's most essential skill.* Sounds True.

McLaren, R. M., & Solomon, D. H. (2008). Appraisals and distancing responses to hurtful messages. *Communication Research, 35,* 339–367.

McLaughlin, M. (1984). *Conversation: How talk is organized.* SAGE.

McLaughlin, M. L., & Cody, M. J. (1982). Awkward silences: Behavioral antecedents and consequences of conversational lapse. *Human Communication Research, 8,* 299–316.

Mead, G. H. (1922). The genesis of self and social control. *International Journal of Ethics, 35,* 251–277.

Mead, G. H. (1934). *Mind, self, and society: From the standpoint of a social behaviorist.* The University of Chicago Press.

Mehra, A., Kilduff, M., & Brass, D. J. (2001). The social networks of high and low self-monitors: Implications for workplace performance. *Administrative Science Quarterly, 46,* 121–146.

Meir, S. C., Sharp, C., Michonski, J., Babcock, C. J., & Fitzgerald, K. (2013). Romantic relationships of female-to-male trans men. A descriptive study. *International Journal of Transgenderism, 14,* 75–85.

Menzies-Toman, D. A., & Lydon, J. E. (2005). Commitment-motivated benign appraisals of partner transgressions: Do they facilitate accommodation? *Journal of Social and Personal Relationships, 22,* 111–128.

Merolla, A. J. (2014). The role of hope in conflict management and relational maintenance. *Personal Relationships, 21,* 365–386.

Messman, S. J., Canary, D. J., & Hause, K. S. (2000). Motives to remain platonic, equity, and the use of maintenance strategies in opposite-sex friendships. *Journal of Social and Personal Relationships, 10,* 273–283.

Metts, S. (1991, February). *The wicked things you say, the wicked things you do: A pilot study of relational transgressions* [Paper presentation]. The Annual Meeting of the Western States Communication Association, Phoenix, AZ, United States.

Metts, S. (1994). Relational transgressions. In W. R. Cupach & B. H. Spitzberg (Eds.), *The dark side of interpersonal communication* (pp. 217–240). Lawrence Erlbaum.

Metts, S. (1997). Face and facework: Implications for the study of personal relationships. In S. Duck (Ed.), *Handbook of personal relationships: Theory, research and interventions* (pp. 373–390). Wiley.

Meyer, I. H. (2003). Prejudice, social stress, and mental health in lesbian, gay, and bisexual populations: Conceptual issues and research evidence. *Psychological Bulletin, 129,* 674–697.

Midgette, A., & Mulvey, K. L. (2021). Unpacking young adults' experiences of race- and gender-based microaggressions. *Journal of Social and Personal Relationships, 38,* 1350–1370. https://doi.org/10.1177/0265407521988947

Mikal, J. P., Rice, R. E., Abeyta, A., & DeVilbiss, J. (2013). Transition, stress, and computer-mediated social support. *Computers in Human Behavior, 29,* A40–A53.

Mikkelson, A. C., Myers, S. A., & Hannawa, A. F. (2011). The differential use of relational maintenance behaviors in adult sibling relationships. *Communication Studies, 62,* 258–271.

Millar, M. (2002). Effects of a guilt induction and guilt reduction on door in the face. *Communication Research, 29*(6), 666–680. https://doi.org/10.1177/009365002237831

Millar, R., Crute, V., & Hargie, O. (2017). *Professional interviewing.* Routledge.

Miller, D. T., & McFarland, C. (1987). Pluralistic ignorance: When similarity is interpreted as dissimilarity. *Journal of Personality and Social Psychology, 53*(2), 298–305. https://doi.org/10.1037/0022-3514.53.2.298

Miller, D. T., & McFarland, C. (1991). When social comparison goes awry: The case of pluralistic ignorance. In J. Suls & T. A. Wills (Eds.), *Social comparison: Contemporary theory and research* (pp. 287–313). Erlbaum.

Miller, G. R. (1978). The current status of theory and research in interpersonal communication. *Human Communication Research, 4,* 164–178.

Miller, G. R. (1980). On being persuaded: Some basic distinctions. In M. E. Roloff & G. R. Miller (Eds.), *Persuasion: New directions in theory and research* (pp. 11–28). SAGE.

Miller, G. R., Boster, F., Roloff, M., & Seibold, D. R. (1977). Compliance-gaining message strategies: A typology and some findings concerning effects of situational differences. *Communication Monographs, 44,* 37–51.

Miller, G. R., & Steinberg, M. (1975). *Between people.* Science Research Associates.

Miller, J., Donner, S., & Fraser, E. (2004). Talking when talking is tough: Taking on conversations about race, sexual orientation, gender, class and other aspects of social identity. *Smith College Studies in Social Work, 74*(2), 377–392.

Miller-Ott, A., Kelly, L., & Duran, R. (2012). The effect of cell phone usage rules on satisfaction in romantic couples. *Communication Quarterly, 60,* 17–34.

Mills, J. H. (2003). *Making sense of organizational change.* Routledge.

Mills, R. S. L., Nazar, J., & Farrell, H. M. (2002). Child and parent perceptions of hurtful messages. *Journal of Social and Personal Relationships*, 19, 731–754.

Minniear, M., & Soliz, J. (2019). Family communication and messages about race and identity in Black families in the United States. *Journal of Family Communication*, 19(4), 329–347.

Mongeau, P. A., & Henningsen, M. L. M. (2015). Stage theories of relationship development: Charting the course of interpersonal communication. In D. O. Braithwaite & P. Schrodt (Eds.), *Engaging theories in interpersonal communication: Multiple perspectives* (2nd ed., pp. 389–402). SAGE.

Mongeau, P. A., Knight, L., Williams, J., Eden, J., & Shaw, C. (2013). Identifying and explicating variation among friends with benefits relationships. *Journal of Sex Research*, 50, 37–47.

Mongeau, P. A., & Schulz, B. E. (1997). What he doesn't know won't hurt him (or me): Verbal responses and attributions following sexual infidelity. *Communication Reports*, 10, 143–152.

Mongeau, P. A., Serewicz, M. C., & Theirren, L. F. (2004). Goals for cross-sex first dates: Identification, measurement and the influence of contextual factors. *Communication Monographs*, 71, 121–147.

Monin, B. (2003). The warm glow heuristic: When liking leads to familiarity. *Journal of Personality and Social Psychology*, 85, 1035–1048.

Monsour, M., Harvey, V., & Betty, S. (1997). A balance theory explanation of challenges confronting cross-sex friendships. *Sex Roles*, 37(11–12), 825–845.

Montagu, A. (1978). *Touching: The human significance of the skin*. Harper & Row. (Original work published 1971)

Montgomery, B. M., & Baxter, L. A. (1998). Dialogism and relational dialectics. In *Dialectical approaches to studying personal relationships* (pp. 155–183). Lawrence Erlbaum.

Montgomery, L. (1993). Relationship maintenance vs. relationship change: Dialectical dilemma. *Journal of Social and Personal Relationships*, 10, 205–224.

Moore, M. R., & Stambolis-Ruhstorfer, M. (2013). LGBT sexuality and families at the start of the twenty-first century. *Annual Review of Sociology*, 39, 439–507.

Moran, C. M., Diefendorff, J. M., & Greguras, G. J. (2013). Understanding emotional display rules at work and outside of work: The effects of country and gender. *Motivation and Emotion*, 37, 323–334.

Morse, C. R., & Metts, S. (2011). Situational and communicative predictors of forgiveness following a relational transgression. *Western Journal of Communication*, 75, 239–258.

Motley, M. T. (1990). On whether one can (not) not communicate: An examination via traditional communication postulates. *Western Journal of Communication*, 54, 1–20.

Mowen, J. C., & Cialdini, R. B. (1980). On implementing the door-in-the-face compliance technique in a business context. *Journal of Marketing Research*, 17(2), 253–258. https://doi.org/10.2307/3150936

Muise, A., Christofides, E., & Desmarais, S. (2009). More information than you ever wanted: Does Facebook bring out the green-eyed monster of jealousy? *CyberPsychology and Behavior*, 12, 441–444.

Munro, L., Travers, R., & Woodford, M. R. (2019). Overlooked and invisible: Everyday experiences of microaggressions for LGBTQ adolescents. *Journal of Homosexuality*, 66, 1439–1471. https://doi.org/10.1080/00918369.2018.1542205

Murphy, N. A., Hall, J. A., Ruben, M. A., Frauendorfer, D., Mast, M. S., Johnson, K. E., & Nguyen, L. (2019). Predictive validity of thin-slice nonverbal behavior from social interactions. *Personality and Social Psychology Bulletin*, 45, 983–993.

Myers, S. A. (2011). "I have to love her, even if sometimes I may not like her": The reasons why adults maintain their sibling relationships. *North American Journal of Psychology*, 13, 51–62.

Myers, S. A., Black, J., Bukaty, A., Callin, A., Davis, L. A., Fairbanks, S. L., Gieron, M. E., Ferry, M. F., Kappenman, K., King, M., McGuire, M., Nix, F. D., Saniuk, J., Tracy, M. M., Triolo, T. N., & Valentino, T. (2001). Relational maintenance behaviors in the sibling relationship. *Communication Quarterly*, 49, 19–34.

Myers, S. A., Brann, M., & Rittenour, C. E. (2008). Interpersonal communication motives as a predictor of early and middle adulthood siblings' use of relational maintenance behaviors. *Communication Research Reports*, 25, 155–167.

Myers, S. A., Byrnes, K. A., Frisby, B. N., & Mansson, D. H. (2011). Adult siblings' use of affectionate communication as a strategic and routine relational maintenance behavior. *Communication Research Reports*, 28, 151–158.

Myers, S. A., & Glover, N. P. (2007). Emerging adults' use of relational maintenance behaviors with their parents. *Communication Research Reports*, 24, 257–264.

Nabi, R. L., Prestin, A., & So, J. (2013). Facebook friends with (health) benefits? Exploring social network site use and perceptions of social support, stress, and well-being. *Cyberpsychology, Behavior, and Social Networking*, 16, 721–727.

Nelson, L. J., Padilla-Walker, L. M., Carroll, J. S., Madsen, S. D., Barry, C. M., & Badger, S. (2007). "If you want me to treat you like an adult, start acting like one!" Comparing the criteria that emerging adults and their parents have for adulthood. *Journal of Family Psychology*, 21, 665–674.

Nelson, S., Dickson, D., & Hargie, O. (2003). Learning together, living apart: The experiences of university students in Northern Ireland. *International Journal of Qualitative Studies in Education*, 16, 777–795.

Newman, P. R., & Newman, B. M. (1976). Early adolescence and its conflict: Group identity versus alienation. *Adolescence*, *11*(42), 261.

Newton, D. A., & Burgoon, J. K. (1990a). Nonverbal conflict behaviors: Functions, strategies, and tactics. In D. D. Cahn (Ed.), *Intimates in conflict: A communication perspective* (pp. 77–104). Lawrence Erlbaum.

Newton, D. A., & Burgoon, J. K. (1990b). The use and consequences of verbal influence strategies during interpersonal disagreements. *Human Communication Research*, *16*, 477–518.

Noah, T., Schul, Y., & Mayo, R. (2018). When both the original study and its failed replication are correct: Feeling observed eliminates the facial-feedback effect. *Journal of Personality and Social Psychology*, *114*, 657–664.

Nofsinger, R. (1991). *Everyday conversation*. Waveland Press.

Noller, P. (1980). Misunderstandings in marital communication: A study of couples' nonverbal communication. *Journal of Personality and Social Psychology*, *39*, 1135–1148.

O'Braithwaite, D., & Baxter, L. A. (2006). "You're my parent but you're not": Dialectical tensions in stepchildren's perceptions about communicating with the nonresidential parent. *Journal of Applied Communication Research*, *34*, 30–48. https://doi.org/10.1080/00909880500420200

Ogolsky, B. G., & Bowers, J. R. (2013). A meta-analytic review of relationship maintenance and its correlates. *Journal of Social and Personal Relationships*, *30*, 343–367.

Ogolsky, B. G., Monk, J. K., Rice, T. M., Theisen, J. C., & Maniotes, C. R. (2017). Relationship maintenance: A review of research on romantic relationships. *Journal of Family Theory & Review*, *9*, 275–306.

O'Keefe, D. J., & Hale, S. L. (1998). The door-in-the-face influence strategy: A random effects meta-analytic review. In M. E. Roloff (Ed.), *Communication Yearbook, 21* (pp. 1–33). SAGE.

Oldenburg, R. (1989). *The great good place: Cafés, coffee shops, community centers, beauty parlors, general stores, bars, hangouts, and how they get you through the day*. Marlowe & Company.

Omdahl, B. L. (1995). *Cognitive appraisal, emotion, and empathy*. Lawrence Erlbaum.

Orbe, M. P. (1998). *Constructing co-cultural theory: An explication of culture, power, and communication*. SAGE.

Orbe, M. P., & Roberts, T. L. (2012). Co-cultural theorizing: Foundations, applications, and extensions. *Howard Journal of Communications*, *23*, 293–311.

Orbe, M., & Spellers, R. (2005). From the margins to the center. In *Theorizing about intercultural communication* (pp. 173–210). SAGE.

O'Sullivan, P. B., & Carr, C. T. (2018). Masspersonal communication: A model bridging the mass-interpersonal divide. *New Media & Society*, *20*(3), 1161–1180. https://doi.org/10.1177/1461444816686104

Oswald, D. J., & Clark, E. M. (2006). How do friendship maintenance behaviors and problem-solving styles function at the individual and dyadic levels. *Personal Relationships*, *3*, 333–348.

Oswald, D. J., Clark, E. M., & Kelly, C. M. (2004). Friendship maintenance: An analysis of individual and dyad behaviors. *Journal of Social and Clinical Psychology*, *23*, 413–441.

Oswald, D. L., & Clark, E. M. (2003). Best friends forever?: High school best friendships and the transition to college. *Personal Relationships*, *10*, 187–196.

Overall, N. C., Fletcher, G. J. O., Simpson, J. A., & Sibley, C. G. (2009). Regulating partners in intimate relationships: The costs and benefits of different communication strategies. *Journal of Personality and Social Psychology*, *96*, 620–639.

Owen, M. (1981). Conversational units and the use of 'well...'. In P. Werth (Ed.), *Conversation and discourse* (pp. 99–116). Croom Helm.

Owens, R. A. (2003). *Friendship features associated with college students' friendship maintenance and dissolution following problems* [Unpublished doctoral dissertation, West Virginia University], .

Oyamot, C. M., Fuglestad, P., & Snyder, M. (2010). Balance of power and influence in relationships: The role of self-monitoring. *Journal of Social and Personal Relationships*, *27*, 23–46.

Oyserman, D., & Markus, H. R. (1998). Self as social representation. In U. Flick (Ed.), *The psychology of the social*. Cambridge University Press.

Pacanowsky, M. E., & O'Donnel-Trujillo, N. (1982). Communication and organizational cultures. *Western Journal of Speech Communication*, *46*, 115–130.

Park, H. S., Smith, S. W., Klein, K. A., & Martell, D. (2011). College students' estimation and accuracy of other students' drinking and believability of advertisements featured in a social norms campaign. *Journal of Health Communication*, *16*, 504–518 .

Parks, M. R. (2007). *Personal relationships and personal networks*. Lawrence Erlbaum Associates.

Parks, M. R., & Adelman, M. B. (1983). Communication networks and the development of romantic relationships: An expansion of uncertainty reduction theory. *Human Communication Research*, *10*, 55–79.

Parsons, C. K., & Liden, R. C. (1984). Interviewer perceptions of applicant qualifications: A multivariate field study of demographic characteristics and nonverbal cues. *Journal of Applied Psychology*, *69*, 557–568.

Pascual, A., Dagot, L., Valee, B., & Guéguen, N. (2009). Compliance without pressure, mediatization of a Tsunami and charitable donation: Compared effectiveness of the door-in-the-face and "you are free of...techniques". *European Review of Applied Psychology*, *59*, 79–84.

Patterson, C. J., Sutfin, E. L., & Fulcher, M. (2004). Division of labor among lesbian and heterosexual parenting couples: Correlates of specialized versus shared patterns. *Journal of Adult Development, 11*(3), 179–189.

Patterson, M. L. (1983). *Nonverbal behavior: A functional perspective.* Springer Science & Business Media.

Pederson, J. R., & McLaren, R. M. (2016). Managing information following hurtful experiences: How personal network members negotiate private information. *Journal of Social and Personal Relationships, 33*, 961–983.

Pederson, J. R., & McLaren, R. M. (2017). Indirect effects of supportive communication during conversations about coping with relational transgressions. *Personal Relationships, 24*, 804–819.

Pedler, M. (2011). Leadership, risk, and the imposter syndrome. *Action Learning, Research and Practice, 8*, 89–91.

Pena, J., & Brody, N. (2014). Intentions to hide and unfriend Facebook connections based on perceptions of sender attractiveness and status updates. *Computers in Human Behavior, 31*, 143–150.

Pennington, D. (2000). *African-American women quitting the workplace.* Edwin Mellon.

Pennycook, A. (2006). *Global Englishes and transcultural flows.* Routledge.

Pennycook, G., Ross, R. M., Koehler, D. J., & Fugelsang, J. A. (2017). Dunning-Kruger effects in reasoning: Theoretical implications of the failure to recognize incompetence. *Psychonomic Bulletin & Review, 24*, 1774–1784. https://doi.org/10.3758/s13423-017-1242-7

Perlman, D., & Sprecher, S. (2012). Sex, intimacy, and dating in college. In R. D. McAnulty (Ed.), *Sex in college.* Praeger.

Perras, M. T., & Lustig, M. W. (1982, February). *The effects of intimacy level and intent to disengage on the selection of relational disengagement strategies* [Paper presentation]. The Annual Meeting of the Western Speech Communication Association, Denver, CO, United States.

Peterson, M. S. (1997). Interviewers' perceptions of the importance and adequacy of applicants' communication skills. *Communication Education, 46*, 287–291.

Petronio, S. (2002). *Boundaries of privacy: Dialectics of disclosure.* State University of New York Press.

Pierro, A., Cicero, L., & Raven, B. H. (2008). Motivated compliance with bases of social power. *Journal of Applied Social Psychology, 38*, 1921–1944.

Pines, A. M., & Zaidman, N. (2003). Gender, culture, and social support: A male-female, Israeli Jewish-Arab comparison. *Sex Roles, 49*, 571–586. https://doi.org/10.1023/B:SERS.0000003128.99279.94

Planalp, S., DeFrancisco, V. L., & Rutherford, D. (1996). Varieties of cues to emotion in naturally occurring settings. *Cognition and Emotion, 10*, 137–153.

Planalp, S., Rutherford, D. K., & Honeycutt, J. M. (1988). Events that increase uncertainty in personal relationships II: Replication and extension. *Human Communication Research, 14*, 516–547.

Planalp, S., & Tracy, K. (1980). Not to change the topic but...: A cognitive approach to the study of conversation. *Communication Yearbook, 4*, 237–258.

Platt, L. F., & Bolland, K. S. (2018). Relationship partners of transgender individuals: A qualitative exploration. *Journal of Social and Personal Relationships, 35*, 1251–1272.

Pollock, J. (2012). The halo effect: The influence of attractiveness on perceived promiscuity. *Sentience, 7*, 34–37.

Posthuma, R. A., Morgeson, F. P., & Campion, M. A. (2002). Beyond employment interview validity: A comprehensive narrative review of recent research and trends over time. *Personnel Psychology, 55*, 1–81.

Powers, P. (2007). Persuasion and coercion: A critical review of philosophical and empirical approaches. *HEC Forum, 19*, 125–143.

Pratkanis, A. R. (2007). *The science of social influence: Advances and future progress.* Psychology Press.

Prescott, M. E., & La Poire, B. A. (2002). Eating disorders and mother-daughter communication: A test of inconsistent nurturing as control theory. *The Journal of Family Communication, 2*, 59–78.

Prickett, T., Gada-Jain, N., & Bernieri, F. J. (2000, May). *The importance of first impressions in a job interview* [Paper presentation]. The Annual Meeting of the Midwestern Psychological Association, Chicago, IL, United States.

Pruitt, D. G. (1983). Strategic choice in negotiation. *American Behavioral Scientist, 27*, 167–194.

Pulakos, E. D., & Schmitt, N. (1995). Experience-based and situational interview questions: Studies of validity. *Personnel Psychology, 48*, 289–308.

Putnam, L. L., & Fairhurst, G. T. (2015). Revising "organizations as discursive constructions": 10 years later. *Communication Theory, 25*, 375–392.

Putnam, L. L., & Wilson, C. E. (1982). Communicative strategies in organizational conflicts: Reliability and validity of a measurement scale. In M. Burgoon (Ed.), *Communication yearbook 6* (pp. 629–652). SAGE.

Quan-Haase, A., Nevin, A. D., & Lukacs, V. (2018). Romantic dissolution and Facebook life: A typology of coping strategies for breakups. In B. Wellman, L. Robinson, C. Brienza, W. Chen, & S. R. Cotton (Eds.), *Networks, hacking and media-CITAMS@ 30: Now and then and tomorrow, Studies in media and communications* (Vol. 16, pp. 73–98). Emerald Publishing Limited.

Rahim, M. A. (1983). A measure of styles of handling interpersonal conflict. *Academy of Management Journal, 26*, 368–376.

Ralston, S. M., & Brady, R. (1994). The relative influence of interview communication satisfaction on applicants' recruitment interview decisions. *Journal of Business Communication*, *31*(1), 61–77. https://doi.org/10.1177/002194369403100104

Ramirez, A., Jr. (2008). An examination of the tripartite approach to commitment: An actor-partner interdependence model analysis of the effect of relational maintenance behavior. *Journal of Social and Personal Relationships*, *25*(6), 943–965.

Ramirez, A., Jr., & Broneck, K. (2009). "IM Me": Instant messaging as relational maintenance and everyday communication. *Journal of Social and Personal Relationships*, *26*, 291–314.

Ramirez, A., Summer, E. M., Fleuriet, C., & Cole, M. (2015). When online dating partners meet offline: The effect of modality switching on relational communication between online daters. *Journal of Computer-Mediated Communication*, *20*(1), 99–114.

Ramirez, A., Jr., & Zhang, S. (2007). When on-line meets off-line: The effect of modality switching on relational communication. *Communication Monographs*, *74*, 287–310.

Rapanata, C., & Hample, D. (2015). Orientations to interpersonal arguing in the United Arab Emirates, with comparisons to the United States, China, and India. *Journal of Intercultural Communication Research*, *44*(4), 263–287. https://doi.org/10.1080/17475759.2015.1081392

Raven, B. H. (1965). Social influence and power. In I. D. Steiner & M. Fishbein (Eds.), *Current studies in social psychology* (pp. 371–381). Holt, Rinehart, Winston.

Raven, B. H., Schwarzwald, J., & Koslowsky, M. (1998). Conceptualizing and measuring a power/interaction model of interpersonal influence. *Journal of Applied Social Psychology*, *28*, 307–332.

Rawlins, W. (1992). *Friendship matters: Communication, dialectics, and the life course*. Transaction Publishers.

Rawlins, W. K. (1983). Openness as problematic in ongoing friendships: Two conversational dilemmas. *Communication Monographs*, *50*, 1–13.

Rawlins, W. K. (1994). Being there and growing apart: Sustaining friendships through adulthood. In D. J. Canary & L. Stafford (Eds.), *Communication and relational maintenance* (pp. 275–294). Academic Press.

Ray, G. B., & Floyd, K. (2006). Nonverbal expressions of liking and disliking in initial interaction: Encoding and decoding perspectives. *Southern Communication Journal*, *71*, 45–64.

Real, K., & Rimal, R. N. (2007). Friends talk to friends about drinking: Exploring the role of peer communication in the theory of normative social behavior. *Health Communication*, *22*(2), 169–180. https://doi.org/10.1080/10410230701454254

Redmond, M. V., & Virchota, D. A. (1994, November). *The effects of varying lengths of initial interaction on attraction and uncertainty reduction* [Paper presentation]. The Annual Meeting of the Speech Communication Association, New Orleans, LA, United States.

Reitz, H. J., Wall, J. A., Jr., & Love, M. S. (1988). Ethics in negotiation: Oil and water or good lubrication? *Business Horizons*, *41*, 5–14.

Reyes, M., Afifi, W., Krawchuk, A., Imperato, N., Shelley, D., & Lee, J. (1999, June). *Just (don't) talk: Comparing the impact of interaction style on sexual desire and social attraction* [Paper presentation]. The Joint Conference of the International Network on Personal Relationships and the International Society for the Study of Personal Relationships, Louisville, KY, United States.

Rhodes, G. (2006). The evolutionary psychology of facial beauty. *Annual Review of Psychology*, *57*, 199–226.

Rhodes, G., Lie, H. C., Thevaraja, N., Taylor, L., Iredell, N., Curran, C., Tan, S. Q. C., Carnemola, P., & Simmons, L. W. (2011). Facial attractiveness ratings from video-clips and static images tell the same story. *PLoS One*, *6*(11), e26653.

Rhodes, G., Proffitt, F., Grady, J. M., & Sumich, A. (1998). Facial symmetry and the perception of beauty. *Psychonomic Bulletin & Review*, *5*, 659–669.

Ricciardelli, L. A., McCabe, M. P., & Ridge, D. (2006). The construction of the adolescent male body through sport. *Journal of Health Psychology*, *11*, 577–587.

Riegel, K. F. (1979). *Foundations of dialectical psychology*. Academic Press.

Riggio, R. E. (1986). Assessment of basic social skills. *Journal of Personality and Social Psychology*, *51*, 649–660.

Riggio, R. E. (2006). Nonverbal skills and abilities. In V. Manusov & M. L. Patterson (Eds.), *The SAGE handbook of nonverbal communication* (pp. 79–95). SAGE.

Riggio, R. E. (2010). Before emotional intelligence: Research on nonverbal, emotional, and social competences. *Industrial and Organizational Psychology*, *3*, 178–182.

Riggle, E. D. B., Rothblum, E. D., Rostosky, S. S., Clark, J. B., & Balsam, K. F. (2016). "The secret of our success": Long-term same-sex couples' perceptions of their relationship longevity. *Journal of GLBT Family Studies*, *12*, 319–333.

Rind, B., & Strohmetz, D. (1999). Effect on restaurant tipping of a helpful message written on the back of customers' checks. *Journal of Applied Social Psychology*, *29*, 139–144.

Ritter, C. R., Barker, B. A., & Scharp, K. M. (2020). Using attribution theory to explore the reasons adults with hearing loss do not use their hearing aids. *PLoS One*, *15*(9), e0238468.

Robins, R. W., Spranca, M. D., & Mendelsohn, G. A. (1996). The actor-observer effect revisited: Effects of individual differences and repeated social interactions on actor and observer attributions. *Journal of Personality and Social Psychology*, *71*(2), 375–389.

Roets, A., Kruglanski, A. W., Kossowska, M., Pierro, A., & Hong, Y. Y. (2015). The motivated gatekeeper of our minds: New directions in need for closure theory and research. In M. P. Zanna (Ed.), *Advances in experimental social psychology* (Vol. 52, pp. 221–283). Academic Press.

Rogers, R. A. (2006). rom cultural exchange to transculturation: A review and reconceptualization of cultural appropriation. *Communication Theory*, *16*(4), 474–503. https://doi.org/10.1111/j.1468-2885-2006.00277.x

Roloff, M. E., & Cloven, D. H. (1990). The chilling effect in interpersonal relationships: The reluctance to speak one's mind. In D. D. Cahn (Ed.), *Intimates in conflict: A communication perspective* (pp. 49–76). Lawrence Erlbaum.

Roloff, M. E., & Ifert, D. E. (2000). Conflict management through avoidance: Withholding complaints, suppressing arguments, and declaring topics taboo. In S. Petronio (Ed.), *Balancing the secrets of private disclosures* (pp. 151–163). Lawrence Erlbaum.

Rose, H., & Galloway, N. (2019). *Global Englishes for language teaching*. Cambridge University Press.

Rose, S. M. (1984). How friendships end: Patterns among young adults. *Journal of Social and Personal Relationships*, *1*, 267–277.

Rose, S. M. (1985). Same- and cross- sex friendships and psychology of homosociality. *Sex Roles*, *12*, 63–74.

Rose, S., & Serafica, F. C. (1986). Keeping and ending casual, close and best friendships. *Journal of Social and Personal Relationships*, *3*, 275–288.

Rosenfeld, M. J., & Thomas, R. J. (2010). *Meeting online: The rise of the Internet as a social intermediary* [Unpublished manuscript, Department of Sociology, Stanford University].

Rowatt, W. C., Cunningham, M. R., & Druen, P. B. (1998). Deception to get a date. *Personality and Social Psychology Bulletin*, *24*, 1228–1242.

Rubin, Z. (1970). Measurement of romantic love. *Journal of Personality and Social Psychology*, *16*, 265–273.

Ruppel, E. K., & Burke, T. J. (2015). Complementary channel use and the role of social competence. *Journal of Computer-Mediated Communication*, *20*(1), 37–51. https://doi.org/10.1111/jcc4.12091

Rusbult, C. E. (1980). Commitment and satisfaction in romantic associations: A test of the investment model. *Journal of Experimental Social Psychology*, *16*, 172–186.

Rusbult, C. E. (1983). A longitudinal test of the investment model: The development (and deterioration) of satisfaction and commitment in heterosexual involvements. *Journal of Personality and Social Psychology*, *45*, 101.

Rusbult, C. E., Agnew, C., & Arriaga, X. (2011). The investment model of commitment processes. In P. A. M. Van Lange, A. W. Kruglanski & E. T. Higgins (Eds.), *The handbook of theories of social psychology* (Vol. 2, pp. 218–231). SAGE.

Rusbult, C. E., Arriaga, X. B., & Agnew, C. R. (2001). Interdependence in close relationships. In G. J. O. Fletcher & M. S. Clark (Eds.), *Blackwell handbook of social psychology: Interpersonal processes* (pp. 359–387). Blackwell.

Rusbult, C. E., Drigotas, S. M., & Verette, J. (1994). The investment model: An interdependence analysis of commitment processes and relationship maintenance phenomena. In D. J. Canary & L. Stafford (Eds.), *Communication and relational maintenance* (pp. 115–139). Academic Press.

Rusbult, C. E., Martz, J. M., & Agnew, C. R. (1998). The investment model scale: Measuring commitment level, satisfaction level, quality of alternatives, and investment size. *Personal Relationships*, *5*, 357–387.

Rusbult, C. E., Olsen, N., Davis, J. L., & Hannon, P. (2001). Commitment and relationship maintenance mechanisms. In J. H. Harvey & A. Wenzel (Eds.), *Close romantic relationships: Maintenance and enhancement* (pp. 87–113). Lawrence Erlbaum.

Rusbult, C. E., Verette, J., Whitney, G. A., Slovik, L. F., & Lipkus, I. (1991). Accommodation processes in close relationships: Theory and preliminary empirical evidence. *Journal of Personality and Social Psychology*, *60*(1), 53–78.

Russell, J. A. (1994). Is there universal recognition of emotion from facial expression? A review of the cross-cultural studies. *Psychological Bulletin*, *115*, 102–141.

Ryan, A. M., & Sackett, P. R. (1989). Exploratory study of individual assessment practices: Interrater reliability and judgments of assessor effectiveness. *Journal of Applied Psychology*, *74*, 568–579.

Rykov, Y., Koltsova, O., & Sinyavskaya, Y. (2020). Effects of user behaviors on accumulation of social capital in an online social network. *PLoS One*, *15*, e0231837.

Saarimäki, H., Gotsopoulos, A., Jääskeläinen, I. P., Lampinen, J., Vuilleumier, P., Hari, R., Sams, M., & Nummenmaa, L. (2016). Discrete neural signatures of basic emotions. *Cerebral Cortex*, *26*, 2563–2573.

Sacks, H., Schegloff, E. A., & Jefferson, G. (1978). A simplest systematics of the organization of turn taking for conversation. In J. Schenkein (Ed.), *Studies in the organization of conversational interaction*. Academic Press.

Sadalla, E. K., Kenrick, D. T., & Vershure, B. (1987). Dominance and heterosexual attraction. *Journal of Personality and Social Psychology*, *52*, 730–738.

Sagrestano, L. M., Heavey, C. L., & Christensen, A. (2006). Individual differences versus social structural approaches to explaining demand-withdraw and social influence behaviors. In K. Dindia & D. J. Canary (Eds.), *Sex differences and similarities in communication* (2nd ed., pp. 379–395). Lawrence Erlbaum.

Sahlstein, E., & Dun, T. (2008). "I wanted time to myself and he wanted to be together all the time": Constructing breakups as managing autonomy-connection. *Qualitative Research Reports in Communication*, *9*, 37–45.

Salazar, L. R. (2016). The relationship between compassion, interpersonal communication apprehension, narcissism, and verbal aggressiveness. *The Journal of Happiness & Well-Being*, *4*, 1–14.

Salovey, P., & Mayer, J. D. (1990). Emotional intelligence. *Imagination, Cognition and Personality*, *9*, 185–211.

Santor, D. A., Messervey, D., & Kusumakar, V. (2000). Measuring peer pressure, popularity, and conformity in adolescent boys and girls: Predicting school performance, sexual attitudes, and substance abuse. *Journal of Youth and Adolescence*, *29*(2), 163–182. https://doi.org/10.1023/a:1005152515264

Sapolin, D. (2013, November 25). The lost art of conversation and connection. *Forbes*.

Schaffer, D. R., Smith, J. E., & Tomarelli, M. (1982). Self-monitoring as a determinant of self-disclosure reciprocity during the acquaintance process. *Journal of Personality and Social Psychology*, *43*, 163–175.

Scharp, K. M. (2006). Parent–child estrangement: Conditions for disclosure and perceived social network member reactions. *Family Relations*, *65*, 688–700.

Scharp, K. M., Thomas, L. J., & Paxman, C. G. (2015). "It was the straw that broke the camel's back": Exploring the distancing processes communicatively constructed in parent–child estrangement backstories. *Journal of Family Communication*, *15*, 330–348.

Schegloff, E. A., & Sacks, H. (1973). Opening up closings. *Semiotica*, *8*, 289–327. https://doi.org/10.1515/semi.1973.8.4.289

Schein, E. H. (2004). *Organizational culture and leadership* (3rd ed.). Jossey-Bass.

Scherer, K. R., & Wallbott, H. G. (1994). Evidence for universality and cultural variation of differential emotion response patterning. *Journal of Personality and Social Psychology*, *66*, 310–328.

Schutz, W. C. (1966). *The interpersonal underworld*. Science and Behavior Books.

Scott, C., & Myers, K. K. (2005). The socialization of emotion: Learning emotion management at the fire station. *Journal of Applied Communication Research*, *33*(1), 67–92. https://doi.org/10.1080/0090988042000318521

Searle, J. (1969). *Speech acts: An essay in the philosophy of language*. Cambridge University Press.

Serewicz, M. C. M., Dickson, F. C., Morrison, J. H. T. A., & Poole, L. L. (2007). Family privacy orientation, relational maintenance, and family satisfaction in young adults' family relationships. *Journal of Family Communication*, *7*, 123–142.

Shackelford, T. K., & Buss, D. M. (1996). Betrayal in mateships, friendships, and coalitions. *Personality and Social Psychology Bulletin*, *22*, 1151–1164.

Shannon, C. E., & Weaver, W. (1949). *The mathematical theory of communication*. University of Illinois Press.

Sharabi, L. L., & Caughlin, J. P. (2019). Deception in online dating: Significance and implications for the first offline date. *New Media & Society*, *21*, 229–247.

Sheldon, P. (2010). Pressure to be perfect: Influences on college students' body esteem. *Southern Communication Journal*, *75*, 277–298.

Sheldon, P., Gilchrist-Petty, E., & Lessley, J. A. (2014). You did what? The relationship between forgiveness tendency, communication of forgiveness, and relationship satisfaction in married and dating couples. *Communication Reports*, *27*, 78–90.

Shelton, J. N., Trail, T. E., West, T. V., & Bergsieker, H. B. (2010). From strangers to friends: The interpersonal process model of intimacy in developing interracial friendships. *Journal of Social and Personal Relationships*, *27*(1), 71–90. https://doi.org/10.1177/0265407509346422

Sherif, M. (1936). *The psychology of social norms*. Harper.

Shimoda, K., Argyle, M., & Bitti, P. R. (1978). The intercultural recognition of emotional expressions by three national racial groups: English, Italian and Japanese. *European Journal of Social Psychology*, *8*, 169–179.

Short, J. A., Williams, E., & Christie, B. (1976). *The social psychology of telecommunication*. John Wiley & Sons.

Shuler, S., & Sypher, B. D. (2000). Seeking emotional labor: When managing the heart enhances the work experience. *Management Communication Quarterly*, *14*, 50–89.

Shulman, H. C., Dixon, G. N., Bullock, O. M., & Colón Amill, D. (2020). The effects of jargon on processing fluency, self-perceptions, and scientific engagement. *Journal of Language and Psychology*, *39*, 579–597. https://doi.org/10.1177/0261927X20902177

Sichel, M. (2007). *Estranged family: Dealing with a family rift*. http://www.sideroad.com/Family_Life/estranged-family.html

Siegert, J. R., & Stamp, G. H. (1994). "Our first big fight" as a milestone in the development of close relationships. *Communication Monographs*, *61*, 345–360.

Sillars, A., & Canary, D. J. (2013). Conflict and relational quality in families. In A. L. Vangelisti (Ed.), *Routledge handbook of family communication* (2nd ed., pp. 338–357). Routledge.

Sillars, A. L. (1980). Attributions and communication in roommate conflicts. *Communication Monographs*, *47*, 180–200.

Sillars, A. L., Canary, D. J., & Tafoya, M. (2004). Communication, conflict, and the quality of family relationships. In A. L. Vangelisti (Ed.), *Handbook of family interaction* (pp. 413–446). Lawrence Erlbaum.

Singh, D. (2004). Mating strategies of young women: Role of physical attractiveness. *Journal of Sex Research*, *41*, 43–54.

Smith, C. A., & Lazarus, R. S. (1990). Emotion and adaptation. In L. A. Pervin (Ed.), *Handbook of personality: Theory and research* (pp. 609–637). Guilford Press.

Snyder, M. (1974). Self-monitoring of expressive behavior. *Journal of Personality and Social Psychology, 30*, 526–537.

Snyder, M. (2002). Psychology of self-monitoring. In N. J. Smelser & P. B. Baltes (Eds.), *International encyclopedia of the social and behavioral sciences* (pp. 13841–13844). Elsevier.

Snyder, M., & Copeland, J. (2013). Self-monitoring processes in organizational settings. In R. A. Giacalone & P. Rosenfeld (Eds.), *Impression management in the organization* (pp. 7–19). Lawrence Erlbaum.

Sobré-Denton, M., & Bardhan, N. (2013). *Cultivating cosmopolitanism for intercultural communication: Communicating as global citizens*. Routledge.

Soliz, J., & Giles, H. (2014). Relational and identity processes in communication: A contextual and meta-analytical review of communication accommodation theory. *Annals of the International Communication Association, 38*(1), 107–144. https://doi.org/10.1080/23808985.2014.11679160

Solomon, D. H., & Knobloch, L. (2004). A model of relational turbulence: The role of intimacy, relational uncertainty, and interference from partners in appraisal of irritations. *Journal of Social and Personal Relationships, 21*, 795–816.

Solomon, D. H., & Samp, J. A. (1998). Power and problem appraisal: Perceptual foundations of the chilling effect in dating relationship. *Journal of Social and Personal Relationships, 15*, 191–209.

Solomon, D. H., & Theiss, J. A. (2008). A longitudinal test of the relational turbulence model of romantic relationship development. *Personal Relationships, 15*, 339–357.

South Richardson, D. (2014). Everyday aggression takes many forms. *Current Directions in Psychological Science, 23*(3), 220–224. https://doi.org/10.1177/0963721414530143.

Speer, R. B., & Trees, A. R. (2007). The push and pull of stepfamily life: The contribution of stepchildren's autonomy and connection-seeking behaviors to role development in stepfamilies. *Communication Studies, 58*(4), 377–394.

Spinoza, B. (1982). In S. Feldman (Ed.), *The ethics and selected letters* (S. Shirley, Trans.). Hackett. (Orig. 1677)

Spitzberg, B. H. (2014). A model of intercultural communication competence. In L. A. Samovar, R. E. Porter, E. R. McDaniel, & C. S. Roy (Eds.), *Intercultural communication: A reader* (pp. 343–355). Cengage Learning.

Spitzberg, B. H. (2015). The composition of competence: Communication skills. In A. F. Hannawa & B. H. Spitzberg (Eds.), *Communication competence* (pp. 237–269). De Gruyter Mouton.

Spitzberg, B. H., & Cupach, W. R. (1984). *Interpersonal communication competence*. SAGE.

Spitzberg, B. H., & Cupach, W. R. (1989). *Handbook of interpersonal competence research*. Springer-Verlag.

Spitzberg, B. H., & Cupach, W. R. (2011). Interpersonal skills. In M. L. Knapp & J. A. Daly (Eds.), *Handbook of interpersonal communication* (4th ed., pp. 481–524). SAGE.

Spitzberg, B. H., & Cupach, W. R. (2012). *Handbook of interpersonal competence research*. Springer Science & Business Media.

Sprecher, S. (1998). Social exchange theories and sexuality. *Journal of Sex Research, 35*, 32–43.

Sprecher, S., Zimmerman, C., & Abrahams, E. M. (2010). Choosing compassionate strategies to end a relationship. Effects of compassionate love for a partner and the reason for the breakup. *Social Psychology, 41*, 66–75.

Stafford, L. (2003). Maintaining romantic relationships: Summary and analysis of one research program. In D. J. Canary & M. Dainton (Eds.), *Maintaining relationships through communication: Relational, contextual, and cultural variations* (pp. 51–77). Lawrence Erlbaum.

Stafford, L. (2008). Social exchange theories. In L. A. Baxter & D. O. Braithwaite (Eds.), *Engaging theories in interpersonal communication: Multiple perspectives* (pp. 377–389). SAGE.

Stafford, L. (2011). Measuring relationship maintenance behaviors: Critique and development of the revised relationship maintenance behavior scale. *Journal of Social and Personal Relationships, 28*(2), 278–303.

Stafford, L., & Canary, D. J. (1991). Maintenance strategies and romantic relationship type, gender and relational characteristics. *Journal of Social and Personal relationships, 8*(2), 217–242.

Stafford, L., Kline, S., & Dimmick, J. (1999). Home e-mail: Relational maintenance and gratification opportunities. *Journal of Broadcasting & Electronic Media, 43*, 659–669.

Stafford, L., Merolla, A. J., & Castle, J. D. (2006). When long-distance dating partners become geographically close. *Journal of Social and Personal Relationships, 23*, 901–919.

Sternberg, R. J. (1986). A triangular theory of love. *Psychological Review, 93*, 119–135.

Sternberg, R. J. (1987). Liking versus loving: A comparative evaluation of theories. *Psychological Bulletin, 102*, 331–345.

Stewart, G. L., Dustin, S. L., Barrick, M. R., & Darnold, T. C. (2008). Exploring the handshake in employment interviews. *Journal of Applied Psychology, 93*(5), 1139–1146. https://doi.org/10.1037/0021-9010.93.5.1139

Stewart, J. (2012). *Bridges not walls: A book about interpersonal communication* (11th ed.). McGraw-Hill.

Stiff, J. B., & Mongeau, P. A. (2003). *Persuasive communication* (2nd ed.). The Guilford Press.

Stone, D., Heen, S., & Patton, B. (2010). *Difficult conversations: How to discuss what matters most*. Penguin.

Strohmetz, D. B., Rind, B., Fisher, R., & Lynn, M. (2002). Sweetening the till: The use of candy to increase restaurant tipping 1. *Journal of Applied Social Psychology, 32*, 300–309.

Strough, J., Mehta, C. M., McFall, J. P., & Schuller, K. L. (2008). Are older adults less subject to the sunk-cost fallacy than younger adults? *Psychological Science, 19*(7), 650–652. https://doi.org/10.1111/j.1467-9280.2008.02138.x

Strough, J., Schlosnagle, L., & DiDonato, L. (2011). Understanding decisions about sunk costs from older and younger adults' perspectives. *The Journals of Gerontology B: Psychological Sciences and Social Sciences, 66*, 681–686.

Sue, D. W. (2013). Race talk: The psychology of racial dialogues. *American Psychologist, 68*(8), 663–672.

Sue, D. W., Capodilupo, C. M., Torino, G. C., Bucceri, J. M., Holder, A. M. B., Nadal, K. L., & Esquilin, M. (2007). Racial microaggressions in everyday life. *American Psychologist, 62*, 271–286.

Sue, D. W., & Spanierman, L. B. (2020). *Microaggressions in everyday life* (2nd ed.). Wiley.

Suedfeld, P., Bochner, S., & Mata, C. (1971). Petitioner's attire and petition signing by peace demonstrations: A field experiment. *Journal of Applied Social Psychology, 1*, 278–283.

Suler, J. (2004). The online disinhibition effect. *CyberPsychology and Behavior, 7*, 321–326.

Sunnafrank, M. (1986). Predicted outcome value during initial interactions: A reformulation of uncertainty reduction theory. *Human Communication Research, 13*, 3–33.

Sunnafrank, M. (1990). Predicted outcome value and uncertainty reduction theories: A test of competing perspectives. *Human Communication Research, 17*, 76–103.

Sunnafrank, M. (1991). Interpersonal attraction and attitude similarity: A communication-based assessment. In J. A. Anderson (Ed.), *Communication yearbook 14* (pp. 451–483). SAGE.

Sunnafrank, M. (1992). On debunking the attitude similarity myth. *Communication Monographs, 59*, 164–179.

Sunnafrank, M., & Ramirez, A., Jr. (2004). At first sight: Persistent relational effects of get-acquainted conversations. *Journal of Social and Personal Relationships, 21*, 361–379.

Surra, C. A., & Hughes, D. K. (1997). Commitment processes in accounts of the development of premarital relationships. *Journal of Marriage and the Family, 59*, 5–21.

Tarico, V. S., Altmaier, E. M., Smith, W. L., Franken, E. A., & Berbaum, K. S. (1986). Development and validation of an accomplishment interview for radiology residents. *Journal of Medical Education, 61*, 845–847.

Tashiro, T. Y., & Frazier, P. (2003). "I'll never be in a relationship like that again": Personal growth following romantic relationship breakups. *Personal Relationships, 10*, 113–128.

Taylor, J. R., & Van Every, E. J. (2000). *The emergent organization: Communication as its site and surface*. Lawrence Erlbaum.

Taylor, L. A., & Shuter, R. (2004). American women's visions of workplace conflict: A metaphorical analysis. *The Howard Journal of Communications, 15*, 169–183. https://doi.org/10.1080/10646170490479787

Taylor, S. H., & Bazarova, N. N. (2018). Social media and well-being: A relational perspective. In Z. Papacharissi (Ed.), *A networked self and love* (pp. 86–112). Routledge.

Teven, J. J., Richmond, V. P., McCroskey, J. C., & McCroskey, L. L. (2010). Updating relationships between communication traits and communication competence. *Communication Research Reports, 27*, 263–270.

Theiss, J. A., & Solomon, D. H. (2007). Communication and the emotional, cognitive, and relational consequences of first sexual encounters between partners. *Communication Quarterly, 55*, 179–206.

Thibaut, J. W., & Kelley, J. J. (1959). *The social psychology of groups*. Wiley.

Thieme, A., & Rouse, C. (1991, November). *Terminating intimate relationships: An examination of the interactions among disengagement strategies, acceptance, and causal attributions* [Paper presentation]. The Annual Meeting of the Speech Communication Association, Atlanta, GA, United States.

Thomas, K. W. (2006). Conflict and conflict management: Reflections and update. *Journal of Organizational Behavior, 13*, 265–274.

Ting-Toomey, S. (1988). Intercultural conflicts: A face-negotiation theory. In Y. Y. Kim & W. B. Gudykunst (Eds.), *Theories in intercultural communication* (pp. 213–235). SAGE.

Ting-Toomey, S. (2005). The matrix of face: An updated face-negotiation theory. In W. B. Gudykunst (Ed.), *Theorizing about intercultural communication* (pp. 71–92). SAGE.

Ting-Toomey, S. (2009). Intercultural conflict competence as a facet of intercultural competence development. Multiple conceptual approaches. In D. K. Deardoff (Ed.), *The SAGE handbook of intercultural competence* (pp. 100–120). SAGE.

INDEX